James Paterson

The Intoxicating Liquor Licensing Acts, 1872, 1874

Tenth Edition

James Paterson

The Intoxicating Liquor Licensing Acts, 1872, 1874
Tenth Edition

ISBN/EAN: 9783337141066

Printed in Europe, USA, Canada, Australia, Japan

Cover: Foto ©ninafisch / pixelio.de

More available books at **www.hansebooks.com**

# THE
Intoxicating Liquor Licensing Acts, 1872, 1874.

TOGETHER WITH ALL

THE ALEHOUSE, BEERHOUSE, REFRESHMENT HOUSE, WINE AND BEER-HOUSE, INLAND REVENUE, AND SUNDAY CLOSING ACTS RELATING THERETO,

WITH INTRODUCTION, NOTES, AND INDEX.

Tenth Edition.

BY

JAMES PATERSON, Esq., M.A.,

BARRISTER-AT-LAW,

Editor of "*Archbold's Justice of the Peace*," "*The Fishery Acts*," "*The Game Acts*," "*The Bastardy Acts*," &c.

LONDON:
SHAW & SONS, FETTER LANE & CRANE COURT, E.C.
Law Printers and Publishers.

1894.

LONDON: SHAW AND SONS, FETTER LANE AND CRANE COURT, E.C.

PREFACE TO THE TENTH EDITION.

SINCE the publication of the Ninth Edition of this Work the cases on the Licensing Acts have been numerous and important. This is partly due to the decision of the House of Lords in the case of *Sharp* v. *Wakefield*, which is reported at length in the Appendix. The Author has included every reported decision up to the present date. The subjects of Refreshment House, Theatre, Music and Dancing Licenses, Billiard Licenses, and the Rights and Duties of Innkeepers have been kept equally in view owing to their increasing interest. A new departure having been taken owing to the Courts adopting recent reforms in procedure from the Summary Jurisdiction Acts, more minute references to the various changes thereby brought to bear on licensing subjects have been necessitated and will be found in their proper places. Scarcely any topic which one would expect to be noticed in a Work with this title will be found to be omitted. And to make the Work practically useful, the copious Index and Table of References have been revised.

The plan of the Work is that which experience and the recommendations of judges and practitioners attest to be most useful in practice, namely, to give the first place to the two Licensing Acts, 1872 and 1874, as now being the leading Statutes, explained by copious notes and cross references, and then to arrange by way of Appendix, in chronological order, all the earlier as well as later series of outstanding enactments on licensing matters, each, in the same manner, accompanied with notes and cross-references. By this method, those who consult the Work have the great advantage of readily seeing the sequence of sections in each Statute, and at the same time have the materials for referring to every other enactment modifying them. Besides this list of Chronological Statutes, there are other enactments more or less referred to in the notes, and of these there is a separate table of sections to be found at the commencement of the Book.

J. P.

GOLDSMITH BUILDING, TEMPLE,
January, 1894.

PREFACE TO THE FIRST EDITION.

THE Licensing Act, 1872, recently passed, and which has made so many important changes in the laws relating to the sale of Intoxicating Liquors, was intended to settle some questions of domestic policy long agitated, confessed to be extremely difficult of treatment, and probably destined after a few years to be again and again made the subject of discussion. It was originally desired by the Government to introduce a consolidation of the multifarious laws on the subject; but practical difficulties prevented the realisation of so desirable an object, and the present Act thus adds one to a group of somewhat incongruous Statutes, and increases the difficulty of its own interpretation.

The Editor, after much consideration, has embodied his views of the leading difficulties that will arise under the new Act, and has suggested some solution of most of them. This Edition also contains a complete collection of the existing statutory law on the subject.

J. P.

GOLDSMITH BUILDING, TEMPLE,
22nd August, 1872.

CHRONOLOGICAL TABLE.

OF THE

STATUTES RELATIVE TO THE LICENSING ACTS, 1872, 1874.

	PAGE
9 Geo. 4, c. 61 (Alehouse Act, 1828)	212
11 Geo. 4 & 1 Will. 4, c. 64 (Beerhouse Act, 1830)... ...	247
4 & 5 Will. 4, c. 85 (Beerhouse Act, 1834)	258
3 & 4 Vict. c. 61 (Beerhouse Act, 1840)	263
5 & 6 Vict. c. 44 (Alehouse Act, 1842)	269
23 Vict. c. 27 (Refreshment Houses Act, 1860)	273
24 & 25 Vict. c. 21 (Revenue (No. 1) Act, 1861)	291
24 & 25 Vict. c. 91 (Revenue (No. 2) Act, 1861)	292
25 & 26 Vict. c. 22 (Revenue Act, 1862)	295
25 & 26 Vict. c. 38 (Tippling Act, 1862)	297
26 & 27 Vict. c. 33 (Revenue Act, 1863)	299
26 & 27 Vict. c. 41 (Innkeepers Liability Act, 1863) ...	302
27 & 28 Vict. c. 18 (Revenue (No. 1) Act, 1864)	305
27 & 28 Vict. c. 64 (Refreshment House Closing Act, 1864)	307
28 & 29 Vict. c. 77 (Refreshment House Closing Act, 1865)	309
30 & 31 Vict. c. 90 (Revenue Act, 1867)	310
32 & 33 Vict. c. 27 (Wine and Beerhouse Act, 1869) ...	312
33 & 34 Vict. c. 29 (Wine and Beerhouse Act, 1870) ...	326
33 & 34 Vict. c. 111 (Beerhouse Act, 1870)	333
35 & 36 Vict. c. 94 (LICENSING ACT, 1872)	1
37 & 38 Vict. c. 49 (LICENSING ACT, 1874)	168
41 & 42 Vict. c. 38 (Innkeepers Act, 1878)	335

	PAGE
43 Vict. c. 6 (Beer Dealers Retail Act, 1880)	337
43 & 44 Vict. c. 20 (Revenue Act, 1880)	340
43 & 44 Vict. c. 24 (Spirits Act, 1880)	346
44 & 45 Vict. c. 61 (Sunday Closing (Wales) Act, 1881)	350
45 & 46 Vict. c. 34 (Beer Dealers Retail Act, 1882)	352
46 & 47 Vict. c. 31 (Payment of Wages in Public Houses Act, 1883)	353
47 & 48 Vict. c. 29 (Licensing (Evidence) Act, 1884)	358
49 & 50 Vict. c. 56 (Liquors Sale to Children Act, 1886)	359
52 & 53 Vict. c. 44 (Cruelty to Children Act, 1889)	360

INDEX OF STATUTES.

GENERAL OUTLINE ARRANGED IN GROUPS.

	PAGE
Licensing Act, 1872, 35 & 36 Vict. c. 94	1
Preliminary	1
Illicit sales	2
Offences against public order	23
Repeated convictions	67
Registers	73
As to grant of licenses	75
Legal proceedings	107
Miscellaneous	132
Saving clauses	143
Definitions	149
Repeal	160
Application to Ireland	165
Licensing Act, 1874, 37 & 38 Vict. c. 49	168
Preliminary	168
Hours of closing	168
Record of convictions and penalties	185
Regulations as to entry on premises	194
Occasional licenses	197
Miscellaneous	199
Definitions and repeal	206
Licensing (Evidence) Act, 1884, 47 & 48 Vict. c. 29	358
Alehouse Act, 1828, 9 Geo. 4, c. 61	212
1842, 5 & 6 Vict. c. 44	269
Beerhouse Act, 1830, 11 Geo. 4 & 1 Will. 4, c. 64	247
1834, 4 & 5 Will. 4, c. 85	258
1840, 3 & 4 Vict. c. 61	263
1870, 33 & 34 Vict. c. 111	333

	PAGE
Beer Dealers Retail Licenses Act, 1880, 43 Vict. c. 6 ...	337
1882, 45 & 46 Vict. c. 34	352
Closing Acts (Refreshment Houses)	307
1864, 27 & 28 Vict. c. 64	307
1865, 28 & 29 Vict. c. 77	309
Sunday Closing (Wales) Act, 1881, 44 & 45 Vict. c. 61 ...	350
Refreshment Houses Act, 1860, 23 Vict. c. 27	273
Revenue Act, 1861, 24 & 25 Vict. c. 21	291
1861, 24 & 25 Vict. c. 91	292
1862, 25 & 26 Vict. c. 22	295
1862, 25 & 26 Vict. c. 38	297
1863, 26 & 27 Vict. c. 33	299
1864, 27 & 28 Vict. c. 18	305
1867, 30 & 31 Vict. c. 90	310
1880, 43 & 44 Vict. c. 20	340
1880, 43 & 44 Vict. c. 24	346
Wine and Beerhouse Act, 1869, 32 & 33 Vict. c. 27... ...	312
1870, 33 & 34 Vict. c. 29... ...	326
Innkeepers Act, 1863, 26 & 27 Vict. c. 41	302
1878, 41 & 42 Vict. c. 38	335
Forms of Licenses and Certificates	368

TABLE OF SECTIONS.

Licensing Act, 1872 (35 & 36 Vict. c. 94).

SECTION		PAGE
1	Short title	1
2	Extent of Act	1
3	Selling liquors without license	2
	Dealers' licenses	4
	Clubs supplying liquors	5
	Selling under void license	6
	Selling in premises enlarged	7
	Hawking spirits	8
	The punishment	8
	Selling by retail	9
	Selling without excise license	10
	Selling by executor, &c.	11
4	Occupiers of unlicensed premises	12
5	Drinking on premises contrary to license	12
6	Evasion of law as to this	15
7	Sale of spirits to children	17
8	Sale by standard measures	18
9	Internal communication with unlicensed premises	20
10	Illicit storing of liquor	21
11	Name of licensed persons on premises	21
12	Persons found drunk	23
13	Permitting drunkenness on premises	26
	Liability for manager's acts	27
14	Keeping disorderly house	29
	As to harbouring of prostitutes and thieves	30
	As to seditious meetings	32
	As to music and dancing in London	33
	Procedure as to in London	36
	Racecourse licenses	37
	Country music and dancing licenses	38
	When music, &c., license required	41

TABLE OF SECTIONS.

SECTION		PAGE
15	Permitting premises to be a brothel	42
16	Harbouring a constable	44
17	Permitting gaming	45
	As to gaming houses	47
	As to betting houses	49
18	Excluding drunkards from premises	54
23	Closing premises in riot	56
25	Persons found on premises in prohibited hours	57
26	Exemption from closing	61
27	Refreshment houses to close same time as inns	64
28	Closing of refreshment houses at 9 and 10 P.M.	65
29	Local authorities granting occasional licenses	66
30	Forfeiting licenses on repeated convictions	67
31	Disqualification of premises	69
32	Conviction five years' back	71
33	Omission to record conviction	72
34	Defacing record of conviction	72
36	Register of licenses to be kept	73
37	Licensing committee in counties	75
38	Licensing committee in boroughs	78
39	Stipendiary magistrates may act in licensing	82
40	Notices before new and transferred licenses	82
41	Licenses withheld wrongfully	86
42	Applications for renewal of license	87
	Grounds of opposition	90
43	Opposing confirmation of license	93
44	Disqualification for licenses	94
45	Qualification as to value of new premises	95
46	Qualification as to value of old premises	97
47	Definition of annual value	99
48	Forms of licenses	101
49	Six-day licenses	102
50	Removal of licenses	105
51	Procedure for penalties	107
	Summary procedure	109
	Imprisonment for non-payment of money	110
	Payment by instalments of penalties	111
	Power to discharge without punishment	112
	Power to award costs	113

TABLE OF SECTIONS. XV

SECTION		PAGE
51 (cont.)	Power to issue distress	113
	Proof of conviction	115
52	Appeal to quarter sessions	116
	Later procedure on appeal to quarter sessions	119
	Application of the provisions to prior Acts...	120
	Appeal by special case stated...	122
53	Temporary renewal of license during appeal ...	124
54	No conviction quashed on *certiorari*	125
55	Recording convictions on license	126
56	Protection of owners of premises	127
57	Conviction for several offences on one day	130
58	Evidence of endorsements and register...	131
59	Double remedy for offences	131
60	Disqualification of justices	132
61	Jurisdiction over piers and shores	134
62	Evidence of selling and consuming liquors	135
63	Excise license to be void on forfeiture...	136
64	Production of licenses by holders	136
65	Population how estimated	137
66	Moiety of penalties to police superannuation ...	137
67	Mitigation of penalties (repealed)	138
68	Dealer's retail spirit licenses	139
69	Retail spirit and liqueur licenses	140
70	Service of notices by post	141
71	Schedule to be part of Act	142
72	Saving of certain privileges	143
	As to theatre licenses...	144
	Selling liquors at theatres	146
73	Cases not requiring justices' license	148
74	Definition of terms	149
	Grant by way of renewal	155
	New and renewed licenses	156
	When premises enlarged	158
75	Billiard licenses ...	160
	As to keeping open billiard tables under 8 & 9 Vict. c. 109, s. 13 ...	163
	As to offences at billiards	163
76-90	Sections as to Ireland	165
	Schedules of repealed enactments	166

Licensing Act, 1874 (37 & 38 Vict. c. 49).

SECTION		PAGE
1	Preliminary and short title	168
2	Commencement of Act	168
3	Hours of closing premises	168
	As to Sunday entertainments	172
4	Exemptions as to theatres repealed	173
5	Exemptions extended to beerhouses, &c.	173
6	Justices varying hours on Sunday afternoon	173
7	Early closing licenses	176
8	Abatement of duty on same	178
9	Selling in prohibited hours	179
10	Selling to *bonâ fide* travellers	180
11	Hours of closing night-houses	185
12	Mitigation of penalties	185
13	Record of convictions	185
14	Recording convictions for adulteration	188
	Adulterating beer	190
	Procedure, Sale of Food Act	191
15	Continuance of forfeited licenses	192
16	Entry of constable on premises	194
17	Search warrant for illicit liquor	195
18	Occasional licenses at fairs and races	197
19	Occasional licenses and time of closing	198
20	Occasional licenses and offences	198
21	Joint committee for borough licenses	199
22	Provisional licenses for unbuilt premises	199
23	One justice's license for several excise licenses	201
24	No confirmation for out-door licenses	202
25	Rules by joint committee	202
26	Notice to oppose renewal of licenses	202
27	No appeal against refusing new certificates	204
28	Licensing justices to decide as to name, &c., on premises	204
29	Definition of "owner," &c.	205
30	Licensed persons entertaining friends	205
32	Definition of terms	206
33	Repeal of sections of Act, 1872	210
	Schedule defining metropolitan district	211

TABLE OF SECTIONS. xvii

Alehouse Act, 1828 (9 *Geo.* 4, *c.* 61).

SECTION   PAGE
1   General annual licensing meeting and adjournments... 212
     Application for licenses 213
     Discretion of justices 213
     Mandamus to justices 215
     Certiorari and prohibition 217
     Licensing in boroughs... 218
     Precepts to constable 221
2   Appointment of general meeting 219
3   Adjournment of meeting 221
4   Special transfer sessions 222
5   Notice of adjournment 223
6   Disqualified justices ... ... · 223
7, 8 Justices in liberties and cinque ports 224
9   Grants by majority of justices 226
12 Applicant unable to attend licensing meeting ... 226
13 Form of licenses 227
14 Transfer of licenses 227
     Discretion of justices 230
     Appeal to quarter sessions 231
     Cases as to transfers 232
     Contracts for sale of premises 235
15 Fees for licenses 236
16 Persons disqualified 237
17 No excise license without justices' license 237
27-29 Appeal to quarter sessions 238
     Statement of special case 242
     Costs on appeal 243
36 Saving as to universities, &c. 245
37 Definitions 246

Beerhouse Act, 1830 (11 *Geo.* 4 *and* 1 *Will.* 4, *c.* 60).

1-3 Licenses to retail beer 247
7   Selling without license 248
10 Partners holding license... 250
30 Licenses to sell cider and perry... 252
31 Covenants against using land for beerhouse 253
32 Definitions of terms 257

TABLE OF SECTIONS.

Beerhouse Act, 1830 (4 & 5 Will. 4, c. 85).

SECTION		PAGE
1	Licenses preceded by certificate of character	258
5	Billeting of soldiers	258
	Army Act, 1881, as to billeting	258
	Liability to provide billets	259
	Offences by keepers of victualling-houses	259
11	Penalties of 1 Will. 4, c. 64, to extend	260
13-15	Excise duty to be paid	260
17	Selling without license	261
20	Selling spirits or wine without license	262

Beerhouse Act, 1834 (3 & 4 Vict. c. 61).

1	Valuation qualification for beerhouses	263
7	Licenses void for felony, &c.	266
8	Death of licensed person, business to continue	266
9	Entry of premises with excise	267
11	Excise officers may enter table-beer houses	267
12	Excise officers may enter premises	267
18	Exemption of then licensed houses as to value	268

Alehouse Act, 1842 (5 & 6 Vict. c. 44).

1	Justices at petty sessions endorsing a transfer	270
2	Lost licenses	271
5	Selling liquors in boats and packets on Sundays	272

Refreshment Houses Act, 1860 (23 Vict. c. 27).

1, 2	Excise duties for refreshment houses	273
3	Shops entitled to wine licenses	273
4	What is selling by retail	274
6	Certain houses required to take licenses	275
7	Confectioners entitled to wine licenses	276
8	Valuation qualification for indoor wine license	276
9	Keeping houses without license	277
10, 11	Forms of licenses and durations	277
12	Death of licensed person	278

TABLE OF SECTIONS.　　　xix

SECTION		PAGE
16	List of licensed persons	... 279
18	Constable visiting refreshment houses... ...	... 280
19	Selling wine without license	... 280
21	Definition of wine and spirits	... 281
22	License void for felony	... 281
23	Entering house with excise	... 281
24	Excise officers may enter wine houses	... 282
25	Having spirits on premises	... 282
30	Penalties recoverable	... 283
31	Adjudging premises disqualified	... 284
32	Penalties on refreshment houses	... 284
33	Mitigating penalties	... 284
34	Appeal to quarter sessions	... 285
35	Costs on appeal	... 286
36	Constable to carry on appeal	... 287
37	Summoning witnesses	... 288
38	Penalty on witnesses	... 288
41	Penalty on drunkards	... 289
42	Procedure for penalties	... 289
43	How excise penalties recovered...	... 290
44	Covenant against using land for public house	... 290

Revenue (No. 1) Act, 1861 (24 & 25 Vict. c. 21).

2	Dealers in spirits additional retail license ...	... 291
3	Table-beer license	... 291

Revenue (No. 2) Act, 1861 (24 & 25 Vict. c. 91).

8	Compulsory license for late refreshment houses	... 292
9	Duty according to valuation of premises ...	... 292
10	Beerhouses may have wine licenses	... 293
11	Beer license exempt from penalties for wine ...	... 294
13	Beer or spirits at fairs and races	... 294
14	Licenses to expire on 10th October	... 294

Revenue Act, 1862 (25 & 26 Vict. c. 22).

12	Beer, &c., at races or fairs	... 295
13	Occasional licenses from two justices	... 295
15	Transfer of license by excise	... 296

b 2

Tippling Act, 1862 (25 & 26 Vict. c. 38).

SECTION		PAGE
1	No action for less than 20s. of spirits	297
	Tippling Act (24 Geo. 2, c. 40, s. 12)	298

Revenue Act, 1863 (26 & 27 Vict. c. 33).

1	Beer dealer's additional retail license	299
18	Wine license to include sweets	300
19	Altering duty on occasional license	300
20	Altering law as to occasional license	301
21	As to fairs and races	301

Innkeepers Liability Act, 1863 (26 & 27 Vict. c. 41).

1	Innkeeper not liable beyond 30l.	302
2	Obligation to receive guests	304
3	Notice to be exhibited	304
4	Interpretation of terms	305

Revenue (No. 1) Act, 1864 (27 & 28 Vict. c. 18).

5	Occasional licenses	305

Public House Closing Act, 1864 (27 & 28 Vict. c. 64).

3, 4	Definitions	307
5	Closing night refreshment house	307
7	Occasional license	308
8	Definition of local authority	308
10	Not to apply to railway stations	309

Public House Closing Act, 1865 (28 & 29 Vict. c. 77).

2	License to accommodate trades	309
3	Withdrawing license	310
5	Justices to grant licenses	310

Revenue Act, 1867 (30 & 31 Vict. c. 90).

SECTION		PAGE
17	Soliciting orders for spirits	311
18	Duty on methylated spirits	311

Wine and Beerhouse Act, 1869 (32 & 33 Vict. c. 27).

2	Definition of beer and cider	313
4	Excise license certificate...	313
5	By whom certificates granted	313
6	Form of certificate	314
7	Notice before new certificate	314
8	Justices to refuse certificate for out-door licenses on certain grounds only	317
11	Forgery of certificate	321
19	Renewal of existing licenses	323
20	Saving of privileges	324
21	Repeal of prior enactments	325
	Schedule thereof...	326

Wine and Beerhouse Act, 1870 (33 & 34 Vict. c. 29).

3	Definition of terms	327
4	Amendment of 32 & 33 Vict. c. 27, ss. 5, 6, 7, 8, 9	327
7	Amendment of 32 & 33 Vict. c. 27, s. 19	330
10	Beer dealer's additional retail license	331
11	Postponing grants and renewals	331
14	Convicted of felony cannot sell spirits...	332
16	Repeal of brewer's retail license	333

Beerhouse Act, 1870 (33 & 34 Vict. c. 111).

1	Valuation of some premises in townships	333

Innkeepers Act, 1878 (41 & 42 Vict. c. 38, s. 1).

	Landlord may dispose of goods left after six weeks	335

Beer Dealer's Retail Licenses Act, 1880
(43 Vict. c. 6).

SECTION		PAGE
1	Justices to have discretion as to beer dealer's retail licenses...	337
2	Licenses at annual meetings only	339

Revenue Act, 1880 (43 & 44 Vict. c. 20).

34	Beer brewed for domestic use	340
41, 42	Duties on excise licenses for retailing cider, sweets, beer, wine	341
43	Duties on retailing of spirits	342
45	Duties on sale of liquors in boats	344
47	Meaning of excisable liquors	345

Spirits Act, 1880 (43 & 44 Vict. c. 24).

101	Situation of retailer's premises	346
102	Restrictions on sale	346
103	Penalty for excess in stock	347
104	Meaning of sale by retail	347
145	Unlawfully removing spirits	348
146	Hawking spirits	348
147	Sale for unlawful purposes	348
148	Unlawful purchase	349
149	Possessing spirits duty not paid	349
155	Informers	349
156	Procedure	349

Sunday Closing (Wales) Act, 1881
(44 & 45 Vict. c. 61).

1	Premises in Wales closed on Sunday	350
2	Application of Licensing Acts	350
3	Commencement of Act	351
4	Sale of liquors at railway stations	351

Beer Dealer's Retail Licenses Act, 1882
(45 & 46 Vict. c. 34).

1	Justices' discretion as to off beer licenses	352
2	Certificates at annual meeting only	353

TABLE OF SECTIONS. xxiii

Payment of Wages in Public Houses Act, 1883
(46 & 47 Vict. c. 31).

SECTION	PAGE
2 Definition of workman	... 354
4 No wages to be paid in public-houses	... 355
4 Penalties	... 356
Polls and elections in inns	... 356

Licensing (Evidence) Act, 1884
(47 & 48 Vict. c. 29).

Extension of 35 & 36 Vict. c. 94, s. 41... 358

Sale to Children Act, 1886 (49 & 50 Vict. c. 56).

1 Sale to children illegal 359
2 Construed with Licensing Acts... 359

Cruelty to Children Act, 1889
(52 & 53 Vict. c. 44).

3 Employing children in licensed premises 361

Form of dealer's excise license 363
Form of excise publican's license 365
Form of excise temporary license 365
Form of justices' consent to occasional license 365
Form of occasional license 366
Form of refreshment house license 366
Forms of justices' licenses and certificates 368
Case of *Sharp* v. *Wakefield* 374

TABLE OF STATUTES AND SECTIONS.

[NOTE.—*Those statutes which are in the Appendix have only the first page stated here.*]

	PAGE
21 Jas. 1, c. 7	23
16 Geo. 2, c. 8, s. 12	147
24 Geo. 2, c. 40, s. 12	298
25 Geo. 2, c. 36, s. 2	34
s. 3	35
s. 4	35
21 Geo. 3, c. 49, ss. 1, 2, 3, 5	172
35 Geo. 3, c. 113, s. 1	12
s. 9	10
39 Geo. 3, c. 79, s. 14	33
51 Geo. 3, c. 36	225
57 Geo. 3, c. 19	33
6 Geo. 4, c. 81	4, 147, 250
7 & 8 Geo. 4, c. 53, s. 78	250, 267
s. 22	197
9 Geo. 4, c. 47	147
9 Geo. 4, c. 61	212
1 Will. 4, c. 51, s. 22	147
11 Geo. 4 and 1 Will. 4, c. 64	247
1 & 2 Will. 4, c. 32, ss. 18, 26	300, 305
4 & 5 Will. 4, c. 51	250, 267
4 & 5 Will. 4, c. 75, s. 10	147
4 & 5 Will. 4, c. 85	258
5 & 6 Will. 4, c. 39, s. 7	35, 144, 146
2 & 3 Vict. c. 14, s. 29	144
2 & 3 Vict. c. xciv., s. 27	17
s. 29	20
s. 30	144
s. 37	25
2 & 3 Vict. c. 47, s. 14	82
s. 43	17

TABLE OF STATUTES AND SECTIONS.

	PAGE
2 & 3 Vict. c. 47, s. 45	20, 144
s. 46	144
s. 58	25
2 & 3 Vict. c. 71, s. 14	82
2 & 3 Vict. c. 93, s. 16	45
3 & 4 Vict. c. 61	263
5 & 6 Vict. c. 44	269
6 & 7 Vict. c. 68	144
s. 2	144
ss. 3, 5, 7, 9, 11	145
ss. 12—15, 19, 20	145
s. 23	145
7 & 8 Vict. c. 33, s. 7	220
8 & 9 Vict. c. 109, ss. 3, 6, 7	48
s. 10	161
s. 11	47, 162
s. 12	163
s. 13	164
s. 14	163
s. 18	49
s. 20	164
10 & 11 Vict. c. 89, s. 29	25
s. 34	45
s. 35	29
11 & 12 Vict. c. 43, s. 5	27
s. 18	113
s. 19	9, 113, 115
s. 20	113
s. 21	113, 115
s. 22	113
s. 24	26
s. 27	243, 245
s. 31	138
11 & 12 Vict. c. 49	307
11 & 12 Vict. c. 121, s. 9	9
12 & 13 Vict. c. 45, s. 1	120, 239
s. 2	120
s. 5	243
s. 18	244

TABLE OF STATUTES AND SECTIONS. xxvii

	PAGE
12 & 13 Vict. c. 92, s. 2	33
16 & 17 Vict. c. 68, s. 6	355
16 & 17 Vict. c. 119, s. 1	49
s. 2	49
s. 3	50
ss. 4—6	52
s. 7	53
s. 11	53
s. 12	54
s. 13	54
17 & 18 Vict. c. 38, s. 3	48
s. 4	48
ss. 5, 6	48
ss. 10, 11	49
18 & 19 Vict. c. 38, s. 3	146
18 & 19 Vict. c. 48	225
18 & 19 Vict. c. 118	307
18 & 19 Vict. c. 120, ss. 249, 250	97, 211
20 & 21 Vict. c. 43, s. 2	122, 124
s. 14	123
21 & 22 Vict. c. 73, s. 5	114
s. 7	82
22 Vict. c. 32	116, 138
23 Vict. c. 27	273
23 & 24 Vict. c. 113	9, 227
24 & 25 Vict. c. 21	291
24 & 25 Vict. c. 91	292
25 Vict. c. 22, s. 16	144
s. 19	144
25 & 26 Vict. c. 22	295
25 & 26 Vict. c. 38	297
25 & 26 Vict. c. 102, ss. 42, 112	97, 211
26 & 27 Vict. c. 33	299
26 & 27 Vict. c. 41	302
27 & 28 Vict. c. 18	305
27 & 28 Vict. c. 64	307
28 & 29 Vict. c. 77	309
30 & 31 Vict. c. 90, s. 12	144
s. 17	310

xxviii   TABLE OF STATUTES AND SECTIONS.

	PAGE
30 & 31 Vict. c. 90, s. 18	147
32 & 33 Vict. c. 14	304
32 & 33 Vict. c. 27	312
32 & 33 Vict. c. 47, s. 1	220, 221
ss. 2, 3	221
s. 7	220
32 & 33 Vict. c. 53	225
33 & 34 Vict. c. 29	326
33 & 34 Vict. c. 111	333
34 & 35 Vict. c. 103, s. 31	305
34 & 35 Vict. c. 112, s. 10	31, 120
s. 18	131
35 & 36 Vict. c. 77, s. 9	354
35 & 36 Vict. c. 79, s. 4	208
35 & 36 Vict. c. 92, s. 7	237
35 & 36 Vict. c. 94	1, 186
36 & 37 Vict. c. 18, s. 4	304
37 & 38 Vict. c. 15, s. 3	53
37 & 38 Vict. c. 49	168
37 & 38 Vict. c. 68	144
37 & 38 Vict. c. 96	269
38 & 39 Vict. c. 21, s. 1	36
38 & 39 Vict. c. 23, s. 9	341
38 & 39 Vict. c. 55	209
s. 128	358
38 & 39 Vict. c. 60	295
38 & 39 Vict. c. 63, s. 2	191
s. 6	189
s. 8	189
ss. 13, 14, 17, 21	189, 191
s. 25	192
38 & 39 Vict. c. 66, Sched.	225
38 & 39 Vict. c. 80, s. 1	172
38 & 39 Vict. c. 90, s. 10	354
39 & 40 Vict. c. 16, s. 4	273
s. 5	305
39 & 40 Vict. c. 20, s. 5	32, 113
41 & 42 Vict. c. 38	335
41 & 42 Vict. c. 32, ss. 11, 12	146

TABLE OF STATUTES AND SECTIONS.

	PAGE
41 & 42 Vict. c. 49, ss. 22, 28, 45, 46, 48	19
41 & 42 Vict. c. 77, s. 26	24
41 & 42 Vict. c. 79	267
42 & 43 Vict. c. 18, ss. 2, 4, 7	37, 38
42 & 43 Vict. c. 30, s. 6	189
s. 10	191
42 & 43 Vict. c. 49, s. 4	110, 116
s. 5	110, 111
s. 7	112
s. 8	112
s. 16	112
s. 17	8, 113
s. 19	212
s. 21	115
s. 22	8, 116
s. 31	119, 228
s. 32	120
s. 33	121, 122, 123, 125
s. 39	110, 115
s. 41	116
s. 43	115
s. 46	135
43 Vict. c. 6	337
43 & 44 Vict. c. 9, s. 1	172, 179
43 & 44 Vict. c. 20	340
43 & 44 Vict. c. 24, ss. 102—104	10, 147, 346
s. 146—156	348
44 Vict. c. 12, s. 3	144
44 & 45 Vict. c. 58, ss. 103, 104	258
s. 107	258
s. 110	258, 259
s. 174	147
44 & 45 Vict. c. 61	350
45 & 46 Vict. c. 34	352
45 & 46 Vict. c. 50, ss. 6, 7	221
s. 23	24
s. 154	219
s. 155	219
s. 160	219, 355

TABLE OF STATUTES AND SECTIONS.

	PAGE
45 & 46 Vict. c. 50, s. 165	241
s. 221	138
s. 246	218
ss. 248, 256	219, 225
46 & 47 Vict. c. 18, ss. 13, 14	225
46 & 47 Vict. c. 31	305
46 & 47 Vict. c. 39, Sched.	166, 288
46 & 47 Vict. c. 51, s. 20	225, 357
s. 38	75, 356
47 & 48 Vict. c. 29	358
47 & 48 Vict. c. 43, s. 5	115, 250
s. 12	122
s. 31	51
47 & 48 Vict. c. 70, s. 16	356
s. 23	357
s. 36	357
48 & 49 Vict. c. 51	147, 190
s. 4	341
ss. 8, 9	190, 191
48 & 49 Vict. c. 69, s. 13	43
48 & 49 Vict. c. 75, s. 2	195
49 & 50 Vict. c. 56	359
50 & 51 Vict. c. 46, s. 4	357
50 & 51 Vict. c. 55, s. 14	357
50 & 51 Vict. c. 58, s. 11	354
51 & 52 Vict. c. 41, s. 3	33, 38, 41, 146
s. 7	144
s. 20	341
s. 40	35
s. 66	244
s. 85	24
51 & 52 Vict. c. 43, s. 182	298
52 Vict. c. 3, s. 7	34, 146, 148
52 Vict. c. 7, s. 3	144
52 & 53 Vict. c. 42, ss. 26, 27	10, 311, 341
52 & 53 Vict. c. 44, s. 3	360
52 & 53 Vict. c. 63, s. 3	175
s. 13	110, 117

TABLE OF STATUTES AND SECTIONS.   xxxi

	PAGE
52 & 53 Vict. c. 63, s. 26	119, 142
s. 33	... 132
53 Vict. c. 8, s. 7	... 341
s. 9	... 5
s. 31	... 147
53 & 54 Vict. c. 21, s. 21	5, 147
s. 32	... 5
s. 35	... 285
53 & 54 Vict. c. 33, s. 31	... 147
53 & 54 Vict. c. 45, s. 16	... 138
53 & 54 Vict. c. 51	... 147
53 & 54 Vict. c. 59, ss. 3, 6, 7...	...38, 41
s. 36	... 41
s. 51	... 40
54 & 55 Vict. c. 76, s. 63	... 358
55 Vict. c. 4	... 53
55 Vict. c. 9	... 49
56 & 57 Vict. c. 54	144, 185

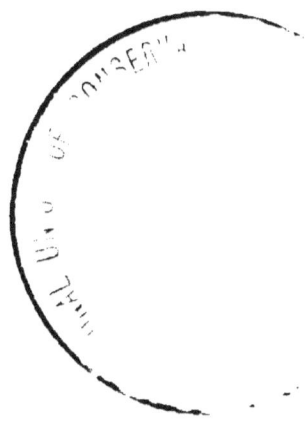

TABLE OF CASES CITED.

A

	PAGE
Abrahams v. Deakin	303
Addy v. Blake	19
Allen v. Lamb	6
Allen v. Smith	336
Allport v. Nutt	47
Angus v. Maclachlan	337
Annandale, re	77, 94
Anon	213
Archer v. Waldegrave	41
Armistead v. Wilde	302
Atkinson v. Sellers	182
Austin, ex parte	125
Authers, re	8, 120, 134, 148
Avards v. Dance	46

B.

Bailey, re	125
Baker v. Marsh	265
Baldwin v. Dover	234
Ballam v. Willshire	7
Banks v. Goodwin	124
Barnes v. Akroyd	28
Barnes v. Chip	192
Barnes v. Rider	191
Barnoyat v. Hutchinson	298
Bassett v. Goodchild	214, 215, 240
Bath v. White	13, 16
Baxter v. Langley	41, 172
Belasco v. Hannant	30
Bellis v. Beal	42
Bellis v. Burghall	41
Belton v. London County Council	235
Bendall, ex parte	90, 317
Bent v. Lister	164
Betts v. Armstead	191
Bew v. Harston	47
Blake v. Beach	48
Bond v. Evans	46, 184
Boodle v. Birmingham	235
Bosley v. Davis	46
Bowman v. Blyth	241
Bows v. Fenwick	51
Bowyer v. Percy Club	6
Brewer v. Shepherd	180
Brigden v. Heighes	59, 141, 171
Britnor, re	11, 236
Briton, re	218
Broad v. Perkins	218
Broadwood v. Granara	336
Brooker v. Wood	249
Brookes v. Drysdale	236, 256
Brown, re	9
Brown v. Foot	28, 191

	PAGE
Brown v. Nicholson	218
Brown v. Nugent	42
Buckle v. Fredericks	147, 257
Budenberg v. Roberts	123

C.

Caminada v. Hulton	53
Candlish v. Simpson	218
Carter v. Williams	254
Cashill v. Wright	302
Caswell v. Hundred JJ.	194
Cates v. South	179
Catt v. Tourle	255
Chamberlain, ex parte	161
Chambers v. Smith	315
Chisholm v. Doulton	28
Clark v. Hague	33
Clark v. Searle	41
Claydon v. Green	235
Clegg v. Hands	255
Clew, re	9
Cole v. Coulton	24, 29, 30
Cooper v. Osborne	47, 59, 206
Cooper v. Turbill	255
Copley v. Burton	182, 184
Corbett v. Haigh	59, 206
Core v. James	28
Cotterill v. Lempriere	26, 179
Coulbert v. Troke	184
Cowles v. Gale	7, 11, 235, 236
Cox v. Andrews	53
Crabtree v. Hole	46
Crofts v. Taylor	190
Crooksbank v. Rose	298
Cross v. Watts	13
Crowther v. Boult	124
Cullen v. Lancashire	42
Cundy v. Le Cocq	27
Curtis v. Buss	117, 241
Curtis v. Marsh	172, 179

D.

Dames v. Bond	183
Danford v. Taylor	46
Dansey v. Richardson	303, 338
Daun v. City of London Brewery	257
Daun v. Simmons	215, 303
Davis, ex parte	20, 24
Davis v. Stephenson	51
Dawson v. Remnant	298
Day v. Bather	30?
Day v. Lukke	335

c

TABLE OF CASES CITED.

	PAGE
Day v. Simpson	41, 146
Deal v. Schofield	13
D'Eresby, ex parte	236
Devine v. Keeling	67
Diggle v. Higgs	49
Dixon v. Birch	215, 303
Dixon v. Steele	266
Dixon v. Wells	191
Drake, re	222, 315
Duffell v. Curtis	275
Dyke v. Gower	191
Dyson v. Mason	46, 47

E.

Eastwood v. Miller	51
Eddleston v. Barnes	132
Edmunds v. James	27
Edwards v. Roberts	123
Edwick v. Hawkes	255
Elder v. Smithson	192
Elstone v. Rose	218
Embleton v. Brown	135
Empson v. Metropolitan Board	315
Ethelstone, ex parte	27
Evans, ex parte	225, 241
Evans v. Hemingway	5

F.

Fairclough v. Roberts	4, 262, 300
Farmers v. Stevenson	192
Fell v. Knight	337
Fielden v. Slater	254
Finch v. Blundell	180
Fisher v. Howard	182
Fleetwood v. Hull	188, 256
Foot v. Baker	46
Foot v. Butler	48, 50
Forsdike v. Colquhoun	172, 351
Foster v. Foster	217
Frailing v. Messenger	42
Francis v. Hayward	236
Fredericks v. Payne	145
Freeman v. Read	244

G.

Gage v. Elsey	190
Gallimore v. Goodall	183
Galloway v. Marles	51
Garford v. Esam	192
Garrett v. Messenger	42
Garrett v. Middlesex	107, 205, 240
Garrety v. Potts	100, 242, 265
Garton v. Southampton	225
Gay v. Mathews	243
Gill v. Bright	8, 21, 197
Girdlestone v. Brighton	172
Gordon v. Silber	336
Gould v. Haynes	357
Graff v. Evans	5

	PAGE
Great North R. v. Inett	124
Green v. Botheroyd	41
Gregory v. Tuffs	41, 42
Greig v. Bendeno	30, 43
Griffiths v. Lancashire	91
Guaglieni v. Mathews	42

H.

Halgh v. Sheffield	51
Hale v. Cole	189
Hall v. Box	254
Hall v. Green	42
Hampden v. Walsh	49
Hanbury v. Cundy	255
Hannant v. Foulger	300
Hare v. Osborne	47, 59, 184, 206
Hargrave v. Dawson	157, 324
Harman v. Powell	188, 257
Harris v. Jonns	154, 281
Harris v. May	192
Harrington, ex parte	145
Harrison v. Leaper	28
Harrison v. McL'Meel	149, 195
Harrison v. Richards	192
Hawthorn v. Hammond	103
Hay v. Tower JJ.	6, 333
Hayward v. Holland	197
Hazell v. Middleton	231
Herbert v. Markwell	304
Higgins v. Hall	191
Hoare v. Metropolitan Board of Works	236
Hocking v. Powell	241
Hoffman v. Bond	42
Holder v. Soulby	303, 338
Holt v. Collyer	255
Hope v. Warburton	27
Horder v. Scott	192
Hornsby v. Raggett	50
Hotchin v. Hindmarsh	191
Howell v. Jackson	103
Howes v. Inland Revenue	275
Howorth v. Minns	154, 313
Hoyle v. Hitchman	191
Hughes v. Done	298
Huntley v. Bedford	303
Huxham v. Wheeler	252, 294

J.

James, ex parte	85
Jefferson v. Richardson	180
Jenks v. Turpin	47
Jennings v. Manchester	265
Johnson v. Colam	42
Jones v. Bone	254, 291
Jones v. Cooper	160
Jones v. Jackson	304
Jones v. Osborne	303
Jones v. Thurloe	337
Jones v. Whittaker	161
Josselyn v. Parson	148
Joynt, ex parte	59, 141, 171

K.

	PAGE
Kay v. Over-Darwen	353
Keurly v. Tyler	28, 191
Kelloway v. MacDougal	275
Kemp v. Bird	254
Kenyon, ex parte	125
Kerwin v. Hines	43
Kirk v. Coates	191
Knight v. Bowers	192
Knight v. Halliwell	123
Knight v. Lee	49

L.

Langrish v. Archer	24
Lea v. Whittaker	236
Leader v. Yell	266
Leah v. Minns	313
Lester v. Torrens	25
Levy v. Yates	41
Llewellyn v. Rutherford	235, 236
Loudman v. Cragg	25
Lockhart v. St. Albans	123
Lon. & N. W. Rail. v. Garnett	254
London, &c., Co. v. Field	254
Luff v. Leaper	46
Luker v. Dennis	255

M.

Macbeth v. Ashley	377
Mackenzie v. Day	197
Mackinnell v. Robinson	48
MacWilliam v. Dawson	50
Mahon v. Gaskell	7, 158
Markham, ex parte	123
Marks v. Benjamin	41
Marshall v. Fox	32
Marson v. London & C. Rail. Co.	158, 215
Martin, ex parte	90
Martin v. Barker	146, 149, 171
Martin v. Pridgeon	25
Marwick v. Codlin	155, 210
Maugham, ex parte	222, 291
Maw v. Hindmarsh	130, 256
Mayer v. Harding	124
Mayhew v. Suttle	215
Medawar v. Grand Hotel	302, 304
Menzies v. Lightfoot	257
Mercantile Co. v. International	315
Meux v. Humphries	249
Minett, ex parte	233
Modlen v. Snowball	235
Moody v. Steggles	236
Moore v. Robinson	256
Moore v. Smith	262
Morgan, ex parte	90, 241
Morgan v. Edwards	124
Morgan v. Palmer	236
Morgan v. Ravey	302
Morley v. Greenhalgh	33
Morris v. Askew	190
Morris v. Johnson	190

	PAGE
Moufflet v. Cole	236, 256
Muir v. Hoare	123
Muir v. Keay	275
Mulliner v. Florence	336
Mullins v. Collins	45
Murray v. Freer	92, 231, 323, 328
Murray v. Thompson	186

N.

Newell v. Hemingway	5
Newman v. Bendyshe	179
Newman v. Earl of Hardwicke	57
Newman v. Jones	5
Nichol v. Fenning	255
Norton v. Salisbury	315
Nunn v. Southall	275

O.

Oldham v. Ramsden	50
Oppenheim v. White Lion	304
Ormerod v. Chadwick	85
Osborne v. Hare	47, 59
Ovenden v. Raymond	59, 164, 184, 206
Overton v. Hunter	179
Owen v. Langford	4
Owens v. Porter	298

P.

Paine v. Boughtwood	191
Palmer v. Thatcher	3, 123, 148, 213, 274
Parker v. Flint	213
Parker v. Green	30
Parsons v. Alexander	49
Pashler v. Stevenill	189
Patman v. Harland	255
Patten v. Rhymer	46, 47
Payne v. Hack	191
Payne v. Thomas	19
Peache v. Coleman	184
Peacock v. R.	123
Pearse v. Gill	180
Pearson v. Broadbent	7, 314
Pease v. Coates	254
Penn v. Alexander	183
Peplow v. Richardson	182
Petherick v. Sargent	135, 179
Phillips, ex parte	87, 271
Philpott v. Jones	298
Piddlesden, ex parte	265
Pigeon v. Legge	55
Pine v. Barnes	184, 206
Pinnett, ex parte	235
Portingell, ex parte	89
Preston v. Buckley	265, 334
Price v. James	87, 121, 123, 242, 271
Proctor v. Nicholson	298
Pulbrook v. Ashby	296
Purkis v. Huxtable	30

xxxvi   TABLE OF CASES CITED.

Q.

Quaglieni v. Mathews 42

R.

Railway Sleepers Co., In re 120, 315
R. v. Aberdare 315
—— Allmey 265
—— Andover JJ. 117, 205
—— Anglesey JJ. 89
—— Anglesey (56 J. P. 532)......120, 241
—— Archdall 144, 252
—— Ashton 47, 319
—— Athay 214
—— Aulton 19
—— Barrett........................... 43
—— Barton 215
—— Beckley 225
—— Belton 215, 226, 241
—— Binney 244
—— Birley 315
—— Birmingham 91, 317
—— Bishop 274
—— Blackburn 85, 299
—— Bodmin 217
—— Boteler................... 214, 375
—— Bolton 125
—— Bristol 241
—— Bristol JJ. (57 J. P. 486)....121, 242
—— Bryan 218
—— Byrde 121
—— Cambridge Union............ 241
—— Carnarvon 215, 226
—— Caulfield 315
—— Charlesworth 264
—— Cheshire JJ. 117, 251
—— Congleton JJ. 92, 203, 216
—— Cox 215, 226
—— Crewkerne JJ. 104, 177, 210, 217
—— Cumberland 97, 137, 319
—— Curzon 157, 233, 324
—— Dale 138
—— Davidson 244
—— Davis 216
—— Deal 218
—— Deane 240
—— De Rutzen 274, 291, 299
—— Devonport JJ. 244
—— Devonshire JJ. 161
—— Dobbins 194
—— Downs 7, 218
—— Eales 91, 203
—— Edwards 213
—— Ely JJ. 244
—— Essex JJ. 89, 338
—— Essex (56 J. P. 375) 218
—— Exeter JJ. 99, 217
—— Farquhar 91, 216
—— Farrant 218
—— Ferguson 218
—— Fletcher (L. R. 1 C. C. 320) 26
—— Fletcher (48 J. P. 407)........... 26
—— Fraser 217

R. v. Garrett................... 107, 205
—— Gibbon 218
—— Gillyard 125
—— Glamorgan (24 Q. B. D. 675) .. 120
—— Glamorganshire (56 J. P. 100).. 117, 121, 123, 241
—— Glamorganshire (22 Q. B. D. 623) 10, 286
—— Glamorganshire (1 Q. B. D. 55) 265, 274, 291, 299
—— Gloucester JJ................ 216
—— Goodall 244
—— Great Yarmouth 218
—— Grove 85, 159, 229
—— Handley 26, 218
—— Hanley 317
—— Hannay 35
—— Hants JJ............... 7, 158, 244
—— Harries....................... 215
—— Henley 218
—— Hereford 90, 157
—— Herts JJ. 193
—— Holland JJ. 43
—— Holland 215, 216
—— Holmes....................... 214
—— Hopkins 9
—— Howard 92, 203, 216, 217
—— Huddersfield 318
—— Hughes 25, 48, 85
—— Hughes (1893) 153
—— Hull JJ. 231
—— Huntley 244
—— Inland Revenue........... 35, 146
—— Ivens......................... 103
—— Jenkins........... 5, 10, 147, 178
—— Kensington.............. 258, 265
—— Kent JJ. 91, 216, 218
—— King .. 92, 216, 294, 318, 323, 338, 353
—— Kirkdale JJ. 222, 291
—— Knapp........................ 174
—— Lancashire JJ. (L. R. 6 Q. B. 97) 214, 382
—— Lancashire JJ. (41 J. P. 293) .. 120
—— Lancashire (55 J. P. 580) .. 91, 317, 318
—— Langridge 265, 249
—— Lawrence 93, 125, 156, 222, 230, 233
—— Leader 266, 317
—— Lee........................... 218
—— Liverpool JJ. (52 J. P. 376) 106
—— Liverpool JJ. 93, 125, 156, 222, 230, 233
—— London County Council......37, 226
—— London JJ 201
—— Long......................... 244
—— Lucilin...................... 103
—— Mainwaring 241
—— Manchester JJ..... 92, 216, 294, 318, 323, 338, 353
—— Mann................... 99, 217
—— Market Bosworth...... 93, 157, 210
—— Marshall 218
—— Maule 236

TABLE OF CASES CITED. xxxvii

	PAGE
R. v. Merthyr Tydvil	89, 91, 317
—— Meyer	218, 226
—— Middlesex JJ.	77, 94, 232, 240
—— Milledge	218
—— Minshul	6, 249
—— Miskin Higher	91, 93, 231
—— Monmouth	215
—— Monmouthshire	215, 226, 274, 318
—— Montagu	101, 222, 318
—— Moore	193
—— Morison	317
—— Mortlock	244
—— Newborough	217
—— Newcastle (42 J. P. 598)	9
—— Newcastle JJ. (51 J. P. 244)	93, 203, 217, 222, 233
—— Newcastle JJ. (3 Q. B. D. 545)	9
—— Newton	44, 123
—— North	179
—— North Riding JJ.	241
—— Northumberland JJ.	230, 234
—— Over Darwen	299
—— Oxfordshire JJ.	120
—— Padwick	244
—— Pawlett	120, 240
—— Penkridge JJ.	315
—— Pilgrim	241, 324
—— Pirehill	216, 217
—— Powell	217, 230, 234
—— Pownal	94, 201
—— Pownall (1893), (2 Q. B. 158)	77
—— Raffles	7, 158
—— Rand	218
—— Reading JJ.	117, 241
—— Redditch	89, 91, 318
—— Rice	43, 47
—— Riley	85, 315
—— Rogers	215, 226
—— Rogier	47
—— Rosenthal	145
—— Rowell	232
—— Rymer	55, 303, 337
—— Sainsbury	216
—— Salford	260
—— Schneider	353
—— Scott	92, 140, 216, 319, 338
—— Shropshire	315
—— Smith (37 J. P. 214)	140, 204, 216, 318, 320
—— Smith (31 J. P. 259)	7, 158
—— Smith (42 J. P. 295)	90, 157
—— Southport JJ.	140, 204, 216, 318, 320
—— South Holland	217
—— Staffordshire	216
—— Stannard	43
—— Stephens	28
—— Strugnell	145
—— Surrey JJ.	217
—— Surrey JJ. (3 Q. B. D. 374)	92, 319
—— Surrey JJ. (52 J. P. 423)	214, 217, 240, 275
—— Surrey JJ. (L. R. 5 Q. B. 466)	217

	PAGE
R. v. Sykes	7, 158, 318
—— Sylvester	214, 376
—— Taylor	232
—— Thomas	93, 216, 230, 234
—— Tooke	218
—— Tott	195
—— Tucker	42
—— Upper Osgoldcross	230, 234
—— Vine	6, 333
—— Waghorn	265
—— Walsall	214
—— West Riding JJ. (21 Q. B. D. 258)	6, 42, 69, 157, 210, 229, 233, 324
—— West Riding JJ. (11 Q. B. D. 417)	193, 240, 333
—— West Riding JJ. (L. R. 5 Q. B. 33)	222, 315, 331
—— Welby	232
—— Wilkinson	214
—— Williams	216
—— Willoughby	55
—— Wilts JJ.	85, 159, 229
—— Withyham	258, 376
—— Wolfe	42
—— York (Mayor)	77
—— Young	216, 240
Rawnsley v. Hutchinson	241, 244
Read v. Anderson	49
Redgate v. Haynes	46
Reigate, Mayor of, v. Hart	138
Rice v. Slee	264
Richards v. Banks	274, 281
Richards v. MacBride	351
Richards v. Rivett	254
Richards v. Swansea	158, 215
Ritchie v. Smith	7, 12
Roberts v. Humphries	183
Roberts v. Woodward	28
Robinson v. Waddington	315
Robinson v. Walter	337
Rookes' Case	375
Rose v. Frogley	11
Rowell v. Norfolk JJ.	232
Ruddick v. Liverpool	91, 240
Rushworth, ex parte	222, 315
Rutter v. Daniel	236, 256
Rutter v. St. Albans	123

S.

Saint Albans v. Battersby	256
Saunders v. Baldy	132
Sandford v. Clarke	43
Sandys v. Florence	303
Sandys v. Small	190, 191
Salford, ex parte	265
Scatchard v. Johnson	14, 27, 136
Scott v. Gilmore	298
Senger v. White	109, 136
Searle v. Reynolds	28
Sewell v. Taylor	20, 24
Sharp v. Hughes	31

c 3

TABLE OF CASES CITED.

	PAGE
Sharp v. Wakefield	90, 203, 214, 231
Sharratt v. Scotney	260
Shaw v. Morley	51
Sheasby v. Oldham	183
Shepheard v. Walker	256
Shelley v. Bethell	145
Shoolbred v. St. Pancras	300
Short, ex parte	322
Shutt v. Lewis	41
Simmonds v. Blackheath JJ.	193, 231, 319, 328
Simpkin v. Birmingham JJ.	232
Simpkins, ex parte	124
Sims v. Pay	51, 132
Smith, ex parte	92, 318
Smith v. Dearlove	302, 336
Smith v. Hereford	90, 157, 378, 382
Smith v. Land Corporation	236
Smith v. Redding	264
Smith v. Vaux	180
Snead v. Watkins	336
Snow v. Hill	51
Somerset v. Hart	46
Somerset v. Miller	192
South Staffordshire v. Stone	123
Spice v. Bacon	304
Spicer v. Martin	257
Squire v. Wheeler	302
Stace v. Smith	192
Stacey v. Milne	171, 178
Stallard v. Marks	4, 274
Stancliffe v. Clarke	255
Stanhope v. Thorsby	123
Stevens v. Eupson	6, 218, 296
Stevens v. Green or Sharnbrook JJ.	183, 210, 230, 240, 333
Stevens v. Marston	255
Stevens v. Wood	5
Strauss v. County Hotel	303
Stringer v. Huddersfield	7, 138
Stuchberry v. Spencer	4, 274
Sunbolf v. Alford	337
Syers v. Conquest	41

T.

Tabarth, ex parte	157
Taite v. Gosling	256
Tarling v. Fredericks	145
Tassell v. Ovenden	141, 171
Tatam v. Reeve	49
Taylor v. Goodwin	24
Taylor v. Humphries	182
Taylor v. Oram	213, 275
Tennant v. Cumberland	179
Terry v. Brighton	172
Thomas v. Hayward	256
Thomas v. Powell	60
Thompson v. Greig	180
Thompson v. Harvey	6, 260, 265

	PAGE
Thompson v. Lacy	303, 338
Thornton v. Clegg	232, 234
Thornwall v. Johnson	255
Threlfall v. Borwick	336
Tippet v. Hart	340
Todd, re	229, 233
Tranter v. Lancashire	92, 319
Traynor v. Jones	231, 235
Turnbull v. Appleton	20
Turner v. Johnson	110, 137
Turrill v. Crawley	336
Tyson, re	214

U.

Ulttzer v. Nichols	303

V.

Vine v. Leeds	6, 333

W.

Walker v. Midland Railway Co.	303
Warden v. Tye	27
Warner v. Brighton	172
Washington v. Scott	264
Washington v. Young	19
Watkins, ex parte	244
Watt v. Glenister	183
Watteau v. Fenwick	304
Webb v. Catchlove	43
Webb v. Knight	190
Wells v. Attenborough	144
Wells v. Choyncy	55
West v. Potts	242
Wemyss v. Hopkins	132
Westbrook v. Griffith	337
Westmore v. Payne	123
Wheeker v. Webb	192
Whiffen v. Malling	91, 320
White v. Coquetdale	233
Whitehurst v. Fincher	50
Whitfield v. Bainbridge	30
Wigan v. Strange	146
Wilson v. Hart	254
Wilson v. Rastall	375
Wilson v. Stuart	27
Windsor v. Jeffrey	264
Winn v. Mossman	138, 244
Woodhouse v. Woods	124
Wooler v. Knott	188, 256
Wray v. Toke	28, 31
Wright v. Harris	218
Wynne v. Ronaldson	124

Y.

Young v. Higgin	315

INTRODUCTION.

The sale of Intoxicating Liquors by retail is now dealt with mostly in five separate statutes, or groups of statutes.

The Alehouse Act, 1828, 9 Geo. 4, c. 61, amended by 5 & 6 Vict. c. 44, and qualified by provisions in the Municipal Corporations Act, 1882, dealt with the houses known as inns, alehouses, and victualling-houses where intoxicating liquors are consumed on the premises, the leading feature of which was, that before intoxicating liquors could be sold in such houses, a license from the justices at the general annual licensing meeting or the adjournment was necessary. And there were numerous miscellaneous offences arising out of the conduct of such houses. The first of these statutes is still the root of the jurisdiction of licensing justices.

The Beerhouse Acts, 1830, 1 Will. 4, c. 64 ; 1834, 4 & 5 Will. 4, c. 85 ; 1840, 3 & 4 Vict. c. 61 ; 1870, 33 & 34 Vict. c. 111 ; 43 Vict. c. 6, and 45 & 46 Vict. c. 34, dealt with the houses or rather shops for the sale of beer and cider by retail both for consumption on the premises and off the premises, and at first such houses were allowed to be opened and carried on without requiring any guarantee of character, though after a few years a certificate of good character. signed by a few neighbours, and of a very imperfect nature, was required as a basis for the excise license. A rating and now a valuation qualification was next added. But up to 1869 no justices' license or certificate was required, and thus an important guarantee of character had been omitted, which was then supplied.

The Wine and Refreshment Houses Act, 23 Vict. c. 27, amended and added to by Revenue Acts, 1861 (No. 1), 24 & 25 Vict. c. 21; 1861 (No. 2), 24 & 25 Vict. c. 91; 1862 (No. 1), 25 & 26 Vict. c. 22; 1862 (No. 2), 25 & 26 Vict. c. 38; 1863, 26 & 27 Vict. c. 33; 1864, 27 & 28 Vict. c. 18; 1880, 43 & 44 Vict. c. 20, followed the analogy of the Beerhouse Acts, and not of the Alehouse Acts.

At last the Wine and Beerhouse Acts, 1869, 1870, 32 & 33 Vict. c. 27; 33 & 34 Vict. c. 29, were passed with a view to supplement the conspicuous deficiency of the Acts as to beer-houses, wine and refreshment houses, by requiring thereafter a certificate from justices for the sale of all intoxicating liquors by retail, and which certificate was tantamount to the alehouse license granted by justices, though not identical in all respects. One or two other retail licenses not included in the Beerhouse or Wine Licenses Acts were also included in the Wine and Beer-house Act of 1869, and treated in the same manner—so far, at least, as to require in all the cases a justices' certificate as a preliminary condition. And the discretion of justices in dealing with beer licenses was again changed by later statutes of 43 Vict. c. 6, and 45 & 46 Vict. c. 34.

It may be also added that, in addition to the four groups of statutes already mentioned, there was a separate group which dealt with the closing of all such houses on *Sundays*, and to some extent also on week-days during the night. These Acts at first applied to all licensed houses, but now are confined to refreshment houses which do not supply intoxicating liquors.

The Licensing Act of 1872, while repealing entirely the Sunday Acts, as regards all houses licensed to sell liquor, though not as

INTRODUCTION. xli

regards refreshment houses where no intoxicating liquor is sold, and substituting new provisions as to Sunday, Christmas Day, and Good Friday, left a considerable portion of all the other Acts untouched. It introduced more uniformity into the management of houses, by requiring a justices' license or certificate (these being now practically equivalent terms) substantially in all cases where intoxicating liquor is sold by retail. Numerous miscellaneous offences connected with such management were singled out for separate treatment, and the punishment generally was increased. In an Act of that kind, however, which was not a consolidation Act, but was designed merely to supplement the more important deficiencies of former Acts, the process of recasting and moulding anew the enactments had been attended with some losses and anomalies which were almost inevitable, and these were further increased by the necessity of references and cross-references between so many statutes, from each of which the others borrowed something.

The Licensing Act, 1874, did not attempt to disturb the settlement contained in the Act of 1872, but merely corrected one or two anomalies which had attracted prominent notice, and added a few minor details supplementary to those in the prior Act.

The leading provisions of the outstanding enactments as to the grant of licenses and certificates may be conveniently classed under the following heads, and will be found noticed in greater detail under the following references :—

Publicans' licenses (new or old). Discretion unlimited.
    9 Geo. 4, c. 61, s. 1.

    „   transfer. Discretion unlimited.
        9 Geo. 4, c. 61, ss. 4, 14.

    „   renewal. Discretion unlimited.
        9 Geo. 4, c. 61, s. 1.
        Licensing Act, 1872, s. 42.

Beer license, new (off and on). Discretion unlimited.
9 Geo. 4, c. 61.
32 & 33 Vict. c. 27, s. 8.
33 & 34 Vict. c. 29, s. 5.
43 Vict. c. 6.
45 & 46 Vict. c. 34.

„ renewal (off and on). Discretion unlimited.

„ transfer (off and on). Discretion unlimited.

„ if existing since 1869 (on). Discretion limited.
32 & 33 Vict. c. 27, s. 19.

Cider license, new (on) license. Discretion unlimited.
35 & 36 Vict. c. 94, s. 45.

„ renewal and transfer (on). Discretion unlimited.
„ if existing since 1869 (on). Discretion limited.
„ new (off). Discretion limited.
32 & 33 Vict. c. 27, s. 8.

„ renewal and transfer (off) license. Discretion limited.

Wine license, new (on) license. Discretion unlimited.
35 & 36 Vict. c. 94, s. 45.

„ renewal and transfer (on). Discretion unlimited.

„ if existing since 1869 (on) renewal and transfer. Discretion limited.

„ new (off) license. Discretion limited.
32 & 33 Vict. c. 27, s. 8.

„ renewal and transfer (off). Discretion limited.

Spirits and liqueurs, new (off) license. Discretion limited.
Licensing Act, 1872, section 69.
32 & 33 Vict. c. 27, s. 8.

„ renewal and transfer (off). Discretion limited.
Licensing Act, 1872, section 69.
32 & 33 Vict. c. 27, s. 8.
33 & 34 Vict. c. 29, s. 4.

Sweets, new (off) license. Discretion limited.
Licensing Act, 1872, section 74.
32 & 33 Vict. c. 27, s. 8.

„ renewal and transfer (off). Discretion limited.

„ new (on) license. Discretion unlimited.
Licensing Act, 1872, sections 45 and 74.
23 Vict. c. 27, s. 7.
32 & 33 Vict. c. 27, s. 8.

INTRODUCTION. xliii

Sweets, renewal and transfer (on). Discretion unlimited.
    ,,   if existing since 1869 (on) renewal and transfer.
            Discretion limited.
Valuation qualification—new publicans' licenses since 1872.
        Licensing Act, 1872, section 45.
    ,,   since 1872 (on), beer, cider, wine, sweets.
            Licensing Act, 1872, sections 45, 47.
    ,,   if existing before 1872, beer and cider (on).
            3 & 4 Vict. c. 61.
            33 & 34 Vict. c. 29, s. 10.
            Licensing Act, 1872, sections 46, 47.
    ,,   if existing before 1872, wine and sweets (on).
            23 Vict. c. 27, s. 8.
            Licensing Act, 1872, sections 46, 47.
    ,,   beer and cider (off).
            3 & 4 Vict. c. 61, s. 1.
            Licensing Act, 1872, sections, 46, 47.
General annual licensing meeting for *all new and renewal licenses*, time of holding.
        32 & 33 Vict. c. 27, s. 8.
        9 Geo. 4, c. 61, s. 1.
        33 & 34 Vict. c. 29, s. 4.
Transfer sessions, when held and cases entertained.
        9 Geo. 4, c. 61, ss. 4, 14.
        33 & 34 Vict. c. 29, s. 4.
        Licensing Act, 1874, section 15.
Petty sessions, temporary license between transfer sessions.
        5 & 6 Vict. c. 44.
Notices by applicants for new license.
        Licensing Act, 1872, section 40.
        32 & 33 Vict. c. 27, s. 7.
    ,,   for transfer in a few cases.
            Licensing Act, 1872, section 40.
            9 Geo. 4, c. 61, ss. 4, 14.
No notices for renewal licenses.
Notices of opposition to renewals.
        Licensing Act, 1872, section 42.
        Licensing Act, 1874, section 26.
Confirmation of all new (on) licenses.
        Licensing Act, 1872, sections 38, 39, 43.
        Licensing Act, 1874, section 24.
No confirmation for new (off) licenses.
        Licensing Act, 1874, section 24.

INTRODUCTION.

Provisional grants.
: Licensing Act, 1872, section 50 ; Act, 1874, s. 22.

Removal grants.
: Licensing Act, 1872, section 50 ; Act, 1874, s. 22.

Six-day licenses.
: Licensing Act, 1872, section 49.

Early closing licenses.
: Licensing Act, 1874, section 7.

Excise temporary license.
: Licensing Act, 1872, section 53.

Exemption orders.
: Licensing Act, 1872, sections 26, 29.

Occasional licenses for other places.
: 24 & 25 Vict. c. 22, s. 13.
  26 & 27 Vict. c. 33, s. 20.
  27 & 28 Vict. c. 18, s. 5.

" licenses for fairs and races.
: 25 & 26 Vict. c. 22, s. 13.
  26 & 27 Vict. c. 33, ss. 19, 21.
  27 & 28 Vict. c. 18, s. 5.
  Licensing Act, 1874, sections 19, 20.

No appeal to quarter sessions against refusal of new licenses.
: 35 & 36 Vict. c. 94, sec Schedule.
  37 & 38 Vict. c. 49, s. 27.

Appeal as to all renewals and transfers of licenses and certificates.
: 9 Geo. 4, c. 61, s. 27.
  32 & 33 Vict. c. 27, s. 8.
  33 & 34 Vict. c. 29, s. 4.

Closing on Sundays, Christmas Day, and Good Friday.
: 37 & 38 Vict. c. 49, ss. 3, 9.
  44 & 45 Vict. c. 61 (Welsh).
  27 & 28 Vict. c. 64 (Refreshment Houses).

The various particulars relating to other details will be found in the Index under their appropriate heads.

THE LICENSING ACTS.

INTOXICATING LIQUOR LICENSING ACT, 1872.

35 & 36 Vict. Cap. 94.

AN ACT for Regulating the Sale of Intoxicating Liquors. [10th August, 1872.]

WHEREAS it is expedient to amend the law for the sale by retail of intoxicating liquors, and the regulation of public houses and other places in which intoxicating liquors are sold, and to make further provision in respect of the grant of new licenses for the sale of intoxicating liquors, and the better prevention of drunkenness.

Be it enacted by the Queen's most excellent Majesty, by and with the advice and consent of the Lords Spiritual and Temporal, and Commons, in this present Parliament assembled, and by the authority of the same, as follows :—

Preliminary.

1. *Short title.*] This Act may be cited as "The Licensing Act, 1872."

2. *Extent of Act.*] This Act shall not extend to Scotland.

Sect. 3. **3.** *Prohibition of sale of intoxicating liquors without license.*] No person shall sell or expose for sale by retail any intoxicating liquor without being duly licensed to sell the same, or at any place where he is not authorised by his license to sell the same. Any person selling or exposing for sale by retail any intoxicating liquor which he is not licensed to sell by retail, or selling or exposing for sale any intoxicating liquor, at any place where he is not authorised by his license to sell the same, shall be subject to the following penalties; that is to say,—

> (1.) For the first offence he shall be liable to a penalty not exceeding fifty pounds, or to imprisonment with or without hard labour for a term not exceeding one month:
>
> (2.) For the second offence he shall be liable to a penalty not exceeding one hundred pounds, or to imprisonment with or without hard labour for a term not exceeding three months, and he may, by order of the court by which he is tried, be disqualified for any term not exceeding five years from holding any license for the sale of intoxicating liquors:
>
> (3.) For the third and any subsequent offence he shall be liable to a penalty not exceeding one hundred pounds, or to imprisonment with or without hard labour for any term not exceeding six months, and may, by order of the court by which he is tried, be disqualified for any term of years or for ever from holding any license for the sale of intoxicating liquors:

In addition to any other penalty imposed by this **Sect. 3.** section any person convicted of a second or any subsequent offence under this section shall, if he be the holder of a license, forfeit such license, and in the case of a conviction of any offence under this section, the court may, if it think expedient so to do, declare all intoxicating liquor found in the possession of any such person as last aforesaid, and the vessels containing such liquor, to be forfeited.

No penalty shall be incurred under this section by the heirs, executors, administrators, or assigns of any licensed person who *dies* before the expiration of his license, or by the trustee of any licensed person who is adjudged a *bankrupt*, or whose affairs are liquidated by arrangement before the expiration of his license in respect of the sale or exposure for sale of any intoxicating liquor, so that such sale or exposure for sale be made on the premises specified in such license, and take place prior to the special sessions then next ensuing, or (if such special session be holden within fourteen days next after the death of the said person or the appointment of a trustee in the case of his bankruptcy, or the liquidation of his affairs by arrangement) take place prior to the special session holden next after such special session as last aforesaid.

Selling liquors without a license.] This section applies to all public-houses, alehouses, houses included in the Wine and Beerhouse Acts, and all those requiring a justices' license. In some cases grocers or wine merchants holding a wine dealer's license may sell wine by retail, not to be consumed on the premises, under an additional retail license, though having no justices' license, being exempted under section 73 : *Palmer* v. *Thatcher*, 3 Q. B. D. 46 ; 47 L. J. M. C. 54 ; 37 L. T. 784 ; 42 J. P. 213. So as to spirit dealers in some cases, see notes to

Sect. 3. *Dealers' Licenses.*

NOTE. section 73, *post*. As to the evidence of sale, see section 62. As to occasional licenses, see section 29, *post*. Where the license holder goes abroad and is not heard of, a person entering and selling for his own profit is not protected, unless and until he gets a temporary or final transfer license: *Owen* v. *Langford*, 55 J. P. 484.

As to alehouses, the offence of selling without a license was dealt with by 9 Geo. 4, c. 61, s. 18. Under that section the penalty was put on "selling, bartering, exchanging, or for valuable consideration otherwise disposing of the liquor, or permitting" those things to be done. Here the offence is "selling or exposing for sale" only, and these words are not so extensive as the words in 9 Geo. 4, c. 61, s. 18, which section is now repealed. But "bartering or exchanging" will now be treated as in the nature of sale under section 62, *post*, and so equally within this penalty. The punishment under this section is much more severe than under 9 Geo. 4, c. 61, s. 18.

Dealers' licenses.] The dealers' or wholesale licenses for liquors are granted by the excise authorities under 6 Geo. 4, c. 81. By section 2, the license is obtained by beer dealers who sell strong beer only, in casks containing not less than four-and-a-half gallons imperial measure, or not less than two dozen reputed quart bottles, at one time, to be consumed elsewhere than on the premises. Each dealer's license excludes any selling for consumption on the premises. A *dealer* in liquors not by retail requires no justices' license, but only an *excise* license; and there may be a difficulty in deciding whether a licensed dealer in wines and spirits who has agencies in other towns requires a license also for the place where the agent takes orders: *Stallard* v. *Marks*, 3 Q. B. D. 412; 42 J. P. 359; 47 L. J. M. C. 91; 38 L. T. 566; 26 W. R. 694. The rule seems to be, that if the dealer keeps premises and stores elsewhere, and has an agent to take orders, he requires to be licensed there also; but if an agent elsewhere is not provided with premises, and takes orders as a traveller, then the dealer need not have a license at the agent's address: *Stuchberry* v. *Spencer*, 51 J. P. 181; 55 L. J. M. C. 141.

A beer dealer who, by 4 & 5 Will. 4, c. 85, and 26 & 27 Vict. c. 33, s. 1, is entitled to sell not less than four-and-a-half gallons or not less than two dozen reputed quart bottles at one time cannot be treated as selling without a license because he sells in pint bottles instead of quart bottles, provided the quantity sold at one time is the same: *Fairclough* v. *Roberts*, 24 Q. B. D. 350; 54 J. P. 421; 59 L. J. M. C. 54; 62 L. T. 700; 38 W. R. 330. All dealers in liquors by wholesale are excepted out of the restrictions

35 & 36 VICT. C. 94, S. 3.

Clubs supplying Liquors.   Sect. 3.
of the Licensing Acts as to times of selling, &c. See section 72,   NOTE.
post; *R.* v. *Jenkins*, 55 J. P. 824; 61 L. J. M. C. 57; 65 L. T. 857;
40 W. R. 318.

The general rule now is that every *excise license* to carry on any trade or business (except that of an appraiser, auctioneer, or hawker) shall only authorise the person to whom the license is granted to carry on the trade or business mentioned therein in one set of premises to be specified in the license: 53 Vict. c. 8, s. 9. And now, in most cases, no proceeding to recover an excise penalty before justices can be commenced without the order of the commissioners and the name of their officer or of the Attorney-General: 53 & 54 Vict. c. 21, s. 21. And informers may be rewarded by the commissioners: *Ibid.* s. 32.

Clubs supplying liquors.] The sale here meant is such a sale as takes place between buyer and seller in ordinary shops; and where there is a club or association of persons, on the footing of a subscription club, the committee of which buy liquor for the whole body, and then distribute it among the members according to rules and bye-laws of their own, this is not a sale: *Graff* v. *Evans*, 8 Q. B. D. 373; 46 J. P. 262; 51 L. J. M. C. 25; 46 L. T. 347. And for the same reason, if a limited company keep a club for the use of the company, and the directors purchase liquor and direct the manager or servant to distribute it among the shareholders according to a fixed tariff, what he does is not a sale within the meaning of this section: *Newell* v. *Hemingway*, 53 J. P. 324; 58 L. J. M. C. 314; 60 L. T. 544. Where there was a workman's subscription club, and a stranger entered and a member wrote down the stranger's name in the visitors' book, and took the money from the stranger, who asked for ale and it was supplied, the member was held liable for selling without a license: *Stevens* v. *Wood*, 54 J. P. 742. If the club is only a sham club, the person selling or distributing the liquor may be liable to the penalty: *Evans* v. *Hemingway*, 52 J. P. 134. Where a club is managed by a committee, who give express instructions to the manager not to sell liquor to non-subscribers, and he does so, the committeemen will not be liable, though the manager may be so: *Newman* v. *Jones*, 17 Q. B. D. 132; 50 J. P. 373; 55 L. J. M. C. 113; 55 L. T. 327. As to proprietary clubs, the rule would be different, and the proprietor or any servant actually managing the club would be deemed the person selling his own or his employers' liquors without a license. Thus, where a limited company kept a proprietary club and supplied members thereof with intoxicating liquor, keeping all the profits to the

Sect. 3.   *Void Licenses.*

NOTE. company, it was held that the company were liable for selling without a license: *Bowyer* v. *Percy Club*, 57 J. P. 470; (1893), 2 Q. B. 154.

Selling under a void license.] A distinction is drawn between a license which purports on the face of it to be regular, and one which is intrinsically void. Thus, where a justice of the petty sessional division only was authorised to grant an occasional license under 25 & 26 Vict. c. 22, s. 13, to sell at other places than the inn, and a justice not of the proper division granted it, the holder was held not liable for selling without a license: *Stevens* v. *Empson*, 1 Ex. D. 100; 40 J. P. 484; 45 L. J. M. C. 63; 33 L. T. 821. So an excise license granted without the overseers' certificate, contrary to 3 & 4 Vict. c. 61, s. 2, was held not void, though it would have been if the holder was not the real resident holder and occupier: *Thompson* v. *Harvey*, 4 H. & N. 254; 28 L. J. M. C. 163; 23 J. P. 150. And where a license was produced, but one of the signatures of the justices was suggested to be forged, though not by the license holder, the justices rightly refused to admit evidence of forgery, and held the license valid: *R.* v. *Minshul*, 1 N. & M. 278. So a beer license granted to a person who does not reside on the premises cannot usually be treated as void, though it may be voidable after obtaining a writ of *certiorari* under certain circumstances. And where a married woman clandestinely sold liquors without a license, the husband, who was not shown to know of her conduct, could not be treated as liable for her acts and so charged with the offence of selling without a license: *Allen* v. *Lumb*, 57 J. P. 376.

On the other hand, some licenses, though on the face of them regular, are treated as utterly void. Thus, a license granted to a person who had been previously convicted of felony, though no one but himself was aware of the felony, and a formal transfer had been subsequently obtained regularly by a third party, was held void in the hands of such third party: *Vine* v. *Leeds*, *R.* v. *Vine*, L. R. 10 Q. B. 195; 39 J. P. 213; 44 L. J. M. C. 60; 31 L. T. 842; 23 W. R. 649. But if the convicted felon has received a free pardon, this wipes out the disqualification as if it had never existed: *Hay* v. *Tower JJ.*, 24 Q. B. D. 557; 59 L. J. M. C. 79; 54 J. P. 500; 62 L. T. 290; 38 W. R. 414. If a license is forfeited on conviction for using licensed premises as a brothel, it is void from that moment for all purposes: *R.* v. *West Riding JJ.*, 52 J. P. 455; 21 Q. B. D. 258; 57 L. J. M. C. 103; 36 W. R. 258. So a license to a dead man would be void, and the executors would get into difficulties by renewing in a dead man's name;

35 & 36 VICT. c. 94, s. 3.

Selling in Premises Enlarged.   Sect. 3.

Cowles v. *Gale,* L. R. 7 Ch. 12 ; 41 L. J. Ch. 14 ; 25 L. T. 524 ;   NOTE.
20 W. R. 70. So a license granted by justices not at the general annual meeting, or an adjournment, would be void : 9 Geo. 4, c. 61, s. 13. And before that Act a license granted by justices under the then existing Acts, sitting in private instead of in public, was also void : *R.* v. *Downs,* 3 T. R. 569. Where the parties, the justices, and the excise all acted on the notion that an enactment was unrepealed, and a license was granted, the court held it void, notwithstanding the mistake : *Pearson* v. *Broadbent,* 36 J. P. 485. So a beer and wine license obtained by forgery would be void (32 & 33 Vict. c. 27, s. 11), and licenses granted to persons who are declared to be disqualified (9 Geo. 4, c. 61, s. 16 ; 1 Will. 4, c. 64, s. 2 ; 3 & 4 Vict. c. 61, s. 7 ; 23 Vict. c. 27, s. 22 ; this Act, s. 44, *post*).

An agreement of a licensed person to sub-let a room to an unlicensed person to sell liquors therein, contrary to 9 Geo. 4, c. 61, is contrary to public policy, and void : *Ritchie* v. *Smith,* 6 C. B. 462 ; 12 J. P. 822 ; 18 L. J. C. P. 9.

Selling in premises which have been enlarged.] The case also sometimes arises where during the licensing year the license holder has rebuilt his premises on a larger site, or annexed adjoining premises. In such a case the High Court seldom interferes with the discretion of justices, and considers that it is for justices on the occasion of a renewal, or of a prosecution under this section, to determine whether the altered or enlarged premises are substantially the same as the original premises. Whichever way the justices determine, the High Court declines to interfere, even though the premises have been doubled in size : *R.* v. *Smith,* 31 J. P. 259 ; 15 L. T. 178 ; *R.* v. *Hampshire, Ballam* v. *Wiltshire,* 44 J. P. 72 ; *R.* v. *Ruffles,* 1 Q. B. D. 207 ; 40 J. P. 68 ; 45 L. J. M. C. 61 ; 34 L. T. 180 ; 24 W. R. 536. A license holder, like other traders, may enlarge and improve his premises at his own discretion, subject to the risk of the justices treating the alterations as substantial when a renewal is applied for : *R.* v. *Sykes* or *Stringer* v. *Huddersfield,* 1 Q. B. D. 52 ; 40 J. P. 22 ; 45 L. J. M. C. 39 ; 33 L. T. 568. And the High Court has refused to interfere even where he was convicted of selling in part of the ground held along with the licensed premises, and which they might well have treated as being part of such premises : *Mahon* v. *Gaskell,* 42 J. P. 583. Though this is usually a question of fact, yet in many cases there may be a question of law involved ; and hence in case of a conviction or refusal of license, the justices may be required to state a case for the opinion of the High Court. See further, sections 52, 74, and notes, *post.*

LICENSING ACT, 1872, S. 3.

Sect. 3.   *Punishment for Unlicensed Selling.*

NOTE.   *Hawking and selling spirits.*] If any person hawks, sells, or exposes to sale any spirits otherwise than on premises for which he is licensed to sell spirits, he shall incur a fine of 100*l.*, and the spirits shall be forfeited. In default of payment of the fine on summary conviction, the offender shall be imprisoned with or without hard labour. Any person may arrest a person found committing an offence against such section : 43 & 44 Vict. c. 24, s. 146, *post.* And a like penalty is incurred for knowingly selling or delivering spirits to the end that they may be unlawfully retailed or consumed : *Ibid.* s. 147. And the same penalty is incurred if any person receives, buys, or procures any spirits from a person not having authority to sell or deliver the same : *Ibid.* s. 148.

The punishment.] The forfeiture of the license on a second or subsequent offence is not a matter of discretion in the justices. On the third offence, as the term of imprisonment exceeds three months, the defendant may demand a trial by jury under the Summary Jurisdiction Act, 1879, 42 & 43 Vict. c. 49, s. 17. The previous conviction may be proved by a certified extract from the register kept by the clerk of the convicting court : 42 & 43 Vict. c. 49, s. 22. See notes to section 51, *post.*

The forfeiture of liquor and of the vessels is discretionary in the justices on any conviction under this section. Before, however, the liquor found in possession can be forfeited, it seems an opportunity must be given to the person convicted to show cause, for there may be good reason for the liquor not being forfeited as being unjust to third parties : *Gill* v. *Bright*, 41 L. J. M. C. 22 ; 25 L. T. 591 ; 20 W. R. 248 ; 36 J. P. 168. And for a like reason the justices may well refuse to decide anything as to this matter of forfeiture.

The disqualification of the convicted person on a *second* or subsequent offence must be ordered by the court which adjudicates on the offence, and at the time the penalty or imprisonment is awarded, and is discretionary in the court. A second offence means a second under the Licensing Acts, and hence the justices were held to act without jurisdiction who treated one offence against this section, coupled with another prior offence against the excise enactment in 4 & 5 Will. 4, c. 85, s. 17, as a second offence : *Re Authers*, 53 J. P. 116 ; 22 Q. B. D. 355 ; 58 L. J. M. C. 62 ; 37 W. R. 320.

Notice of the forfeiture and disqualification must be sent by the clerk of the court to the licensing officer of the district, and to the clerk of the justices (if a different person), along with the forfeited license : see section 55, *post.*

35 & 36 VICT. c. 94, s. 3.

Selling by Retail.

Sect. 3.

NOTE.

The imprisonment authorised by this section as the alternative punishment does not mean an imprisonment in default of payment of any penalty imposed, for if a penalty be imposed there must be in the conviction the usual clause of distress before the imprisonment can be directed : *Re Clew*, 8 Q. B. D. 54 ; 51 L. J. M. C. 140 ; 46 J. P. 534 ; 46 L. T. 482 ; 30 W. R. 704 ; *R.* v. *Hopkins*, 57 J. P. 152 ; (1893), 1 Q. B. 621. And the procedure mentioned in section 51 of this Act before it was repealed did not apply to imprisonment when made the alternative punishment for this offence : *Re Brown, R.* v. *Newcastle JJ.*, 3 Q. B. D. 545 ; 42 J. P. 598 ; 47 L. J. M. C. 108 ; 38 L. T. 682 ; 26 W. R. 757. The defendant may appeal to quarter sessions against the imprisonment under section 52, *post*.

The mode of enforcing the penalty hereby imposed is set forth in 11 & 12 Vict. c. 43, s. 19, supplemented by 42 & 43 Vict. c. 49, s. 21, namely, by distress, and if it appear that there are no goods or insufficient goods, or it would be injurious to distrain, then instead of issuing warrant of distress, by commitment to prison without hard labour according to the scale of terms set forth in 42 & 43 Vict. c. 49, s. 5, the maximum term being three months : 47 & 48 Vict. c. 43, s. 5. See these Acts in notes to this Act, 1872, s. 51, *post*.

Selling by retail.] The Alehouse Act, 9 Geo. 4, c. 61, did not define what is meant by selling by retail, and this Act gives no definition of that expression beyond what is contained in section 74, *post*, and which in effect says that that expression shall have the meaning which any of the Liquor Acts has assigned to it in reference to the particular kind of liquor. That section seems to extend to alehouses the definition contained in 4 & 5 Will. 4, c. 85, s. 19, *post*, and confined formerly to beerhouses, and therefore whenever beer, cider, or perry is sold in a less quantity than four-and-a-half gallons it will be a selling by retail. As regards spirits, the sale of spirits in any quantity less than two gallons, or than one dozen reputed quart bottles, shall be deemed sale by retail : 43 & 44 Vict. c. 24, ss. 102, 104. A selling of foreign wines in less quantity than two gallons or in less than one dozen reputed quart bottles at one time, shall be deemed to be a selling by retail : 23 Vict. c. 27, s. 4. And so is selling of sweets in those quantities : 26 & 27 Vict. c. 33, s. 18. These quantities will apply to public-house keepers when selling the same liquors. Sweets are also said to be sold wholesale if sold above two gallons or one dozen quarts : 11 & 12 Vict. c. 121, s. 9 ; 23 & 24 Vict. c. 113, s. 7. Sweets or made wines mean any liquor made

LICENSING ACT, 1872, S. 3.

Sect. 3.

NOTE.

Extent of Third Section.

by fermentation from fruit and sugar, or from fruit or sugar mixed with any other material, and which has undergone a process of fermentation in the manufacture thereof: 52 & 53 Vict. c. 42, s. 28. And sweets include made wines, mead, and metheglin: 33 & 34 Vict. c. 29, s. 3; 43 & 44 Vict. c. 20, s. 40. Moreover, all persons making entry at the excise office as alehouse keepers, victuallers, or retailers, are deemed sellers by retail of such liquors to all intents and purposes: 35 Geo. 3, c. 113, s. 9.

The usual dealer's license granted by the excise, as contradistinguished from a retail license granted by justices and excise, is not called in the Excise Act, 6 Geo. 4, c. 81, a wholesale license, though it is so called in common parlance: *R.* v. *Jenkins*, 55 J. P. 824; 61 L. J. M. C. 57; 65 L. T. 857; 40 W. R. 318. See a form of such license in Appendix, *post.*

Selling without excise license.] As to beerhouses not holding excise licenses, the former enactments on this subject were 1 Will. 4, c. 64, s. 7; 4 & 5 Will. 4, c. 85, s. 17, and as to winehouses the enactment was 23 Vict. c. 27, s. 19, neither of which is repealed expressly. Those enactments will still apply to the houses which have no excise license, while the present enactment will apply to the houses for which no justices' certificate has been obtained; but these, of necessity, must, under 32 & 33 Vict. c. 27, s. 4, be now always found co-existing. The penalties in those sections are thus concurrent, and do not interfere with this third section of the Licensing Act, 1872, or with the 5th and 6th sections, subject to this, that a person cannot (by section 59) be punished under both Acts. The penalty for contravening the terms of an excise license, not specially provided for otherwise, is the same as for having no excise license: 52 & 53 Vict. c. 42, s. 24. And the appeal to quarter sessions against a conviction for selling without an excise license is now held to be regulated for some purposes by the Summary Jurisdiction Acts like ordinary appeals under this Act: *R.* v. *Glamorganshire*, 53 J. P. 294; 22 Q. B. D. 628; 58 L. J. M. C. 93.

As to the rule that excise licenses must be for separate premises, and as to prosecuting offences, see *ante,* p. 5.

But if the justices' license is void under any provision of this Act the excise license becomes void also. See section 63, *post.* Sweets and spirits off-licenses are on the same footing as wine: see sections 69, 74, *post.*

Extent of third section.] This section seems to apply to those who sell anywhere by retail (that is, in the small quantities above referred to) any kind of intoxicating liquor without a

35 & 36 VICT. C. 94, S. 3.

Death, &c., of License Holder.   Sect. 3.

license or certificate for that liquor, or who, though licensed, sell   NOTE.
at a place not covered by their license, and for which the owner
has not any occasional license : Licensing Act, 1874, s. 17.
There may be often a difficulty in deciding whether an offence
comes within the 3rd or 5th or 6th sections. See notes to those
sections.

Selling by executor or trustee of licensed person.]
The last paragraph in this section is a re-enactment of the
proviso in 9 Geo. 4, c. 61, s. 18, now repealed, but is not identical
in language. Nor is it identical with the similar enactment as to
wine licenses in 23 Vict. c. 27, s. 12, and beer licenses in 3 & 4
Vict. c. 61, s. 8, which were excise licenses only. This enactment
extends to certificates for all the houses included in the Wine
and Beerhouse Acts, and the sale of spirits and liquors by retail
for consumption off the premises, also the sale of sweets, as well
as to alehouse licenses, and provides for the temporary interval
between death or bankruptcy of the licensed person, and the
application of the personal representative or trustee to the next
special transfer sessions under 9 Geo. 4, c. 61, s. 14. But the
exemption from the penalty is confined under this section to the
two cases of death and bankruptcy of the licensed person during
the currency of his license or certificate. The exemption will not
continue after the next special sessions or the next after, though
it will not be necessary to obtain during that interval any
indorsement at petty sessions. Where the license holder dies
intestate during the licensing year, the person who has a *primâ
facie* right to apply for letters of administration does not commit
the offence of selling without a license for continuing the sale of
liquors until the next special transfer sessions, for his right to do
so is here recognised : *Rose* v. *Frogley*, 57 J. P. 376. As to all
the other grounds for applying for transfer mentioned in 9 Geo. 4,
c. 61, s. 14, it will be necessary to get an indorsement at petty
sessions, until the next special sessions, in order to exempt the
transferee or succeeding occupier from penalties : 5 & 6 Vict. c. 44,
s. 1. By the 3 & 4 Vict. c. 61, s. 8, and 23 Vict. c. 27, s. 12, the
executor is entitled to enjoy the excise license for the rest of the
yearly term without further payment.

Care must be taken not to renew a license in the name of a
dead person : *Cowles* v. *Gales*, L. R. 7 Ch. 12 ; 41 L. J. Ch. 14 ; 25
L. T. 524 ; 20 W. R. 70.

Where a licensee became bankrupt, and by the covenant of his
lease was bound on its determination to assign the license to the
lessor, it was held that the license was not "property" of the
lessee, and did not pass to the trustee, but ought to be assigned
to the lessor : *Re Britnor*, 46 L. J. Bk. 85 ; 25 W. R. 560.

Sect. 4. **4.** *Occupier of unlicensed premises liable for sale of liquor.*] The occupier of any unlicensed premises on which any intoxicating liquor is sold, or if such premises are occupied by more than one person, every occupier thereof, shall, if it be proved that he was privy or consenting to the sale, be subject to the penalties imposed upon persons for the sale of intoxicating liquors without license.

This section deals separately with all occupiers of houses not licensed, in which liquors are sold by third parties without license, if such occupiers are aware of the fact. The previous section includes occupiers who sell without a license as well as non-occupiers; but there may be a few cases where the occupier is not the person who sells, though he allows another to sell, or consents to his selling, in which event both are to be punished alike.

This section supersedes what was provided for in the repealed 18th section of 9 Geo. 4, c. 61, as to persons permitting unlicensed selling, and it was held that any agreement of a licensed person to allow an unlicensed person to sell in part of his premises, was contrary to public policy and void: *Ritchie* v. *Smith*, 6 C. B. 462; 12 J. P. 822; 18 L. J. C. P. 9. The Excise Act, 35 Geo. 3, c. 113, s. 1, which also prohibits persons permitting unlicensed selling in one's house, outhouse, yard, garden, orchard, or other place, under a penalty of 20*l.*, seems still in force.

5. *Seller liable for drinking on premises contrary to license.*] If any purchaser of any intoxicating liquor from a person who is not licensed to sell the same to be drunk on the premises drinks such liquor on the premises where the same is sold, or on any highway adjoining or near such premises, the seller of such liquor shall, if it shall appear that such drinking was with his privity and consent, be subject to the following penalties (that is to say) :—

For the first offence he shall be liable to a penalty not exceeding ten pounds :

For the second and any subsequent offence he shall Sect. 5.
be liable to a penalty not exceeding twenty pounds.

For the purposes of this section the expression " premises where the same is sold " shall include any premises adjoining or near the premises where the liquor is sold if belonging to the seller of the liquor or under his control, or used by his permission.

[Any conviction for an offence under this section shall be recorded on the license of the person convicted.]

This section and the next are enactments superseding corresponding sections in previous Acts, 4 &. 5 Will. 4, c. 85, s. 4; 32 & 33 Vict. c. 27, s. 14; 33 & 34 Vict. c. 29, s. 6, and much difficulty has hitherto been felt in meeting the offences aimed at, as was seen in *Cross* v. *Watts*, 13 C. B. (N.S.) 239; 27 J. P. 18; 32 L. J. M. C. 73; 7 L. T. 463; 11 W. R. 210; *Deal* v. *Schofield*, L. R. 3 Q. B. 8; 32 J. P. 181; 37 L. J. M. C. 15; 17 L. T. 143; 16 W. R. 77; 8 B. & S. 760. The word "not" in the second line was probably intended to be put before "to be drunk" in the third line. A person "not licensed to sell liquor to be drunk on the premises" may mean either a person who has no license at all of any kind, or one who has a license to sell liquor, but only " liquor not to be drunk on the premises." The enactment seems to have been intended to meet this latter case only, and hence the word "not" is misplaced.

The present section is confined entirely to the circumstances described in the first four lines, which collectively constitute a condition precedent to the offence. (1) The premises on which the liquor is drunk must be premises on which the person selling has no license to sell the same in order to be drunk on such premises; (2) The sale must be on such premises; and (3) The liquor must also be drunk on the premises, or on a highway near such premises, or in a third party's premises adjoining or near, if under the seller's control. These conditions existing, the seller of such liquor is to be liable to penalties, but only if he was privy or consenting to such drinking. If the liquor is taken to neighbouring premises (not being the seller's), a few yards distant and drunk on such premises and partly on the highway, this cannot be treated as an offence with the seller's privity: *Bath* v. *White*, 3 C. P. D. 175; 42 J. P. 375; 26 W. R. 617.

LICENSING ACT, 1872, S. 5.

Sect. 5.
NOTE.

The consent or *privity* must refer to some premises as to which the seller's consent would be matter of legal right, for he could not be said to consent to something he cannot prevent or control. Hence, if, for example, the field of a third person adjoins the house, and if the seller has no interest in it, and the purchaser gets into the field and there drinks the liquor, it will be difficult to hold that he did so with the privity or consent or permission of the seller since the seller will not be able either to give or take away the permission to go into another's field. Such a case as this seems not covered by this section. If the last paragraph of section 6 had been applicable to the 5th section, this difficulty would have been met.

Another difficulty may arise when the man who purchases the liquor does not drink it himself, but hands it over to a third person, who drinks it on the premises or near them ; the penalty seems not to apply in such a case. The justices may, however, in such a case, hold that the real purchaser was the one who drank the liquor, and the other, or nominal purchaser, was his agent, if the facts warrant the inference ; for, under section 62, the consumer is *primâ facie* a purchaser. And this view was acted on as to an offence under section 13, *post: Scatchard* v. *Johnson*, 52 J. P. 389 ; 57 L. J. M. C. 41. And the seller may be liable under the 3rd section.

This penalty seems to be cumulative to that mentioned in the 3rd section, unless the construction above suggested is adopted, viz.; that it applies only to persons having a license of some kind ; for otherwise it would be somewhat singular that a person who sells liquor on premises without a license will be liable on proof of those facts alone to the heavy penalties of the 3rd section, and yet, if the same person, in addition to the above facts, let the purchaser drink the liquor on the premises, he would only be liable to the much milder penalties of the 5th section.

It seems that there is no penalty incurred by a purchaser who, against the will of a licensed person (whose license is only to sell liquor "not to be consumed on the premises"), insists on drinking the liquor on such premises immediately after buying it ; though he may in some cases be brought within the 18th section. The above 5th section seems intended to prevent any encouragement being given to such purchasers, who, if not checked, might practically turn a house which was not licensed for consumption on the premises into one which was so licensed.

The part *within brackets* was repealed by Licensing Act, 1874, section 33, but see that Act, section 13. The justices may order this conviction to be recorded.

35 & 36 VICT. C. 94, S. 6.

6. *Evasion of law as to drinking on premises contrary to license.*] If any person having a license to sell intoxicating liquors not to be drunk on the premises, himself takes or carries, or employs or suffers any other person to take or carry, any intoxicating liquor out of or from the premises of such licensed person for the purpose of being sold on his account, or for his benefit or profit, and of being drunk or consumed in any other house, or in any tent, shed, or other building of any kind whatever, belonging to such licensed person, or hired, used, or occupied by him, or on or in any place whether enclosed or not, or whether or not a public thoroughfare, such intoxicating liquor shall be deemed to have been consumed by the purchasers thereof on the premises of such licensed person, with his privity and consent, and such licensed person shall be punished accordingly in manner provided by this Act.

Sect. 6.

[Any conviction for an offence under this section shall be recorded on the license of the person convicted.]

In any proceeding under this section it shall not be necessary to prove that the premises or place or places to which such liquor is taken to be drunk belonged to, or were hired, used, or occupied by the seller, if proof be given to the satisfaction of the court hearing the case that such liquor was taken to be consumed thereon or therein with intent to evade the conditions of his license.

_{This section seems to be an attempt to explain more fully the circumstances which will amount to the offence described in section 5. It attempts to punish any evasion of the statute which consists in allowing people to drink liquor on other premises, for the profit of the seller, when the license is one for the sale of}

Sect. 6.
NOTE.

liquor "not to be drunk on the premises." It seems to prevent the holder of a particular license doing substantially the very thing which his license forbids; for if his customers could drink the liquor in the immediate neighbourhood the house would be used practically in the same way as if licensed for consumption on the premises.

This section is confined to cases where the seller has a license "not to be drunk on the premises," and the liquor is consumed in some other premises, or building, but sufficiently near to be used as if they were the same premises.

The words at the end of the first paragraph, "shall be punished accordingly in manner provided by this Act," must mean that the penalties incurred are those in the 5th section. See notes to that section.

The whole section seems not to apply to the case where the liquor was sold before leaving the premises, but only where it was not then actually sold and was taken to be hawked or to be sold in some neighbouring place. If, for example, a previous order was given for liquor to be sent to premises this would be a lawful sale except where the liquor was understood to be drunk as in section 5. To make out the offence, the liquor must have been sold for the profit of the licensed person, and the place of intended consumption of the liquor must have been in contemplation of the seller before the consumption was effected. The place of consumption may be : (1) Any tent, shed, or other building than the licensed place, if belonging to or hired or used by the seller; and *primâ facie* proof of hiring or using will be the fact of the consumption in such place, with the seller's knowledge or intent; but this *primâ facie* evidence may be rebutted; (2) The place of consumption may also be "any place, whether enclosed or not, and whether or not a public thoroughfare." As these words would *primâ facie* include the whole world, there must of necessity be some implied restriction. The highway must obviously be adjacent to the house, or within view of the house, otherwise the connection between the sale and consumption will be too remote. The "enclosed place" cannot include the purchaser's own house, or tent, or shed, otherwise the liquor never could in any conceivable place be legally consumed. Thus, where the purchaser's premises adjoin, his drinking the beer obtained on the highway close to his own premises, as well as to the licensed premises, is no offence : *Bath* v. *White*, 3 C. P. D. 175 ; 42 J. P. 375 ; 26 W. R. 617. The liquor sold need not be the same as that which the license authorises to be sold.

As to proof of consumption, see also section 62, *post*.

With regard to the proof mentioned in the last paragraph, that the liquor was taken to be consumed therein, *i.e.*, on other

premises, the only reasonable construction seems to be, that it **Sect. 6.** was intended by the seller that the liquor should be taken by the consumer for the purpose of consuming it on premises which, NOTE. according to this section, must be deemed equivalent to the seller's own premises, and thus of doing what the statute meant to prohibit. The liquor must have been taken "with intent," and the intent must mean "the intent of the seller," for the buyer may, in defiance of the seller, drink it on the premises, and the seller could not be held liable; at least, if he had no reasonable expectation that this defiance of law would be perpetrated there.
The part *within brackets* was repealed by Licensing Act, 1874, section 33, but see that Act, section 13. The justices may order this conviction to be recorded.

7. *Sale of spirits to children.*] Every holder of a license who sells or allows any person to sell, to be consumed on the premises, any description of spirits to any person apparently under the age of sixteen years, shall be liable to a penalty not exceeding twenty shillings for the first offence, and not exceeding forty shillings for the second and any subsequent offence.

This is an application of the enactment 2 & 3 Vict. c. 47, s. 43 (now repealed by this Act, and formerly confined to the metropolitan police district), to England. In the city of London a similar enactment still seems to be in force (2 & 3 Vict. c. xciv., s. 27), and applicable to all excisable liquors.

By 49 & 50 Vict. c. 56, *post* (which is to be construed as one with the Licensing Acts, 1872 and 1874), section 1, every holder of a license who knowingly sells or allows any person to sell any description of intoxicating liquors to any person under the age of thirteen years, for consumption on the premises by any person under such age as aforesaid, shall be liable to a penalty not exceeding 20s. for the first offence, and not exceeding 40s. for the second and any subsequent offence.

Under the first enactment it is immaterial who consumes the spirits. Under the second enactment the liquor must be consumed on the premises by some person under thirteen.

The words "any person apparently under the age of sixteen years," leave it to the discretion of the justices to find that fact, and in arriving at their conclusion, they may be guided by the opinion of witnesses, as well as their own judgment, though their own view will be sufficient. If, at the hearing, it be proved that,

C

Sect. 7.
Note.

though apparently under sixteen, the person is above sixteen, then the justices will not be justified in convicting; but such a ground would not be sufficient for quashing a conviction after it had been once made on the best judgment the justices could arrive at for the time being.

With regard to any kind of liquor sold to a person under thirteen, in order to convict the holder of the license or his manager, it must be proved that he knowingly sold to such person; that the person is under thirteen years of age; and that it was for consumption on the premises by a person under thirteen (not necessarily the same person under thirteen). As to proof of age under thirteen, it seems that the jurisdiction to convict will not depend on the mere fact of the age, but, as in the former enactment, on the apparent age, or, in other words, the knowledge of the license holder or manager as to that fact. The words of both enactments seem not to throw the risk of finding out the age on the licensed person as in sections 13 and 16. See notes to those sections.

As to restrictions on the *employment of children* under ten, and boys under fourteen and girls under sixteen in licensed premises, see statute 52 & 53 Vict. c. 44, in Appendix.

8. *Sale to be by standard measure.*] Every person shall sell all intoxicating liquor which is sold by retail and not in cask or bottle, and is not sold in a quantity less than half a pint, in measures marked according to the imperial standards.

Every person who acts or suffers any person under his control or in his employment to act in contravention of this section shall be liable to a penalty not exceeding, for the first offence, ten pounds, and not exceeding for any subsequent offence twenty pounds, and shall also be liable to forfeit the illegal measure in which the liquor was sold.

The penalty in this section is incurred only by the person who sells or suffers his servants to sell and act in contravention of the section. There may be cases where the keeper of the house shows successfully that he did not suffer his servants to sell in

35 & 36 VICT. c. 94, s. 8.

measures not marked, as where the servant has, in disregard of his orders, so sold. This penalty will apply to unlicensed as well as licensed persons selling, and is a cumulative penalty. A publican who uses earthen mugs, and serves customers with them, impliedly represents them to be of imperial measure, and if they are unstamped they will be liable to seizure: *R.* v. *Aulton*, 30 L. J. M. C. 129; 3 E. & E. 568; 25 J. P. 69; 3 L. T. 699; 9 W. R. 278; *Washington* v. *Young*, 19 L. J. Exch. 348; 5 Ex. 403. And it has been held that if a customer asks for a quantity of liquor, not under any usual denomination of imperial capacity, but by some local name, and the quantity supplied equals or exceeds half-a-pint, as, for example, a blue of beer, which is about one-third of a quart, the seller is liable under this section, notwithstanding the Weights and Measures Act, 41 & 42 Vict. c. 49, s. 22; *Payne* v. *Thomas*, 60 L. J. M. C. 3; 63 L. T. 456; 39 W. R. 240; 54 J. P. 824. But where the customer asks for a glass or other quantity which is not a known legal measure of capacity, and which does not exceed or equal a half-pint, then no offence will be committed by the seller, whatever may be the capacity of the glass.

The forfeiture of the illegal measure is discretionary in the justices under this section.

In *Addy* v. *Blake*, 19 Q. B. D. 478; 51 J. P. 599; 56 L. T. 711; 35 W. R. 719, B. went into a licensed house of A. and asked for a pint of beer. A. went into a back parlour, poured the liquor into a stamped measure not seen by B., and then into a jug and delivered the jug to B., and the court held that this was not a selling by imperial measure, as the measure was not seen by B., and therefore A. had committed the offence under this section.

The Weights and Measures Act, 41 & 42 Vict. c. 49, s. 22, does not subject any one to a fine under that Act if the vessel is not represented as containing any amount of imperial measure, or if he does not use or intend to use it as a measure. But every measure of capacity shall have the denomination thereof stamped on the outside of such measure in legible figures and letters (section 28). A measure stamped by an inspector is a legal measure (section 45). A measure for liquids partly of glass and partly of metal or other transparent medium may have the capacity indicated by a level line drawn through the transparent part (section 46). The inspector, if authorised in writing by a justice of the peace, may inspect measures and seize unjust measures, and to refuse examination subjects him to a fine of 5*l.* (section 48). All appeals against convictions under the Weights and Measures Act are now regulated by the Summary Jurisdiction Act, 47 & 48 Vict. c. 43, sched. See notes to section 52 of this Act, *post*.

Sect. 8.
NOTE.

Sect. 9.

9. *Penalty on internal communication between licensed premises and house of public resort.*] Every person who makes or uses, or allows to be made or used, any internal communication between any licensed premises and any unlicensed premises which are used for public entertainment or resort, or as a refreshment house, shall be liable to a penalty not exceeding ten pounds for every day during which such communication remains open.

In addition to any penalty imposed by this section any person convicted of an offence under this section shall, if he be the holder of a license, forfeit such license.

A similar enactment and more extensive is in the Metropolitan Police Act, 2 & 3 Vict. c. 47, s. 45, and the City of London Act, 2 & 3 Vict. c. xciv. s. 29.

This penalty is imposed on the occupier of the unlicensed as well as of the licensed premises. There seems no reason why the internal communication should be large enough to allow persons to pass through.

A place of public resort may be any ordinary shop; it may be an auction room: *Sewell* v. *Taylor*, 7 C. B. (N.S.) 160; 29 L. J. M. C. 50; 1 L. T. 37; or a cricket ground : *Turnbull* v. *Appleton*, 45 J. P. 69; or a railway platform : *Ex parte Davis*, 2 H. & N. 149; 26 L. J. M. C. 178; 21 J. P. 280.

A place of public entertainment may be a public dancing-room, or music-room, as to which see notes to section 14, *post;* and as to theatre, see notes to section 72, *post.*

As to what is a refreshment-house, see 23 Vict. c. 27, s. 6, and notes, *post.*

The forfeiture of the license of the licensed person convicted is imperative, or rather follows on the conviction by operation of the statute; and the justices have no discretion in the matter. As to the effect of it, and as to how the landlord may protect himself against the consequences of a conviction for this offence of his tenant, see Licensing Act, 1874, section 15, *post.*

This section does not interfere with the natural right of any licensed person to enlarge his premises by adding other premises so long as both are used as one house. See section 74 and notes.

35 & 36 VICT. C. 94, S. 11.

10. *Penalty on illicit storing of liquor.*] If any licensed person has in his possession on the premises in respect of which his license is granted any description of intoxicating liquor which he is not authorised to sell, unless he shall account for the possession of the same to the satisfaction of the court by which he is tried, he shall forfeit such liquor and the vessels containing the same, and shall be liable to a penalty not exceeding for the first offence, ten pounds, and not exceeding for any subsequent offence, twenty pounds.

Sect. 10.

This section is confined to the case of a person being licensed to sell only some kinds of liquor and having a different kind of liquor in his premises, in which case, unless he can account for the possession of such last-mentioned liquor, he will incur the penalty. If, for example, a beerhouse keeper has a cask of spirits or wine in his premises and is summoned under this section, it will be for the justices to judge whether the cask of wine or spirits was for his own personal use only, as it may well be. The justices must decide whether his account is only a pretence. In any event he must have an opportunity of giving his account of the matter before the liquor is forfeited: *Gill* v. *Bright*, 36 J. P. 168; 41 L. J. M. C. 22; 25 L. T. 591; 20 W. R. 248.

A power to search for liquors not only in licensed premises, but in any place where such liquors are not authorised to be sold, is given by the Licensing Act, 1874, s. 17, *post*. See notes to that section.

See also enactment as to wine sellers having spirits in their premises: 23 Vict. c. 27, s. 25, *post*.

11. *Names of licensed persons to be affixed to premises.*] Every licensed person shall cause to be painted or fixed, and shall keep painted or fixed on the premises in respect of which his license is granted, in a conspicuous place and in such form and manner as the [licensing justices] may from time to time direct, his

Sect. 11. name, with the addition after the name of the word "licensed," and of words sufficient, in the opinion of the said [justices] to express the business for which his license has been granted, and in particular of words expressing whether the license authorises the sale of intoxicating liquor to be consumed on or off the premises only, as the case may be; and no person shall have any words or letters on his premises importing that he is authorised as a licensed person to sell any intoxicating liquor which he is not in fact duly authorised to sell. Every person who acts in contravention of the provisions of this section shall be liable to a penalty not exceeding for the first offence ten pounds, and not exceeding for the second and any subsequent offence twenty pounds.

The words *within brackets* were inserted by the Licensing Act, 1874, section 28, *post*.

This section makes it the duty of the party licensed to apply to the licensing justices for information as to what form and manner of publication they have directed. But if none is directed, each party is nevertheless forbidden to state that he sells any kind of liquor which he is not in fact authorised to sell, and he will incur the penalty for this misstatement alone. It will be for the justices to decide, as matter of law, whether the words or letters "import" that the person sells other liquors than he is entitled to do. In general, before conviction, the person is entitled to notice from the justices, who should lay down some general rule on the subject, clear and minute, so that parties may be able to comply with it. Should the license be a six-day license, there must be words indicating that such license is for six days only. See section 49, *post*. And if the license is an early closing license, this must be stated. See Act, 1874, section 7, *post*. The not keeping up of the name and license is a continuing offence.

The obligation to "keep fixed" implies the duty to renew the words if defaced.

As to who are the licensing justices in this and other sections, see section 74 (definition of those words) and notes thereon; also Act, 1874, section 6, and notes, *post*.

35 & 36 VICT. C. 94, S. 12.

Sect. 12.

Offences against Public Order.

12. *Penalty on persons found drunk.*]. Every person found drunk in any highway or other public place, whether a building or not, or on any licensed premises, shall be liable to a penalty not exceeding ten shillings, and on a second conviction within a period of twelve months shall be liable to a penalty not exceeding twenty shillings, and on a third or subsequent conviction within such period of twelve months be liable to a penalty not exceeding forty shillings.

Every person who in any highway or other public place, whether a building or not, is guilty while drunk of riotous or disorderly behaviour, or who is drunk while in charge on any highway or other public place of any carriage, horse, cattle, or steam-engine, or who is drunk when in possession of any loaded fire-arms, may be apprehended, and shall be liable to a penalty not exceeding forty shillings, or, in the discretion of the court, to imprisonment, with or without hard labour, for any term not exceeding one month.

Where the court commits any person to prison for non-payment of any penalty under this section, the court may order him to be imprisoned with hard labour.

This section applies to premises having an *occasional* license: Licensing Act, 1874, section 20.

By section 60, a justice who is a brewer, &c., may take part in the disposal of cases under this section if the offence do not relate to premises in which he is interested, as defined by that section.

The statute 21 Jas. 1, c. 7, as to drunkenness, being repealed by the second schedule, this section is now the general enactment dealing with the punishment of drunkenness.

Sect. 12.

NOTE.

Public place.] The words "or other public place, whether a building or not," coming after the word "highway," confine this offence to a highway, or a street, or a building like a market or pier, where the public have a right to be. The words "public place" have been held to include a railway carriage while carrying passengers : *Langrish* v. *Archer*, 10 Q. B. D. 44 ; 47 J. P. 295 ; 47 L. T. 548. The description of place here given is not quite so extensive as the words "place of public resort," used in section 9, which have been held, for example, to include a railway station : *Ex parte Davis*, 2 H. & N. 149 ; 21 J. P. 280 ; 26 L. J. M. C. 178 ; a house where an auction was held : *Sewell* v. *Taylor*, 7 C. B. (N.S.) 160 ; 23 J. P. 792 ; 29 L. J. M. C. 50 ; and also an alehouse itself : *Cole* v. *Coulton*, 2 E. & E. 695 ; 29 L. J. M. C. 125 ; 2 L. T. 216 ; 8 W. R. 412 ; 24 J. P. 596. If the party is drunk in the licensed premises, he is now expressly made liable by this section ; but if he is found drunk in a place merely of public resort, not being a highway or street, or some enlargement thereof, and *ejusdem generis*, then the penalty is not incurred.

Drunk and riotous, &c.] The only exceptions where this offence may be committed, though not on a highway or street, or public place, are where the person is in possession of loaded firearms when drunk, and where he is drunk on licensed premises. Probably, it was not intended that the offence as to fire-arms should be on a different footing from the others, but owing to the position of the clause in the sentence, this offence may be committed anywhere, whether in a public place or in a private house or ground. And there is nothing to require any evidence of any person being endangered by the drunken man.

The Highways and Locomotives Act, 1878, 41 & 42 Vict. c. 77, s. 26, the Municipal Corporations Act, 1882, 45 & 46 Vict. c. 50, s. 23, and the Local Government Act, 1888, 51 & 52 Vict. c. 41, s. 85, having all been passed since the Licensing Act, 1872, the question whether this word "carriage" includes a bicycle, &c., is not affected by those Acts ; and it has not yet been decided whether "carriage," as used in this 12th section, would include a bicycle. See *Taylor* v. *Goodwin*, 4 Q. B. D. 228 ; 43 J. P. 653 ; 40 L. T. 458 ; 48 L. J. M. C. 104 ; 27 W. R. 489.

Found drunk.] The penalty is incurred if the person is found drunk "on any licensed premises," that is to say, in an alehouse, or any house mentioned in the Wine and Beerhouse Acts, &c., and for which a license is in force either for consumption on or off the premises. See section 74. If he is found drunk in unlicensed premises he incurs no penalty. If he is drunk in licensed premises but is not "found" in the state of drunkenness, he escapes the penalty. It seems not necessary that he should be "found" by a constable, for any one may be the prosecutor, but the prosecutor must prove that the defendant was found drunk in the places specified. If the drunken person, before being found, has staggered out of the licensed premises into an adjoining field he seems to escape the penalty. And if the licensed premises are his own house, the drunken person would obviously not be liable, except he was found drunk during open hours and in the public part of the premises: *Lester* v. *Torrens*, 2 Q. B. D. 403; 41 J. P. 521; 25 W. R. 691; 46 L. J. M. C. 280.

Sect. 12.
———
NOTE.

As to the words "found on the premises," see notes to section 25, *post*.

A person "found drunk" under the first paragraph of this section cannot be apprehended by a constable under the authority of this Act, though a constable, or indeed any private person, would be justified in taking a drunken person into any house or station to keep him out of danger, so long as he is not imprisoned therein against his will; and a drunken person generally has not a "will" until he becomes sober. Those found under the second paragraph, including a drunken person in possession of fire-arms, may be apprehended. There may, however, be power to apprehend given by other Acts in both cases: see the Towns Police Clauses Act, 10 & 11 Vict. c. 89, s. 29; the Metropolitan Police Act, 2 & 3 Vict. c. 47, s. 58; and the City of London Act, 2 & 3 Vict. c. xciv., s. 37.

Drunk in the Metropolis.] Thus the Metropolis Police Act, 2 & 3 Vict. c. 47, s. 58, enacts: Every person who shall be found drunk in any street or public thoroughfare within the said district, and who while drunk shall be guilty of any violent or indecent behaviour, and also every person who shall be guilty of any violent or indecent behaviour in any police station-house shall be liable to a penalty of not more than forty shillings for every such offence, or may be committed if the magistrate before whom he shall be convicted shall think fit instead of inflicting on him any pecuniary penalty to the house of correction for any time not more than seven days.

Punishment.] The offences in the first and second paragraphs of this 12th section must be kept separate, and a person charged with one cannot be found guilty of another (*Martin* v. *Pridgeon*, 1 E. & E. 778; 7 W. R. 412; 28 L. J. M. C. 179; 23 J. P. 630; *Loadman* v. *Cragg*, 26 J. P. 743), unless the justices amend the summons and adjourn the hearing; or unless the defendant has waived the objection by appearing and taking part in defending himself: *R.* v. *Hughes*, 4 Q. B. D. 614; 43 J. P. 556; *R.* v.

Sect. 12.

Permitting or Selling.

NOTE. *Fletcher*, 40 L. J. M. C. 128; 35 J. P. 789; L. R. 1 C. C. R. 320; *R.* v. *Fletcher*, 48 J. P. 407. A single justice can dispose of the charges in the first paragraph. See section 51. The length of imprisonment for default of payment of penalty under the first part of the section will be according to the Summary Jurisdiction Act, 1879, 42 & 43 Vict. c. 49, s. 5. Where the punishment under the second clause is imprisonment merely, the commitment will be under 11 & 12 Vict. c. 43, s. 24, and the form in Summary Jurisdiction Rules, 1886.

And though the punishment may be the same, the conviction will be bad if it states two offences in the alternative or does not define which of the offences it is: *Cotterill* v. *Lempriere*, 24 Q. B. D. 634; 59 L. J. M. C. 133; 54 J. P. 583; 63 L. T. 695.

The offence may be committed in premises having an *occasional* license: Licensing Act, 1874, section 20.

The words "on a third or subsequent conviction" must be read with the words implied "for the same offence under this Act." And the person's conviction may be proved by a certified extract from the register kept by the clerk of the convicting court (42 & 43 Vict. c. 49, s. 22), or in some cases by a certified copy from the register of licenses: see section 58, *post*.

13. *Penalty for permitting drunkenness.*] If any licensed person permits drunkenness or any violent, quarrelsome, or riotous conduct to take place on his premises, or sells any intoxicating liquor to any drunken person, he shall be liable to a penalty not exceeding for the first offence ten pounds, and not exceeding for the second and any subsequent offence twenty pounds.

[Any conviction for an offence under this section shall be recorded on the license of the person convicted, unless the convicting magistrate or justices shall otherwise direct.]

Permitting or selling.] The offence here is in terms confined to a licensed person who permits or sells. Where the only evidence was that a person had been drinking in a licensed house,

Liability of a Manager.   Sect. 13.

and three-quarters of an hour later was found drunk in a ditch   NOTE.
about 100 yards distant, it was held that there was some evidence on which the justices might convict the keeper of the licensed house under this section: *Ex parte Ethelstane*, 32 L. T. 339 ; 40 J. P. 39. Where the customer is really drunk the license holder cannot set up the defence that he and his potman considered the customer not to be drunk, for the risk of discovering the fact rests with the license holder: *Cundy* v. *Le Cocq*, 13 Q. B. D. 207 ; 48 J. P. 599 ; 53 L. J. M. C. 125 ; 51 L T. 265 ; 32 W. R. 769. Moreover, if a drunken man and a sober man enter together, and the latter orders liquor for both, this will be deemed a selling to the drunken man: *Scatchard* v. *Johnson*, 57 L. J. M. C. 41 ; 52 J. P. 389. So to supply drink to one already drunk is to permit drunkenness: *Edmunds* v. *James* (1892), 1 Q. B. 18 ; 56 J. P. 40 ; 61 L. J. M. C. 56 ; 40 W. R. 140 ; 65 L. T. 675. And where a drunken person is found on licensed premises, and is known to be so by the license holder, the latter is liable, though no drink may have been supplied by such license holder: *Hope* v. *Warburton* (1892), 2 Q. B. 134; 61 L. J. M. C. 147; 56 J. P. 328; 66 L. T. 589 ; 40 W. R. 510. At the same time, to permit implies that there was power to prevent ; and if a customer becomes drunk, but is not allowed to remain in the house, the license holder cannot be deemed to permit it. A licensed person cannot be convicted under this section for being drunk on his own premises, for any charge of that kind must be made under section 12, *ante*: *Warden* v. *Tye*, 2 C. P. D. 74 ; 41 J. P. 120 ; 46 L. J. M. C. 111 ; 35 L. T. 852.

Liability for manager's acts.] Any servant, wife, or manager of the house will not be liable to be convicted for doing the acts here prohibited ; but they may make the license holder liable, and may themselves also in some cases be convicted as aiders and abettors, under 11 & 12 Vict. c. 43, s. 5 ; *Wilson* v. *Stuart*, 32 L. J. Q. B. 311 ; 3 B & S. 913 ; 27 J. P. 661 ; 8 L. T. 277 ; and their acts will render the licensed person liable unless there is strong evidence that the latter gave express orders to the contrary, and did what he could to enforce his orders. The courts will hold this to be one of the excepted cases—where the master is responsible criminally for the act of his servant or manager ; if it be held otherwise, the statute may be very easily evaded. It may be reasonably assumed that the law requires some responsible person to be always on such premises, and in charge of them, who represents the master in the conduct of the house ; and though a master is not usually responsible for the crimes of his servant, this may well be deemed to be an

Sect. 13.   *Liability of a Manager.*

NOTE. exception ; and it has been so held in cases under sections 15, 16, and 17. See notes to those sections. In some cases, where the act done by a servant is done for the master's benefit in the course of the business, and causes a nuisance either to an individual or the public, the master, though taking no part, may be indictable in respect of the act done : *R.* v. *Stephens,* L. R. 1 Q. B. 702 ; 35 L. J. M. C. 251 ; 14 L. T. 593 ; 14 W. R. 859 ; 30 J. P. 822. In other Acts, such as the Cattle Diseases Act, the Bread Act, the Nuisances Removal Act, and the Mines Act, cases have occurred which have been mostly decided according to the general rule that the master is not liable if the servant alone, without the master's knowledge or against his express orders, has committed the act prohibited. At the same time, there must be some one on licensed premises to conduct the house, and the master must in that view be the person liable for acts done knowingly by the servant or manager in contravention of many of these enactments. See a case of a chimney sending forth black smoke, the servant having lighted the fire, and the master was held liable : *Barnes* v. *Akroyd,* L. R. 7 Q. B. 474 ; 41 L. J. M. C. 110 ; 36 J. P. 280 ; 26 L. T. 437 ; 20 W. R. 671. As to adulterating milk, see *Brown* v. *Foot,* 56 J. P. 85 ; 61 L. J. M. C. 110 ; 66 L. T. 649 ; *Kearley* v. *Tyler,* 56 J. P. 72 ; 65 L. T. 261. On the other hand, if the master has done all in his power to make a furnace consume its own smoke, and has appointed a careful servant, he is not liable : *Chisholm* v. *Doulton,* 22 Q. B. D. 736 ; 53 J. P. 292 ; 58 L. J. M. C. 133. So where a baker was held not liable for alum being in bread, neither baker nor servant having any knowledge of it : *Core* v. *James,* L. R. 7 Q. B. 135 ; 41 L. J. M. C. 19 ; 36 J. P. 519. So where a tradesman sold coals, and his servant, without his knowledge, misrepresented the weight of a sack : *Roberts* v. *Woodward,* 55 J. P. 116 ; 25 Q. B. D. 412 ; 63 L. T. 200. See a case of a servant neglecting to disinfect premises, and the master held liable : *Searley* v. *Reynolds,* 7 B. & S. 704 ; 14 L. T. 518 ; 31 J. P. 4 ; *R.* v. *Handley,* 9 L. T. 827. It is absolutely necessary that there should be some evidence of knowledge on the part of the master or servant, as was held where the servant of H., by direction of a customer of H., placed a portable steam engine in a place prohibited by statute, and the master was not liable : *Harrison* v. *Leaper,* 5 L. T. 640 ; 26 J. P. 373.

In a conviction under this section it will not be necessary to state the names of the persons who were permitted to be drunk : *Wray* v. *Toke,* 17 L. J. M. C. 183 ; 12 Q. B. 492 ; 12 J. P. 804.

Harbouring Prostitutes.   Sect. 13.

The second and third offence need not be for precisely the same NOTE. offence as the former. Thus, one may be for permitting drunkenness, another may be for permitting quarrelsome conduct, or riotous, &c. But the offences must all be under this section of the Licensing Acts.

The part *within brackets* was repealed by Licensing Act, 1874, section 33 ; but see that Act, section 13. The justices may order this conviction to be recorded.

14. *Penalty for keeping disorderly house.*] If any licensed person knowingly permits his premises to be the habitual resort of or place of meeting of reputed prostitutes, whether the object of their so resorting or meeting is or is not prostitution, he shall, if he allow them to remain thereon longer than is necessary for the purpose of obtaining reasonable refreshment, be liable to a penalty not exceeding for the first offence ten pounds, and not exceeding for the second and any subsequent offence twenty pounds.

[Any conviction for an offence under this section shall, unless the convicting magistrate or justices shall otherwise direct, be recorded on the license of the person convicted.]

This offence may be equally committed while there is an *occasional* license for the place : Licensing Act, 1874, section 20.

The part *within brackets* was repealed by Licensing Act, 1874, section 33 ; but see that statute, section 13, *post*. The justices may order this conviction to be recorded.

A penalty is also imposed by the Towns Police Act, 10 & 11 Vict. c. 89, s. 35, for suffering prostitutes or thieves to assemble, which applies to alehouses : *Cole* v. *Coulton*, 2 E. and E. 695 ; 24 J. P. 596 ; 29 L. J. M. C. 125 ; 2 L. T. 216 ; 8 W. R. 412.

The same remarks as were made in the notes to the 13th section apply to the above 14th section as regards the liability of the licensed person for his servant or manager disobeying the statute, except that owing to the word "knowingly" being here used,

Sect. 14. *Resort of Prostitutes.*

NOTE. the evidence of knowledge ought to be much more cogent, in order to make the master liable for his servant or manager's knowledge.

Resort of Prostitutes.] In order to prove the offence it must be shown : (1) That the licensed person, or at least his manager, knew the women were reputed prostitutes, and the justices will inquire into the grounds of belief of witnesses as to this evil reputation ; (2) That he allowed them to remain longer than necessary for reasonable refreshment, which is partly a matter of arithmetic, the nature of the meal or refreshment being generally the best materials for showing whether they remained longer than was necessary for its consumption.

There are previous cases on the subject, under similar enactments of *Greig* v. *Bendeno*, E. B. E. 133 ; 27 L. J. M. C. 294 ; *Purkis* v. *Huxtable*, 1 E. & E. 780 ; 28 L. J. M. C. 221 ; *Whitfield* v. *Bainbridge*, 30 J. P. 644. The constable having seen prostitutes previously in the house is some evidence of the keeper's knowledge of their character : *Parker* v. *Green*, 2 B. & S. 299 ; 31 L. J. M. C. 133 ; 26 J. P. 247 ; 10 W. R. 316 ; *Belasco* v. *Hannant*, 3 B. & S. 13 ; 31 L. J. M. C. 225 ; 26 J. P. 823 ; 6 L. T. 577 ; 10 W. R. 867 ; *Cole* v. *Coulton*, 2 E. & E. 695 ; 29 L. J. M. C. 125 ; 24 J. P. 596 ; 2 L. T. 216 ; 8 W. R. 412. The cases decided under the previous statutes show that prostitutes are entitled, like other people, to refreshment, and that it cannot be reasonably implied from the fact of the licensed person supplying them with refreshment that he permits them to assemble in an unlawful manner.

This present section has been considerably altered in its language from the previous enactments. Unless the woman had remained longer on the premises than is necessary for the purpose of refreshment, it seems that, though her object may be prostitution, yet the penalty will not be incurred by the licensed person till the time for her refreshment has ceased. It is only after that time that her remaining on the premises can be inquired into ; but for whatever purpose she is there after that time is immaterial. And if she do not resort for refreshment at all, then if the landlord allow her to remain for any length of time, however short, he will be liable to the penalty. The licensed person has power to turn her out under the 18th section, and if he fails to do so he will run the risk of the penalty.

An objection, founded on the conduct of licensed houses as to serving prostitutes, being often raised to the renewal of a license, in one case there was evidence given that several times seventeen

35 & 36 VICT. C. 94, S. 14.

Harbouring Thieves. Seditious Meetings, &c. Sect. 14.
Note.

prostitutes were found in the house at one time and this was known to the license holder, and he produced no evidence that they were there for purposes of refreshment, the licensing justices were held justified, after due notice of opposition being proved, in refusing to renew the license : *Sharp* v. *Hughes*, 57 J. P. 104.

It is not essential that the prostitutes who "meet" should be the same persons; it is enough that persons of their class frequently come to the house, and that one is there, though for the first time, if known as to character. And in any summons or conviction it is not necessary to name the disorderly persons : *Wray* v. *Toke*, 12 Q. B. 492 ; 17 L. J. M. C. 183 ; 12 J. P. 804.

Forfeiture of license for harbouring thieves, &c.] A penalty is imposed on keepers of licensed houses for harbouring thieves, &c., of a kindred character to the above, as follows :

The *Prevention of Crimes Act*, 1871, 34 & 35 Vict. c. 112, s. 10, enacts as follows :—Every person who occupies or keeps any lodging-house, beer-house, public-house, or other house or place where intoxicating liquors are sold, or any place of public entertainment or public resort, and knowingly lodges or knowingly harbours thieves or reputed thieves, or knowingly suffers them to meet or assemble therein, or knowingly allows the deposit of goods therein, having reasonable cause for believing them to be stolen, shall be guilty of an offence against this Act, and be liable to a penalty not exceeding ten pounds, and in default of payment to be imprisoned for a period not exceeding four months, with or without hard labour, and the court before which he is brought may, if it think fit, in addition to or in lieu of any penalty, require him to enter into recognizances, with or without sureties, and if in Scotland to find caution, for keeping the peace or being of good behaviour during twelve months : provided that—

> (1.) No person shall be imprisoned for not finding sureties or cautioners in pursuance of this section for a longer period than three months ; and
>
> (2.) The security required from a surety or cautioner shall not exceed twenty pounds :

And any license for the sale of any intoxicating liquors, or for keeping any place of public entertainment or public resort, which has been granted to the occupier or keeper of any such house or place as aforesaid, may, in the discretion of the court, be forfeited on his first conviction of an offence under this section, and on his second conviction for such an offence his license shall be forfeited and he shall be disqualified for a period of two years from

Sect. 14. *Forfeiture of License for Holding Seditious Meetings.*

NOTE. receiving any such license; moreover, where two convictions under this section have taken place within a period of three years in respect of the same premises, whether the persons convicted were or were not the same, the court shall direct that for a term not exceeding one year from the date of the last of such convictions no such license as aforesaid shall be granted to any person whatever in respect of such premises; and any license granted in contravention of this section shall be void.

Any licensed person brought before a court in pursuance of this section shall produce his license for examination, and if such license is forfeited shall deliver it up altogether, and if such person wilfully neglects or refuses to produce his license he shall, in addition to any other penalty under this section, be liable on summary conviction to a penalty not exceeding five pounds: 34 & 35 Vict. c. 112, s. 10.

Any person convicted under 34 & 35 Vict. c. 112, s. 10, shall have a *right of appeal* against such conviction in the same manner in all respects as a person may appeal who feels aggrieved by a conviction made by a court of summary jurisdiction under the Licensing Act, 1872, and all the provisions of such last-mentioned Act and of any Act amending the same relating to an appeal from a conviction made by a court of summary jurisdiction under such last-mentioned Act shall apply accordingly: 39 & 40 Vict. c. 20, s. 5. One consequence of this last enactment is that a convicted person must appeal to the quarter sessions of the borough or city and not to the county sessions as he would do in case of a refusal of a renewal or transfer of a license. See section 52 of Licensing Act, 1872, *post.*

The mode of *proving a previous conviction* is set forth in 34 & 35 Vict. c. 112, s. 18. The proceeding to convict is under the Summary Jurisdiction Act, 42 & 43 Vict. c. 49, s. 17. See also the provision on that subject in 42 & 43 Vict. c. 49, s. 22, in notes to 50th section of Licensing Act, 1872, *post.*

A meeting by circular at an ale-house to get up a subscription for the wife and children of a convicted thief, several thieves being in the company, is an assembling of thieves within 34 & 35 Vict. c. 112, s. 10: *Marshall* v. *Fox,* L. R. 6 Q. B. 370; 24 L. T. 751; 40 L. J. M. C. 142; 19 W. R. 1108; 35 J. P. 631.

Forfeiture of license for holding seditious meetings.]
It shall be lawful for any two or more justices of the peace acting for any county, stewartry, riding, division, city, town, or place, upon evidence on oath that any meeting of any society (or club), hereby declared to be an unlawful combination and confederacy

35 & 36 VICT. C. 94, S. 14.

Music and Dancing Licenses.   Sect. 14.

or any meeting for any seditious purpose hath been held after the   NOTE.
passing of this Act, at any house, room, or place licensed for the
sale of ale, beer, wine, or spirituous liquors [with the knowledge
and consent of the person keeping such house, room, or place], to
adjudge and declare the license or licenses for selling ale, beer,
wine, or spirituous liquors granted to the person or persons keeping such house, room, or place to be forfeited; and the person or
persons so keeping such house, room, or place shall from and after
the day of the date of such adjudication and declaration be subject and liable to all and every the penalties and forfeitures for
any act done after that day which such person or persons would
be subject to if such license or licenses had expired or otherwise
determined on that day : 39 Geo. 3, c. 79, s. 14. There is now
no particular form of adjudicating the forfeiture of such license :
47 & 48 Vict. c. 43. The above 14th section of 39 Geo. 3, c. 79,
is repeated in identical words (but including the words as above
in brackets), by the statute 57 Geo. 3, c. 19. And see 53 & 54
Vict. c. 33.

Other similar offences by license holders.] The offences
which may be committed by license holders in reference to *gaming*
and *betting* are set forth in the Licensing Act, 1872, section 17,
and notes, *post*. A cock fight took place in a bowling alley of a
public-house, and the court held that the keeper could not be
convicted under the Cruelty to Animals Act, 12 & 13 Vict. c. 92,
s. 2, of assisting, as it was not a place kept for such fighting;
Clarke v. *Hague*, 24 J. P. 517 ; 29 L. J. M. C. 105 ; 2 E. & E. 280 ;
8 W. R. 363 ; *Morley* v. *Greenhalgh*, 3 B. & S. 374 ; 32 L. J. M. C.
93 ; 7 L. T. 624 ; 11 W. R. 263 ; 27 J. P. 197.

There are also offences by keepers of licensed houses as to
wages paid in public-houses. See *post*, 46 & 47 Vict. c. 31, s. 3,
and notes, where also offences as to *holding polls* and election
committee rooms in public-houses (16 & 17 Vict. c. 68, s. 6 ;
46 & 47 Vict. c. 51, s. 20 ; 47 & 48 Vict. c. 20, s. 16) are
collected.

For public entertainments on *Sunday*, see 37 & 38 Vict. c. 49,
s. 3, and notes, *post*.

*Music, dancing, and race-course licenses in and within
twenty miles of London and Westminster.*] By the Local
Government Act, 51 & 52 Vict. c. 41, s. 3, the licensing of houses
for music and dancing and race-courses within the metropolitan
area was transferred to the London County Council. Subject
thereto, in places in and within twenty miles of London and
Westminster the following enactments apply :

D

Sect. 14.

NOTE.

Music and Dancing Licenses.

Unlicensed music and dancing places within twenty miles, &c., deemed disorderly houses.] Whereas the multitude of places of entertainment for the lower sort of people is another cause of thefts and robberies, as they are thereby tempted to spend their small substance in riotous pleasures, and in consequence are put on unlawful methods of supplying their wants, and renewing their pleasures: In order, therefore, to prevent the said temptation to thefts and robberies, and to correct as far as may be the habit of idleness, which is become too general over the whole kingdom, and is productive of much mischief and inconvenience: Be it enacted by the authority aforesaid, that from and after the 1st day of December, 1752, any house, room, garden, or other place kept for public dancing, music, or other public entertainment of the like kind, in the cities of *London and Westminster or within twenty miles thereof*, without a license had for that purpose, from the last preceding Michaelmas quarter sessions of the peace, to be holden for the county, city, riding, liberty, or division in which such house, room, garden, or other place is situate (who are hereby authorised and empowered to grant such licenses as they in their discretion shall think proper), signified under the hands and seals of four or more of the justices there assembled, shall be deemed a disorderly house or place; and every such license shall be signed and sealed by the said justices in open court, and afterwards be publicly read by the clerk of the peace, together with the names of the justices subscribing the same; and no such license shall be granted at any adjourned sessions; nor shall any fee or reward be taken for any such license; and it shall and may be lawful to and for any constable, or other person, being thereunto authorised, by warrant under the hand and seal of one or more of His Majesty's justices of the peace of the county, city, riding, division, or liberty where such house or place shall be situate, to enter such house or place, and to seize every person who shall be found therein, in order that they may be dealt with according to law: and every person keeping such house, room, garden, or other place, without such license as aforesaid, shall forfeit the sum of 100*l.* to such person as will sue for the same, and be otherwise punishable as the law directs in cases of disorderly houses: 25 Geo. 2, c. 36, s. 2.

Though this statute is confined to the metropolitan district, yet most of the Local Improvement Acts of the large towns in the country contain an enactment nearly in the same words.

Notwithstanding the above Act, the Secretary of State or the Admiralty may give authority to manage or conduct any recreation room for public dancing, music, or other public entertainment without any license: 52 Vict. c. 3, s. 7.

35 & 36 VICT. C. 94, S. 14.

Music and Dancing Licenses.   Sect. 14.

Licensed music and dancing places within twenty miles,   NOTE.
&c., to have an inscription over them.] Provided always, and it is hereby further enacted by the authority aforesaid, that in order to give public notice what places are licensed pursuant to this Act, there shall be affixed and kept up in some notorious place over the door or entrance of every such house, room, garden, or other place kept for any of the said purposes, and so licensed as aforesaid, an inscription in large capital letters, in the words following : *videlicet,* " Licensed pursuant to Act of Parliament of the twenty-fifth of King George the Second ;" and that no such house, room, garden, or other place kept for any of the said purposes, although licensed as aforesaid, shall be open for any of the said purposes before the hour of [noon] ; and that the affixing and keeping up of such inscription as aforesaid, and the said limitation or restriction in point of time, shall be inserted in, and made conditions of, every such license ; and in case of any breach of either of the said conditions, such license shall be forfeited, and shall be revoked by the justices of the peace in their next general or quarter sessions, and shall not be renewed ; nor shall any new license be granted to the same person or persons, or any other person on his or their or any of their behalf, or for their use or benefit, directly or indirectly, for keeping any such house, room, garden, or other place, for any of the purposes aforesaid : 25 Geo. 2, c. 36, s. 3. The wôrd in *brackets* was substituted by 38 & 39 Vict. c. 21, s. 1 : see next page.

Where a music and dancing license has been granted under 25 Geo. 2, c. 36, the inland revenue are not bound to grant a license under 5 & 6 Will. 4, c. 39, s. 7, to the proprietors to sell liquors therein, as the exemption from the necessity of a justices' license conferred by the Licensing Act, 1872, s. 72, applies only to theatres, but not to places of public entertainment ; *R.* v. *Inland Revenue*, 21 Q. B. D. 569 ; 52 J. P. 390 ; 57 L. J. M. C. 92 ; 59 L. T. 378 ; 36 W. R. 696. Regulations for these places made by the London County Council are obligatory : 41 & 42 Vict. c. 32, s. 12 ; 51 & 52 Vict. c. 41, s. 40 ; *R.* v. *Hannay* (1891), 2 Q. B. 709 ; 56 J. P. 151 ; 60 L. J. M. C. 167 ; 40 W. R. 14.

Theatres excepted.] Provided always that nothing in this Act contained shall extend, or be construed to extend, to the *theatres* royal in Drury Lane and Covent Garden, or the theatre commonly called the King's Theatre in the Haymarket, or any of them ; nor to such performances and public entertainments as are or shall be lawfully exercised and carried on under or by virtue of letters patent, or license of the Crown, or the license of

D 2

Sect. 14. *Music and Dancing Licenses.*

NOTE. the Lord Chamberlain of His Majesty's Household ; anything herein contained notwithstanding : 25 Geo. 2, c. 36, s. 4.

The rules as to *theatre* licenses are stated in notes to Licensing Act, 1872, s. 72, *post.*

Time of keeping open music and dancing rooms within twenty miles, &c.] By the *Public Entertainments Act,* 1875, 38 & 39 Vict. c. 21, s. 1, section 3 of the recited Act, 25 Geo. 2, c. 36, shall be construed as if, instead of the proviso, "that no such house, room, garden, or other place kept for any of the said purposes, although licensed as aforesaid, shall be opened for any of the said purposes before the hour of five in the afternoon," there were substituted the proviso "that no such house, room, garden, or other place kept for any of the said purposes, although licensed as aforesaid, shall be open for any of the said purposes before the hour of noon." Provided, that if on any special occasion an occasional license of exemption shall have been granted under the twenty-ninth section of the Licensing Act, 1872, in respect of any house, room, garden, or other place licensed under the recited Act, no penalty or forfeiture shall be incurred for contravention of section 3 of the recited Act, as hereby amended, on account of such house, room, garden, or other place being kept open for any of the purposes aforesaid on such special occasion from midnight until the hour specified in such occasional license as the hour for closing : 38 Vict. c. 21, s. 1.

Rules of procedure for music, dancing, and theatre licenses in County of London.] The following rules of procedure were settled by the London County Council on 16th of October, 1889, for applications to them as the licensing authority for music, dancing, and theatre licenses :—

1. No person shall be heard in opposition to the renewal of an old license in cases where the licensing committee have, without opposition, recommended it.

2. No person shall be heard in opposition to the grant of a new license in cases where the licensing committee have recommended it, unless such person shall have given notice of objection to the person applying for such new license, in the manner prescribed by the rules of the council, fourteen days at least before the day appointed for the hearing by the committee, and shall have appeared before the committee.

3. Any person intending to oppose a recommendation of the licensing committee, "that the license be not granted," shall send in notice to the clerk of the council, at Spring Gardens, twenty-

Race-course Licenses.   **Sect. 14.**

four hours at least before the day appointed for the council to sit   NOTE.
as the licensing authority.

4. The order of procedure in opposed cases before the London County Council shall be as follows :—
 (a) Each case shall be called in the order in which it appears in the report of the committee.
 (b) If the committee have recommended that the license shall be refused, the applicant for the license shall be first heard, and his evidence (if any) put in.
 (c) The parties objecting to the license shall then be heard in defence of the recommendation, and their evidence (if any) put in.
 (d) The applicant shall then be heard in reply.
 (e) If the committee have recommended that the license shall be granted, the objectors shall open the case and reply, and the applicant be heard in defence.
 (f) Parties may be heard in person or by counsel, but only one speaker shall address the council on behalf of each party in the opening or in the defence, or in the reply.
 (g) No party shall be allowed to call witnesses unless he shall show to the satisfaction of the council that he was prevented from calling or tendering such witnesses before the committee by surprise, want of notice, or other sufficient cause.

5. Members of the council may, during the hearing, put questions through the chairman.

6. At any time after the reply has been finished the chairman may declare that the hearing of the case is closed, and, upon such declaration being made, the council shall deliberate upon it at once.

It has been held that members of the county council are not entitled to take up the position of active opponents and to be represented by counsel, and at the same time vote as a judge with the other members : *R.* v. *London County Council* (1892), 1 Q. B. 190 ; 40 W. R. 285 ; 66 L. T. 168 ; 56 J. P. 8. But those actually opposing must abstain from appearing on the bench or near it.

Race-course licenses.] All race-courses within ten miles from Charing Cross] must be licensed pursuant to 42 & 43 Vict. c. 18, s. 2. And the application for a license was directed to be made

LICENSING ACT, 1872, s. 14.

Sect. 14.   *Country Music and Dancing Licenses.*

NOTE. to the justices at the Michaelmas quarter sessions in the same manner as for the music and dancing licenses : section 4. A horse-race not so licensed is deemed a nuisance : section 7. These licenses are now granted by the London County Council : 51 & 52 Vict. c. 41, s. 3.

Music and dancing licenses twenty miles distant from London and Westminster.] Where the distance from London and Westminster is twenty miles or upwards, music and dancing licenses may now be granted by the licensing justices of the petty sessional division or borough, &c., in which the local authority's district is situated as follows, provided the Public Health Amendment Act, 1890, 53 & 54 Vict. c. 59, has been adopted by the local authority under the provisions of that Act. When the part of the Act has been so adopted as prescribed, the resolution of the local authority is to be published in the local newspapers and on the doors of churches and chapels, a copy of the resolution is to be sent to the Secretary of State, and then a copy of the advertisement shall be conclusive evidence of the resolution having been passed : 53 & 54 Vict. c. 59, s. 3. The enactments which will then be applicable to country licenses will be as follows :—

Regulation of music and dancing licenses twenty miles from London.] For the regulation of places ordinarily used for public *dancing* or *music*, or *other public entertainment* of the like kind, the following provisions shall have effect (namely) :—

1. After the expiration of six months from the adoption of this part of this Act, a house, room, garden, or other place, whether licensed or not for the sale of wine, spirits, beer, or other fermented or distilled liquors, shall not be kept or used for public dancing, singing, music,(a) or other public entertainment of the like kind without *a license* for the purpose or purposes for which the same respectively is to be used first obtained from .the licensing justices of the licensing district in which the house, room, garden, or place is situate, and for the registration thereof a *fee* of five shillings shall be paid by the person applying therefor :

(a) It is to be noticed that the words as to the metropolitan counties differ slightly from these, viz., "any house kept for public dancing, music, or other public entertainment of the same kind :" 25 Geo. 2, c. 36, s. 2. The word "singing" in 53 & 54 Vict. c. 59, s. 51, is mentioned separately, and hence capable of a separate license.

35 & 36 VICT. C. 94, S. 14.

Country Music and Dancing Licenses.   Sect. 14.

2. Such justices may, under the hands of a majority of them assembled at their general annual licensing meeting or at any adjournment thereof or at any special session convened with fourteen days' previous notice, *grant licenses* to such persons as they think fit to keep or use houses, rooms, gardens, or places for all or any of the purposes aforesaid, upon such terms and conditions, and subject to such restrictions as they by the respective licenses determine, and every license shall be in force for one year or for such shorter period as the justices on the grant of the license shall determine, unless the same shall have been previously revoked as hereinafter provided :

3. Such justices may from time to time at any such special session aforesaid *transfer* any such license to such person as they think fit :

4. Each person shall in each case give *fourteen days' notice* to the clerk of the licensing justices and to the chief officer of police of the police district in which the house, room, garden, or place is situated, of his intention to apply for any such license or for the transfer of any such license :

5. Any house, room, garden, or place kept or used for any of the purposes aforesaid *without such license* first obtained shall be deemed a *disorderly* house, and the person occupying or rated as occupier of the same shall be liable to a penalty not exceeding five pounds for every day on which the same is kept or used for any of the purposes last aforesaid :

6. There shall be *affixed* and kept up in some conspicuous place on the door or entrance of every house, room, garden, or place so kept or used and so licensed as aforesaid, an inscription in large capital letters in the words following : " Licensed in pursuance of Act of Parliament for   ," with the addition of words showing the purpose or purposes for which the same is licensed :

7. Any house, room, garden, or place so kept or used, although so licensed as aforesaid, shall not be opened for any of the said purposes except on the *days* and between the *hours* stated in the license :

8. The affixing and keeping up of such inscription as aforesaid, and the observance of the days and hours of opening and closing, shall be inserted in and made a condition of every such license :

NOTE.

Sect. 14.
NOTE.

Inspection of Dancing, &c., Rooms.

9. In case of any breach or disregard of any of the terms or conditions upon or subject to which the license was granted, the holder thereof shall be liable to a penalty not exceeding twenty pounds, and to a daily penalty not exceeding five pounds, and such license shall be *liable to be revoked* by the order of a court of summary jurisdiction :

10. No notice need be given under sub-section four of this section when the application is for a *renewal* of any existing license held by the applicant for the same premises :

11. The justices in any petty sessions may, if and as they think fit, grant to any person applying for the same a license to keep or use any house, room, garden, or place for any purpose within the meaning of this section for any period not exceeding *fourteen days* which they shall specify in such *license*, notwithstanding that no notices shall have been given under sub-section four of this section.

12. This section shall not apply within *twenty miles* of the cities of London or Westminster :

13. In this section the expressions "licensing justices," "licensing district," and "clerk of the licensing justices," have respectively the same meanings as in the Licensing Acts, 1872—1874 ; the expression "police district" means any area for which a separate police force is maintained ; and the expression "chief officer of police" means the chief constable, head constable, or other officer, by whatever name called, having the chief command of such separate police force : 53 & 54 Vict. c. 59, s. 51.

Convenient access to and inspection of public dancing, &c., rooms.] Every building which after the adoption of this Part of this Act (Part III.) in any urban district is used as a place of public resort shall to the satisfaction of the urban authority be substantially constructed and supplied with ample safe and convenient means of ingress and egress for the use of the public, &c. (3) An officer authorised in writing by the urban authority and producing his authority if so required may at all reasonable times enter any such building to see that the provisions of this section are carried into effect. (4) Any person who being the occupier or manager uses the same, or suffers the same to be used, in contravention of this section, or fails to comply with the provisions of this section in respect thereof, shall for every such offence be liable to a penalty not exceeding twenty pounds. (6) For the purposes of this section the expression

35 & 36 VICT. C. 94, S. 14.

Music and Dancing Licenses.   Sect. 14.

"place of public resort" means a building, &c., used as a theatre,   NOTE.
public hall, public concert room, or as a public place of assembly
for persons admitted thereto by tickets or by payment, or used or
constructed or adapted to be used either ordinarily or occasionally
for any other public purpose, but shall not include a private
dwelling-house used occasionally or exceptionally for any of those
purposes : 53 & 54 Vict. c. 59, s. 36.

Appeal as to licenses twenty miles from London.] No
appeal is given against the refusal of the justices to grant, transfer,
or renew these licenses for music, dancing, singing, or other
public entertainment. But where there has been a conviction
for a penalty under the above section there is an appeal to
quarter sessions : 53 & 54 Vict. c. 59, s. 7. Offences are prosecuted, and penalties, costs, and expenses are recovered in a
summary manner under the Public Health Acts : 53 & 54 Vict.
c. 59, s. 6.

The power to grant these licenses, not within 53 & 54 Vict.
c. 59, s. 51, was *transferred* to the county council : 51 & 52 Vict.
c. 41, s. 3.

When music and dancing rooms require licenses.] The
music and dancing license does not authorise stage plays, as these
require the theatre license : *Levy* v. *Yates*, 8 A. & E. 129 ; *Day*
v. *Simpson*, 18 C. B. (N.S.) 680 ; 34 L. J. M. C. 149 ; 13 W. R.
748 ; 12 L. T. 386. As to theatre license, see *post*, section 72 and
notes.

In construing the Act of 25 Geo. 2, c. 36, and similar Acts, it
has been held that some habitual use or several instances of so
using the premises must be shown in order to render a license
necessary : *Marks* v. *Benjamin*, 5 M. & W. 565. Thus an occasional concert given in a licensed theatre on Ash Wednesday is
not within this Act : *Syers* v. *Conquest*, 37 J. P. 342 ; 28 L. T.
402 ; 21 W. R. 524 ; nor a room where a lecture and sacred music
are given : *Baxter* v. *Langley*, 32 J. P. 805 ; 38 L. J. M. C. 1.
An ordinary dancing school does not require a license : *Bellis* v.
Burghall, 2 Esp. 722. A temporary use of a room for dancing on
the occasion of a festival does not require a license : *Shutt* v.
Lewis, 5 Esp. 128 ; *Gregory* v. *Tuffs*, 6 C. & P. 271, 281. But it
is no defence that the dancing was in a public-house which had
a public-house license : *Green* v. *Botheroyd*, 3 C. & P. 471 ; nor
that the dancing was kept comparatively private : *Clarke* v. *Searle*,
1 Esp. 25 ; nor that no money was charged for admission, being
a room in a public-house : *Archer* v. *Waldegrave*, 4 Esp. 186 ;

Sect. 14.   *Gregory* v. *Tuffs*, 6 C. & P. 271 ; *Frailing* v. *Messenger*, 16 L. T.
NOTE. (N.S.) 497 ; 31 J. P. 423. And a room kept for public dancing
or music without a license is a disorderly house though no disorderly or improper conduct is allowed : *R.* v. *Wolfe*, 13 J. P.
428. The music license may be granted separately from the
dancing license: *Brown* v. *Nugent*, L. R. 6 Q. B. 693 ; 40 L. J.
M. C. 166 ; 26 L. T. 880 ; 20 W. R. 89 ; 36 J. P. 22. It is
immaterial that the house or room was not kept exclusively for
dancing ; *Bellis* v. *Beale*, 3 Esp. 592. If the music or dancing is
subsidiary to something else, and is no substantial part of the
entertainment, a license is not required : *Guaglieni* v. *Mathews*, 6
B. & S. 474 ; 34 L. J. M. C. 116 ; 29 J. P. 439 ; *Hall* v. *Green*,
9 Ex. 247 ; 23 L. J. M. C. 15. A skating rink with band of
music comes within the statute, for the music was as important
as the skating, and skating was *ejusdem generis* with dancing :
R. v. *Tucker*, 46 L. J. M. C. 197 ; 41 J. P. 294 ; 2 Q. B. D. 417 ;
36 L. T. 478 ; 25 W. R. 697.

If a local Act say a dancing house shall not be kept without a
license, the justices will act rightly by granting a license only for
one year : *Hoffmann* v. *Bond*, 40 J. P. 5 ; 32 L. T. 775.

One penalty only is recoverable, though several performances
have occurred within six months on separate days : *Garrett* v.
Messenger, L. R. 2 C. P. 583 ; 36 L. J. C. P. 337 ; 31 J. P. 423 ;
10 Cox, 498.

15. *Penalty for permitting premises to be a brothel.*] If any licensed person is convicted of permitting his premises to be a brothel he shall be liable to a penalty not exceeding twenty pounds, and shall forfeit his license, and he shall be disqualified for ever from holding any license for the sale of intoxicating liquors.

This enactment seems impliedly to confer a jurisdiction on
justices to convict the keeper of a licensed house in a summary
way of an offence which is otherwise indictable at common law.
As to a case of implied jurisdiction under the former Contagious
Diseases (Animals) Act, see *Cullen* v. *Justices of Lancashire*, L. R.
7 Q. B. 416 ; 37 J. P. 115 ; 41 L. J. M. C. 132 ; 26 L. T. 691 ;
20 W. R. 691 ; *Johnson* v. *Colam*, L. R. 10 Q. B. 544 ; 40 J. P.
135 ; 44 L. J. M. C. 185 ; 32 L. T. 725 ; 23 W. R. 697.

The same kind of evidence seems to be required under this
section as in the case of a person being indicted for keeping a

35 & 36 VICT. C. 94, S. 15.

Criminal Law Amendment Act Offences.   Sect. 15.

brothel, but, according to section 59, either remedy may be resorted to with this qualification, that if one remedy be pursued, the party cannot be punished again for the same offence. As regards the evidence necessary to prove the offence, it is not material that there was no outward sign of indecency : *R* v *Rice*, L. R. 1 C. C. R. 21 ; 35 L. J. M. C. 93 ; 13 L. T. 382 ; 14 W. R. 56 ; or that there was no actual disorderly conduct : *Greig* v. *Bendeno*, E. B. E. 133 ; 27 L. J. M. C. 294. If there is a conviction, the forfeiture and disqualification follow of course, and the excise license is also, by section 63, forfeited. One consequence of the forfeiture is, that no new tenant can apply either for a transfer or a renewal of the license, the forfeiture dating from the conviction : *R.* v. *West Riding JJ.*, 21 Q. B. D. 258 ; 52 J. P. 455 ; 57 L. J. M. C. 103 ; 36 W. R. 258.

Where a licensed person or his manager permits people to use the premises for purposes of prostitution *once*, this is some evidence to support the charge of permitting the premises to be used as a brothel : *R.* v. *Justices of Parts of Holland*, 46 J. P. 312. In one case the constable, who was the prosecutor, refused to say where he was standing when he discovered that the place was used as a brothel, and the court held that he was bound to answer on cross-examination as to this, as it had an important bearing on his credibility : *Webb* v. *Catchlove*, 50 J. P. 795.

This offence may be committed on premises having at the time an *occasional* license : Licensing Act, 1874, section 19.

Criminal Law Amendment Act offences.] The Criminal Law Amendment Act, 1885, 48 & 49 Vict. c. 69, s. 13, declares, in nearly the same words as the above, that any person who, being the occupier of premises, knowingly permits such premises to be used as a brothel, shall be liable, on summary conviction, to a penalty of 20*l.*, or three months' imprisonment with hard labour. The only difference is the word "knowingly" in this last enactment.

Though formerly a landlord could not be indicted for keeping a bawdy house merely because he did not give notice to quit to a tenant using the premises for such a purpose (*R.* v. *Stannard*, 1 L. & C. 349 ; 33 L. J. M. C. 61 ; 9 L. T. 428 ; 12 W. R. 208 ; 28 J. P. 20 ; *R.* v. *Barrett*, 1 L. & C. 263 ; 32 L. J. M. C. 36 ; 7 L. T. 435 ; 11 W. R. 124) ; yet now a landlord who lets [or relets] with such knowledge may be convicted summarily : 48 & 49 Vict. c. 69, s. 13 ; *Sandford* v. *Clarke*, 21 Q. B. D. 398 ; 52 J. P. 773. And the procedure now against keepers of brothels may be either by indictment or summary : *Kerwin* v. *Hines*, 52 J. P. 230. And

Sect. 15.
Note.
where a brothel keeper is proceeded against summarily and a summons is issued, the justices are bound at once to issue a warrant against the defendant in the same way as if a prosecutor had entered into recognizance to prosecute. *R.* v. *Newton,* 56 J. P. 408; (1892), 1 Q. B. 648; 66 L. T. 830.

16. *Penalty for harbouring constable.*] If any licensed person—

(1.) Knowingly harbours or knowingly suffers to remain on his premises any constable during any part of the time appointed for such constable being on duty, unless for the purpose of keeping or restoring order, or in execution of his duty; or

(2.) Supplies any liquor or refreshment, whether by way of gift or sale, to any constable on duty unless by authority of some superior officer of such constable; or

(3.) Bribes or attempts to bribe any constable,

he shall be liable to a penalty not exceeding for the first offence ten pounds, and not exceeding for the second or any subsequent offence twenty pounds. [Any conviction for an offence under this section shall, unless the convicting magistrate or justices shall otherwise direct, be recorded on the license of the person convicted.]

This offence was formerly confined to the circumstances stated in the 1st sub-section, and the penalty was only 20s.: 23 Vict. c. 27, s. 39. The two last sub-sections increase the stringency of the punishment. Now a licensed person cannot lawfully serve a constable, while the latter is on duty, with any refreshment, except on the order of a superior officer. A constable will be in the execution of his duty in assisting to exclude drunkards under

35 & 36 VICT. C. 94, S. 17.

section 18, *post*, or in demanding the names of persons unlawfully **Sect. 16.**
on the premises under section 25, *post*, or in preventing or detect- ──
ing offences under Act, 1874, section 16, *post*. **NOTE.**
If a servant or manager of the premises knowingly serve a
constable on duty the master may be convicted, though personally
having nothing to do with the matter: *Mullins* v. *Collins*, L. R. 9
Q. B. 292; 43 L. J. M. C. 67; 29 L. T. 838; 22 W. R. 297; 38
J. P. 629. But in all cases either the master or servant must know
that the person is a constable on duty; and his being in uniform,
and not being asked if he was on duty, &c., is good *primâ facie*
evidence of such knowledge. See also notes on this subject to
sections 13—15, *ante*, and section 17, *post*.

There are similar enactments in 2 & 3 Vict. c. 93, s. 16, and
10 & 11 Vict. c. 89, s. 34.

The offence may be committed on premises having only an
occasional license: Licensing Act, 1874, section 20.

The part *within brackets* was repealed by Licensing Act, 1874,
section 33, but see that Act, section 13. The justices may order
this conviction to be recorded.

17. *Penalty for permitting gaming.*] If any licensed person—

(1.) Suffers any gaming or any unlawful game to be carried on in his premises; or

(2.) Opens, keeps, or uses, or suffers his house to be opened, kept, or used in contravention of the Act 16 & 17 Vict. c. 119, intituled "An Act for the Suppression of Betting Houses,"

he shall be liable to a penalty not exceeding for the first offence ten pounds, and not exceeding for the second and any subsequent offence twenty pounds.

[Any conviction for an offence under this section shall, unless the convicting magistrate shall otherwise direct, be recorded on the license of the person convicted.]

This offence may be committed on premises having an *occasional* license: Licensing Act, 1874, section 20.

Sect. 17. *Gaming.*

NOTE. This 1st sub-section is substantially the same as the usual clause in the original form of alehouse licenses.

Playing for money.] The rule is, that no game, however lawful in itself, if played for money, or money's worth, can be permitted in licensed premises. Thus nine-pins or skittles played for beer are unlawful: *Danford* v. *Taylor,* 20 L. T. 483; 33 J. P. 612. And it is immaterial whether the beer is drunk on the premises or not: *Luff* v. *Leaper,* 36 J. P. 773. So if cards are played for money: *Patten* v. *Rhymer,* 3 E. & E. 1; 29 L. J. M. C. 189; 24 J. P. 342; 2 L. T. 352; 8 W. R. 496. It is no defence that the game, such as skittle-pool, is said to be mostly a game of skill, if it is played for money: *Dyson* v. *Mason,* 22 Q. B. D. 351; 58 L. J. M. C. 55; 53 J. P. 261; 60 L. T. 265. Moreover, if the license holder were to lend money to a guest to play for money, the former could not recover it: *Foot* v. *Baker,* 6 Scott N. R. 301; 5 M. & Gr. 335.

How far knowledge of the gaming must be proved.] If the game is played without the knowledge of the licensed person or the manager, and is a mere casual frolic, no penalty is incurred by him: *Avards* v. *Dance,* 26 J. P. 437. But if the conduct of the landlord is such that he leaves the management of the house to a servant, and either he or such servant closes his eyes to what is going on, the landlord will be guilty of the offence, his gross negligence or wilful shutting of his own or his manager's eyes being equivalent to "suffering the gaming to be carried on:" *Bosley* v. *Davies,* 1 Q. B. D. 84; 45 L. J. M. C. 27; 33 L. T. 528; 24 W. R. 140; 40 J. P. 550; *Redgate* v. *Haynes,* 1 Q. B. D. 89; 41 J. P. 86; 33 L. T. 779; 45 L. J. M. C. 65. Thus where the manager goes to bed and leaves the house under the management of "the boots" during late hours, and gaming goes on, the licensed person may be rightly convicted: *Crabtree* v. *Hole,* 43 J. P. 799. And where the skittle-alley was in charge of a separate attendant, who allowed gambling, though directed generally by the license holder never to do so, the latter was held to be rightly convicted: *Bond* v. *Evans,* 21 Q. B. D. 249; 52 J. P. 613; 57 L. J. M. C. 105; 59 L. T. 411; 36 W. R. 767. But where all that was shown was, that the potman, who was not proved to be in charge, saw some gambling, and did nothing to prevent it, and the master was in another part of the building and knew nothing whatever about the matter, and the justices refused to convict, the High Court held they were right: *Somerset* v. *Hart,* 12 Q. B. D. 360; 53 L. J. M. C. 77; 48 J. P. 327.

35 & 36 VICT. C. 94, S. 17.

Gaming Houses.   Sect. 17.

Some games illegal per se.] There are some games illegal in themselves; others are illegal only when played for money. See an enumeration of illegal games in *Jenks* v. *Turpin*, 13 Q. B. D. 505; 53 L. J. M. C. 161; 50 L. T. 808; 48 J. P. 489. Thus cards and dice are not in themselves unlawful: *Allport* v. *Nutt*, 1 C. B. 989; 14 L. J. C. P. 272; nor dominoes: *R.* v. *Ashton*, 1 E. & B. 286; 16 J. P. 790; 22 L. J. M. C. 1. The games may be lawful, as being mostly games of skill: *Bew* v. *Harston*, 3 Q. B. D. 454; 47 L. J. M. C. 121; 26 W. R. 915; 42 J. P. 808; yet if played for money they are equally gaming: *Dyson* v. *Mason, ante*, p. 46.

NOTE.

Friends of license holder.] The licensed keeper cannot set up any exemption from this enactment on the ground that the persons playing at the game were his own private friends, and not customers: *Patten* v. *Rhymer*, 3 E. & E. 1; 29 L. J. M. C. 189; 24 J. P. 342; 2 L. T. 352; 8 W. R. 496. And though the Act, 1874, section 30, *post*, allows him to keep private friends in his house after closing hours, he is still liable under this section if he allows them to game: *Hare* v. *Osborne*, 34 L. T. (N.S.) 294; *Osborne* v. *Hare*, 40 J. P. 759; *Cooper* v. *Osborne*, 35 L. T. (N.S.) 347; 40 J. P. 759.

There is no penalty imposed by this Act on the persons who may be allowed to game in the house, unless, perhaps, the justices were to find as a fact that they were on the premises for the sole purpose of gaming, in which case see section 25, *post*.

With regard to *billiards*, though an alehouse keeper is exempt by 8 & 9 Vict. c. 109, s. 11, from requiring a special license to keep a table, yet if the customers play for money the play comes under the description of gaming. As to playing billiards after closing hours, see *post*, section 75, and notes.

The part *within brackets* was repealed by Licensing Act, 1874, section 33; but see that statute, section 13. The justices may order this conviction to be recorded.

Unlawful gaming houses.] The question what is an unlawful game under the Gaming Act, 8 & 9 Vict. c. 109, and the Betting Houses Act, 17 & 18 Vict. c. 38, was discussed in *Jenks* v. *Turpin*, 13 Q. B. D. 505; 53 L. J. M. C. 161; 50 L. T. 808; 48 J. P. 489, where the game of baccarat, as played, was held to be more a game of chance than of skill, and illegal. In *R.* v. *Rogier*, 1 B. & C. 272; 2 D. & Ry. 431, the court said if the gaming tended to injure public morals it was illegal and indictable. And a keeping of a common gaming house was said to be illegal at common law: *R.* v. *Rice*, L. R. 1 C. C. R. 21; 35 L. J.

Sect. 17.   *Wagers on Games.*

NOTE.   M. C. 93; 14 W. R. 56; 13 L. T. 382. But mere excessive gaming not in a common gambling house is not unlawful. HAWKINS, J., said that the result of the statutes now is, that somes games are expressly declared to be absolutely forbidden, and to the gaming at which a penalty is attached. Such are ace of hearts, pharoah (faro), bassett, and hazard (*Mackinnell* v. *Robinson*, 3 M. & W. 434), passage, and every other game with a die or dice (except backgammon) and roulet (or roly-poly), [and any other mere game of chance. The other games are unlawful only when played in common gaming houses. Thus, bowling, coyting, cloysh-cayls, half-bowl, tennis, dicing table, or carding, were unlawful till 1845, after which games of mere skill were said not to be illegal. The Gaming Houses Act, 17 & 18 Vict. c. 38, was said by HAWKINS, J., to treat games of chance, or of chance and skill combined, as unlawful ; but the keeping of a common gaming house is in itself a nuisance and indictable.

   Punishment for unlawful gaming houses.] The keeper of a house for unlawful gaming forfeits 500*l.* : 17 & 18 Vict. c. 32, s. 4. Justices, except in the metropolitan police district, may by special warrant authorise constables to enter places in which it is suspected that unlawful games are holden and arrest persons found therein : 8 & 9 Vict. c. 109, s. 3 ; 17 & 18 Vict. c. 38, s. 3. And like provisions are made for the metropolitan district : 8 & 9 Vict. c. 109, ss. 6, 7. The obstruction of constables is punished by 17 & 18 Vict. c. 38, ss. 1, 2. And persons found in gaming houses are dealt with as set forth in 8 & 9 Vict. c. 109 ; 17 & 18 Vict. c. 38, ss. 5, 6.

   If two separate acts of betting and keeping of betting books are proved, this is some evidence of the offence of keeping a common gaming house : *Foote* v. *Butler*, 41 J. P. 292.

   When a person is arrested and brought before a justice he is entitled to demand an information and summons before going into a defence : *Blake* v. *Beach*, 45 L. J. 111 ; 40 J. P. 678 ; 1 Ex. D. 320. See *R.* v. *Hughes*, 4 Q. B. D. 614, *ante*, p. 25.

   Parties convicted may appeal to quarter sessions under the Summary Jurisdiction Act, 47 & 48 Vict. c. 43, sched. And as imprisonment may be ordered for six months they may, before the hearing, demand a trial by jury : 42 & 43 Vict. c. 49, s. 17. See this Act, 1872, ss. 51, 52, *post*.

   Wagers on games.] All contracts by way of gaming or wagering are void ; but such enactment does not apply to any subscription or contribution, or agreement to subscribe or con-

35 & 36 VICT. c. 94, s. 17.

Betting Houses. Sect. 17.

tribute, for or towards any plate, prize, or sum of money to be awarded to the winner or winners of any lawful game, sport, pastime or exercise : 8 & 9 Vict. c. 109, s. 18. This enactment makes void a wager on a game of billiards, as it is not within the proviso : *Parsons* v. *Alexander*, 5 E. & B. 263. The loser of a wager may, before the stakes have been paid over, repudiate the wager and recover his money from the stakeholder : *Hampden* v. *Walsh*, 1 Q. B. D. 189 ; *Diggle* v. *Higgs*, 2 Ex. D. 422 ; 43 J. P. 245. And commission agents were able to sue for money paid on the principal's bets : *Read* v. *Anderson*, 13 Q. B. D. 779. But the Gaming Act, 1892, 55 Vict. c. 9, made promises to pay money under a contract which was rendered null and void by 8 & 9 Vict. c. 109, or to pay commission in respect of gaming contracts, null and void, and no action should be brought to recover such sums. This later Act was not retrospective : *Knight* v. *Lee* (1893), 1 Q. B. 41 ; 57 J. P. 118 ; 67 L. T. 686. Now the Act prohibits an action for money paid by an agent to settle his principal's bets : *Tatam* v. *Reeve* (1893), 1 Q. B. 44 ; 67 L. T. 683 ; 57 J. P. 118.

NOTE.

Keeping a betting house.] No house, office, room, or other place shall be opened, kept, or used for the purpose of the owner, occupier, or keeper thereof,—or any person using the same,—or any person procured or employed by or acting for or on behalf of such owner, occupier, or keeper, or person using the same,— or of any person having the care or management or in any manner conducting the business thereof,—betting with persons resorting thereto ;—or for the purpose of any money or valuable thing being received by or on behalf of such owner, occupier, keeper, or person as aforesaid, as or for the consideration for any assurance, undertaking, promise, or agreement, express or implied, to pay or give thereafter any money or valuable thing on any event or contingency of or relating to any horse-race or other race, fight, game, sport, or exercise —or as or for the consideration for securing the paying or giving by some other person of any money or valuable thing on any such event or contingency as aforesaid ; and every house, office, room, or other place opened, kept, or used for the purposes aforesaid, or any of them, is hereby declared to be a common nuisance and contrary to law : 16 & 17 Vict. c. 119, s. 1.

And every house, room, office, or place opened, kept, or used for the purposes aforesaid, or any of them, shall be taken and deemed to be a common gaming house within the meaning of 8 & 9 Vict. c. 109 ; 16 & 17 Vict. c. 119, s. 2.

LICENSING ACT, 1872, S. 17.

Sect. 17. *Betting Houses.*

NOTE. *Penalty for keeping betting house.*] Any person who being the owner or occupier of any house, office, room, or other place, or a person using the same, shall open, keep, or use the same for the purposes hereinbefore mentioned, or either of them;—and any person who, being the owner or occupier of any house, room, office, or other place, shall knowingly and wilfully permit the same to be opened, kept, or used by any other person for the purposes aforesaid, or either of them;—and any person having the care or management of, or in any manner assisting in conducting the business of, any house, office, room, or place, opened, kept, or used for the purposes aforesaid, or either of them,—shall, on summary conviction thereof before any two justices of the peace, be liable to forfeit and pay such penalty, not exceeding 100l., as shall be adjudged by such justices, and may be further adjudged by such justices to pay such costs attending such conviction as to the said justices shall seem reasonable; and on the non-payment of such penalty and costs, or in the first instance, if to the said justices it shall seem fit, may be committed to the common gaol or house of correction, with or without hard labour, for any time not exceeding six calendar months; 16 & 17 Vict. c. 119, s. 3; 47 & 48 Vict. c. 43, sched.

If the defendant choose he may, before the charge is gone into, demand a trial by jury: 42 & 43 Vict. c. 49, s. 17.

If two separate acts of betting with strangers are proved and betting books kept, this is some evidence of keeping a betting house: *Foote* v. *Butler*, 41 J. P. 792. But if the betting takes place between members of a club this is not an offence within these sections: *Oldham* v. *Ramsden*, 44 L. J. C. P. 309; 32 L. T. 825; 39 J. P. 583.

A person who goes into the bar of a public-house, and not casually but for several days habitually bets with people he meets there on horse-racing, though he has no interest in the room or house, may be convicted under 16 & 17 Vict. c. 119, s. 3; *MacWilliam* v. *Dawson*, 56 J. P. 182.; *Whitehurst* v. *Fincher*, 62 L. T. 433; 54 J. P. 565. And the license holder who knows of a bookmaker using the bar of his house for the purpose of betting with the customers may also be convicted of suffering, &c.: *Hornsby* v. *Raggett* (1892), 1 Q. B. 20; 66 L. T. 21; 40 W. R. 111; 55 J. P. 708. Where a stranger stood on a piece of waste ground near but not belonging to a public-house, and received bets in sealed packets, and these packets were fetched at intervals by a servant of the house, who kept them in the house till the stranger entered, and opened them, but the stranger had no interest in the house, it was held that the license holder could not be

35 & 36 VICT. C. 94, S. 17.

Betting Houses.   Sect. 17.

convicted of suffering the stranger to use the house as a betting   NOTE.
house: *Davis* v. *Stephenson*, 24 Q. B. D. 529; 54 J. P. 565; 59
L. J. M. C. 73; 62 L. T. 436; 38 W. R. 492.
ɪ ɪWhere the grounds of a public-house are used for races or
matches, much depends on the kind of user and the relation
between the owner of the place and those who bet there. In
Shaw v. *Morley*, L. R. 3 Ex. 137; 32 J. P. 391, the owner of the
ground allowed a betting man to receive bets in a palisade, 44
yards long and 2 yards wide, and the latter was held to keep a
place. In *Bows* v. *Fenwick*, L. R 9 C. P. 339; 43 L. J. C. P. 107;
30 L. T. 524; 22 W. R. 804; 38 J. P. 440, B. stood on a stool
on a raceground, and was held to keep a place. In *Eastwood* v.
Miller, L. R. 9 Q. B. 440; 43 L. J. M. C. 139; 30 L. T. 716;
22 W. R. 799; 38 J. P. 647, a bookmaker who stood in a field of
three acres during a pigeon match, was held to keep a place. In
Haigh v. *Sheffield*, L. R. 10 Q. B. 102; 44 L. J. M. C. 17; 31
L. T. 536; 23 W. R. 547; 39 J. P. 230, bookmakers standing on
chairs at a foot race betting were held to keep a place. In *Gallo-
way* v. *Maries*, 8 Q. B. D. 275; 46 J. P. 326, the bookmaker who
stood in the ring at a grand stand during the races was held to
keep a place. In *Snow* v. *Hill*, 14 Q. B. D. 588; 54 L. J. M. C.
95; 52 L. T. 859; 33 W. R. 475; 49 J. P. 440, S. went into a
field where dog races were held, but only walked up and down
and stood in no one spot making bets, and he was held not to
keep a place.

This provision of section 3 of this Act (16 & 17 Vict. c. 119)
is not impliedly repealed as regards license holders by the Licensing Act, 1872, section 17, the only effect being that one cannot
be punished under both enactments: *Sims* v. *Pay*, 58 L. J. M. C.
39; 53 J. P. 420; 60 L. T. 602.

Agreeing to pay money on the event of a race, fight, &c.]
Any person being the owner or occupier of any house, office,
room, or place opened, kept, or used for the purposes aforesaid, or
either of them, or any person acting for or on behalf of any such
owner or occupier, or any person having the care or management
or in any manner assisting in conducting the business thereof,
who shall receive, directly or indirectly, any money or valuable
thing as a deposit on any bet on condition of paying any sum of
money or other valuable thing on the happening of any event or
contingency of or relating to a horse-race or any other race, or any
fight, game, sport or exercise, or as or for the consideration for
any assurance, undertaking, promise or agreement, express or
implied, to pay or give thereafter any money or valuable thing on

LICENSING ACT, 1872, s. 17.

Betting Houses.

any such event or contingency—and any person giving any acknowledgment, note, security, or draft on the receipt of any money or valuable thing so paid or given as aforesaid, purporting or intended to entitle the bearer or any other person to receive any money or valuable thing on the happening of any such event or contingency as aforesaid—shall, upon summary conviction thereof before two justices of the peace, forfeit and pay such penalty, not exceeding 50*l*., as shall be adjudged by such justices, and may be further adjudged by such justices to pay such costs attending such conviction as to the said justices shall seem reasonable ; and on the non-payment of such penalty and costs, or in the first instance, if to such justices it shall seem fit, may be committed to the common gaol or house of correction, with or without hard labour, for any time not exceeding three calendar months : 16 & 17 Vict. c. 119, s. 4 ; 47 & 48 Vict. c. 43, sched.

And any money or valuable thing received by any such person aforesaid as a deposit on any bet, or as or for the consideration for any such assurance, undertaking, promise, or agreement as aforesaid, shall be deemed to have been received to or for the use of the person from whom the same was received ; and such money or valuable thing, or the value thereof, may be recovered accordingly, with full costs of suit, in any court of competent jurisdiction : 16 & 17 Vict. c. 119, s. 5.

But nothing in this Act contained shall extend to any person receiving or holding any money or valuable thing by way of stakes or deposit to be paid to the winner of any race, or lawful sport, game, or exercise, or to the owner of any horse engaged in any race : 16 & 17 Vict. c. 119, s. 6.

Advertising betting houses.] Any person exhibiting or publishing, or causing to be exhibited or published, any placard, handbill, card, writing, sign, or advertisement whereby it shall be made to appear that any house, office, room, or place is opened, kept, or used for the purpose of making bets or wagers, in manner aforesaid, or for the purpose of exhibiting lists for betting, or with intent to induce any person to resort to such house, office, room, or place for the purpose of making bets or wagers in manner aforesaid, or any person who, on behalf of the owner or occupier of any such house, office, room, or place, or person using the same, shall invite other persons to resort thereto for the purpose of making bets or wagers in manner aforesaid, shall, upon summary conviction thereof before two justices of the peace, forfeit and pay a sum not exceeding 30*l*., and may be further adjudged by such justices to pay such costs attending such

35 & 36 VICT. C. 94, S. 17.

Betting Houses.   Sect. 17.

conviction as to the said justices shall seem reasonable; and on the non-payment of such penalty and costs, or in the first instance, if to such justices it shall seem fit, may be committed to the common gaol or house of correction, with or without hard labour, for any time not exceeding two calendar months: 16 & 17 Vict. c. 119, s. 7.

Those who send, exhibit, or publish, or cause to be published, any letter, circular, telegram, placard, handbill, card, or advertisement offering information or advice as to bets or wagers, or to induce people to apply for information or advice, or to invite shares in such bet or wager, shall be subject to the penalties in the 7th section above quoted: 37 & 38 Vict. c. 15, s. 3. This enactment only refers to betting in betting houses: *Cox* v. *Andrews*, 12 Q. B. D. 126; 48 J. P. 247. And a person who publishes and sells lists of races and offers prizes for those who guess the winners of several races seems to commit no offence either within 16 & 17 Vict. c. 119, or under the Lottery Act, 4 Geo. c. 60: *Caminada* v. *Hulton*, 64 L. T. 572; 55 J. P. 727.

Inciting infants to bet or wager.] It is now a misdemeanour for anyone who, for the purpose of earning commission, &c., to send circulars, &c., inviting an infant to make any bet or wager. The Betting and Loans (Infants) Act, 1892, 55 Vict. c. 4.

Warrant to search suspected betting houses.] It shall be lawful for any justice of the peace, upon complaint made before him on oath that there is reason to suspect any house, office, room, or place to be kept or used as a betting house or office, contrary to this Act, to give authority by special warrant under his hand, when in his discretion he shall think fit, to any constable or police officer, to enter with such assistance as may be found necessary into such house, office, room, or place, and, if necessary, to use force in making such entry, whether by breaking open doors or otherwise, and to arrest, search, and bring before a justice of the peace all such persons found therein, and to seize all lists, cards, or other documents relating to racing or betting found in such house or premises; and any such warrant may be according to the form given in the first schedule annexed to the beforementioned 8 & 9 Vict. c. 109; 16 & 17 Vict. c. 119, s. 11. See *ante,* p. 47, tit. "Gaming House."

And if any superintendent belonging to the metropolitan police force shall report in writing to the commissioners of police of the metropolis that there are good grounds for believing, and that he does believe, that any house, office, room, or place within the

Sect. 17. *Excluding Drunkards.*

NOTE. metropolitan police district is kept or used as a betting house or office, contrary to this Act, it shall be lawful for either of the said commissioners, by order in writing, to authorise the superintendent to enter any such house, office, room, or place, with such constables as shall be directed by the commissioner to accompany him, and, if necessary, to use force for the purpose of effecting such entry, whether by breaking open doors or otherwise, and to take into custody all persons who shall be found therein, and to seize all lists, cards, or other documents relating to racing or betting found in such house or premises: 16 & 17 Vict. c. 119, s. 12. See *ante*, p. 47, tit. " Gaming House."

Appeal to quarter sessions.] Those who are convicted may appeal to quarter sessions under the Summary Jurisdiction Acts: 16 & 17 Vict. c. 119, s. 13; 47 & 48 Vict. c. 43, sched. See notes to 35 & 36 Vict. c. 94, s. 52, *post.*

18. *Power to exclude drunkards from licensed premises.*] Any licensed person may refuse to admit to and may turn out of the premises in respect of which his license is granted any person who is drunken, violent, quarrelsome, or disorderly, and any person whose presence on his premises would subject him to a penalty under this Act.

Any such person who, upon being requested in pursuance of this section by such licensed person, or his agent or servant, or any constable, to quit such premises, refuses or fails so to do, shall be liable to a penalty not exceeding five pounds, and all constables are required on the demand of such licensed person, agent, or servant to expel or assist in expelling every such person from such premises, and may use such force as may be required for that purpose.

The court committing any person to prison for nonpayment of any penalty under this section may order him to be imprisoned with hard labour.

This offence may be committed on premises having an *occasional* **Sect. 18.**
license : Licensing Act, 1874, section 20. **NOTE.**
In turning out a person who is drunken, violent, quarrelsome,
or disorderly, no more force can be lawfully used than is necessary
to overcome the resistance of the person to be turned out. And
a request to leave peaceably should always be first made to such
person, and proved on the hearing of the charge. And the constable acts usually as the agent of the licensed person, unless he
has witnessed some violation of the Act. The persons whose
presence on the premises would subject them to a penalty will be,
for example, persons acting contrary to section 14 to 17 inclusive.
If the licensed person turn out a person who is not drunken,
violent, quarrelsome, or disorderly, or whose presence would not
subject him to a penalty, then such person when turned out
cannot be convicted under this section. Where a chimney-sweep
in his working dress came to the public-house bar amongst the company and refused to leave, it was held that he could be excluded
by force, even though the premises were an inn : *Pigeon* v. *Legge*,
21 J. P. 743. And the same where a person had a large dog
accompanying him, which caused reasonable alarm : *R.* v. *Rymer*,
2 Q. B. D. 136 ; 46 L. J. M. C. 108 ; 41 J. P. 199 ; 25 W. R. 415.
See, further, as to the right of excluding persons, sections 49 and
notes, *post*.

A person cannot be convicted under the second paragraph of
this section unless he has been drunken, violent, quarrelsome,
disorderly, &c., and a previous request to leave addressed to him
by the licensed person, his agent or servant, or a constable, is
proved, and also a failure and refusal to leave thereupon. Where
several persons are charged on one information for refusing to
quit, this is a mere irregularity, and may be waived, and a
separate conviction of each would be right : *Wells* v. *Cheney*,
36 J. P. 198.

The power to commit to prison for non-payment of the penalty
only arises after insufficient distress, pursuant to 42 & 43 Vict.
c. 49, s. 21 ; 47 & 48 Vict. c. 43, s. 5, and the time of imprisonment must be regulated by the same Acts. See notes to section
51, *post*.

Where one of two drunken soldiers came to a publican's house
after being already refused, and being refused admission a second
time, rushed in and demanded beer, and on being collared by the
landlord and put out, the other attacked the landlord with a sharp
instrument, and gave a wound which caused death, the judge held
both were guilty of murder, for the landlord acted within his
rights : *R.* v. *Willoughby*, 1 East P. C. 288.

LICENSING ACT, 1872, s. 23.

Sect. 19. **19.** Penalty on *adulteration* of intoxicating *liquors* (*repealed* by Licensing Act, 1874, section 33. See that Act, section 14, and notes).

20. *Possession* of adulterated liquor or deleterious ingredients (*repealed* by Licensing Act, 1874, sections 33 and 14, *post*).

21. Schedule of *deleterious ingredients* (*repealed* by Licensing Act, 1874, sections 33 and 14, *post*).

22. Analysis of *intoxicating liquor* (*repealed* by Licensing Act, 1874, sections 33 and 14, *post*).

Closing Licensed Premises in Case of Riot.

23. *Power of justices to close licensed premises in case of riot.*] Any two justices of the peace acting for any county or place where any riot or tumult happens or is expected to happen may order every licensed person in or near the place where such riot or tumult happens or is expected to happen to close his premises during any time which the justices may order; and any person who keeps open his premises for the sale of intoxicating liquors during any time at which the justices have ordered them to be closed shall be liable to a penalty not exceeding fifty pounds; and it shall be lawful for any person acting by order of any justices to use such force as may be necessary for the purpose of closing such premises.

This section is a re-enactment in language somewhat varied of 9 Geo. 4, c. 61, s. 20, and is now applied not only to alehouses but also to beerhouses, and all houses for which a justices' certificate is necessary. The penalty is increased from five pounds to fifty pounds. It is essential in any conviction under this section to allege and prove specifically two things: 1. That the justices during a riot or tumult, &c., ordered the house to be closed, and such order was served on the license holder; 2. What were the hours or days when the premises were so ordered to be closed, so that it may be seen whether there was any excess of jurisdiction. A conviction which merely alleged that the defendant kept open his premises "during a time at which the justices ordered them to be closed" was held bad as being too vague: *Newman* v. *Earl of Hardwicke*, 9 A. & E. 124.

Sect. 23.
NOTE.

24. *Times of closing.*] (*Repealed* by Licensing Act, 1874, section 33. See that Act, sections 3, 5, 6, 9, 10, 31, and notes.)

25. *Penalty on person found on premises during closing hours.*] If during any period during which any premises are required under the provisions of this Act to be closed, any person is found on such premises, he shall, unless he satisfies the court that he was an inmate, servant, or a lodger on such premises, or a *bonâ fide* traveller, or that otherwise his presence on such premises was not in contravention of the provisions of this Act with respect to the closing of licensed premises, be liable to a penalty not exceeding forty shillings.

Any constable may demand the name and address of any person found on any premises during the period during which they are required by the provisions of this Act to be closed, and if he has reasonable ground to suppose that the name or address given is false, may require evidence of the correctness of such name and address, and may, if such person fail upon such demand

Sect. 25. to give his name or address, or such evidence, apprehend him without warrant, and carry him, as soon as practicable, before a justice of the peace.

Any person required by a constable under this section to give his name and address, who fails to give the same, or gives a false name or address, or gives false evidence with respect to such name and address, shall be liable to a penalty not exceeding five pounds.

Every person who by falsely representing himself to be a traveller or a lodger, buys or obtains, or attempts to buy or obtain, at any premises any intoxicating liquor during the period during which such premises are closed in pursuance of this Act, shall be liable to a penalty not exceeding five pounds.

This section is a re-enactment in different language of the repealed sections of 32 & 33 Vict. c. 27, s. 16, and 33 & 34 Vict. c. 29, s. 6.

Found on premises not in contravention of Act.] The offence created by the first paragraph of the section is, the person being found on licensed premises during prohibited hours, and not satisfying the court that he is an inmate, servant, lodger, traveller, or otherwise not contravening the section. In order to convict the person found on the premises, it is not necessary that the keeper of the house should have committed any offence. Nor, on the other hand, is it necessary, in order to convict, that the person found should have consumed or purchased any liquor during the prohibited hours. The mere presence of the person found is sufficient *primâ facie* evidence of the offence, unless explained. The explanation, which will no doubt be generally given, will be, that the person found is a "friend of the family," and is on a visit of friendship or condolence or mutual admiration. It was under this Act, before the Act of 1874 passed, not unlawful for a licensed person to entertain a visitor or friend even during prohibited hours, and in order to define the circumstances under which the friend will escape liability, it is necessary to consider what meaning is to be given to the words "in contravention of the provisions of this Act with respect to closing."

35 & 36 VICT. C. 94, S. 25.

Sect. 25.
NOTE.

The only object of the provisions as to closing as declared by the Act, 1874, section 9, is to prevent the selling or exposing for sale of liquor, or keeping open the premises for the sale of liquors, during those hours, or allowing liquors already sold to be consumed there, or permitting anything equivalent to a sale or consumption, as explained by section 62; therefore the provisions will not be contravened if there is no selling and no keeping open, or exposing to sale, or consumption, of liquors on the premises during those hours by persons of the class of customers or purchasers. It would seem to follow that if a person is found on the premises, and is a private friend, or has any lawful business there, the mere fact of the licensed person giving (not selling) liquor to such visitor would not amount to an offence, while, on the other hand, if the liquor was actually sold to, or consumed by, one who is there as a customer, and not as a private friend, it would. This view of the construction of this section has been more clearly supported by the Act, 1874, section 30, which expressly exempts from any penalty a licensed person who during prohibited hours entertains his private friends *bonâ fide* at his own expense. It will thus be a delicate inquiry in such cases for the justices to discriminate between sham friendships and real hospitality, or lawful business. A "private friend" is a somewhat vague phrase, but justices may, from the explanations, easily settle its meaning in each case. Not only private friends, however, but persons having other lawful business on the premises would also be exempt, however difficult it may be to describe the conditions of their being lawfully there. If, for example, people have been frequenting the house, and paying for their liquor in the ordinary way, and being about to leave on the closing hour arriving, the licensed person says he will treat them as his private friends, and allows them to remain later, this will usually be treated as a mere device, and the host will be held liable to the penalty : *Corbett* v. *Haigh*, 5 C. P. D. 50; 42 L. T. (N.S.) 185; 44 J. P. 39; 28 W. R. 430. The mere fact of persons being private friends, and lawfully on the premises during closing hours, does not entitle the landlord to allow them to carry on gaming : *Hare* v. *Osborne*, 34 L. T. (N.S.) 294 ; *Osborne* v. *Hare*, 40 J. P. 759 ; *Cooper* v. *Osborne*, 34 L. T. (N.S.) 347 ; 40 J. P. 759 ; nor to play at billiards : *Ovenden* v. *Raymond*, 40 J. P. 727.

Another instance of no penalty being incurred will occur in grocers' and tobacconists' shops, where customers after closing hours are *bonâ fide* purchasing other articles, as tea, sugar, cigars, which a licensed person is not prohibited from selling. See *Brigden* v. *Heighes*, 1 Q. B. D. 330 ; 40 J. P. 661 ; 45 L. J. M. C. 58 ; 34 L. T. 242 ; 24 W. R. 58; *Ex parte Joynt*, 38 J. P. 390. And see notes to section 69.

Sect. 25.

NOTE.

And this section obviously cannot apply to persons at or near a railway station refreshment room, which need not at any time be closed, if there are persons arriving at or departing from the station by railroad. See Act, 1874, section 10, *post*, and notes.

Where P. was seen, by a constable standing about twelve yards distant, to go into licensed premises during prohibited hours, and in three minutes to come out with a bottle of gin, it was held that P. may be treated as " found on the premises," and so rightly convicted under this section : *Thomas* v. *Powell*, 57 J. P. 329.

Constable demanding visitor's address.] The visitor found on the premises during prohibited hours is bound to give his name and address, on request, to a constable ; but he is not bound to give it to any other person. As to the constable requiring evidence of the correctness of the name and address given, it is difficult to define what this means. The person found cannot be expected to do more that assert his correct name and residence ; at the same time, if the name and address given turn out to be false, the constable, acting at his peril, will be able to justify the apprehension, if made. The more prudent course for the constable will be to proceed against the visitor if the name and address be refused or be false, and not apprehend on the last ground, namely, " giving false evidence with respect to such name or address," which must be a very vague and uncertain ground to proceed upon, so far as he is concerned, and will require great judgment to work out within the limits of the law.

The offence committed under the third paragraph seems distinct from that under the first paragraph, and they are cumulative. In order to establish the offence, a previous request by the constable must be proved ; and in all cases the reasonableness and truth of the information given will be important.

No power is given to the constable to turn out the visitor found on the premises, or detain him till inquiries] are made ; and though he may, in the circumstances stated, apprehend the visitor, and carry him before a justice, this will be at the risk of the constable.

Found on unlicensed premises.] There is also a penalty imposed on persons found on unlicensed premises, or where liquor is found for unlawful sale. See Act, 1874, section 17, *post*.

False representations by travellers.] The penalty on persons falsely representing themselves to be travellers or lodgers, and attempting to buy liquor, is new, but was needed in order to prevent the easy evasion of the enactment. The false representation must be made to the licensed person, or his servant or manager, and it is immaterial whether the attempt to get liquor was successful. It may be doubted whether the "traveller" here mentioned includes a "person arriving at or departing from a railway station by railroad," as described in Act, 1874, section 10, *post*. If the pretended traveller does not ask for liquor, the last clause of the section does not touch him.

Sect. 25.
———
NOTE.

26. *Exemption from closing by order of local authority in respect of certain trades.*] The local authority of any licensing district, upon the production of such evidence as such authority may deem sufficient to show that it is necessary or desirable so to do for the accommodation of any considerable number of persons attending any public market, or following any lawful trade or calling, may grant, if such authority think fit, to any licensed victualler or licensed keeper of a refreshment house [or any person licensed to sell beer or cider by retail to be consumed upon the premises], in respect of premises in the immediate neighbourhood of such market, or of the place where the persons follow such lawful trade or calling, an order exempting such person from the provisions of this Act with respect to the closing of his premises on such days and during such time, except between the hours of one and two of the clock in the morning, as may be specified in such order.

The holder of an order under this section shall not be liable to any penalty for not closing his premises on such days and during such time as may be specified in such order; but he shall not be exempt from any other penalty under this or any other Act, or otherwise.

A notice in such form as may be prescribed by the

Sect. 26. local authority, stating the days and hours during which the premises are permitted to be open under such order of exemption shall be affixed and kept affixed in a conspicuous position outside the premises; and if the holder of the order of exemption make default in affixing or in keeping affixed such notice in manner aforesaid during any part of the time for which his exemption is granted, he shall be liable to pay a penalty not exceeding five pounds.

Every person who keeps affixed to his premises any such notice when he does not hold an order under this section, shall be liable to a penalty not exceeding ten pounds.

Any such local authority as aforesaid may at any time, if it seem fit to them, withdraw an order under this section, or alter the same by way of extension or restriction, as such authority may deem necessary or expedient, so, however, as not to render any person liable to any penalty for anything done under such order before the holder was informed of such withdrawal or alteration.

The following persons and bodies of persons shall be deemed to be local authorities of licensing districts for the purposes of this Act, that is to say,—

> (1.) In the *metropolitan police district*, the commissioner of police for the metropolis, subject to the approbation of one of Her Majesty's principal Secretaries of State:
>
> (2.) In the *city of London* and the liberties thereof, so far as they are not included in the metropolitan police district, the commissioner of

city police, subject to the approbation of the Lord Mayor of the said city:

Sect. 26.

(3.) In *any other place*, two justices of the peace in sessions assembled.

The words *in brackets* were inserted by the Licensing Act, 1874, sections 4, 5.

The exemption order.] This section contemplates the granting of a permanent exemption order, intended to last some months, or it may be years, or indefinitely, without any period specified. The object is to confer this exemption on certain houses, so as to allow them to be open during part of the prohibited hours, without incurring the usual penalty. The hours of exemption must be specified in the order of the local authority. The power of exemption is conferred not only as to licensed victuallers' houses, that is, alehouses licensed under 9 Geo. 4, c. 61, and refreshment houses licensed under 23 Vict. c. 27, but also on houses licensed for beer and cider to be consumed on the premises. Out-door licensed houses are not entitled to this exemption order. The premises must be in the "immediate neighbourhood" of the market or place where the persons follow their trade or calling. The commissioner or justices are to decide what is a considerable number of persons, and what is the immediate neighbourhood; probably all that is meant is that the premises be near and convenient, though the local authority is not restricted to select the nearest house, nor to limit the order to a single house. Though all persons attending a theatre were included in the original enactment, but are now excluded by the Licensing Act, 1874, section 4, still the persons following the calling of servants, attendants, or actors at a theatre will come within the words.

The local authority.] It is entirely discretionary in the local authority to grant this exemption order, though all the conditions are fulfilled. It is also to be obtainable without notice, so that any one of the public would have no right to be heard or to oppose the granting or altering of such order. And for a like reason, no appeal seems to be given against the refusal, at least as regards the commissioners of police.

The local authority is not bound to follow any rules of evidence on this subject, but the order should recite the ground on which the exemption is conferred—for example, in respect of what market, trade, or calling the exemption is given, and should state

Sect. 26.
NOTE.
that the person exempted is a licensed victualler, or refreshment-house keeper, or licensed beerhouse keeper, and the precise days and hours of the exemption.

Fixing a notice up.] To keep affixed on the premises a notice implies the duty to renew the notice.

The license holder should apply to the local authority to define the form of the notice to be affixed.

The fifth paragraph makes the order revocable at will by the local authority, and no reason need be given for the withdrawal, and no particular mode of giving notice of the withdrawal is prescribed. It may be, however, assumed that the order will be withdrawn in the same way as it was made, with the addition of serving the notice of withdrawal on the party holding the order of exemption. The order should not specify any period during which it shall be in force, since it can be revoked at any time, and in general will cease at the end of the licensing year, unless the same person continues to hold the license.

The holder of this exemption order is liable to a penalty for not producing it on a lawful demand: section 64, *post*.

As to occasional exemption orders intended to last only for a day, or one or two days at a time, see *post*, section 29, and notes.

As to occasional licenses authorising a sale of liquor at other places than the licensed premises, see *post*, 25 & 26 Vict. c. 22, s. 13; 26 & 27 Vict. c. 33, s. 20; 27 & 28 Vict. c. 18, s. 5.

27. *Intoxicating liquors not to be drunk at refreshment house during the hours when the house would be closed if it were an inn.*] No intoxicating liquor shall be consumed upon premises licensed as a refreshment house, but not for the sale of any intoxicating liquor, during the hours during which the same premises would, if they were the licensed premises of licensed victuallers, be closed by law for the sale and consumption of intoxicating liquor.

If any person, licensed to keep such refreshment house, allows any intoxicating liquor to be consumed on the premises in contravention of this section, he shall be

35 & 36 VICT. C. 94, S. 28.

liable for the first offence to a penalty not exceeding ten pounds, and for any subsequent offence to a penalty not exceeding twenty pounds.

Sect. 27.

This section is confined to refreshment houses not licensed for the sale of intoxicating liquors. These houses are governed by the Acts 23 Vict. c. 27, and 24 & 25 Vict. c. 91, s. 8; 27 & 28 Vict. c. 64 ; 28 & 29 Vict. c. 77, *post*. See also Licensing Act, 1874, section 11, as to night houses.

As to what is a refreshment house, see 23 Vict. c. 27, s. 6, in Appendix, and notes, *post*.

The penalty can only refer to liquor which had been sent for by a guest to be consumed during the ordinary prohibited hours.

28. *Amendment of law as to refreshment houses.*] Every refreshment house in respect of which a license is granted for the sale therein by retail of foreign wine, upon which license an abatement of duty has been allowed under 24 & 25 Vict. c. 91, s. 9 (*post*), intituled "An Act to amend the Laws relating to the Inland Revenue," shall be *closed* every night *at ten* of the clock ; and if any person keeping any such refreshment house as is mentioned in this section sells or exposes for sale in such refreshment house, or opens or keeps open any such refreshment house for the sale of intoxicating liquor during the time that such house is directed to be closed by this section, or during such time as aforesaid allows any intoxicating liquor to be consumed on such premises, he shall for the first offence be liable to a penalty not exceeding ten pounds, and for any subsequent offence to a penalty not exceeding twenty pounds.

[Any conviction for an offence against this section shall be recorded on the license of the person convicted

F

Sect. 28. unless the convicting magistrate or justices shall otherwise direct.]

> This section applies only to refreshment houses selling by retail foreign wine for which abatements for license duty are obtained on the condition of the house not being kept open after 10 P.M. : 24 & 25 Vict. c. 91, s. 9, *post.*
> The part *within brackets* was repealed by Licensing Act, 1874, section 33 ; but see that Act, section 13. The justices may record the conviction on the license.
> Part of the original section has been left out, being repealed by 46 & 47 Vict. c. 39, sched.

29. *Local authority may grant occasional licenses exempting from provisions relating to closing during certain hours.*] If any licensed victualler or keeper of a refreshment house in which intoxicating liquors are sold [or any person licensed to sell beer or cider by retail to be consumed on the premises], applies to the local authority of a licensing district for a license exempting him from the provisions of this Act relating to closing of premises on any special occasion or occasions, it shall be lawful for such local authority, if in his discretion he thinks fit so to do, to grant to the applicant an occasional license exempting him from the provisions of this Act relating to closing of premises during certain hours, and on the special occasion or occasions to be specified in the license ; and no licensed victualler or keeper of a refreshment house [or person licensed to sell beer or cider to be consumed on the premises] to whom an occasional license has been granted under this section shall be subject to any penalty for the contravention of the provisions of this Act relating to the closing of premises

during the time to which his occasional license extends, **Sect. 29.**
but he shall not be exempted by such occasional license
from any penalty to which he may be subject by any
other provision of this or any other Act of Parliament.

The words *within brackets* were inserted by the Licensing Act,
1874, section 5.

As to who is the *local authority* of a licensing district, see section 26 and notes, *ante*, p. 62.

The holder of this occasional exemption order is bound under
a penalty to produce it on a lawful demand : section 64, *post*.

An occasional license to sell liquors at *places other than the
licensed premises* was authorised by 25 & 26 Vict. c. 22, s. 13, and
26 & 27 Vict. c.'33, ss. 19—21 ; 27 & 28 Vict. c. 18, s. 5 ; and see
Licensing Act, 1874, sections 18—20.

Special occasion.] The nature of the "special occasion" is
left to the local authority, and the usual occasion is some local
festival or entertainment, as to which the discretion of the
authority seems unlimited and without appeal. The High Court
accordingly will not interfere, even though justices treat Christmas Eve and New Year's Eve as special occasions : *Devine* v.
Keeling, 50 J. P. 551 ; 34 W. R. 718. The application refers to
keeping open the licensed premises during some part of the
ordinary prohibited hours on account of the local festival, such
as a fair, race, ball, &c. It is to be noticed that the exemption
extends only to "the provisions of this Act relating to closing
of premises during certain hours," which are now those in the
Licensing Act, 1874, section 2. And the license can only be
granted to houses for in-door consumption.

By 38 & 39 Vict. c. 21, s. 1, the holder of an occasional license
under this 29th section shall not be liable under the Act 26 Geo. 2,
c. 36 (the Music and Dancing Licenses Act for London and Westminster, and 20 miles round), *ante*, p. 36, to any penalty for being
open from midnight to the hour for closing specified in the
occasional license.

Repeated Convictions.

30. *Forfeiture of license on repeated convictions.*] If any licensed person on whose license two
convictions for offences committed by him against this

Sect. 30. Act have been recorded, is convicted of any offence which is directed by this Act to be recorded on his license, the following consequences shall ensue ; that is to say,—

    (1.) The license of such licensed person shall be forfeited, and he shall be disqualified for a term of five years from the date of such third conviction from holding any license ; and

    (2.) The premises in respect of which his license was granted shall, unless the court having cognizance of the case in its discretion thinks fit otherwise to order, be disqualified from receiving any license for a term of two years from the date of such third conviction :

Provided that nothing in this section contained shall prevent the infliction by the court of any pecuniary penalty or any term of imprisonment to which such licensed person would otherwise be liable, or shall preclude the court from exercising any power given by any other section of this Act of disqualifying such licensed person or such premises for a longer period than the term mentioned in this section.

    A "licensed person" does not include a mere refreshment-house keeper : section 74, *post*.

    The convictions here mentioned must be convictions for offences committed by the same persons against and therefore subsequent to this Act, though they need not be of the same description. There is no limit of time specified between the three convictions, but by the next section (section 31) a partial limit is defined for some purposes. And by section 32, no conviction is to count for some purposes after the lapse of five years from its date.

    The previous conviction may be proved by a certified extract from the register kept by the clerk of the convicting justices : 42 & 43 Vict. c. 49, s. 22 ; or in some cases from the register of licenses under section 58. See also 34 & 35 Vict. c. 112, s. 18.

The effect of a forfeiture of a license is, that from the date of **Sect. 30.** conviction the house ceases for all purposes to be licensed, and no person can thereafter apply during the current licensing year **NOTE.** either for a transfer or a renewal: *R.* v. *West Riding JJ.*, 52 J. P. 455; 21 Q. B. D. 258; 57 L. J. M. C. 103; 36 W. R. 258.

The words "which is directed by this Act to be recorded on his license" are interpreted by the Licensing Act, 1874, section 13, to mean "which is directed by the justices to be recorded," and thus an ambiguity under the original Act, 1872, is avoided. But those convictions recorded by compulsion of law since the Act, 1872, and before the Act, 1874, will remain in force.

The justices seem to have no power to alter the period of disqualification of the person from five years or of the premises from two years to shorter periods respectively. But they may by the order prevent the disqualification of premises altogether. The license or certificate becomes void when the disqualification takes effect: section 44, and see section 63, *post*.

The effect of a person being disqualified for five years seems to be that any license granted or transferred to him by inadvertence during that period would be void. But after the lapse of the five years he might obtain a transfer, like other persons.

Where a conviction is such that if repeated the premises may be liable to be disqualified, the clerk of the licensing justices is to serve notice thereof on the owner. See section 56, *post*. And the order to record is appealable: Act, 1874, s. 13, *post*.

31. *Disqualification of premises.*] The following additional provisions shall be enacted with respect only to convictions of persons who may hereafter become licensed in respect of the premises, and shall not apply to a conviction of any person licensed for any premises at the passing of this Act so long as he is licensed in respect of the same premises; viz.:

(1.) The second and every subsequent conviction recorded on the license of any one such person shall also be recorded in the register of licenses against the premises:

(2.) When four convictions (whether of the same or of different licensed persons) have within five years been so recorded against premises, those

Sect. 31.
premises shall during one year be disqualified for the purposes of this Act :

(3.) If the licenses of two such persons licensed in respect of the same premises are forfeited within any period of two years, the premises shall be disqualified for one year from the date of the last forfeiture :

Provided that where any premises are disqualified under this section notice of such disqualification shall be served upon the owner of the premises in like manner as an order of disqualification is required to be served under this Act, and the regulations for the protection of the owner of premises in case of an order of disqualification shall, so far as the same are applicable, extend to the case of disqualification under this section.

This section applies only to persons who had no license or certificate on the 10th August, 1872, in respect of the same premises. Those who had such license or certificate will continue exempt from the section so long only as they continue to be licensed for the same premises.

It is to be borne in mind that no conviction can be recorded on the license except where directed to be recorded by the justices, and who always have a discretion on that matter and there is an appeal. See Act, 1874, s. 13, *post*.

It is the second recorded conviction only that is to be the first recorded against the premises in the register.

It is of no consequence, under sub-section (2), whether the successive convictions be for the same offence or by the same person. When five convictions have been recorded against the successive licensed occupiers of the same premises within five years (which count four against the premises), the premises shall by the operation of law become disqualified for one year. So, under sub-section (3), if the licenses of two successive tenants are forfeited in two years, the same disqualification will attach by operation of law. All persons who purchase licensed houses will thus, besides requiring the usual legal title, require to search the register of licenses to discover the moral character of " the premises."

35 & 36 VICT. C. 94, S. 32.

Disqualification during one year.] The effect of premises being disqualified for one year will be that if by inadvertence the justices should renew the license it would be void. Another effect would be as to in-door beerhouses licensed since 1869, that the justices in future would not be bound by the four grounds. See 32 & 33 Vict. c. 27, s. 19, *post.* Under sub-section (2), as well as sub-section (3), the one year will count from the date of the last conviction.

Sect. 31.
NOTE.

As to the consequences to the owner, see section 56.

As to the effect of Licensing Act, 1874, section 13, regarding recording a conviction, see notes to that section.

The proceedings as to serving orders of disqualification are stated in section 56.

The notice to the owner can only be served personally, or, if by post, by registered letter. See section 70, *post.*

32. *Conviction after five years not to increase penalty.*] A conviction for any offence under this Act shall not after five years from the date of such conviction be receivable in evidence against any person for the purpose of subjecting him to an increased penalty or to any forfeiture.

The conviction under this Act after five years loses its recording power, and is to be deemed non-existent, but only for the purpose of increasing the penalty or causing forfeiture. It might have been doubted whether, if the words " or to any forfeiture " had not been added, the word " penalty " would not have been deemed to be used in the popular sense, and to include such a consequence as forfeiture of license and disqualification of person and of premises, but owing to the last four words that view seems untenable. According to the literal and technical meaning, the word "penalty" applies only to a sum of money, and does not include imprisonment, forfeiture, disqualification, and other consequences of a conviction. As the word is obviously used here not to include forfeiture, it seems to follow that so far as regards the consequences described by section 30, the convictions recorded will count, though they are more than five years old, for the purpose of disqualification of person and premises. And, of course, it may operate seriously against all persons applying for transfers or new grants of licenses. This section, therefore, practically does not apply to disqualifications, subject to the express restrictions on that head in section 31.

Sect. 33. **33.** *Omission to record conviction on license.*] Where a conviction for an offence is by this Act directed to be recorded on the license of any person, the fact of no such record having been made shall not, if such conviction be otherwise proved to the satisfaction of the court having cognizance of any case under this Act, exempt such person or the premises occupied by him from any penalty to which such person or premises would have been subject if such record had been duly made. And on such proof being given the omitted conviction may be recorded accordingly, and shall be deemed to have been duly recorded in accordance with this Act.

This section practically makes the provision as to recording convictions on a license one which executes itself, and the omission is of little consequence, since it can be cured at any time. The Licensing Act, 1874, section 13, makes this apply to all cases in which a license was formerly recorded by operation of the Act instead of by express order of justices. The recording of convictions is provided for in section 55, *post.* Though the not recording of a conviction is not allowed to be relied upon by the person convicted, still it may be an important matter to the owner of the premises, or at least to the purchaser of such property in future, to be able to search the register, so as to ascertain the value of the premises, and the risk of disqualification.

34. *Penalty for defacing record of conviction on license.*] If any person defaces or obliterates, or attempts to deface or obliterate, any record of a conviction on his license, he shall be liable to a penalty not exceeding five pounds.

As the practice will be in future to renew a license or certificate by endorsement under section 48, this section may be of use. But the register of licenses (section 36) will probably be found to render any attempt to deface a record of conviction

35 & 36 VICT. C. 94, S. 36.   73

nugatory. Every person summoned for an offence must produce **Sect. 34**
his license under section 55.
The justices cannot order this conviction to be recorded on the **NOTE.**
license.

35. *Entry on premises by constable.*] *(Repealed* by Licensing Act, 1874, section 33. See now the Act, 1874, s. 16, *post.*)

Registers.

36. *Register of licenses to be kept in licensing district.*] There shall be kept in every licensing district by the clerk of the licensing justices of that district a register to be called the register of licenses, in such form as may be prescribed by such justices, containing the particulars of all licenses granted in the district, the premises in respect of which they were granted, the names of the owners of such premises, and the names of the holders for the time being of such licenses. There shall also be entered on the register all forfeitures of licenses, disqualifications of premises, records of convictions, and other matters relating to the licenses on the register.

Every person applying for a new license, or the renewal of a license, shall state the name of the owner of the premises in respect of which such license is granted or renewed, and such name shall be endorsed on the license, and the person whose name is so stated shall, subject as hereinafter mentioned, be deemed for the purposes of this Act to be the owner of the premises.

A court of summary jurisdiction may, on the application of any person who proves to the court that he

LICENSING ACT, 1872, s. 36.

is entitled to be entered as owner of any premises in place of the person appearing on the register to be the owner, make an order substituting the name of the applicant, and such order shall be obeyed by the clerk of the licensing justices, and a corresponding correction may be directed to be made on the license granted in respect of the premises in which such applicant claims to be the owner.

Any ratepayer, any owner of premises to which a license is attached, and any holder of a license within a licensing district, shall upon payment of a fee of one shilling, and any officer of police, and any officer of Inland Revenue in such district, without payment, shall be entitled at any reasonable time to inspect and take copies of or extracts from any register kept in pursuance of this section for such district; and the clerk of the licensing justices and every other person who prevents the inspection or taking copies of or extracts from the same, or demands any unauthorised fee therefor, shall be liable to a penalty not exceeding five pounds for each offence.

The licensing justices may, if they think fit, cause the register kept in pursuance of this section to be divided into parts, and assign a part to any portion of the licensing district; and there shall be paid by each licensed person to the clerk in respect of such registration the sum or fee of one shilling for every license granted or renewed.

This register is a convenient mode of enabling the owners and purchasers of premises to ascertain the position of their tenant in respect of misconduct, since disqualification of premises may follow on almost every kind of offence, if repeated. If there are more than one person who is clerk of the licensing justices, the justices shall determine which of them is to keep this register: see *post*, section 74. As to using the register as evidence, see section 58, *post*.

Sect. 36.
NOTE.

The words "records of convictions" in the first paragraph do not mean "records of convictions ordered to be recorded on the license," but records of convictions of any holder of the premises for the time being, whether ordered to be recorded on the license or not: see section 55, *post*. In this register also must be entered any conviction for bribery or treating, or any report respecting a licensed person: 46 & 47 Vict. c. 51, s. 38, *post*.

For definition of *owner*, see section 74, *post*, and Licensing Act, 1874, section 29. By the Licensing Act, 1874, section 29, the owner may demand to have his name put on the register. Before justices should substitute the name of the applicant for the name of the person entered, notice should be given to the latter that he might show cause and oppose the change; and either may appeal under section 52, *post*.

The right to demand inspection of the register is confined to ratepayers, owners of licensed premises, license holders in the district, constables, and Inland Revenue officers.

The fee of one shilling is in addition to the fees payable on grants of licenses and certificates as well as transfers, as to which see 9 Geo. 4, c. 61, s. 15; 33 & 34 Vict. c. 29, s. 4, sub-section 5. And this fee is payable on renewals as well as new grants.

Amendment of Law as to Grant of Licenses.

37. *Licensing committee of justices in counties.*] In counties a grant of a *new license* shall not be valid unless it is confirmed by a standing committee of the county justices, in this Act called the *county licensing committee*.

The justices in quarter sessions assembled for every county shall annually appoint from among themselves for the purpose of this Act a *county licensing committee*, or they may appoint more than one such committee, and assign to any such committee such area of jurisdiction as they may think expedient.

Sect. 37. A county licensing committee shall consist of not less than three nor more than twelve members.

The *quorum* of a county licensing committee shall be *three* members.

Any vacancies arising in any such committee from death, resignation, or other causes may be from time to time filled up by the justices in quarter sessions by whom the committee is appointed.

A county licensing committee shall be deemed to be a standing committee of the quarter sessions by whom they are appointed for the year succeeding their appointment, and their jurisdiction and proceedings shall not be affected by the termination of the sessions at which they were appointed. The members of a committee retiring at the end of the year may be re-appointed; and if from any cause members have not been appointed in any year to succeed the retiring members, such retiring members may continue to act as the committee until their successors are appointed.

The justices in quarter sessions shall make such regulations with respect to the meetings of any such committee and the transaction of business thereat as they may think fit.

The clerk of the peace of the county shall, by himself or his deputy, be the clerk of the county licensing committee or committees, and shall perform all such duties in relation to any such committee or committees as he is required by law to perform in relation to the justices in quarter sessions assembled.

[The rest *repealed* by 46 & 47 Vict. c. 39, Sched.]

No confirmation of a new certificate for houses licensed for consumption off the premises is now required: Licensing Act, 1874, section 24.

35 & 36 VICT. C. 94, S. 37.

Discretion of confirming authority.] The confirming authority have the same discretion which the licensing justices have—neither more nor less; and now in all cases that require confirmation their discretion is absolute. They need give no reasons, and there is no appeal against their decision: *Re Annandale JJ.*, 37 J. P. 85; *R.* v. *Middlesex JJ.*, 42 J. P. 469; *R.* v. *Pownall*, 57 J. P. 424; (1893), 2 Q. B. 158. They are bound, like the licensing justices, to hear all competent objections, such as that there are too many licensed houses, that the annual value of premises is insufficient, that the applicant is of bad character, &c. The only qualification is that the confirming authority is not bound to hear any party who did not object before the licensing justices. See *post*, section 43. The confirming authority does not stand towards the licensing justices in the position of a court of appeal; they are merely to go over the same ground, and to exercise their independent judgment on the same materials, or such materials as the applying and objecting parties placed before them. They cannot reverse, and they are not bound merely to register the conclusion come to by the licensing justices: *R.* v. *Mayor of York*, 1 E. & B. 588.

The origin of the power of justices to grant a new license, as well as a renewal of a license, is found in 9 Geo. 4, c. 61, s. 1, *post*. This 37th section deals with new licenses only so far as the functions of the licensing committee in counties as the confirming authority are concerned. Transfers of licenses come before the general body of justices (including those that are members of the licensing committee) who sit at transfer sessions, which are appointed under 9 Geo. 4, c. 61, s. 4, and require no confirmation. As regards renewal of current licenses, all the justices take part in these, including those who form the licensing committee, and no confirmation is necessary.

Grant of new licenses.] The grant of a new license or certificate is still to be made as before this Act in counties by the justices at the general annual licensing meeting, but that grant will not be valid until confirmed by the county licensing committee. As to the general duties and powers of justices as to grants, see 9 Geo. 4, c. 61, s. 1, *post*, and notes.

A *mandamus* will lie to the justices in quarter sessions to appoint a county licensing committee.

There is, as already stated, no appeal to quarter sessions against the refusal of a new grant of a license or certificate. See second schedule, which repealed 9 Geo. 4, c. 61, s. 27, as to new licenses. See also Licensing Act, 1874, section 27, to the same effect, as to cases of wine and beerhouse certificates.

Sect. 37.
NOTE.

Sect. 37.

NOTE.

Object of confirming authority.] The *confirmation* by the licensing committee is a sufficient check on new grants, and if the first body of justices refuse the application for a new grant, their decision is now final so far as quarter sessions are concerned. The appeal to quarter sessions, however, remains as regards applications for renewals or transfers of licenses or certificates. The first body of justices can, moreover, only refuse applications for certificates for out-door wine, spirit, sweets, and cider licenses under the Wine and Beerhouse Acts for certain reasons. See 32 & 33 Vict. c. 27, s. 8, *post*, and notes, and this Act, sections 69, 74.

The applicants, therefore, for new licenses or certificates for in-door consumption cannot obtain an excise license under 9 Geo. 4, c. 61, s. 17, and 32 & 33 Vict. c. 27, s. 4, until they have not only obtained the justices' license, but also the committee's confirmation of the license; while no confirmation is needed for out-door licenses.

Procedure before confirming authority.] The mode of obtaining confirmation of a new license by the committee is regulated by section 43, and is subject to regulations to be made as to the proceedings by the justices in quarter sessions. See also Act, 1874, section 25. These regulations must be consulted in each county as to what is required to be done by the applicants, and the clerk of the peace will give such information.

The *fee* payable to the clerk of the justices in respect of a new license remains the same as before. See 9 Geo. 4, c. 61, s. 15. As to certificates under the Wine and Beerhouse Acts, the same fee is also due: 32 & 33 Vict. c. 27, s. 8. And see sect. 36, *ante*, p. 74.

Notices before new grants.] The notices by applicants for new licenses are regulated by 32 & 33 Vict. c. 27, s. 7, which was extended to all cases by Licensing Act, 1872, section 40.

38. *Licensing committee of justices in boroughs.*] In boroughs in which, at the commencement of the time appointed for the annual appointment of a licensing committee in this section mentioned, there are *ten justices* acting in and for such borough or upwards, new licenses shall be granted by a *committee,* who shall, for the purpose of such new licenses, perform all the duties and be subject to the obligations of licensing justices. Sect. 38.

In every such borough as aforesaid the justices, acting in and for such borough, shall annually in the fortnight preceding the commencement of the period during which the general annual licensing meeting for such borough may be held, appoint from among themselves for the purposes of this Act a committee of not less than three nor more than seven in number, but no justice shall be appointed a member of such committee unless he is qualified to act under this Act.

Any vacancies arising in such committee (in this Act referred to as the borough licensing committee) from death, resignation, or other causes, may be from time to time filled up by the justices by whom the committee is appointed.

The *quorum* of a borough licensing committee shall be *three* members.

The members of the borough licensing committee retiring at the end of the year may be re-appointed, and if from any cause members have not been appointed in any year to succeed the retiring members, such retiring members may continue to act as the borough licensing committee until their successors are appointed.

The grant of a new license by the borough licensing committee shall not be valid unless it is confirmed by the whole body of borough justices, who would, if this Act had not passed, have been authorised to grant licenses, or by a majority of such body present at any

Sect. 38. meeting assembled for the purpose of confirming such licenses.

In boroughs in which there are *not ten justices* acting in and for such borough at such time as aforesaid, new licenses shall be granted by the qualified borough justices, but the grant of a new license by such justices shall not be valid unless it is confirmed by a joint committee appointed in respect of such borough in manner hereinafter mentioned :—

> A *joint committee* for any such borough as last aforesaid shall consist of three justices of the county in which such borough is situate, and three justices of the borough [or if there are not three such borough justices, then the deficiency is to be supplied by county justices, to be appointed by the county licensing committee], but no justice shall be appointed a member of such committee unless he is qualified to act under this Act. The three county justices on a joint committee shall be appointed by the county licensing committee. The same county justices may be appointed members of more than one joint committee under this section. The borough justices on a joint committee shall be appointed by the justices of the borough for which they act, or by the majority of such justices assembled at any meeting held for that purpose. Any casual vacancy arising in the joint committee from death, resignation, or other cause, may from time to time be filled up by the justices by whom the person creating such vacancy was appointed. The *quorum* of the joint committee shall be five members. The senior

magistrate on the joint committee present at any Sect. 38. meeting shall be its chairman; and in the event of an equal division of the committee the chairman shall have a second vote.

(A part here was *repealed* by 46 & 47 Vict. c. 39, Sched.)
No objection shall be made to any licenses granted or confirmed in pursuance of this section on the ground that the justices or committee of justices who granted or confirmed the same were not qualified to make such grant or confirmation.

From and after the passing of this Act, the justices of a county shall not for licensing purposes, save in so far as respects the power of appointing members of a joint committee, have any jurisdiction in a borough in which the borough justices have for such purposes concurrent jurisdiction.

The words *within brackets* were inserted by Licensing Act, 1874, section 21.

No grant of a new certificate to sell liquors not to be consumed on the premises requires any confirmation: Licensing Act, 1874, section 24.

The powers of licensing committees.] This section makes the important distinction as regards boroughs with ten justices, that the whole body of justices cannot exercise the power to grant a new license, the committee being substituted for the whole body in respect to that matter. There being, however, nothing said as to transfers and renewals, the whole body of justices may deal with these as before.

Boroughs having a separate commission of the peace are divided into those which have ten justices acting for the borough, and those which have less. The word "borough" is defined in section 74, *post.*

In the former case, the grants of new licenses and certificates are to be made by the borough licensing committee, and confirmed

G

Sect. 38.
NOTE.
by the whole body of borough justices, that is to say, by the majority of those who attend a meeting for the purpose of confirming such licenses or certificates. The "commencement of the time appointed for the annual appointment of a licensing committee" is "the fortnight preceding the commencement of the period during which the general annual licensing meeting may be held for the borough." Therefore, in the country, this is the fortnight before the 20th of August, and in Middlesex and Surrey before the 1st of March, and at the commencement of such fortnight, if ten justices exist, the licensing committee is to be appointed.

In boroughs which have less than ten acting justices, the grant of new licenses or certificates is to be made by the borough justices, and confirmed by a joint committee of three county justices and three borough justices, and if the borough justices are deficient, then by county justices, as stated above.

A justice who is a brewer, &c., will count as one of the ten, though he is disqualified by section 60, *post*, from acting in most cases.

As to fees, see notes to last section.

As to jurisdiction of justices in boroughs, see also notes to 9 Geo. 4, c. 61, s. 1, *post*.

It is important to notice that a license cannot be objected to for non-qualification of the justices.

39. *Stipendiary magistrates may act as licensing justices.*] Beyond the limits of the jurisdiction of the metropolitan police courts a metropolitan police or stipendiary magistrate may act as one of the justices empowered to grant or confirm licenses so far as regards any licensing district wholly or partly within his jurisdiction.

This removes partly a disqualification in 2 & 3 Vict. c. 71, s. 14, and 21 & 22 Vict. c. 73, s. 7. The word "grant" is obviously used in its popular sense, so as to include transfers and renewals respectively. See as to some metropolitan magistrates indorsing licenses under 5 & 6 Vict. c. 44, s. 1, *post*.

40. *Regulations as to new licenses and transfer of licenses.*] Every person intending to apply for a new license, or to apply for the transfer of a license, shall publish notice of such application as follows ; that is to say,— Sect. 40.

(1.) In the case of a *new license*, he shall cause notice thereof to be given and to be affixed and maintained in manner directed by section seven of the " Wine and Beerhouse Act, 1869," *post*, and any enactment amending the same, and shall advertise such notice in some paper circulating in the place in which the premises to which the notice relates are situate, on some day not more than four and not less than two weeks before the proposed application, and on such day or days (if any) as may be from time to time fixed by the licensing justices :

(2.) In the case of the *transfer of a license* he shall, fourteen days prior to one of the special sessions appointed by the justices for granting transfers of such licenses, serve a notice of his intention to transfer the same upon one of the overseers of the parish, township, or place in which the premises in respect of which his application is to be made are situate, and on the superintendent of police of the district. This notice shall be signed by the applicant or by his authorised agent, and shall set forth the name of the person to whom it is intended that such license shall be transferred, together with the place of his residence, and his trade or

Sect. 40. calling during the six months preceding the time of serving such notice:

(3.) Any license may be *authenticated* in manner in which a certificate may be authenticated in pursuance of sub-section two of section four of "The Wine and Beerhouse Act Amendment Act, 1870," and the provisions of the said sub-section shall apply accordingly:

[Part here *repealed* by 46 & 47 Vict. c. 39, Sched.]

The provisions of this section as to notices shall extend to all cases where, under the Intoxicating Liquors Act, 1828, notices are required to be served in a like form to or in the same manner as notices for new licenses.

Notices before new licenses.] As to the meaning of "new license," see definition in section 74, *post*, and notes thereon; and Licensing Act, 1874, s. 2, *post*. The notice before application for a *new* license was regulated by 9 Geo. 4, c. 61, s. 10, *post*. That section is now repealed and superseded by the corresponding section in the Wine and Beerhouse Act, 32 & 33 Vict. c. 27, s. 7, *post*. Besides complying with the last-mentioned section, the applicant must advertise his notice as above in a local newspaper. He is at liberty to select his newspaper if there are several circulating in the place; but the justices may fix the days on which the advertisement shall appear, as to which the clerk of the licensing justices will give information to applicants. They will be guided by the days of publication of the appropriate newspaper. There is no precise form given by any of the statutes for a notice, but it must state in substance the name of the applicant, describe his place of residence, house for which the license is asked, the kind of license applied for, and time of the general annual meeting or adjournment at which the application is to be made. It is for the justices to decide whether the notices have been given pursuant to the statutes, and as the giving of notices is a condition precedent to the jurisdiction to grant licenses, questions may arise as to the validity of licenses granted in contravention of the statutory notices: *Ormerod* v. *Chadwick*, 2 N. Sess. 697; 16 M. & W. 367;

35 & 36 VICT. C. 94, S. 40.

Ex parte James, 12 J. P. 262. The justices were held to have **Sect. 40.** rightly decided that service of notice on the superintendent of police was bad where the service was at one of the police offices of **Note.** his district, and not at his own residence : *R.* v. *Riley*, 53 J. P. 452. A notice is not bad for describing the license as one to sell beer, though the justices can only grant a license which authorises the excise to grant such a license : *R.* v. *Blackburn JJ.*, 42 J. P. 775 ; 43 J. P. 111 ; 39 L. T. (N.S.) 444. And see further as to notices, 32 & 33 Vict. c. 27, s. 7, and notes, *post.*

This latter enactment as to a newspaper advertisement, which is new, will apply to certificates under the Wine and Beerhouse Acts, as well as to alehouse licenses. The notice for a new alehouse license is now, therefore, identical with that for a new certificate under the Wine and Beerhouse Acts.

Notices before transfer.] The notice previous to the application for a *transfer* of license was regulated by 9 Geo. 4, c. 61, s. 11, which is repealed, and the provision in clause (2) of this section is substituted. It increases the length of the notice. There is a proviso at the end of 9 Geo. 4, c. 61, s. 14, which is not repealed. The words at the end of this 40th section say, however, that this section shall apply to all cases in that proviso, which required notices like those of a new license. Hence in those cases of transfer which come within the words used in the proviso, the same notice is to be given as is prescribed by this 40th section for a new license, and not as required by the 9 Geo. 4, c. 61, s. 11.

It has been held that the word "transfer" in sub-section 2 applies only to those cases included in 9 Geo. 4, c. 61, ss. 4, 14, where the outgoing licensee formally applies to the justices in his own name ; and that in all the other cases, if the proposed transferee only applies without the outgoing tenant's assistance, this section does not apply, and there being no other provision requiring a notice, none is necessary : *R.* v. *Grove*, 57 J. P. 454 ; *R.* v. *Hughes*, 62 L. J. M. C. 150 ; 57 J. P. 500. In future, therefore, it is not likely that any notice will ever be given by an applicant under 9 Geo. 4, c. 61, ss. 4, 14, as there is no object to be gained by the out-going tenant taking the initiative in these applications for a transfer.

This section will apply also to transfers of certificates under the Wine and Beerhouse Act, 33 & 34 Vict. c. 29, s. 4, sub-sect. 5, *post.*

As to the mode of *authenticating* the license or certificate, see 33 & 34 Vict. c. 29, s. 4, and notes, *post.* The *form of license* and certificate is regulated by the Secretary of State. See section 48, and the official forms at the end of this volume.

As to the mode of *computing* the days, see notes to 32 & 33 Vict. c. 27, s. 7, *post.* The words "14 days prior" to transfer sessions

Sect. 40.
NOTE.
mean "14 clear days;" so that the day of notice and the day of sessions are to be excluded. See further as to computation, 32 & 33 Vict. c. 27, s. 7, and notes, *post.*
All these notices may be served by post : see section 70, *post.*
As to the *discretion of justices* in granting or refusing new licenses, the law is stated in the notes to 9 Geo. 4, c. 61, s. 1, and 32 & 33 Vict. c. 27, s. 8 ; 43 Vict. c. 6 ; 45 & 46 Vict. c. 34, *post.* And as to the discretion of justices on applications for transfers, see 9 Geo. 4, c. 61, s. 14, *post,* and notes.

41. *Amendment of 5 & 6 Vict. c. 44, with respect to licenses wilfully withheld.*] Whereas by the 5 & 6 Vict. c. 44, s. 2, the magistrates or justices in petty sessions are empowered in the event of a license being lost or mislaid to receive a copy of such license, and to deal therewith in manner in the said section mentioned : And whereas it is expedient to extend the power of such magistrates or justices to the reception of a copy of a license in the event of a license being wilfully withheld by the holder thereof : Be it enacted, that such section shall be construed as if after the words "lost or mislaid," there were inserted the words "or if the application is for the grant of a license [or the transfer of a license], has been wilfully withheld by the holder thereof."

The words *in brackets* were inserted by 47 & 48 Vict. c. 29, *post.*
The provisions of 5 & 6 Vict. c. 44, ss. 2, 3, which originally were confined to alehouse licenses, were extended to certificates under the Wine and Beerhouse Acts by 33 & 34 Vict. c. 29, s. 4, the fee for endorsing the copy of a lost license being 2s. 6d. These sections are now extended to the case of a license " wilfully withheld by the holder." It had been held that justices sitting at petty sessions under 5 & 6 Vict. c. 44, were not compellable to receive a copy of the license if the outgoing licensee, owing to a quarrel with his landlord, would not give up the original, as the provision was held to apply only to applications for *grants* of licenses, but not to applications for endorsement or transfer : *Ex parte Phillips,* 42 J. P. 279. The holder of a license is bound by section 64 to produce the license to justices and constables.

35 & 36 VICT. C. 94, S. 42.

Sect. 41.
NOTE.

It is not to be inferred from this section, and 5 & 6 Vict. c. 44, that justices at petty sessions are incapable of granting a temporary transfer, unless the identical piece of paper on which the current license was written is produced, for now by the aid of the register of licenses, under sections 36 and 58, justices can always ascertain with certainty all the particulars of a current license,. and can exercise their power in regard to temporary transfers without the aid of the original document, the importance of which in most cases is trifling.

It has been held that the person obtaining a temporary license or authority under 5 & 6 Vict. c. 44, does not come within the description of a licensed person mentioned in the next section (section 42), and hence, that he is not entitled to receive any notice of opposition to the renewal of the license in respect of the house as to which he obtains the temporary license : *Price* v. *James* (1892), 2 Q. B. 28 ; 56 J. P. 471 ; 57 J. P. 148; 61 L. J. M. C. 203 ; 67 L. T. 543 ; 41 W. R. 57.

42. *Provisions as to renewal of licenses.*] Where a licensed person applies for the renewal of his license the following provisions shall have effect :—

(1.) He need not attend in person at the general annual licensing meeting, unless he is required by the licensing justices [for some special cause personal to himself] so to attend :

(2.) The justices shall not entertain any objection to the renewal of such license, or take any evidence with respect to the renewal thereof, unless written notice of an intention to oppose the renewal of such license [and stating in general terms the grounds of opposition] has been served on such holder not less than seven days before the commencement of the general annual licensing meeting : Provided that the licensing justices may, notwithstanding that no notice has been given, on an objection being made, adjourn the granting of any license to a future day, and require the attendance of the holder of the license on such day, when the case will be heard and the objection considered, as if the notice hereinbefore prescribed had been given :

(3.) The justices shall not receive any evidence with respect to the renewal of such license which is not given on oath.

Subject as aforesaid, licenses shall be renewed and the powers and discretion of justices relative to such renewal shall be exercised as heretofore.

The words *in brackets* were inserted by the Licensing Act, 1874, s. 26.

The Alehouse Act, 9 Geo. 4, c. 61, s. 12, *post*, authorised a sick or infirm person, &c., to apply for the grant of a license, the legislature having assumed that the justices would not be likely to grant a license to a person whom they had not seen. But there was nothing in the other parts of the Act 9 Geo. 4, c. 61, to prevent them granting a license to such person if they chose.

The renewal of licenses is the same as before, subject to the provisions as to notice of opposition, and no confirmation by a licensing committee is necessary. As to how a renewal is distinguished from a new license, see section 74 and note.

No notice by applicant for renewal.] No notice is required to be given by the applicant on an application to renew a certificate under the Wine and Beerhouse Act, 32 & 33 Vict. c. 27, s. 7, *post*. And there was nothing in the Alehouse Act, 9 Geo. 4, c. 61, s. 10, requiring such notice as to renewal of alehouse licenses, and, though that section is repealed, there is no such obligation still.

The justices who renew licenses.] The justices who *renew* are the *same justices* who entertain the new applications. In boroughs with ten justices, the licensing committee now, under section 38, *ante*, alone exercise the jurisdiction as to new licenses.

35 & 36 VICT. C. 94, S. 42.

Nevertheless, there seems to be nothing expressly to prevent the whole of the borough justices joining in the hearing of applications for renewal, though the licensing committee in the larger boroughs sitting by themselves can alone deal with the applications for new licenses, as stated in section 38.

Sect. 42.
―――
NOTE.

Proof of service of notice of opposition.] As service of notice of opposition is a condition precedent to the jurisdiction of justices to entertain any objections to renewal the objector must first prove the notice. Though the words "served upon" are apt words, and are so used in all the Procedure Acts and rules to denote personal service, the Court of Appeal has held that personal service is not necessary, and that it must be a question for the justices in each case to decide whether there is reasonable or at least *primâ facie* evidence, that the notice reached the hands of the license holder within the time : *Ex parte Portingell* (1892), 1 Q. B. 15 ; 65 L. T. 603 ; 40 W. R. 102 ; 56 J. P. 276 ; 61 L. J. M. C. 1. The license holder may, however, rebut any *primâ facie* evidence by proving that the notice did not reach him. It has been held, that if the person in possession of the licensed house, has nothing but a temporary license or authority under 5 & 6 Vict. c. 44, he does not come within the description of a "licensed person" (see notes to section 41, *ante*). In a large county, where the general meeting was always adjourned to another town to suit local applicants, the notice was held good if served before the adjournment day ; *R.* v. *Anglesea JJ.* (1892), 1 Q. B. 850 ; 56 J. P. 440 ; 61 L. J. M. C. 149.

Burden of proof of opposition.] Though this section throws the *onus* of proving the objection to the renewal of both licenses and certificates on the objecting party, the licensing justices have an entire discretion in most cases as to the subject-matter of objection, subject only to an appeal on the part of the applicant under 9 Geo. 4, c. 61, ss. 27—29, which sections are unrepealed in so far as regards renewal of licenses and certificates. What the justices have to see to is that some one has served in due time notice of opposition, stating grounds, seven days before the general annual meeting. But this objection can be overcome by the justices starting the objection in open court, and then adjourning under the latter part of the second sub-section : *R.* v. *Merthyr Tydvil JJ.*, 49 J. P. 213 ; 14 Q. B. D. 584 ; 54 L. J. M. C. 78 ; *R.* v. *Redditch*, 50 J. P. 246 ; *R.* v. *Essex JJ.*, 46 J. P. 761. Hence, this section renders it no longer necessary, as was required under the Wine and Beerhouse Acts, for the applicant for a renewal of a certificate, if unopposed, to give affirmative evidence

Sect. 42.

NOTE.

of good character : '*Ex parte Morgan*, 35 J. P. 37 ; 23 L. T. 650. The burden of proof is thrown on the parties objecting to a renewal of a license or certificate. It appears that any person may oppose the renewing of a license or certificate. The evidence must now be on oath in all cases where the applicant is a licensed person. And by the Licensing Act, 1874, s. 26, even the justices are prohibited from requiring the applicant to attend, except for some special cause personal to the applicant. The meaning of the words "personal cause" seems not to be confined to misconduct, but rather to something which applies to the applicant's house as distinguished from other houses. It was held that where notice of opposition was duly served, and the only reason given by the justices for their refusal to renew was that the public-house was too far removed from police supervision, this was a valid ground for refusing a renewal : *Sharp* v. *Wakefield* (1891), 1 App. Cas. 473 ; 55 J. P. 197 ; 60 L. J. M. C. 238 ; 64 L. T. 180 ; 37 W. R. 187 ; *R.* v. *Smith* or *Smith* v. *Hereford*, 42 J. P. 295 ; 48 L. J. M. C. 38 ; 39 L. T. 606. But whatever be the meaning of "personal cause," the jurisdiction as to renewals is precisely the same on the merits as in cases of new applications, the personal cause being only a reason for calling on the applicant to attend in person or by advocate, and to explain away the ground of opposition.

The legislature seems to have assumed that the licensing justices would renew all licenses as a matter of course, unless there should be proved some misconduct or other objection personal to the applicant. And though it is now only in cases of some personal objection that a requisition can be served on the applicant to attend the justices on the occasion of a renewal, yet the joint effect of this section, and of the Act, 1874, section 26, has not been to cut down the absolute discretion of justices as to refusing to renew alehouse and nearly all other licenses, with or without reasons given : *Sharp* v. *Wakefield*, *supra; Ex parte Martin*, 40 J. P. 133 ; *Ex parte Bendall*, 42 J. P. 88.

The grounds of opposition.] The enactment does not define the nature of the ground of opposition that may be raised to a renewal. The ground must not be so utterly frivolous and capricious that the discretion of the justices, in giving effect to it, can be called no exercise of a judicial discretion at all ; but as they are not bound to give reasons in most cases for their decision, it is difficult by *certiorari* or *mandamus* to correct the decision, as there is no appeal on the merits except to quarter sessions, and the High Court will not lay down rules as to what is or is not a judicial discretion : *Sharp* v. *Wakefield*, *supra*. The circumstance that the house was too far removed from police supervision was held a good and relevant objection on the merits : *Ibid.* So it has been held that keeping the house shut during a negotiation for sale was a relevant objection : *Griffiths* v. *Lancashire JJ.*, 51 J. P. 453 ; 35 W. R. 732. And if the renewal is opposed merely on the ground that the holder was convicted of an offence, the court will treat this as equivalent to an objection to the character of the applicant : *R.* v. *Lancashive JJ.*, 55 J. P. 580 ; *R.* v. *Birmingham JJ.*, 40 J. P. 132. If notice be given that the house is disorderly, this allows evidence of convictions against previous license holders : *R.* v. *Miskin Higher*, 57 J. P. 263 ; (1893), 1 Q. B. 225 ; 67 L. T. 680.

Sect. 42.
—
NOTE.

Justices starting objection without notice.] When the justices themselves start an objection to renewing such license, which must be done in open court, it is their duty not to decide then and there, but to give notice to the applicant, and adjourn the further hearing, and request him to attend and answer the objection : *R.* v. *Farquhar*, L. R. 9 Q. B. 258 ; 39 J. P. 166. And the court has quashed an order of quarter sessions for disregarding this matter : *Ruddick* v. *Justices of Liverpool*, 42 J. P. 406. At the same time, if both parties act on the assumption that an objection has been duly made and time given to answer it, then it will be taken that they waived literal compliance with the section : *R.* v. *Kent Justices*, 41 J. P. 263. Moreover, when the justices start the objection and give an opportunity to the party to answer it, they must apparently still hear the evidence on oath : *R.* v. *Eales*, 44 J. P. 553 ; 42 L. T. 735. The justices, as above stated, must not only see that the objection is stated in open court, but that notice of it was duly served, and also that an order to attend had been served on the license holder : *R.* v. *Merthyr Tydvil JJ.*, 49 J. P. 213 ; 54 L. J. M. C. 78 ; 14 Q. B. D. 584. The objection need not be stated in writing in open court, but it should at least be stated in the seven days' notice to attend which the justices themselves should cause to be served on the holder : *R.* v. *Redditch JJ.*, 50 J. P. 246. No third party is entitled after such adjournment to serve the notice of opposition in his own name, but he must be authorised by the justices to do so in their name, and if the notice does not purport to come from the justices to the license holder, the latter need not pay any attention to it : *Whiffin* v. *Malling* or *Bligh*, 56 J. P. 325 ; (1892), 1 Q. B. 362 ; 66 L. T. 333 ; 40 W. R. 292 ; 61 L. J. M. C. 82. Yet, if such notice be served by a third party and the applicant attend and show cause against the objection, he will be taken to have waived the informality, and he cannot afterwards be heard to object to the defect : *Ibid.*

Mandamus *to re-hear.*] Should the justices refuse a renewal, though no notice of objection had been served or though none

Sect. 42. started by justices, and a *mandamus* issues to re-hear, the objec-
NOTE. tions may be then made and heard on the merits at the re-hearing:
R. v. *Howard* or *Congleton JJ.*, 23 Q. B. D. 502; 60 L. T. 960;
37 W. R. 617; 53 J. P. 454. See also 9 Geo. 4, c. 61, s. 1, and
notes, *post*.

As to some renewals, justices' discretion limited.] As
regards renewal of certificates for some out-door licenses, the
justices have not the same wide discretion as they have in reference to alehouse or publican's licenses, for they cannot refuse to
renew a certificate to sell wines, spirits, sweets, or cider not to be
consumed on the premises, except on one of the grounds set forth
in 32 & 33 Vict. c. 27, s. 8, *post*. See *R.* v. *Scott*, 22 Q. B. D. 481;
53 J. P. 119; 58 L. J. M. C. 78; 60 L. T. 231; 37 W. R. 301.
And the justices must in such cases state the grounds of refusal:
Ex parte Smith, R. v. *Surrey JJ.*, 3 Q. B. D. 374; 47 L. J. M. C.
104; 42 J. P. 598; 26 W. R. 682; *Tranter* v. *Lancashire JJ.*,
51 J. P. 454. As regards certificates to sell beer, cider, or wine to
be consumed on the premises, if the house was licensed on 1st
May, 1869, and the justices have not since made any order taking
away the privilege, and the privilege has not been lost, then the
justices cannot refuse such renewal except on one of the grounds
already specified: 32 & 33 Vict. c. 27, s. 19; 33 & 34 Vict. c. 29,
s. 7. See notes. *R.* v. *King* or *Manchester JJ.*, 20 Q. B. D. 430;
52 J. P. 199; 57 L. J. M. C. 20; 58 L. T. 607; 36 W. R. 600.
And it has been held that if the license run out and no application for transfer be made till after the expiration of license, then
the privilege as to the four grounds is lost and the justices have
an entire discretion as to transfer: *Murray* v. *Freer*, (1893), 1 Q. B.
635; 57 J. P. 101, 583; 67 L. T. 507; 62 L. J. M. C. 33. On
the other hand, if the house had no in-door license on 1st May,
1869, then the justices may refuse to renew the on-certificate in
cases of beer, cider, or wine without stating reasons, subject only
to the appeal to quarter sessions. See 32 & 33 Vict. c. 27, s. 19;
33 & 34 Vict. c. 29, s. 7; 43 Vict. c. 6; 45 & 46 Vict. c. 34,
post.

If the justices refuse to renew the license, and the applicant
appeals, he may get a temporary license from the Inland Revenue
until the appeal is determined. See section 53. And if the
application fail for some inadvertence or misadventure, the
justices may postpone the application: 33 & 34 Vict. c. 29, s. 11.

Fees on renewal.] The *fee* on a renewal of an alehouse license
is the same as the grant of a new license, namely, 7*s*. 6*d*. See 9
Geo. 4, c. 61, s. 15. The fee on the renewal of a certificate is 4*s*.
to the justices' clerk, and 1*s*. to the constable: 33 & 34 Vict. c. 29,

s. 4. In each case 1s. is to be added for registration fee. See section 36, *ante*, p. 74.

Sect. 42.
———
NOTE.

Renewal by endorsement.] The renewal of a license or certificate may now be endorsed on the license or certificate, or on a copy thereof. See section 48, *post.*

Appeal against refusal to renew.] It is to be borne in mind that there is always an appeal to the quarter sessions of the county in all cases against a refusal of the justices to renew, as the 9 Geo. 4, c. 61, s. 27, which was extended to all licenses, was not repealed by this Licensing Act. See schedule. And in some cases a person may be entitled to appeal, though he was not a licensed person, and therefore not entitled to the notice of opposition and other requirements stated in this section : *R.* v. *Market Bosworth JJ.,* 51 J. P. 438 ; 57 L. T. 56 ; 35 W. R. 734 ; 56 L. J. M. C. 96 ; *R.* v. *Newcastle JJ.,* 51 J. P. 244 ; *R.* v. *Lawrence or Liverpool JJ.,* 11 Q. B. D. 638 ; 47 J. P. 596 ; 52 L. J. M. C. 114 ; 49 L. T. 244 ; 32 W. R. 20 ; *R.* v. *Thomas,* 56 J. P. 151 ; (1892), 1 Q. B. 426 ; 61 L. J. M. C. 141 ; 66 L. T. 289 ; 40 W. R. 472. See further as to appeals, 9 Geo. 4, c. 61, s. 27, *post.*

Where a rule *nisi* was granted for a *mandamus* to justices to hear an application to renew, and before cause was shown another general annual meeting was held, the court gave power to the justices to hear the application as if for the next following year : *R.* v. *Miskin Higher JJ.,* 50 J. P. 247.

43. *Confirmation of licenses.*] Any person who appears before the licensing justices and opposes the grant of a new license, and no other person, may appear and oppose the confirmation of such grant by the confirming authorities in counties or boroughs ; and the confirming authority may award such costs as they shall deem just to the party who shall succeed in the proceedings before them. In a county the justices in quarter sessions assembled, and in a borough the borough justices [and in cases where a joint committee is appointed, then the joint committee] shall make rules as to the proceedings to be adopted for confirmation of new licenses and the costs to be incurred in

Sect. 43. any such proceedings, and the person by whom such costs are to be paid.

The words *in brackets* were inserted by the Licensing Act, 1874, section 25.

The *procedure* before the confirming authority is to be regulated by the justices or joint committee, so far as regards the proceedings and the costs before the confirming authority, as to which application for information should be made to the clerk of the peace or clerk of the licensing justices. In either case, by this section no person is to be allowed to oppose the grant of a new license or certificate before the confirming authority who did not appear before the licensing justices. Any person is entitled to appear and oppose the grant of a new license. But if the same objecting party appears, he may call additional evidence and new witnesses before the confirming authority. The proceedings will be similar in many respects to an appeal, but the confirming authority has nothing to do with the reasons acted on by the licensing justices, for the object is, that the applicant shall satisfy two independent bodies of justices that there are good reasons for his application.

The rules made regulating procedure before the confirming body may be objected to if *ultra vires*. But in the exercise of their jurisdiction the discretion of the confirming authority on the merits is absolute : *R.* v. *Middlesex JJ.*, 42 J. P. 469 ; *Re Annandale JJ.*, 37 J. P. 85 ; *R.* v. *Pownall*, 57 J. P. 263 ; (1893), 1 Q. B. 273 ; 67 L. T. 680. See *ante*, p. 77.

With regard to any *costs* ordered to be paid, these may be recovered as stated in section 51, *post*, namely, under 11 & 12 Vict. c. 18, s. 18, and 42 & 43 Vict. c. 49.

44. *Disqualification for licenses.*] No license shall be granted under the Intoxicating Liquor Licensing Acts to any person or in respect of any premises declared by or in pursuance of any of the Intoxicating Liquor Licensing Acts or in this Act to be disqualified persons or disqualified premises during the continuance of such disqualification. Any license held by any person so disqualified, or attached to premises so disqualified, shall be void.

The expression " Intoxicating Liquor Licensing Acts" means 9 Geo. 4, c. 61, and the Wine and Beerhouse Acts, 32 & 33 Vict.

c. 27, and 33 & 34 Vict. c. 29, *post*. See section 74. The disqualification of premises is always limited to a term of years, but in one case (section 3) the disqualification of the person may be made for life. See, as to disqualification of persons, 9 Geo. 4, c. 61, s. 16 ; 1 Will. 4, c. 64, s. 2 ; 3 & 4 Vict. c. 61, s. 7 ; 23 Vict. c. 27, s. 22 ; 32 & 33 Vict. c. 27, s. 11 ; 33 & 34 Vict. c. 29, s. 14 ; and this Act, sections 3, 15, 19, 30. As to disqualification of premises, see this Act, sections 3, 19, 30, 31.

Sect. 44.
———
NOTE.

45. *Qualification of premises for licenses.*] Premises to which at the time of the passing of this Act no license under the Acts recited in the Wine and Beerhouse Act, 1869, authorising the sale of beer and wine for consumption thereupon is attached, shall not be subject to any of the provisions now in force prescribing a certain rent or value or rating as a qualification for receiving any such license.

Premises not at the time of the passing of this Act licensed for the sale of any intoxicating liquor for *consumption thereupon* shall not be qualified to receive a license authorising such sale unless the following conditions are satisfied :—

> (*a*.) The premises, unless such premises are a railway refreshment room, shall be of not less than the following annual value :—
>
>> If situated within the city of London or the liberties thereof, or any parish or place subject to the jurisdiction of the Metropolitan Board of Works, or within the four miles radius from Charing Cross, or within the limits of a town containing a population of not less than *one hundred thousand* inhabitants, *fifty* pounds per annum ; or if the license do not authorise

Sect. 45.

the sale of spirits, *thirty* pounds per annum.

If situated elsewhere and within the limits of a town containing a population of not less than *ten thousand* inhabitants, *thirty* pounds per annum ; or if the license do not authorise the sale of spirits, *twenty* pounds per annum.

If situated elsewhere and not within any such town as above mentioned, *fifteen* pounds per annum ; or if the license do not authorise the sale of spirits, *twelve* pounds per annum.

(*b.*) The premises shall be, in the opinion of the licensing authority, structurally adapted to the class of license for which a certificate is sought : Provided that no house, not licensed at the time of the passing of this Act, for the sale of any intoxicating liquor for consumption on the premises, shall be qualified to have a license attached thereto authorising such sale, unless such house shall contain, exclusive of the rooms occupied by the inmates of such house, if the license authorise the sale of spirits, two rooms, and if the license do not authorise the sale of spirits, one room, for the accommodation of the public.

The obscure clause at the commencement of this section was capable of being construed as impliedly repealing all valuation qualifications for out-door wine and beer licenses. But it has now been decided that it does not repeal that qualification ; and whatever meaning it has is confined to indoor licenses : *R.* v.

Cumberland JJ., 8 Q. B. D. 369 ; 51 L. J. Q. B. D. 142 ; 46 J. P. Sect. 45. 7 ; 30 W. R. 178.

NOTE.

There are houses, namely, table-beer houses, under 24 & 25 Vict. c. 21, s. 3, and houses licensed to sell wine for consumption off the premises under 23 Vict. c. 27, ss. 1, 8, and also for liqueurs and sweets under sections 69, 74, of this Act, which never were subject to any rating or value qualification, and as to which this paragraph could not apply.

New in-door licenses.] The second paragraph of the section is not so obscure. It says in effect as to all houses (alehouses or public-houses, beerhouses and winehouses) to be licensed for the first time after 10th August, 1872, for the sale of liquor to be consumed on the premises, that the valuation qualification in this clause is to be applicable, that is to say, in the metropolis and towns above 100,000 population, 50*l*. annual value, &c. And they are also to have at least one public room if for sale of beer, and two public rooms if for sale of spirits. As to structural adaptation, as no rules are laid down, the justices will be the sole judges of what this means ; but the number of rooms is stated only as a minimum qualification. In cases of premises covering a considerable area, there seems no reason why the several rooms should be under one roof. As regards alehouses or public-houses licensed under 9 Geo. 4, c. 61, there was no valuation qualification required by that or any other Act. Though, therefore, all alehouses licensed for the first time since 1872 will require the valuation in the latter part of the section, still those which were licensed on 10th August, 1872, will continue to be exempt from such valuation qualification.

The area of the jurisdiction of the Metropolitan Board of Works is set forth in 18 & 19 Vict. c. 120, ss. 249, 250, Scheds. A., B., C. : 25 & 26 Vict. c. 102, ss. 42, 112.

The word "town" was defined in this Act, section 74, and the definition was amended by Licensing Act, 1874, section 32. The old definition in section 74 of this Act was also repealed for certain purposes set forth in Act, 1874, section 33.

The words "annual value" are explained in the 47th section.

As to the "census," as a test of population, see section 65, *post*, and notes.

46. *Annual value necessary for obtaining grant of license.*] Whereas in certain cases a license under the Wine and Beerhouse Acts, 1869 and 1870, is

H

Sect. 46. not to be granted unless the house and premises in respect of which such license is granted are of such rent and value, or are rated to the poor rate on a rent or annual value of such amount as is respectively in that behalf stated in the Acts recited in the Wine and Beerhouse Act, 1869 ; and it is expedient to substitute in such cases "annual value" for the said rent, value, or rating, and to provide for the ascertaining the annual value of such house and premises : Be it therefore enacted that in cases not provided for by the last preceding section—

A license under the Wine and Beerhouse Acts, 1869 and 1870, shall not be granted in respect of any premises which are not, in the opinion of the licensing justices who grant such license, of such annual value as is mentioned in that behalf in the Acts recited by the Wine and Beerhouse Act, 1869 ; and those Acts shall be construed as if "annual value" were therein substituted for "rent," "value," "rated on a rent or annual value," and other like expressions.

If at the first general annual licensing meeting after the passing of this Act the licensing justices are of opinion that any premises which are licensed for the sale of intoxicating liquors at the passing of this Act are not of such annual value as authorises the grant of a license for such premises, they may, notwithstanding, renew such license upon the condition, to be expressed in the license, that the holder thereof, before the next general annual licensing meeting, improves the premises so as to make them of sufficient annual value, and if the holder fail to comply with such condition the license

35 & 36 VICT. C. 94, S. 47.

shall not be renewed at such next general annual licensing meeting.

Sect. 46.

In cases not provided for in last section.] This section applies to all houses for the sale of liquor to be consumed on the premises which already had a certificate under the Wine and Beerhouse Acts on 10th August, 1872, namely, beerhouses, ciderhouses, wine and refreshment houses, those to be licensed for the first time after 1872 being subject to the qualification in the latter part of the 45th section. The "annual value" of these houses licensed in 1872 is, however, to be taken instead of the "rent" or "rating," &c.; and the Acts 3 & 4 Vict. c. 61, and 23 Vict. c. 27, s. 8, will be read as if the "annual value" was substituted. If the houses licensed in 1872 could not stand this new test, then the justices were to require the houses to be improved in value, otherwise the license or certificate was not to be renewed in 1873. And this power still continues, though it is so expressed as if it was intended to be acted on in 1873; it may be exercised at any future general annual licensing meeting as the occasion requires.

The outdoor beerhouses and ciderhouses, whether licensed in 1872 or not, will still require the same valuation as before, under 3 & 4 Vict. c. 44, and 33 & 34 Vict. c. 29, s. 10, the value being arrived at as stated in the next (47th) section.

As to out-door winehouses and table-beer houses (and sweets and spirits and liqueur houses, which are on the same footing as wine) they never required a valuation qualification, and do not now require it.

It was decided on a *certiorari* to quash part of a license in *R.* v. *Exeter JJ.*, *R.* v. *Mann*, 42 L. J. M. C. 35; 37 J. P. 212; L. R. 8 Q. B. 235; 27 L. T. 847; 21 W. R. 329, that this section does not apply to alehouses which had been before this Act licensed under 9 Geo. 4, c. 61, but is confined to houses licensed under the Wine and Beerhouse Acts, 32 & 33 Vict. c. 27; 33 & 34 Vict. c. 29, *post.*

47. *Mode of ascertaining annual value.*] The licensing justices shall take such means as may seem to them best for ascertaining the annual value of any premises for the purposes of this Act, and may, if they think fit, order a valuation to be made of such premises by a competent person appointed by them for the pur-

Sect. 47. pose, and may order the costs of such valuation to be paid by the applicant for a license.

The annual value of premises for the purposes of this Act shall be the annual rent which a tenant might be reasonably expected, taking one year with another, to pay for the same, if he undertook to pay all tenants' rates and taxes, and tithe commutation rentcharge (if any), and if the landlord undertook to bear the cost of the repairs and insurance and other expenses (if any) necessary to maintain the premises in a state to command the said rent, and if no license were granted in respect thereof; but no land shall be included in such premises other than any pleasure grounds or flower or kitchen garden, yard, or curtilage usually held and occupied and used by the persons residing in and frequenting the house.

> The justices are entitled under this section to take their own way of ascertaining the annual value, and are not bound to accept the valuation list or any other valuation, even by their own valuer. But they must have some evidence on which to support the conclusion they may arrive at. The actual rent paid is not necessarily a conclusive test of annual value. They may order the premises to be re-valued at the expense of the applicant.
>
> The valuations satisfactory to justices may not coincide with the valuations of the Excise authorities for their own purpose.
>
> The mode of recovering the costs of a valuation of the premises is pointed out at the end of section 51; but in all cases the party will, no doubt, deem it expedient to volunteer such a payment, which can seldom be considerable in amount.
>
> The premises are to be valued at the same rent as if they had no license attached to them, and in the manner described.
>
> As a beer or cider-house requires to be a dwelling-house, where there is a real resident holder and occupier, if the house is used also as a shop or place of business for other purposes, the value of the whole premises must be taken: *Garratty* v. *Potts*, L. R. 6 Q. B. 86; 35 J. P. 168; 40 L. J. M. C. 1; 23 L. T. 554; 19 W. R. 127.

The test of valuation is to be taken as at the time of the hearing of the application; hence, where the valuation was not sufficient at the date of the general annual meeting, but was made sufficient at the adjournment day, when the case was heard, the court held this sufficient: *R.* v. *Montague,* 49 J. P. 55. And where adjoining premises are added, and used with the original premises, the annual value may always be properly increased, so as to make up the required amount.

Sect. 47.
NOTE.

48. *Regulations as to form of licenses.*] The following regulations shall be made with respect to licenses:

(1.) Every license granted after the commencement of this Act shall be in such form as may from time to time be prescribed by a Secretary of State.

(2.) A renewal of a license may be made by an endorsement on the license, or by the issue of a copy of the old license, but in the latter case there shall be endorsed on such copy all convictions made within the previous five years which are endorsed on the old license.

The Commissioners of Inland Revenue may alter the form of any license granted by them for the sale of intoxicating liquors in such manner as they may think expedient, for the purpose of bringing such form into conformity with the law for the time being in force.

The *forms of justices' licenses* were soon after the passing of this Act issued by the Secretary of State, and will be found in the Appendix.

The second clause as to licenses or certificates provides a way of preserving the continuity of the character of the licensee. In the eye of the law a license ceases to exist at the end of the licensing year, and what becomes of the paper on which it was written is of no consequence. It is not important, for by the

Sect. 48.
Note.
aid of the register of licenses the character and previous convictions of the party licensed may be traced. But it is, nevertheless, very convenient (as this section permits) to have one paper embodying the license, which lasts for years, and is renewable by endorsement, so as to save trouble, and show at a glance the conduct of the holders during the previous years. The licenses and certificates granted for 1872 may be continued hereafter by endorsements, though a new piece of paper can always be substituted at any of the annual licensing meetings.

See a *form of Inland Revenue license* in Appendix.

49. *Provisions as to six-day licenses.*] Where on the occasion of an application for a new license or transfer or renewal of a license, which authorises the sale of any intoxicating liquor for consumption on the premises, the applicant, at the time of his application, applies to the licensing justices to insert in his license a condition that he should keep the premises in respect of which such license is or is to be granted, closed during the whole of Sunday, the justices shall insert the said condition in such license.

The holder of a license in which such condition is inserted (in this Act referred to as a six-day license) shall keep his premises closed during the whole of Sunday and the provisions of this Act with respect to the closing of licensed premises during certain hours on Sunday shall apply to the premises in respect of which a six-day license is granted as if the whole of Sunday were mentioned in those provisions instead of certain hours only.

The holder of a six-day license may obtain from the Commissioners of Inland Revenue any license granted by such commissioners which he is entitled to obtain in pursuance of such six-day license, upon payment of

six-seventh parts of the duty which would otherwise Sect. 49.
be payable by him for a similar license not limited to
six days; and if he sell any intoxicating liquor on
Sunday he shall be deemed to be selling intoxicating
liquor without a license.

The notice which a licensed person is required to
keep painted or fixed on his premises shall, in the
case of a license under this section, contain words indicating that such license is for six-days only. In calculating the amount to be paid for a six-day license any
fraction of a penny shall be disregarded.

This section applies to alehouses, beerhouses, and all the
houses included in this Act, where liquors are consumed on the
premises.

Right of license holder to close his house.] This section
seems to be based on the notion that there is some binding obligation on the keeper of licensed premises to keep his house open
all the year round for the sale of liquors. For this notion,
however, there seems no authority. It is true that, at common
law, if a man keeps an inn, that is, a house of entertainment
for man and beast, or rather for travellers, he is bound, if he has
accommodation, to receive and procure food for, the traveller,
and may be indicted, or liable to an action, if he refuses to receive
the traveller when he has accommodation, and can make no
reasonable objection : *R.* v. *Ivens*, 7 C. & P. 213 ; *R.* v. *Luellin*, 12
Mod. 445 ; 1 Show. 270 ; *Hawthorn* v. *Hammond*, 1 C. & K. 404 ;
Howell v. *Jackson*, 6 C. & P. 725 ; see further, 26 & 27 Vict. c. 41,
post. But this obligation is confined to travellers and to food
or meat, and would not necessarily extend to the supply of
intoxicating liquors. An innkeeper, whether licensed or not, is
liable to this extent, but no further, and as to all the other
licensed persons, they are merely in the position of shopkeepers
who sell a certain article, but may, if they please, shut up their
shops at any hour or day when it suits their convenience. All
that they require to do is to take care not to sell intoxicating
liquors without a license, and not to sell during the times when
such persons are prohibited from selling, and not to commit the
other offences relating to licensed houses. Beyond those limits
they are their own masters. There is no declaration in the

Sect. 49.

NOTE.

statutes that the holders of licenses, as such, are bound to keep open all the times that they are not forbidden to do so. Nor is there any penalty imposed on them by any statute expressly or impliedly for not supplying intoxicating liquors to any person. They keep open as long as they can merely for their own convenience and profit. At the same time, if they shut up their houses at unexpected times, and so put to inconvenience the public or neighbours, this might be a good reason for the licensing justices at the next general annual licensing meeting refusing to renew the license, as they may always do, with or without reason, as regards nearly every license for in-door consumption. The general rule is, therefore, as to all intoxicating liquors, that though the licensed person is prohibited from selling within certain hours, he is nevertheless not bound to sell during the hours not prohibited, unless he keeps an inn, and in that case he is only bound to find board and meat and drink, which drink need not, however, in all cases, be intoxicating drink.

This section, however, though founded on a fundamental mistake as to the obligations of licensed persons, must be interpreted so as to give effect to its provisions. A person may, if he choose, put himself in the position of holding a six-day license. The chief advantage will be that he will pay only six-sevenths of the usual duty to the Inland Revenue ; and if he make it also an early closing house under the Act, 1874, section 8, he will be entitled to a license on paying five-sevenths of the usual duty ; but, on the other hand, he will render himself liable to heavy penalties (including the penalty under section 3) for selling or keeping his house open for sale of liquors during any part of Sunday.

Effect of six-day license.] It has been held that if a license holder at any time, either on an application for a new license, or a transfer or renewal thereof, apply for a condition as to six days to be inserted in the license, this is an election which will preclude himself and any succeeding licensee from ever again obtaining a renewal or transfer of the license without such condition inserted. Thus, if a license is for the first time granted as a six-day license, the justices cannot be in any way compelled, on application for a renewal, to grant a seven-day or ordinary license, leaving out this condition : *R.* v. *Crewkerne JJ.,* 21 Q. B. D. 85 ; 52 J. P. 372 ; 57 L. J. M. C. 127 ; 60 L. T. 84 ; 36 W. R. 629.

And in like manner, if the holder of a license, held for years as a seven-day license, happen to ask the six-day condition to be inserted, he and any successor will be for ever precluded from demanding by way of renewal the original form of the license to be restored : *R.* v. *Liverpool JJ.,* 52 J. P. 376.

35 & 36 VICT. C. 94, S. 50.

It is to be observed that this section applies only to licenses which authorise the sale of "liquor for consumption *on the premises*," that is to say, alehouse or public-house licenses under 9 Geo. 4, c. 61, and beerhouse, ciderhouse, and refreshment-house licenses for consumption of liquor on the premises. And when an alehouse keeper obtains a six-day license under 9 Geo. 4, c. 61, he seems still bound, like other innkeepers, to afford meat and usual refreshment to travellers on Sundays if he so holds himself out. He cannot, however, owing to the express enactment in the Act, 1874, section 10, sell liquors on Sunday to travellers, or any person whatever, except to those lodging in his house; and therefore to that extent gets rid of the common law duty.

As to Christmas Day and Good Friday, see notes to Act, 1874, section 3, *post*.

This section was extended to the United Kingdom by 43 & 44 Vict. c. 20, s. 44, *post*.

Sect. 49.
———
NOTE.

50. *Licenses may be removed from one part of a district to another, &c.*] Licenses may be removed from one part of a licensing district to another part of the same district, or from one licensing district to another licensing district within the same county, in manner following :—

The application for an order sanctioning removal shall be made by the person desiring to be the holder of the license when removed, and shall be made at a general annual licensing meeting, or any adjournment thereof, to the justices authorised to grant new licenses in the licensing district in which the premises are situated to which the license is to be removed.

Notice of the intended application shall be given in the same manner as notice is given of an application for the grant of a new license.

A copy of the notice shall be personally served upon or sent by registered letter to the owner of the

Sect 50. premises from which the license is to be removed, and the holder of the license, unless he is also the applicant.

The justices to whom the application is made shall not make an order sanctioning such removal unless they are satisfied that no objection to such removal is made by the owner of the premises to which the license is attached, or by the holder of the license, or by any other person whom such justices shall determine to have a right to object to the removal.

Subject as aforesaid, such justices shall have the same power to make an order sanctioning such removal as they have to grant new licenses; but no such order shall be valid unless confirmed by the confirming authority of the licensing district.

The removal of a license was a novelty introduced in 1871, when the justices could not grant a new license, as was the case under the Intoxicating Liquor Licenses Suspension Act of 1871, now repealed. But now that the justices are subdivided into two bodies—one a licensing and the other a confirming body, and without any restriction on their absolute joint discretion as to granting new licenses (except as regards some of the houses mentioned in the Wine and Beerhouse Acts) there seems little occasion for continuing this practice. Moreover, as the application for removal of a license or certificate is put on the same footing as an application for a new license, it is difficult to see what advantage is to be gained by applying for a removal. It is not compulsory in the justices to grant it. If they refuse it, there is no appeal. If they grant it, it must still be confirmed (unless an off-license) by the confirming authority. In the case of an off-wine, off-spirit, off-sweets, or off-cider license, the justices cannot refuse unless on one of the four grounds set forth in 32 & 33 Vict. c. 27, s. 8. The fact that if the license or certificate be removed, there will be no addition to the aggregate number of licensed houses, is the only circumstance which may tell in its favour, but if a new license were applied for, and it were shown, as it may be, that somebody else did not intend to apply for a renewal, the

35 & 36 VICT. C. 94, S. 51.

same circumstances would exist in favour of an application for a new license. No confirmation is required if it is an off-license: Licensing Act, 1874, s. 24.

Sect. 50.
———
NOTE.

As a removal license is put on the same footing as a new license, it follows that any person is entitled to oppose the grant of this license both before the general annual licensing meeting and the confirming authority, subject to the qualification that no one will be allowed to be heard against the confirmation who did not oppose before the licensing justices.

The consents of the persons specified in this section are something in the nature of a condition precedent to the jurisdiction.

The words, "or by any other person whom such justices shall determine to have a right to object to the removal," seem to contemplate the case of a mortgagee or other person having a legal interest in the premises, as was seen in *Garrett* v. *Middlesex JJ.*, or *R.* v. *Garrett*, 12 Q. B. D. 620; 48 J. P. 358; 53 L. J. M. C. 81; 32 W. R. 646.

The party applying for a removal may combine with his application one for a provisional grant to a house not yet built, but about to be built. See Act, 1874, s. 22.

Legal Proceedings.

51. *Summary proceedings for offences under this Act, &c.*] Except as in this Act otherwise expressly provided, every offence under this Act may be prosecuted, and every penalty and forfeiture may be recovered and enforced, in manner provided by the Summary Jurisdiction Act, 1848, subject to the following provisions:—

(1.) The court of summary jurisdiction when hearing and determining an information or complaint, other than in a case where the offence charged is that of being found drunk in any highway or other public place, or any licensed premises, shall be constituted either of two or more justices of the peace in petty sessions sitting at a place appointed for holding petty

Sect. 51. sessions, or of a stipendiary magistrate or some other officer for the time being empowered by law to do alone any act authorised to be done by more than one justice of the peace, sitting alone or with others at some court or other place appointed for the administration of justice:

(2.) (*Repealed* by 47 & 48 Vict. c. 43, Sched.)

(3.) (*Repealed* by 47 & 48 Vict. c. 43, Sched.)

(4.) (Part of this sub-section *repealed* by 47 & 48 Vict. c. 43, Sched.)

In all cases of summary proceedings under this Act, the *defendant* and his *wife* shall be competent to give evidence.

(5.) All *forfeitures* shall be sold or otherwise disposed of in such manner as the court may direct, and the proceeds of such sale or disposal (if any) shall be applied in the like manner as penalties, but the court may direct that such proceeds may be applied in the first instance in paying the expenses of and incidental to any search and seizure which resulted in such forfeiture:

(6.) Penalties and forfeitures under this Act shall not for the purpose of any Act respecting the application of such penalties, or the costs, charges, and expenses attending proceedings for recovery of such penalties or of forfeitures, be deemed to be penalties or forfeitures under any Act relating to the Inland Revenue.

Any officer appointed by the Commissioners of In- **Sect. 51.**
land Revenue may sue for any penalties under this
Act, and when so sued for, any penalties which may
be recovered shall be applied in the manner in which
excise penalties are for the time being applicable
by law.

Where under this Act any sum for costs (other than
costs upon a conviction or order of dismissal of an information) or for compensation, or both, is ordered or
awarded to be paid by any person, the amount thereof
shall be recovered in manner directed by "The Summary Jurisdiction Act, 1848," for the recovery of
costs awarded upon the dismissal of an information or
complaint.

The offences specified in sub-section 1 are those in section 12, *ante*, p. 23.

Defendant and wife as witnesses.] The allowing of a defendant (clause 4), in a criminal proceeding, and his wife to give evidence was a novelty; but it has since been applied to many other cases. Being competent witnesses, the defendant and his wife are also compellable witnesses, and are on the same footing as other married witnesses. Where the wife is the licensed person, and is summoned, she as well as her husband may both give evidence: *Seager* v. *White*, 48 J. P. 436; 51 L. T. 261.

The Summary Jurisdiction Acts.] In all Acts, whether passed before or after 1st January, 1890, the expression "Summary Jurisdiction Act, 1848," shall mean 11 & 12 Vict. c. 43; and the expression "The Summary Jurisdiction (England) Acts" shall mean 11 & 12 Vict. c. 43; 42 & 43 Vict. c. 49; 47 & 48 Vict. c. 43, and any Act, past or future, amending those Acts or either of them.

And the expression "court of summary jurisdiction" shall mean any justice or justices of the peace or other magistrate, by whatever name called, to whom jurisdiction is given by or who is authorised to act under the Summary Jurisdiction Acts, whether

Sect. 51. "*Summary Procedure.*"

NOTE. in England, Wales, or Ireland, and whether acting under the Summary Jurisdiction Acts, or any of them, or under any other Act, or by virtue of their commission or under the common law: 52 & 53 Vict. c. 63, s. 13.

Procedure under Summary Jurisdiction Acts.] This *section* having been partly repealed is now replaced by the *Summary Jurisdiction Acts*, 11 & 12 Vict. c. 43 ; 42 & 43 Vict. c. 49; 47 & 48 Vict. c. 43, which contain the following enactments :—

Description of offence and proof of exceptions, &c.] (1) The description of any offence in the words of the Act, or any order, bye-law, regulation, or other documents creating the offence, or in similar words, shall be sufficient in law. (2.) Any exception, exemption, proviso, excuse, or qualification, whether it does or does not accompany, in the same section, the description of the offence, in the Act, order, bye-law, regulation, or other document creating the offence, may be proved by the defendant, but need not be specified or negatived in the information or complaint ; and if so specified or negatived no proof in relation to the matter so specified or negatived shall be required on the part of the informant or complainant : 42 & 43 Vict. c. 49, s. 39. The general rule is that a person who relies on his license as a defence is bound to prove it : *Turner* v. *Johnson*, 51 J. P. 22.

The *summons* in all cases where a licensed person is accused shall state that the production of his license will be required, as the clerk of the court may have to indorse some particulars upon the license : Licensing Act, 1872, section 55, *post.*

Mitigation of punishment.] Where a court of summary jurisdiction can impose imprisonment or fine, that court may impose the imprisonment without hard labour, and reduce the prescribed period, or do either of those Acts, and in case of fine, if in respect of a first offence, may reduce the prescribed amount : 42 & 43 Vict. c. 49, s. 4. See also Licensing Act, 1874, section 12, *post.*

Scale of imprisonment for non-payment of money.] The period of imprisonment imposed by a court of summary jurisdiction under this Act, or under any other Act, whether past or future, in respect of the non-payment of any sum of money adjudged to be paid by a conviction, or in respect of the default of a sufficient distress to satisfy any such sum, shall, notwithstanding any enactment to the contrary in any past Act, be such

"Summary Procedure."   Sect. 51.

period as in the opinion of the court will satisfy the justice of the case, but shall not exceed in any case the maximum fixed by the following scale; that is to say,—   NOTE.

Where the amount of the sum or sums of money, adjudged to be paid by a conviction, as ascertained by the conviction.	The said period shall not exceed
Does not exceed ten shillings	Seven days.
Exceeds ten shillings but does not exceed one pound	Fourteen days.
Exceeds one pound but does not exceed five pounds	One month.
Exceeds five pounds but does not exceed twenty pounds	Two months.
Exceeds twenty pounds	Three months.

And such imprisonment shall be without hard labour, except where hard labour is authorised by the Act on which the conviction is founded, in which case the imprisonment may, if the court thinks the justice of the case requires it, be with hard labour, so that the term of hard labour awarded do not exceed the terms authorised by the said Act: 42 & 43 Vict. c. 49, s. 5.

Payment by instalments of or security taken for payment of money.] A court of summary jurisdiction, by whose conviction or order any sum is adjudged to be paid, may do all or any of the following things, namely,—

(1.) Allow time for the payment of the said sum; and

(2.) Direct payment to be made of the said sum by instalments; and

(3.) Direct that the person liable to pay the said sum shall be at liberty to give to the satisfaction of that court, or of such other court of summary jurisdiction, or such person as may be specified by that court, security with or without a surety or sureties for the payment of the said sum or of any instalment thereof and such security may be given and enforced in manner provided by this Act.

Where a sum is directed to be paid by instalments and default is made in the payment of any one instalment, the same proceedings may be taken as if default had been made in payment of all the instalments then remaining unpaid.

A court of summary jurisdiction directing the payment of a sum or of an instalment of a sum may direct such payment to be made at such time or times, and in such place or places, and to

Sect. 51.   *" Summary Procedure."*

NOTE. such person or persons, as may be specified by the court; and every person to whom any such sum or instalment is paid, where not the clerk of the court of summary jurisdiction, shall as soon as may be account for and pay over the same to that clerk: 42 & 43 Vict. c. 49, s. 7.

Provisions as to costs in the case of small fines.] Where a fine adjudged by a conviction by a court of summary jurisdiction to be paid does not exceed *five shillings*, then, except so far as the court may think fit to expressly order otherwise, an order shall not be made for payment by the defendant to the informant of any costs; and the court shall, except so far as they think fit to expressly order otherwise, direct all fees payable or paid by the informant to be remitted or repaid to him; the court may also order the fine or any part thereof to be paid to the informant in or towards the payment of his costs: 42 & 43 Vict. c. 49, s. 8.

Power of court to discharge accused without punishment.] If upon the hearing of a charge for an offence punishable on summary conviction under this Act, or under any other Act, whether past or future, the court of summary jurisdiction think that though the charge is proved the offence was in the particular case of so trifling a nature that it is inexpedient to inflict any punishment, or any other than a nominal punishment,—

(1.) The court, without proceeding to conviction, may dismiss the information, and, if the court think fit, may order the person charged to pay such damages, not exceeding forty shillings, and such cost of the proceeding, or either of them, as the court think reasonable; or

(2.) The court upon convicting the person charged may discharge him conditionally on his giving security, with or without sureties, to appear for sentence when called upon, or to be of good behaviour, and either without payment of damages and costs, or subject to the payment of such damages and costs, or either of them, as the court think reasonable :

Provided that this section shall not apply to an adult convicted in pursuance of this Act of an offence of which he has pleaded guilty, and of which he could not, if he had not pleaded guilty, be convicted by a court of summary jurisdiction: 42 & 43 Vict. c. 49, s. 16.

35 & 36 VICT. C. 94, S. 51.

"Summary Procedure."   Sect. 51.

Right to claim trial by jury in some summary offences.] NOTE.
A person when charged with an offence for which an offender is liable on summary conviction to be imprisoned for a term exceeding *three* months, and which is not an assault, may, on appearing before the court and before the charge is gone into, but not afterwards, claim to be tried by a jury, and thereupon the court of summary jurisdiction shall deal with the case in all respects as if the accused were charged with an indictable offence, and the offence shall be deemed to be an indictable offence: 42 & 43 Vict. c. 49, s. 17.

Power to award costs of conviction or dismissal.] In all cases of summary convictions or of orders, it shall be lawful for the justice or justices making the same in his or their discretion to award and order that the defendant shall pay to the prosecutor or complainant such costs as shall seem just and reasonable in that behalf. And where such justice or justices shall dismiss the information or complaint, it shall be lawful for him or them in his or their discretion in and by his or their order of dismissal to award and order that the prosecutor or complainant respectively shall pay to the defendant such costs as to such justice or justices shall seem just and reasonable, and the sums so allowed for costs shall in all cases be specified in such conviction or order of dismissal aforesaid, and the same shall be recoverable by distress, &c.: 11 & 12 Vict. c. 43, s. 18.

The costs, for example, ordered by the confirming authority under the Licensing Act, 1872, section 43, *ante*, p. 94, are to be recovered as set out in the above section of 11 & 12 Vict. c. 43, s. 18.

Power to justices to issue warrant of distress and commitment.] Where a conviction adjudges a pecuniary penalty or where an order requires the payment of a sum of money, and no mode of raising or levying such penalty, compensation, or sum of money, or of enforcing the payment of the same is stated or provided, any justice of the same county, division, borough, &c., may issue his warrant of distress under his hand and seal; and in case of insufficient distress, another justice may, by indorsement on the warrant, authorise distress and sale of defendant's goods within such other county or place: 11 & 12 Vict. c. 43, s. 19. Until such warrant of distress is executed the defendant may be suffered to go at large, or be detained unless he give sufficient security to appear at the time and place for the return of the warrant: *Ibid.* s. 20. If, on return of such warrant of distress,

I

LICENSING ACT, 1872, s. 51.

Sect. 51.

NOTE.

" Summary Procedure."

no sufficient distress is found, the justice may order the constable to convey the defendant to the house of correction or common gaol, to be imprisoned [and kept to hard labour] for the time directed by the statute : *Ibid.* s. 21. Where the statute in that behalf provides no further remedy in default of distress, or where the distress is insufficient, or where no mode of enforcing payment of the penalty, &c., the defendant may be committed to imprisonment for three calendar months : *Ibid.* s. 22 ; 21 & 22 Vict. c. 73, s. 5.

Mitigation of warrant of distress and commitment.] (1.) A court of summary jurisdiction, to whom application is made either to issue a warrant of distress for any sum adjudged to be paid by a conviction or order, or to issue a warrant for committing a person to prison for non-payment of a sum of money adjudged to be paid by a conviction, or in the case of a sum not a civil debt by an order, or for default of sufficient distress to satisfy any such sum may, if the court deem it expedient so to do, postpone the issue of such warrant until such time and on such conditions, if any, as to the court may seem just.

(2.) The wearing apparel and bedding of a person and his family, and to the value of 5*l.* the tools and implements of his trade, shall not be taken under a distress issued by a court of summary jurisdiction.

(3.) Where a person is adjudged by the conviction of a court of summary jurisdiction or in the case of a sum not a civil debt by an order of the court to pay any sum of money, and in default of payment of such sum, a warrant of distress is authorised to be issued, and it appears to the court of summary jurisdiction to whom application is made to issue such warrant, that such person has no goods whereon to levy the distress, or that in the event of a warrant of distress being issued his goods will be insufficient to satisfy the money payable by him, or that the levy of the distress will be more injurious to him or his family than imprisonment, such court, instead of issuing such warrant of distress may, if it think fit, order the said person, on non-payment of the said sum, to be imprisoned for any period not exceeding the period for which he is liable under such conviction or order to be imprisoned in default of sufficient distress.

(4.) Where on application to a court of summary jurisdiction to issue a warrant for committing a person to prison for non-payment of a sum adjudged to be paid by a conviction of any court of summary jurisdiction or in the case of a sum not a civil

" Summary Procedure."   Sect. 51.

debt, by an order of such court or for default of sufficient distress to satisfy such sum, it appears to the court to whom application is made, that either by payment of part of the said sum whether in the shape of instalments or otherwise, or by the net proceeds of the distress, the amount of the sum so adjudged has been reduced to such an extent that the unsatisfied balance if it had constituted the original amount adjudged to be paid by the conviction or order would have subjected the defendant to a maximum term of imprisonment, less than the term of imprisonment to which he is liable under such conviction or order, the court shall, by its warrant of commitment, revoke the term of imprisonment, and order the defendant to be imprisoned for a term not exceeding such less maximum term instead of for the term originally mentioned in the conviction or order: 42 & 43 Vict. c. 49, s. 21.

NOTE.

The *forms* of warrants of *distress* and *commitment* are now contained in the Summary Jurisdiction Rules, 1886.

A *warrant of commitment* is not to be void for a defect if it be alleged therein that the offender has been convicted and there is a valid conviction or order: 42 & 43 Vict. c. 49, s. 39.

A *warrant of distress* will not be void for a defect if it allege that a conviction or order has been made, and there is a good and valid conviction or order: 42 & 43 Vict. c. 49, s. 39. The mode of executing a warrant of distress is set forth in 42 & 43 Vict. c. 49, s. 43.

Where no method of recovery of penalty provided.] In all cases where no method of recovery of a penalty or fine is provided the above enactments of 11 & 12 Vict. c. 43, ss. 19, 21, and 42 & 43 Vict. c. 49, s. 21, shall apply to such recovery. Thus, it is declared that where by virtue of the repeal enacted by this Act (47 & 48 Vict. c. 43), or otherwise, any statute authorising the infliction by any justice or justices of a penalty or fine, either as a sole punishment or as an alternative punishment for imprisonment, provides no method for the recovery of such penalty or fine; sections 19, 21 of 11 & 12 Vict. c. 43, as amended by section 21 of 42 & 43 Vict. c. 41, shall apply to the recovery of such penalty or fine: 47 & 48 Vict. c. 43, s. 5.

Proof of summary conviction.] (1.) The clerk of every court of summary jurisdiction shall keep a register of the minutes or memorandums of all the convictions and orders of such court.

Sect. 51. *"Summary Procedure."*

NOTE. (2.) Such register, and also any extract from such register certified by the clerk of the court keeping the same to be a true extract, shall be *primâ facie* evidence of the matters entered therein for the purpose of informing a court of summary jurisdiction, acting for the same county, borough, or place as the court, whose convictions, orders, and proceedings are entered in the register; but nothing in this section shall dispense with the legal proof of a previous conviction for an offence when required to be proved against a person charged with another offence. (6.) Every such register shall be open for inspection without fee or reward by any justice of the peace, or by any person authorised in that behalf by a justice of the peace, or by a Secretary of State: 42 & 43 Vict. c. 49, s. 22. See also as to proof of conviction in other cases, 34 & 35 Vict. c. 112, s. 18.

Proof of service of process, notices, &c.] A solemn declaration before a justice of the peace as to service is a *primâ facie* evidence of service: 42 & 43 Vict. c. 49, s. 41.

Forfeitures sold.] The above provision as to sale of forfeitures will apply to the liquor declared by section 3 of Act, 1872, also by Act, 1874, section 17, to be forfeited.

Penalties.] The mitigation of penalties is provided for in Licensing Act, 1874, section 12, *post*, and notes thereon; also by the Summary Jurisdiction Act, 1879, 42 & 43 Vict. c. 49, s. 4, *ante*, p. 110. As to application of penalties, see this Act, 1872, section 66, and notes, *post*. The Crown may remit the penalty: 22 Vict. c. 32.

52. *Appeal to quarter sessions.*] If any person feels aggrieved by any order or conviction made by a court of summary jurisdiction, the person so aggrieved may appeal therefrom, subject to the conditions and regulations following:—

(1.) The appeal shall be made to the *next* court of quarter sessions. [The rest of this section was *repealed* by 47 & 48 Vict. c. 43, Sched.]

Procedure in Summary Jurisdiction Acts.] The effect of the Summary Jurisdiction Acts, 42 & 43 Vict. c. 9, s. 31;

35 & 36 VICT. C. 94, S. 52.

47 & 48 Vict. c. 43, s. 6, and Sched.; and 52 & 53 Vict. c. 63, **Sect. 52.**
s. 13, sub-sect. (11), has been held to be such, that appeals against
refusal of licensing justices to renew or transfer a license are now **Note.**
governed as regards serving notice of appeal by the procedure in
the Summary Jurisdiction Acts : *R.* v. *Glamorganshire JJ.* (1892),
1 Q. B. 363, 621 ; 61 L. J. M. C. 1 ; 67 L. T. 543 ; 41 W. R. 57 ;
56 J. P. 100. See further on this subject, 9 Geo. 4, c. 61, s. 27,
and notes, *post*.

Under this section, as originally drawn, it was held necessary
to serve each of the convicting justices with notice of appeal, and
that to serve the clerk of the justices only was not then sufficient:
Curtis v. *Buss*, 3 Q. B. D. 13 ; 41 J. P. 87 ; 37 L. T. (N.S.) 533 ;
47 L. J. M. C. 35 ; 26 W. R. 210. And this last was the rule in
all like cases of convictions: *R.* v. *Reading*, 10 L. J. M. C. 126 ;
R. v. *Cheshire JJ.*, 11 A. & E. 139 ; 3 P. & D. 23*n*. But see now
42 & 43 Vict. c. 49, s. 31, below, which has been declared to substitute for service on each justice a service on their clerk in all
appeals against refusals of licenses.

The person aggrieved.] The person aggrieved is the person
who has been convicted, or against whom an order has been made,
or whose license has been refused. Where a license holder was
convicted, it was held that the landlord has no right to appeal to
quarter sessions though his interest may be indirectly affected by
the conviction : *R.* v. *Andover Justices*, 16 Q. B. D. 711 ; 50 J. P.
549 ; 55 L. J. M. C. 143 ; 55 L. T. 33 ; 34 W. R. 456. But when
a license has been refused the owner is deemed sufficiently
aggrieved to entitle him to join in the appeal or to appeal in his
own right.

Summary Jurisdiction Acts, 1879 *and* 1884, *as to
appeals.*] The procedure as to *appeals* against summary convictions and orders under the Licensing Acts is now regulated by the
Summary Jurisdiction Acts, 1879, 42 & 43 Vict. c. 49; 1884,
47 & 48 Vict. c. 43 ; 52 & 53 Vict. c. 63, s. 13, sub-section (11).

Procedure on appeal to general or quarter sessions.]
Where any person is authorised (some words here struck out by
47 & 48 Vict. c. 43, sched.) to appeal from the conviction or order
of a court of summary jurisdiction to a court of general or quarter
sessions, he may appeal to such court, subject to the conditions
and regulations following :

(1.) The appeal shall be made to the prescribed court of general
or quarter sessions, or if no court is prescribed, to the
next practicable court of general or quarter sessions having

Sect. 52.
NOTE.

Procedure on Appeal.

jurisdiction in the county, borough, or place for which the said court of summary jurisdiction acted, and holden not less than fifteen days after the day on which the decision was given upon which the conviction or order was founded ; and

(2.) The appellant shall, within the prescribed time, or if no time is prescribed within *seven days after* the day on which the said decision of the court was given, give notice of appeal by serving on the other party and on the clerk of the said court of summary jurisdiction notice in writing of his intention to appeal, and of the general grounds of such appeal ; and

(3.) The appellant shall, within the prescribed time, or if no time is prescribed within *three days* after the day on which he gave notice of appeal, enter into a *recognizance* before a court of summary jurisdiction, with or without a surety or sureties, as that court may direct, conditioned to appear at the said sessions and to try such appeal, and to abide the judgment of the court of appeal thereon, and to pay such costs as may be awarded by the court of appeal, or the appellant may, if the court of summary jurisdiction before whom the appellant appears to enter into a recognizance think it expedient instead of entering into a recognizance, give such other security, by deposit of money with the clerk of the court of summary jurisdiction or otherwise, as that court deems sufficient ; and

(4.) Where the appellant is in *custody*, the court of summary jurisdiction before whom the appellant appears to enter into a recognizance may, if the court think fit, on the appellant entering into such a recognizance or giving such other security as aforesaid, release him from custody ; and

(5.) The court of appeal may adjourn the hearing of the appeal, and upon the hearing thereof may confirm, reverse, or *modify* the decision of the court of summary jurisdiction, or remit the matter, with the opinion of the court of appeal thereon, to a court of summary jurisdiction acting for the same county, borough, or place as the court by whom the conviction or order appealed against was made, or may make such other order in the matter as the court of appeal may think just, and may by such order exercise any power which the court of summary

35 & 36 VICT. C. 94, S. 52.

Procedure on Appeal.   Sect. 52

jurisdiction might have exercised, and such order shall have the same effect, and may be enforced in the same manner, as if it had been made by the court of summary jurisdiction. The court of appeal may also make such order as to costs to be paid by either party as the court may think just; and

NOTE.

(6.) Whenever a decision is *not confirmed by the court of appeal,* the clerk of the peace shall send to the clerk of the court of summary jurisdiction from whose decision the appeal was made, for entry in his register, and also indorse on the conviction or order appealed against, a memorandum of the decision of the court of appeal, and whenever any copy or certificate of such conviction or order is made, a copy of such memorandum shall be added thereto, and shall be sufficient evidence of the said decision in every case where such copy or certificate would be sufficient evidence of such conviction or order; and

(7.) Every *notice* in writing required by this section to be given by an appellant shall be in writing signed by him, or by his agent on his behalf, and may be transmitted as a registered letter *by the post* in the ordinary way, and shall be deemed to have been served at the time when it would be delivered in the ordinary course of the post : 42 & 43 Vict. c. 49, s. 31.

The notice may be served by registered letter. On this subject the meaning of "*service by post*" in statutes passed after 1890 has been declared to be this:—Where an Act passed after the commencement of this Act (1st January, 1890) authorises or requires any document to be served by post, whether the expression "serve" or the expression "give" or "send," or any other expression is used, then, unless the contrary intention appears, the service shall be deemed to be effected by properly addressing, prepaying, and posting a letter containing the document, and unless the contrary is proved, to have been effected at the time at which the letter would be delivered in the ordinary course of post : 52 & 53 Vict. c. 63, s. 26.

The "prescribed court of quarter sessions," in case of convictions and orders made under this Act, is in boroughs having a court of quarter sessions to the recorder. But where the license is refused the appeal lies in all cases not to the borough sessions, but to the county sessions, as directed by 9 Geo. 4, c. 61, s. 27, *post.* And the same Act prescribes five days as the time for bringing the appeal : 9 Geo. 4, c. 61, s. 27. The same Act, 9

Sect. 52. *Procedure on Appeal.*

NOTE. Geo. 4, c. 61, s. 27, qualified by 12 & 13 Vict. c. 45, s. 1 (now repealed), prescribes that the appeal was to be to a quarter sessions, sitting not sooner than twelve days after the decision. Whether this Act, 42 & 43 Vict. c. 49, s. 31, now substitutes fifteen days for twelve days seems doubtful. The recognisance was prescribed by 9 Geo. 4, c. 61, s. 27, to be entered into within five days, and this is still the proper time. It is irregular to fix the deposit in lieu of recognisance before notice of appeal has been served: *R.* v. *Anglesea JJ.* (1892), 2 Q. B. 29; 56 J. P. 552; 67 L. T. 322. The recognisance, though entered into too late, may yet be estreated: *R.* v. *Glamorgan*, 24 Q. B. D. 675; 63 L. T. 730; 55 J. P. 39.

The quarter sessions always have power to dismiss the appeal on the ground of the notice being bad: 12 & 13 Vict. c. 45, s. 2; *R.* v. *Lancashire JJ.*, 41 J. P. 293. The notice of appeal is not invalid though addressed only to the justices' clerk: *R.* v. *Essex JJ.* (1892), 1 Q. B. 190; 56 J. P. 375; 66 L. T. 676. Service on the solicitor who last acted for the other party is not sufficient: *R.* v. *Oxfordshire JJ.* (1893), 2 Q. B. 149; 57 J. P. 409. A person convicted under the Prevention of Crimes Act, 34 & 35 Vict. c. 112, s. 10, of harbouring thieves, *ante*, p. 31, is entitled to appeal in the same way as if he were convicted under the Licensing Acts: 39 & 40 Vict. c. 20, s. 5, *ante*, p. 32. The appeal from excise convictions is now also governed by the procedure under these Acts: *Re Authers*, 22 Q. B. D. 355; 53 J. P. 116; 58 L. J. M. C. 62; 37 W. R. 320. The quarter sessions cannot add further restrictions on the appeal: *R.* v. *Pawlett*, L. R. 8 Q. B. 491; 37 J. P. 775; 29 L. T. 390.

Application of provisions respecting appeals to quarter sessions to appeals under prior Acts.] [The previous part of this section was *repealed* by 47 & 48 Vict. c. 43, sched.]

Where any past Act, so far as unrepealed, prescribes that any appeal from the conviction or order of a court of summary jurisdiction shall be made to the next court of general or quarter sessions, such appeal may be made to the next practicable court of general or quarter sessions having jurisdiction in the county, borough, or place for which the court of summary jurisdiction acted, and held not less than *fifteen days* after the day on which the decision was given upon which the conviction or order appealed against was founded: 42 & 43 Vict. c. 49, s. 32. The period of "not less than fifteen days" means "fifteen clear days:" *Re Railway Sleepers Company*, 29 Ch. D. 204. See also notes to 32 & 33 Vict. c. 27, s. 7, *post*.

35 & 36 VICT. C. 94, S. 52.

Procedure by Special Case Stated.   Sect. 52.

Special case stated by licensing justices.] As recent cases   NOTE.
have brought the decisions of licensing justices to a large extent
within the procedure formerly supposed to be confined to appeals
against orders and convictions in proceedings commenced by
complaint and information, it is necessary to keep in view how
far those cases have gone.

The first case of *R.* v. *Glamorganshire JJ.* (1892), 1 Q. B. 363,
621 ; 56 J. P. 232, 437 ; 67 L. T. 543 ; 61 L. J. M. C. 169 ; 40
W. R. 102, involved the point whether the notice of appeal prescribed by the Summary Jurisdiction Act, 42 & 43 Vict. c. 49, s. 31,
applied to appeals under 9 Geo. 4, c. 61, s. 27, against refusals of
licenses, or whether the latter appeals were still governed by the
procedure set forth in 9 Geo. 4, c. 61. And the Court of Appeal
decided that, having regard to 42 & 43 Vict. c. 49, s. 31 ; 47 & 48
Vict. c. 43 ; and 52 & 53 Vict. c. 63, s. 13, sub-sect. (11), these
later Acts impliedly repealed the former Act as regards the mode
of serving notice of appeal. Hence the notice of appeal may now
be served by giving the notice thereof to the clerk of the licensing
justices instead of as formerly serving notice on each of the
justices.

The next case of *R.* v. *Byrde*, which was heard and decided by
the Court of Appeal at the same time as *R.* v. *Glamorganshire*,
involved the point whether the licensing justices who refused a
license were in the same position as justices at petty sessions
when adjudicating on summonses under the Summary Jurisdiction Acts, and therefore whether the applicant could demand a
case to be stated on a point of law pursuant to 42 & 43 Vict. c. 49,
s. 33, and Summary Jurisdiction Rules, 1886. And the court
held that they were in the same position, and that the aggrieved
applicant might demand a case giving notices as the statute
requires.

The next case of *Price* v. *James* (1892), 2 Q. B. 428 ; 61 L. J.
M. C. 203 ; 56 J. P. 471 ; 57 J. P. 148 ; 67 L. T. 543 ; 41 W. R.
57, involved the point whether, if the licensing justices agreed to
state a case and the superintendent of police had been a party
opposing and consented to be made a respondent in the case that
is stated, the superintendent was entitled to be heard by counsel
in the High Court and to his costs, if he succeeded. And the
court decided that he was so entitled.

The next case of *R.* v. *Bristol Justices*, 57 J. P. 486 ; 68 L. T.
225, involved the point whether, if the superintendent of police
opposed the renewal of a license and the applicant appealed to
quarter sessions, the appellant was bound to serve notice of the
appeal on the superintendent and treat him as "the other party"

Sect. 52. *Procedure by Case Stated.*

NOTE. mentioned in 42 & 43 Vict. c. 49, s. 31, and therefore that if he failed to serve such notice the quarter sessions may refuse to hear the appeal. The court held he was so bound.

Who may demand a special case.] Under the first statute of 20 & 21 Vict. c. 43, either the prosecutor or the defendant could demand a special case. The later statute, 42 & 43 Vict. c. 49, enacts as follows :—(1.) Any person aggrieved who desires to question a conviction, order, determination, or other proceeding of a court of summary jurisdiction, on the ground that it is erroneous in point of law, or is in excess of jurisdiction, may apply to the court to state a special case setting forth the facts of the case and the grounds on which the proceeding is questioned, and if the court decline to state the case, may apply to the High Court of Justice for an order requiring the case to be stated.
(2.) The application shall be made and the case stated within such time and in such manner as may be from time to time directed by rules under this Act, and the case shall be heard and determined in manner prescribed by rules of court made in pursuance of the Supreme Court of Judicature Act, 1875, and the Acts amending the same ; and, subject as aforesaid, the Act 20 & 21 Vict. c. 43, intituled " An Act to improve the administration of the law so far as respects summary proceedings before justices of the peace," shall, so far as it is applicable, apply to any special case stated under this section, as if it were stated under that Act : Provided that nothing in this section shall prejudice the statement of any special case under that Act : 42 & 43 Vict. c. 49, s. 33. The definition of " court of summary jurisdiction," 52 & 53 Vict. c. 62, s. 13, sub-section (11), which is to be taken in connection with the 33rd section, is stated, *ante*, p. 109.

The Summary Jurisdiction Act, 1884, 47 & 48 Vict. c. 43, s. 12, authorised the Lord Chancellor to make rules in relation to the forms to be used. The Summary Jurisdiction Rules, 1886 (signed 12th December, 1879), contained the following :—

Rule 17. An application to a court of summary jurisdiction under section 33 of 42 & 43 Vict. c. 49, to state a special case, shall be made in writing, and may be made at any time within *seven days* from the date of the proceeding to be questioned, and the case shall be stated within three calendar months after the date of the application.

The *demand of a case* for the opinion of the High Court, under 20 & 21 Vict. c. 43, s. 2, and 42 & 43 Vict. c. 49, must be made in writing to " the court," which has been interpreted to mean each and all the convicting or ordering justices, that is to say, the

Procedure by Case Stated. Sect. 52.
written notice must be served personally or at the residence of NOTE.
those justices, and also a copy must be served on the clerk to the
justices: *South Staffordshire JJ.* v. *Stone,* 19 Q. B. D. 168; 51
J. P. 662; 56 L. J. M. C. 122; 57 L. T. 368; 36 W. R. 76;
Lockhart or *Rutter* v. *St. Albans,* 21 Q. B. D. 188; 52 J. P. 420;
57 L. J. M. C. 118; 36 W. R. 420; *Westmore* v. *Payne,* 55 J. P.
440; 64 L. T. 55; (1891), 1 Q. B. 482; *Edwards* v. *Roberts*
(1891), 1 Q. B. 302; 55 J. P. 439.

Not merely the person aggrieved but either party to the proceeding may demand a case to be stated for the opinion of the High Court under 20 & 21 Vict. c. 43, s. 2, when the proceeding is commenced by information or complaint and by summons. But under 42 & 43 Vict. c. 49, s. 33, which is the enactment relied on by applicants whose license is refused, it is only a person aggrieved who can demand a case: *R.* v. *Glamorganshire* (1892), 1 Q. B. 363, 621; 56 J. P. 232, 437; 67 L. T. 543; 61 L. J. M. C. 169; 40 W. R. 102. It has also been held that as the licensing justices act only as judges and not as parties, it is competent and proper for the justices, when stating the case, to use the name of the opponent, such as the superintendent of police, when he is consenting to act as respondent: *Price* v. *James,* 56 J. P. 471; 57 J. P. 143; (1892), 2 Q. B. 428; 61 L. J. M. C. 203; 67 L. T. 543; 41 W. R. 57. It has not been decided how, in case of several opponents, one may be selected or whether all stand on the same footing.

Conditions as to case stated.] In demanding a case the applicant is not bound to state the point of law with which he is dissatisfied: *R.* v. *Newton,* 43 J. P. 351; *Ex parte Markham,* 34 J. P. 150. The recognizance will be in time if entered into before delivery of the case: *Stanhope* v. *Thorsby,* L. R. 1 C. P. 423; 35 L. J. M. C. 182; 30 J. P. 342. And the appellant may take points not taken in the court below, if it is a question of law arising on the facts: *Knight* v. *Halliwell,* L. R. 9 Q. B. 412; 38 J. P. 470. The justices may, after deciding that they have no jurisdiction, state a case: *Muir* v. *Hoare,* 47 L. J. M. C. 17; 37 L. T. 315; 41 J. P. 471. The application for costs should be made immediately after the disposal of the case: *Budenberg* v. *Roberts,* L. R. 2 C. P. 292.

By asking a case to be stated, an appeal to quarter sessions is waived: 20 & 21 Vict. c. 43, s. 14. And a *certiorari* is also usually waived, unless great delay has occurred: *Palmer* v. *Thatcher,* 3 Q. B. 346; 47 L. J. M. C. 54; 42 J. P. 213; 37 L. T. 786.

The computation of days includes Sunday: *Peacock* v. *R.,*

Sect. 52. *Procedure by Case Stated.*

NOTE. 4 C. B. (N.S.) 264 ; 27 L. J. M. C. 224 ; 22 J. P. 403 ; 31 L. T. 101 ; *Ex parte Simpkins,* 29 L. J. M. C. 23 ; *Wynne* v. *Ronaldson,* 29 J. P. 566.

The party demanding the case shall, within three days after receiving such case, transmit the same to [the Crown Office], first giving notice in writing of such appeal, with a copy of the case so stated and signed, to the other party to the proceeding in which the determination was given, hereinafter called the respondent : 20 & 21 Vict. c. 43, s. 2.

The statutory conditions of transmitting the case to the Crown Office set forth in 20 & 21 Vict. c. 43, s. 2, are conditions precedent to the hearing of the case by the High Court, unless the appellant found it impossible to comply with them : *Morgan* v. *Edwards,* 20 L. J. M. C. 108 ; 5 H. & N. 415 ; 24 J. P. 245 ; *Woodhouse* v. *Woods,* 29 L. J. M. C. 149 ; 23 J. P. 759 ; 1 L. T. 59 ; *Banks* v. *Goodwin,* 27 J. P. 404 ; *Mayer* v. *Harding,* L. R. 2 Q. B. 410 ; 31 J. P. 376 ; 16 L. T. 429. If the appellant does not proceed in the case the respondent may apply to strike out the case with costs : *Great Northern Railway Company* v. *Inett,* 2 Q. B. D. 284 ; 41 J. P. 294 ; 25 W. R. 584 ; *Crowther* v. *Boult,* 13 Q. B. D. 680 ; 49 J. P. 135 ; 33 W. R. 150.

53. *Continuance of license during pendency of appeal against justices' refusal to renew.*] Where the justices refuse to renew a license, and an appeal against such refusal is duly made, and such license expires before the appeal is determined, the Commissioners of Inland Revenue may, by order, permit the person whose license is refused to carry on his business during the pendency of the appeal upon such conditions as they think just ; and, subject to such conditions, any person so permitted may, during the continuance of such order, carry on his business in the same manner as if the renewal of the license had not been refused.

Where a license is forfeited on or in pursuance of a conviction for an offence, and an appeal is duly made against such conviction, the court by whom the conviction was made may, by order, grant a temporary license to be in force during the pendency of the appeal upon such conditions as they think just.

Sect. 53.

This section is similar to 33 & 34 Vict. c. 29, s. 9, now repealed, and extends to alehouses as well as to the houses mentioned in the Wine and Beerhouse Acts.

The words "refuse to renew" are obviously used not in the technical sense given to the words "renewal of a license" as used in section 42, and as defined in section 74, but in the popular sense adopted in *R.* v. *Lawrence* or *Liverpool*, 11 Q. B. D. 638; 47 J. P. 596; 52 L. J. M. C. 114; 49 L. T. 244; 32 W. R. 20, namely, "refuse to continue a license for the same house," whether the same person held such license or not. Hence this section must obviously include transfers as well as renewals. And the words "appeal against such refusal," now that it is declared that a special case may be demanded, must be taken to apply to all those cases where, instead of appealing to quarter sessions, the applicant has chosen the other equivalent remedy of appealing by way of special case under 42 & 43 Vict. c. 49, s. 33.

54. *Conviction, &c., not to be quashed for want of form, or removed by* certiorari.] No conviction or order made in pursuance of this Act, originally or on appeal, relative to any offence, penalty, forfeiture, or summary order, shall be quashed for want of form, or if made by a court of summary jurisdiction, be removed by *certiorari* or otherwise at the instance of the Crown or of any private party, into any superior court. [The rest of this section *repealed* by 47 & 48 Vict. c. 43.]

If the conviction has been wrongly drawn up, a fresh conviction may be drawn up before filing with the clerk of the peace: *Ex parte Austin*, 45 J. P. 302; *Ex parte Kenyon*, 45 J. P. 303.

This section does not take away the *certiorari* where want of jurisdiction or fraud is shown by affidavit: *R.* v. *Bolton*, 1 Q. B. 66; *Re Bailey*, 3 E. & B. 607; *R.* v. *Gillyard*, 12 Q. B. 527.

Sect. 55.

55. *As to record of convictions of licensed persons for offences under Act.*] With respect to the record of convictions of licensed persons for offences under this Act committed by them as such, the following provisions shall have effect in cases where this Act requires the conviction to be recorded on the license; that is to say :—

(1.) The court before whom any licensed person is accused shall require such person to produce and deliver to the clerk of the court the license under which such person carries on business, and the summons shall state that such production will be required :

(2.) If such person is convicted, the court shall cause the short particulars of such conviction and the penalty imposed, to be endorsed on his license before it is returned to the offender :

(3.) The clerk to the licensing justices shall enter the particulars respecting such conviction, or such of them as the case may require, in the register of licenses kept by him under this Act :

(4.) If the clerk to the court be not the clerk to the licensing justices, he shall send forthwith to the last-mentioned clerk notice of such conviction, and of the particulars thereof :

(5.) Where the conviction of any such person has the effect of forfeiting the license, or of disqualifying any person or premises for the purposes of this Act, the license shall be retained by the clerk of the court, and notice of such forfeiture

and disqualification shall be sent to the licensing **Sect. 55.**
officer of the district, and if the clerk to the
court is not the clerk to the licensing justices,
to such last-mentioned clerk, together with the
forfeited license.

As this section first stood in the Act, 1872, the rule was that
the justices were compelled to record some convictions on the
license, and in other cases had the power to do so if they thought
fit. But now, by the Act, 1874, section 13, the justices in all
cases have a discretion as to recording the conviction on a license.
As to the keeping of the register of licenses, see section 36, *ante*,
p. 73, and notes. See also section 58, as to extracts therefrom
being given in evidence; also Act, 1874, section 13, *post*.

The holder of the license is subject to a penalty for refusing
to deliver his license when demanded by certain persons. See
section 64, *post*.

This section enables the court to get possession of the license
or certificate when the Act requires the conviction to be recorded.
But if for any cause the license cannot be got, the same effect is
produced if the justices order a conviction to be recorded. See
section 33, *ante*, p. 72.

The Summary Jurisdiction Act, 1879, 42 & 43 Vict. c. 49, s. 22,
ante, p. 116, also contains provisions as to justices' clerks register-
ing all convictions, and as to certified copies of extracts used in
evidence.

56. *For protection of owners of licensed premises in cases of offences committed by tenants.*]
Where any tenant of any licensed premises is convicted
of any offence against this Act, and such offence is one
the repetition of which may render the premises liable
to be disqualified from receiving a license for any
period, it shall be the duty of the clerk of the licensing
justices to serve, in manner provided by this Act,
notice of every such conviction on the owner of the
premises.

Where any order of a court of summary jurisdiction,

Sect. 56. declaring any licensed premises to be disqualified from receiving a license for any period has been made, the court shall cause such order to be served on the owner of such premises, where the owner is not the occupier, with the addition of a statement that the court will hold a petty sessions at a time and place therein specified, at which the owner may appear and appeal against such order on all or any of the following grounds, but on no other grounds :—

(*a.*) That notice, as required by this Act, has not been served on the owner, of a prior offence, which on repetition renders the premises liable to be disqualified from receiving a license at any period ; or

(*b.*) That the tenant by whom the offence was committed held under a contract made prior to the commencement of this Act, and that the owner could not legally have evicted the tenant in the interval between the commission of the offence, in respect of which the disqualifying order was made, and the receipt by him of the notice of the immediate preceding offence which on repetition renders the premises liable to be disqualified from receiving a license at any period ; or

(*c.*) That the offence in respect of which the disqualifying order was made, occurred so soon after the receipt of such last-mentioned notice that the owner, notwithstanding he had legal power to evict the tenant, could not with reasonable diligence have exercised that power in the interval which occurred between the said notice and the second offence.

Sect. 56.

If the owner appear at the time and place specified, and at such sessions, or any adjournment thereof, satisfy the court that he is entitled to have the order cancelled on any of the grounds aforesaid, the court shall thereupon direct such order to be cancelled, and the same shall be void. (The rest of this section was *repealed* by Act, 1874, section 33.)

This section is intended to protect the owner of licensed premises from the consequences of the offences committed by the tenant or occupier. See the definition of owner in section 74, and Licensing Act, 1874, section 29. The clerk of the licensing justices gets, as a matter of course, by the 55th section, notice of the conviction from the clerk of the convicting court. The first words, "where any tenant of any licensed premises is convicted of an offence against this Act, and such offence is one the repetition of which may render the premises liable to be disqualified," apply to all those offences which, by the exercise of the discretion of the justices, would be recorded on the license or certificate. Convictions can now only be recorded if the justices think fit; though, under the Act, 1872, it was otherwise. See Licensing Act, 1874, section 13. Whenever a conviction, which might have been recorded under the Act, 1872, *i.e.*, under sections 5, 6, 13, 14, 16, 17, 28, occurs, the clerk of the licensing justices is to send notice to the owner. Under the 30th section the premises become disqualified if the justices do not say the contrary. Under the 31st section the premises become disqualified whether the justices say anything on the subject or not. Both cases are included here. As to the offences in section 31, sub-section (3), which will cause forfeiture in the first instance, and thereafter as consequential thereupon disqualification of premises by the operation of that section, it seems the clerk would not require to give notice as to these; but there seems no reason why he should not give the notice in those cases also.

The clerk obtains the name and residence of the owner by the 36th section, which obliges the applicant for a grant or renewal to state the owner's name, and by section 70, which obliges the owner himself to give his name and address to the clerk. See also Licensing Act, 1874, section 29.

K

Sect. 56.

NOTE.

The second paragraph refers only to the cases where the order of the court "declares licensed premises to be disqualified ;" but in those cases where the premises become disqualified under this Act, whether the justices declare them to be so or not, such second paragraph seems not to apply, except in the cases specified in section 31.

An offence by a licensed person under the *Sale of Food Act* is treated as an offence under the Licensing Acts. See Licensing Act, 1874, section 14, *post*, and this Act, section 55, *ante*, p. 126.

If the tenant has forfeited his license for a single offence, the owner may in some cases apply for a continuance of the license. See Licensing Act, 1874, section 15.

As to service of notices, see section 70, *post*.

On the letting of a public-house there is no implied agreement on the part of the tenant not to do acts which may cause a forfeiture of the license : *Maw* v. *Hindmarsh*, 28 L. T. 644.

57. *As to conviction of licensed persons of more than one offence on same day.*] Where a licensed person is convicted of more offences than one, committed on the same day, the convictions for which are by this Act directed to be recorded on his license, the court by whom he is convicted may, in their discretion, order that one or some only of such convictions shall be recorded.

The offences here referred to need not be the same kind of offences. The words, "by this Act directed to be recorded," now include those offences which the justices directed to be recorded, or could have directed to be recorded, and thus all those under sections 5, 6, 13, 14, 16, 17, 28, are included. See Licensing Act, 1874, section 13. When two or more recordable convictions occur in one day, the justices who have convicted may reduce to one the number to be recorded. And it seems they may now say that none shall be recorded, for in all cases it is discretionary in the justices to record any conviction : Licensing Act, 1874, section 13. Nor does this power apply to other than recordable convictions. It is obvious that the justices are intended to exercise their power of reduction and selection in recording several convictions, when the last of the convictions has been made.

58. *Evidence of endorsements of register.*] Sect. 58.
The registers of licenses kept in pursuance of this Act shall be receivable in evidence of the matters required by this Act to be entered therein. Every endorsement upon a license, and every copy of an entry made in the register of licenses in pursuance of this Act, purporting to be signed by the clerk to the licensing justices and (in case of a copy) to be certified to be a true copy, shall be evidence of the matters stated in such endorsement and entry, without proof of the signature or authority of the person signing the same.

The register of licenses is regulated by section 36. See also sections 31, 33, and Licensing Act, 1874, section 13.

This section gives a convenient and easy mode of proving the endorsements by the official copy signed by the clerk to the licensing justices.

See also a convenient mode of proving all convictions under the Summary Jurisdiction Act, 1879, 42 & 43 Vict. c. 49, s. 22, *ante*, p. 115, and the same under the Prevention of Crimes Act, 1871, 34 & 35 Vict. c. 112, s. 18.

59. *Saving for indictments, &c., under other Acts.*] Nothing in this Act shall prevent any person from being liable to be indicted or punished under any other Act, or otherwise, so that he be not punished twice for the same offence.

This section prevents the implied repeal of previous enactments dealing with the same offence, and practically gives the prosecutor the election to proceed under either, subject to this condition, that after punishing the offender under either, he cannot afterwards punish him under the other enactment. See an example of this double remedy under section 17. See also sections 3, 5, 6; and 4 & 5 Will. 4, c. 85, ss. 17, 20; 3 & 4 Vict. c. 61, s. 7; 23 Vict. c. 27, s. 22. See also section 8, and Acts there referred to. The enactment seems to include "any other

K 2

Sect. 59.
NOTE.

Act" to be passed after 1872, and therefore will apply to section 10 of this Act, as compared with the Licensing Act, 1874, section 17.

The general rule is that no person can be convicted twice in respect of the same subject matter : *Wemyss* v. *Hopkins*, L. R. 10 Q. B. 378; 44 L. J. M. C. 101 ; 39 J. P. 549 ; 32 L. T. 9 ; 23 W. R. 691 ; *Eddleston* v. *Barnes*, 1 Ex. D. 67 ; 40 J. P. 89; 45 L. J. M. C. 73 ; 34 L. T. 497 ; *Sims* v. *Pay*, 58 L. J. M. C. 39 ; 53 J. P. 420. Nevertheless, a revenue offence and a general statutory offence may arise out of the same facts ; *Saunders* v. *Baldy*, 6 B. & S. 791 ; L. R. 1 Q. B. 87 ; 30 J. P. 148 ; 14 W. R. 177 ; 13 L. T. 322.

The general law is now repeated by 52 & 53 Vict. c. 63, s. 33, thus : Where an act or omission constitutes an offence under two or more Acts, or both under an Act, and at common law, whether any such Act was passed before or after the commencement of this Act (1st Jan., 1890), the offender shall, unless the contrary intention appears, be liable to be prosecuted, and punished under either or any of those Acts or at common law, but shall not be liable to be punished twice for the same offence.

Miscellaneous.

60. *Disqualification of justices to act under this Act.*] No justice shall act for any purpose under this Act, or under any of the Intoxicating Liquor Licensing Acts, except in cases where the offence charged is that of being found drunk in any highway or other public place, whether a building or not, or on any licensed premises, or of being guilty while drunk of riotous or disorderly conduct, or of being drunk while in charge, on any highway or other public place, of any carriage, horse, cattle, or steam-engine, or of being drunk when in possession of loaded fire-arms, who is or is in partnership with or holds any share in any company which is a common brewer, distiller, maker of malt for sale, or retailer of malt or of any intoxicating liquor in the licensing district, or in the district or dis-

tricts adjoining to that in which such justice usually Sect. 60.
acts ; and no justice shall act for any purpose under
this Act, or under any of the Intoxicating Liquor
Acts, in respect of any premises in the profits of which
such justice is interested, or of which he is wholly or
partly the owner, lessee, or occupier, or for the owner,
lessee, or occupier, of which he is the manager or
agent.

Any justice, hereby declared not to be qualified to
act under this Act, who knowingly acts as a justice for
any of the purposes of this Act, shall for every such
offence be liable to a penalty not exceeding one hundred
pounds, to be recovered by action in one of Her Majesty's
superior courts at Westminster :

Provided that—

(1.) No justice shall be disqualified under this section
to act in respect of any premises by reason of
his having vested in him a legal interest only
and not a beneficial interest, in such premises
or the profits thereof :

(2.) No justice shall be liable to a penalty for more
than one offence committed by him under this
section before the institution of any proceedings for the recovery of such penalty :

(3.) No act done by any justice disqualified by this
section shall by reason only of such disqualifi-
tion be invalid.

The offences referred to are contained in section 12, *ante*,
p. 23.

"Acting under any of the Intoxicating Liquor Licensing Acts,"
mean, by section 74, the statutes 9 Geo. 4, c. 61 ; 32 & 33 Vict.
c. 27 ; 33 & 34 Vict. c. 29, *post*. The Beerhouse Acts are not

Sect. 60.
NOTE.

included in this description, and hence convictions such as that in *Re Authers*, 22 Q. B. D. 355 ; 53 J. P. 116 ; 58 L. J. M. C. 62 ; 37 W. R. 320 ; which proceeded on 4 & 5 Will. 4, c. 85, s. 17, would not come within this section.

If the justice be a shareholder in a company, which is a hotel company, or of a railway or other company, which carries on a hotel by a manager in the district or is part owner or lessee of the premises, that would, under this section, disqualify such justice.

It is no disqualification if the business in which the justice is interested is carried on in a different county or place within another licensing district in England or Wales, unless it is an adjoining district, or his premises are the subject of the proceedings.

The former disqualification of justices, under 9 Geo. 4, c. 61, s. 6, was more extensive than under the present Act, for it was equally a disqualification if the business was carried on anywhere in England.

A justice who is a brewer, &c., may act in the cases excepted in the third line of this section, namely, in adjudicating on charges of drunkenness, subject to the exception as to interestedness defined by this section.

61. *Extension of jurisdiction of justices over river, water, &c.*] For all the purposes of this Act any pier, quay, jetty, mole, or work extending from any place within the jurisdiction of any licensing justices or court of summary jurisdiction into or over any part of the sea, or any part of a river within the ebb and flow of the tide, shall be deemed to be within the jurisdiction of such justices and court.

For the purpose of jurisdiction in any proceeding under this Act, any river or water which runs between or forms the boundary of two or more licensing districts or of the jurisdiction of two or more courts of summary jurisdiction shall be deemed to be wholly within each such licensing district and the jurisdiction of each of such courts.

The jurisdiction of justices, irrespective of this enactment, extends over the shore between high and low water mark :

35 & 36 VICT. C. 94, S. 62.

Embleton v. *Brown*, 3 E. & E. 234 ; 30 L. J. M. C. 1. Hence, if
a booth or tent were erected on the sea-shore where there are
races, and used under an occasional license, and an offence were
committed, the justices would have jurisdiction.
The Summary Jurisdiction Act, 1879, 42 & 43 Vict. c. 49, s. 46,
enlarges this section, and makes any offence committed within
500 yards of a boundary, or begun in one jurisdiction and completed within another, triable by either court ; and in the case
of an offence in respect of a carriage or vessel, any court through
whose district the same passes during the journey has jurisdiction.

Sect. 61.
―――
NOTE.

62. *Evidence of sale or consumption of intoxicating liquors.*] In proving the sale or consumption of intoxicating liquor for the purpose of any proceeding relative to any offence under this Act, it shall not be necessary to show that any money actually passed or any intoxicating liquor was actually consumed, if the court hearing the case be satisfied that a transaction in the nature of a sale actually took place, or that any consumption of intoxicating liquor was about to take place, and proof of consumption, or intended consumption, of intoxicating liquor on premises to which a license under this Act is attached, by some person other than the occupier of or a servant in such premises, shall be evidence that such liquor was sold to the person consuming, or being about to consume or carrying away the same by or on behalf of the holder of such license.

The sections with reference to which this enactment will be most used will be sections 3, 5, 6, 7, 8, *ante*, and Act, 1874, section 9, and the enactment meets the case where, for example, the person gives liquor in exchange for some valuable consideration. But if a pure gift is established, it will not be within this or the other sections : *Petherick* v. *Sargent*, 26 J. P. 135 ; 6 L. T. 48. The evidence referred to in the latter part of the section means *primâ facie* or admissible, but not conclusive evidence, and it will still

Sect. 62.
NOTE.

be open for the defendant to rebut such evidence. It has been held that where a drunken man accompanies a sober man who orders liquor, which is consumed by the drunken man, on licensed premises, this is evidence of selling to the drunken man : *Scatchard* v. *Johnson*, 52 J. P. 389 ; 57 L. J. M. C. 41.

Where a wife held a license, and the husband carried liquor to a private house, and sold it at a raffle there going on, and brought back the money and gave it to the wife, she may be convicted of selling at an unlicensed place, contrary to section 3 : *Seager* v. *White*, 51 L. T. 261 ; 48 J. P. 436.

63. *Avoidance of excise license on forfeiture of license.*] Where a license is forfeited in pursuance of this Act, or becomes void under any of the provisions of this Act, any license for the sale of intoxicating liquors granted by the Commissioners of Inland Revenue to the holder of such license shall be void.

When justices refuse to renew a license and the applicant appeals or takes steps to keep alive the license, the Inland Revenue may grant a temporary license under section 53. And also where the license is forfeited, and an appeal is duly made, the convicting court may grant a temporary license : Section 53. In cases of forfeiture for felony or selling spirits without license (see 3 and 4 Vict. c. 61, s. 7 ; 23 Vict. c. 27, s. 22 ; 33 & 34 Vict. c. 29, s. 14), a remedy is pointed out where a tenant for the first time is disqualified or forfeits the license. See Licensing Act, 1874, section 15.

64. *Production of license by holder, and penalty on non-production.*] Every holder of a license or of an order of exemption made by a local authority, in pursuance of this Act, shall, by himself, his agent, or servant, produce such license or order within a reasonable time after the production thereof is demanded by a justice of the peace, constable, or officer of Inland Revenue, and deliver the same to be read and examined

35 & 36 VICT. C. 94, S. 66. 137

by him. Any person who acts in contravention of this section shall be liable to a penalty not exceeding ten pounds. Sect. 64.

The order of exemption from closing hours, permanently or temporarily by a local authority, is dealt with in sections 26, 29, *ante*, pp. 61, 66.

This penalty will not be incurred unless a previous demand has been made by a person authorised to demand, namely, a justice of the peace, constable, or officer of Inland Revenue, and the license has not been produced within a reasonable time. The holder is entitled to have the license returned to him after it has been read and examined, unless, as may happen, the clerk of the justices is authorised to retain it in his hands for certain further purposes, as under section 55, sub-section (5). Every person summoned must also produce his license to the justices' clerk : Section 55, sub-section (1), *ante*, p. 126.

The burden of proof of a license as a defence lies on the defendant, according to 42 & 43 Vict. c. 49, s. 39 : *Turner* v. *Johnson*, 51 J. P. 22.

65. *Population to be according to last census.*] The population of any area for the purposes of this Act shall be ascertained according to the last published census for the time being.

This section has reference to section 45, *ante*, p. 95 ; also to Licensing Act, 1874, section 32, *post*.

In the Beerhouse Act, 3 & 4 Vict. c. 61, s. 1, the test of population is said to be "according to the last parliamentary census," omitting the word "published," and that Act is not incorporated in this Act. Hence, where a census depending on that Act was not published, though otherwise known, the justices might act upon it. See *R.* v. *Cumberland JJ.*, 8 Q. B. D. 369 ; 46 J. P. 7 ; 51 L. J. Q. B. 142 ; 30 W. R. 178.

66. *Moiety of penalties may be awarded to police superannuation fund.*] Any part not exceeding a moiety of any penalty recovered under this Act may, if the court shall so direct, be paid to the super-

Sect. 66. annuation fund of the police establishment within whose jurisdiction the offence in respect of which such penalties are imposed shall have occurred.

As to the application of penalties, see also section 51, and 11 & 12 Vict. c. 43, s. 31. In boroughs having no court of quarter sessions, but a separate commission of the peace, or neither one nor the other, the penalties, if not otherwise disposed of, were to be paid to the treasurer of the county : *Winn* v. *Mossman*, L. R. 4 Exch. 292 ; 38 L. J. Exch. 200 ; 33 J. P. 743 ; 20 L. T. 672 ; *Mayor of Reigate* v. *Hart*, L. R. 3 Q. B. 244 ; 37 L. J. M. C. 70 ; 18 L. T. 237 ; 16 W. R. 896 ; 9 B. & S. 129 ; 32 J. P. 342 ; *R.* v. *Dale*, 17 J. P. 342 ; 22 L. J. M. C. 44 ; 1 Dearsl. 37.

The *Municipal Corporations Act*, 45 & 46 Vict. c. 50, s. 221, lays down the following rules for some boroughs :

Application of penalties in quarter sessions boroughs.] (1) Where by an Act passed or to be passed any fine, penalty, or forfeiture is made recoverable in a summary manner before any justice or justices, and payable to the Crown or to any body corporate, or to any person whomsoever, the same if recovered and adjudged before any justice of a borough having a separate court of quarter sessions, shall, notwithstanding anything in the Act under which it is recovered, be recovered for and adjudged to be paid to the treasurer of the borough.

(2) But this section shall not apply to a fine, penalty, or forfeiture, or part thereof, where the Act under which it is recovered,

(*a*) Directs payment thereof to the informer, or to any person aggrieved :

(*b*) If passed since the Municipal Corporations Act, 1835, directs that the same shall go in any other manner and not to the borough funds :

(*c*) Relates to the customs, excise, or post office, or to trade or navigation, or to any branch of the revenue of the Crown.
The Crown may remit the penalty : 22 Vict. c. 32.
The *Police Act*, 1890 (53 & 54 Vict. c. 45), s. 16, enacts :—(1) There shall be a pension fund of every police force and there shall be carried to that fund (*b*) the fines imposed by a court of summary jurisdiction when imposed on constables in the force, and the fines or portions of fines imposed by a court of summary jurisdiction for other offences and awarded to informers being constables in the

35 & 36 VICT. C. 94, S. 68. 139

force, and (c) such fines or portions of fines, and such fees payable to or received by constables as by any Act are directed or authorised to be carried to the superannuation or pension fund of the police force; (2) unless the authority having control of the fund otherwise resolve, and except so far as subject to the foregoing provisions of this section, there shall be carried to the pension fund of every police force, &c., (k) the fines imposed by a court of summary jurisdiction for offences under the Licensing Acts, 1872 and 1874, when committed within the police area, or for any offence under a general or local Act similar to any of the above offences.

Sect. 66.
———
NOTE.

67. *Limit of mitigation of penalties.*] Repealed by Licensing Act, 1874, section 12: see that section, also 42 & 43 Vict. c. 49, s. 4, *ante*, p. 110.

68. *Regulations as to retail licenses of wholesale dealers.*] No person shall sell by retail liqueurs or spirits under the authority of any retail license which such person shall have obtained as a wholesale spirit dealer from the Commissioners of Inland Revenue, except in premises occupied and used exclusively for the sale therein of intoxicating liquor, and which premises have no communication with the premises of nor are in any way occupied by a person who is carrying on any other trade or business, unless such person shall have first obtained from the licensing justices a license authorising such sale in premises not exclusively so occupied and used.

The additional retail license here referred to is allowed to licensed dealers in spirits by 24 & 25 Vict. c. 21, s. 2, *post*; and see notes thereto.

As to the spirit dealer's license, see notes to section 3, *ante*, p. 4, and Spirits Act, 1880, 43 & 44 Vict. c. 24, *post*.

The foreign or British spirits are to be sold in any quantity not less than one reputed quart bottle, or as to foreign liqueurs, in the bottles in which the same may have been imported.

Sect. 68.
NOTE.
The premises, if used exclusively for the sale of intoxicating liquor, are exempted from any license by section 73, *post*.

69. *Licenses for sale of liqueurs, &c., by retail not to be consumed on the premises.*] A license for the sale of liqueurs or spirits by retail not to be consumed on the premises, may, where such license is required by this Act, be granted in the same manner in all respects in which a license for selling wine not to be consumed on the premises may by law be granted, and an application for such a license shall not be refused except upon one or more of the grounds on which a certificate in respect of a license to sell by retail beer, cider, or wine not to be consumed on the premises may be refused. (Part of the section *repealed* by 46 & 47 Vict. c. 39, sched.)

Provided also, that nothing in this Act contained as to the requirements of a justices' license shall affect the sale of liqueurs or spirits or sweets under any excise license granted before the passing of this Act during the continuance of such excise license.

As to the license for selling wine not to be consumed on the premises, see 23 Vict. c. 27, s. 3; and 32 & 33 Vict. c. 27, s. 8.

As the applicants for spirit and liqueur licenses for consumption off the premises are put on the same footing as wine licenses under 32 & 33 Vict. c. 27, and 33 & 34 Vict. c. 29, it follows that they must give notice before applying as required by 32 & 33 Vict. c. 27, s. 7, and by Licensing Act, 1872, s. 40. They can only apply at the general annual licensing meeting or its adjournment. See section 74, "Definition of License." The justices can only refuse the license or its renewal or transfer on the three first grounds stated in 32 & 33 Vict. c. 27, s. 8 : *R.* v. *Scott*, 22 Q. B. D. 481 ; 53 J. P. 119 ; 58 L. J. M. C. 78 ; 60 L. T. 231 ; 37 W. R. 301 ; *R.* v. *Smith* or *Southport JJ.*, L. R. 8 Q. B. 146 ; 37 J. P. 214; 42 L. J. M. C. 146 ; 28 L. T. 129 ; 21 W. R. 382.

35 & 36 VICT. C. 94, S. 70.   141

The fourth ground of refusal mentioned in 32 & 33 Vict. c. 27, s. 8, has no application to these licenses, for they were never subject to any valuation qualification before 32 & 33 Vict. c. 27; and that statute does not impose any new qualification of that kind. The license or certificate may be transferred in case of death, bankruptcy, &c., as in the case of other licenses: 33 & 34 Vict. c. 29, s. 4. See also this Act, section 3, *ante*, p. 11.

Sect. 69.

NOTE.

As regards the *closing of such premises*, though they must comply with the hours set forth in the Licensing Act, 1874, sections 3, 9, yet the keepers can only be convicted for selling and keeping open, &c., for the sale of liquors. As they usually sell other articles than liquors they may keep open after prohibited hours for the sale of other articles, provided they neither sell nor expose for sale nor keep open for the sale of liquors. They should therefore cover up the liquors in some way so as not to expose them to view of customers during the closing hours, and justices would not in that case be warranted in convicting unless they found that the keeping open for the sale of other articles than liquors was only a pretence. See *Tassell* v. *Ovenden*, 2 Q. B. D. 284; 41 J. P. 710; 46 L. J. M. C. 228; 36 L. T. 696; 25 W. R. 692; *Brigden* v. *Heighes*, 1 Q. B. D. 330; 40 J. P. 661; 45 L. J. M. C. 58; 34 L. T. 242; 24 W. R. 272; *Ex parte Joynt*, 38 J. P. 390.

70. *Notices may be sent by post.*] All notices and documents required by this Act to be served or sent may, unless otherwise expressly provided, be served and sent by post, and, until the contrary is proved, shall be deemed to have been served and received respectively at the time when the letter containing the same would be delivered in the ordinary course of post; and in proving such service or sending it shall be sufficient to prove that the letter containing the notice or document was prepaid, and properly addressed.

Where any officer or other person interested in any licensed premises is entitled to receive notice of a conviction under this Act, he shall supply his address to the clerk or other person required to send such notice,

Sect. 70. and any notice sent to such address shall be deemed to be duly served ; and where no notice is supplied in pursuance of this section, all notices shall be deemed to be duly served if sent to any address which such clerk or other person in the exercise of his discretion believes to be the address of the person to whom the notice was so sent.

Provided that any notice of any offence required by this Act to be sent to the owner of licensed premises shall be either served personally or sent by registered letter.

> The service of notices by registered letter was allowed by 33 & 34 Vict. c. 29, s. 4, in cases of application for a new certificate under 32 & 33 Vict. c. 27, s. 7. The same mode of serving notice has also been extended to all applications under this Act for new licenses or transfer licenses under 9 Geo. 4, c. 61, and the Beerhouse Acts, as stated by section 40, *ante*, p. 82. All these notices may now be served by ordinary letter, and need not be by registered letter, except that the notices mentioned in the last paragraph must be by registered letter if not personally served.
> The notice to the *owner* here referred to is required by section 31. Another notice to owner of a removed license is provided for by section 50.
> The notices *of appeal* under this Act against convictions and orders may also be served by post, and by virtue of the Summary Jurisdiction Act, 1879, 42 & 43 Vict. c. 49, s. 31, *ante*, p. 119, may be served on the clerk of the convicting justices instead of on the justices themselves.
> In all statutes passed after 1890 the words "service by post" will be interpreted as set forth in 52 & 53 Vict. c. 63, s. 26.

71. *Schedules to be part of Act.*] The schedules to this Act shall be construed and have effect as part of this Act.

> The schedules have since been repealed, but leaving the law unaffected : see sched., *post*.

Saving Clauses.

72. *Saving of certain privileges, rights, &c.*] Nothing in this Act shall affect or apply to—

1. The privileges at the date of the passing of this Act enjoyed by any *university* in England, or the respective chancellors or scholars of the same or their successors:

2. The privileges at the date of the passing of this Act enjoyed by the mayor or burgesses of the borough of St. Albans, in the county of Hertford, or their successors, or the exemptions from the obligation to take out a license as defined by this Act, or a license from the Commissioners of Inland Revenue enjoyed by the company of the master, wardens, and commonalty of *vintners* of the city of London:

3. The sale of *spruce* or black beer:

4. The sale of intoxicating liquor by proprietors of *theatres* in pursuance of the Acts in that behalf:

5. The sale of intoxicating liquor in *packet boats*, in pursuance of the Acts in that behalf:

6. The sale of intoxicating liquor on *special occasions* in pursuance of the provisions in that behalf enacted:

7. The sale of spirits in *canteens*, in pursuance of any Act regulating the same:

8. The sale of medicated or *methylated* spirits or spirits made up in medicine and sold by medical practitioners or chemists and druggists:

Sect. 72. 9. The sale of intoxicating liquor by *wholesale:*

10. Any penalties recoverable by or on behalf of the Commissioners of *Inland Revenue* or any laws relating to the excise.

(1) The privileges of the *universities* are also referred to in 9 Geo. 4, c. 61, s. 36; 5 & 6 Vict. c. 44, s. 6; 1 Will. 4, c. 64, s. 29; 3 & 4 Vict. c. 61, s. 22; 23 Vict. c. 27, s. 45; 32 & 33 Vict. c. 27, s. 20; *R.* v. *Archdall,* 8 A. & E. 281; 3 N. & P. 696.

(2) The privileges relating to St. Albans are also referred to in 23 Vict. c. 27, s. 45; 32 & 33 Vict. c. 27, s. 20.

The privileges of the *vintners* of London are noticed in Vaugh. 330, 359; Levinz. 217, 221; 9 Geo. 4, c. 61, s. 36; 32 & 33 Vict. c. 27, s. 20; also in Metropolitan Police Act, 2 & 3 Vict. c. 47, s. 45; The City of London Police Act, 2 & 3 Vict. c. 14, s. 29. As to entry of premises, see 30 & 31 Vict. c. 90, s. 12; 25 Vict. c. 22, s. 16.

The word "vintner" is not restricted to the selling of wine to be consumed on the premises: *Wells* v. *Attenborough,* 24 L. T. 312; 19 W. R. 465.

The privilege of selling wine as a freeman of the Vintners' Company extends only to persons whose freedom has been obtained by patrimony or servitude and their widows: Board's Order, 26th February, 1830. Order of Vintners' Company, 12th March, 1839.

(3) The sale of *spruce* beer is noticed in 25 Vict. c. 22, s. 19. The duty on spruce beer and Berlin white beer is set forth in 44 Vict. c. 12, s. 3; 52 Vict. c. 7, s. 3.

(4) The sale of liquors in *theatres* is regulated by 5 & 6 Will. 4, c. 39, s. 7; 6 & 7 Vict. c. 68. See also 2 & 3 Vict. c. 47, s. 46, as to metropolitan police district, and 2 & 3 Vict. c. 94, s. 30, as to the city of London. As to Ireland, see 37 & 38 Vict. c. 68, s. 7; 56 & 57 Vict. c. 54.

Theatre licenses.] The licensing of houses or places for the public performance of stage plays was transferred to county councils by 51 & 52 Vict. c. 41, s. 7. It shall not be lawful for any person to have or keep any house or other place of public resort in Great Britain for the public performance of stage plays without authority by virtue of letters patent from Her Majesty, or without license from the Lord Chamberlain or from the justices of the peace; the offender incurs a penalty not exceeding 20*l.* for every day on which the house or place is kept open: 6 & 7 Vict. c. 68, s. 2. The Lord Chamberlain's license is required for all

Theatre Licenses.   Sect. 72.

theatres within the cities of London and Westminster and the boroughs of Finsbury, Marylebone, Tower Hamlets, Lambeth, and Southwark, and places where Her Majesty shall occasionally reside; also New Windsor and Brighton: *Ibid.* s. 3. In other places applications might be made to the justices of the peace, and these are within twenty-one days to hold a special session for granting licenses for theatres: *Ibid.* s. 5. The license was only to be granted by the Lord Chamberlain or justices to the actual and responsible manager for the time being: *Ibid.* s. 7. There was no appeal against the refusal by justices of a theatre license: *Ex parte Harrington*, 4 *Times* L. R. 435. The Lord Chamberlain may in certain circumstances suspend the license or order the theatre to be closed: *Ibid.* s. 8. The justices also could make suitable rules for insuring order and decency, for regulating the times of keeping open theatres in their jurisdiction, and in some circumstances to order the theatre to be closed: *Ibid.* s. 9. A penalty of 10*l.* per day is incurred by every person who for hire shall act or permit, or cause, permit, or suffer to be acted or presented any part in any stage play in any place not being a patent theatre or duly licensed as a theatre: *Ibid.* s. 11. And this penalty is incurred by acting a stage play in a booth: *Tarling* v. *Fredericks*, 28 L. T. 814; 21 W. R. 785; 38 J. P. 197; *Fredericks* v. *Payne*, 1 H. & C. 584; 32 L. J. M. C. 14; 27 J. P. 104.

Stage play includes every tragedy, comedy, farce, opera, burlesque, interlude, melodrama, pantomime, or other entertainment of the stage or any part thereof: *Ibid.* s. 23.

A copy of every new stage play and every act, scene, &c., intended to be produced and acted in any theatre in Great Britain shall be sent to the Lord Chamberlain, who may allow or forbid the acting, and a penalty of 50*l.* is incurred for acting these without their having been allowed: *Ibid.* ss. 12—15. The penalties are recoverable by action or summarily before justices: *Ibid.* s. 19. And there is an appeal to quarter sessions against a conviction: *Ibid.* s. 20.

A theatre license under section 2 is required only for places not casually but permanently used for stage plays, while section 11 deals with those casually using a place: *R.* v. *Strugnell*, *R.* v. *Rosenthal*, L. R. 1 Q. B. 93; 35 L. J. M. C. 78; 13 L. T. 433; 14 W. R. 193; 30 J. P. 101. But a theatre built and used in a private house for a public performance requires a license: *Shelley* v. *Bethell*, 12 Q. B. D. 11; 53 L. J. M. C. 16; 49 L. T. 779; 32 W. R. 276; 48 J. P. 244.

The question, whether a representation given in a house licensed for music and dancing is such as to amount to a stage

LICENSING ACT, 1872, s. 72.

Sect. 72.　　　　　　　*Theatre Licenses.*

NOTE. play, and so that a theatre license would be necessary, is mainly one of fact, and the decision of justices would not usually be interfered with : *Wigan* v. *Strange,* L. R. 1 C. P. 175 ; 35 L. J. M. C. 31 ; 29 J. P. 774 ; *Day* v. *Simpson,* 18 C. B. (N.S.) 680 ; 34 L. J. M. C. 149 ; 12 L. T. 386 ; 13 W. R. 748.

A recreation room managed under the authority of a Secretary of State or the Admiralty may be used for the public performance of stage plays without a license : 52 Vict. c. 3, s. 7.

Theatres within twenty miles of London.] The power to regulate metropolitan theatres and music halls was given to the Metropolitan Board of Works by 41 & 42 Vict. c. 32, ss. 11, 12, and is now transferred to the London County Council : 51 & 52 Vict. c. 41. The rules of procedure on applications for theatre licenses within the county of London are set forth, *ante*, p. 36.

License to sell intoxicating liquors at theatres.] It shall be lawful for the commissioners and officers of excise, and they are hereby authorised and empowered to grant retail licenses to any persons to sell beer, spirits, and wine in any theatre established under a royal patent, or in any theatre or other place of public entertainment licensed by the Lord Chamberlain or by justices of the peace, without the production by the person applying for such license or licenses, of any certificate or authority for such person to keep a common inn, alehouse, or victualling-house, anything in any Act or Acts to the contrary notwithstanding : 5 & 6 Will. 4, c. 39, s. 7. The above section of 35 & 36 Vict. c. 94, s. 72, only exempts theatres strictly so-called from having a justices' license, but does not exempt places of public entertainment : *R.* v. *Inland Revenue,* 21 Q. B. D. 569 ; 57 L. J. M. C. 92 ; 59 L. T. 378 ;. 36 W. R. 696 ; 52 J. P. 390.

As to the duty payable, see Inland Revenue Act, 1880, 43 & 44 Vict. c. 20, s. 43, *post.*

Though *theatre* bars require no justices' licenses, yet the *hour of closing* set forth in 37 & 38 Vict. c. 49, ss. 3, 9, applies to all premises in which intoxicating liquors are sold by retail without any exception of theatres : *Martin* v. *Barker,* 50 L. J. M. C. 109 ; 45 L. T. (N.S.) 214 ; 45 J. P. 749 ; 29 W. R. 789. And as to the time of opening and keeping open, the natural meaning of the statutory exemption seems to be, that the selling at the theatre bar is incidental to the time of performance at the theatre, and a reasonable time before and after, but always subject to the time of closing set forth in 37 & 38 Vict. c. 49, ss. 3, 9, *post.*

Where the lessee of a theatre bought a piece of ground adjoin-

35 & 36 VICT. C. 94, S. 72.

Theatre Licenses.   Sect. 72.

ing, on which he erected additional exits, and also a refreshment NOTE.
bar; and where such piece of ground was subject to a covenant
against the retail of wine, spirits, and beer, it was held that this
was a breach of the covenant, though the retailing was used only
as incidental to the theatre : *Buckle* v. *Fredericks,* 44 Ch. D. 244 ;
62 L. T. 884 ; 55 J. P. 214; 38 W. R. 742.

(5.) As to the sale in *packet boats,* see 9 Geo. 4, c. 47 ; 4 & 5
Will. 4, c. 75 ; 5 & 6 Vict. c. 44, s. 5 ; 43 & 44 Vict. c. 20, s. 45 ;
53 & 54 Vict. cc. 21, 33.

(6.) As to sale on *special occasions,* see section 29, where temporary exemptions from closing hours may be obtained. There are also occasional licenses granted to sell at other than the ordinary licensed places under the authority of 25 & 26 Vict. c. 22, s. 13; 26 & 27 Vict. c. 33, s. 20 ; 27 & 28 Vict. c. 18, s. 5, *post.* See also Licensing Act, 1874, sections 18—20.

(7.) As to sale of liquors in *canteens*, the Army Act, 44 & 45 Vict. c. 58, s. 174, enacts—(1.) When a person holds a canteen under the authority of a Secretary of State or the Admiralty, it shall be lawful for any two justices, within their respective jurisdictions, to grant, transfer, or renew any license for the time being required to enable such person to obtain or hold any excise license for the sale of any intoxicating liquor, without regard to the time of the year, and without regard to the requirements as to notices, certificates, or otherwise of any Acts for the time being in force affecting such licenses ; and excise licenses may be granted to such persons accordingly. (2.) For the purposes of this section the expression "license" includes any license or certificate for the time being required by law to be granted, renewed, or transferred by any justices of the peace, in order to enable any person to obtain or hold any excise license for the sale of any intoxicating liquor.

(8.) The sale of *methylated spirits* is regulated by 18 & 19 Vict. c. 38, s. 3; 24 & 25 Vict. c. 91, ss. 1, 2; 30 & 31 Vict. c. 90, s. 18; 43 & 44 Vict. c. 24 ; 53 Vict. c. 8, s. 31. For spirits made up in medicines by chemists, &c., see 16 Geo. 2, c. 8, s. 12.

(9.) See several statutes as to *dealers,* referred to in notes to section 3, *ante,* p. 4 ; also 43 & 44 Vict. c. 20 ; 43 & 44 Vict. c. 24 ; 1 Will. 4, c. 51, s. 22 ; 6 Geo. 4, c. 81 ; 48 & 49 Vict. c. 51 ; 53 & 54 Vict. c. 51 ; *R.* v. *Jenkins,* 55 J. P. 824 ; 61 L. J. M. C. 57 ; 65 L. T. 857 ; 40 W. R. 318.

(10.) Where a penalty such as the *excise penalty,* declared by 4 & 5 Will. 4, c. 85, s. 17, is recovered, it will not count as a

Sect. 72.
NOTE.

conviction under section 3, *ante*, p. 2, as regards an increase of punishment there directed : *Re Authers*, 22 Q. B. D. 345; 58 L. J. M. C. 62; 53 J. P. 116; 37 W. R. 320. As to prosecuting for excise penalties, see *ante*, pp. 5, 10.

Any recreation room managed or conducted under the authority of a Secretary of State or the Admiralty, may be used for public dancing, music, or other public entertainment of the like kind, or for the public performance of stage plays without any license: 52 Vict. c. 3, s. 7.

73. *Licenses as defined by this Act not required for certain retail sales.*] A license as defined by this Act shall not be required for—

1. The sale of wine by retail, not to be consumed on the premises, by a wine merchant in pursuance of a wine dealer's license granted by the Commissioners of Inland Revenue; or

2. The sale of liqueurs or spirits by retail, not to be consumed on the premises, by a wholesale spirit dealer whose premises are exclusively used for the sale of intoxicating liquors, in pursuance of a retail license granted by the Commissioners of Inland Revenue, under the provisions of the twenty-fourth and twenty-fifth years of Her present Majesty, chapter twenty-one, intituled "An Act for granting to Her Majesty certain duties of excise and stamps."

The exceptions from the necessity of a license or certificate are—

1. A retail license to sell *wine* obtained by a wine dealer. And a grocer who takes out a wine dealer's license fulfils the description of a wine merchant: *Palmer* v. *Thatcher*, 3 Q. B. D. 46; 42 J. P. 213; 47 L. J. M. C. 54; 26 W. R. 314; 37 L. T. (N.S.) 784. A wine merchant may be said to be one who sells goods not produced by himself: *Josselyn* v. *Parsons*, L. R. 7 Ex. 127; 41

35 & 36 VICT. C. 94, S. 74.   149

L. J. Ex. 60; 36 J. P. 455; 25 L. T. 912; 20 W. R. 316. Though **Sect. 73.**
a license of justices is not required in this case, still the holder of NOTE.
the license is subject to the ordinary penalties for keeping open
his premises during the closing hours set forth in 37 & 38 Vict.
c. 49, s. 3;. *Martin* v. *Barker*, 50 L. J. M. C. 109; 45 J. P. 749;
45 L. T. 214. Whether he would be liable as a licensed person
to other offences set forth, as, for example, in sections 7, 11, and
other sections, no decision of the court as to this has yet
occurred.

2. A retail *spirit* license by a spirit dealer, provided his premises are used exclusively for the sale of intoxicating liquors.
See section 68. The same remark as in the last case applies to
this license. As such, a spirit dealer does not require a justices'
license to sell under his additional retail license, and his premises
are not licensed premises within the meaning of section 74. A
constable has no right of entry under 37 & 38 Vict. c. 49, s. 16:
Harrison v. *Mac L'Meel*, 48 J. P. 469; 50 L. T. (N.S.) 210.

Definitions.

74. *Interpretation of terms, &c.*] In this Act,
if not inconsistent with the context, the following expressions have the meanings hereinafter respectively
assigned to them; that is to say:—

" *Intoxicating Liquor Licensing Act*, 1828 " (now
  called the Alehouse Act, 1828: 55 Vict. c. 10),
  means 9 Geo. 4, c. 61, intituled " An Act to regulate the granting of licenses to keepers of inns,
  alehouses, and victualling houses in England," and
  includes the Acts amending the same :(a)

" *Wine and Beerhouse Acts* " means the Wine and
  Beerhouse Act, 1869, 32 & 33 Vict. c. 27, and the
  Wine and Beerhouse Act Amendment Act, 1870,
  33 & 34 Vict. c. 29:

" *Intoxicating Liquor Licensing Acts* " means the
  Intoxicating Liquor Licensing Act, 1828, and the

Sect. 74.   Wine and Beerhouse Acts, *i.e.*, 9 Geo. 4, c. 61; 32 & 33 Vict. c. 27; 33 & 34 Vict. c. 29:

"*Intoxicating liquor*" means spirits, wine, beer, porter, cider, perry, and sweets, and any fermented, distilled, or spirituous liquor, which cannot, according to any law for the time being in force, be legally sold without a license from the Commissioners of Inland Revenue :(*b*)

"*License*" means a license for the sale of intoxicating liquors granted by justices in pursuance of the Intoxicating Liquor Licensing Act, 1828 (now called the Alehouse Act, 1828: 55 Vict. c. 10), including a certificate of justices granted under the Wine and Beerhouse Acts, and including a license for the sale of sweets which is hereby authorised to be granted in the same manner as if sweets were wine, and including a license for the retail of spirits granted to a wholesale spirit dealer by the justices in pursuance of this Act :(*c*)

"*A new license*" means a license granted at a general annual licensing meeting in respect of premises not theretofore licensed for the sale of intoxicating liquors: (See also 37 & 38. Vict. c. 49, s. 32.)

"*The renewal of a license*" means a license granted at a general annual licensing meeting by way of renewal :(*d*)

"*The transfer of a license*" means a transfer made in special sessions in exercise of the power granted to justices by the fourth section of the said Act of 9 Geo. 4, c. 61 :(*e*)

" *Licensed person* " means a person holding a license as defined by this Act:

Sect. 74.

" *Licensed premises* " means premises in respect of which a license as defined by this Act has been granted and is in force:

" *Unlicensed premises* " means premises in respect of which a license as defined by this Act has not been granted or is not in force:

" *Owner of licensed premises* " means the person for the time being entitled to receive, either on his own account or as mortgagee, or other incumbrancer in possession, the rackrent of such premises:(*f*)

" *Licensing district* " means the area for which a general annual licensing meeting is held in pursuance of the Intoxicating Liquor Licensing Act, 1828 (now called the Alehouse Act, 1828: 55 Vict. c. 10):

" *Licensing justices* " means the justices having jurisdiction in respect of the grant of new licenses in a licensing district ander the last-mentioned Act as amended by this Act:(*g*)

" *Licensing officer* " means any officer appointed by the Commissioners of Inland Revenue to issue or superintend the issue of licenses under this Act in any place:

" *Sale by retail* " in respect of any intoxicating liquor, means the sale of that liquor in such quantities as is declared to be a sale by retail by any Acts relating to the sale of intoxicating liquors:(*h*)

Sect. 74. "*County*" does not include a county of a city or a county of a town, but means any county, riding, parts, division, or liberty of a county having a separate commission of the peace and a separate court of quarter sessions:

"*Borough*" means a county of a city, county of a town, city, municipal borough, cinque port and its liberties, town corporate, or other place in which a general annual licensing meeting is held in pursuance of the Intoxicating Liquor Licensing Act, 1828, exclusive of a petty sessional division of a county:

Where a liberty of a county, as defined by this Act, is not divided into petty sessional divisions, such liberty shall, so far as respects the provisions of this Act with respect to the grant of new licenses, stand in the same position as if it were a petty sessional division of the county in which it is geographically situate, or with which it has the longest common boundary:

"*Clerk of the licensing justices*" means where the licensing district is a county or petty sessional division of a county, the clerk of the petty sessions for such division; and where the licensing district is a county of a city, county of a town, city, municipal borough, town corporate, or other place not a county or a petty sessional division of a county, means the clerk to the justices of such county of a city, county of a town, city, borough, town corporate, or place, or other person performing analogous duties to such clerk; and where there

are more persons than one, in any county, petty Sect. 74.
sessional division, or other place filling the office
of clerk of the licensing justices as hereinbefore
defined, the licensing justices shall determine by
which of such persons the register of licenses shall
be kept:

"*Town*" means any parliamentary or municipal
borough, Improvement Act district, local government district, or other place having a known legal
boundary, and wherever two or more of the above-mentioned places occupy portions of the same area,
"town" shall be taken to mean such one of such
places as is the largest in area; and any premises
situate in more than one town shall, for the purposes of this Act, be deemed to be in such one of
the towns as is the largest in area (see Act, 1874,
s. 32, *post*) :(*i*)

"*Local government district*" means any area subject
to the jurisdiction of a local board constituted in
pursuance of the Local Government Act, 1858:

"*Improvement Act district*" means any area for the
time being subject to the jurisdiction of any commissioners, trustees, or other persons entrusted by
any local Act, not being a Turnpike Act or Highway
Act, with powers of improving, cleansing, or paving
any part of such district:

"*Court of summary jurisdiction*" means any justice
or justices of the peace, metropolitan police magistrate, stipendiary or other magistrate, or officer,
by whatever name called, to whom jurisdiction is

Sect. 74. given by the Act of the session of the eleventh and twelfth years of the reign of Her present Majesty, chapter forty-three, intituled "An Act to facilitate the performance of the duties of justices of the peace out of sessions within England and Wales with respect to summary convictions and orders," in this Act referred to as "The Summary Jurisdiction Act, 1848," and any Acts amending the same:

"*Quarter sessions*" includes general sessions:

[Part here *repealed* by 46 & 47 Vict. c. 39, Sched.]

"*Secretary of State*" means one of Her Majesty's principal Secretaries of State.

(*a*) The usual name given to the Act 9 Geo. 4, c. 61, was the Alehouse Act, which was a much shorter and more convenient name than that here used; and that short name is now restored by 55 Vict. c. 10, so that in future the Act will be referred to as "The Alehouse Act, 1828."

(*b*) Spirits is defined, as to degree of strength, in 23 Vict. c. 27, s. 21. Beer is defined in 1 Will. 4, c. 64, s. 32; 32 & 33 Vict. c. 27, s. 2; and see 43 & 44 Vict. c. 20, ss. 2, 40; 48 & 49 Vict. c. 51, s. 4; *Howarth* v. *Minns*, 51 J. P. 7; 56 L. T. 316. Beer includes cider, and cider includes perry: 43 & 44 Vict. c. 20, s. 40; 32 & 33 Vict. c. 27, s. 2. Sweets is defined in 33 & 34 Vict. c. 29, s. 3; also 43 & 44 Vict. c. 20, s. 40. It was held that justices were right in treating British wine as wine, when a chemist proved that it contained a large proportion of alcohol: *Harris* v. *Jenns*, 9 C. B. (N.S.) 152; 30 L. J. M. C. 183; 3 L. T. 408; 9 W. R. 36.

(*c*) *License.*] The word "license" in this Act includes a certificate granted under the Wine and Beerhouse Acts. It would have been better to have now discontinued the use of the word "certificate" altogether; and it might have been called in future the justices' license to distinguish it from the excise license.

But throughout the notes to this Act the word "certificate" has been used to prevent mistake.

35 & 36 VICT. C. 94, S. 74.

The fact that wine dealers and spirit dealers may sell wines and spirits by retail in some cases without a justices' license has been entirely overlooked in this definition of the word "license." And the same oversight has been committed in the definition of "licensed person."

Sect. 74.
———
NOTE.

Sweets.] The definition of license contains the authority to justices to give licenses for sweets, and these are put on the same footing as wine. If the sale of sweets is for consumption on the premises the justices can refuse a new certificate without reasons; but if the consumption is to be off the premises, then the justices cannot refuse the certificate, except on the first three grounds stated in 32 & 33 Vict. c. 27, s. 8. See the notes to section 69, which apply equally to sweets. Though there may be a separate license for sweets, yet when a wine license is obtained it includes sweets as part thereof: 43 & 44 Vict. c. 20, s. 40.

New license.] This definition has been amended by the Licensing Act, 1874, s. 32, *post*.

(*d*) *Grant by way of renewal of license.*] The definition of a new license has been amended, and is now contained in Licensing Act, 1874, section 32. See note to that section. But the former definition meant the same in effect: *Marwick* v. *Codlin*, L. R. 9 Q. B. 509; 38 J. P. 518: 43 L. J. M. C. 169; 30 L. T. 719; 22 W. R. 823.

It is to be observed that a renewal of a license or certificate naturally implies two things. 1. That it is the same person who previously held the license or certificate, and who now applies for the renewal; 2. That the premises are the same, or substantially the same, in both cases. The phrase "renewal of license" is, however, sometimes popularly used to denote that a person applies for a license or a certificate for the same house which some other person was previously licensed to use as an alehouse or beerhouse, &c. This distinction, though unimportant, when justices could either grant or renew licenses without any reasons given, will prove to be of considerable importance now that justices must deal very differently with the grant of a new and the renewal of an old license.

The Alehouse Act, 9 Geo. 4, c. 61, did not explain which of the above meanings belongs to the phrase "renewal of a license." As to the Wine and Beerhouse Acts, the words "renewal of certificate" are also left undefined. It is true that as regards the 19th section of the Act, 1869, 32 & 33 Vict. c. 27, it may be taken, since 33 & 34 Vict. c. 29, s. 7, that the words "renewal of

Sect. 74.

Note.

license" means a continuous renewal of the license in respect of the same house, though different persons may have held the license since 1st May, 1869. That meaning is the one which must be used in applying the 19th section, but it does not follow that it is the meaning for other purposes. An alehouse license is only in operation for one year, when it expires by effluxion of time; so it is as to a certificate under the Wine and Beerhouse Acts. If after the expiration of the license or certificate a new tenant comes in and applies for a license, he must usually apply, not for a renewal, but for a new license. It is true that during the currency of the license there may be a transfer or transmission of a license or certificate, in the various circumstances set forth in the Act 9 Geo. 4, c. 61, s. 14, and extended to the Wine and Beerhouse Acts by 33 & 34 Vict. c. 29, s. 4. If such transferree had held the license or certificate up to the expiration thereof, and seeks again to renew the license, this case will come strictly within the meaning of an application by way of renewal. An opportunity for inquiry into the character of the transferree was given under the transfer clauses of the Alehouse Act, and since 33 & 34 Vict. c. 29, s. 4, also under the Wine and Beerhouse Acts, and it is the same under the Licensing Act, 1872, section 40. And, therefore, when the transferree has acquired the same or equivalent premises, and a legal title to the privileges and duties incident to the holding of the license or certificate which his predecessor held in respect of the same premises, it is a renewal and not a new license or certificate which he applies for at the end of the licensing year.

Renewals not to a licensed person.] Several instances, however, may occur of a renewal being rightly asked for, though the person entitled to ask it has not acquired by transfer the current license. Thus, the Court of Appeal held, in *R.* v. *Lawence* or *Liverpool JJ.*, 11 Q. B. D. 638; 52 L. J. M. C. 114; 49 L. T. 244; 32 W. R. 20; 47 J. P. 596, that a new tenant who had entered in June, and was in possession at the date of the general annual licensing meeting in September, might apply for a "license to continue," and if he did not so apply, he may be treated as a person "neglecting to apply," so that any succeeding tenant entering after 10th October would be entitled to make an application under 9 Geo. 4, c. 61, s. 14. The effect of this decision seems to be that a license to *continue*, though not identical with a renewal, may be applied for by an incoming tenant who is in possession at the date of the annual general meeting, for in those circumstances nobody but the tenant in possession would be in a position to do anything. Thus, the Court of Appeal seems in some respects to have treated a renewal as if

35 & 36 VICT. C. 94, S. 74.

it were a renewal in respect of the house, whether the person applying was the person holding the license or not. Hence also, where the justices wrongfully refused to renew P.'s license, while no statutory notice of opposition had been served, and P. did not appeal, but would not quit the house till next June, and C., a new tenant, then entered, and at the next general annual meeting in September applied for a renewal, it was held that this was a competent application : *R.* v. *Market Bosworth JJ.*, 51 J. P. 439 ; 57 L. T. 56 ; 35 W. R. 734 ; 56 L. J. M. C. 96.

Sect. 74.
———
NOTE.

Where application must be for a new license.] In all other cases than those mentioned it must be a new license or certificate, and not a renewal which is applied for. Thus, where a house had been closed for more than a year owing to difficulties about mortgages and a tenant absconding, so that there had been a break in renewing the license, it was held that, when a new tenant applied, he must apply for a new license : *Ex parte Tabrath*, 39 J. P. 101 ; 31 L. T. 513. So where a holder forfeited his license in May and nobody applied at the general meeting, but at the next again a new tenant applied, it was held that his application must be for a new license : *Hargraves* v. *Dawson*, 35 J. P. 342 ; 24 L. T. 428. So where during rebuilding of the premises no license had been granted for three years, it was held that the next application must be for a new license : *R.* v. *Curzon*, L. R. 8 Q. B. 400 ; 42 L. J. M. C. 155 ; 37 J. P. 774 ; 29 L. T. 32 ; 21 W. R. 886. And the same is true whenever a holder of a license forfeits the same, for the license ceases entirely at the date of the forfeiture : *R.* v. *West Riding JJ.*, 21 Q. B. D. 358 ; 52 J. P. 455 ; 57 L. J. M. C. 103 ; 36 W. R. 258. On the other hand, where a licensed person entitled to take out the usual excise licenses had not done so for a year, but intended to do so next year, what he required to apply for was not a new license but a renewal, for the taking out of an excise license does not affect the substance of his application : *Smith* v. *Hereford JJ., R.* v. *Smith*, 42 J. P. 295 ; 48 L. J. M. C. 38 ; 39 L. T. 604.

Summary as to new and renewed licenses.] The result, therefore, of the various enactments in the Alehouse Act, and the Wine and Beerhouse Acts, and this Act, seems to be as follows :—

Where the person applying for a license or certificate has at the time a license or certificate respectively in force in respect of the same premises, whether he acquired such license or certificate at the previous general annual licensing meeting, or its adjournment, or since that time by virtue of transfer on one of the

Sect. 74.
Note.

grounds specified in 9 Geo. 4, c. 61, s. 14, and 33 & 34 Vict. c. 29, s. 4, or if he has not got a transfer but has entered upon possession under one of the grounds specified in 9 Geo. 4, c. 61, s. 14, before the general annual meeting or its adjournment, then he is in the position of one applying for a grant by way of renewal. But all other persons are in the position of applying at such meeting for a new license or certificate.

Where premises enlarged or altered, if renewal can be asked.] In some cases, where the *premises* have been *enlarged* by taking in another house, the justices will treat the application as one of renewal if the premises are not materially altered except by enlargement : *R.* v. *Smith*, 31 J. P. 259 ; 15 L. T. 178. This is always a question of degree, and as to the relative extent of the old premises and the new additions. As a general rule, it is a right of an owner, incident to all businesses, to extend his premises from time to time, and the enlarged area is for the time being the place of business : *Richards* v. *Swansea*, 9 Ch. D. 425. And a house includes the curtilage or a piece of ground in front : *Marson* v. *London and Chatham Railway Company*, L. R. 6 Eq. 101. If the licensee were to add several houses to one, the justices may hold that the premises are different, but in general, where a smaller or an equal extent has been added, they will rightly treat this as merely an enlargement of the existing premises, and not different premises, and so they will renew the old license, and not insist on new notices and a new license : *R.* v. *Raffles*, 1 Q. B. Div. 207 ; 40 J. P 68 ; 45 L. J. M. C. 61 ; 34 L. T. 180; 24 W. R. 536. Sometimes the justices specify by metes and bounds the exact extent of the licensed premises, and there is nothing irregular in this ; but it is doubtful whether this controls the natural right of the licensee to extend his premises : *Stringer* v. *Huddersfield JJ.*, *R.* v. *Sykes*, 40 J. P. 22 ; 33 L. T. 568 ; 24 W. R. 141. In one case the justices convicted a licensed person for selling in an outlying part of his premises, holding that the original license did not extend to all the outhouses, and the court would not interfere, treating this as usually a question of fact for the justices alone to determine : *Mahon* v. *Gaskell*, 42 J. P. 583. On the other hand, where a licensed person had added an adjoining house nearly as large as the original premises, and converted the whole into one set of premises, and sold liquors in the new part, and the licensing justices treated the next application at the general annual meeting as a renewal and not as a new grant, the High Court would not interfere, treating it as a question of fact for the licensing justices exclusively : *R.* v. *Justices of Hants*, 44 J. P. 72.

See also notes to 32 & 33 Vict. c. 27, s. 19, *post.*

(e) *Transfer of license.*] This definition should have in- Sect. 74.
cluded section 14 as well as section 4 of 9 Geo. 4, c. 61, for in ———
reality they are one section. All licenses and certificates can be Note.
transferred under the conditions and circumstances set forth in
9 Geo. 4, c. 61, s. 14, *post*, and under the circumstances set forth
in 37 & 38 Vict. c. 49, s. 15. And a temporary transfer can in all
classes of cases be obtained at petty sessions under 5 & 6 Vict.
c. 44, *post*.

A very limited meaning has, however, been adopted by the
court, so as to restrict the word "transfer" to the case where the
outgoing licensee himself applies to the justices for a grant of a
license to the incoming tenant under 9 Geo. 4, c. 61, s. 14 ; *R.* v.
Grove or *Wilts JJ.*, 57 J. P. 454 ; *R.* v. *Hughes* (1893), 2 Q. B.
; 57 J. P. 454 ; 62 L. J. M. C. 150.

(f) *Owner of licensed premises.*] This expression has been
further defined in Licensing Act, 1874, section 29. See also
section 56 of this Act.

(g) *Licensing justices.*] This expression was used in section 24, now repealed, and section 43. See another use of it in
Licensing Act, 1874, section 6, and notes, *post*.

(h) *Sale by retail.*] The words "sale by retail" had different
definitions in different Acts. This clause seems to import that if
the sale by retail of beer was defined by the Beerhouse Acts, the
same definition as to beer will apply to all houses which sell beer
under this Act. So as to sale of wines, spirits, &c., respectively.
But it does not mean that "sale by retail" denotes a uniform
quantity of all intoxicating liquors. See notes to section 3,
ante, p. 9.

(i) *Town.*] In fixing the valuation qualification of in-door
licensed houses which are to be licensed for the first time, the
words used in 3 & 4 Vict. c. 61, s. 1, namely, "any town corporate, parish, or place," have been discontinued, and the word
"town" substituted, with a definition which seems more easily
applied. The Act 3 & 4 Vict. c. 61, s. 1, is now only in force as
to the beerhouses that had certificates for in-door consumption on
10th August, 1872, and for all out-door beerhouses and cider
houses. See section 45 and notes. This word "town" as used in
the Beerhouse Acts must be taken according to the definition of
those Acts and not of this Act. And this definition of the word
"town" is repealed by the Licensing Act, 1874, section 33, *post*,
and another definition substituted by the same Act, section 32,
post.

Sect. 75.

Repeal.

75. *Repeal of Acts mentioned in the second schedule.*] (Part here *repealed* by 46 & 47 Vict. c. 39, Sched.)

Provided also, that in the case of persons intending to apply for *billiard licenses* under the Act of the eighth and ninth years of the reign of Her present Majesty, chapter one hundred and nine, intituled "An Act to amend the law concerning games and wagers," or for the transfer of such licenses, the same notices shall be given as are by this Act required in the case of licenses as defined by this Act, or as near thereto as circumstances admit ; and any person convicted of an offence against the tenor of a billiard license, or of any offence declared by the last-mentioned Act to be an offence against the tenor of a license as defined by this Act, shall be punished under this Act in the same manner in all respects as a licensed person within the meaning of this Act is punishable under this Act for suffering any gaming or any unlawful game to be carried on on his premises ; and in construing the last-mentioned Act any reference to the Intoxicating Liquor Licensing Act, 1828, shall be construed to refer to that Act as amended by this Act.

It was held that the various new offences and penalties took effect on the passing of this Act on all the current licenses, and that these were not saved from the operation of the Act by subsection 3 : *Jones* v. *Cooper*, 37 J. P. 613 ; 28 L. T. 496 ; 21 W. R. 732.

Billiard licenses.] The Act 8 & 9 Vict. c. 109, s. 10, provided that the like notices should be given for applications for billiard

35 & 36 VICT. C. 94, S. 75.

Billiard Licenses.   Sect. 75.

licenses as in case of alehouse licenses. The billiard license   NOTE.
includes billiard tables and bagatelle boards, or instruments used
in any game of a like kind. The same section of 8 & 9 Vict.
c. 109, also enacted that transfers of billiard licenses may be
obtained at the same transfer sessions as public-house licenses,
viz., under 9 Geo. 4, c. 61, ss. 4, 14. The duration of the billiard
licenses is also the same, those in Middlesex and Surrey ending
on 5th April, and elsewhere on 10th October. The fees payable
by licensees are 5s. for the clerk to the justices, and 1s. for services of constable. The penalty for demanding or receiving
more than these two fees is 5l.

The above 75th section of the Licensing Act, 1872, thus
extends to billiard licenses the same notices as for public-house
licenses. Therefore, for new grants and transfers the notices are
those specified in 32 & 33 Vict. c. 27, s. 7, *post*, and this
Licensing Act, 1872, s. 40, *ante*, p. 82. There is no notice required for renewals.

The justices have the same absolute discretion as to granting or
refusing a billiard license as in the case of public-house licenses,
under 9 Geo. 4, c. 61, s. 1, *post*.

There is no appeal against a refusal to grant a billiard license :
R. v. *Devonshire JJ.*, 21 J. P. 773 ; *Ex parte Chamberlain*, 8 E. &
B. 644.

The license prohibits the consumption of excisable liquors on
the premises, and beer is not now an excisable liquor : *Jones* v.
Whittaker, L. R. 3 Q. B. 541 ; 22 L. T. 534 ; 39 L. J. M. C. 139 ;
34 J. P. 663 ; 18 W. R. 1197. And the same meaning of excisable liquor is preserved in the Inland Revenue Act, 1880, 43 &
44 Vict. c. 20, s. 47, *post*.

Form of the billiard license.] "At the general annual
licensing meeting [*or* an adjournment of the same annual
licensing meeting, *or* at a special petty session] of Her Majesty's
justices of the peace acting for the division [*or* liberty, &c., *as the
case may be*] of ——, in the county of ——, holden at ——, on
the —— day of ——, in the year ——, for the purpose of granting
billiard licenses, we, being —— of Her Majesty's justices of the
peace acting for the said county [*or* liberty, &c., *as the case may be*],
and being the majority of those assembled at the said session, do
hereby authorise and empower A. L., now dwelling at ——, in
the parish of ——, to keep a house for public billiard playing at
[*here specify the house*], provided that he [*or* she] put and keep up
the words "licensed for billiards," legibly printed in some conspicuous place near the door and on the outside of the said house,

M

Sect. 75.   *Billiard Licenses.*

NOTE. and do not wilfully or knowingly permit drunkenness or other disorderly conduct in the said house, and do not knowingly allow the consumption of excisable liquors therein by the persons resorting thereto, and not knowingly suffer any unlawful games therein, and do not knowingly suffer persons of notoriously bad character to assemble and meet together therein, and do not open the said house for play, or allow any play therein after one and before eight of the clock in the morning, or keep it open or allow any play therein on Sundays, Christmas Day, or Good Friday, or on any day appointed for a public fast or thanksgiving, but do maintain good order and rule therein : And this license shall continue in force from the —— day of —— next, until the —— day of —— then next following, and no longer.

"Given under our hands and seals on the day and at the place first written" : 8 & 9 Vict. c. 109, Sched.

Keeping billiard table, &c., without license.] Every house, room, or place kept for public billiard playing, or where a public billiard table or bagatelle board, or instrument used in any game of the like kind, is kept at which persons are admitted to play (except in houses or premises specified in any license granted under 9 Geo. 4, c. 61, hereinafter called a victualler's license), shall be licensed under this Act ; and every person keeping any such public billiard table or bagatelle board, or instrument used in any game of the like kind for public use, without being duly licensed so to do, and not holding a victualler's license for the house or premises where such billiard table, bagatelle board, or other instrument as aforesaid is kept or used,—and also every person licensed under this Act, who shall not during the continuance of such billiard license put and keep up the words "*licensed for billiards*," legibly printed in some conspicuous place near the door on the outside of the house specified in the license,—shall be liable to be proceeded against as the keeper of a common gaming-house, and besides any penalty or punishment to which he may be liable if convicted of keeping a common gaming-house, shall, on conviction of keeping such unlicensed billiard table, bagatelle board, or other instrument as aforesaid, by his own confession, or by the oath of one or more credible witnesses, before any police magistrate or any two justices of the peace, be liable to pay such penalty, not more than 10*l.* for every day on which such billiard table, bagatelle board, or instrument as aforesaid shall be used, as shall be adjudged by the magistrate or justices before whom he shall be convicted, or, in the discretion of the magistrate or justices, may be committed to the house of correction, with or

Billiard Licenses.

Sect. 75.

without hard labour, for any time not more than one calendar month; but no person who shall have been summarily convicted of any such offence shall be liable to be further proceeded against by indictment for the same offence : 8 & 9 Vict. c. 109, s. 11.

NOTE.

Offences against the tenor of billiard license.] By 8 & 9 Vict. c. 109, s. 12, and the 75th section of the Licensing Act, 1872, every person licensed under this Act, who shall be convicted, before a police magistrate or two justices acting in and for the division or place in which shall be situated the house kept, or theretofore kept by such person, of any offence against the tenor of the license to him granted, shall be liable to the same penalties and punishments [as if he were a licensed person convicted under the Licensing Act, 1872, section 17]. See notes to Act, 1872, section 17, *ante*, p. 45.

Constable to visit licensed billiard houses.] And it shall be lawful for all constables and officers of police to enter into any house, room, or place where any public table or board is kept for playing at billiards, bagatelle, or any game of the like kind, when and so often as such constables and officers shall think proper; and every person licensed under 9 Geo. 4, c. 61, or this Act, who shall refuse to admit, or who shall not admit, any such constable or officer of police into such house, room, or place, shall, on conviction thereof before a police magistrate, or any two justices of the peace, be deemed guilty of an offence against the tenor of his license, whether the same be a billiard license or a victualler's license : 8 & 9 Vict. c. 109, s. 14.

Keepers of billiard tables not to allow play at certain times—penalty.] Every person keeping any public billiard table or bagatelle board, or instrument used in any game of the like kind, whether he be the holder of a victualler's license or licensed under this Act, who shall allow any person to play at such table, board, or instrument, after one or before eight o'clock in the morning of any day, or at any time on Sunday, Christmas Day, or Good Friday, or any day appointed to be kept as a public fast or thanksgiving; and every person holding a victualler's license who shall allow any person to play at such table, board, or instrument kept on the premises specified in such victualler's license, at any time when such premises are not by law allowed to be open for the sale of wine, spirits, or beer, or other fermented or distilled liquors, shall be liable to the penalties herein provided

M 2

Sect. 75. *Billiard Licenses.*

NOTE. in the case of persons keeping such public billiard table, bagatelle board, or instrument as aforesaid for public use without license ; and during those times when play at such table, board, or instrument is not allowed by this Act, every house licensed under this Act, and every billiard room in every house specified in any victualler's license, shall be closed, and the keeping of the same open or allowing any person to play therein or thereat, at any of the times or on any of the days during which such play is not allowed by this Act, shall be deemed in such case an offence against the tenor of the license of the person so offending : 8 & 9 Vict. c. 109, s. 13.

It has been held that this section applies only to persons holding publican's licenses under 9 Geo. 4, c. 61, and not to beerhouse keepers : *Bent* v. *Lister*, 52 J. P. 389.

It has been held that persons staying as lodgers in licensed premises where there is a billiard table cannot lawfully play at billiards after the hours of closing the licensed premises for sale of liquor, though they are entitled to be supplied with liquor after such hours, and the landlord may be convicted of allowing gaming if he allow them at such hours to play at billiards : *Ovenden* v. *Raymond*, 40 J. P. 727 ; 34 L. T. 698.

Appeal by billiard license holder against convictions.] Any person who shall be summarily convicted under this Act may appeal to the next general or quarter sessions of the peace [part here *repealed* by 47 & 48 Vict. c. 43, sched.] ; and it shall be lawful for the magistrate or justices by whom such conviction shall have been made to bind over the witnesses who shall have been examined, in sufficient recognizances, to attend and be examined at the hearing of such appeal ; and that every such witness, on producing a certificate of being so bound, under the hand of the said magistrate or justices, shall be allowed compensation for his or her time, trouble, and expenses in attending the appeal, which compensation shall be paid in the first instance by the treasurer of the county or place, in like manner as in cases of misdemeanor, under the provisions of 7 Geo. 4, c. 64 ; and in case the appeal shall be dismissed, and the order of conviction affirmed, the reasonable expenses of all such witnesses attending as aforesaid, to be ascertained by the court, shall be repaid to the said treasurer by the appellant : 8 & 9 Vict. c. 109, s. 20.

For procedure as to appeal see Licensing Act, 1872, section 52, *ante*, p. 116, and notes.

35 & 36 VICT. C. 94, S. 84.   165

Application of certain of the preceding Provisions of this Act to Ireland.   Sect. 76.

76. *Mode of reference to particular provisions of Acts.*] A reference to the words forming a heading to any of the provisions of this Act shall be deemed to be a reference to all the provisions under such heading, unless otherwise specially provided.

77. *Application to Ireland of certain provisions of Act, with modifications.*]

78. *Closing of premises in Ireland at certain hours on Sunday, Christmas Day, Good Friday, &c.*]

79. *Recovery and application of penalties in Ireland.*]

80. *Repeal of section 4 of 34 & 35 Vict. c. 88.*] (*Repealed* by 46 & 47 Vict. c. 39, Sched.)

81. *Interpretation of " spirit grocer," " excise license," &c., as applying to Ireland.*]

82. *No renewal of license to be granted to spirit grocers in Ireland without certificate of justices.*]

83. *Penalty on spirit grocer in Ireland if liquor drunk on or near to the premises.*]

84. *Penalty on evasion of law as to drinking on premises of spirit grocer in Ireland.*]

Sect. 85. **85.** *Penalty on internal communication between premises of spirit grocer and house of public resort in Ireland.*]

86. *Limitation of hours during which spirit grocers may sell intoxicating liquors in Ireland.*]

87. *Justices and constables may enter premises of spirit grocer in Ireland during prohibited hours.*]

88. *Provisions as to repeated convictions to apply to spirit grocers in Ireland, &c.*]

89. *Application of provisions as to legal proceedings, penalties, &c., in Ireland.*]

90. *No license to be granted to disqualified person or for disqualified premises in Ireland.*]

SCHEDULES to which the Act refers.

FIRST SCHEDULE.

(*Repealed* by Licensing Act, 1874, section 33.)

SECOND SCHEDULE.

NOTE.—This schedule was *repealed* by 46 & 47 Vict. c. 39, sched., but is here retained for convenient reference. Each statute and the extent of its repeal is mentioned in the text.

The effect of the repeal was, that it did not revive anything not existing at the date of the repeal, so that the schedule as it stood is still a record of the existing law, and shows how the previous statutes were dealt with. See 46 & 47 Vict. c. 39, s. 1.

21 James 1, c. 7 : So much as is unrepealed.

35 & 36 VICT. C. 94, SCHED.

Sched.

9 Geo. 4, c. 61: Section 6; section 10; section 11; so much of section 13 as relates to the form of license; sections 18 and 19; section 20; section 21; section 22; section 23; section 25; section 26; also section 27, section 28, section 29, except in so far as the three last-mentioned sections relate to the *renewal* of licenses or to the *transfer* of licenses under sections 4 and 14 of the same Act; also section 31; section 32; section 33; section 34.

11 Geo. 4 and 1 Will. 4, c. 64: Section 6; section 11; section 12; section 13; section 15; section 16; section 17; section 18; section 19; section 20; section 21; section 22; section 25; section 26; section 27; so much of section 30 as incorporates or applies any repealed enactment.

4 & 5 Will. 4, c. 85: Section 4; section 7; section 10; so much of section 11 as incorporates or applies any repealed enactment; section 18; section 22.

2 & 3 Vict. c. 47: Section 41, from "and in the case of any offence" to end of section; section 42; section 43.

3 & 4 Vict. c. 61: Section 10; section 13; section 15; section 16; section 17; section 19; also so much of section 21 as incorporates or applies any repealed enactment.

11 & 12 Vict. c. 49: The whole Act so far as it relates to England.

18 & 19 Vict. c. 118: The whole Act.

23 & 24 Vict. c. 27: Section 5; section 17; section 20; section 26; section 27; section 28; section 29; section 31; also sections 18, 30, 31, 32, 33, 34, 35, 36, 37, 38, 41, and 42, so far as such sections relate to the sale of intoxicating liquors or any offences connected therewith; also section 39; section 40.

23 & 24 Vict. c. 113: Section 41.

27 & 28 Vict. c. 64: The whole Act, except in so far as it relates to refreshment houses in which intoxicating liquors are not sold.

28 & 29 Vict. c. 77: The whole Act, except in so far as it relates to refreshment houses in which intoxicating liquors are not sold.

32 & 33 Vict. c. 27: So much of section 6 as relates to the form of certificate; section 12; section 13; section 14; section 15; section 16; section 17; section 18; so much of section 19 as relates to offences; section 22.

33 & 34 Vict. c. 29: Section 5; section 6; section 7, from "the second and third provisoes" to the end of section; section 8; section 9; section 12; section 13; section 15; section 17.

34 & 35 Vict. c. 88: The whole Act.

LICENSING ACT, 1874.

37 & 38 Vict. Cap. 49.

AN ACT to amend the Laws relating to the Sale and Consumption of Intoxicating Liquors.

[30th July, 1874.]

WHEREAS it is expedient to amend the Licensing Act, 1872, in this Act referred to as the principal Act:

Preliminary.

Sect. 1. **1.** *Construction and short title of Act, 35 & 36 Vict. c. 94.*] This Act and the principal Act shall, so far as is consistent with the respective tenors of such Acts, be construed as one Act, and may be cited together as "The Licensing Acts, 1872-1874 ;" but this Act may, if necessary, be cited separately as "The Licensing Act, 1874."

2. *Commencement of Act.*] (*Repealed by 56 & 57 Vict. c. 54.*)

Hours of Closing.

3. *Hours of closing premises licensed for sale of intoxicating liquors.*] All premises in which intoxicating liquors are sold by retail shall be closed as follows (that is to say),

(1.) If situate within the metropolitan district—

(*a.*) On Saturday night from midnight until one

o'clock in the afternoon on the following Sunday ; and

(*b.*) On Sunday night from eleven o'clock until five o'clock on the following morning ; and

(*c.*) On all other days from half-an-hour after midnight until five o'clock on the same morning; and

(2.) If situate beyond the metropolitan district and in the metropolitan police district or in a town or in a populous place as defined by this Act ;

(*a.*) On Saturday night from eleven o'clock until half-an-hour after noon on the following Sunday ; and

(*b.*) On Sunday night from ten o'clock until six o'clock on the following morning ; and

(*c.*) On the nights of all other days from eleven o'clock until six o'clock on the following morning ; and

(3.) If situate elsewhere than in the metropolitan district or the metropolitan police district or such town or populous place as aforesaid,—

(*a.*) On Saturday night from ten o'clock until half-an-hour after noon on the following Sunday ; and

(*b.*) On Sunday night from ten o'clock until six o'clock on the following morning ; and

(*c.*) On the night of all other days from ten o'clock until six o'clock on the following morning.

Such premises wherever situate shall, save as hereinafter mentioned, be closed on Sunday afternoon from

Sect. 3.

Sect. 3. three or half-past two according as the hour of opening shall be one o'clock in the afternoon or half-an-hour after noon until six o'clock.

Such premises wherever situate shall be closed on Christmas Day and Good Friday, and on the days preceding Christmas Day and Good Friday respectively, as if Christmas Day and Good Friday were respectively Sunday, and the preceding days were respectively Saturday, but this provision shall not alter the hours during which such premises shall be closed on Sunday when Christmas Day immediately precedes or succeeds Sunday.

The "metropolitan district" is defined by section 32 and the schedule, *post*. "Town" and "populous place" are also defined in section 32, *post*.

Under the repealed 24th section of the Act, 1872, the justices out of the metropolitan district could *vary* the hours very considerably both on Sundays and week-days, but under this enactment the hours are fixed both in the metropolitan district and out of it, except that by the 6th section the justices can, in extra-metropolitan districts, turn the period of closing between half-past 12 and half-past 2 into the period between 1 P.M. and 3 P.M. If they do not vary the hours then this 3rd section fixes the period absolutely for the extra-metropolitan districts as between half past 12 P.M. and half-past 2 P.M. See section 6 and notes, *post*. If, therefore, the justices do nothing under section 6, the hours remain as fixed by this section.

As regards Christmas Day and Good Friday, the day preceding each is to be deemed a Saturday, and, therefore, in the metropolis the houses must be closed on the preceding night at midnight and in extra-metropolitan districts at 11 P.M. and 10 P.M. according to the population.

Grocers' premises.] Where premises are kept for two different purposes, as, for example, where a house is sub divided into two parts, one for selling liquors and the other for groceries, and at the closing hour for liquors the part used for selling liquors is closed by shutters, and all communication with the grocer's shop is cut off, no offence is committed by continuing to sell groceries and other articles in the other part of the premises unless the grocer's shop is kept open merely as a blind for the other purpose, as to which last matter of fact it will be for justices to decide: *Brigden* v. *Heighes*, 1 Q. B. D. 330 ; 40 J. P. 661 ; 45 L. J. M. C. 58 ; 34 L. T. 242 ; 24 W. R. 272 ; *Ex parte Joynt*, 38 J. P. 390. So where the large wooden case in which all the liquors were kept was shut up and locked : *Tassell* v. *Ovenden*, 2 Q. B. D. 284 ; 41 J. P. 710 ; 46 L. J. M. C. 228 ; 36 L. T. 696 ; 25 W. R. 692.

Sect. 3.
NOTE.

Where sold only under excise license.] Where wine or spirits are sold under an excise retail license, though no justices' licenses may be required and is not taken out, these hours of closing equally apply : *Martin* v. *Barker*, 50 L. J. M. C. 109 ; 45 L. T. 214 ; 45 J. P. 749.

Local customs.] There can be no such thing as a local custom, as, for example, Mid-Lent Sunday, dispensing with the prohibitions here laid down : *Stacy* v. *Milne*, 39 J. P. 103.

Six-day licenses.] The case of the six-day licensed houses has been entirely forgotten in this section. Nothing was said expressly in the Act, 1872, section 49, as to how these houses were to be situated as to Christmas Day and Good Friday ; but as to Sunday these houses were to be closed the whole day. This section says that premises wherever situated shall be closed on Christmas Day and Good Friday as if these days were Sunday, and they cannot be treated as Sunday unless these six-day premises are closed the whole day. The legislature probably forgot to provide for the six-day houses, and the question is what is the result of the enactments. If this section is confined to the seven-day houses, then there will be no enactment requiring the six-day houses to close on Christmas Day or Good Friday any more than week days. If this section had said, " as if Christmas Day and Good Friday were respectively Sunday *as above described*," then it would have made the six-day Christmas Day and Good Friday the same as the seven-day Christmas Day and Good Friday. There being, however, no such words as "*as above described*," and nothing to limit the general words " shall be closed as if Christmas Day and Good Friday were Sunday," it seems to follow that the six-day houses must be closed the whole of Christmas Day and Good Friday, the same as on Sunday. Nevertheless, owing to the apparent hardship, if it be a hardship, or at least the oversight, justices may fairly use their discretion as to how they will treat this enactment as regards the six-day houses, and may refuse to convict, thereby leaving it to those interested to take the opinion of the High Court.

LICENSING ACT, 1874, S. 3.

Sect. 3.

Closing Hours.

NOTE. *Welsh Sunday Act.*] Under the *Welsh Sunday Act,* 44 & 45 Vict. c. 61, *post,* it has been held that that Act did not interfere with the previous law as to Christmas Day or Good Friday, whatever that may be, but only dealt with Sunday: *Forsdike* v. *Colquhoun,* 11 Q. B. D. 71; 49 L. T. 136; 47 J. P. 393.

Computation of time.] Formerly the justices were not bound to follow Greenwich time, but followed the medium time of the place, as in *Curtis* v. *Marsh,* 3 H. & N. 866; 23 J. P. 663; 28 L. J. M. C. 36. But now, whenever any expression of time occurs in any Act of Parliament, deed, or other legal instrument, unless it is otherwise specifically stated, this shall mean in Great Britain Greenwich time: 43 & 44 Vict. c. 9, s. 1.

Sunday public entertainments.] A house, room, or other place which shall be opened or used for public entertainment, or amusement, or for publicly debating on any subject whatsoever upon any part of the Lord's Day, called Sunday, and to which persons shall be admitted by the payment of money or by tickets sold for money, shall be deemed a disorderly house or place, and the keeper, &c., shall forfeit 200*l.* for every day so opened or used to such person as shall sue for the same; and the person managing or conducting, &c., shall forfeit 100*l.*, and every doorkeeper, servant, &c., shall forfeit 50*l.*: 21 Geo. 3, c. 49, s. 1. Any person behaving as master, mistress, or manager, shall be deemed the keeper, though not the real owner, and each of several joint owners shall be deemed the keeper. And any house, room, or place where tea, coffee or other refreshment of eating or drinking on the Lord's Day at any greater prices than the usual prices on other days shall be deemed a house, &c., to which persons are admitted on payment of money, though no money is taken for admittance: *Ibid.* s. 2. Persons advertising such places are also liable to 50*l.* penalty: *Ibid.* s. 3. Actions for penalties to be brought within six months: *Ibid.* s. 5.

Where only sacred music is performed the place is not subject to this Act: *Baxter* v. *Langley,* L. R. 4 C. P. 21; 38 L. J. M. C. 1; 32 J. P. 805. But an aquarium, where a brass band plays music, is within the Act: *Terry* v. *Brighton Aquarium,* L. R. 10 Q. B. 306; 39 J. P. 519; 44 L. J. M. C. 173; 32 L. T. 458; *Warner* v. *Brighton Aquarium,* L. R. 10 Ex. 291. A verdict in an action by a friendly informer cannot be set up as a defence: *Girdlestone* v. *Brighton Aquarium,* 4 Ex. D. 107; 43 J. P. 428.

The Crown may remit the whole or any part of the penalty incurred under this Act: 38 & 39 Vict. c. 80, s. 1.

4. *Exemptions as to theatres repealed.*] An exemption from the above-mentioned hours of closing shall not be granted in respect of premises in the neighbourhood of a theatre, for the accommodation of persons attending the same. (Part of this section *repealed* by 46 & 47 Vict. c. 39, Sched.)

Sect. 4.

The words in the 26th section of the Licensing Act, 1872, *ante*, p. 58, hereby repealed, have been altered in that section in the way pointed out by this section. See notes to that section, *ante*, p. 61.

5. *Exemptions as to beerhouses.*] The grant of an order of exemption under the said twenty-sixth section amended as aforesaid may be made to any person licensed to sell beer or cider by retail, to be consumed upon the premises, as well as to any licensed victualler or licensed keeper of a refreshment house.

Further exceptions as to beerhouses.] The grant of a license under the twenty-ninth section of the principal Act may be made to any person licensed to sell beer or cider by retail, to be consumed upon the premises, as well as to any licensed victualler or keeper of a refreshment house in which intoxicating liquors are sold.

The 26th and 29th sections of the Licensing Act, 1872, *ante*, pp. 61, 66, have been altered in the way pointed out by this section. See the notes to those sections.

6. *Power to vary on Sunday afternoon hours of closing premises for sale of intoxicating liquors.*] Notwithstanding anything in this or in any local Act

Sect. 6. contained, the licensing justices may, if they think fit, as respects premises in which intoxicating liquors are sold, when situate in any place beyond the metropolitan district, for the purpose of accommodating the hours of closing on Sunday, Good Friday, and Christmas Day to the hours of public worship in such place, by order direct that such premises shall remain closed until one o'clock in the afternoon instead of half an hour after noon, and in that case such premises shall be closed in the afternoon from three until six o'clock, instead of from half-past two until six o'clock.

Any order made by the licensing justices under this section shall not come into operation until the expiration of one month after the date thereof, and shall be advertised in such manner as the licensing justices direct, and shall be in force until the same is revoked; the expense of any such advertisement may be defrayed in like manner as the expenses of advertising the sittings of such justices are defrayed.

This section gives a discretion to the licensing justices to alter, by half an hour, the closing of premises on one part of Sunday, Christmas Day, and Good Friday, but not on public fasts or thanksgiving days. The discretion can only be exercised in one way, namely, by turning half-past 12 P.M. into 1 P.M. No intermediate time can be fixed on; it must be 1 P.M. or nothing. There is no necessity for saying in the order that the houses shall close at 3 P.M., for that will follow as a matter of course both by the third and this section. The purpose of altering the hours is stated to be for accommodating the hours of closing to the hours of public worship, but that is a vague phrase and cannot be deemed to limit the discretion of the justices.

It was held that where a penalty was formerly put on opening during the hours of Divine service, there could be no conviction if there was no Divine service: *R. v. Knapp*, 2 E. & B. 447; 22 L. J. M. C. 139; 17 J. P. 599. But under this and the 3rd section the penalty is put on opening during fixed hours, subject to the trifling variations made in this section.

Sect. 6.

NOTE.

How order is to be made.] In the corresponding enactment in the 24th section of the Act, 1872, now repealed, the justices could only make an order altering the hours for closing at the general annual licensing meeting or an adjournment, and after giving twenty-one days' notice, but nothing is said in this section either as to the giving of any preliminary notice or as to the time of making the order. This gives rise to a difficulty. As no time is specified, the natural interpretation is that the justices may make the order at any time, and are not bound to give any public notice. As, however, it is left to the discretion of the justices they will, no doubt, exercise that discretion much in the same manner as they did under the Act of 1872, by giving some preliminary notice, and also hearing parties on the subject if they desire it. Probably the legislature thought the power of altering was so trifling in extent that it was not necessary to prescribe any conditions, more especially as the time of public worship is usually fixed in each locality, and therefore it is rather a matter of arithmetic in each case than of public policy. And as the time of public worship may vary in each district, it seems competent for the justices to alter the hours in one part of the district, and not in another part. When the order is made it is not to come into force till the expiration of one month after the date. The better opinion seemed to be that they could not make such an order before the 10th October, 1874. Month means calendar month : 52 & 53 Vict. c. 63, s. 3.

And the justices have no discretion as to when the order shall come into force. The mode of advertising the order is in the discretion of the justices, but should be such as to give ample notice to all the people in the district affected.

Who are licensing justices.] The order altering the closing hours can only be made by the licensing justices, who, by the 74th section of the Licensing Act, 1872, are "the justices having jurisdiction in respect of the grant of new licenses in a licensing district, under 9 Geo. 4, c. 61, as amended by this Act." There is some ambiguity in this definition, since the justices now acting with regard to new licenses are divided into two bodies, both of whom must join in most new grants. But the better construction is, that the justices who are to make the order to vary the closing are not the confirming body, but the body who initiate the grant. The confirming body have no jurisdiction to initiate a new grant ; they at most can only veto or assent to a new grant already

Sect. 6.

Note.

initiated, and hence have no more jurisdiction in respect of new grants than the High Court might have in some cases when, by *certiorari* or *mandamus*, that court may treat a new grant as no grant. If the confirming justices are not licensing justices, then, in counties, the county justices are the justices to make the order. In boroughs having ten justices it is the borough licensing committee, and in boroughs with less than ten justices it is the borough justices who alone can make the order. This construction seems to follow from the words "new grant," and the last words in the above definition of licensing justices, namely, "as amended by this Act." If these words had been omitted from the definition then in all cases it would have been the whole body of justices. But as the Act of 9 Geo. 4, c. 61, is to be taken as amended, *i.e.*, by turning the whole body into a more limited body in boroughs having ten justices, this implies the distinction mentioned, and the Licensing Act, 1872, section 43, and this Act, section 22, confirm it. Though, however, this seems to be the correct construction, yet the law officers of the Crown in 1873, are said to have given their opinion that "licensing justices" meant the whole body of justices in all cases. See 37 J. P. 639.

7. *Early closing licenses.*] Where, on the occasion of an application for a new license, or the removal or renewal of a license which authorises the sale of any intoxicating liquor for consumption on the premises, the applicant applies to the licensing justices to insert in his license a condition that he shall close the premises in respect of which such license is or is to be granted one hour earlier at night than that at which such premises would otherwise have to be closed, the justices shall insert the said condition in such license.

The holder of a license in which such condition is inserted (in this Act referred to as an *early closing license*) shall close his premises at night one hour earlier than the ordinary hour at which such premises would be closed under the provisions of this Act, and the provisions of this Act and the principal Act shall apply to the premises as if such earlier hour were the hour at which the premises are required to be closed.

The holder of an early closing license may obtain from the Commissioners of Inland Revenue any license granted by such commissioners which he is entitled to obtain in pursuance of such early closing license, upon payment of a sum representing six-sevenths of the duty which would otherwise be payable by him for a similar license not limited to such early closing as aforesaid. In calculating the six-sevenths, fractions of a penny shall be disregarded.

The notice which a licensed person is required by section eleven of the principal Act to keep painted or fixed on his premises shall, in the case of an early closing license, contain such words as the licensing justices may order for giving notice to the public that an early closing license has been granted in respect of such premises.

This section is an imitation of the 49th section of the Licensing Act, 1872, as to six-day licenses, though the words are slightly altered. The application cannot be refused by the justices, but they have only power to grant it on an application for a new or a renewal of an old license, and cannot grant it on a transfer of the license as can be done with reference to a six-day license.

This section, as well as the 49th section of the Act, 1872, is founded on the mistaken notion that a license holder cannot close his premises at any hour he thinks proper, and all the remarks on that subject in the notes in section 49 of the Act, 1872, *ante*, p. 102, apply to this section.

As, however, the courts have decided that when once a license holder has asked for the six-day condition to be inserted, the justices can never afterwards be compelled to omit the condition, though requested, on future renewals, the same rule will apply to early closing licenses : *R.* v. *Crewkerne JJ.*, 21 Q. B. D. 85 ; 52 J. P. 372 ; 57 L. J. M. C. 127 ; 60 L. T. 84 ; 36 W. R. 629.

Sect. 8. **8.** *Remission of duty in case of six-day and early closing license.*] A person who takes out a license containing conditions rendering such license a six-day license, as well as an early closing license, shall be entitled to a remission of two-sevenths of the duty.

The duties upon retailing liquors are now regulated by the Inland Revenue Act, 43 & 44 Vict. c. 20, s. 43, *post*.

9. *Penalty for infringing Act as to hours of closing.*] Any person who—

During the time at which premises for the sale of intoxicating liquors are directed to be closed by or in pursuance of this Act, sells or exposes for sale in such premises any intoxicating liquor, or opens or keeps open such premises for the sale of intoxicating liquors, or allows any intoxicating liquors, although purchased before the hours of closing, to be consumed in the premises,—

shall, for the first offence, be liable to a penalty not exceeding ten pounds, and for any subsequent offence, to a penalty not exceeding twenty pounds.

This enactment overrules all local customs : *Stacy* v. *Milne*, 39 J. P. 103. But the sale of liquors by wholesale dealers is specially exempted from the restrictions of this Act by Act of 1872, s. 72, *ante*, p. 143. *R.* v. *Jenkins*, 55 J. P. 824 ; 61 L. J. M. C. 57 ; 65 L. T. 857 ; 40 W. R. 318.

This section is in substantially the same words as those used in the 24th section of the Licensing Act, 1872, now repealed, except that the words are introduced, "although purchased before the hours of closing." When the liquor is purchased before the hours of closing, but not to be consumed on the premises, there seems to be no offence, and customers may call at the house for liquor after closing hours, if previously purchased.

The offence of selling during prohibited hours is different from that of keeping open the premises for the sale of liquor during such hours, and the evidence, which might be sufficient to prove one offence, may be insufficient to prove the other. Great care is therefore required in selecting the proper clause under which to proceed. A keeper of a licensed house was not precluded by the former Acts from having friends as guests during the prohibited hours, and supplying them was neither selling nor keeping open the house for sale : *Overton* v. *Hunter*, 23 J. P. 808 ; 1 L. T. 360. But under this section the consumption of liquor previously purchased is not to take place on the premises after the closing hour—at least in all cases as between an ordinary customer and the license holder. A gift of liquor during those hours, if the gift be clearly established, was, however, formerly held not to be within the penalty : *Petherick* v. *Sargent*, 26 J. P. 135 ; 6 L. T. 48. And this exception is now expressly recognised and extended by the 30th section of this Act. But a barter may be treated as in the nature of a sale in many cases. See Act, 1872, section 62, *ante*, p. 135. In ascertaining the hour, the justices were not bound to follow Greenwich time : *Curtis* v. *Marsh*, 23 J. P. 663 ; 3 H. & N. 365 ; 28 L. J. Exch. 36. But now Greenwich time is meant by all statutes and deeds in Great Britain, if not stated to the contrary : 43 & 44 Vict. c. 9. A conviction should state clearly which offence is found, as this may affect future consequences and proceedings against the licensed person. See *Newman* v. *Bendyshe*, 10 A. & E. 11 ; 2 P. & D. 340 ; *R.* v. *North*, 6 D. & Ry. 143 ; *Cotterill* v. *Lempriere*, 24 Q. B. D. 634 ; 54 J. P. 583 ; 59 L. J. M. C. 133.

Selling or keeping open.] The following cases illustrate the distinction between selling and keeping open :—

In *Tennant* v. *Cumberland*, 1 E. & E. 401 ; 23 J. P. 57, T., a beerhouse keeper, was charged with opening his house for the sale of beer before a certain hour on Sunday. The evidence was that the door was shut at twelve on Saturday night, but about two on Sunday morning a constable saw the beerhouse keeper and another man drinking ale inside, and soon afterwards the man came out. There was no proof of selling beer, and the Court of Queen's Bench held there was no evidence of the offence of keeping open his house, though there was some of selling beer during the time. In *Cates* v. *South*, 23 J. P. 739 ; 1 L. T. 365, an alehouse keeper was charged with keeping open the house for sale of spirits during the prohibited hours. The only evidence was that guests remained in the house after the hour of closing, but there was no selling of liquor after the hour of closing. The court

Sect. 9.
NOTE.

held there was no evidence of keeping open, and that an alehouse keeper was not bound to turn his guests out when the clock struck twelve. In *Pearse* v. *Gill*, 41 J. P. 742, some country farmers had met to transact business as to letting some grass fields, and remained after the hours of closing, the outer door being open, and the court held there was evidence to support a conviction for keeping open. In *Thompson* v. *Greig*, 34 J. P. 214, an alehouse keeper was charged with opening his house in prohibited hours. The door was kept partly open. During the prohibited hours some men were found inside with glasses before them and liquor, and the court held that this was some evidence to support the charge. In *Jefferson* v. *Richardson*, 35 J. P. 470, an alehouse keeper was charged with opening and keeping open on Sunday. Men were seen to come out of a side door, though the front door was shut, but there was no evidence that liquor had been sold during the prohibited hours. It was held there was no evidence to support the charge. In *Brewer* v. *Shepherd*, 36 J. P. 373, a beerhouse keeper was charged with keeping his house open. A man was seen to go into the house after the hour of closing, and to come out with a bottle of beer. It was explained that he had previously called before the hour of closing and paid for the beer, and went to get shaved, and then returned to fetch the beer. But the justices, disbelieving the explanation, convicted, and the Court of Queen's Bench held there was some evidence to support the conviction and so allowed it. A constable entering during prohibited hours, found two men secreted, one having a pot of fresh beer in his hand ; the outer doors were shut, and the men not seen to enter ; held, some evidence of opening the house for sale : *Finch* v. *Blundell*, 5 L. T. 672 ; 26 J. P. 71. During prohibited hours the street door was found open, and men, not lodgers or travellers, drinking inside, but there was no evidence as to when the liquor was sold ; held, some evidence of keeping open for sale : *Smith* v. *Vaux*, 6 L. T. 46 ; 26 J. P. 134.

See also notes to section 3, *ante*, p. 170.

Excise license and grocers' license.] Where premises require no justices' license for the sale by retail of liquors, they are nevertheless subject to the closing hours specified in Act, 1874, and section 3, and notes, *ante*, p. 171. And where grocers and others carry on other business, the premises do not require to be closed so far as the other business is concerned. See notes to Act, 1874, section 3, *ante*, p. 170.

10. *Saving as to* bonâ fide *travellers and lodgers.*] Nothing in this Act or in the principal Act contained shall preclude a person licensed to sell any Sect. 10. intoxicating liquor to be consumed on the premises from selling such liquor at any time to *bonâ fide* travellers or to persons lodging in his house: Provided that no person holding a six-day license shall sell any intoxicating liquor on Sunday to any person whatever not lodging in his house.

Nothing in this Act contained as to hours of closing shall preclude the sale at any time, at a *railway station*, of intoxicating liquors to persons arriving at or departing from such station by railroad.

If in the course of any proceedings which may be taken against any licensed person for infringing the provisions of this Act, or the principal Act relating to closing, such person (in this section referred to as the defendant) fails to prove that the person to whom the intoxicating liquor was sold (in this section referred to as the purchaser) is a *bonâ fide* traveller, but the justices are satisfied that the defendant truly believed that the purchaser was a *bonâ fide* traveller, and further that the defendant took all reasonable precautions to ascertain whether or not the purchaser was such a traveller, the justices shall dismiss the case as against the defendant, and if they think that the purchaser falsely represented himself to be a *bonâ fide* traveller, it shall be lawful for the justices to direct proceedings to be instituted against such purchaser under the twenty-fifth section of the principal Act.

A person for the purposes of this Act and the principal Act shall not be deemed to be a *bonâ fide* traveller unless the place where he lodged during the preceding night is at least three miles distant from the place

Sect. 10. where he demands to be supplied with liquor, such distance to be calculated by the nearest public thoroughfare.

Sale of liquor at railway stations.] Premises licensed for sale of liquors at railway stations are exempt from the ordinary rule as to valuation and the number of public rooms. See Act, 1872, section 45, *ante*, p. 97. And in many cases there are no premises exclusively used as refreshment rooms so as to render it possible to convict persons under the Act, 1872, section 25, *ante*, p. 57. And there is no clear limit to the hours of closing, for at any time during day or night there may be persons waiting to depart from the station, so that strictly speaking no hours of closing are defined. The exemption of railway travellers arriving at or departing from the station was already established. Thus it was held that persons supplied ten minutes before the train started were travellers. It was also held that the fact of two non-travellers being amongst other travellers supplied, was not of itself evidence of the offence : *Fisher* v. *Howard,* 34 L. J. M. C. 42 ; 11 L. T. 373 ; 29 J. P. 246 ; 13 W. R. 145 ; *Copley* v. *Burton,* L. R. 5 C. P. 489 ; 39 L. J. M. C. 141 ; 22 L. T. 888. This express exemption extends to travellers whether living near the railway station or not, if they have just arrived from or are about to depart from such station. The distance of the journey by railway seems immaterial. And the words "persons arriving at or departing from such station by railroad" are obviously wider than the ordinary word "travellers."

Sale of liquor to travellers and lodgers.] The exemption from the penalty on the ground of serving a traveller is confined to houses licensed to sell liquor "to be consumed on the premises ;" and keepers of houses licensed to sell liquor not to be consumed on the premises are not mentioned, so that they cannot claim any exemption. The question as to who was a traveller within the meaning of the exemption depended very much on his distance from home, and the courts had held that a person walking or driving two-and-a-half miles from home sufficiently comes within the description of a traveller : *Peplow* v. *Richardson,* 33 J. P. 407 ; L. R. 4 C. P. 168 ; 17 W. R. 410. Whether business or pleasure is the object of the traveller is wholly immaterial : *Atkinson* v. *Sellers,* 5 C. B. (N.S.) 442 ; 28 L. J. M. C. 12 ; 23 J. P. 71 ; *Taylor* v. *Humphries,* 30 L. J. M. C. 242 ; 10 C. B. (N.S.) 429 ; 9 W. R. 705 ; 4 L. T. 514 ; *Taylor* v. *Humphries,* 34 L. J. M. C. 1 ; 28 J. P. 793.

O. with others travelled in a vehicle to a town 20 miles off on Sunday, and went to a publichouse where they got refreshment, and remained three hours. They then went to see the town, and visited a second publichouse where they took refreshment during prohibited hours, staying fifteen minutes, after which they returned to the first house, from which they proceeded home. It was held that O. did not cease to be a traveller while he was in the second house, and was there entitled to refreshment : *Sheasby* v. *Oldham*, 55 J. P. 214 ; 60 L. J. M. C. 81. Where D., a publican, invited C., a friend, who lived seven miles off, to sing at a concert at D.'s house, and C. performed there till after closing hours, and C. then before starting home was supplied with a bottle of whiskey, it was held that C. was a *bonâ fide* traveller, and continued such till he returned home : *Dames* v. *Bond*, 55 J P. 503.

Sect. 10.
———
NOTE.

Where P.'s licensed house was three-and-a-half miles from N., a large town, and about 131 persons on being asked stated that they had walked from N. on Sunday, and were then served in prohibited hours with a pint of beer and left the house of P. immediately, the justices, on P. being charged with opening in prohibited hours, found as a fact that the travellers had gone there solely to get beer, and were not *bonâ fide* travellers; the court held that the decision of justices who convicted P. could not be interfered with : *Penn* v. *Alexander* (1893), 1 Q. B. 522 ; 57 J. P. 118 ; 68 L. T. 355.

In any proceeding against the keeper of a licensed house for supplying liquor to persons during the prohibited hours, it was held in *Roberts* v. *Humphreys*, 42 L. J. M. C. 147 ; 29 L. T. 387 ; 21 W. R. 885 ; 38 J. P. 135 ; L. R. 8 Q. B. 483, that it lay on the defendant to prove that the person supplied was a traveller, If, however, the stranger, being unknown to the housekeeper, is asked and answers that he is a traveller, and states the place he slept at on the previous evening, and there is no reason for disbelieving him, that will be enough to justify the supply of refreshment.

Where about sixty persons were found sitting in an alehouse in prohibited hours, let in at a back door, of whom three had travelled four miles, but had sat more than two hours, all the rest of the company being travellers, it was held the justices might fairly draw the inference that all the people were not *bonâ fide* travellers : *Gallimore* v. *Goodall*, 38 J. P. 597. But where a large number of supposed excursionists were served near a railway station, and one or two persons living a mile off were served, but without the license holder being aware who they were, the court held there was no evidence of the offence : *Watt* v. *Glenister*, 40 J. P. 181 ; 32 L. T. 856. And where one or two non-travellers

Sect. 10.
NOTE.

are among travellers supplied, this will not justify a conviction in the absence of any evidence of intention : *Peache* v. *Colman*, L. R. 1 C. P. 324 ; 35 L. J. M. C. 118 ; 14 W. R. 439.

The three mile limit.] By the latter part of this section no person shall now be deemed a traveller unless he is three miles from his place of sleeping on the previous night. And it has been decided that the three miles are to be measured by the nearest public thoroughfare, whether by land or water. Thus, where by sailing in a boat across a public navigable lake or arm of the sea the distance would be less than three miles, while round by land it would be eight miles, the landlord would be liable for serving such traveller, for the way by sea was within the prohibited distance : *Coulbert* v. *Troke*, 1 Q. B. D. 1 ; 40 J. P. 533 ; 45 L. J. M. C. 7 ; 33 L. T. 340 ; 24 W. R. 41. Nothing is said as to the length of time that has elapsed since the journey began. Though, however, the person slept three miles off the previous night, it does not follow that he is entitled to be served, the justices having still to find whether he had come to the place for the sole object of obtaining the liquor, and this may depend on the intervening period of time between the sleeping and the application. See *Penn* v. *Alexander*, *ante*, p. 183. The lodging-place includes the traveller's own or any friend's house, and is not confined to a lodging-house ; otherwise an absurdity would arise.

The mere neglect of a servant, contrary to his or her instructions, to ask if the person supplied was a traveller, will not render the keeper of the house liable : *Copley* v. *Burton*, L. R. 5 C. P. 489 ; 22 L. T. 888 ; 39 L. J. M. C. 141. But it will depend on whether the servant was a manager of that department of the business : *Bond* v. *Evans*, 21 Q. B. D. 249 ; 52 J. P. 613 ; 57 L. J. M. C. 105 ; 59 L. T. 411 ; 36 W. R. 767 ; and see notes to Act, 1872, ss. 16, 17.

Lodger gaming.] A lodger in the licensed premises is not allowed to play at billiards after the closing hour for sale of liquors : *Ovenden* v. *Raymond*, 34 L. T. 698 ; 40 J. P. 727 ; see *ante*, p. 164, nor can he be allowed to carry on gaming : *Hare* v. *Osborne*, 34 L. T. 294 ; 40 J. P. 759, *ante*, p. 59. But there is nothing to prevent a lodger or traveller entertaining his friends, so long as there is no selling to such friends, and the lodger pays for them : *Pine* v. *Barnes*, 20 Q. B. D. 221 ; 52 J. P. 199 ; 57 L. J. M. C. 28 ; 58 L. T. 520 ; 36 W. R. 473.

If the person falsely represents himself to be a traveller or lodger, he will, under section 25 of the Licensing Act, 1872, incur a penalty of 5*l*. See notes to that section.

37 & 38 VICT. C. 49, S. 12.   185

11. *Hours of closing night-houses.*] Whereas Sect. 11.
by the Act of 27 & 28 Vict. c. 64, it is provided that no
person within the limits of that Act shall open or keep
open any refreshment house, to which that Act so far as
it is unrepealed applies, or sell or expose for sale or
consumption in any such refreshment house any refreshment or any article whatsoever *between the hours of one
and four o'clock in the morning:* And whereas it is
expedient to amend the provisions of the said Act: Be
it therefore enacted that the said Act, so far as it is
unrepealed, shall be construed as if there were substituted therein for the hour of *one o'clock* in the
morning "the hour of the night or morning at which
premises licensed for the sale of intoxicating liquors by
retail situate in the same place as such refreshment
house are required to be closed," and as if the whole of
England were within the limits of the Act [and as if the
expression "district" in the Act included any place in
which such refreshment house is situate. These last
words repealed by 56 & 57 Vict. c. 54].

This section relates to the Night-house Closing Act (27 & 28
Vict. c. 64), which was confined to the metropolis and certain
boroughs, and which was repealed by the Licensing Act, 1872, as
to houses licensed to sell intoxicating liquors. See the Act, *post*.
This Act is now extended to England and Wales, and no night-house is to be open after the prohibited hours for licensed houses,
and till 4 A.M. following.

Records of Convictions and Penalties.

12. *Mitigation of penalties.*] When any person
holding a license under this or the principal Act is
convicted of any offence against this or the principal
Act, or against any of the Acts recited or mentioned

Sect. 12. therein, the court may not, except in the case of a first offence, reduce the penalty to less than twenty shillings, nor shall the penalty, whether of excise or police, be reduced in any case to less than the minimum authorised by any other Act.

This section repealed 35 & 36 Vict. c. 94, s. 67, and in substitution thereof allows justices on a first offence committed after this Act to reduce the penalty to any amount, except where any other Act forbids it.

The Commissioners of Inland Revenue may mitigate any fine or penalty, and after judgment may remit any fine or penalty relating to Inland Revenue. And so may the Treasury : 53 & 54 Vict. c. 21, s. 35. See *Murray* v. *Thompson*, 53 J. P. 70 ; 22 Q. B. D. 142 ; 60 L. T. 151, as to former law.

The Summary Jurisdiction Act, 1879 (42 & 43 Vict. c. 49, s. 4), gave power to mitigate any penalty for a first offence : and by section 53, extended that Act to Inland Revenue proceedings.

13. *Record of convictions on licenses.*] Where any licensed person is convicted of any offence against the principal Act which by such Act was to have been or might have been indorsed upon the license, or of any offence against this Act, the court before whom the offender is brought shall cause the register of licenses in which the license of the offender is entered, or a copy of the entries therein relating to the license of the offender, certified in manner prescribed by section fifty-eight of the principal Act, to be produced to the court before passing sentence, and after inspecting the entries therein in relation to the license of the offender or such copy thereof as aforesaid, the court shall declare, as part of its sentence, whether it will or will not cause the conviction for such offence to be recorded on the license of the offender, and if it decide that such record is to be made, the same shall be made accordingly.

37 & 38 VICT. C. 49, S. 13.

A declaration by the court that a record of an offence **Sect. 13.**
is to be made on a license shall be deemed to be part of
the conviction or order of the court in reference to such
offence, and shall be subject accordingly to the jurisdiction of the Court of Appeal.

A direction by the court that a conviction for an
offence is to be recorded on the license of the offender
shall, for the purposes of the principal Act, be deemed
equivalent to a direction or requirement by the Act that
such conviction is to be recorded ; and all the provisions
of the principal Act importing that convictions are
required or directed by the Act to be recorded on the
license of an offender shall be construed accordingly.

This section removes the distinction contained in the Licensing
Act, 1872, between certain convictions which were recorded by
operation of law and those which were recorded only by the
exercise of a discretion on the part of the justices. Of the first
class were sections 5 and 6 of the Act, 1872 ; of the second were
sections 13, 14, 16, 17, 28. This section puts them both on the
same footing in future, and leaves it to the discretion of the
justices in all cases to order the conviction to be recorded. But
those convictions which were recorded by operation of law since
the Act of 1872, and before the Act of 1874, will keep their place
on the license and on the register, subject to the qualification
specified in Act, 1872, s. 32, *ante*, p. 71, as to increasing the
penalty.

The corresponding parts of those sections referred to are expressly repealed by this Act, section 33, and there would, therefore, be no power now in the justices at all to record any of those
convictions if it were not for the words in the first part of this
section, which restores the power. The power to record extends
also to all the offences under this Act.

The part of this section as to the court ordering the register of
licenses or copies of entries to be produced seems merely directory,
and is not a condition precedent to their causing a conviction to
be recorded. The court is to declare as part of its sentence
whether each of those offences is or is not to be recorded ; but
such declaration is only deemed part of the conviction or order, if
the court resolves that the conviction shall be recorded. The

Sect. 13. *Adulteration of Liquors.*

NOTE. register referred to is regulated by Act, 1872, s. 36, *ante*, p. 73, and the register is, by Act, 1872, s. 58, *ante*, p. 131, admissible evidence of the matters stated therein.

In leases of licensed houses it is sometimes stipulated that the tenant shall do nothing that will affect, lessen, or make void the license. In such cases if the tenant has been convicted, but the justices have not ordered the conviction to be recorded, the tenant will not have committed a breach of his covenant ; but it will be different if the convictions shall be recorded : *Wooler* v. *Knott*, 1 Ex. D. 265 ; 40 J. P. 788 ; 35 L. T. 121 ; 45 L. J. Ex. 884 ; 24 W. R. 1004 ; *Fleetwood* v. *Hull*, 23 Q. B. D. 35 ; 54 J. P. 229 ; 58 L. J. M. C. 341 ; 37 W. R. 320 ; *Harman* v. *Powell*, 60 L. J. Q. B. 628 ; 65 L. T. 255 ; 56 J. P. 150.

14. *Record of conviction for adulteration.*] Where a licensed person is convicted of any offence against the provisions of any Act for the time being in force relating to the adulteration of drink, such conviction shall be entered in the proper register of licenses, and may be directed to be recorded on the license of the offender in the same manner as if the conviction were for an offence against this Act, and when so recorded shall have effect as if it had been a conviction for an offence against this Act.

This section replaces sections 19—22 of the Licensing Act, 1872, which are repealed by this Act, section 33. The offence of adulteration of liquors will be dealt with under the Sale of Food and Drugs Act, 1875, 38 & 39 Vict. c. 63 ; and 42 & 43 Vict. c. 30.

Sale of food not of the proper nature, substance, and quality.] No person shall sell to the prejudice of the purchaser any article of food or any drug which is not of the nature, substance, and quality of the article demanded by such purchaser, under a penalty not exceeding 20*l.* ; provided that an offence shall not be deemed to be committed under this section in the following cases ; that is to say,

(1.) Where any matter or ingredient not injurious to health has been added to the food or drug because the same is

37 & 38 VICT. C. 49, S. 14.

Adulteration of Liquors.   Sect. 14.

required for the production or preparation thereof as an   NOTE.
article of commerce, in a state fit for carriage or consumption, and not fraudulently to increase the bulk, weight, or measure, of the food or drug, or conceal the inferior quality thereof: 38 & 39 Vict. c. 63, s. 6.

Selling articles with label.] Provided that no person shall be guilty of any such offence as aforesaid in respect of the sale of an article of food or drug mixed with any matter or ingredient not injurious to health, and not intended fraudulently to increase its bulk, weight, or measure, or conceal its inferior quality, if at the time of delivering such article or drug he shall supply to the person receiving the same a notice, by a label distinctly and legibly written or printed on or with the article or drug, to the effect that the same is mixed: 38 & 39 Vict. c. 63, s. 8.

Any inspector or police constable may procure a sample and submit the same to the analyst of the district: 38 & 39 Vict. c. 63, s. 13. The person purchasing is forthwith to notify to the seller or his agent his intention to have the same analysed by the public analyst, and shall offer to divide the article into three parts to be separated and sealed up: *Ibid.* s. 14. If the inspector or constable shall apply to purchase any article of food exposed to sale by retail and tender the reasonable price, and the person exposing the same refuse to sell he shall be liable to a penalty not exceeding 10l.: *Ibid.* s. 17. The certificate of the analyst is *primâ facie* evidence as to the facts therein stated: *Ibid.* s. 21. The seller may, in defence, prove that the article is the same as when he bought it, and that he has a written warranty with it: *Ibid.* s. 25. It is not necessary as a condition precedent to prove that a constable was directed by the local authority to prosecute: *Hale* v. *Cole*, 55 J. P. 376.

Adulteration of liquors.] The Sale of Food Act, 1879, 42 & 43 Vict. c. 30, s. 6, now enacts that in determining whether an offence has been committed under section 6 of the Act 38 & 39 Vict. c. 63, by selling to the prejudice of the purchaser spirits not adulterated otherwise than by the admixture of water, it shall be a good defence to prove that such admixture has not reduced the spirit more than twenty-five degrees under proof, for brandy, whisky, or rum, or thirty-five degrees under proof for gin.

In *Pashler* v. *Stevenill*, 41 J. P. 136; 35 L. T. 862, a publican sold a bottle of gin without specifying any quality. When analysed it contained 44 per cent. of water. The court held there was

Sect. 14. **Adulteration of Liquors.**

NOTE. evidence to support a conviction for unlawfully selling gin not of the nature, substance, and quality demanded. So where the gin was 43 below proof: *Webb* v. *Knight,* 2 Q. B. D. 530; 46 L. J. M. C. 264 ; 26 W. R. 14 ; 41 J. P. 726 ; 36 L. T. 791. In another case of *Sandys* v. *Small,* 3 Q. B. D. 449 ; 42 J. P. 550 ; 47 L. J. M. C. 115 ; 39 L. T. 118 ; 26 W. R. 814, the publican stuck up a notice in his house in the smoke-room and bar, "all spirits sold here are mixed," and the court held that as the purchaser bought it with his eyes open, though it contained 30 per cent. of water, no offence was committed. So where a notice was stuck up "all spirits sold are diluted, no alcoholic strength guaranteed :" *Gage* v. *Elsey,* 10 Q. B. D. 518 ; 47 J. P. 391 ; 48 L. T. 226 ; 52 L. J. M. C. 44 ; 31 W. R. 500. Where such a notice was stuck up in the bars and the kitchen, but not in a room to which customers went and were served, it was held that the license holder could not be convicted if the customers knew of the notice or the practice of the house : *Morris* v. *Johnson,* 54 J. P. 612. See also *Morris* v. *Askew,* 57 J. P. 724.

Prohibition against adulteration of beer.] (1.) A brewer of beer for sale shall not adulterate beer, or add any matter or thing thereto (except finings for the purpose of clarification or other matter or thing sanctioned by the Commissioners of Inland Revenue) before the same is delivered for consumption, and any beer found to be adulterated or mixed with any other matter or thing (except as aforesaid) in the possession of a brewer of beer for sale shall be forfeited, and the brewer shall incur a fine of 50*l.*

(2.) A dealer in or retailer of beer shall not adulterate or dilute beer, or add any matter or thing thereto (except finings for the purpose of clarification), and any beer found to be adulterated or diluted or mixed with any other matter or thing (except finings) in the possession of a dealer in or retailer of beer shall be forfeited, and he shall incur a fine of 50*l.*: 48 & 49 Vict. c. 51, s. 8.

To mix good beer with an inferior quality of beer is adulteration: *Crofts* v. *Taylor,* 19 Q. B. D. 324 ; 51 J. P. 789 ; 56 L. J. M. C. 137 ; 57 L. T. 310; 36 W. R. 47.

Provisions to be applied to allowances and penalties.] The powers and provisions contained in any Act relating to excise allowances, or to penalties or forfeitures under Excise Acts, and now or hereafter in force, shall respectively be of full force and effect with respect to the allowances mentioned in this part of this Act, and the penalties and forfeitures thereby imposed, so far as the same are applicable and are consistent with the provisions of this Act, as fully and effectually as if the same had

Adulteration of Liquors.   Sect. 14.

been herein specially enacted with reference to the last mentioned   NOTE.
allowances, penalties, and forfeitures respectively : 48 & 49 Vict.
c. 51, s. 9.

Procedure under Sale of Food Acts.] The word "food" includes every article used for food or drink by man other than drugs or water: 38 & 39 Vict. c. 63, s. 2. The proceedings to recover penalties are under the Summary Jurisdiction Acts : *Ibid.* s. 20. But all summonses for the offence must be served within a reasonable time, and in the case of perishable articles, not exceeding twenty-eight days from the date of purchase, and the summons must state the prosecutor's name and particulars of the offence, and must be made returnable in not less than seven days after service : 42 & 43 Vict. c. 30, s. 10 ; *Dixon* v. *Wells,* 54 J. P. 725 ; 25 Q. B. D. 249 ; 62 L. T. 812 ; *Barnes* v. *Rider,* 68 L. T. 447 ; 57 J. P. 473.

It is not necessary to prove that the seller knew of the adulteration : *Betts* v. *Armstead,* 20 Q. B. D. 721 ; 52 J. P. 471 ; 57 L. J. M. C. 100 ; 58 L. T. 811 ; 38 W. R. 720 ; *Pain* v. *Boughtwood,* 24 Q. B. D. 353 ; 55 J. P. 469. And the master does not escape liability, though the servant acted contrary to orders in selling adulterated food : *Hotchin* v. *Hindmarsh* (1891), 2 Q. B. 181 ; 55 J. P. 775 ; 65 L. T. 149 ; *Kearly* v. *Tyler,* 56 J. P. 72 ; 65 L. T. 261 ; 60 L. J. M. C. 159 ; *Brown* v. *Foot,* 56 J. P. 84 ; 66 L. T. 649 ; *Dyke* v. *Gower,* 65 L. T. 760 ; 56 J. P. 168. The false representation must be made at the time of the sale and not at a prior time : *Kirk* v. *Coates,* 16 Q. B. D. 49 ; 50 J. P. 148 ; 55 L. J. M. C. 182 ; 54 L. T. 178 ; 34 W. R. 295.

The sale is deemed to be to the prejudice of the purchaser unless the purchaser is told of the mixture and makes no objection : *Sandys* v. *Small,* L. R. 3 Q. B. 49 ; 42 J. P. 550 ; 26 W. R. 814 ; *Higgins* v. *Hall,* 51 J. P. 293. And it is equally to the purchaser's prejudice, though the purchaser is an inspector using the ratepayers' money : *Hoyle* v. *Hitchman,* 4 Q. B. D. 233 ; 43 J. P. 430. It is no defence that the purchaser bought only for analysis : 42 & 43 Vict. c. 30, s. 2.

Where an inspector of constabulary had been authorised by quarter sessions to act in the execution of the Sale of Food Acts, and called at P.'s public-house not in uniform, and not known to P. as duly authorised, and demanded to be supplied with gin, the court held that P. was bound on request to supply the inspector under 38 & 39 Vict. c. 63, s. 17, with gin, and also was bound to serve him with the liquor from the same bottle as that from which the inspector had already been supplied : *Payne* v. *Hack,* 57 J. P. 325.

Sect. 14.   *Adulteration of Liquors.*

NOTE.   When an inspector sends a messenger into the place of sale and waits outside, the inspector is the purchaser: *Stace* v. *Smith,* 45 J. P. 141 ; *Horder* v. *Scott,* 5 Q. B. D. 552 ; 49 L. J. M. C. 78 ; 42 L. T. 660 ; 44 J. P. 520 ; 28 W. R. 918 ; *Somerset* v. *Miller,* 54 J. P. 614 ; *Garford* v. *Esam,* 56 J. P. 85. The purchaser must notify the intention to have the article analysed : *Barnes* v. *Chipp,* 3 Ex. D. 176 ; 47 L. J. M. C. 85 ; 38 L. T. 570 ; 26 W. R. 635. But calling the analyst the county instead of the public analyst, if he is both, is no objection : *Wheeker* v. *Webb,* 51 J. P. 661. If there is no evidence to contradict the analyst's certificate the justices are bound to act upon it: *Harrison* v. *Richards,* 45 J. P. 552.

When a defence is made under 38 & 39 Vict. c. 63, s. 25, that the article had been purchased by the seller with a written warranty as to its nature, the warranty must be specific and not general : *Harris* v. *May,* 12 Q. B. D. 97 ; 48 J. P. 281 ; 32 W. R. 595 ; 53 L. J. M. C. 39 ; *Farmers* v. *Stevenson,* 60 L. J. M. C. 70 ; 63 L. T. 776 ; 55 J. P. 407 ; *Elder* v. *Smithson,* 57 J. P. 740. The offence under section 6 is not confined to adulteration, but extends to articles when they are different in substance and quality : *Knight* v. *Bowers,* 14 Q. B. D. 845 ; 49 J. P. 614 ; 54 L. J. M. C. 108 ; 53 L. T. 234 ; 33 W. R. 613.

15. *Temporary continuance of licenses forfeited for single offences.*] Where any licensed person is convicted for the first time of any one of the following offences :—

1, Making an internal communication between his licensed premises and any unlicensed premises :

2. Forging a certificate under the Wine and Beerhouse Acts, 1869 and 1870 ;

3. Selling spirits without a spirit license ;

4. Any felony ;

and in consequence either becomes personally disqualified or has his license forfeited, there may be made by

37 & 38 VICT. C. 49, S. 15.

or on behalf of the owner of the premises an application to a court of summary jurisdiction for authority to carry on the same business on the same premises until the next special sessions for licensing purposes, and a further application to such next special sessions for the grant of a license in respect of such premises, and for this purpose the provisions contained in the Intoxicating Liquor Licensing Act, 1828, with respect to the grant of a temporary authority, and to the grant of licenses at special sessions, shall apply as if the person convicted had been rendered incapable of keeping an inn, and the person applying for such grant was his assignee.

Sect. 15.

This section refers to making an internal communication contrary to the Licensing Act, 1872, section 9; forging a certificate contrary to 32 & 33 Vict. c. 27, s. 11; selling spirits without a license contrary to Licensing Act, 1872, section 3, and a conviction for felony forfeiting a license, as to both of which see 3 & 4 Vict. c. 61, s. 7; 23 Vict. c. 27, s. 22; and 33 & 34 Vict. c. 29, s. 14. The words "where any person is convicted" imply that the conviction must take place after this Act. This section in future brings these cases expressly within the words "incapable of keeping an inn," as used in 9 Geo. 4, c. 61, s. 14. But the court has decided that in the case of a conviction for felony, the landlord and new tenant have not all the remedies of new tenants under 9 Geo. 4, c. 61, s. 14, but are restricted to the two remedies above stated, namely, an application to petty sessions under 5 & 6 Vict. c. 44, and then a further application to the next transfer sessions: *Stevens* v. *Sharnbrook JJ.*, 23 Q. B. D. 143; 58 L. J. M. C. 167; 61 L. T. 240; 37 W. R. 605; 53 J. P. 423.

The court has decided that the justices have the same but not a greater discretion as to granting or refusing the transfer license to the landlord or new tenant, when the licensed person has been convicted of felony: *R.* v. *Moore* or *Hertfordshire JJ.*, 7 Q. B. D. 542; 45 J. P. 768; 50 L. J. M. C. 121. And he is equally entitled to appeal to quarter sessions: *R.* v. *West Riding*, 11 Q. B. D. 417; 52 L. J. M. C. 99; 48 J. P. 149. As to those cases where the justices on renewal or a new grant have a discretion limited to the four grounds, the same limit will, in most cases, apply to applications for transfer: *Simmonds* v. *Blackheath JJ.*, 17 Q. B. D. 765; 50 J. P. 742; 55 L. J. M. C. 166; 35 W. R. 167.

O

LICENSING ACT, 1874, S. 16.

Regulations as to Entry on Premises.

16. *Constable to enter on premises for enforcement of Act.*] Any constable may, for the purpose of preventing or detecting the violation of any of the provisions of the principal Act or this Act which it is his duty to enforce, at all times enter on any licensed premises, or any premises in respect of which an occasional license is in force.

Every person who, by himself, or by any person in his employ, or acting by his direction or with his consent, refuses or fails to admit any constable in the execution of his duty demanding to enter in pursuance of this section, shall be liable to a penalty not exceeding for the first offence five pounds, and not exceeding for the second and every subsequent offence ten pounds.

Though under this section the constable seems not bound to give special reasons to the licensed person before entering a licensed house, yet in case of dispute as to the right of entry he will not be justified, without being able to show some reasonable ground to the court for thinking that the statute was about to be or had been violated. And on proving the offence in the second paragraph the constable must allege and prove some reasonable ground for entering. If, however, the constable says he wants to see if there was anything wrong in the house as he was going a round of visiting all the licensed houses, this will be deemed a sufficient reason for demanding entry: *R.* v. *Dobbin,* 48 J. P. 182. There is no limit as to the hour of demanding entry, but justices will always consider whether the time was reasonable.

Where a constable had visited C.'s house twenty minutes previously, but hearing a noise again demanded an entry, &c., and C.'s wife being at the door and saying he should not get in till he had heard her opinion of him, yet after some abuse he was allowed to go in, the husband (C.) knowing nothing of what had taken place outside, it was held this was no evidence that C. had refused admittance, as he was not bound by the acts of the wife as his manager: *Caswell* v. *Hundred JJ.,* 54 J. P. 87.

37 & 38 VICT. C. 49, S. 17.   195

The word "premises" includes outhouses : *R.* v. *Tott,* 30 L. J. **Sect. 16.**
M. C. 177 ; 4 L. T. 306 ; 25 J. P. 327 ; 9 W. R. 663.
The right of a constable to enter is confined to licensed premises, that is to say, premises licensed by the justices ; for if a spirit dealer under a dealer's retail license sells spirits not to be consumed on the premises under 24 & 25 Vict. c. 21, s. 2, and so is exempt from a justice's license under section 73, then the constable has no right to enter : *Harrison* v. *MacL'Meel,* 48 J. P. 469 ; 50 L. T. 210.

NOTE.

The Prevention of Crimes Act, 1871, 34 & 35 Vict. c. 112, s. 12, which imposed higher penalties upon all who assault or wilfully obstruct any constable, now extends to all cases of resisting or wilfully obstructing any constable in the execution of his duty, providing the penalty on a first conviction shall not be greater than 5*l.*, and the imprisonment in default not more than two months : 48 & 49 Vict. c. 75, s. 2.

17. *Search warrant for detection of liquors sold or kept contrary to law.*] Any justice of the peace if satisfied by information on oath that there is reasonable ground to believe that any intoxicating liquor is sold by retail or exposed or kept for sale by retail at any place within his jurisdiction, whether a building or not, in which such liquor is not authorised to be sold by retail, may in his discretion grant a warrant under his hand, by virtue whereof it shall be lawful for any constable named in such warrant, at any time or times within one month from the date thereof, to enter, and, if need be by force, the place named in the warrant, and every part thereof, and examine the same and search for intoxicating liquor therein, and seize and remove any intoxicating liquor found therein which there is reasonable ground to suppose is in such place for the purpose of unlawful sale at that or any other place, and the vessels containing such liquor ; and in the event of the owner or occupier of such premises being convicted

o 2

Sect. 17. of selling by retail or exposing or keeping for sale by retail any liquor which he is not authorised to sell by retail, the intoxicating liquor so seized and the vessels containing such liquor shall be forfeited.

When a constable has entered any premises in pursuance of any such warrant as is mentioned in this section, and has seized and removed such liquor as aforesaid, any person found at the time on the premises shall, until the contrary is proved, be deemed to have been on such premises for the purpose of illegally dealing in intoxicating liquor, and be liable to a penalty not exceeding forty shillings.

Any constable may demand the name and address of any person found on any premises on which he seizes or from which he removes any such liquor as aforesaid, and if he has reasonable ground to suppose that the name or address given is false, may examine such person further as to the correctness of such name and address, and may, if such person fail upon such demand to give his name or address, or to answer satisfactorily the questions put to him by the constable, apprehend him without warrant, and carry him as soon as practicable before a justice of the peace.

Any person required by a constable under this section to give his name and address who fails to give the same, or gives a false name or address, or gives false information with respect to such name and address, shall be liable to a penalty not exceeding five pounds.

<small>Under this section the liquor and vessels can only be forfeited in the event of the owner or occupier being convicted, and the conviction would be under Act, 1872, s. 3; but the forfeiture follows as a direct consequence of the conviction. The forfeited</small>

articles may be sold under section 51 of the Licensing Act, 1872. **Sect. 17.**
But before sale the owner should have an opportunity of being
heard: *Gill* v. *Bright*, 41 L. J. M. C. 28; 36 J. P. 168; 25 L. T. **Note.**
591; 20 W. R. 248.

The officers of Inland Revenue can enter licensed houses under such sections as 7 & 8 Geo. 4, c. 53, s. 22; 3 & 4 Vict. c. 61, ss. 11, 12; and 23 Vict. c. 27, s. 24.

The two last paragraphs are similar to those in section 25 of the Licensing Act, 1872. There is a like penalty imposed by that section on persons found on licensed premises during closing hours in contravention of the Act, 1872. See Act, 1872, s. 25, and notes, *ante*, p. 57. The words "illegally dealing" make the consumer of the liquor punishable: *Mackenzie* v. *Day* (1893), 1 Q. B. 289; 57 J. P. 216; 62 L. J. M. C. 49; 68 L. T. 345.

Occasional Licenses.

18. *Occasional license required at fairs and races.*] Any person selling or exposing for sale any intoxicating liquor in any booth, tent, or place within the limits of holding any lawful and accustomed fair or any races without an *occasional license* authorising such sale shall, notwithstanding anything contained in any Act of Parliament to the contrary, be deemed to be a person selling or exposing for sale by retail intoxicating liquor at a place where he is not authorised by his license to sell the same, and be punished accordingly.

Provided that this section shall not apply to any person selling or exposing for sale intoxicating liquors in premises in which he is duly authorised to sell the same throughout the year although such premises are situate with the limits aforesaid.

This section abolishes an exemption long enjoyed under a series of statutes by keepers of some licensed houses of frequenting fairs and races to sell liquors in booths (see *Hayward* v. *Holland*, 28 L. T. 702; 21 W. R. 920; 37 J. P. 376), and renders it necessary for them henceforth in all cases to obtain a justices'

Sect. 18.
NOTE.
occasional license, otherwise the penalty of selling without a license is incurred under Act, 1872, s. 3. See 24 & 25 Vict. c. 91, s. 13; 25 & 26 Vict. c. 22, s. 13; 26 & 27 Vict. c. 33, ss. 19, 24; 27 & 28 Vict. c. 18, s. 5, and next section of this Act.

As to the exception formerly preserved in favour of beerhouses and fairs, see 1 Will. 4, c. 64, s. 29, *post*.

19. *Occasional licenses—Extension of time for closing.*] Whereas by 25 & 26 Vict. c. 33, s. 20, it is provided that the hours during which an *occasional license* shall authorise the sale of any beer, spirits, or wine shall extend from sunrise until one hour after sunset: Be it enacted, that the said section shall be construed as if in place of the words "sunrise until one hour after sunset" there were inserted the words "such hour not earlier than sunrise until such hour not later than ten o'clock at night as may be specified in that behalf in the consent given by the justice for the granting of such occasional license."

See 26 & 27 Vict. c. 33, s. 20, *post*; 27 & 28 Vict. c. 18, s. 5, *post*.

20. *Offences on premises with occasional license.*] For the purpose of so much of the principal Act as relates to offences against public order, that is to say, sections twelve to eighteen, both inclusive, and the sections for giving effect to the same, a person taking out an occasional license shall be deemed to be a licensed person within the meaning of the said sections, and the place in which any intoxicating liquors are sold in pursuance of the occasional license shall be deemed to be licensed premises, and to be the premises of the person taking out such license.

See sections 12 to 18 of Licensing Act, 1872, and notes.

37 & 38 VICT. C. 49, S. 22. 199

Sect. 21.

Miscellaneous.

21. *Supply of deficiency in quota of borough justices on joint committee.*] Where from any reason there are not for the time being three qualified borough justices to form the quota of a joint committee for such borough, in pursuance of section thirty-eight of the principal Act, the deficiency in the number of such borough justices shall be supplied by qualified county justices to be appointed by the county licensing committee.

See section 38 of the Licensing Act, 1872, where the necessary amendment is made, and notes.

22. *Provisional grant and confirmation of licenses to new premises.*] Any person interested in any premises about to be constructed or in course of construction for the purpose of being used as a house for the sale of intoxicating liquors to be consumed on the premises may apply to the licensing justices and to the confirming authority for the provisional grant and confirmation of a license in respect of such premises; and the justices and confirming authority, if satisfied with the plans submitted to them of such house, and that if such premises had been actually constructed in accordance with such plans they would, on application, have granted and confirmed such a license in respect thereof, may make such provisional grant and order of confirmation accordingly.

A provisional grant and order of confirmation shall not be of any validity until it has been declared to be

Sect. 22. final by an order of the licensing justices made after such notice has been given as may be required by the justices at a general annual licensing meeting or a special sessions held for licensing purposes. Such declaration shall be made if the justices are satisfied that the house has been completed in accordance with such plans as aforesaid, and are also satisfied that no objection can be made to the character of the holder of such provisional license.

A provisional grant and confirmation of a license shall be subject to the same conditions as to the giving of notices and generally as to procedure to which such grant and confirmation would be subject if they respectively were not provisional, with this exception, that where a notice is required to be put up on a door of a house such notice may be put up in a conspicuous position on any part of the premises.

This section shall, with the necessary variations, extend to the provisional removal to any premises of an existing license under section fifty of the principal Act.

> This was a new provision, though under the previous law it was competent to justices under 9 Geo. 4, c. 61, to grant a license to persons about to keep an inn though the inn was not finished. This section expressly recognises the practice, and allows it in all cases of houses to be licensed for consumption on the premises.
>
> It is imperative on the justices to grant the final license after the provisional grant is made if satisfied that the plan has been carried out, and as to the character of the applicant. But the justices cannot be said to be merely acting ministerially when called on to confirm the provisional order. In one case the justices assented to the grant subject to an alteration suggested as to the site, which alteration was agreed to at the time; but justices never met again nor assented to any other site, and it

was held that the applicant was entitled to act upon the original Sect. 22.
plan shown to the justices: *R.* v. *Cox*, 48 J. P. 440. The
licensing justices, at the time of the provisional grant being NOTE.
applied for and allowed, should specify what notice an applicant
is to give before coming before them for the final order, for the
licensing justices may obviously make this final order at any
period of the year between the general annual meetings. But
there is nothing in this or the other Acts to make it compulsory
on the justices to renew the license thereafter when made final,
any more than in ordinary cases. Should the building be not
completed within the licensing year, the owner is entitled to apply
for a renewal as in other cases, and to appeal to quarter sessions
if such renewal is refused: *R.* v. *London County Justices*, 54 J. P.
213; 24 Q. B. D. 341; 59 L. J. M. C. 71; 62 L. T. 700; 38
W. R. 330. The licensing justices are to make the final order,
and the confirming authority need not again confirm the final
license.

The application for a provisional grant must be made at the
general annual licensing meeting, or the adjourned meeting,
though the final license may be made at any time, and what
notice is to be given on the latter case may be fixed at a special
transfer sessions. There seems to be no limit of time within
which the applicant *must* apply for the final order; but a reasonable time may be said to be implied, for if delayed the interests
of third parties, who would otherwise apply, may be interfered
with.

Where the plan approved by the justices had been designed for
a level site, and the owner, when about to build, asked the justices to allow certain small alterations adapted to a sloping site,
which they refused, the court held the owner was entitled to
make the alterations on his own authority, as they were not material: *R.* v. *London County Justices*, 54 J. P. 213; 24 Q. B. D. 341;
59 L. J. M. C. 71; 62 L. T. 700; 38 W. R. 330. And in the
same case the justices refusing to make a final order because the
original plan had been confirmed by the confirming authority, the
court held that the licensing justices had power, without consent
of the confirming authority, to make a final order, notwithstanding
the alterations, as these were not substantial alterations: *R.* v.
Pownal, 62 L. T. 418; 54 J. P. 438.

This application may be combined with the application for
removal as authorised by Act, 1872, section 50, *ante*, p. 105.

23. *One license of justices may extend to several excise licenses.*] Separate licenses of justices

Sect. 23. shall not be required in the case of separate excise licenses, and a license of justices shall comprehend a permission to the licensee to take out as many excise licenses as may be specified in such license of the justices.

The effect of this section will be to make only one fee payable instead of a fee applicable to each separate license.

24. *Confirmation of license to sell liquor not to be consumed on the premises not required.*] A license to sell any intoxicating liquor for consumption only off the premises shall not require confirmation by any authority.

The Act, 1872, laid down the rule that no new license, whether an off-license or an on-license, should be valid until it was confirmed by the confirming authority. There is now an exception to the necessity of a confirmation as regards off-licenses: see Licensing Act, 1872, sections 37, 38; and the same applies also to off-licenses removed under section 50, *ante*, p. 105.

25. *Joint committee to make rules under section 43 of principal Act.*] Where the confirming authority is a joint committee, that committee shall make rules in pursuance of section forty-three of the principal Act as to the proceedings to be adopted for the confirmation of new licenses, and as to the costs of such proceedings, and the persons by whom such costs are to be paid.

See Licensing Act, 1872, section 43, where the necessary amendment here directed is made, and notes, *ante*, p. 93.

26. *Notices of adjourned brewster sessions and of intention to oppose.*] Whereas by section forty-two

37 & 38 VICT. c. 49, s. 26.

of the principal Act it is enacted that a licensed person **Sect. 26.**
applying for the renewal of his license need not attend
in person at the general annual licensing meeting unless
he is required by the licensing justices so to attend :
Be it enacted, that such requisition shall not be made,
save for some special cause personal to the licensed
person to whom such requisition is sent.

It shall not be necessary to serve copies of notices of
any adjournment of a general annual licensing meeting
on holders of licenses or applicants for licenses who are
not required to attend at such adjourned annual general
licensing meeting.

A notice of an intention to oppose the renewal of a
license served under section forty-two of the principal
Act shall not be valid unless it states in general terms
the grounds on which the renewal of such license is to
be opposed.

See Licensing Act, 1872, section 42, and notes, *ante,* p. 87.

This section takes from the justices the power of compelling
the attendance of parties seeking a renewal of their licenses or
certificates, unless for some cause personal to the applicants. Nor
need applicants be served, as a matter of course, with notice to
attend. The word "personal" is flexible, and is capable of a
very wide signification, as to which see *Sharp* v. *Wakefield* (1891),
1 App. Cas. 473 ; 60 L. J. M. C. 8 ; 55 J. P. 197 ; 64 L. T. 180 ;
39 W. R. 561. It is not to be assumed, however, that the
applicant is not to make application at each renewal, which
he must always do, either by himself or by some authorised
messenger. See *R.* v. *Newcastle JJ.,* 51 J. P. 244. And each
holder of a license is entitled to have notice served upon him of
the time and place of the original or general annual meeting :
9 Geo. 4, c. 61, s. 2.

When the justices themselves start the objection and give an
opportunity to the party to answer it, they are bound to receive
the evidence on oath : *R.* v. *Eales,* 44 J. P. 553 ; 42 L. T. 735.
See also *R.* v. *Howard, Justices of Congleton,* 53 J. P. 454 ; 23
Q. B. D. 502 ; 60 L. T. 960 ; 37 W. R. 617.

LICENSING ACT, 1874, S. 28.

Sect. 27.   **27.** *No appeal to quarter sessions in certain cases.*] No appeal shall be had to quarter sessions from any act of any justice with respect to the grant of new certificates under the Wine and Beerhouse Acts, 1869 and 1870. (Some words at the beginning *repealed* by 46 & 47 Vict. c. 39, Sched.)

> This section was necessary in consequence of the court holding, in *R.* v. *Smith, R.* v. *Southport JJ.*, L. R. 8 Q. B. 146; 37 J. P. 214; 42 L. J. M. C. 46; 28 L. T. 129; 21 W. R. 382; that the enactments incorporated in 32 & 33 Vict. c. 27, s. 8, though themselves repealed, kept alive the power of appeal to quarter sessions against the refusal of new certificates.
>
> This does not affect the right of appeal to quarter sessions, which still applies to all refusals of transfers, or of renewals of certificates or licenses under the Wine and Beerhouse Acts. See 9 Geo. 4, c. 61, ss. 27—29; Act, 1872, Sched.; 32 & 33 Vict. c. 27, s. 8.

28. *Substitution of licensing justices for Commissioners of Inland Revenue as respects certain notices.*] [Whereas by 35 & 36 Vict. c. 94, s. 11 (*ante*, p. 21), it is provided that every licensed person shall cause to be printed or fixed, and shall keep painted or fixed, on the premises in respect of which his license is granted, in a conspicuous place, and in such form and manner as the Commissioners of Inland Revenue may from time to time direct, his name, with such additions as in the said Act mentioned; and whereas it is expedient to substitute in the said section the licensing justices for the Commissioners of Inland Revenue: this recital repealed by 56 & 57 Vict. c. 54.]

> In the said eleventh section the expression "licensing justices" shall be deemed to be substituted for the expression "Commissioners of Inland Revenue,"

37 & 38 VICT. C. 49, S. 30.

and the word "justices" for the word "com- Sect. 28.
missioners."

The Licensing Act, 1872, section 11, *ante*, p. 21, has been altered in the way here pointed out. See notes to that section.

29. *Definition of term " owner.*] Any person possessing an estate or interest in premises licensed for the sale of intoxicating liquors, whether as owner, lessee, or mortgagee, prior or paramount to that of the immediate occupier, shall on payment of a fee of one shilling to the clerk of the licensing justices, be entitled to be registered as owner or one of the owners of such premises : Provided that when such estate or interest is vested in two or more persons jointly, one only of such persons shall be registered as representing such estate or interest.

See the Licensing Act, 1872, section 36, and notes : also sections 56, 70, 74.

A mortgagee has been held to be sufficiently aggrieved by the refusal of the renewal of the tenant's license to be able to appeal to quarter sestions if the mortgage deed made the mortgagee attorney for the license holder in that respect : *Garrett* v. *Middlesex JJ.*, or *R.* v. *Garrett*, 12 Q. B. D. 620 ; 53 L. J. M. C. 81 ; 48 J. P. 357 ; 32 W. R. 357. But in general the landlord, as such, is a stranger to the license (except in those cases where notice of a conviction is to be sent to him), and cannot insist on appealing in his own right to quarter sessions against a conviction of the license holder : *R.* v. *Andover JJ.*, 16 Q. B. D. 711 ; 50 J. P. 549 ; 55 L. J. M. C. 143 ; 55 L. T. 23 ; 34 W. R. 456. Where, however, the renewal or transfer of a license is refused to his tenant, the landlord may join with the applicant in an appeal to quarter sessions, as he is an aggrieved party under 9 Geo. 4, c. 61, s. 27.

30. *Persons not to be liable for supplying liquor to private friends without charge.*] No person keeping a house licensed under this or the

Sect. 30. principal Act shall be liable to any penalty for supplying intoxicating liquors, after the hours of closing, to private friends *bonâ fide* entertained by him at his own expense.

> This section recognises as law what was already in effect declared by the courts to be the law under the previous Acts. The words "private friends" seem to include those who are not in the relative situation of customers. The justices have nothing to do with the occasion of the entertainment, except as throwing light on the fact whether the friends were pretended friends only and really paid for their entertainment in some substantial way, by exchange or otherwise, in the nature of a sale, as defined by the Licensing Act, 1872, section 62. The license holder, it is true, cannot obtain the benefit of this enactment by saying to the ordinary customers when the hour of closing arrives that if they stay he will treat them as private friends, as this may be an evasion of the Act : *Corbett* v. *Haigh*, 5 C. P. D. 50 ; 44 J. P. 39 ; 42 L. T. 185 ; 28 W. R. 430. And where a lodger in the house has invited friends, and entertains them at his own expense the license holder is not liable under section 9, *ante*, p. 178, merely because liquor is supplied to and consumed by the friends after closing hours : *Pine* v. *Barnes*, 20 Q. B. D. 221 ; 52 J. P. 199 ; 57 L. J. M. C. 28 ; 58 L T. 520 ; 36 W. R. 473. The entertainment must be in the licensed premises. Though the private friends may be lawfully on the premises during closing hours, yet the license holder will commit an offence if he allow them to carry on gaming, and it seems the friends themselves cannot be convicted of aiding in the offence : *Hare* v. *Osborne*, 34 L. T. 294 ; 40 J. P. 759 ; *Cooper* v. *Osborne*, 35 L. T. 347 ; 40 J. P. 759. And for a like reason he will be liable if he allows his friends to play at billiards : *Ovenden* v. *Raymond*, 40 J. P. 727 ; 34 L. T. 727.

31. *Additional retail license may be granted at special sessions for licensing.*] (*Repealed* by 43 Vict. c. 6, s. 2, *post*, which see.)

Definitions and Repeal.

32. *Definitions.*] In this Act, if not inconsistent with the context, the following expressions have the

meanings hereinafter respectively assigned to them; Sect. 32.
that is to say,—

"*The metropolitan district.*"] "The metropolitan district" means the area in that behalf mentioned in the schedule hereto.

"*Town.*"] "Town" means an urban sanitary district as described for the purposes of the Public Health Act, 1872; and any collection of houses adjacent to a town as so defined shall, for the purposes of the provisions of this Act with respect to the closing of premises, be deemed to be part of such town after it has been declared so to be by an order of the county licensing committee having jurisdiction in the place where such houses are situated: Provided that no urban sanitary district, whether including such adjacent houses or not shall be deemed a town, unless it contains one thousand inhabitants.

"*Populous place.*"] "Populous place" means any area with a population of not less than one thousand, which, by reason of the density of such population, the county licensing committee may by order determine to be a populous place.

At a meeting especially convened for that purpose in manner provided by any regulations in that behalf, or in default of such regulations, by the clerk of the peace, as soon as may be after the passing of this Act, and not later than the first day of September, one thousand eight hundred and seventy-four, the county licensing committee shall consider all the cases within their jurisdic-

Sect. 32. tion with respect to which it is incumbent upon them to make orders in pursuance of this section, and they shall make orders accordingly, and shall specify therein the boundaries of such towns or populous places.

The county licensing committee may adjourn any meeting held in pursuance of this section, and may also, at any subsequent meeting especially convened for that purpose, make with respect to any town or populous place within their jurisdiction any like order not restrictive of any order previously made.

Provided that as soon as may be after the publication of each census the county licensing committee shall, at a meeting to be especially convened for the purpose, revise the orders then in force within their jurisdiction, constituting areas either parts of towns or populous places, and may alter or cancel any of the said orders, or may make such further orders, if any, as they shall deem necessary to give effect to the provisions of this Act.

"*Occasional license.*"] "Occasional license" means a license to sell beer, spirits, or wine, granted in pursuance of 25 & 26 Vict. c. 22, s. 13, and 27 Vict. c. 18, s. 5, and the Acts amending the same in relation to the licenses therein mentioned, or of any such Acts.

"*A new license.*"] "A new license" means a license for the sale of any intoxicating liquor, granted at a general annual licensing meeting in respect of premises in respect of which a similar license has not theretofore been granted.

Town.] This definition of "*town*" refers to the Public Health Act, 1872 (35 & 36 Vict. c. 79, s. 4). That Act is now repealed and superseded by the Public Health Act, 1875 (38 & 39 Vict. c. 55), and though the Act, 1872, is incorporated in this Act, still the definition of urban sanitary district is repeated almost *verbatim* in the Public Health Act, 1875, and thus no difference is caused by the subsequent repeal. Both Acts define an urban sanitary district as (1) any borough constituted such either before or after the passing of that Act; (2) an Improvement Act district, constituted such before that Act (*i.e.*, before 10th August, 1872), and having no part of its area situate within a borough or local government district; (3) any local government district, constituted such either before or after that Act, having no part of its area situated within a borough and not coincident in area with a borough or Improvement Act district. The definition of "town" in Act, 1872, s. 74, was repealed by this Act, section 33, *post*.

Sect. 32.

NOTE.

Populous place.] As to the definition of "*populous place*," which is used in this Act, section 3, *ante*, p. 169, for regulating the closing time of licensed houses, the county licensing committee might meet before 1st September, 1874, and decide whether any part of their district could be called a populous place. The only limit to their discretion in this matter was, that they should not declare any place to be populous which had less than a population of 1,000. And the last published census was the test of population according to Act, 1872, section 65, *ante*, p. 137. The area was, however, left undefined as to extent, and it was for the justices to define it. The "regulations in that behalf" for the meeting of the county licensing committee are those made in pursuance of the Licensing Act, 1872, section 37. Where an order as to a populous place has been once made there is no power given to restrict it, *i.e.*, to reduce the area of the operation of the order till the next census. But there seems nothing to prevent the county licensing committee acting from time to time after 1st September, 1874, and declaring new places, or increasing places, as populous places within the meaning of this section.

Occasional license.] As to *occasional* licenses authorising the sale of liquor at other places than licensed premises, see 25 & 26 Vict. c. 22, s. 13, *post;* 26 & 27 Vict. c. 33, ss. 19—21, *post;* 27 & 28 Vict. c. 18, s. 5, *post;* and the 18th, 19th, and 20th sections of this Act of 1874.

New license.] The new definition of "*new license*" contains the word "similar," which can scarcely be construed as meaning "identically the same." The word seems properly to imply that

P

the license must be for the same kind of liquor, and the same general character as regards its being in-door or out-door, and as to any particular qualification attached to it. Different kinds of liquor have been dealt with by separate statutes, and yet all licenses have some points identical. Yet an alehouse license under 9 Geo. 4, c. 61, is not similar to a beerhouse license under 1 Will. 4, for the former includes wines and spirits: *Marwick* v. *Codlin*, L. R. 9 Q. B. 509; 38 J. P. 518; 43 L. J. M. C. 169; 30 L. T. 719; 22 W. R. 823. It may now be taken that a six-day license is not similar to an ordinary seven-day license, though the liquors sold may be identical: *R.* v. *Crewkerne JJ.*, 21 Q. B. D. 85; 52 J. P. 372; 57 L. J. M. C. 127; 60 L. T. 84; 36 W. R. 629. The word "theretofore" does not necessarily mean that the previous license must be subsisting continuously, at least if this was owing to no default of the occupier of the premises: *R.* v. *Market Bosworth*, 51 J. P. 438; 57 L. T. 56; 35 W. R. 734; 56 L. J. M. C. 96. But if the license has been forfeited for some offence, the next application must usually be for a new license: *R.* v. *West Riding JJ.*, 52 J. P. 455; 21 Q. B. D. 258; 57 L. J. M. C. 103; 36 W. R. 258; unless in those cases specified in this Act, section 15, *ante*, p. 192; *Stevens* v. *Green*, or *Sharnbrook JJ.*, 53 J. P. 423; 23 Q. B. D. 143; 58 L. J. M. C. 167; 61 L. T. 240; 37 W. R. 605.

33. *Repeal.*] [There are hereby repealed the sections of the principal Act (35 & 36 Vict. c. 94) relating to the following matters; that is to say,—

(1.) Sections 19 to 22, both inclusive, relating to adulteration, and the first schedule to the principal Act;

(2.) Section 24, relating to hours of closing; and

(3.) Section 35, relating to entry on premises by constable; and

(4.) So much of sections 5, 6, 13, 14, 16, 17, and 28, as relates to the records of conviction on licenses, and of section 74, as contains the definition of a town for the purposes of the provisions with respect to closing and of a new license.

37 & 38 VICT. C. 49, SCHED. 211

(5.) The last paragraph of section 56, beginning with words, "In a county the justices," to the end of the section :]   Sect. 33.

This section was repealed by 46 & 47 Vict. c. 39, Sched., but is here retained for convenience of showing the mode of dealing with some sections in the Act, 1872.

SCHEDULE.

METROPOLITAN DISTRICT.

The Metropolitan District.] The city of London or the liberties thereof, or any parish or place for the time being subject to the jurisdiction of the Metropolitan Board of Works, or within the area contained within a circle the radius of which is four miles from Charing Cross.

[The jurisdiction of the Metropolitan Board of Works was defined by 18 & 19 Vict. c. 120, s. 249 ; 25 & 26 Vict. c. 120, s. 42.]

APPENDIX

OF RELATIVE STATUTES IN CHRONOLOGICAL ORDER.

THE ALEHOUSE ACT, 1828.

9 GEO. 4, CAP. 61.

AN ACT to regulate the granting of Licenses to Keepers of Inns, Alehouses, and Victualling Houses in England.(a)
[15th July, 1828.]

General licensing meetings to be held annually—Time of holding such meetings.] In every division of every county and riding, and of every division of the county of Lincoln, and in every hundred of every county, not being within any such division, and in every liberty, division of every liberty, county of a city, county of a town, city, and town corporate in that part of the United Kingdom called England, there shall be annually holden a special session of the justices of the peace (to be called the general annual licensing meeting), for the purpose of granting licenses to persons keeping or being about to keep inns, alehouses, and victualling houses, to sell excisable liquors by retail, to be drunk or consumed on the premises therein specified; and such meetings shall be holden in the counties of Middlesex and Surrey within the first ten days of the month of March, and in every other county on some day between the twentieth day of

---

(a) This Act was described in the Licensing Act, 1872, s. 74, as "The Intoxicating Liquor Licensing Act, 1828," but now it is to be known as "The Alehouse Act, 1828 :" 55 Vict. c. 10.

The recital and some words in this and other sections were struck out by the Statute Revision Act, 53 & 54 Vict. c. 33.

August and the fourteenth day of September inclusive; and it shall be lawful for the justices acting in and for such county or place assembled at such meeting, or at any adjournment thereof, and not as hereinafter disqualified from acting, to grant licenses for the purposes aforesaid, to such persons as they, the said justices, shall, in the execution of the powers herein contained, and in the exercise of their discretion, deem fit and proper.(b)

Appndx.

(b) *General effect of this Act.*—This is now the enactment governing all the houses requiring a justices' license or certificate. It applied primarily only to inns, alehouses, and victualling houses, but was extended to all the other houses by 32 & 33 Vict. c. 27, ss. 5, 8, and 33 & 34 Vict. c. 29, s. 4, and Licensing Act, 1872, ss. 68, 74. It repealed all the former statutes on the subject, and which are enumerated in section 35, *post*. The general result, therefore, is that nearly all retail licenses to sell intoxicating liquor are now subject to the same rules as to the justices who grant licenses, the times at which the meetings of justices are held, the duration of licenses, the fees payable, the rights of appeal so far as these exist, the mode of transferring and renewing the licenses. The Act, however, being modified by the Licensing Acts, 1872—74, the result is, that there is now no appeal against the refusal of a new license, but only against refusals to transfer or renew existing licenses, and the discretion of justices at the various stages is not uniform, the discretion being now absolute as to the great majority of licenses, and limited to four grounds as regards a few of the licenses. Moreover, nearly all the offences relating to licensed houses are now provided for in the two Licensing Acts, 1872—74, exclusively.

Justices' license, how far necessary.] The general rule now is, that a justices' license is necessary before an excise license can be obtained. But there is an exception where a wine dealer obtains an additional retail license from the excise to sell wine not to be consumed on the premises. And a grocer may be a wine dealer to that extent: *Palmer* v. *Thatcher*, 3 Q. B. D. 46; 42 J. P. 213; 47 L. J. M. C. 54; 46 L. T. 347. And a spirit dealer may also in some cases not require a justices' license to sell spirits by retail. See Act, 1872, s. 73, and notes, *ante*, p. 148. And wherever the house is situated it must be licensed by some authority. Thus, a license is necessary to sell in a desert island some miles from the county: *Wright* v. *Harris*, 49 J. P. 180. But it is not an indictable offence to keep an inn without a publichouse license: *Anon.*, 3 Salk. 25; *R.* v. *Edwards*, 3 Salk. 27. And a boarding-house keeper who merely sends out for liquors as agent of the guest does not require a license: *Parker* v. *Flint*, 12 Mod. 254; 1 L. Raym. 479; *Taylor* v. *Oram*, 1 H. & C. 370; 31 L. J. M. C. 252; 27 J. P. 8; 7 L. T. 68; 10 W. R. 800.

Mode of justices exercising discretion.] At the general annual licensing meeting and its adjournment, the justices sit in public and

ALEHOUSE ACT, 1828, S. 1.

Discretion of Justices.

act judicially, and are bound to hear the applications of all persons within their division who desire to have licenses, and who have complied with the statutes as to notices, and who can prove the requisite qualifications. At the same time, any one of the public is entitled to oppose the grant of a new license; and every applicant is bound to state the name of the owner of the house to be licensed: Licensing Act, 1872, section 36, *ante*, p. 73. The justices at the general annual licensing meeting have, as a general rule, an absolute discretion to refuse a grant of a new license for an inn under this Act, or for in-door beer and wine houses, first licensed after 1872, without stating reasons. This discretion of the justices must, however, be a judicial discretion and not a mere capricious act, regardless of the special circumstances of each application: *R.* v. *Boteler*, 4 B. & S. 959; 33 L. J. M. C. 101; 28 J. P. 453. As to some out-door certificates and in-door certificates, the justices have only a limited discretion: 32 & 33 Vict. c. 27, ss. 8, 19. Yet they act judicially, and an appeal to quarter sessions lies, except against their refusing a new grant, for the appeal against refusing new licenses was entirely taken away by the Act, 1872, though retained when the refusal is of a transfer or a renewal of the license. See Licensing Act, 1872, Schedule. No action lies against the justices for refusal: *Basset* v. *Goodchild*, 3 Wils. 121. They may rightly refuse a license under this Act, on the ground that there are already too many alehouses: *R.* v. *Lancashire JJ., Re Tyson*, 35 J. P. 170; 40 L. J. M. C. 17; L. R. 6 Q. B. 97; 23 L. T. 461; 19 W. R. 204; or that the house is too far removed from police supervision: *Sharp* v. *Wakefield* (1891), 1 App. C. 473; 55 J. P. 212; 60 L. J. Q. B. 209; 64 L. T. 180; 39 W. R. 561. They do wrong, however, to lay down a rule before hearing the applications, such as that they will refuse all licenses, except the party will promise to take out an excise license to sell spirits: *R.* v. *Sylvester*, 31 L. J. M. C. 93; 26 J. P. 151; 2 B. & S. 322; 5 L. T. 794; 8 Jur. (N.S.) 484. Nor can they lay down any general rule beforehand to fetter their discretion, for they ought to consider the circumstances of each case independently: *R.* v. *Walsall*, 24 L. T. (O.S.) 111; 18 J. P. 757; 3 C. L. R. 100. Nor can justices annex a condition to the license, such as that, for example, the applicant must pay a debt to some third person: *R.* v. *Athay*, 2 Burr. 653.

The justices have in most cases a large discretion both as to the kind of person and the kind of house to be licensed, and are bound to see that the requirements of the statutes have been complied with. The power of the licensing justices is limited so far that they cannot grant a license except to a person about to keep an inn, &c.: *R.* v. *Wilkinson*, 10 L. T. 370; 28 J. P. 597. But they may treat a confectioner's house where luncheons are provided as a victualling-house, and so within the express words of this section: *R.* v. *Surrey JJ.*, 52 J. P. 423.

Where the house is occupied by a tenant the landlord *quâ* landlord is not qualified to receive the license in his own name: *R.* v. *Holmes*,

Discretion of Justices.

45 J. P. 372. But in most cases the license holder need not reside on the premises, and he may manage the house by means of servants; yet it may be difficult in some cases to distinguish whether a manager is a servant or a tenant: *Mayhew* v. *Suttle,* 4 E. & B. 347; 19 J. P. 38; 24 L. J. Q. B. 54.

Where a firm or company are the owners or occupiers of an inn, the license is frequently applied for and held by a manager or servant who resides on the premises. And it may happen that one person holds the license, and the company, his employers, being the real innkeepers, are liable to guests for the loss of luggage: *Dixon* v. *Birch,* L. R. 8 Ex. 135; 42 L. J. Ex. 135; 28 L. T. 360; *Daun* v. *Simmons,* 41 L. T. 783; 28 W. R. 129; 44 J. P. 264.

If the justices are *equally divided* they should adjourn the hearing to another day, when some additional justices may be present; if they do not adjourn the case the application will be deemed to be refused: *R.* v. *Cox,* 48 J. P. 440; *R.* v. *Carnarvon,* 4 B. & Ald. 86; *R.* v. *Monmouthshire JJ.,* 4 B. & C. 844; 8 B. & C. 137; *R.* v. *Belton,* 11 Q. B. 380; 17 L. J. M. C. 70; *R.* v. *Rogers,* 56 J. P. 183. And see notes to section 7, *post.*

Extent of licensed premises.] When a license is granted to a house without defining the metes and bounds, the house includes the curtilage and a piece of land in front: *Marson* v. *London and Chatham Railway Company,* L. R. 6 Eq. 101; *Richards* v. *Swansea,* 9 Ch. D. 425.

As to treating *alterations* and enlargements of premises and when these require new licenses, see Act, 1872, section 74, and notes, *ante,* p. 158.

Mandamus to licensing justices.] As justices derive all their authority to grant licenses from this statute of 9 Geo. 4, c. 61, modified by later statutes, they are bound to hear and determine all applications on the merits, and if they fail to do so, and thereby some applicant has not been duly heard, the only remedy usually is for the High Court to grant a *mandamus* directing the justices to hear the application over again. The fact that the justices made a mistake in law sometimes is a ground for a *mandamus,* but usually is treated as a misfortune which cannot be remedied. The justices, like other judges, are not personally liable for making a mistake in exercising their jurisdiction: *R.* v *Barton,* 14 J. P. 738; *Basset* v. *Goodchild,* 3 Wils. 121; *R.* v. *Holland,* 1 T. R. 692.

A *mandamus* will lie to command the justices to hear an application for a new license, if they refuse to entertain it; but when once the justices hear and adjudicate, there is often no remedy, if they refuse to grant a new license of any kind, though in some cases there may be a remedy by *mandamus* owing to the neglect of some preliminary condition: *R.* v. *Monmouth,* L. R. 5 Q. B. 251; 34 J. P. 566; 39 L. J.

Appndx.

Note.

Mandamus.

Q. B. 77; 21 L. T. 748. If the quarter sessions refuse to hear an appeal owing to some mistake in law, a *mandamus* may be applied for, but care must be taken to do so within two calendar months after the sitting of the sessions: *R.* v. *Gloncestershire JJ.*, 54 J. P. 519. Should a *mandamus* be granted, and the justices seek to evade it, the prosecutor may traverse the return which they make in answer to the writ of *mandamus*: *R.* v. *Staffordshire JJ., R.* v. *Pirehill,* 14 Q. B. D. 13; 54 L. J. M. C. 17; 51 L. T. (N.S.) 534; 49 J. P. 36; 33 W. R. 205. Thus, in one case, a *mandamus* issued to the justices and they heard the case over again and came to the same conclusion, and the applicant, by pleading, raised an issue for trial as to whether the justices really heard the case or merely pretended to hear it over again: *R.* v. *Pirehill Justices,* 49 J. P. 453. And this course of traversing the return is always open to the applicant: *R.* v. *King* or *Manchester JJ.,* 20 Q. B. D. 430; 52 J. P. 164; 57 L. J. M. C. 20; 58 L. T. 607; 36 W. R. 600.

When a *mandamus* is issued to justices it is not framed so as to compel them to grant the license, but merely to hear and determine; and the justices on hearing the case again have in most cases the same jurisdiction to entertain all objections to the license, and to hear parties on the merits, as if they had acted regularly on the first occasion: *R.* v. *Howard, Justices of Congleton,* 53 J. P. 454; 23 Q. B. D. 502; 60 L. T. 960; 37 W. R. 617; *R.* v. *Farquhar,* L. R. 9 Q. B. 258; 32 J. P. 166.

If the justices act corruptly, the only remedy is a criminal information against them: *R.* v. *Holland,* 1 T. R. 692; *R.* v. *Young,* 1 Burr. 556; *R.* v. *Harries,* 13 East, 270; *R.* v. *Davis,* 3 Burr. 1317. Thus, refusing a license because the applicant would not vote for a particular candidate for parliament, was a ground of criminal information: *R.* v. *Williams,* 3 Burr. 1317. And it would be the same whether they granted or refused the license on such ground: *R.* v. *Holland,* 1 T. R. 692. If one set of justices were to grant a license which another set of the justices had refused, this would be indictable: *R.* v. *Sainsbury,* 4 T. R. 451.

As to the case of licenses granted or refused by justices who are interested, and the respective remedies of *certiorari* and *mandamus*, see *R.* v. *Kent JJ.,* 44 J. P. 298, and next page.

The writ of *mandamus* is usually issued to justices, who decide or assume that they have an absolute discretion when they have only a limited discretion: *R.* v. *King,* 20 Q. B, D. 43; 52 J. P. 164; 57 L. J. M. C. 20; 58 L. T. 607; 36 W. R. 600; *R.* v. *Scott,* 22 Q. B. D. 481; 53 J. P. 119; 58 L. J. M. C. 78; 37 W. R. 301; 60 L. T. 231.

It is sometimes refused if there was a better remedy by appeal to quarter sessions: *R.* v. *Smith, R.* v. *Southport JJ.,* L. R. 8 Q. B. 146; 37 J. P. 214; 28 L. T. 129; 21 W. R. 382; *R.* v. *Thomas,* 56 J. P. 151; (1892) 1 Q. B. 426; 66 L. T. 289; 61 L. J. M. C. 141; 40 W. R. 478. Where a motion for an order *nisi* for *mandamus* has been once

Certiorari, &c. Appndx.

NOTE.

heard and refused, the court will not allow a second motion for the same thing to be made on amended affidavits: *R.* v. *Bodmin* (1892), 2 Q. B. 21 ; 56 J. P. 504.

When the justices make their return to the writ, this is treated like the statement of defence to an action, and the prosecutor may traverse the fact in the return that they have heard the case, and allege in effect that they merely pretended to hear it, and all the time intended to repeat their judgment: *R.* v. *Pirehill JJ.*, 49 J. P. 453. Or the prosecutor may plead to the return that it is bad in point of law: *R.* v. *Howard* or *Congleton JJ.*, 53 J. P. 454 ; 23 Q. B. D. 502 ; 60 L. T. 960 ; 37 W. R. 617.

Should the Divisional Court refuse or grant a rule for a *mandamus*, or a judge give judgment in favour of the prosecutor on a *mandamus*, there is an appeal to the Court of Appeal and the House of Lords : *R.* v. *King*, 20 Q. B. D. 43 ; 52 J. P. 164, *supra ; R.* v. *Crewkerne JJ.*, 21 Q. B. D. 85 ; 52 J. P. 372 ; 57 L. J. M. C. 127 ; 60 L. T. 84 ; 36 W. R. 629 ; *R.* v. *Newcastle JJ.*, 51 J. P. 244 ; *R.* v. *Powell* (1891), 2 Q. B. 693 ; 56 J. P. 52 ; 60 L. J. Q. B. 594 ; 65 L. T. 210 ; 39 W. R. 630.

Certiorari *and prohibition.*] In some cases a license granted by justices may be granted without jurisdiction, and an application may be made for a writ of *certiorari* to quash it. But this remedy must be applied for within six months, and is sometimes refused owing to the necessity of the application being made by a person aggrieved : *R.* v. *Surrey JJ.*, 52 J. P. 423 ; *R.* v. *Surrey JJ.*, L. R. 5 Q. B. 466 ; *R.* v. *Newborough*, L. R. 4 Q. B. 585. If a license is sought to be quashed the whole license must be quashed, and not merely one part of it : *R.* v. *Exeter JJ. ; R.* v. *Mann*, L. R. 8 Q. B. 235 ; 37 J. P. 212 ; 42 L. J. M. C. 35 ; 27 L. T. 847 ; 21 W. R. 329.

At the most, a *certiorari*, unless applied for by the party aggrieved, is a discretionary writ : *Foster* v. *Foster*, 4 B. & S. 199 ; 32 L. J. Q. B. 314.

And even the party aggrieved may, by his conduct, preclude himself from the remedy : *R.* v. *South Holland*, 8 A. & E. 429.

A *certiorari* or a prohibition is the remedy where the justices, or one of them, was interested in the subject-matter or had a real bias. Where G., a justice, was a member of a voluntary association, one of whose objects was to oppose all licenses, and he was present at a meeting, though he left before the resolution was passed instructing a solicitor to oppose the transfer of a license, and G. sat as one of the justices who heard the application for transfer, and which application was opposed by that solicitor, the Court set aside the order refusing the license: *R.* v. *Fraser*, 57 J. P. 600. So where A., a justice, was one of the county licensing committee, and a new license was granted to D. which required to be confirmed by such committee, and A. had written to the licensing justices to inform them that no such license was necessary, and

218　　　　　ALEHOUSE ACT, 1828, s. 1.

Appndx.　　　　　*Licenses in Boroughs.*
NOTE.

attended at the confirmation and then voted against the confirmation, the order of the confirming authority was quashed on *certiorari*: *R.* v. *Ferguson*, 54 J. P. 101. The grounds for quashing orders of other bodies of justices on account of interest or bias, are shown in the following cases: *R.* v. *Rand*, L. R. 1 Q. B. 230; 30 J. P. 293; *R.* v. *Milledge*, 4 Q. B. D. 332; *R.* v. *Meyer*, 1 Q. B. D. 173; 40 J. P. 645; *R.* v. *Handsley*, 8 Q. B. D. 383; 46 J. P. 119; *R.* v. *Gibbon*, 6 Q. B. D. 168; *R.* v. *Henley* (1892), 1 Q. B. 504; 56 J. P. 391; *R.* v. *Lee*, 9 Q. B. D. 394; *R.* v. *Deal JJ.*, 46 J. P. 71; *R.* v. *Tooke*, 48 J. P. 276; 32 W. R. 753; *R.* v. *Great Yarmouth JJ.*, 8 Q. B. D. 168; 46 J. P. 518; *R.* v. *Farrant*, 20 Q. B. D. 58; 52 J. P. 116; *R.* v. *Kent JJ.*, 44 J. P. 298.

A license is not always void though the justices granting it had no jurisdiction: *Brown* v. *Nicholson*, 5 C. B. (N.S.) 468; 22 J. P. 303; 28 L. J. M. C. 49; *R.* v. *Downs*, 3 T. R. 560; *R.* v. *Bryan*, Andr. 81; *Stevens* v. *Empson*, 1 Ex. D. 100; 40 J. P. 484; 45 L. J. M. C. 63; 33 L. T. 821. In *R.* v. *Marshall*, 1 N. & M. 277, it was decided that, if the license was obtained by fraud, yet it would not be invalid unless the party licensed practised the fraud.

See also notes to Licensing Act, 1872, section 3, *ante*, p. 6.

A *prohibition* is a corresponding remedy, where it is practicable, to prevent justices proceeding in a matter of licensing not yet concluded, over which they have no jurisdiction; but owing to the rapidity with which such applications are disposed of, this remedy is generally too late: *Elstone* v. *Rose*, L. R. 4 Q. B. 4; *Broad* v. *Perkins*, 21 Q. B. D. 533; *Re Briton*, 32 Ch. D. 503.

City of London.] The time of holding the general annual meeting in the city of London was saved by section 36 of this Act, and is still the second Monday of March.

Licensing meetings in boroughs.] Disputes formerly existed in boroughs not having a separate court of quarter sessions between the county or borough justices, where there was no intromittant clause in the charter of the borough: *Candlish* v. *Simpson*, 1 B. & S. 357; 25 J. P. 662; *Brown* v. *Nicholson*, 5 C. B. (N.S.) 468; 28 L. J. M. C. 49; 22 J. P. 803. But these disputes were put an end to by a statute of 24 & 25 Vict. c. 75, which is now repealed. By the *Municipal Corporations Act*, 1882, 45 & 46 Vict. c. 50, s. 246, it is enacted that in 9 Geo. 4, c. 61, the expressions "town corporate," "county or place," and "division or place" include every borough having a separate commission of the peace, and the expression "high constable" includes any constable of any such borough to whom the justices of the borough direct their precept under that Act. See also notes to Act, 1828, section 2, *post*.

The Licensing Act, 1872, section 38, *ante* p. 78, points out who are the licensing justices in boroughs having a separate commission of the

2. Time and place how to be appointed—Notice of meetings to be given.] And be it further enacted, that in every such division or place as aforesaid there shall be holden, twenty-one days at the least before each such general annual licensing meeting, a petty sessions of the justices acting for such county or place, the majority of whom then present shall, by a precept under their hands, appoint the day, hour, and place upon and in which such general annual licensing meeting for such division or place shall be holden, and shall direct such precept to the high

Appndx.

---

peace, and divides the boroughs into those which have ten justices acting in and for the borough, and those which have not ten justices.

The general rule laid down by the *Municipal Corporations Act*, 1882, section 154, is, that where a borough has not a separate court of quarter sessions, the justices of the county in which the borough is situated shall exercise the jurisdiction of justices in and for the borough as fully as they can or ought in and for the county. And no part of a borough having a separate court of quarter sessions shall be within the jurisdiction, exercisable out of quarter sessions, of the justices of a county where the borough was exempt therefrom before the passing of the Municipal Corporations Act, 1835. And by section 155, the mayor of a borough shall, by virtue of his office, be a justice for the borough, and shall, unless disqualified to be mayor, continue to be such a justice during the year next after he ceases to be mayor, and he shall have precedence over all other justices acting in and for the borough, and be entitled to take the chair at all meetings of justices held in the borough at which he is present by virtue of his office of mayor.

No room in a house licensed for the sale of intoxicating liquors may be used for the business of borough justices: 45 & 46 Vict. c. 50, s. 160. See notes to 46 & 47 Vict. c. 31, *post*.

Penalties in quarter sessions boroughs.] The Municipal Corporations Act, 1882, 45 & 46 Vict. c. 50, s. 221, lays down certain rules as to application of penalties adjudged before borough justices. See that section quoted, *ante*, p. 138.

Licensing meetings in the Cinque Ports.] By the Municipal Corporations Act, 1882, 45 & 46 Vict. c. 50, s. 248, the justices for the five boroughs of Hastings, Sandwich, Dover, Hythe, and Rye, shall have all the jurisdiction, powers, and authorities of justices for a county relating to the granting of licenses or authorities to persons to keep inns, alehouses, or victualling houses, or to sell excisable liquors by retail within any of the corporate or non-corporate members or liberties of the five boroughs respectively not being within the limits of a borough having a separate commission of the peace. See also 9 Geo. 4, c. 61, s. 8, *post*, and notes, where further provisions are contained as to the cinque ports, and where the local statutes relating to those ports are mentioned.

ALEHOUSE ACT, 1828, s. 2.

Appndx. constable of the division or place for which such meeting is to be holden, requiring him, within five days next ensuing that on which he shall have received such precept, to order the several petty constables or other peace officers within his constablewick to affix or cause to be affixed on the door of the church or chapel, and where there shall be no church or chapel on some other public and conspicuous place within their respective districts, a notice of the day, hour, and place at which such meeting is appointed to be holden, and to give to or leave at the dwelling-house of each and every justice acting for such division or place, and of each and every person keeping an inn, or who shall have given notice of his intention to keep an inn, and to apply for a license to sell excisable liquors by retail, to be drunk or consumed on the premises, within their respective districts, a copy of such notice.(a)

(a) As to the *precept* to the high constable, see 32 & 33 Vict. c. 47, s. 3, which abolishes the office of high constable, and substitutes the justices' clerk as the party to receive the precept. But this does not apply to the metropolitan police district or the city of London.

The notice of holding special sessions may be signed by any one justice and sent by post to the other justices : 7 & 8 Vict. c. 33, s. 7.

The *High Constables* Abolition Act, 32 & 33 Vict. c. 47, s. 2, directed justices in quarter sessions to put an end to the office of high constable in certain cases, and enacted as follows :—

How notices are to be sent.] It shall be the duty of the clerk to the justices of the peace in each petty sessional division, other than those which are either wholly or partly within the metropolitan police district or the city of London, to send by post to the proper parties in such division all notices of the holding of special or other sessions, of days of appeal, and of any other matter or thing (except such as relate to claims against the hundred or other like district, or to parliamentary or municipal elections, or the registration of electors), of which notices are now by law or custom served upon or sent to any parochial officer or other person by high constables, and no precept or notice to perform any such duty in any such division shall hereafter be issued to any high constable, after the passing of this Act : 32 & 33 Vict. c. 47, s. 3.

When part of any hundred or other like district is within the limits of any borough or place having separate police jurisdiction, such hundred or district shall, for the purposes of this Act, be deemed to be in the county in which the other part of such hundred or district is situate : 32 & 33 Vict. c. 47, s. 7.

Interpretation of terms.] For the purposes of this Act the words "high constable" shall include any constable of any hundred or other like district, and any officer discharging the duties usually performed by high constables by whatever name such officer shall be called ; and

3. *Adjournment of meetings.*] And be it further enacted, **Appndx.** that it shall be lawful for the justices acting at the general annual licensing meeting, and they are hereby required to continue such meeting by adjournment to such day or days, and to such place or places within the division or place for which such meeting shall be holden, as such justices may deem most convenient and sufficient for enabling persons keeping inns within such division or place to apply for such license: Provided, nevertheless, that the adjourned meeting to be holden next after such general annual licensing meeting shall not be so holden in or upon any of the five days next ensuing that on which such general annual licensing meeting shall have been holden as aforesaid, and that every adjournment of the said general annual licensing meeting shall be holden within the month of March in the counties of Middlesex and Surrey, and of August or September in every other county.(*b*)

---

the word "county" shall include any riding, division, liberty, and place having separate quarter sessions of the peace: 32 & 33 Vict. c. 47, s. 1.

As to precepts relating to borough licenses.] The Municipal Corporations Act, 1882, specially provides for boroughs in respect to these precepts as follows:—

In the 9 Geo. 4, c. 61, the expressions "town corporate," "county or place," and "division or place," include every borough having a separate commission of the peace; and the expression "high constable" includes any constable of any such borough to whom the justices of the borough direct their precept under that Act: 45 & 46 Vict. c. 50, s. 246.

The word "borough" includes every city or town to which the Municipal Corporations Act, 1835, 5 & 6 Will. 4, c. 76, applied, and every town, district, or place subsequently incorporated: 46 & 47 Vict. c. 50, ss. 6, 7.

Hence all boroughs having a separate commission of the peace, whether these have a separate quarter sessions or not, and whether ten justices or not are appointed for such borough, are under the above 246th section as regards this matter.

(*b*) The justices are bound under this section to appoint at least one adjourned meeting, though they may appoint more than one, and may appoint any convenient place or places for such adjournment. The legislature seems in 1870 to have thought that justices should facilitate applications, and even where these fail from some inadvertence, should appoint adjournments to enable statutory requirements to be complied with: 33 & 34 Vict. c. 29, s. 11. Nevertheless, in 1872, the legislature took away altogether the right of appeal to quarter sessions against the refusal of any new license: 35 & 36 Vict. c. 94, Sched. The justices may and should so arrange the adjournment days as to allow a

Appndx.
—

4. *Special sessions for transferring licenses to be appointed.*] And be it further enacted, that the justices assembled at the general annual licensing meeting in every year, shall appoint not less than four nor more than eight special sessions, to be holden in the division or place for which each such meeting shall be holden in the year next ensuing such general annual licensing meeting, at periods as near as may be equally distant, at which special session it shall be lawful for the justices then and there assembled, in the case and in the manner and for the time hereinafter directed,(*a*) to license such persons intending to keep

person who has not given notice for the general annual licensing meeting to give such notice in time for the adjournment day: *Re Drake*; *R.* v. *West Riding JJ.*, 34 J. P. 4; L. R. 5 Q. B. 33; 39 L. J. M. C. 17; 10 B. & S. 840. And where, for example, an applicant applied at the general meeting for a spirit dealer's retail license, and failed because he had not then taken out the dealer's license, it was held that he might take out such dealer's license, and give fresh notices for the adjournment day: *Ex parte Maugham*; *R.* v. *Kirkdale JJ.*, 1 Q. B. D. 49; 40 J. P. 39; 45 L. J. M. C. 36; 33 L. T. 603; 24 W. R. 205. So where premises were not of sufficient annual value at the date of the general meeting, they may be made sufficient in time for the adjournment: *R.* v. *Montagu*, 49 J. P. 55.

Where, however, the justices have heard and decided the case at the general licensing meeting, they may decline to re-hear the same application on the same materials at the adjournment day, though a fresh notice has been given: *Ex parte Rushworth*, 23 L. T. 120; 34 J. P. 676.

If justices sit more than one day to dispose of the business at the general meeting, their sitting on the second and subsequent days will not be adjournment days within the meaning of this section.

The justices sitting at a general meeting or an adjournment cannot adjourn any matter to a special transfer sessions, as these are two distinct sessions dealing with different classes of business: *R.* v. *Newcastle JJ.*, 51 J. P. 244.

(*a*) These words "in the cases, and in the manner, and for the time hereinafter directed," refer to section 14, *post*, and practically make this section and section 14 operate as one section, the latter part of this section being a mere recital of what will be found in the 14th section at greater length.

The justices ought to fix the transfer sessions at convenient times occurring between 10th October and the following 10th October, especially so as to meet the difficulties likely to arise between the annual general meeting, which is held some weeks previous and the 10th October. This is, however, now of less importance since the decision of *R.* v. *Lawrence* or *Liverpool JJ.*, 11 Q. B. D. 638; 47 J. P. 596; 52 L. J. M. C. 114; 49 L. T. 244; 32 W. R. 20, noticed in the notes to section 14, *post*, which allows the applications for transfer to be made after the expiry of the current license.

inns theretofore kept by other persons being about to remove from such inns as they, the said justices, shall in the execution of the powers herein contained, and in the exercise of their discretion, deem fit and proper persons under the provisions hereinafter enacted, to be licensed to sell excisable liquors by retail, to be drunk or consumed on the premises.(*b*)

5. *Notice to be given of the adjournment of the general annual licensing meeting and special sessions.*] And be it further enacted, that whenever the justices shall have ordered any such adjournment of the general annual licensing meeting, or shall have appointed such special sessions as aforesaid, the day, hour, and place for holding every such adjourned meeting and every such special sessions shall be appointed by precept of the majority of the said justices directed to the high constable, requiring notices similar in form to those given at the general annual licensing meeting, to be affixed on the door of the church or chapel, or on some other public and conspicuous place, and to be served upon the same parties.(*c*)

6. *What justices shall be disqualified from acting.*] [And be it further enacted, that no justice who shall be a common brewer, distiller, maker of malt for sale, or retailer of malt or of

---

The words "transfer sessions" are usually applied to these intermediate special sessions, though the statute does not in the 4th and 14th sections so describe them, but the word "transfer" was used in the 11th section and the schedule now repealed, and is a convenient description of the object of the sessions. The notice required to be given before all transfer applications is set forth in Licensing Act, 1872, s. 40, but see note to section 14 of the present Act, *post*. And the circumstances under which a transfer license is granted are stated in section 14, *post*.

(*b*) Power is also given to petty sessions to give a temporary authority in the interval between any two special transfer sesssions. See 5 & 6 Vict. c. 44, *post*.

(*c*) With regard to the parties who are applicants only for renewals of licenses or certificates, and who are not specially required by the justices to attend pursuant to a notice of opposition served under Licensing Act, 1872, section 42, *ante*, p. 83, no such notice need now be given to them for the purpose of their attending, though a notice must always be served as to the time and place of the general annual meeting on each holder of a license: 9 Geo. 4, c. 61, s. 2. But an application must always be made by some person duly authorised; hence, if such application has not been made at the general meeting, it will be useful to continue this notice in those cases in order to remind them: Licensing Act, 1874, section 26.

Appndx. any excisable liquor, or who shall be concerned in partnership with any common brewer, distiller, maker of malt for sale, or retailer of malt or of any excisable liquor, shall act in, or be present at any general annual licensing meeting, or at any adjournment thereof, or at any special session for granting or transferring licenses under this Act, or shall take part in the discussion or adjudication of the justices, upon any application for a license or upon any appeal therefrom; and no justice shall act upon any of the aforesaid occasions in the case of any house licensed, or about to be licensed, under this Act, of which such justice shall be the owner, or for the owner of which he shall be manager or agent, or of any house being in whole or in part the property of any common brewer, distiller, maker of malt for sale, or retailer of malt, or of any excisable liquor, to whom such justice shall be either by blood or by marriage, the father, son, or brother, or of whom such justice shall be the partner in any other trade or calling; and that every justice who, being hereby disqualified, shall knowingly or wilfully so offend, shall for every such offence forfeit and pay the sum of 100*l*.: Provided always, that nothing herein contained shall extend to disqualify any justice (not otherwise disqualified, and having no beneficial interest in the house licensed or about to be licensed under this Act) from acting on any of the occasions aforesaid by reason of the legal estate in such house being vested in him as trustee for any person or persons, or for any charitable or public use or purpose whatever.](*a*)

7. *When in liberties, &c., two justices not disqualified do not attend, the county justices may act.*] And be it further enacted, that whenever at any of the meetings to be holden as aforesaid for any liberty, county of a city, county of a town, city, or town corporate, there shall not be present at least two justices acting in and for any such liberty, county of a city, county of a town, city, or town corporate, who are not disqualified, it shall be lawful for the justices acting in and for the county or counties adjoining to such liberty, county of a city, county of a town, city, or town corporate, and not disqualified from acting, to act within such liberty or place, and with the justice or justices thereof not as hereinbefore disqualified who shall be present at any such meeting as aforesaid, for the purpose of granting or transferring licenses under or of hearing complaints as to offences against

---

(*a*) This section was repealed by the Licensing Act, 1872, Schedule, but is here retained as a means of comparison with the substituted enactment in Licensing Act, 1872, section 60.

this Act, any law, custom, or usage to the contrary notwithstanding.(b)

Appndx.

8. *Powers hereby given to the justices of the county not to extend to the Cinque Ports.*] Provided always, that nothing herein contained shall extend to give the justices of the county or any division thereof any power or authority for the putting of the provisions of this Act in execution within any of the cinque ports, or either of the two ancient towns, or any of the corporate or other members or liberties of the cinque ports or two ancient towns, but that it shall be lawful for the justices of and for each of the principal cinque ports and two ancient towns, and not as hereinbefore disqualified from acting, and none other, to act within and for the same and the liberties thereof not corporate respectively as they have been accustomed, and for them or any of them (not so as last aforesaid disqualified) to act within each of the corporate members immediately belonging or subordinate to such principal cinque port or ancient town, with the justice or justices of each such corporate member (not so as last aforesaid disqualified), for the purpose of granting or transferring licenses under or of hearing complaints as to offences against this Act, in all such cases in which the justices of the county are hereinbefore empowered or authorised to act with the justice or justices of any liberty, county of a city, county of a town, city, or town corporate.(c)

(b) The disqualification here mentioned is now set forth for the purposes of this Act in Licensing Act, 1872, section 60. The adjoining county to a town corporate seems to be read distributively, and no great nicety would be required as to which of several adjoining counties a justice may for this purpose be taken from. The rule is that a justice for a county or borough can sit at any sessions within his county or borough : *R.* v. *Beckley*, 20 Q. B. D. 187 ; 52 J. P. 120.

Where the justices who hear the case do not all vote in deciding it, the whole of the justices who were present, whether voting or not in the final decision, must be counted in order to discover whether there is a majority for or against the license. And if the justices do not adjourn the hearing and they are equally divided, the result is a refusal of the renewal or transfer of the license : *Garton* v. *Southampton JJ.*, 57 J. P. 328. Whether, when the justices at quarter sessions are equally divided, the applicant can compel the justices to adjourn the hearing so as to constitute a court in which there shall be a majority, see *Ex parte Evans*, 57 J. P. 488.

(c) The Cinque Ports Acts are 51 Geo. 3, c. 36 ; 18 & 19 Vict. c. 48 ; 32 & 33 Vict. c. 53 ; 38 & 39 Vict. c. 66, Sched. ; 45 & 46 Vict. c. 50, ss. 248, 256 ; 46 & 47 Vict. c. 18, ss. 13, 14 ; 46 & 47 Vict. c. 39, Sched.

Appndx.   **9.** *Questions respecting licenses to be determined, and licenses to be signed, by the majority of justices at the meeting.*] And be it further enacted, that when (at any of the meetings aforesaid) any question touching the granting, withholding, or transferring any license, or the fitness of the person applying for such license, or of the house intended to be kept by such person, shall arise, such question shall be determined by the majority of justices not disqualified, who shall be present when such question shall arise; and every license granted under the authority of this Act shall be signed by the majority of the justices not disqualified who shall be present when such license shall be granted.(*a*)

10. *Notice of application* for a license to keep a house as an inn, not previously kept as such. *Repealed* by Licensing Act, 1872. See Schedule.(*b*)

11. *Notice of application* to *transfer* a license. *Repealed* by Licensing Act, 1872. See Schedule.(*b*)

12. *Any person hindered from attending any licensing meeting by sickness may authorise another person to attend for him.*] And be it further enacted, that if any person intend-

---

The disqualification referred to formerly set forth in section 6 is now that substituted by Licensing Act, 1872, section 60.

See also note to 9 Geo. 4, c. 61, s. 1, *ante*, p. 219.

(*a*) A justice is not bound to vote, but if he does not intend to vote, or cannot vote, he should not sit on the bench with other justices, as confusion and irregularity may result from this : *R.* v. *Meyer*, 1 Q. B. D. 173 ; 40 J. P. 645 ; *R.* v. *London County Council* (1892), 1 Q. B. 190 ; 56 J. P. 8.

If the justices are equally divided they should adjourn the matter so that other justices may attend; if they do not, the result is equivalent to a refusal, and the applicant may appeal accordingly. See *R.* v. *Cox*, 48 J. P. 440 ; *R.* v. *Carnarvon*, 4 B. & Ald. 86 ; *R.* v. *Monmouthshire*, 4 B. & C. 844 ; 8 B. & C. 137 ; *R.* v. *Belton*, 11 Q. B. 380. In one case there being an equality of votes, half of the justices being under the impression that the chairman had by law a casting vote, nominally consented to a judgment accordingly, and the court refused to quash the adjudication : *R.* v. *Rogers*, 56 J. P. 68.

The mode of signing the license is now alternative. See 33 & 34 Vict. c. 29, s. 4, sub-sect. 2 ; Licensing Act, 1872, section 40, sub-sect. 3.

(*b*) There is no particular form of notice specified in any of the statutes, but the requirements both as to notices for new licenses and for some transfers of licenses are now contained in the Licensing Act, 1872, section 40, *ante*, and in 32 & 33 Vict. c. 27, s. 7, *post*.

9 GEO. 4, C. 61, S. 14. 227

ing to apply at the general annual licensing meeting, or at any **Appndx.** adjournment thereof, or at any special session, for any license to be granted under the authority of this Act, or for the transfer of any such license, shall be hindered by sickness or infirmity, or by any other reasonable cause, from attending in person at any such meeting, it shall be lawful for the justices there assembled to grant or transfer such license to such person so hindered from attending, and to deliver the same to any person then present who shall be duly authorised by the person so hindered from attending to receive the same, proof being adduced to the satisfaction of such justices, who are hereby empowered to examine upon oath into the matter of such allegation, that such person is hindered from attending by good and sufficient cause.(c)

13. *Form of license.*] And be it further enacted, that every license which shall be granted under the authority of this Act shall be according to the form in the schedule hereunto annexed (marked C), and shall be in force in the counties of Middlesex and Surrey from the fifth day of April, and elsewhere from the tenth of October, after the granting thereof, for one whole year thence respectively next ensuing, and no longer ; and every license for the purposes aforesaid, which shall be granted at any other time or place or in any other form than that hereby directed, except as hereinafter excepted, shall not entitle any person to obtain an excise license for selling excisable liquors by retail to be drunk or consumed on the premises of the person licensed, and shall be utterly void to all intents and purposes.(d)

14. *Provision for death, change of occupancy, or other contingency—Duration of license granted in event of such contingency—Notice required.*] If any person duly licensed

---

(c) This was extended to certificates under the Wine and Beerhouse Acts, 33 & 34 Vict. c. 29, s. 4, and is further extended by Licensing Act, 1872, section 42. By this Act of 1828, and previous Acts, it was assumed to be essential that each applicant should appear in person at the general meeting, whether he applied for a new license, or a renewal of a license. That is now rendered unnecessary as to renewals in most cases. See Licensing Act, 1872, s. 42: *Sharp* v. *Wakefield* (1891), 1 App. Cas. 473 ; 55 J. P. 197 ; 60 L. J. M. C. 8 ; 64 L. T. 180 ; 39 W. R. 630. But though the applicant need not appear in person, he must send an authorised messenger, otherwise the justices need not renew the license, and it would drop.

(d) This section is *repealed* so far as regards the form of license. See Licensing Act, 1872, schedule and section 48. The *forms* issued by the Secretary of State are in the Appendix at the end of this volume.

Q 2

Appndx. under this Act shall (before the expiration of such license) die, or shall be by sickness or other infirmity rendered incapable of keeping an inn, or shall become bankrupt, or if any person so licensed, or the heirs, executors, administrators, or assigns of any person so licensed, shall remove from or yield up the possession of the house specified in such license; or if the occupier of any such house, being about to quit the same, shall have wilfully omitted or shall have neglected to apply at the general annual licensing meeting, or at any adjournment thereof, for a license to continue to sell excisable liquors by retail, to be drunk or consumed in such house; or if any house, being kept as an inn by any person duly licensed as aforesaid, shall be or be about to be pulled down or occupied under the provisions of any Act for the improvement of the highways or for any other public purpose, or shall be, by fire, tempest, or other unforeseen and unavoidable calamity, rendered unfit for the reception of travellers and for the other legal purposes of an inn: *it shall be lawful* for the justices assembled as aforesaid at a special session holden under the authority of this Act for the division or place in which the house so kept or having been kept shall be situate in any one of the above-mentioned cases, and in such cases only, to grant to the heirs, executors, or administrators of the person so dying, or to the assigns of such person becoming incapable of keeping an inn, or to the assignee or assignees of such bankrupt, or to any new tenant or occupier of any house having so become unoccupied, or to any person to whom such heirs, executors, administrators, or assigns, shall by sale or otherwise have *bond fide* conveyed or otherwise made over his or their interest in the occupation and keeping of such house, a license to sell excisable liquors by retail, to be drunk or consumed in such house or the premises thereunto belonging: or to grant to the person whose house shall as aforesaid have been or shall be about to be pulled down or occupied for the improvement of the highways or for any other public purpose, or have become unfit for the reception of travellers, or for the other legal purposes of an inn, and who shall open and keep as an inn some other fit and convenient house, a license to sell excisable liquors by retail, to be drunk or consumed therein: *Provided* always, that every such license shall *continue in force* only from the day on which it shall be granted until the fifth day of April or the 10th day of October then next ensuing, as the case may be: *Provided* also, that every person intending to apply, in any of the above-mentioned cases, at any such special session, for a license to sell excisable liquors by retail, to be drunk or consumed in a house or premises thereunto belonging in which excisable liquors shall not have been sold by retail, to be drunk or consumed on the premises by virtue of a license granted at the general annual licensing meeting next before such special session, shall on some one Sunday within the six weeks next before such special session, at some time between the hours of ten in the forenoon and of four in the afternoon, affix or cause to be affixed on the door of such house, and on the door of the church or chapel of the parish or place in which such house shall be situate, and where there shall be no church or chapel on some other public and conspicuous place within such parish and place, such and *the like notice* as is hereinbefore directed to be affixed by every person intending to apply at the general annual licensing meeting for a license to sell excisable liquors by retail, to be drunk or consumed in a house not theretofore kept as an inn, and shall in like manner serve copies of the said notice on one of the overseers of the poor and on one of the constables or other peace officers of such parish or place.(*a*)

[Some words were *repealed* by 51 & 52 Vict. c. 57, Schedule, and are omitted in the text.]

(*a*) This section applies not only to publicans' licenses, but to all certificates under the Wine and Beerhouse Acts, 33 & 34 Vict. c. 29, s. 4, sub-section 5 ; and to certificates for spirits and liqueurs, Licensing Act, 1872, section 69 ; and for sweets, Licensing Act, 1872, section 74. It is the only enactment which provides for transfers of justices' licenses, that is to say, the substitution of a new person or a new house, when some one of the incidents here mentioned occurs during the currency of a license.

Time for applying for transfer and notice.] The authority to appoint certain days for transfer sessions not exceeding eight during the licensing year, is given by section 4, *ante*, and the cases that may be dealt with are here set out. Before any application can be made notices need only be given pursuant to Licensing Act, 1872, section 40, sub-section 2, in those cases where the outgoing licensee makes the application under section 4, *ante*, and, therefore, no notice need be given before the applications under the 14th section : *R.* v. *Grove* or *Wilts JJ.*, 57 J. P. 454 ; *R.* v. *Hughes*, 57 J. P. 500 ; 62 L. J. M. C. 150. See notes to that section, *ante*, p. 85. The notice at the end of this section may sometimes be required if the house has not been licensed before. See notes, *ante*, p. 86.

Where a new tenant has come into the premises and has failed to obtain a transfer, there is nothing to prevent a second new incoming tenant making a second application, and so on, during the licensing year, for the justices may accept one person though they may have rejected another, and the license once granted continues in existence till 10th October : *Re Todd*, 3 Q. B. D. 407 ; 42 J. P. 662 ; 47 L. J. M. C. 89. It is true that if the license has been forfeited no such application can be made : *R.* v. *West Riding JJ.*, 21 Q. B. D. 258 ;

Appndx.

NOTE.

52 J. P. 455 ; 57 L. J. M. C. 103 ; 36 W. R. 258. But in the additional cases specified in Licensing Act, 1874, s. 15, *ante*, p. 192, there seems to be a doubt whether a succession of new incoming tenants could apply one after the other: *Stevens* v. *Sharnbrook JJ.*, 53 J. P. 423 ; *ante*, p. 193.

The application under this section is usually made before the expiration of the license which is proposed to be transferred or transmitted, the object being to provide for some contingency happening between the general annual licensing meetings, at which alone a license or a renewal can be obtained, and which license positively lapses on a defined day in the year. If, however, the events mentioned have all happened during the current year, such as the death or removal of one tenant or the entry of another into the licensed premises, then the application may be made at any time after the expiration of the current license, or at least within the year next after the lapse of the current license, the jurisdiction depending on the happening of events, and not on the date at which the remedy is asked for : *R.* v. *Lawrence* or *Liverpool JJ.*, 11 Q. B. D. 638 ; 47 J. P. 596 ; 52 L. J. M. C. 114 ; 40 L. T. 244 ; 32 W. R. 20. Though it has been usual to call the license granted under this section a transfer, and it has been so described in the Licensing Act, 1872, s. 74, *ante*, p. 159, yet it is in strictness simply the grant of a license to some person different from the person who held it before, or to the same person in respect of a different house, and which is authorized when the events happen which are described in this 14th section. In some cases it may be useful to postpone the application ; for if the justices make the transfer before the 10th of October, the license so transferred will end on the 10th : *R.* v. *Northumberland JJ.*, 43 J. P. 271 ; and a second application for a transfer for the ensuing year must be made. In one case the new tenant entered a day or two before the adjourned meeting, and as he did not apply to that meeting for a renewal, it was held that he could not apply a second time under section 14, for what covered the same period : *R.* v. *Powell* (1891), 1 Q. B. 718 ; 2 Q. B. 693 ; 55 J. P. 422 ; 56 J. P. 52 ; 65 L. T. 210 ; 60 L. J. Q. B. 594 ; 39 W. R. 630.

It is not uncommon for a tenant whose renewal has been refused to surrender the premises, and if this is done before 10th October in country licenses, or 5th April in Middlesex and Surrey, and a new tenant enters, the latter is entitled to apply for a transfer, and the justices cannot refuse to hear his application on the ground that they had already refused a renewal to the outgoing tenant, as this is not a case of *res judicata: R.* v. *Upper Osgoldcross*, 53 J. P. 823 ; 62 L. T. 112 ; *R.* v. *Thomas*, 56 J. P. 151 ; (1892), 1 Q. B. 426 ; 66 L. T. 289 ; 61 L. J. M. C. 141 ; 40 W. R. 472.

Discretion of justices as to transfers.] The general rule is, that justices have the same discretion, but not more, as to the grant of transfers, as they have as to new and renewal licenses, and that discretion is, as to the great majority of cases, absolute, as, for example, as to publicans' licenses, and all in-door beer and wine licenses first granted since 1869. The leading rule as to publicans' licenses was discussed in *Sharp* v. *Wakefield*, 22 Q. B. D. 239 ; 53 J. P. 20 ; 58 L. J. M. C. 57 ; 60 L. T. 130 ; 37 W. R. 187, *supra*, p. 90 ; and is equally applicable to transfers of publicans' licenses : see notes to section 1, *ante*, p. 214.

Appndx.
—
NOTE.

But there are several exceptions where the justices have only a discretion limited to the four grounds specified in 32 & 33 Vict. c. 27, s. 8, *post* ; and the rule being, that if the discretion was limited as to renewals, or new licenses, then it is equally limited as to transfers : *Simmonds* v. *Blackheath*, 17 Q. B. D. 765 ; 50 J. P. 742 ; 55 L. J. M. C. 166 ; 35 W. R. 167. But where the current license had come to an end before any application for a transfer, or grant under section 14 was made to special transfer sessions, the court held that the justices were no longer restricted to the four grounds : *Murray* v. *Freer* (1893), 1 Q. B. 635 ; 57 J. P. 101, 583 ; 67 L. T. 507 ; 62 L. J. M. C. 33. And it has also been held that where an in-door beerhouse has been taken for public purposes, and the licensee applies to have the license transferred to another house, the discretion of the justices is no longer limited to the four grounds : *Traynor* v. *Jones*, 57 J. P. 724. And the same limit would extend to applications to petty sessions for an endorsement or temporary license under 5 & 6 Vict. c. 44. Accordingly the discretion of justices is limited to the four grounds as to in-door beerhouses, in-door winehouses, and in-door ciderhouses, licensed in 1869 : 32 & 33 Vict. c. 37, s. 19, subject to the case last cited.

With regard to out-door licenses for wine or spirits, or cider, or sweets, the discretion of justices is still limited to the four grounds, both as to new licenses and renewal licenses : 32 & 33 Vict. c. 27, s. 8 ; 35 & 36 Vict. c. 94, ss. 69, 74 ; and hence equally limited as to transfers : *Simmonds* v. *Blackheath*, *supra*.

Where a spinster who held a license married, and the husband applied for a transfer to himself under section 14, it was held to be unnecessary as the license remained valid : *Hazell* v. *Middleton*, 45 J. P. 540.

In applications for transfers, as notice must be given pursuant to 35 & 36 Vict. c. 94, s. 40, before all applications under section 4, *ante*, though not before applications under this section 14, still the character of the transferree requires to be proved, and is usually a leading requirement. Any person may oppose the applicant for transfer, and sometimes does so by evidence as to misconduct of previous license holders. Where the discretion of justices is limited to four grounds, the transfer can only be opposed on one or other of those four grounds set forth in 32 & 33 Vict. c. 27, s. 8. In general, evidence as to the bad character of a previous outgoing tenant ought not to have weight on a transfer application : *R.* v. *Hull JJ.*, 47 J. P. 820 ; but see *R.* v. *Miskin Higher* (1893), 1 Q. B. 275 ; 57 J. P. 263 ; 67 L. T. 680, *ante*, p. 91.

Appeal to quarter sessions.] There is, however, in all applications for transfer an appeal to the county quarter sessions, if the transfer is refused, so that any injustice may be corrected and additional evidence given on both sides : see section 27, *post*.

In one case on refusal of a transfer the applicant appealed to quarter

Appndx.

NOTE.

sessions, and the sessions refused to hear him on the ground that the case came within section 14, and that by the definition of "transfer of license" in 35 & 36 Vict. c. 94, s. 74, that Act allowed no appeal, except the case was within 9 Geo. 4, c. 61, s. 4. The court held that section 4 and section 14 of 9 Geo. 4, c. 61, were one and the same, and that in all cases under section 14 there was an appeal to quarter sessions : *Thornton* v. *Clegg*, 24 Q. B. D. 132 ; 53 J. P. 742 ; 58 L. J. M. C. 6 ; 61 L. T. 562 ; 38 W. R. 160.

Where a transfer had been refused and there was an appeal to quarter sessions, and the sessions on a wrong ground dismissed the appeal, but stated a special case, and before the High Court disposed of the special case and reversed the judgment of the sessions, a new licensing year had begun, it was held that the applicant for a transfer might renew his application to a transfer sessions, and need not pursue his remedy against the quarter sessions further : *R.* v. *Welby*, 54 J. P. 183.

Cases as to transfers.] The following cases further illustrate this section as to applications for transfers :

The holder of a certificate for a beer license in Middlesex removed on 14th February. The next general annual licensing meeting was held on 6th March. The old tenant, without the new tenant's knowledge, then applied for renewal, but was refused. The new tenant, who entered on 14th February, did not apply on 6th March, but, after proper notices, applied, under 9 Geo. 4, c. 61, s. 14, at the special transfer sessions on 12th April. He was held entitled to apply for the certificate under 9 Geo. 4, c. 61, s. 14, and 33 & 34 Vict. c. 29, s. 4, subsection 5 : *R.* v. *Middlesex JJ.*, 40 L. J. M. C. 184 ; L. R. 6 Q. B. 781 ; 25 L. T. 41 ; 35 J. P. 599 ; 19 W. R. 960.

W., the holder of a country beerhouse license, at the general annual licensing meeting on the previous 25th August, applied for renewal of certificate, but was refused. He occupied till 13th October, and was succeeded by S., who then applied at the next special sessions on 4th January, under 9 Geo. 3, c. 61, s. 14. Held, that the special sessions had no jurisdiction, as W. had remained in possession till after the license expired : *Simpkin* v. *Birmingham JJ.*, 41 L. J. M. C. 102 ; L. R. 7 Q. B. 482 ; 26 L. T. 620 ; 20 W. R. 702 ; 36 J. P. 709.

T., a new tenant of an alehouse in Middlesex, applied at the adjourned general meeting for a license and was refused. At that date he could have appealed to quarter sessions but did not do so, and after the current license expired applied again to transfer sessions. Held, his only remedy being the appeal, he could not apply under section 14 : *R.* v. *Taylor*, L. R. 7 Q. B. 487 ; 37 J. P. 101 ; 42 L. J. M. C. 13.

R., a new tenant in a country publichouse, who had entered on 4th September, applied at the special transfer sessions on 20th November, 1871, when the justices refused. R. then appealed to quarter sessions, but they refused also. The court held it was discretionary in the justices both at special sessions and at quarter sessions to refuse the license : *R.* v. *Rowell*, *Rowell* v. *Norfolk JJ.*, 37 J. P. 103 ; L. R. 7 Q. B. 490 ; 41 L. J. M. C. 175 ; 26 L. T. 732.

9 GEO. 4, c. 61, s. 14.

Appndx.
NOTE.

The holder of a country license gave up possession on 11th September to B., who entered and applied to the transfer sessions on 25th September, and was refused. B. left the house on 28th September, and G. entered and applied to the transfer sessions on 23rd October, and was refused. T. next entered on 29th November, and applied to the transfer sessions on 22nd January, and was refused for want of jurisdiction, and the Q. B. held the justices right: *Re Todd*, 3 Q. B. D. 407; 47 L. J. M. C. 89; 42 J. P. 662. But this case has been overruled by *R.* v. *Liverpool JJ.*, *R.* v. *Lawrence, ante*, p. 230.

C., having a lease of country licensed premises at M. till July, 1879, began in 1876 to build a new house of his own at I., for which he got a provisional license and then a confirmation of that license in 1877, and then dropped the license at M. A new tenant entered M. in 1879 and duly applied for a new license in 1879, and in each year till 1883, and was always refused. After the decision of *R.* v. *Lawrence*, 11 Q. B. D. 638, the same new tenant applied for a transfer of the license at M., which had expired in 1877. Held, that the justices had a discretion to refuse the transfer, and could not be compelled by *mandamus* to hear the application: *Ex parte Minett*, 51 J. P. 84.

The country licensee died on 27th September. No new tenant entered till after 10th October, and an application was not made for a transfer till the 4th December, and the court held there was no jurisdiction, as the license had been allowed to lapse: *White* v. *Coquetdale*, 7 Q. B. D. 238; 50 L. J. M. C. 128; 44 L. T. 715; 45 J. P. 539. This case has, however, been overruled by *R.* v. *Liverpool JJ.*, *R.* v. *Lawrence*, see below.

The new tenant, Mrs. B., of a country publichouse entered in June, and applied before August for transfer, and was refused. Mrs. B. remained in possession till after the general annual meeting, and did not apply for renewal, and went out in September. The new tenant entered in November and was refused a transfer. Another new tenant entered in January, and the court held that he was entitled to apply for transfer though the current license had expired on 10th October preceding: *R.* v. *Lawrence* or *Liverpool*, 11 Q. B. D. 638; 47 J. P. 596; 52 L. J. M. C. 114; 49 L. T. 244; 32 W. R. 20.

If the license has been forfeited, there can be no application thereafter for a transfer: *R.* v. *West Riding JJ.*, 21 Q. B. D. 258; 52 J. P. 455; 57 L. J. M. C. 103; 36 W. R. 258. So if the license has been discontinued for a year or more there can be no application for a renewal or transfer, but only one for a new license: *R.* v. *Curzon*, L. R. 8 Q. B. 400; 42 L. J. M. C. 155; 37 J. P. 774; 29 L. T. 32; 21 W. R. 886.

K., the license holder, abandoned possession, and at next general meeting landlord asked for a renewal in K.'s name or his own, which justices refused. P., a new tenant, entered after general meeting, and at next transfer sessions asked for transfer, which was refused, and P. appealed to quarter sessions and was again refused. Held, that the decision of quarter sessions standing, P. could not apply again at next annual meeting for renewal: *R.* v. *Newcastle JJ.*, 51 J. P. 244.

Appndx.

Note.

G., a country publican, left the premises in December, 1890. A new tenant, W., in May, 1891, applied for a transfer, was refused, and did not appeal. A second new tenant, K., entered, and on 9th September, 1891, applied for renewal, was refused, and did not appeal. A third new tenant, B., entered, and applied on 1st March, 1892, for a transfer under 9 Geo. 4, c. 61, s. 14. Held, that B. was entitled to apply, and the justices were bound to hear him, and had jurisdiction to grant the transfer license: *Baldwin* v. *Dover JJ.* (1892), 2 Q. B. 421; 56 J. P. 423; 61 L. J. M. C. 215.

Where a country publican left his house in April, and F., a new tenant, applied for transfer on 31st August, which was refused, and also applied for a new license on 28th September, and was refused, W., a new tenant, entered on 7th October, and applied on 2nd November for a transfer under 9 Geo. 4, c. 61, s. 14. Held, the justices were bound to hear W., and could not refuse on the ground of *res judicata*: *R.* v. *Upper Osgoldcross*, 53 J. P. 823; 62 L. T. 112.

Where S., the licensee of an indoor beerhouse of 1869, on receiving notice of opposition, did not apply for renewal, and left the house on the adjournment day of the general meeting, and T., a new tenant, entered and applied for transfer under 9 Geo. 4, c. 61, s. 14, at next special transfer sessions, and was refused. Held, T. was entitled to appeal to quarter sessions, and that an appeal lay against all refusals under section 14: *Thornton* v. *Clegg*, 24 Q. B. D. 132; 53 J. P. 742; 58 L. J. M. C. 6; 61 L. T. 562; 38 W. R. 160.

Where the tenant of a country beerhouse gave up possession on 2nd September, and a new tenant entered on 5th September, and obtained a transfer which lasted till 10th October. He did not apply at the adjourned general meeting of 27th September for a renewal, but instead thereof applied on 3rd January following for a second transfer, under 9 Geo. 4, c. 61, s. 14. Held, that the second application was incompetent, because he ought to have applied for a renewal on 27th September. Held, also, by Kay, L.J., that if he had had no opportunity of applying for renewal then he might have made a second application under section 14: *R.* v. *Powell* (1891), 2 Q. B. 693; 60 L. J. M. C. 594; 65 L. T. 210; 39 W. R. 630; 55 J. P. 422; 56 J. P. 52.

O., the holder of in-door beer license dated before 1869, got notice of opposition, and was refused a renewal on 26th August. O. did not appeal, but went out, and K. entered into possession on 19th September, and at the adjourned general meeting on 23rd September, applied for renewal. The justices refused the application on the ground of *res judicata*, as O.'s application for the same house had been heard and refused. Held, that the justices were wrong, and ought to have heard K.'s application and rule for *mandamus* made absolute: *R.* v. *Thomas*, 56 J. P. 151; (1892), 1 Q. B. 426; 66 L. T. 289; 61 L. J. M. C. 141; 40 W. R. 472.

A licensed house had been pulled down for public improvements, and the licensed person chose another house in all respects well fitted for the business but the justices when asked to make the transfer considered that there were already sufficient houses in the new locality

Appndx.
NOTE.

and refused to transfer on that ground alone, and the High Court held that their discretion could not be interfered with: *Boodle* v. *Birmingham JJ.*, 45 J. P. 635.

Where a licensed house was pulled down in order to anticipate public improvements in a locality, this was held not to come within the powers of the justices to grant a transfer: *R.* v. *Northumberland JJ.*, 43 J. P. 271.

Where an indoor licensed beerhouse of 1869 was taken down for public improvements, and the licensee applied under this section for a transfer of the license to another house, the court held that the justices were no longer bound by the four grounds but had an unlimited jurisdiction: *Traynor* v. *Jones*, 57 J. P. 724.

In estimating the price to be paid as compensation for compulsorily taking the reversionary interest in a public-house after the end of twenty-five years' lease, it was held that evidence was properly received as to the possibility of such interest being enhanced by still having a license attached to the premises: *Belton* v. *London County Council*, 68 L. T. 411; 57 J. P. 185.

The notice at the end of the 14th section means the notice for new license under Licensing Act, 1872, s. 40, in those cases. See Act, 1872, s. 40, and notes, *ante*, p. 84.

Contracts of sale of licensed houses.] Cases of transfer of licenses are often mixed up with the sale of the business of a publican. In *Claydon* v. *Green*, L. R. 3 C. P. 511; 37 L. J. C. P. 236; 18 L. T. 607; 16 W. R. 1126, the vendor of a public-house agreed to sell the business and assign the license on 5th February, 1867. It turned out that the licenses were held in the name of the vendor's son, who had gone to America, and was not heard of, and the business had been carried on in the name of another son, no indorsement or application for transfer being deemed possible. The court held that the vendor not being able to perform his contract, the purchaser was entitled to recover back his deposit. In *Day* v. *Lukke*, L. R. 5 Eq. 336; 37 L. J. Ch. 330; 16 W. R. 719; 32 J. P. 499, a vendor covenanted to transfer the license on a given day. At the day in question the holder of the license could not be got to authorise an application to justices, and so a transfer was not obtained. It was held that the vendor having failed to carry out the contract, the purchaser could repudiate the contract. So when the license cannot be secured, the contract for sale of the public-house as a going concern may always be repudiated: *Cowles* v. *Gale*, 41 L. J. Ch. 14; L. R. 7 Ch. 12; 25 L. T. 524; 20 W. R. 70. And where parties contract on the footing of a license being in force and it appears that the existing license is subject to qualifications, the contract cannot be enforced: *Modlen* v. *Snowball*, 4 De G. F. & J. 143.

At the expiration of the lease the licensee may be entitled to the goodwill according to his covenant, in which case the goodwill may require to be valued. See *Llewellyn* v. *Rutherford*, L. R. 10 C. P. 456; 44 L. J. C. P. 281; 32 L. T. 610. Or the goodwill may be

Appndx. **15.** *Fees to be paid for license—Penalty for taking larger fees.*] And be it further enacted, that it shall be lawful for the clerk of the justices, as well at the general annual licensing meeting as also at any special sessions to be holden under this Act, to demand and receive from every person to whom a license shall be granted under this Act, for the trouble of such clerk, and for all expenses connected therewith, the sums following, and no more : *videlicet*, for the petty constable, or other peace officer, for serving notices, and for all other services hereby required of such petty constable or other peace officer, the sum of one shilling ; for the clerk of the justices, for the license, the sum of five shillings ;

---

declared to go with the house : *Ex parte Pinnett*, 16 Ch. D. 226 ; 50 L. J. Ch. 212 ; 44 L. T. 226 ; 29 W. R. 129. But the goodwill carries the right to get transfer of license, if procurable : *Rutter* v. *Daniel*, 46 L. T. 684 ; 30 W. R. 801.

A covenant is often given by the vendor of the goodwill not to carry on business within a certain distance. Such distance is, unless the context varies it, measured in a straight line : *Moufflet* v. *Cole*, L. R. 8 Ex. 32 ; 42 L. J. Ex. 8 ; 27 L. T. 678 ; 21 W. R. 175.

On a sale of a public-house, as time is of the essence of the contract, the sale may go off for want of justices' license. *Cowles* v. *Gale*, L. R. 7 Ch. 12 ; 41 L. J. Ch. 14 ; 25 L. T. 524 ; 20 W. R. 70. If lease contains covenant to leave assignment with ground landlord's solicitor, the sale goes off : *Brookes* v. *Drysdale*, 3 C. P. D. 52 ; 37 L. T. 467 ; 26 W. R. 331. If at termination of lease goodwill is to be allowed to tenant, the tenant may sue landlord for the same : *Llewellyn* v. *Rutherford*, L. R. 10 C. P. 456 ; 44 L. J. C. P. 281 ; 32 L. T. 610. If there is a covenant on bankruptcy of lessee for landlord to re-enter, the license does not pass to the trustee of bankrupt, for a license is not property : *Re Britnor*, 46 L. J. Bk. 85 ; 25 W. R. 560. See a sale set aside describing hotel as "let to a most desirable tenant :" *Smith* v. *Land Corporation*, 28 Ch. D. 7 ; 49 J. P. 182 ; 51 L. T. 718. As to sale of trade fixtures in a public-house, see *Lea* v. *Whittaker*, L. R. 8 C. P. 70 ; 27 L. T. 676 ; 37 J. P. 183 ; 21 W. R. 230.

A *signboard* of a public-house erected on a post by the wayside is usually an incorporeal hereditament which passes with the house: *Hoare* v. *Metropolitan Board of Works*, L. R. 9 Q. B. 296 ; 38 J. P. 535. So a signboard may be affixed to an adjoining house : *Moody* v. *Steggles*, 12 Ch. D. 261 ; *Francis* v. *Hayward*, 22 Ch. D. 177 ; 47 J. P. 517.

A valuable picture painted by an artist and fixed outside an inn as a signboard was held to belong to the landlord as a fixture : *Ex parte D'Eresby*, 44 L. T. 781 ; 29 W. R. 527.

A power given in a lease to distrain for non-payment of goods supplied was held to be a bill of sale : *Pulbrook* v. *Ashby*, 60 L. J. Q. B. 376 ; 35 W. R. 779.

See also, further, as to covenants, 1 Will. 4, c. 64, s. 31, and notes, *post*.

and for preparing the precepts to be directed to the high constable, and notices to be delivered by the petty constable, as required by this Act, the sum of one shilling and sixpence ; and every such clerk who shall demand or receive from any person for such respective fees in his behalf any greater sum or anything of greater value than the sums hereinbefore specified, being in the whole the sum of seven shillings and sixpence, shall for every such offence, on conviction before one justice, forfeit and pay the sum of five pounds.(*a*)

Appndx.

16. *Persons disqualified to hold licenses.*] And be it further enacted, that no sheriff's officer, or officer executing the legal process of any court of justice in any county or place, shall be capable of receiving or using any license under this Act ; and that every license granted or transferred to any person exercising any such office shall be void to all intents and purposes.(*b*)

17. *No excise license to be granted except to a person licensed under this Act.*] And be it further enacted, that no license for the sale of any excisable liquors by retail, to be drunk or consumed on the premises of the person licensed, shall be granted by the commissioners of excise, or by any officer of excise, to any person whatsoever, unless such person shall have previously obtained from the justices a license under this Act, and which said license of such justices shall be retained by such person, after being produced to the commissioners or officers of excise ; and every license granted by the commissioners of excise, or by any officer of excise, contrary to this provision, shall be null and void to all intents and purposes.(*c*)

(*a*) This includes the fees of transfers and renewals as well as new licenses. Besides these fees there is a fee of 1*s*. for registration : Licensing Act, 1872, section 36. These fees apply to certificates for beer, cider, and winehouse and spirits and sweets licenses, except that on renewals of these a fee of 4*s*. and 1*s*. only beside the registration fee is to be paid : 33 & 34 Vict. c. 29, s. 4, sub-section 3. As to the constable's fees, see 35 & 36 Vict. c. 92, s. 7.

In one case a mayor claimed a fee of 4*s*. over and above those statutory fees as due under the ancient custom of the borough, but the court held all such customs impliedly repealed, and the sum was recovered back by the licensee : *Morgan* v. *Palmer*, 2 B. & C. 729.

There is no appeal to quarter sessions against any conviction under this section owing to the repeal of section 27 as to convictions.

(*b*) Disqualifications are also declared as to beerhouses by 1 Will. 4, c. 64, s. 2 ; 3 & 4 Vict. c. 61, s. 7. And when felony is committed, see 3 & 4 Vict. c. 61, s. 7 ; 23 Vict. c. 27, s. 22 ; 33 & 34 Vict. c. 29, s. 14.

(*c*) A similar enactment has been extended to beerhouses, cider

ALEHOUSE ACT, 1828, s. 27.

18. Penalty for selling excisable liquors by retail *without license*. Repealed by Licensing Act, 1872. See Schedule, and section 3.

19. Licensed persons to use *standard measures* in sale of liquors. Repealed by Licensing Act, 1872. See Schedule, and section 8.

20. Houses to be *closed* by order of justices in case of *riot, &c.* Repealed by Licensing Act, 1872. See Schedule, and section 23.

21. Penalties for *offences* against tenor of licenses. Repealed by Licensing Act, 1872. See Schedule.(a)

22. Proceedings at the session in certain cases to be carried on by the petty constable. Repealed by Licensing Act, 1872. See Schedule.

23. Penalty on witness not attending. Repealed by Licensing Act, 1872. See Schedule.

24. Penalties of justices how to be recovered and applied. Repealed by 51 & 52 Vict. c. 27, Schedule.

25. Other penalties, how to be recovered. Repealed by Licensing Act, 1872. See Schedule.

26. How penalties are to be applied. Repealed by Licensing Act, 1872. See Schedule.

27. *Appeal may be made to the quarter sessions—Judgment of quarter sessions to be final.*] And be it further enacted, that any person who shall think himself aggrieved by any act of any justice done in or concerning the execution of this Act, may appeal against such Act to the next general or quarter sessions of the peace holden for the county or place wherein the cause of such complaint shall have arisen, unless such sessions

---

houses, wine licenses, off-spirit licenses, and sweets. And the rule is as to all justices' licenses, that when such licenses become void or are forfeited, the excise license becomes void also: Licensing Act, 1872, s. 63, *ante*, p. 136.

(*a*) Nearly all offences are now set forth in Licensing Acts, 1872, 1874.

9 GEO. 4, c. 61, s. 27. 239

shall be holden within twelve days next after such act shall have **Appndx.**
been done, and in that case to the next subsequent sessions holden
as aforesaid, and not afterwards, provided that such person shall
give to such justice notice in writing of his intention to appeal
and of the cause and matter thereof within five days next after
such act shall have been done, and *seven days*(b) at the least before
such session, and shall within such five days enter into a recognizance, with two sufficient sureties, before a justice acting in and
for such county or place as aforesaid, conditioned to appear at the
said session, and to try such appeal, and to abide the judgment
of the court thereupon, and to pay such costs as shall be by the
court awarded; and upon such notice being given, and such recognizance being entered into, the justices before whom the same
shall be entered into shall liberate such person, if in custody for
any offence in reference to which the act intended to be appealed
against shall have been done; and the court at such session shall
hear and determine the matter of such appeal, and shall make
such order therein, *with or without costs*, as to the said court shall
seem meet; and in case the act appealed against shall be the
refusal to grant or to transfer any license, and the judgment under
which such act was done be reversed, it shall be lawful for the
said court to grant or to transfer such license in the same manner
as if such license had been granted at the general annual licensing
meeting, or had been transferred at a special sessions; and the
judgment of the said court shall be final and conclusive to all
intents and purposes; and in case of the *dismissal of such appeal*,
or of the affirmance of the judgment on which such act was done,
and which was appealed against, the said court shall adjudge and
order the said judgment to be carried into execution, and *costs*
awarded to be paid, and shall, if necessary, issue process for
enforcing such order: Provided that no justice shall act in the
hearing and determination of any appeal to the general or quarter
sessions as aforesaid from any act done by him in or concerning
the execution of this Act: Provided also, that when any cause of
complaint shall have arisen within any liberty, county of a city,
county of a town, city, or town corporate, it shall be lawful for
the person who shall think himself so as aforesaid aggrieved, to

---

(b) This, so far as regards the *seven* days, was repealed by 47 & 48
Vict. c. 43, which repeals 12 & 13 Vict. c. 45, s. 1, as regards appeals
and now requires 15 clear days (the period mentioned in 42 & 43 Vict.
c. 49, s. 31) to intervene between the day of decision and the sitting of
the quarter sessions. See also *R.* v. *Maule*, 35 J. P. 596. There is,
however, a doubt whether the " prescribed quarter sessions " in 42 & 43
Vict.c.49,s.31, means not only the particular county quarter sessions, but
also such a quarter sessions as sits not less than fifteen days distant.

Appndx. appeal against any such act as aforesaid, if he shall think fit, to the quarter sessions of the county within or adjoining to which such liberty or place shall be situate, subject to all the provisions hereinbefore contained.(*a*)

(*a*) This section is repealed so far as relates to appeals against the refusal to grant a new license, and in all other respects, except that it remains in force as regards appeals against a refusal of the renewal or transfer of licenses.

A person aggrieved includes a person whose license has been refused, and he may always appeal in those cases where an appeal still exists: *R.* v. *Deane,* 2 Q. B. 96. But a rival who has already a licensed house near a house newly licensed cannot appeal against such new license, for he is not a person aggrieved in this sense: *R.* v. *Middlesex JJ.,* 3 B. & Ad. 938; *R.* v. *Surrey JJ.,* 52 J. P. 423.

When the owner may appeal.] The owner may join in the appeal against a refusal of renewal along with the license holder who is his tenant; and it has been held that a mortgagee of the premises may appeal against a refusal of the renewal of the license if the licensee expressly authorised such mortgagee to take all steps to preserve the license, even though the licensee declines to appeal himself: *Garrett* v. *Middlesex JJ.,* 12 Q. B. D. 620; 53 L. J. M. C. 81; 48 J. P. 358; 32 W. R. 646. But the owner is not entitled to ask a license in his own name unless he is about to keep the premises as a licensed house: 9 Geo. 4, c. 91, s. 1. In the cases, however, mentioned in Licensing Act, 1874, s. 15, *ante,* p. 192, the owner is expressly authorised to apply for a transfer, and he may appeal in his own name: *R.* v. *West Riding JJ.,* 11 Q. B. D. 417; 48 J. P. 149; 52 L. J. M. C. 99; *Stevens* v. *Sharnbrook JJ.,* 53 J. P. 423; 23 Q. B. D. 142; 58 L. J. M. C. 167.

An appeal is the only redress against the refusal of a renewal or transfer of a license on the merits where the facts are in controversy, and the justices cannot be sued by action, at least, if no corrupt motive can be proved: *Bassett* v. *Gadshall,* 3 Wils. 121; nor can a criminal information be filed for like reasons: *R.* v. *Young,* 1 Burr. 556. See notes to section 1, *ante,* p. 214. But there may be a remedy by way of *mandamus,* as to which see *Ruddick* v. *Liverpool JJ.,* 42 J. P. 406, and notes to section 1, *ante,* p. 215, and notes to Licensing Act, 1872, s. 42, *ante,* p. 91.

An appellant cannot be deprived of his appeal by a rule made at quarter sessions that the court will hear no appeal unless entered three days before the first day of sitting: *R.* v. *Pawlett,* L. R. 8 Q. B. 491; 37 J. P. 775; 29 L. T. 390.

Where H., being refused his renewal license though he had not received any notice of opposition under 35 & 36 Vict. c. 94, s. 42, and though the justices had not adjourned the hearing as therein directed, gave notice of appeal to quarter sessions, and the superintendent of police, who had opposed the renewal, served a seven days' notice of opposition, stating grounds, upon H. before the hearing of the appeal,

9 GEO. 4, c. 61, s. 28.

28. *Justices to bind parties to appear to give evidence at quarter sessions.*] And be it further enacted, that when any Appndx.

the court held the notice was too late, and that the quarter sessions had no jurisdiction to enter upon any question as to the character of H.: *Hocking* v. *Powell*, 55 J. P. 358.

To what sessions appeal lies.] The appeal lies to the county quarter sessions, and not to the recorder of a borough, against the refusal to transfer or renew a license : *R.* v. *Deane*, *R.* v. *Reading JJ.*, 2 Q. B. 96 ; *R.* v. *Recorder of Bristol*, 4 E. & B. 265 ; 24 L. J. M. C. 43 ; 19 J. P. 342. The Municipal Corporations Act, 1882, 45 & 46 Vict. c. 50, s. 165, expressly enacts that the recorder shall not by virtue of his office have power to grant any license or authority to any person to keep an inn, alehouse, or victualling house to sell excisable liquors by retail. The county quarter sessions to which the appeal is taken must decide it, and cannot adjourn the hearing to a subsequent sessions : *R.* v. *Belton*, 11 Q. B. 379 ; 12 J. P. 232 ; 17 L. J. M. C. 70 ; *Bowman* v. *Blyth*, 7 E. & B. 47 ; 22 J. P. 5 ; 26 L. J. M. C. 57. But there is nothing to prevent the quarter sessions from adjourning a particular case for a few days if necessary, so long as they decide it before the next following quarter sessions : *R.* v. *Cambridge Union*, 1 B. & S. 61 ; 30 L. J. M. C. 137 ; 4 L. T. 212 ; 9 W. R. 599 ; *R.* v. *Mainwaring*, E. B. & E. 474 ; 47 L. J. M. C, 278 ; *Rawnsley* v. *Hutchinson*, L. R. 6 Q. B. 303 ; 40 L. J. M. C. 97 ; 35 J. P. 501.

When the licensing justices refuse the license on the ground that good character was not sufficiently proved, the appellant may give new and additional evidence of good character : *R.* v. *Pilgrim*, L. R. 6 Q. B. 89 ; 40 L. J. M. C. 3; 23 L. T. 410 ; 19 W. R. 99 ; 35 J. P. 167 ; *Ex parte Morgan*, 23 L. T. 605 ; 35 J. P. 37. The court has held that there is no obligation on the justices to adjourn the hearing so that the court may be so constituted that there shall be a majority : *Ex parte Evans*, 56 J. P. 488.

Notice of appeal.] The recognisances should not be entered into till the notice of appeal has been served : *R.* v. *Anglesey* (1892), 2 Q. B. 29 ; 56 J. P. 552.

When an appeal is competent the notice of appeal used to be served on at least two of the justices who joined in the decision : *R.* v. *Cheshire JJ.*, 11 A. & E. 139. And service on the clerk to the justices was deemed to be not sufficient : *Ex parte Curtis* ; *Curtis* v. *Buss*, 3 Q. B. D. 13 ; 41 J. P. 87 ; 37 L. T. 533 ; 47 L. J. M. C. 35 ; 26 W. R. 210. The service on the justice might always be either personal or at his dwelling-house : *R.* v. *North Riding JJ.*, 7 Q. B. 154 ; 14 L. J. M. C. 91. And now it has been held that the procedure of the Summary Jurisdiction Acts, as regards service of notice of appeal, applies to this class of appeals, and hence service need only be on the clerk of the licensing justices, and not on the justices themselves : 42 & 43 Vict. c. 49, s. 31 ; *R.* v. *Glamorganshire* (1892), 1 Q. B. 363, 621 ; 56 J. P. 232, 437 ; 61 L. J. M. C. 169 ; 67 L. T. 543 ; 41 W. R. 57.

R

Appndx. person shall have given notice of his intention to appeal as aforesaid, and shall have entered into recognizance as hereinbefore directed, it shall be lawful for the justice before whom such recognizance shall have been entered into to summon any person whose evidence shall appear to him to be material, and to require such person to be bound in recognizance to appear at the said general or quarter sessions, and to give evidence on such appeal; and in case any such person as aforesaid shall neglect or refuse to obey such summons, or shall refuse to enter into such recognizance,

Not only must notice of appeal be served on the clerk of the licensing justices, but also on the person who opposed the license at the general annual meeting, for such person comes within the words "the other person" in 42 & 43 Vict. c. 49, s. 31 : *R.* v. *Bristol JJ.*, 57 J. P. 486; 68 L. T. 355.

It has not yet been decided whether, if several persons oppose the license at the general meeting, each of those persons is entitled to be served with the notice of appeal. Nor has it been decided whether the opponent after being served with notice of the appeal is entitled to appear at quarter sessions as a party, or to what extent he may be treated by the quarter sessions as a party, either with or without his consent.

As to costs of appeal, see section 29 and notes.

If the justices at quarter sessions are *equally divided*, see notes to section 1, *ante*, p. 226.

Statement of case by justices.] No case could formerly be stated by licensing justices under 20 & 21 Vict. c. 43, as regards granting or refusing a license: *West* v. *Potts*, 34 J. P. 760; *Garrety* v. *Potts*, L. R. 6 Q. B. 88*n*; 40 L. J. M. C. 1; 23 L. T. 554; 19 W. R. 127; 35 J. P. 168. But if an appeal were taken to quarter sessions, the latter court could always state a case for the opinion of the High Court. And now the person aggrieved is entitled to demand from licensing justices a case for the opinion of the High Court on any point of law: 42 & 43 Vict. c. 49, s. 33; 47 & 48 Vict. c. 43, Sched.; 52 & 53 Vict. c. 63, s. 13; *R.* v. *Glamorganshire JJ.*, *ante*, p. 241. And when the justices state a special case, it has been held that if the superintendent of police, being an opponent, desires it, he may be made the respondent in the case so stated and entitled to be heard in the High Court and to costs if he succeed: *Price* v. *James* (1892), 2 Q. B. 28; 61 L. J. M. C. 203; 56 J. P. 471; 57 J. P. 143; 67 L. T. 543; 41 W. R. 57.

As all the convictions for offences relating to the keeping of licensed houses will now take place under the Licensing Act, 1872, and section 52 of that Act provides an appeal, that section and the Summary Jurisdiction Acts, 1879 and 1882, 42 & 43 Vict. c. 49, s. 19, and 47 & 48 Vict. c. 43, will govern the procedure in respect of such appeals.

During the appeal against the refusal to renew or transfer a license or certificate, the Inland Revenue may grant a temporary license: Licensing Act, 1872, section 53.

it shall be lawful for such justice as aforesaid to issue his warrant **Appndx.** to apprehend such person so neglecting or refusing to obey such summons, and to bring him before such justice, and if such person shall continue to refuse to enter into such recognizance, to commit him to the common gaol or house of correction of the county or place for which such justice shall be then acting, there to remain until he shall enter into such recognizance, or shall be otherwise discharged by due course of law.

29. *Court to adjudge costs in certain cases.*] And be it further enacted, that in every case where notice of appeal against the judgment of any justice in or concerning the execution of this Act shall have been given, and such appeal shall have been dismissed, or the judgment so appealed against shall have been confirmed, or such appeal shall have been abandoned, it shall be lawful for the court to whom such appeal shall have been made or intended to be made, and such court is hereby required, to adjudge and order that the party so having appealed, or given notice of his intention to appeal, shall pay to the justice to whom such notice shall have been given, or to whomsoever he shall appoint, such sum by way of costs as shall in the opinion of such court be sufficient to indemnify such justice from all cost and charge whatsoever to which such justice may have been put in consequence of his having had served upon him notice of the intention of such party to appeal; and if such party shall refuse or neglect forthwith to pay such sum, it shall be lawful for the said court to adjudge and order that the party so refusing or neglecting shall be committed to the common gaol or house of correction, there to remain until such sum be paid; and that in every case in which the judgment so appealed against shall be *reversed* it shall be lawful for such court, if it shall think fit, to adjudge and order that the treasurer of the county or place in and for which such justice whose judgment shall have been so reversed shall have acted on the occasion when he shall have given such judgment shall pay to such justice, or to whomsoever he shall appoint, such sum as shall in the opinion of such court be sufficient to indemnify such justice from all costs and charges whatsoever to which such justice may have been so put; and the said treasurer is hereby authorised to pay the same, which shall be allowed to him in his accounts.(*a*)

(*a*) *Payment of costs at quarter sessions.*] The costs awarded to be paid by courts of quarter sessions are now directed to be paid to the clerk of the peace, who is to pay them over to the party entitled: 12 & 13 Vict. c. 45, s. 5; 11 & 12 Vict. c. 43, s. 27; *Gay* v. *Mathews*, 4 B. & S. 440; 33 L. J. M. C. 14; 8 L. T. 674; 14 W. R. 922; 27

Appndx. **30.** *Actions against justices, &c.*] And be it further enacted, that every action against any justice, constable, or other

J. P. 247; *R.* v. *Devonport JJ.*, 33 J. P. 614. But an order directing the costs to be paid to the party would not be bad: *R.* v. *Binney*, 1 F. & B. 810; 22 L. J. M. C. 127; *R.* v. *Ely JJ.*, 5 E. & B. 484; 25 L. J. M, C. 1.

In municipal boroughs having no separate court of quarter sessions, but a separate commission of the peace, the costs are to be paid to the treasurer of the county and not of the borough: *Winn* v. *Mossman*, L. R. 4 Exch. 292; 38 L. J. Exch. 200; 33 J. P. 743; 20 L. T. 672. If not paid, then on the certificate of the clerk of the peace a warrant of distress shall be issued: 11 & 12 Vict. c. 43, s. 27; or upon a certified copy of the order of quarter sessions, such order may be removed to the High Court and enforced like a rule of that court: 12 & 13 Vict. c. 45, s. 18.

The court of quarter sessions have power to give costs against the licensing justices if their decision is reversed: *R.* v. *Devonport*, 33 J. P. 614. But if the justices do not appear the High Court might quash that part of the order: *R.* v. *Davidson*, 43 L. J. 22; 35 J. P. 500; *R.* v. *Goodall*, L. R. 9 Q. B. 557; 38 J. P. 616. But quarter sessions may also, under the above section 29, make an order to indemnify the justices whose decision is reversed. The court may give costs of an appeal though they have no jurisdiction to hear the appeal: *R.* v. *Padwick*, 8 E. & B. 704.

The court of quarter sessions, independently of the above 29th section, may give costs in all cases before them, the Act 12 & 13 Vict. c. 45, s. 5, being a cumulative remedy in that respect: *R.* v. *Huntley*, 3 E. & B. 172; 23 L. J. M. C. 106. And the court may have a standing order about costs following the event which they may competently act upon: *Freeman* v. *Read*, 9 C. B. (N.S.) 301; 30 L. J. M. C. 123; 9 W. R. 141.

Though the costs might not be taxed before the close of the sessions: *R.* v. *Long*, 1 Q. B. 740; *R.* v. *Hants JJ.*, 33 L. J. M. C. 46; 7 L. T. 391; 11 W. R. 122, the opposite party may consent, or if he attends taxation he waives objections: *Freeman* v. *Read*, 9 C. B. (N.S.) 301, *supra*; *R.* v. *Mortlock*, 9 Q. B. 459; *Ex parte Watkins*, 5 L. T. 605; 10 W. R. 249. Or if the costs are taxed before or at an adjournment this will be sufficient: *R.* v. *Hants*, 33 L. J. M. C. 104, *supra*; *Rawnsley* v. *Hutchinson*, 35 J. P. 501; L. R. 6 Q. B. 305.

All *costs incurred* by the quarter sessions or the justices out of session of a county, and all costs incurred by any justice, police officer, or constable in defending any legal proceedings taken against him in respect of any order made or act done in the execution of his duty as such justice, police officer, or constable shall, to such amount as may be sanctioned by the standing committee of the county council and quarter sessions, and so far as they are not otherwise provided for, be paid out of the county fund of the county, and the council of the county shall provide for such payment accordingly: 51 & 52 Vict. c. 31, s. 66.

9 GEO. 4, C. 61, S. 36.

person for or on account of any matter or thing whatsoever done Appndx. or commanded by him in the execution of his duty or office under this Act, shall be commenced within three calendar months after the cause of action or complaint shall have arisen, and not afterwards; and if any person shall be sued for any matter or thing which he shall have done in the execution of this Act, he may plead the general issue, and give the special matter in evidence.(a)

31. Conviction to be on oath of witnesses. *Repealed* by Licensing Act, 1872. See Schedule.

32. Form of conviction. *Repealed* by Licensing Act, 1872. See Schedule.

33. Convictions to be returned to the quarter sessions, and filed of record. *Repealed* by Licensing Act, 1872. See Schedule.

34. Writ of *certiorari* not to be allowed. *Repealed* by Licensing Act, 1872. See Schedule, and section 54.

35. *Commencement of this Act.*] And be it further enacted that this Act shall commence on the tenth day of October next ensuing the passing thereof; and that from and after the commencement of this Act the Acts 5 & 6 Ed. 6, c. 25; 1 Jac. 1, c. 9; 4 Jac. 1, cc. 4 and 5; 7 Jac. 1, c. 10; part of 21 Jac. 1, c. 7; 1 Car. 1, c. 7; 3 Car. 1, c. 3; 9 Geo. 2, c. 23, ss. 14, 15, 20; 24 Geo. 2, c. 40, s. 24; 26 Geo. 2, c. 13, s. 12; 26 Geo. 2, c. 31; 28 Geo. 2, c. 19, s. 2; 29 Geo. 2, c. 12, ss. 23, 24; 30 Geo. 2, c. 24, s. 14; 5 Geo. 3, c. 46, ss. 20—22; 32 Geo. 3, c. 59; 38 Geo. 3, c. 54, s. 13; 39 Geo. 3, c. 86; 48 Geo. 3, c. 143, ss. 7, 10; 4 Geo. 4, c. cxxv., ss. 1—6, shall be and the same are hereby repealed.(*b*)

36. *Act not to affect the two universities; nor to alter time of licensing in London ;—nor any law of excise ;—nor to prohibit the sale of beer at fairs in certain cases.*] Provided always, and be it further enacted, that nothing in this Act contained shall extend to, alter, or in any manner to affect any of the rights or privileges of the universities of Oxford or

---

(*a*) As this Act and these last sections have now nothing to do with convictions or orders, this section seems superfluous.

(*b*) This section was repealed by 36 & 37 Vict. c. 91, Schedule, but is still a useful reference to the series of Acts.

246   ALEHOUSE ACT, 1828, S. 37.

Appndx. Cambridge, or the powers of the chancellors or vice-chancellors of the same, as by law possessed under the respective charters of the said universities or otherwise ; or the master, wardens, freemen, and commonalty of the vintners of the city of London, but not to extend to those freemen of the said company of vintners who have obtained the same by redemption only ; nor to alter the time of granting licenses for keeping inns in the city of London : Provided also, that nothing in this Act contained shall alter any law relating to the revenue of excise, except so far as the same is hereby expressly altered and otherwise provided for ; nor to prohibit any person from selling beer in booths or other places at the time and within the limits of the ground or place in or upon which is holden any lawful fair in like manner as such person was authorised to do before the passing of this Act.(a)

37. *Rules for the interpretation of this Act.*] In this Act, be it enacted, that the word "justice" shall be deemed to mean justice of the peace ; and the words "treasurer of the county or place" shall be deemed to include any officer acting in such capacity, or charged with the receipt and expenditure of moneys from and out of which the cost of public prosecutions have been usually defrayed ; the words "peace officer" shall be deemed to include any petty constable, tithingman, head-borough, beadle, or bailiff ; the words "parish officer" shall be deemed to include any churchwarden, chapelwarden, or overseer of the poor ; and the said words "justice," "treasurer of the county or place," "peace officer," "parish officer," and the words "high constable," and the words "petty constable," and the words "overseer of the poor," and the words "clerk of justices," shall each be deemed to include any person acting as such, and any number of justices, treasurers, peace officers, parish officers, high constables, petty constables, overseers of the poor, and clerks of justices ; and the word "person" and the word "party" shall be deemed to include any number of persons and parties ; and that the meaning of the aforesaid several words shall not be restricted, although the same may be subsequently referred to in the singular number and masculine gender only ; and that the word "notice," and the word "license," and the word "adjournment," and the word "day," and the word "time," and the word "house," and the word "place," shall each be deemed to include any number of notices, licenses, adjournments, days, times, houses, or places ; and the word "county," and the words "county or place," shall

---

(a) As to selling at fairs, see now Licensing Act, 1874, section 18, *ante*, p. 197.

be deemed severally to include any county, riding, division of the **Appndx.**
county of Lincoln, hundred, division of a county, liberty, division
of a liberty, county of a city, county of a town, city, cinque port,
or town corporate; and the words "division or place" shall be
deemed to include any division of a county or riding, liberty,
division of a liberty, county of a city, county of a town, city,
cinque port, or town corporate; and the words "parish or place"
shall be deemed to include any township, hamlet, tithing, vill,
extra-parochial place, or any place maintaining its own poor;
and the word "inn" shall be deemed to include any inn, alehouse,
or victualling-house; and that the words "inn, alehouse, or
victualling-house" shall be deemed to include all houses in which
shall be sold by retail any excisable liquor to be drunk or consumed on the premises; and the words "excisable liquor" shall
be deemed to include any ale, beer, or other fermented malt
liquor, sweets, cider, perry, wine, or other spirituous liquor which
now is or hereafter may be charged with duty either by customs
or excise; and the word "penalty" shall be deemed to include
any fine, penalty, or forfeiture of a pecuniary nature; and the
meaning of the said several words shall not be restricted, although
the same may be subsequently referred to in the singular number
only.

THE BEERHOUSE ACT, 1830.

11 GEO. 4 & 1 WILL. 4, CAP. 64.

*AN ACT to permit the General Sale of Beer and Cider by
Retail in England.* [23rd July, 1830.]

*All persons licensed under this Act may sell beer by
retail.*] Whereas it is expedient, for the better supplying the
public with beer in England, to give greater facilities for the sale
thereof than are at present afforded by licenses to keepers of inns,
alehouses, and victualling-houses: Be it therefore enacted, &c.
It shall and may be lawful for any and every person, who shall
obtain a license for that purpose under the provisions of this Act,
to sell beer, ale, and porter by retail in any part of England, in
any house or premises specified in such license; anything in any
Act or Acts heretofore made, or in force at the time of the passing
of this Act, to the contrary in anywise notwithstanding.(*b*)

(*b*) This is the first of the series of Beerhouse Acts; those following
are 4 & 5 Will. 4, c. 85; 3 & 4 Vict. c. 61; 33 & 34 Vict. c. 111; 43
Vict. c. 6; 45 & 46 Vict. c. 34.

Appndx.

2. *Parties desirous of retailing beer shall take out a license—In London licenses shall be granted by the commissioners of excise, &c.—Elsewhere in England by the collectors and supervisors of excise—No license shall be granted to a sheriff's officer or non-householder—Register of licenses—Licenses shall be produced for the inspection of magistrates.*] It shall be lawful for every and any person, being a householder (other than and except such persons as are hereinafter specially excepted), who shall be desirous of selling beer, ale, and porter by retail under the provisions of this Act, to apply for and to obtain an excise license for that purpose ; and in every application for such license there shall be specified, set forth, and inserted the Christian name and surname of the party applying for such license, and a description of the *house or premises* in which beer, ale, and porter is intended to be sold by retail by such person ; and any and every such license which shall be taken out within the limits of the chief office of excise in London shall be granted under the hands and seals of two or more of the commissioners of excise for the time being, or of such persons as they, the said commissioners of excise, or the major part of them, for the time being shall from time to time authorise, employ, or direct for that purpose ; and any and every such license which shall be taken out in any part of England not within the said limits shall be granted under the respective hands and seals of the several collectors and supervisors of excise within their respective collections and districts ;(*a*) and every such license shall be dated on the day when the same shall be granted ; and every such license shall be duly registered in the proper department of the excise : Provided always, that no such license shall authorise or entitle the party licensed to receive any license to sell or retail wine or spirits, anything in any Act or Acts of Parliament to the contrary thereof notwithstanding ; and that *no* such *license* shall be *granted* to any person being a sheriff's officer, or officer executing the legal process of any court of justice ; and that any license granted to any such person shall be void to all intents and purposes ; and a list or register of every license so granted, specifying the name and place of abode of every person licensed, and the name and description of the house mentioned in such license, shall be kept at the excise office with respect to all licenses granted by the commissioners of excise or any person

---

(*a*) Part of this section is repealed by 32 & 33 Vict. c. 27, Schedule, *post*, as regards the excise license, and other parts by 36 & 37 Vict. c. 91, Schedule, which parts are here omitted.

11 GEO. 4 & 1 WILL. 4, C. 64, S. 6. 249

authorised by them, and at the office or dwelling-house of every collector and supervisor of excise in their and his respective collections and districts; and such list or register shall at all times be produced to and shall be open to the inspection and perusal of any magistrate of the county or place where such license shall be granted and where such house shall be situate; and a copy of such list or register shall once in every calendar month be transmitted by every such collector or supervisor to the clerk of the magistrates for the district in which such license shall be granted; and any copy of or extract from such list or register, which shall or may be at any time required by the clerk to the magistrates, shall be given to him by such collector or supervisor, whenever thereto required.(*b*)

Appndx.
—

3. *License duty shall be under the management of the commissioners of excise, and carried to the consolidated fund.*]

4. Party requiring license shall enter into a bond, with sureties, for payment of penalties. *Repealed* by 30 & 31 Vict. c. 90, s. 13.

5. No person licensed to sell beer shall be competent to be a surety. *Repealed* by 30 & 31 Vict. c. 90, s. 13.

6. Person licensed to retail beer shall put up descriptive boards. *Repealed* by Licensing Act, 1872. See Schedule and section 11.

7. *No person shall sell beer after expiration of his license—License may be renewed yearly—Penalty on selling without license 20l.*] And be it further enacted, that no person shall sell any beer by retail under the provisions of this Act at any time after the expiration of any license granted under this Act,

---

(*b*) This section has also been greatly qualified by the later statutes describing the valuation qualification: see 3 & 4 Vict. c. 61, s. 2, and Licensing Act, 1872, sections 46, 47.
Where the license was obtained under this Act by the fraud of a third party, it was held to be not void: *R.* v. *Minshall*, 1 N. & M. 277. And where a third party carried on the business, using the name of the licensed person, this was held to be not a void license or fraudulent: *Brooker* v. *Wood*, 5 B. & Ad. 1052; *Meux* v. *Humphries*, 1 N. & M. 132.
The date of expiration of license was altered to 10th October by 24 & 25 Vict. c. 91, s. 14, *post*.

Appndx. nor in any house or place not specified in such license: Provided always, that it shall be lawful for any person so licensed to take out a fresh retail license for the selling beer by retail before the expiration of any former retail license, and so from year to year; and if any person not being duly licensed to sell beer as the keeper of a common inn, alehouse or victualling-house, shall sell any beer by retail without having an excise retail license in force authorising such person so to do, or after the expiration of any such license, or without renewing such license in manner aforesaid, or in any house or place not specified in such license, or if any such person so licensed shall deal in or retail any wine or spirits, every such person so offending shall for every such offence forfeit and lose the sum of twenty pounds. [See Licensing Act 1872, sections 3, 63.]

8. *Such penalty may be recovered as other excise penalties.*] (*a*)

9. *Powers of Excise Act, 7 & 8 Geo. 4, c. 53, &c., extended to this Act.*] (*b*)

10. *Proviso for partners—License shall not extend to any other house.*] Provided always, and be it further enacted, that persons trading in partnership, and in one house or premises only, shall not be obliged to take out more than one license in any one year, for selling any beer by retail under the provisions of this Act: provided also, that no one license which shall be granted by virtue of this Act, shall authorise and empower any person or persons to sell any beer, ale, or porter under the provisions of this Act, in any house or place other than the place mentioned in such license for selling beer, ale, and porter by retail under the provisions of this Act, and in respect whereof such license shall be granted.

11. Houses to be closed by order of justices in cases of riot, &c. *Repealed* by Licensing Act, 1872. See Schedule, and section 23.

12. Standard measures to be used. *Repealed* by Licensing Act, 1872. See Schedule, and section 8.

(*a*) See also 42 & 43 Vict. c. 49, ss. 32, 53.
(*b*) See also 6 Geo. 4, c. 81, ss. 25, 28, 32, as to legal proceedings; 7 & 8 Geo. 4, c. 53, ss. 3, 61, 70, 84, 128; 4 & 5 Will. 4, c. 51, ss. 20, 25; 42 & 43 Vict. c. 49; 47 & 48 Vict. c. 43.

13. Penalty on retailers permitting drunkenness, &c., in their houses. *Repealed* by Licensing Act, 1872. See Schedule, and section 13.

Appndx.
—

14. Retailers' house shall not be open before four in the morning, nor after ten in the evening; nor on Sundays between 10 and 1, or 3 and 5 in the day. *Repealed* by 3 & 4 Vict. c. 61, s. 14.

15. Penalties recoverable before two justices in petty sessions, within three months after offence committed. *Repealed* by Licensing Act, 1872. See Schedule.

16. Appeal to the quarter sessions. *Repealed* by Licensing Act, 1872. See Schedule, and section 52.

17. Court to adjudge costs of appeal in certain cases. *Repealed* by Licensing Act, 1872. See Schedule.

18. Proceedings at the sessions in certain cases to be carried on by the petty constable. *Repealed* by Licensing Act, 1872. See Schedule.

19. In default of payment of penalties, proceedings may be had against the sureties. *Repealed* by Licensing Act, 1872. See Schedule.

20. Penalty on witnesses not attending. *Repealed* by Licensing Act, 1872. See Schedule.

21. Penalties may be levied by distress. *Repealed* by Licensing Act, 1872. See Schedule.

22. Application of penalties. *Repealed* by Licensing Act, 1872. See Schedule, and sections 55—57.

23. *If justices of liberties, &c., do not attend at sessions, the county justices may act.*] (c)

24. *Powers hereby given to justices of counties not to extend to the cinque ports.*] (d)

25. Form of conviction. *Repealed* by Licensing Act, 1872. See Schedule.

(c) See 9 Geo. 4, c. 61, s. 7, which is identical.
(d) See notes to 9 Geo. 4, c. 61, ss. 1, 8.

Appndx. **26.** Convictions to be returned to the quarter sessions, and filed of record. *Repealed* by Licensing Act, 1872. See Schedule.

27. Writ of *certiorari* not to be allowed. *Repealed* by Licensing Act, 1872. See Schedule, and section 54.

28. *Actions against justices, &c.*] (a)

29. *Act not to affect the two universities nor the Vintners' Company in London;—nor to prohibit the sale of beer at fairs as heretofore.*] (b)

30. *Licenses to retail cider and perry may be granted under the regulations of this Act, on payment of* 1l. 1s. *duty—Provisions and penalties of this Act with respect to the sale of beer to apply to the sale of cider and perry— Persons licensed to retail beer may also retail cider and perry.*] And whereas it is expedient that the sale of cider and perry by retail should be licensed in like manner and should be subject to the like regulations as the sale of beer : Be it therefore enacted, that from and after the tenth day of October, one thousand eight hundred and thirty, it shall be lawful for any person desirous of selling cider and perry by retail to apply for and to obtain an excise license for that purpose, under the same regulations in all respects (except as hereinafter or otherwise provided) as are in this Act prescribed and contained with respect to persons desirous of selling beer, ale, and porter by retail, and of being licensed for that purpose ; and that all the clauses, regulations, and provisions in this Act contained relating to the sale of beer by retail, and to the licenses for selling the same, and to the sureties for the parties licensed, and to the conduct of the parties licensed, and to all other matters whatever respecting the selling of beer by retail, and the retailers thereof, and the licenses for the same, and the houses where the same are sold, and the penalties against the parties licensed, shall be taken and deemed to be applicable to the sale of cider and perry by retail and to

---

(a) See note to 9 Geo. 4, c. 61, s. 30.
(b) See 9 Geo. 4, c. 61, s. 36, which is identical ; see also Licensing Act, 1872, section 72.
See *R.* v. *Archdall*, 8 A. & E. 281 ; *Huxham* v. *Wheeler*, 3 H. & C. 75. As to *fairs and races*, see Licensing Act, 1874, section 18 ; also 25 & 26 Vict. c. 22, s. 12 ; 26 & 27 Vict. c. 33, s. 21 ; 27 & 28 Vict. c. 18, s. 5.

11 GEO. 4 & 1 WILL. 4, C. 64, S. 31. 253

licenses for the same, and to the sellers of cider and perry by retail, as if cider and perry, and the retailers thereof, were expressly mentioned and specified in and throughout this Act: Provided always, that the person receiving a license for selling cider or perry by retail shall pay for such license a duty of one pound one shilling, and no more, instead of the duty of two pounds two shillings hereinbefore mentioned, and which said duty of one pound one shilling shall be applied in like manner as the said duty of two pounds two shillings is hereinbefore directed to be applied; and every such license shall be according to the form in the schedule annexed to this Act: Provided also, that any person licensed under this Act to sell beer by retail may sell also cider and perry by retail without receiving a separate license for that purpose; but that no person licensed to sell cider and perry by retail, and paying for such license, as herein provided, the sum of one pound and one shilling, shall be at liberty to sell beer by retail.(c)

Appndx.
—

31. *Covenants against houses, &c., being used as public-houses to extend to persons licensed under this Act.*] Provided always, and be it enacted, that any and every covenant or clause of restriction contained in any lease or contract between any landlord and tenant, whereby the trade or business of a victualler or publican is prohibited from being carried on in any house, building, or place mentioned or comprised in such lease or contract, or whereby any such house, building, or place is prohibited from being used as a public-house, or alehouse, shall apply and extend, and shall be construed to apply and extend, to every person who shall be licensed to sell beer, ale, or porter, or cider, or perry, under the provisions of this Act, and to any and every house specified and mentioned in the license granted to such person.(d)

(c) This section is *repealed* so far as it incorporates any repealed enactment: Licensing Act, 1872. See Schedule and 3 & 4 Vict. c. 61, *post.*

(d) *Covenants relating to public-houses, beer-houses, &c.*

The existence of this section has been overlooked in some decisions of the court on this subject.

Where the person applying to the justices for a license to sell intoxicating liquors on his premises is subject to a covenant in his lease or deed of purchase, which prohibits such sale, the covenant is sometimes used as a ground of opposition and the justices may or may not give effect to the objection. But the remedy against the applicant more properly lies in other courts, and it is sometimes a difficult question of

Appndx.

NOTE.

law and fact whether the prohibition is or is not effectual. If the justices grant a license to one who is by law liable to an injunction or action of damages at the suit of his landlord or other party, the license is not void, but nevertheless the applicant may be restrained from making any use of it, for he may be liable to ejectment or injunction or action. And whether the justices refuse an application on that ground or not, their decision is not conclusive, should another court be resorted to.

The following cases have been decided on various kinds of covenants:

Covenant not to build public-house, &c., on land.

Wilson v. *Hart*, L. R. 1 Ch. 43. Covenant not to sell ale, beer, wine, or spirits:—Held, to include sale of beer though only sold in bottles.

Pease v. *Coats*, L. R. 2 Eq. 688 ; 36 L. J. Ch. 57 ; 30 J. P. 819 ; 14 L. T. 886. Covenant not to use as a public-house:—Held, not to include off license for sale of beer.

Fielden v. *Slater*, L. R. 7 Eq. 523 ; 38 L. J. Ch. 379 ; 20 L. T. 485 ; 17 W. R. 485. Covenant not to use "as an inn, public-house, or tap-room, or for the sale of spirituous liquors or ale or beer":—Held, to include off license to sell wine and spirits in bottle.

London and North Western Railway Company v. *Garnett*, L. R. 9 Eq. 26 ; 39 L. J. Ch. 25 ; 21 L. T. 352 ; 18 W. R. 246. Covenant not to use as a beer-house, inn, or public-house, for the sale of spirituous liquors:—Held, not to include off beer licenses.

Jones v. *Bone*, L. R. 9 Eq. 674 ; 39 L. J. Ch. 405 ; 23 L. T. 304 ; 18 W. R. 489 ; 34 J. P. 468. Covenant not to carry on trade of hotel or tavern keeper, publican or beershop keeper, or seller by retail of wine, beer, spirits:—Held, not to include off-license for wine and spirits in bottle.

Carter v. *Williams*, L. R. 9 Eq. 678 ; 39 L. J. Ch, 560 ; 23 L. T. 183 ; 18 W. R. 593. Covenant not to use for an inn, public-house, or beerhouse:—Held, not to extend to tenant of assignee if he got no notice of covenant. As to covenant running with land.

Hall v. *Box*, 18 W. R. 820. Covenant not to erect a shop:—Held, to include a public-house.

Kemp v. *Bird*, 5 Ch. D. 974 ; 46 L. J. Ch. 828 ; 42 J. P. 36 ; 25 W. R. 838. Covenant not to let or demise for eating house:—Held, not the same as permitting tenant to so use it.

Richards v. *Revitt*, 7 Ch. D. 224 ; 44 L. J. Ch. 472 ; 26 W. R. 166 ; 37 L. T. 632. Covenant not to open tavern, beerhouse, or place licensed for sale of liquors:—Held, assignee of land, with notice of the covenant, may be restrained by injunction though no damage shown.

London and Suburban Company v. *Field*, 16 Ch. D. 645 ; 38 L. J. Ch. 549 ; 44 L. T. 444. Covenant not to use as public-house, tavern, or beershop:—Held, to include off-license for beer.

Appndx.
NOTE.

Holt v. *Collyer*, 16 Ch. D. 718; 44 L. T. 214; 45 J. P. 456. Covenant not to use as public-house, tavern, or beerhouse:—Held, not to include off-beer license held by grocer.

Thornewall v. *Johnson*, 50 L. J. Ch. 641; 44 L. T. 768; 29 W. R. 677. Covenant by purchaser not to carry on trade of retailer of wine, spirits, beer :—Held, to apply to sub-lessee of purchaser though having no notice of covenant using off-license.

Patman v. *Harland*, 17 Ch. D. 353; 44 L. T. 728; 29 W. R. 707. Covenant by purchaser not to carry on trade binds purchaser's lessee who is bound to inquire into lessor's title.

Nicoll v. *Fenning*, 19 Ch. D. 258; 45 L. T. 738; 51 L. J. Ch. 166. Covenant by purchaser not to erect tavern, public-house or beershop:—Held, sub-tenant of assignee of purchaser bound not to use off-beer license.

Covenant to take all beer, &c., from landlord.

Catt v. *Tourle*, L. R. 4 Ch. 654; 38 L. J. Ch. 665; 21 L. T. 188; 17 W. R. 662; 33 J. P. 659. Covenant by purchaser of land to take all beer from C., the vendor, who was to have exclusive right to supply. Assignee of purchaser restrained by injunction from taking beer from another than C.

Luker v. *Dennis*, 7 Ch. D. 227; 47 L. J. Ch. 174; 37 L. T. 827; 26 W. R. 167. Covenant by publican to take all beer sold at this house and other house from lessor. Assignee of second house with notice bound by covenant. Covenant to supply beer means good marketable beer. Covenant to take beer and covenant to supply beer, first covenant conditional on second covenant.

Edwick v. *Hawkes*, 18 Ch. D. 199; 50 L. J. Ch. 577; 45 L. T. 168. Covenant by tenant to purchase all beer he sells from landlord implies covenant of landlord to supply the beer and is not broken by tenant buying lessor's beer through agent.

Clegg v. *Hands*, 44 Ch. D. 503; 55 J. P. 180. Covenant by lessee and assigns of public-house to take all beer from lessor and assigns:— Held, the covenant may be enforced by assigns of lessor though beer made at a different brewery:—Held, covenant ran with the land.

Hanbury v. *Cundy*, 58 L. T. 155. Covenant to take all beer required for the business and reduction of rent so long as all beer taken:— Held, the covenant to take all beer was absolute, and that lessee had not the option to deal with a rival brewer and pay the full rent.

Stevens v. *Marston*, 64 L. T. 274; 55 J. P. 404. Covenant by lessor of public-house that lessee shall take all beer from lessor, and that lessor may distrain for unpaid price of beer sold makes the lease a bill of sale and must be registered as such as regards that covenant but lease not void as to other covenants.

See also *Cooper* v. *Turbill*, 3 Camp. 286; *Stancliffe* v. *Clarke*, 7 Ex. 439.

Appndx.

NOTE.

Miscellaneous covenants as to public-house.

Thomas v. *Hayward*, L. R. 4 Ex. 311 ; 38 L. J. Ex. 175. Covenant by lessor of public-house not to keep house for sale of beer or spirits within half a mile :—Held, not to run with land in favour of assignee of lease.

Maw v. *Hindmarsh*, 28 L. T. 644. On parol lease of public-house there is no implied agreement by tenant not to do anything to forfeit licenses.

Moufflet v. *Cole*, L. R. 8 Ex. 32 ; 42 L. J. Ex. 8 ; 21 W. R. 175. Covenant not to carry on public-house within half-a-mile :—Held, half-a-mile means as the crow flies.

Shepheard v. *Walker*, 34 L. T. 230. Agreement for new lease to contain similar covenant to the covenant in old lease (which was to keep up licenses) :—Held, lessor only entitled to a covenant from tenant to do his best to keep up license.

Moore v. *Robinson*, 48 L. J. Q. B. 156 ; 40 L. T. 99 ; 28 W. R. 312. S. agreed to rent beerhouse and covenanted to do nothing to imperil license :—Held, that S. going abroad and leaving a manager was not a breach of the agreement.

Wooler v. *Knott*, 1 Ex. D. 265 ; 45 L. J. Ex. 884 ; 35 L. T. 121 ; 24 W. R. 1004 ; 40 J. P. 788. Covenant by lessee of public-house to do nothing that can or may affect lease or make void any of the licenses. Lessee committed three offences, but none of them was endorsed on license :—Held, no breach of covenant.

Brookes v. *Drysdale*, 3 C. P. D. 52 ; 37 L. T. 467 ; 26 W. R. 331. Agreement to take lease of public-house with usual covenants. One covenant was in case of assignment to register the same with landlord's solicitor paying a fee :—Held, not a usual covenant and purchaser not bound to complete.

St. Albans (Bishop) v. *Battersby*, 3 Q. B. D. 359 ; 47 L. J. Q. B. 571 ; 26 W. R. 678 ; 38 L. T. 685 ; 42 J. P. 581. Covenant not to allow house to be used as a beershop or public-house :—Held, grocer's off-license to sell beer was a breach of covenant.

Taite v. *Gosling*, 11 Ch. D. 273 ; 48 L. J. Ch. 397 ; 40 L. T. 251 ; 27 W. R. 394. Mutual covenants by adjoining owners and assigns not to carry on trade of inn-keeper or retailer of liquors. Assignee of one can enforce covenant against neighbour. Assignee includes lessee.

Rutter v. *Daniel*, 46 L. T. 684 ; 30 W. R. 801. Assignment of goodwill of public-house gives assignee right to get licenses transferred.

Fleetwood v. *Hull*, 23 Q. B. D. 35 ; 58 L. J. Q. B. 341 ; 54 J. P. 229 ; 60 L. T. 790 ; 37 W. R. 714. Lessee of public-house covenanted to do nothing to forfeit or endanger license :—Held, mere conviction by sub-lessee was not a breach :—Held, that such covenant runs with the land, and may be enforced by assignee of reversion.

32. *Rules for the Interpretation of this Act.*] In this Act Appndx. the word "justice" shall be deemed to mean justice of the peace; and the word "person" and the word "party" shall be deemed to include any number of persons and parties; and the word "license," and the word "day," and the word "time," and the word "house," and the word "place," shall each be deemed to include any number of licenses, days, times, houses, or places; and the word "beer" shall in all cases be deemed to include beer, ale, and porter; and the word "cider" shall in all cases be deemed to include cider and perry; and the word "county" and the words "county or place" shall be deemed severally to include any county, riding, division of the county of Lincoln, hundred, division of a county, liberty, division of a liberty, county of a city, county of a town, city, cinque port, or town corporate; and the words "division or place" shall be deemed to include any division of a county or riding, liberty, division of a liberty, county of a city, county of a town, city, cinque port, or town corporate; and the words "parish or place" shall be deemed to include any township, hamlet, tithing, vill, extraparochial place, or any place maintaining its own poor; and the word "penalty" shall be deemed to include any fine, penalty, or forfeiture of a pecuniary nature; and the meaning of the several words in this Act shall not be restricted, although the same may be subsequently referred to in the singular number or masculine gender only.

Spicer v. *Martin*, 14 App. C. 12. Covenant by purchaser not to erect house for trade :—Held, to prevent hotel; covenants by mutual purchasers under building scheme enforceable.

Buckle v. *Fredericks*, 44 Ch. D. 244; 62 L. T. 884; 55 J. P. 214; 28 W. R. 742. Covenant not to carry on trade of innkeeper or retailer of wine, spirits, or beer :—Held, to include the sale of liquors under an excise license held by a theatre proprietor.

Harman v. *Powell*, 65 L. T. 255; 56 J. P. 150. Covenant by tenant not to do act whereby license forfeited or renewal withheld :— Held, that two convictions by tenant endorsed on license were a breach of covenant.

Deposit of publican's lease as security.

Dawn v. *City of London Co.*, L. R. 8 Eq. 155; 20 L. T. 601; 38 L. J. Ch. 454. Deposit by publican with brewer to cover advances past and future :—Held not to take priority of a second mortgage to other parties made before the further advance.

Menzies v. *Lightfoot*, L. R. 11 Eq. 459; 40 L. J. Ch. 561; 24 L. T. 695; 19 W. R. 578. Mortgage of lease by publican to brewer to secure past advance and future advance, then mortgage to distiller for advance, then further advance by brewer :—Held, the distiller has priority over the brewer's further advance.

S

THE BEERHOUSE ACT, 1834.

4 & 5 WILL. 4, CAP. 85.

AN ACT to amend an Act passed in the first year of His present Majesty, to permit the general Sale of Beer and Cider by retail in England.

[15th August, 1834.]

1 *Will. 4, c. 64—Licenses to be granted for sale of beer not to authorise consumption thereof on the premises unless granted upon certificate.*] It shall be lawful for the commissioners of excise or other persons duly authorised, to grant licenses for the sale of beer, ale, porter, cider, or perry, under the provisions of the said Act, 1 Will. 4, c. 64, to any person applying for the same, but such license shall not authorise the person obtaining it to sell beer or cider to be drunk or consumed in the house or on the premises specified in the same license, unless the same be granted on the certificate hereinafter required.

2. Every person applying for a license to sell beer to be drunk on the premises to deposit with the commissioners of excise a certificate of good character, signed by six rated inhabitants of the parish, &c., and certified by one of the overseers. *Repealed* by 32 & 33 Vict. c. 27, Schedule.

3. Penalty on overseer refusing to certify as required. *Repealed* by 32 & 33 Vict. c. 27, Schedule.(*a*)

4. Permitting drinking beer in a neighbouring house or in any shed, &c., with intent to evade, &c. *Repealed* by Licensing Act, 1872. See Schedule.

5. *To what persons provisions for billeting soldiers under Mutiny Act shall extend.*(*b*)

(*a*) Under this section the overseer had a discretion as to certifying: *R*. v. *Kensington*, 12 Q. B. 654; 17 L. J. Q. B. 332; but see *R*. v. *Withyham*, 2 C. L. R. 1657.

(*b*) *Billeting soldiers.*] The law as to billeting soldiers on licensed houses was finally settled by the Army Act, 1881, 44 & 45 Vict. c. 58, which is renewed from year to year. The constable is, by section 107,

Appndx.
NOTE.

to make out an annual list of the victualling and other houses liable, open to inspection, and subject to being amended on complaint to a court of summary jurisdiction. By section 103, the constable is, on request, to give the billets, and the houses are described as follows:—

104. *Liability to provide billets* (1).] The provisions of this part of this Act with respect to victualling-houses shall extend to all inns, hotels, livery stables, or alehouses, also to the houses or sellers of wine by retail, whether British or foreign, to be drunk in their own houses or places thereunto belonging, and to all houses of persons selling brandy, spirits, strong waters, cider, or metheglin by retail; and the occupier of a victualling-house, inn, hotel, livery stable, alehouse, or any such house as aforesaid, shall be subject to billets under this Act, and is in this Act included under the expression "keeper of a victualling house," and the inn, hotel, house, stables, and premises of such occupier are in this Act included under the expression "victualling-house."

(2) Provided that an officer or soldier shall not be billeted—

(*a.*) In any private house; nor

(*b.*) In any canteen held or occupied under the authority of a Secretary of State; nor

(*c.*) On persons who keep taverns only, being vintners of the city of London admitted to their freedom of the said company in right of patrimony or apprenticeship, notwithstanding the persons who keep such taverns have taken out licenses for the sale of any intoxicating liquor; nor

(*d.*) In the house of any distiller kept for distilling brandy and strong waters, so as such distiller does not permit tippling in such house; nor

(*e.*) In the house of any shopkeeper whose principal dealing is more in other goods and merchandise than in brandy and strong waters, so as such shopkeeper does not permit tippling in such house; nor

(*f.*) In a house of a person licensed only to sell beer or cider not to be consumed on the premises; nor

(*g.*) In the house or residence of any foreign consul duly accredited as such.

Sections 102—108 deal further with obligations and remedies of licensed victuallers as to billeting.

110. *Offences by keepers of victualling-houses.*] If a keeper of a victualling-house commits any of the offences following; that is to say,—

(1) Refuses or neglects to receive any officer, soldier, or horse billeted upon him in pursuance of this Act, or to furnish such accommodation as is required by this Act; or

Appndx. 6. Justices of the peace to regulate the time of opening and closing houses. *Repealed* by 3 & 4 Vict. c. 61, s. 14.

7. Empowering constables, &c., to visit licensed houses. *Repealed* by Licensing Act, 1872. See Schedule.

8. Penalty for making or using false certificates. *Repealed* by 32 & 33 Vict. c. 27, Schedule.

9. No license for beer to be drunk on the premises to be granted without a certificate. *Repealed* by 32 & 33 Vict. c. 27. Schedule.(a)

10. Retailers compellable to produce their licenses on requisition of two magistrates. *Repealed* by Licensing Act, 1872. See Schedule.

11. *The powers, provisions, and penalties of* 1 *Will.* 4, *c.* 64, *to apply to persons licensed under this Act, and to their sureties, &c.*] This is *repealed* so far as incorporating repealed enactments. Licensing Act, 1872. See Schedule.

---

(2) Gives or agrees to give any money or reward to a constable to excuse or relieve him from being entered in a list as liable, or from his liability to billets, or any part of such liability ; or

(3) Gives or agrees to give any officer or soldier billeted upon him in pursuance of this Act any money or reward in lieu of receiving an officer, soldier, or horse, or furnishing the said accommodation ;

he shall, on summary conviction, be liable to a fine of not less than forty shillings, and not exceeding five pounds.

The same Act of 1881 and a later Act define the extent of accommodation to be furnished by the keepers of licensed houses, and the rate of payment, and the mode of its recovery.

It has been held under these sections that though the constable must make out a billet list, and state the number of men to be accommodated in each house liable to the billet, yet in the event of the list not being adequate for the total number of troops the licensed victuallers are to provide accommodation for the surplus in the same relative proportions: *Sharratt* v. *Scotney* (1892), 2 Q. B. 479 ; 56 J. P. 680 ; 67 L. T. 472.

(a) Under this section no *certiorari* lay to quash a license granted without certificate : *R.* v. *Salford*, 18 Q. B. D. 687. Nor was the license void merely for want of the certificate : *Thompson* v. *Harvey*, 4 H. & N. 254 ; 28 L. J. M. C. 163 ; 23 J. P. 150.

12. *Recited Act to continue in force, except as hereby* **Appndx.**
altered.] And be it enacted that all the provisions of the said
Act, 1 Will. 4, c. 64, shall be deemed and taken to be in full force,
save and except where the same are altered by this Act; and that
so much of the said Act as relates to the interpretation of certain
words therein mentioned shall be applied to the interpretation of
the same words where used in this Act.

13. *Duties on beer licenses under* 1 *Will.* 4, *c.* 64,
repealed, and new duties granted in lieu thereof.] (b)

14. *Such duties to be under the management of commissioners of excise, and to be recovered and accounted for under the provisions of recited Act.*]

15. *Not to affect duty on licenses to retail cider and perry; but such licenses to state particulars.*] Provided always, and be it further enacted, that nothing herein contained shall affect, or be deemed or construed to affect, the amount of duty payable according to the provisions of the said recited Act on licenses to retail cider and perry; but in every such license shall be specified whether the same is granted for the sale of cider and perry by retail not to be drunk or consumed in or upon the house or premises where sold, or for the retail of cider and perry to be drunk and consumed in or upon the house and premises where sold.(c)

16. *Licenses under this Act not to authorise persons to hold licenses for sale of wine.*] No license to be granted under the said recited Act and this Act for the sale of beer or cider shall authorise any person to take out or hold any license for the sale of wine, spirits, or sweets, or made wines, or mead, or metheglin, and if any person licensed under the said recited Act and this Act to sell beer or cider shall permit or suffer any wine or spirits, sweets or made wines, mead or metheglin, to be brought into his house or premises to be drunk or consumed there, or shall suffer any wine, spirits, sweets, mead, or metheglin, to be drunk or consumed in his house or premises by any person whomsoever, such

---

(b) The duties on beer licenses are now set forth in 43 & 44 Vict. c. 20, s. 41, *post.*
(c) The duties on cider licenses are set forth in 43 & 44 Vict. c. 20, s. 41, *post.*

Appndx. person shall, over and above any excise penalty or penalties to which he may be subject, forfeit 20*l.*, to be levied, mitigated, and applied in the same manner as other penalties (not being excise penalties) are by this Act to be recovered, levied, mitigated, and applied. [See 23 Vict. c. 27, s. 3; 24 & 25 Vict. c. 91, s. 10; 43 & 44 Vict. c. 20, ss. 41, 42.]

17. *Penalty on unlicensed persons selling beer and cider by retail to be drunk off the premises,* 10*l. ; to be drunk on the premises,* 20*l.*] And be it further enacted, that every person not being duly licensed to sell beer, cider, and perry, as the keeper of a common inn, alehouse, or victualling-house who shall sell any beer or cider or perry by retail, not to be drunk or consumed in or upon the house or premises where sold, without having an excise retail license in force authorising him so to do, shall forfeit 10*l.* ; and every person not being duly licensed to sell beer, cider, and perry as the keeper of a common inn, alehouse, or victualling-house, who shall sell any beer, or cider, or perry by retail, to be drunk or consumed in or upon the house or premises where sold, without having an excise retail license in force authorising him so to do, whether such person shall or shall not be licensed to sell beer to be drunk or consumed off the premises where sold, shall forfeit 20*l.* ; which said penalties shall be sued for and recovered, mitigated, and applied by the same means and under the same provisions as any other penalty may be sued for and recovered, mitigated and applied under any law or laws of excise. [See Licensing Act, 1872, section 3, and notes.](*a*)

18. The board over the door to state "not to be drunk on the premises," or "to be drunk on the premises." *Repealed* by Licensing Act, 1872. See Schedule, and section 11.

19. *What is a retailing of beer, cider, or perry.*] Every sale of any beer, or of any cider or perry, in any less quantity than four gallons and a half, shall be deemed and taken to be a selling by retail. [See Licensing Acts, 1872, section 3, and notes.](*b*)

(*a*) It was held under a case stated on a conviction under this section that costs of the appellant could be granted against the Crown under 20 & 21 Vict. c. 43, s. 4 : *Moore* v. *Smith*, 1 E. & E. 597 ; 28 L. J. M. C. 126 ; 23 J. P. 133.

(*b*) Where a dealer has an excise license, he may sell in pint bottles as well as quart bottles, a quantity, if exceeding four and a half gallons at one time : *Fairclough* v. *Roberts*, 24 Q. B. D. 350 ; 54 J. P. 421 ;

20. *Persons licensed to sell beer or cider under this Act* Appndx. *liable to penalties for selling spirits or wine without license.*] . . . All persons licensed under the said recited Act and this Act selling wine or spirits, or any sweets or made wines, or mead or metheglin, shall be liable to and shall incur all the penalties imposed by the laws of excise for selling spirits or wine, sweets or made wines, mead or metheglin, without license.(c) [See 23 Vict. c. 27, s. 3 ; 24 & 25 Vict. c. 91, s. 10 ; 43 & 44 Vict. c. 20, ss. 41, 42.]

21. Certificate not to be required for houses in certain situations, if population exceed 5,000. *Repealed* by 37 & 38 Vict. c. 35.

22. Service of summons or order. *Repealed* by Licensing Act, 1872. See Schedule.

23. *Commencement of Act.*]

THE BEERHOUSE ACT, 1840.

3 & 4 Vict. Cap. 61.

AN ACT to amend the Act relating to the general Sale of Beer and Cider by retail in England.

[7th August, 1840.]

11 *Geo.* 4 & 1 *Will.* 4, *c.* 64—4 & 5 *Will.* 4, *c.* 85— *License to retail beer not to be granted to any but the real resident occupier, nor in respect of any house rated at less than* 15*l. per annum, within the Bills of Mortality, or in cities, towns, &c., containing* 10,000 *inhabitants ; nor less than* 11*l. per annum in places exceeding* 2,500 *inhabitants ; nor less than* 8*l. per annum in places situate elsewhere.*] . . . No license to sell beer or cider by retail under the said recited Acts or this Act shall be granted to any person who shall not be the *real resident holder and occupier* of the dwelling-house in which he shall apply to be licensed, nor shall any such

---

59 L. J. M. C. 54 ; 62 L. T. 700 ; 38 W. R. 330. And see 26 & 27 Vict. c. 33, s. 1, *post.*

(c) The recital of this section was struck out by 53 & 54 Vict. c. 33.

Appndx. license be granted in respect of any dwelling-house which shall not, with the premises occupied therewith, be rated in one sum to the rate for the relief of the poor of the parish, township, or place in which such house and premises are situate on a rent or annual value of fifteen pounds per annum at the least if situated in the cities of London or Westminster, or within any parish or place within the Bills of Mortality, or within any city, cinque port, town corporate, parish, or place, the population of which, according to the last parliamentary census, shall exceed ten thousand, or within one mile, to be measured by the nearest public street or path, from any polling place used at the last election for any town having the like population, and returning a member or members of Parliament ; nor shall any such license be granted in respect of any dwelling-house which shall not, with the premises occupied therewith, be rated in one sum to the rate for the relief of the poor of the parish, township or place in which such house and premises are situated on a rent or annual value of eleven pounds per annum, if situated within any city, cinque port, town corporate, parish, or place, the population of which according to such last parliamentary census shall exceed two thousand five hundred and shall not exceed ten thousand, or within one mile, to be measured as aforesaid, from any polling place used at the last election for any town having the like population as last aforesaid, and returning a member or members of Parliament ; nor shall any such license be granted in respect of any dwelling-house which shall not, with the premises occupied therewith, be rated in one sum to the rate for the relief of the poor of the parish, township, or place in which such house and premises are situate on a rent or annual value of eight pounds, if situated elsewhere than as aforesaid ; and every license granted contrary hereto shall be null and void.(a)

(a) This section still governs the value qualifications of all premises for the sale of beer and cider, 1st, as to all houses for in-door consumption licensed before 1872 ; 2nd, as to all houses for out-door consumption, whether licensed before or after 1872 for the first time. The mode of arriving at the *annual value* is now defined by Licensing Act, 1872, sections 46, 47. Those houses which have been first licensed for in-door consumption under this Act since 1872 are governed by the Licensing Act, 1872, section 45 ; see *ante*, p. 95.

The cases decided under this section show that when a parish is in one of the larger areas of a city, cinque port, or town corporate, then the population of the city or town is the criterion ; and where the parish was not in a city or town, though it contained several townships or hamlets, it was not the population of the particular township or hamlet which was the criterion, but the population of the entire parish : *R.* v. *Charlesworth*, 20 L. J. M. C. 181; *Washington* v. *Scott*, 29 J. P.

2. Person applying to be licensed to produce a certificate of his being the *real resident* occupier of the house, and of the amount at which it is rated. *Repealed* by 32 & 33 Vict. c. 27, Schedule.(*b*).

Appndx.
—

---

598 ; 6 B. & S. 617 ; *Smith* v. *Redding*, 30 J. P. 518 ; L. R. 1 Q. B. 489 ; *Windsor* v. *Jeffrey*, 30 J. P. 552 ; 6 B. & S. 617 ; *Preston* v. *Buckley*, L. R. 5 Q. B. 391 ; 35 J. P. 38 ; 39 L. J. M. C. 105 ; 22 L. T. 653 ; 18 W. R. 1104 ; *Rice* v. *Slee*, L. R. 7 C. P. 378 ; 36 J. P. 454. But see 33 & 34 Vict. c. 111, *post*.

The annual value was held to be the rateable value : *Baker* v. *Marsh*, 19 J. P. 117 ; but it is not so now. See Licensing Act, 1872, section 47, *ante*, p. 99

The house must have been, before the Licensing Act, 1872, sections 46, 47, but need not now be rated in one sum, or at all, to the poor rate. Thus, where it was situated in two parishes or townships and rated to each, this was held not sufficient, though the aggregate rate exceeded the sum mentioned in the statute : *Jennings* v. *Manchester JJ.*, 22 L. T. 412. Now it is enough that the occupant is a real resident holder and occupier, and that the house is of the required valuation.

A house partly used as a grocer's shop and partly as a beerhouse was deemed qualified under this enactment : *Garrety* v. *Potts*, L. R. 6 Q. B. 86 ; 35 J. P. 168 ; 40 L. J. M. C. 1 ; 23 L. T. 554 ; 19 W. R. 127.

But a railway arch used as a beerhouse was not qualified, because no one slept in it, and it was not a dwelling-house : *R.* v. *Allney*, 35 J. P. 534.

This qualification of residence on the premises does not apply to the licenses under 23 Vict. c. 27, s. 3 ; 24 & 25 Vict. c. 21, s. 3 ; 26 & 27 Vict. c. 33, s. 1, to ;sell wine and spirits for consumption off the premises : *R.* v. *Glamorganshire*, 1 Q. B. D. 55 ; 40 J. P. 150 ; 33 L. T. 726 ; 24 W. R. 343 ; 45 L. J. M. C. 57.

See Licensing Act, 1872, sections 45—47, as to future qualification of in-door licensed houses.

(*b*) Under this section an excise license granted without the overseer's certificate was held not to be void, though it would have been if the person were not the real resident holder : *Thompson* v. *Harvey*, 4 H. & N. 254 ; 28 L. J. M. C. 163 ; 23 J. P. 150. The overseer could not be compelled to certify the applicant to be the real resident occupier : *R.* v. *Kensington*, 12 Q. B. 654 ; 12 L. P. 743 ; *R.* v. *Langridge*, 24 L. J. Q. B. 73. But he could be ordered by *mandamus* to inquire and determine : *Ex parte Piddlesden*, 18 J. P. 391. And yet a *certiorari* to quash the excise license would not be granted : *Ex parte Salford*, 16 J. P. 649.

The offence of using a false certificate could only be punished by the justices of the peace where the offence was committed : *R.* v. *Waghorn*, 1 E. & B. 647 ; 22 L. J. M. C. 60. An overseer was held not guilty of uttering a false certificate of character because he knew the beer seller

Appndx. 3. *Provision for new houses occupied since a rate was made.* Repealed by 32 & 33 Vict. c. 27, Schedule.

4. *In extra-parochial places licenses may be granted on the certificate of two inhabitant householders of the required annual values.* Repealed by 32 & 33 Vict. c. 27, Schedule, so far as the certificate was required from inhabitants, but unrepealed so far as requiring a real rent or annual value of 15*l.*, 11*l.*, and 8*l.* respectively.

5. *Penalty on overseers refusing to grant certificates, and on overseers and other persons granting false certificates.* Repealed by 32 & 33 Vict. c. 27, Schedule.

6. *Penalty on forging certificates, or using false certificates.* Repealed by 32 & 33 Vict. c. 27, Schedule.

7. *Licenses to be void on conviction of felony or of selling spirits without license.*] Every person who shall hereafter be lawfully convicted of felony, or of selling spirits without license, shall for ever thereafter be disqualified from selling beer and cider by retail, and no license to sell beer and cider by retail under the said recited Acts or this Act shall be granted to any person who shall be so convicted as aforesaid; and if any such person shall, after having been so convicted as aforesaid, take out or have any license to sell beer or cider by retail under the said recited Acts or this Act, the same shall be void to all intents and purposes, and every person who shall, after being convicted as aforesaid, sell any beer or cider by retail, in any manner whatsoever, shall incur the penalty for so doing without license, and in all such cases in the prosecution for the recovery of such penalty a certificate from the clerk of the peace, or person acting as such, of any such conviction as aforesaid, shall on the trial in such prosecution be legal evidence thereof.(a)

8. *On the death of a licensed person the executors or administrators, or the widow or child, may be authorised to sell for the remainder of the term of license.*] Upon the

---

to be living in concubinage: *Leader* v. *Yell*, 28 J. P. 470; *R.* v. *Leader*, 16 C. B. (N.S.) 584; 33 L. J. M. C. 231; 10 L. T. 632; nor because the amount of rate was anticipated and not yet actually assessed: *Dixon* v. *Steele*, 31 J. P. 564.

(a) See similar sections in 23 Vict. c. 27, s. 22; 33 & 34 Vict. c. 29, s. 14, and notes thereto.

death of any person whatever licensed to sell beer or cider under the said recited Acts or this Act before the expiration of the license, it shall be lawful for the person authorised to grant licenses to authorise and empower, by endorsement or otherwise, as the Commissioners of Excise shall direct, the executors or administrators, or the widow or child of such deceased person, who shall be possessed of and occupy the dwelling-house and premises before used for such purpose, to continue to retail beer and cider in the same house and premises during the residue of the term for which such license was originally granted, without taking out any fresh license, or payment of any additional duty thereon ; and also at the expiration of such license (in case the residue of the said term shall be less than three calendar months from the death of the person licensed) to grant a new license to such executors, administrators, or widow, on payment of the proper license duty [and entering into the usual bond].(*b*)

Appndx.
—·

9. *Persons licensed to retail beer or cider to make entry with the excise—7 & 8 Geo. 4, c. 53—4 & 5 Will. 4, c. 51.*] Every person whatever licensed to retail beer or cider under the said recited Act or this Act shall, in manner directed by 7 & 8 Geo. 4, c. 53, and by 4 & 5 Will 4, c. 51, make entry with the officers of excise of every house, cellar, room, and place for storing, keeping, or retailing beer or cider on pain of forfeiting the penalties imposed by the said last-mentioned Act for making use of any unentered room or place ; and all beer and cider found in any such unentered house, cellar, room, or place shall be forfeited.

10. Penalty on persons licensed to sell beer or cider having wine, spirits, or sweets in their entered premises. *Repealed* by Licensing Act, 1872. See Schedule, and section 10.

11. *Officers of excise empowered to enter the premises of licensed beer retailers.*] It shall be lawful for any officer of excise, at all times during the hours in which any house licensed for the retail of beer or cider may be kept open, to enter into every house, cellar, room, or place entered for the storing, keep-

---

(*b*) The effect of this section, which relates to the excise license and is similar to 23 Vict. c. 27, s. 12, is stated in the notes to the latter section. See also Licensing Act, 1872, section 3.
The words *within brackets* were repealed by 41 & 42 Vict. c. 79, Schedule.

BEERHOUSE ACT, 1840, s. 18.

ing, or retailing of beer or cider, and to make search for and seize all wine and spirits and sweets which may be found in any such house, cellar, room, or place, and to examine all beer or cider kept therein.

12. *And also the houses of persons selling beer at the rate of 1½d. or less the quart.*] It shall be lawful for any officer of excise, during the hours which any house is kept open for the sale of beer at the rate of one penny halfpenny or after a less rate the quart, to enter into every such house, cellar, room, or place for the keeping or retailing such beer, and to make search for and seize all wines, spirits, sweets, and all beer which by law they are not entitled to sell.

13. Additional penalty on unlicensed persons selling beer or cider. *Repealed* by Licensing Act, 1872. See Schedule.

14. 11 Geo. 4 and 1 Will. 4, c. 64, s. 14, and 4 & 5 Will. 4, c. 85, s. 6, repealed. *Repealed* by 11 & 12 Vict. c. 49, s. 15.

15. Hours for opening and closing houses. *Repealed* by Licensing Act, 1872. See Act, 1874, section 3.

16. Justices may mitigate penalties. *Repealed* by Licensing Act, 1872. See Schedule, and section 67.

17. No person to forfeit his license for a first offence ; and no license to be void unless so adjudged. *Repealed* by Licensing Act, 1872. See Schedule.

18. *Licenses may be granted to persons licensed before the passing of the Act whilst they continue the occupiers of the same house, although it is below the qualification.*] Provided always, and be it enacted, that nothing in this Act contained shall prevent any person from obtaining, at the expiration of his existing license, a renewed license in respect of any house in which he shall at the time of the passing of this Act be duly licensed to retail beer or cider under the said recited Acts or either of them, notwithstanding such house may not be of the rent or annual value by this Act prescribed [nor to oblige such person to produce any other certificate (where a certificate is required) for obtaining his license than the certificate required by the said recited Acts] ; but it shall be lawful for the officers of excise duly authorised to grant licenses to renew and continue to Appndx. grant licenses to such person (being in other respects properly qualified) [on the production of such certificate as last aforesaid], so long as such person shall continue to be the resident holder and occupier of the same house, anything in this Act to the contrary notwithstanding.(a)

19. Penalties under this Act, where not otherwise directed, to be recovered under the provisions of the former Acts. *Repealed by Licensing Act, 1872.* See Schedule.

20. *Recited Acts to continue in force, except as hereby altered—Interpretation of words.*]

21. *Powers, provisions, and penalties of* 11 *Geo.* 4 *and* 1 *Will.* 4, *c.* 64, *and* 4 *& 5 Will.* 4, *c.* 85, *to apply to persons licensed under this Act.*] (b)

22. *Act not to affect the two universities.*]

23. *Act may be altered this session.*]

THE ALEHOUSE ACT, 1842.

5 & 6 VICT. CAP. 44.

AN ACT *for the Transfer of Licenses and regulation of Public Houses.* [1st July, 1842.]

Empowering transfer of licenses by justices at petty sessions—9 *Geo.* 4, *c.* 61—*Proviso as to the metropolitan police district.*] At any petty session of justices of the peace holden in and for every division of every county and riding, and in any hundred of every county not being within such division, and in every liberty, city, town, or place within which any inn, alehouse, or victualling-house shall be situated, and for which the said justices shall be acting, at any time when no special sessions shall be holden for any such division, hundred, liberty, city, town, or place, it shall be lawful, *in those cases* where

---

(a) This section may now be deemed spent, unless the holders of a license in 1840 survive and have continued occupiers of the same houses. Words in brackets repealed by 37 & 38 Vict. c. 96.

(b) Repealed so far as incorporating repealed enactments: Licensing Act, 1872, Sched.

Appndx. justices of the peace assembled at a special session are empowered, by 9 Geo. 4, c. 61, to transfer or grant licenses, before the expiration thereof, to sell excisable liquors by retail in *the same house* or premises in respect of which any person had been theretofore duly licensed, for the majority of the justices then present, upon application made to them at any such petty session, by endorsement under their hands and seals on any license which shall have been granted pursuant to the provisions of the said Act at any general licensing meeting, or at any adjournment thereof, to authorise (if they shall deem it proper so to do, after examining upon oath all necessary parties), any person not disqualified by the said Act, to whom it shall be proposed at the time of such application to transfer or grant any such license, to use, exercise, and carry on the business of a licensed victualler at the same house and on the same premises, and there to sell such excisable liquors as might theretofore have been lawfully sold and retailed therein; and thereupon it shall be lawful for the officer of excise empowered to transfer licenses by endorsement on the excise licenses required to be transferred to give the like authority to the persons so authorised by the magistrate or justices; and the authority so granted shall continue and be in force until the then next ensuing special session which shall be holden for the division, hundred, liberty, city, town, or place within which such house and premises shall be situated, and no longer; at which special session the justices then and there assembled, upon application made to them pursuant to the said Act, touching any transfer or grant of license to the party or parties to whom such authority shall have been so given at petty sessions as aforesaid, shall hear and dispose of such application according to the provisions of the said Act : Provided always, that nothing herein contained shall be construed to empower any justices at petty sessions to give any such authority as aforesaid within any of the divisions assigned or to be assigned to any of the police courts already established or to be established within the metropolitan police district, except in the borough of Southwark; but that any such application as is hereinbefore directed to be made at petty sessions shall, when the house and premises in respect whereof any license shall have been obtained under the said Act shall be situated within any of the said police court divisions, and not in the borough of Southwark, be made to one of the police magistrates sitting at any of the said courts, and such magistrate shall in his discretion grant such authority in the manner and for the time hereinafter mentioned : Provided also, that any person or persons who shall be authorised under the provisions of this Act, to continue to carry on the business of a licensed victualler, shall, after the obtaining such authority, and so long as the same shall continue in force, be subject to all the powers, regulations, proceedings, penalties, and provisions declared by or contained in any Act or Acts in force touching the regulation, government, or control of licensed keepers of inns, alehouses, and victualling-houses, in like manner as if the same had been repeated and re-enacted, and that all penalties and forfeitures imposed by any such Act or Acts shall be applied as directed by the same respectively.(*a*)

2. *When licenses are lost a copy may be endorsed and considered valid.*] Whenever it shall be proved to the satisfaction of any such magistrate or justices at petty sessions, upon any application made as aforesaid, that any license granted pursuant to the said Act, 9 Geo. 4, c. 61, has been lost or mislaid [or if the application is for the grant or transfer of a license, has been wilfully withheld by the holder thereof], it shall and may be lawful for the said magistrate or justice to receive a copy of such license, certified to be a true copy under the hand of the clerk to the licensing justices by whom the said license shall have been granted, and to make such endorsement thereon as he or they might make under the provisions of this Act upon the original license; and such endorsement upon the copy so certified shall be as valid and effectual as if the same had been made upon the said license.(*b*)

3. *Fee for endorsing the copy.*] For every such certified copy and every such endorsement a fee of two shillings and sixpence, and no more, shall and may be demanded and taken.

(*a*) This section seems not to cover all the cases provided for in 9 Geo. 4, c. 61, s. 14. As to selling without a license, see Licensing Act, 1872, section 3.

It has been held that a person holding this authority does not come within the words "licensed person" in Act 1872, s. 42, and therefore is not entitled to notice of opposition should he apply for a renewal of the license to himself : *Price* v. *James* (1892), 2 Q. B. 28 ; 61 L. J. M. C. 203 ; 67 L. T. 543 ; 41 W. R. 57 ; 56 J. P. 471 ; 57 J. P. 148.

(*b*) This has been extended to other cases by Licensing Act, 1872, section 41, and 47 & 48 Vict. c. 29, so as to include the words within brackets. Nevertheless, the court has held that where an outgoing tenant wilfully withheld his license owing to a quarrel with his landlord, the justices were not bound to accept a copy : *Ex parte Phillips*, 42 J. P. 279. At the same time, they may exercise their jurisdiction without having the current license, a copy of which can be obtained under Licensing Act, 1872, sections 36, 58.

Appndx. 4. *Disqualified justices not to act at petty sessions.* Repealed by 37 & 38 Vict. c. 96, Sched.]

5. *No wine, &c., to be sold on board any boats or vessels moored or lying at anchor during the time when prohibited to be sold in public-houses.*] And be it enacted, that no wines, spirits, or other excisable liquors shall be sold by retail on board of any boat, steamboat, or other vessel which shall be moored or lying at anchor within the metropolitan police district during the hours and times on Sundays, Good Friday, and Christmas Day on which licensed victuallers are by law obliged to keep their houses closed; and any master, steward, mistress, or stewardess, or any other person on board any such boat, steamboat, or other vessel, who shall, during those hours, on Sundays, Good Friday, and Christmas Day, in which the houses of licensed victuallers shall be closed, sell any wines, spirits, or other excisable liquors, in and on board such boat, steamboat, or other vessel, within the said district, shall be liable to a penalty not exceeding five pounds, which may be recovered before any magistrate of the metropolitan police courts, or if the offence shall be committed beyond the limits of any metropolitan police court, established or to be established, before any two justices of the peace having jurisdiction therein, or shall, in the discretion of the magistrate or justices of the peace before whom the conviction shall take place, be imprisoned for any time not longer than one calendar month in any gaol or house of correction within his jurisdiction; and in every case of the adjudication of such pecuniary penalty and non-payment thereof, it shall be lawful for such magistrate or justices of the peace to commit the offender to such gaol or house of correction for a term not exceeding one calendar month, the imprisonment to cease on payment of the sum due; and such penalty shall be paid to the receiver of the metropolitan police, and be applied by him towards the expenses of the police courts established within the said district.(a)

6. *Act not to extend to Universities of Oxford and Cambridge.*]

(a) The Licensing Act, 1872, does not affect the sale of intoxicating liquor in packet boats: section 72. This subject is also governed by 9 Geo. 4, c. 47; 4 & 5 Will. 4, c. 75, s. 10; 43 & 44 Vict. c. 20, s. 45 *post;* 53 & 54 Vict. c. 33. See *ante*, p. 147.

REFRESHMENT HOUSES ACT, 1860.

Appndx.

23 VICT. CAP. 27.

An Act for granting to Her Majesty certain Duties on Wine Licenses and Refreshment Houses, and for regulating the licensing of Refreshment Houses and the granting of Wine Licenses. [14th June, 1860.]

* * * * * *

1. From and after 1st July, 1860, certain duties to be charged for licenses herein mentioned.(*b*)

2. *Powers and provisions of Excise Acts to apply to the duties granted by this Act.*] The duties by this Act granted shall be deemed to be excise duties, and shall be under the care and management of the Commissioners of Inland Revenue for the time being; and all powers, provisions, and regulations, penalties, and forfeitures contained in or enacted by any Act in force in relation to excise duties, shall, in all cases not herein expressly provided for, and so far as the same are not superseded by and are consistent with the express provisions of this Act, be duly observed, applied, and put in execution, for ascertaining the rent or value of any house or premises in respect of which any license shall be applied for under this Act, and for charging, collecting, and securing the said duties hereby granted, and otherwise relating thereto, as fully and effectually as if the same powers, provisions, and regulations, penalties, and forfeitures, were repeated and re-enacted in the body of this Act with reference to such rent or value and to the said duties hereby granted.

3. *Every person keeping a shop entitled to take out a license to retail wine not to be consumed on the premises.*] Every person who shall keep a shop for the sale of any goods or commodities other than foreign wine, or who shall have taken out a license as a dealer in wine (except persons expressly disqualified by this Act), shall, without producing or having any

---

(*b*) Certain duties were by this section declared on refreshment-houses and on refreshment-houses having a wine license. These duties were altered by 24 & 25 Vict. c. 91, ss. 8—11; 39 & 40 Vict. c. 16, s. 4; and 43 & 44 Vict. c. 20, ss. 41, 42. See 24 & 25 Vict. c. 91, s. 9, *post.*

T

Appndx. other license or authority, be entitled to take out a license under this Act to sell by retail, and in reputed quart or pint bottles only, in such shop, foreign wine not to be consumed on the premises where sold, anything in any former Act to the contrary notwithstanding.(*a*)

4. *What shall be deemed selling by retail.*] Every sale of foreign wine in any less quantity than two gallons, or in less than one dozen reputed quart bottles, at one time, shall be deemed to be selling by retail. [See Licensing Act, 1872, sections 3, 74.]

5. Permitting drinking wine in a neighbouring house, shed, &c., with intent to evade the provisions of this Act, to be deemed

---

(*a*) The Wine and Beerhouse Act, 1869, 32 & 33 Vict. c. 27, s. 4, *post*, afterwards made it compulsory before holding this license to apply for a justices' license or certificate; but the justices could not and cannot now refuse the off-wine license except on four grounds: 32 & 33 Vict. c. 27, s. 8, *post*. Those who hold a wine dealer's license are exempt from the necessity of getting any justices' off-certificate as regards the sale of foreign wine : Licensing Act, 1872, section 73. Thus, a grocer who holds a wine dealer's license does not require a justices' license if he has the excise additional retail license : *Palmer* v. *Thatcher*, 3 Q. B. D. 346 ; 42 J. P. 213 ; 47 L. J. M. C. 54 ; 37 L. T. 94 ; 26 W. R. 314.

Residence on the premises is not a necessary condition for a justices' certificate when such is required : *R.* v. *Glamorganshire ; R.* v. *De Rutzen*, 1 Q. B. D. 55 ; 40 J. P. 150 ; 45 L. J. M. C. 57 ; 33 L. T. 726 ; 24 W. R. 343 ; nor is the rateable value of the premises material for an off-license : *R.* v. *Monmouthshire*, 38 J. P. 807.

The license can only be given to those who keep a shop for other goods than foreign wine. Where the applicant kept a shop only for selling casks of beer of four-and-a-half gallons, this was held to satisfy the description : *R.* v. *Bishop*, 50 J. P. 167. Where wine was sold as "Best Sherry, British," this was held to be foreign wine requiring a license : *Richards* v. *Banks*, 58 L. T. 634 ; 52 J. P. 23.

A license to sell foreign wine by wholesale or by retail now includes authority to sell sweets, or made wines, or mead, or metheglin in any quantity : 38 & 39 Vict. c. 23, s. 9.

When a wine dealer has branch offices in other towns in which he has an agent to receive orders which are sent to the head office and executed there, a license must be taken at each branch office also : *Stallard* v. *Marks*, 3 Q. B. D. 412 ; 42 J. P. 359 ; 47 L. J. M. C. 91 ; 38 L. T. 566 ; 26 W. R. 694. But where the agent has his own office and takes orders there only as a traveller, the dealer need not have a license there : *Stuchberry* v. *Spencer*, 51 J. P. 181 ; 55 L. J. M. C. 141.

drinking on the premises. Penalty. [*Repealed* by Licensing Act, **Appndx.**
1872. See Schedule, and section 6 of that Act.]

6. *Persons keeping houses, &c., herein named required to take out licenses.*] All houses, rooms, shops, or buildings, kept open for public refreshment, resort, and entertainment at any time between the hours of [ten](b) of the clock at night and five of the clock of the following morning, not being licensed for the sale of beer, cider, wine, or spirits respectively, shall be deemed refreshment houses(c) within this Act, and the resident owner, tenant, or occupier thereof shall be required to take out a license under this Act to keep a refreshment house ; and every person who shall keep any house, room, shop, or building, for the purpose of selling therein any victual or refreshment to be consumed on the premises where the same shall be sold (except beer, cider, wine, and spirits sold respectively under a proper license in that behalf), and every person who shall keep any house, room, shop, or building for the consumption therein by the public of any refreshment (except as aforesaid), although the same shall not be sold therein, may, if he shall think fit, take out a license under

---

(b) The word *ten* was substituted for *nine* by 24 & 25 Vict. c. 91, s. 8, *post.*

(c) *What is a refreshment house.*] Where a shop provides lemonade and ginger beer, having no accommodation for visitors to sit down, and nothing but a table or counter at which they stand only for a few minutes, this is deemed a refreshment house within the meaning of this section : *Howes* v. *Inland Revenue*, 1 Exch. D. 385 ; 46 L. J. M. C. 15; 41 J. P. 423 ; 35 L. T. 584 ; 24 W. R. 897. And the same if coffee and cigars were only provided : *Muir* v. *Keay*, L. R. 10 Q. B. 599 ; 44 L. J. M. C. 143 ; 23 W. R. 700 ; 40 J. P. 694 ; 41 J. P. 423. If the refreshments are not kept in the house to be supplied to visitors, but are merely sent for at request of and for behoof of the visitors as required, this seems not a keeping open of the house : per BRAMWELL, B. : *Taylor* v. *Oram*, 1 H. & C. 370 ; 31 L. J. M. C. 252 ; 27 J. P. 8 ; 7 L. T. 58 ; 10 W. R. 800. If the house is a temperance hotel not selling intoxicating liquors, but supplying ordinary refreshments, it is nevertheless a refreshment house: *Kelleway* v. *Macdougal*, 45 J. P. 207.

As to the words "public resort and entertainment," see notes to Act, 1872, s. 9, *ante*, p. 20, and to Act, 1874, s. 3, *ante*, p. 168.

Persons who hold licenses for refreshment houses are subject to the Lord's Day Act, or at least not more exempt than other shopkeepers : *Duffell* v. *Curtis*, 35 L. T. 853.

As to the duty on refreshment houses, see *post*, 24 & 25 Vict. c. 91, s. 9.

As to occasional licenses to refreshment house, see 27 & 28 Vict. c. 18, s. 5, *post.*

Appndx. this Act to keep a refreshment house ; and in all proceedings and upon all occasions whatever it shall be sufficient to describe by the term refreshment house any house, room, shop, or building in which any such article as aforesaid (except as aforesaid) is sold to be consumed, or is consumed as aforesaid, without further or otherwise designating or describing the same.(*a*)

7. *Confectioners and eating-house keepers entitled to take out licenses to sell wine to be drunk on the premises.*] Every person who shall be licensed to keep a refreshment house, and shall pursue therein the trade or business of a confectioner, or shall keep open such house as an eating-house, for the purpose of selling, to be consumed therein, animal food or other victuals wherewith wine or other fermented liquors are usually drunk, shall be entitled (subject to the terms and conditions of this Act, and not being expressly disqualified thereby), to take out a license to sell foreign wine by retail in such refreshment house, to be consumed on the premises where the same shall have been sold, without producing or having any other license or authority than as aforesaid ; and every confectioner and eating-house keeper respectively, who shall have taken out such license to retail wine under this Act, shall not be subject or liable to any penalty or forfeiture under any other Act or Acts by reason or on account of his selling wine by retail or having the same in his possession in his entered premises, anything in any other Act or Acts to the contrary notwithstanding.(*b*)

8. *Wine licenses not to be granted for refreshment houses under a certain rent or annual value—Persons disqualified to hold wine licenses.*] Provided always, that no license to sell

---

(*a*) The 24 & 25 Vict. c. 91, s. 8, *post*, altered the hour of closing as above.

(*b*) This wine license includes sweets and made wines : 26 & 27 Vict. c. 33, s. 18 ; 38 & 39 Vict. c. 23, s. 9. See also note to section 3, *ante*, p. 258.

A refreshment house keeper who supplied travellers with bread and cheese was held to keep an eating house, and entitled to the wine license : *Nunn* v. *Southall*, 26 J. P. 775 ; 7 L. T. 356.

A confectioner who supplied luncheons was held to keep a victualling house, and entitled to the publichouse license under 9 Geo. 4, c. 61, s. 1 : *R.* v. *Surrey JJ.*, 52 J. P. 423.

As to persons licensed to retail beer taking out wine licenses, see 24 & 25 Vict. c. 91, s. 10, *post*.

foreign wine by retail to be consumed on the premises shall be granted for any refreshment house which, with the premises belonging thereto and occupied therewith, shall be under the rent and value of ten pounds a year, nor for any refreshment house situated in any city, borough, town, or place containing a population exceeding ten thousand according to the last parliamentary census, if such refreshment house, with the premises belonging thereto and occupied therewith, shall be under the rent and value of twenty pounds a year; and no sheriff's officer, or officer executing the legal process of any court of justice, shall be capable of receiving or using any license under this Act to sell wine by retail to be consumed on the premises; and every license which shall be granted contrary hereto shall be void to all intents and purposes.(c)

Appndx.
—

9. *Penalty for keeping a refreshment house without license, 20l.*] Every person who shall keep a refreshment house for which a license is required by this Act, without taking out and having in force a proper license in that behalf granted to him under the authority of this Act, shall forfeit a sum not exceeding twenty pounds, which penalty shall be recovered as hereinafter directed.(d)

10. *By whom licenses under this Act shall be granted —Forms of licenses as in schedule to this Act.*] All licenses authorised to be granted under this Act shall be granted by and under the hands of the collector or other person having charge of the excise collection, and the supervisor of excise of the district within which respectively the refreshment house or other house or shop for or relating to which any such license shall be required, or by such other person or persons as the Commissioners of Inland Revenue shall appoint or authorise in that behalf, on payment of the duty chargeable for such licenses respectively; . . . Provided always that it shall be lawful for the Commissioners of Inland Revenue from time to time to make such alteration therein as they may deem to be necessary, in consequence of any alteration

---

(c) This valuation qualification (as to the mode of arriving at which see Licensing Act, 1872, section 47) is confined to in-door licenses. No valuation qualification was put on out-door wine licenses, nor is there any now.

(d) This was made an excise penalty: 23 & 24 Vict. c. 113, s. 42. See notes to Licensing Act, 1872, s. 3, *ante*, p. 10; 27 & 28 Vict. c. 64, *post*.

Appndx. or amendment of the law, in order to make such form of license conformable to the law for the time being.(*a*)

11. *Licenses: date, expiration, and renewal thereof.*] All licenses which shall be granted under the authority of this Act between the thirty-first day of March and the first day of May in any year shall be dated on the first day of April, and all licenses which shall be granted at any other time shall be dated on the day on which the same shall be granted; and all such licenses, whensoever granted, shall have effect on and after the day of the date thereof until the first day of April then next following, and shall be renewed annually on payment of the duty by this Act charged thereon respectively.(*b*)

12. *On death of a licensed person, his representative, or widow, or child, may be authorised to continue the business for which the license was granted for the remainder of the term thereof.*] Upon the death of any person licensed under this Act before the expiration of the license, it shall be lawful for the persons authorised to grant licenses to authorise and empower, by endorsement or otherwise, as the Commissioners of Inland Revenue shall direct, the executors or administrators or the widow or child of such deceased person who shall be possessed of and occupy the dwelling-house and premises before used for such purpose, to continue the business for which such license was granted, and to sell in the same house and premises such articles as by the said license are authorised to be sold therein, during the residue of the term for which such license was originally granted without taking out any fresh license or payment of any additional duty thereon, and the person so authorised and empowered shall then be deemed to be a person licensed under this Act, and accordingly subject to the provisions, conditions, regulations, and penalties contained therein.(*c*)

(*a*) It was afterwards required by the Wine and Beerhouse Act, 1869, 32 & 33 Vict. c. 27, s. 4, *post*, that a justices' license should first be obtained. This section originally prescribed the form of license, but that part of the section was repealed by 38 & 39 Vict. c. 66, Schedule, and the statutory form is now given in the Appendix to this volume.

(*b*) The time of the justices' license being in force was made the same as in other licenses by 33 & 34 Vict. c. 29, s. 4, sub-sect. (5), *post*.

(*c*) Though this enactment, which resembles that in the Beer Act, 3 & 4 Vict. c. 61, s. 8, *ante*, p. 266, applied to the excise license only, it

13. Notice of first application for a wine license for refreshment house. *Repealed* by 32 & 33 Vict. c. 27, s. 27, Schedule. See Licensing Act, 1872, section 40.

Appndx.

14. Notice to be given of application for license to retail wine to be consumed on the premises in a house not previously licensed. *Repealed* by 32 & 33 Vict. c. 27, Schedule. See Licensing Act, 1872, section 40.

15. Justices may object to the renewal of a wine license if they shall see just cause of objection. *Repealed* by 32 & 33 Vict. c. 27, Schedule. See Licensing Act, 1872, section 42.

16. *A list of licenses to be kept by collectors and supervisors for inspection of the justices, and copies of the list to be transmitted to the justices' clerk.*] A list or register of every license granted under the authority of this Act, specifying the name and place of abode of every person licensed, and the name and description of the house for which such license shall be granted, and whether the license shall be to keep a refreshment house or for the sale of wine therein, shall be kept at the office or dwelling-house of every collector and supervisor of excise in their respective collections and districts; and such list or register shall at all times be produced to and shall be open to the inspection and perusal of any justice of the county or place where such license shall be granted and where such house shall be situate, and a copy of such list and register shall, once in every six months, be transmitted by every collector and supervisor of excise to the clerk of the magistrates for the district in which

---

was impliedly repealed by the 32 & 33 Vict. c. 27, s. 4, to some extent. And if the holder of a wine license die, his representative must apply for a transfer under 9 Geo. 4, c. 61, s. 14, as in other cases; though the executor, &c., will still be entitled so far as the excise duty is concerned to be relieved of any further payment. But by the Licensing Act, 1872, section 3, a similar though narrower power is given to the executors, &c., of all licensed persons to continue the business till the next special sessions, and that date only, if there is time for the notices to be given pursuant to Licensing Act, 1872, section 40. The general rule is, that when the justices' license is forfeited or becomes void the excise license ceases also to be valid: Licensing Act, 1872, section 63, *ante*, p. 126; but the mere circumstance of the death of the license holder at most only prevents the license being available till some new tenant acquires a right to hold it. The transfer of the excise license by itself was provided for in 25 & 26 Vict. c. 22, s. 15, *post*.

Appndx. such license shall be granted, and any copy or extract of or from such list or register which shall be at any time required by the clerk to the said justices shall be given to him by such collector or supervisor whenever thereto required.(*a*)

17. In case of complaint, licensed retailers of wine to produce their licenses on requisition of two justices. *Repealed* by Licensing Act, 1872.

18. *Constables empowered to visit licensed refreshment houses.*] It shall be lawful for all constables and officers of police, when and so often as they shall respectively think proper, to enter into all houses licensed as refreshment houses under the authority of this Act, and into and upon the premises belonging thereto; and if any person licensed to keep a refreshment house, or any servant or other person in his employ or by his direction, shall refuse to admit or shall not admit any constable or officer of police demanding admittance into such refreshment house or upon such premises, the person so licensed shall for the first offence forfeit and pay any sum not exceeding five pounds, together with the costs of conviction, to be recovered before one or more justices of the peace, on information or complaint made within seven days next after the day on which such offence was committed; and it shall be lawful for any two or more justices before whom any such person shall be convicted for the second time of any such offence to adjudge (if they shall so think fit) the license or licenses of such offender in respect of such refreshment house to be forfeited, and that he shall be disqualified from having any license granted to him under this Act in respect of such house for the space of two years, or for such shorter space of time as they may think proper to adjudge.(*b*)

19. *Penalty for selling wine by retail without license.*] Every person who shall sell any wine by retail, whether to be consumed on the premises or not, without having a proper license in force duly authorising him in that behalf, shall, over and above any other penalty to which he may be liable, forfeit the sum of twenty pounds, which shall be denominated an excise penalty.(*c*)

(*a*) A register of all licensed houses having a justices' license is now directed to be kept by the Licensing Act, 1872, section 36, *ante*, p. 73, and extracts may be used in evidence by section 58, *ante*, p. 130.

(*b*) Constables are authorised to enter all premises licensed for sale of intoxicating liquors by Licensing Act, 1874, s. 16, *ante*, p. 280.

(*c*) See Licensing Act, 1872, sections 3, 59.

20. Additional penalty on unlicensed person selling wine. **Appndx.** *Repealed* by Licensing Act, 1872. See Schedule.

21. *What shall be deemed foreign wine and what shall be deemed spirits.*] All liquor which shall be sold or offered for sale by any person, whether licensed under this Act or not, as being foreign wine, or under the name by which any foreign wine is usually designated or known, shall, as against the person who shall so sell or offer the same for sale, be deemed and taken to be foreign wine; and any fermented liquor containing a greater proportion than forty per centum of proof spirit shall be deemed and taken to be spirits.(*d*)

22. *License to be void on conviction of felony or selling spirits without license.*] Every person who shall be convicted of felony or of selling spirits without license shall for ever thereafter be disqualified from selling wine by retail, and no license to sell wine by retail under this Act shall be granted to any person who shall have been so convicted as aforesaid; and, if any person shall, after having been so convicted as aforesaid, take out or have any license to sell wine by retail under this Act, the same shall be void to all intents and purposes, and every person who shall, after being convicted as aforesaid, sell any wine by retail in any manner whatsoever, shall incur the penalty for so doing without license; and in all such cases, in the prosecution for the recovery of such penalty, a certificate from the clerk of assize or the clerk of the peace, or person acting as such of any such conviction as aforesaid shall on the trial in such prosecution be legal evidence thereof.(*e*)

23. *Licensed retailers of wine to make entry of houses, &c., with the excise.*] Every person licensed to retail wine under this Act shall, in manner directed by the laws of excise in that behalf, make entry with the proper officer of excise of every house, cellar, room, and place for storing, keeping, or retailing of wine, on pain of forfeiting the penalties imposed by the statutes

---

(*d*) A liquor sold as "British sherry" was held to be foreign wine within this section: *Richards* v. *Banks*, 52 J. P. 23; 58 L. T. 634. British wine which contains a large proportion of alcohol is treated as wine: *Harris* v. *Jenns*, 9 C. B. (N.S.) 152; 30 L. J. M. C. 183; 3 L. T. 408; 9 W. R. 36; 24 J. P. 807. A license to sell foreign wine includes British wines: 38 & 39 Vict. c. 23, s. 9.

(*e*) See similar sections in 3 & 4 Vict. c. 61, s. 7; 33 & 34 Vict. c. 29, s. 14, and note to this last.

Appndx. in that behalf for making use of any unentered room or place ; and all wine found in any such unentered house, cellar, room, or place shall be forfeited.

24. *Excise officers empowered to enter the premises of licensed retailers of wine.*] It shall be lawful for any officer of excise, during the hours in which any house licensed for the retail of wine to be consumed on the premises may be kept open, to enter into every house, cellar, room, or place entered for the storing, keeping, or retailing of wine to be consumed as aforesaid, and to make search for and seize all spirits which may be found in any such house, cellar, room, and place, and to examine all wine kept therein.(*a*)

25. *Penalty on persons licensed to retail wine having spirits in their entered premises.*] If any person licensed to retail wine under this Act shall receive into, or keep, or have in his possession, in any cellar, room, or place entered for storing, keeping, or retailing wine, any spirits, he shall, in addition to all other penalties, forfeit the sum of fifty pounds which shall be denominated an excise penalty ; and all spirits found in any such entered cellar, room, or place shall be forfeited ; and on conviction of any such licensed person in any penalty for having spirits in his possession, or for selling or retailing spirits, the license of such person for retailing wine shall become null and void, and shall be so adjudged.(*b*)

26. *Standard measures* to be used. *Repealed* by Licensing Act, 1872. See section 8.

27. *Hours for opening* and closing. *Repealed* by Licensing Act, 1872. See section 28, and Act, 1874, ss. 3, 9.

28. Houses closed *in case of riot*, &c. *Repealed* by Licensing Act, 1872. See Schedule, and section 23.

29. Penalty on permitting drunkenness. *Repealed* by Licensing Act, 1872. See Schedule and section 13.

(*a*) See power to constables to enter all licensed houses : Licensing Act, 1874, sections 16, 17.

(*b*) See Act, 1872, s. 69, *ante*, p. 140, which puts off-spirit licenses on the same footing as off-wine licenses.

30. *Penalties recoverable before two justices in petty sessions within three months.*] All penalties under this Act, except those denominated excise penalties, shall be recovered upon the information or complaint of a constable or other peace officer before two justices acting in petty sessions, and shall be prosecuted and proceeded for within three calendar months next after the commission of the offence in respect of which such penalty shall be incurred, or within such shorter time as may be herein limited with regard to any particular penalty ; and every person licensed under this Act to retail wine, to be consumed on the premises, who shall be convicted before two justices so acting in and for the division or place in which shall be situate the house kept or theretofore kept by such person, of any offence against the tenor of the license to him granted under this Act, or of any offence for which any penalty is imposed by this Act, shall, unless proof be adduced to the satisfaction of such justices that such person had been theretofore convicted within the space of twelve calendar months next preceding of some offence against the tenor of his license or against this Act, be adjudged to be guilty of a first offence against the provisions of this Act, and to forfeit and pay any penalty by this Act imposed for such offence, or if no specific penalty be so imposed then any sum not exceeding five pounds, together with the costs of the conviction ; and if such proof as aforesaid shall be adduced that such person had been previously convicted within the space of twelve calendar months next preceding of one such offence only, such person shall be adjudged to be guilty of a second offence against the provisions of this Act, and to forfeit and pay any penalty by this Act imposed for such offence, or if no specific penalty be so imposed then any sum not exceeding ten pounds, together with the costs of the conviction ; and if such proof as aforesaid shall be adduced that such person had been previously convicted within the space of eighteen calendar months next preceding of two such separate offences, and if proof shall be adduced to the satisfaction of the justices that such person so charged is guilty of the offence charged against him, such person shall be adjudged to be guilty of a third offence against the provisions of this Act, and to forfeit any penalty imposed by this Act in respect of such offence, or if no such specific penalty shall be so imposed then to forfeit and pay the sum of fifty pounds, together with the costs of the conviction.(c)

Appndx.

31. *Justices may adjudge premises disqualified.*] It shall be lawful for the justices before whom any person holding a

---

(c) This section was repealed by Licensing Act, 1872, as to houses for sale of intoxicating liquors.

Appndx. license under this Act for the sale of wine by retail shall be convicted of any offence against the tenor of the said license, or for which any penalty is imposed by this Act, if proof shall be adduced to their satisfaction that within two years last preceding such conviction two convictions for any such offence of the same person, or of any other person licensed in respect of the same house or premises, have taken place, to declare the license granted in respect of the said house or premises, forfeited and void, and to adjudge that no license for the sale of wine shall be granted to any person whatever in respect of the said house or premises for the term of three years from the date of such adjudication, of which adjudication the justices shall give notice to the supervisor of excise; and any license for the sale of wine that may be granted in respect of the said house or premises during the said term of three years shall be null and void.(*a*)

32. *Penalties for offences in refreshment houses.*] Every person licensed to keep a refreshment house under this Act who shall (without a license for that purpose) sell or permit or suffer to be sold within such refreshment house any intoxicating liquor, or shall knowingly suffer any unlawful games or gaming therein, or knowingly suffer prostitutes, thieves, or drunken and disorderly persons to assemble at or continue in or upon his premises, or do, suffer, or permit any act in contravention of his license, shall, upon conviction thereof before two justices, pay for the first offence a fine not exceeding forty shillings, for the second offence a fine not exceeding five pounds, and for every subsequent offence a fine not exceeding twenty pounds, or be subject to a forfeiture of his license, at the discretion of the justices before whom he shall be convicted; and in case of such forfeiture of his license, such person shall be disqualified for the space of one year then next ensuing from obtaining a fresh license; and such fresh license, if obtained within the said year, shall be absolutely null and void to all intents and purposes.(*b*)

33. *Power to justices to mitigate penalties.*] It shall be lawful for the justices before whom any person shall be convicted of any offence against this Act to mitigate, if they shall see cause, any penalty incurred for such offence; provided that where any

---

(*a*) Repealed by Licensing Act, 1872, as to houses selling intoxicating liquors.
(*b*) Repealed by Licensing Act, 1872, as to houses selling intoxicating liquors.

conviction shall take place on any information exhibited under the laws of excise such penalty shall not be mitigated to any sum less than one-fourth part thereof.(c)

Appndx.

34. *Appeal to the sessions against a second or third conviction.*] Provided always, that it shall be lawful for the party convicted of any such second or third offence to appeal to the general or quarter sessions of the peace then next ensuing, unless such sessions shall be held within twelve days next after such conviction, and in that case to the then next subsequent sessions; and in such case the party so convicted shall, before the convicting justices, forthwith enter into a recognizance, with two sufficient sureties, personally to appear at such general or quarter sessions, and to abide the judgment of the court thereupon, and to pay such costs as shall be by the court awarded, which recognizances such justices are hereby authorised to require and take, or in failure of the party convicted entering into such recognizance, the conviction shall remain good and valid to all intents and purposes; and the said justices who shall take such recognizance from the party convicted are also hereby required to bind the person who shall make such charge in a recognizance to appear at such general or quarter sessions as aforesaid, then and there to give evidence against the person so charged, and in like manner to bind any other person who shall have any knowledge of the circumstances of such offence; and it shall be lawful for such court of general or quarter sessions to adjudge such person to be guilty of any such second or third offence against the provisions of this Act, as the case may be, and such adjudication shall be final to all intents and purposes; and it shall be lawful for such court of general or quarter sessions to punish such offender by fine not exceeding the sum of one hundred pounds, together with the costs of such appeal, or to adjudge the license granted to and held by or on behalf of such offender to be forfeited and void, or to adjudge that no wine shall be sold by retail in the house or premises mentioned in the license of such offender for the term of two years from the date of such adjudication, or to punish such offender by such fine as aforesaid, and to adjudge such premises to be disqualified for the sale of wine as aforesaid, and such license to be forfeited and void, and if such license shall be

---

(c) Repealed by Licensing Act, 1872, as to houses selling intoxicating liquors. See also Licensing Act, 1874, section 12, and notes, *ante*, p. 23. The Commissioners of Inland Revenue and also the Treasury may remit any fine or penalty relating to Inland Revenue: 53 & 54 Vict. c. 21, s. 35.

Appndx. adjudged to be forfeited and void, it shall thenceforth be void accordingly; and whenever in such case or in any other case the license of such offender shall be adjudged to be void, such offender shall from and after such adjudication be deemed and taken to be incapable of selling wine by retail in any house kept by him for the space of two years, to be computed from the time of such adjudication, and any license granted to such person during such term shall be void to all intents and purposes.(a)

35. *Court to adjudge costs of appeal in certain cases.*] Whenever it shall happen that any appeal in pursuance of this Act shall be dismissed, or that the judgment appealed against shall be affirmed, or that such appeal shall be abandoned, it shall be lawful for the court to which such appeal shall have been made or intended to have been made, and such court is hereby required to adjudge and order that the party so having appealed, or having entered into such recognizance, shall pay to the justices against whose judgment such appeal shall have been made or intended to be made, or to whomsoever they shall appoint, such sum by way of costs as shall in the opinion of such court be sufficient to indemnify such justices from all costs and charges whatsoever to which such justices may have been put in consequence of the intention or declared intention of such party to appeal; and if such party shall refuse or neglect to pay forthwith such sum, it shall be lawful for the said court to adjudge and order that the party so refusing or neglecting shall be committed to the common gaol or house of correction, there to remain until such sum be paid, or for any time not exceeding six calendar months, unless such sum be sooner paid; and in every case in which the judgment so appealed against shall be reversed, it shall be lawful for such court (if it shall think fit) to adjudge and order that the treasurer of the county or place in and for which such justices, whose judgment shall have been so reversed, shall have acted on the occasion when they shall have given such judgment shall pay to such justices, or to whomsoever they shall appoint,

---

(a) Repealed by Licensing Act, 1872, as to houses selling intoxicating liquors. The appeal in such cases is now regulated by the Summary Jurisdiction Acts, 42 & 43 Vict. c. 49, and 47 & 48 Vict. c. 43, *ante*, p. 117. And it is the same where the penalties are for excise offences : *R.* v. *Glamorganshire JJ.*, 22 Q. B. D. 628; 53 J. P. 294; 58 L. J. M. C. 93.

such sum as shall in the opinion of such court be sufficient to Appndx. indemnify such justices from all costs and charges whatsoever to which they may have been so put; and the said treasurer is hereby authorised to pay the same, which shall be allowed to him in his accounts.(*b*)

36. *Proceedings on appeal to be carried on by the constable, and the expenses of prosecution to be charged on county rates.*] In every case in which any appeal shall be made by any person convicted of any offence under the provisions of this Act to the general or quarter sessions, it shall be lawful for the convicting justices, if no other fit and proper person shall appear to prosecute such charge, and to carry on such proceedings as may be necessary to obtain at such session an adjudication thereon, to order that a constable of the city of *London* police force, within the city of *London* and liberties thereof, or a constable of the metropolitan police force within the metropolitan police district, or if elsewhere, the superintendent or inspector of police of the district, or the constable or other peace officer of the parish or place in which the house kept by the person charged shall be situate, as to the said justices shall seem fit, shall carry on all proceedings necessary to obtain such adjudication as aforesaid, and to bind any such constable, or the said superintendent or inspector of police, or other peace officer, in a sufficient recognizance so to do; and it shall be lawful for the justices before whom such offender shall have been convicted, to order the treasurer of the county or place in and for which such justices shall then act to pay to such constable, superintendent, inspector, or other peace officer, and to the witnesses on his behalf, such sum or sums of money as to the court shall appear to be sufficient to reimburse them respectively the expenses which they shall have been severally put to in and about such prosecution, which order the clerk of the peace is hereby directed and required forthwith to make out, and to deliver to such constable, superintendent, inspector, or other peace officer and witnesses respectively; and the said treasurer is hereby authorised and required, upon sight of such order, forthwith to pay to the person authorised to receive the same such money as aforesaid, and the said treasurer shall be allowed the same in his accounts.(*b*)

(*b*) Repealed by Licensing Act, 1872, as to houses selling intoxicating liquors. See notes, *ante*, p. 117.

Appndx.

37. *Power to Lord Mayor, alderman, or justices of the peace to summon witnesses.*] It shall be lawful for the said Lord Mayor or alderman, and for the justices of the peace before whom respectively any question shall be dependent touching any objection against the granting or renewing of a license under the provisions of this Act, to summon witnesses on behalf of either party to such question, and to examine all such witnesses on oath, and to do and perform all things necessary for the due and proper hearing and determination of such question, and also to order payment of fees, allowances, and reasonable expenses to their clerks, and to all witnesses, constables, and persons by whom any duties shall have been performed or expenses or loss of time incurred respectively under this Act; and the amount of such fees, allowances, and expenses shall be ascertained according to the tables of fees and allowances for the time being in force in the county, city, or borough respectively within which the refreshment house in question shall be situate; and the order for payment may be made at the discretion of the said Lord Mayor, alderman, or justices, either wholly or partially, on the applicant or on the objector, or, if the equity of the case shall seem so to require, then on the treasurer of the county, city, or borough aforesaid, who shall be reimbursed out of the county or borough rate; and the provisions of the Act passed in the eleventh and twelfth years of the reign of Her Majesty, chapter forty-three, for the recovery of costs ordered by justices in petty sessions to be paid, shall apply to all costs, allowances, and expenses ordered to be paid under this Act.(*a*)

38. *Penalty on witnesses refusing to attend.*] Any person summoned as a witness to give evidence before the said Lord Mayor or alderman, or any justices or sessions, touching any matters arising under this Act either on the part of the complainant or of the person accused, or of any person interested in any such matter, who shall neglect or refuse to appear at the time and place for that purpose appointed, and who shall not make such reasonable excuse for such neglect or refusal as shall be admitted and allowed by such Lord Mayor or alderman or justices or sessions, or who appearing shall refuse to be examined

---

(*a*) Repealed by Licensing Act, 1872, as to houses selling intoxicating liquors. In other respects superseded by repeals in 32 & 33 Vict. c. 27, Sched., and 46 & 47 Vict. c. 39, Sched., and by existing provisions in Summary Jurisdiction Acts.

23 VICT. C. 27, S. 42. 289

on oath or affirmation and give evidence, shall, on conviction, **Appndx.** forfeit and pay any sum not exceeding ten pounds for every such offence.(*b*)

39. *Penalty for harbouring constables.*] (*c*)

40. *Penalty on drunkards guilty of riotous or indecent behaviour.*] (*d*)

41. *Penalty on drunken and disorderly persons refusing to quit.*] Any person who shall be drunk, riotous, quarrelsome, or disorderly in any shop, house, premises, or place licensed for the sale of beer, wine, or spirituous liquors by retail to be consumed on the premises, or for refreshment, resort, and entertainment under the provisions of this Act, and shall refuse or neglect to quit such shop, house, premises, or place upon being requested so to do by the manager or occupier, or his agent or servant, or by any constable, shall, on conviction thereof before one justice, be liable to pay a fine not exceeding forty shillings; and all constables are hereby authorised, empowered, and required, on the demand of such manager, occupier, agent, or servant, to assist in expelling such drunken, riotous, quarrelsome, and disorderly persons from such shop, house, premises, and place.(*e*)

42. *Provisions of 11 & 12 Vict. c. 43, to be applied in the recovery of penalties under this Act.*] And with regard to all penalties incurred under this Act, except the penalties herein denominated excise penalties, all the provisions contained in the Act 11 & 12 Vict. c. 43, relating to proceedings for the recovery of penalties by summary conviction, and to appeals against such convictions, and the levying and enforcing of penalties, and the cost of such proceedings, shall be applied and put in force in relation to the penalties by this Act imposed.(*f*)

(*b*) Repealed by Licensing Act. 1872, as to houses licensed to sell intoxicating liquor.
(*c*) Repealed by Licensing Act, 1872, and see section 16 of that Act.
(*d*) Repealed by Licensing Act, 1872, and see section 12 of that Act.
(*e*) Repealed by Licensing Act, 1872, as to houses selling intoxicating liquors, and see section 18 of that Act.
(*f*) Repealed by Licensing Act, 1872, as to houses selling intoxicating liquors, and see 42 & 43 Vict. c. 49, s. 53.

Appndx.

43. *How excise penalties under this Act are to be recovered, &c.*] The penalties imposed by this Act denominated excise penalties shall be recovered, levied, mitigated, and applied by the same ways, means, and methods, and in like manner, as penalties may be recovered, levied, mitigated, and applied under the laws of excise in that behalf.(*a*)

44. *Covenants against houses, &c., being used as public-houses to extend to persons licensed to sell wine under this Act.*] Provided always, that any covenant or clause of restriction contained in any lease or contract between a landlord and tenant, whereby the trade or business of a vintner is prohibited from being carried on in any house, building or place mentioned or comprised in such lease or contract, or whereby any such house, building, or place is prohibited from being used as a public-house, shall be construed to apply and extend to every person who shall be licensed to sell wine to be consumed on the premises under the provisions of this Act, and to any house specified in the license granted to such person.(*b*)

45. *Act not to affect the two Universities, or the Vintners' Company in London, or the borough of St. Albans.*] (*c*)

46. *Extent of Act.*] This Act shall not extend to Scotland or Ireland.

Form of refreshment house license.] (*d*)

(*a*) The excise penalties also may now be recovered, under the Summary Jurisdiction Acts, 42 & 43 Vict. c. 49, s. 53.
(*b*) See notes to 1 Will. 4, c. 64, s. 31, *ante*, p. 253, as to similar covenants.
(*c*) See a similar section in 9 Geo. 4, c. 61, s. 36, and Licensing Act, 1872, section 72.
(*d*) The Schedule to this Act contained a *form* of a refreshment-house license. See the form now used in Appendix to this volume.

24 & 25 VICT. C. 21, S. 3.

Appndx.

THE REVENUE (No. 1) ACT, 1861.

24 & 25 VICT. CAP. 21.

* * * * *

[28th June, 1861.]

* * * * *

2. *Power to licensed dealers in spirits taking out an additional license to retail and send out foreign or British spirits in less quantities than two gallons.*] Any person duly licensed as a dealer in spirits in England may take out an additional license authorising him to sell by retail foreign or British spirits in any quantity not less than one reputed quart bottle, or, as to foreign liqueurs, in the bottles in which the same may have been imported, not to be drunk or consumed upon the premises (the rest of the section *repealed* by 43 & 44 Vict. c. 24, Sched.).(e)

3. *Licenses may be granted for the sale of table beer by retail not to be drunk on the premises.*] It shall be lawful for any person to take out a license for the sale in any house or shop of table beer, at a price not exceeding the rate of one penny halfpenny the quart, and not to be drunk or consumed on the

---

(e) The schedule to the Act imposed a duty on this additional retail spirit license of 3l. 3s. Residence of the holder of the license on the licensed premises is not a necessary condition to this license: *R.* v. *De Rutzen*; *R.* v. *Glamorganshire JJ.*, 1 Q. B. D. 55; 45 L. J. M. C. 57; 33 L. T. 726; 24 W. R. 343; 40 J. P. 150. The applicant must, before the application, have taken out the dealer's license in respect of the premises for which he seeks the additional license; but he need not have done so before he gave the necessary notices previous to the application. Hence, where at the general licensing meeting the applicant failed for want of the dealer's license, but he immediately gave fresh notices, and then took out the dealer's license before the adjournment day, he was held entitled to the certificate: *Ex parte Maugham*; *R.* v. *Kirkdale JJ.*, 1 Q. B. D. 49; 45 L. J. M. C. 36; 40 J. P. 39; 33 L. T. 603; 24 W. R. 205.

It was held, that a grocer who sells spirits under this license does not commit a breach of the covenant in his lease against using the premises as a public house, or for the retail of spirits: *Jones* v. *Bone*, 39 L. J. Ch. 405; L. R. 9 Eq. 674. But see *ante*, p. 254, 1 Will. 4, c. 64, s. 31, and notes.

U 2

Appndx. premises where sold, and it shall not be necessary to the obtaining of such license that the said house or shop shall be rated to the relief of the poor to any amount.(a)

THE REVENUE (No. 2) ACT, 1861.

24 & 25 VICT. CAP. 91.

* * * * *

[6th August, 1861.]

* * * * *

8. *Persons not compellable to take out refreshment house license for a house not kept open after ten o'clock at night.*]

* * * * *

No person shall be compellable to take out a license under either of the said Acts to keep a refreshment house, whose house, room, shop or building shall not be kept open for public refreshment, resort and entertainment after the hours of ten of the clock at night; and the said Act shall be read and construed as if the word "ten" had been substituted for the word "nine" in the sixth section of the said Acts respectively.(b)

9. *Lower rate of duty on refreshment house licenses for houses under 30l. annual value—Allowance of duty paid for refreshment house license to be made on taking out wine license.*] And in lieu of the duties chargeable under the said last-mentioned Acts respectively for every license to keep a refreshment house there shall be charged the following duties; (that is to say,)—

If the house and premises in respect of which such license shall be granted shall in England be under the rent and value or in Ireland be under the value of thirty pounds a year, the duty of ten shillings and sixpence:

(a) The rest of this section is *repealed* by 32 & 33 Vict. c. 27, Sched. The justices have now an absolute discretion to refuse this license: 32 & 33 Vict. c. 27, s. 8; 45 & 46 Vict. c. 34.

The schedule to the Act imposed a duty of 5s. on this excise table-beer license.

(b) The word "ten" was substituted for "nine" in the section of 23 Vict. c. 27, s. 6, *ante*, p. 275.

And if the same shall be of the rent or value of thirty pounds a year or upwards, the duty of one pound and one shilling: **Appndx.**

And whenever any person who shall have taken out a license to keep a refreshment house, not being a house open after ten o'clock at night, shall apply for and obtain a license under either of the said Acts to sell therein by retail foreign wine to be consumed in such house, he shall be allowed an abatement at the rate per annum hereinafter mentioned from the duty chargeable for such last-mentioned license in respect of the same period of time or portion of the year for which he shall take out the said license to retail wine; (that is to say,)—

	£	s.	d.
Where the house and premises in respect of which such licenses shall be granted shall in England be under the rent and value, or in Ireland under the value of thirty pounds a year, an abatement of	- 0	7	4
And where the same shall be of the rent or value of thirty pounds or upwards an abatement of(c)	- 0	17	10

Provided always, that if any person to whom any such abatement as aforesaid shall have been made on taking out a wine license shall keep open his house as a refreshment house, or shall sell therein any wine or other refreshment after the hour of ten of the clock at night, he shall be deemed to keep a refreshment house without taking out and having in force a proper license in that behalf; and also in respect of any wine sold by him after the hour aforesaid, he shall be deemed to have sold the same without having a proper license in force duly authorising him in that behalf, and shall forfeit the penalties imposed for such offences respectively, by the ninth and nineteenth sections of the said Act of the last session of Parliament, chapter twenty-seven.(d)

10. *Persons licensed to retail beer not precluded from taking out wine licenses.*] * * * * * *
Nothing in the said Act or in any other Act or Acts contained shall be adjudged, deemed, or construed to preclude or disqualify any person from taking out or having granted to him any license for the sale of wine under the said Act of the last session of

---

(c) The above abatement was repealed by 39 & 40 Vict. c. 16, s. 4. See also 43 & 44 Vict. c. 20, *post*, as to the duty.
(d) See Licensing Act, 1872, section 28, as to hour of closing, and sections 45, 46, and 47, as to mode of estimating valuation.

REVENUE (NO. 2) ACT, 1861, s. 14.

Appndx. Parliament, by reason or on account of his being licensed for the sale of beer under any Act or Acts in that behalf.(a)

11. *Persons liable to retail wine not to be subject to penalty under the Beer Acts for having wine or sweets in possession.*] No person licensed for the sale of wine under the Act, 23 Vict. c. 27, shall be subject or liable to any penalty or forfeiture under any Act relating to the retailing of beer by reason or on account of his selling, dealing in, retailing, or receiving into, or having in his possession, any wine, or sweets, or made wines, or mead, or metheglin, anything in any such Act or Acts as last mentioned to the contrary notwithstanding.(b)

* * * * * *

13. *Exemption as to the sale of beer or spirits at fairs or races not repealed by* 23 & 24 Vict. cc. 113, 114.] (c)

14. *All licenses granted under the Acts relating to the retailing of beer to expire on the 10th October in each year.*] Whereas the licenses authorising the retailing of beer granted under the authority of three several Acts, 11 Geo. 4 and 1 Will. 4, c. 64 ; 4 & 5 Will. 4, c. 85, and 3 & 4 Vict. c. 61, are directed by the first of the said Acts to be dated on the day when the same shall be granted, and to expire at the end of twelve calendar months after the day on which such licenses shall be dated, and it is expedient that all such licenses should expire at one and the same period of the year : Be it enacted that every license taken out under the said recited Acts shall be in force from the day of

---

(*a*) And the same rule applies to the spirit dealer's retail licenses as to wine off-licenses : 35 & 36 Vict. c. 94, s. 69.
Some words struck out by 55 & 56 Vict. c. 19.

(*b*) The statute 4 & 5 Will. 4, c. 85, s. 16, provided that those holding licenses to retail beer should not be authorised to hold retail licenses for wine, spirits, or sweets. This section has been said merely not to preclude a beerhouse keeper as such from obtaining a wine license, but that it does not of itself entitle him to it : *R.* v. *King* or *Manchester JJ.*, 20 Q. B. D. 430 ; 52 J. P. 164 ; 57 L. J. M. C. 20 ; 58 L. T. 607 ; 36 W. R. 600. See also Act, 1872, s. 69, *ante*, p. 140.

(*c*) This section kept alive any existing exemptions as to selling at fairs and races, notwithstanding 23 & 24 Vict. cc. 113, 114. The Act 23 & 24 Vict. c. 114, was repealed by 43 & 44 Vict. c. 24. See now as to fairs and races, Licensing Act, 1874, section 19 ; also 25 & 26 Vict. c. 22, s. 13 ; 26 & 27 Vict. c. 33, ss. 19, 21 ; 27 & 28 Vict. c. 18, s. 5.

25 & 26 VICT. C. 22, S. 13. 295

the date of such license until the *tenth* day of *October*, next follow- **Appndx.**
ing the granting thereof; and every person who shall take out a
license under the said Acts for the first time shall be entitled to
the same on payment of a proportionate part of the duty thereon
in the same manner as a person commencing a trade or business
for which an excise license is required, may now take out a
license under the provisions contained in the seventeenth section
of the Act, 6 Geo. 4, c. 81.(*d*)

THE REVENUE ACT, 1862.

25 & 26 VICT. CAP. 22.

*   *   *   *   *   *

12. *So much of any Act as permits sale of beer at fairs, &c., without license repealed.*] So much of any Act as permits the sale of beer, spirits, or wine at fairs or races without an excise license shall be and the same is hereby repealed.(*e*)

13. *Occasional license may be granted to victuallers to sell beer, spirits, &c., at such time and place as the Commissioners of Inland Revenue shall approve.*] It shall be lawful for the Commissioners of Inland Revenue, whenever they shall consider it conducive to public convenience, comfort, and order, and with the consent in writing of two justices of the peace usually acting at the petty sessions for the petty sessional division within which the place of sale is situate, to authorise any officer of excise to grant to any person who shall be duly authorised to keep a common inn, alehouse, or victualling-house, and who shall have taken out the proper excise licenses to sell therein beer, spirits, wine, or tobacco, an occasional license under this Act empowering him to sell the like articles for which he shall have taken out such licenses as aforesaid at any such other place, and for and during such space or period of time, not

---

(*d*) This made all retail beer licenses conform to the rule laid down as to publican's licenses by 9 Geo. 4, c. 61, s. 13, *ante*, p. 227.
Some parts of this section are left out, being repealed by 38 & 39 Vict. c. 60.
(*e*) See 26 & 27 Vict. c. 33, s. 21.
This Act puts an end to all customs in localities to sell at fairs without a license : *Huxham* v. *Wheeler*, 3 H. & C. 75 ; 33 L. J. M. C. 153 ; 10 L. T. 342.

Appndx. exceeding three consecutive days at any one time, as the said commissioners shall approve, and as shall be specified in such occasional license; and any person who shall have taken out such occasional license shall not be liable to any penalty or forfeiture whatever by reason or on account of his selling the articles mentioned in the said license during the time and at the place specified therein; provided that no such occasional license shall authorise the sale of any beer, spirits, or wine, except during the hours after sunrise and before sunset; and provided that the said license shall not protect any such person in the sale of any of the articles herein mentioned, unless he shall at the time of such sale produce such license when requested to do so by any officer of excise, or by any constable or police officer; nor shall any such license be granted for the sale of any of the articles herein mentioned on any Sunday, Christmas Day, or Good Friday, or on any day appointed for a public fast or thanksgiving; provided also, that the provisions of this clause shall not extend to Scotland.(a)

*　　　*　　　*　　　*　　　*　　　*

15. *Licenses granted under* 23 *Vict. c.* 27, *and* 23 & 24 *Vict. c.* 107, *may be transferred as other excise licenses in case of the removal of the licensed person.*] The provisions contained in 6 Geo. 4, c. 81, s. 21, relating to the transfer of excise licenses in the case of the removal of any person from the house or premises at which he shall be licensed under that Act, shall be and the same are hereby extended to licenses granted under the Act 23 Vict. c. 27, and 23 & 24 Vict. c. 107, respectively: Provided that no license granted under either of the two last-mentioned Acts for the sale of foreign wine by retail to be consumed upon the premises where the same shall be sold shall be transferred by the officers of excise, unless the assignee of such license shall be duly licensed to keep a refreshment-house, nor unless he shall produce to such officers a certificate from a justice of the peace acting for the city, borough, town, or place in which the house and premises are situated, that such justice does not object to such

---

(a) See 26 & 27 Vict. c. 33, s. 50, which required only the consent of one justice, and the law was further altered as there stated.

Where a justice, who was not entitled under this section to grant the occasional license, as not "usually acting for the petty sessional division" nevertheless did grant such license, it was held that the licensed victualler could not be convicted of selling without a license, as the license was good on the face of it: *Stevens* v. *Emson*, 1 Ex. D. 100; 40 J. P. 484; 45 L. J. M. C. 63; 33 L. T. 821.

transfer being made, and provided that no such license so transferred shall authorise the assignee to carry on the business mentioned therein, for a longer period than five weeks from the date of such transfer, unless he shall in the meantime have qualified himself to become the holder of a license of the like kind according to the provisions of the said respective Acts.(b)

Appndx.

* * * * * *

THE TIPPLING ACT, 1862.

25 & 26 VICT. CAP. 38.

AN ACT to amend the Laws relating to the Sale of Spirits. [17th July, 1862.]

Recital of section 12 of 24 Geo. 2, c. 40, enacting that no action should be brought to recover any debt for spirituous liquors unless contracted at one time to the amount of 20s.—Recited enactment repealed.] Whereas by 24 Geo. 2, c. 40, s. 12, it is amongst other things enacted, that no person or persons whatsoever shall be entitled unto, or maintain any cause, action, or suit for, or recover either in law or equity, any sum or sums of money, debt, or demands whatsoever for or on account of any spirituous liquors, unless such debt shall have really and *bond fide* been contracted at one time to the amount of twenty shillings or upwards, nor shall any particular article or item in any account or demand for distilled spirituous liquors be allowed or maintained where the liquors delivered at one time, and mentioned in such article or item, shall not amount to the full value of twenty shillings at the least : And whereas it is expedient that the said recited enactment should be repealed so far as is hereinafter mentioned : Be it therefore enacted by the Queen's most Excellent Majesty by and with the advice and consent of the Lords Spiritual and Temporal, and Commons, in this present Parliament assembled, and by the authority of the same, that so much of the said enactment as is hereinbefore

---

(*b*) The 16th section of this statute removed some doubt as to the privileges of free vintners of the city of London. See Licensing Act, 1872, s. 72, and notes.

Appndx. recited shall be and the same is hereby repealed, so far only as relates to spirituous liquors sold to be consumed elsewhere than on the premises where sold, and delivered at the residence of the purchaser thereof in quantities not less at any one time than a reputed quart.(*a*)

(*a*) The Tippling Act referred to in this section enacts (24 Geo. 2, c. 40, s. 12): "No person or persons whatsoever shall be entitled unto, or maintain any cause, action, or suit for, or recover either in law or equity, any sum or sums of money, debt, or demands whatsoever, for or on account of any *spirituous liquors*, unless such debts shall have really and *bonâ fide* been contracted at one time to the amount of 20*s.* or upwards; nor shall any particular article or item in any account or demand for distilled spirituous liquors be allowed or maintained where the liquors delivered at one time, and mentioned in such article or item, shall not amount to the full value of 20*s.* at the least, and that without fraud or covin, and where no part of the liquors so sold or delivered shall have been returned or agreed to be returned directly or indirectly; and in case any retailer of spirituous liquors, with or without a license, shall take or receive any pawn or pledge from any person or persons whatsoever, by way of security for the payment of any sum or sums of money owing by such person or persons for such spirituous liquors or strong waters, every such person or persons offending herein shall forfeit and lose the sum of 40*s.* for each and every pawn or pledge so taken in or received by him or them, to be levied and recovered by warrant under the hand and seal of one justice of the peace where the offence is committed, and that one moiety thereof shall be to the use of the poor of the parish where such offence is committed, and the other moiety to the informer or informers; and the person or persons to whom any such pawn or pledge doth or shall belong, shall have the same remedy for recovering such pawn or the value thereof as if it had never been pledged :" 24 Geo. 2, c. 40, s. 12.

The statute 24 Geo. 2, c. 40, was held to apply to spirits sold to another publican to sell again : *Hughes* v. *Done*, 1 Q. B. 294. If the aggregate of price for several kinds of spirits exceed 20*s.*, the statute did not apply: *Owens* v. *Porter*, 4 C. & P. 367 ; nor did it apply to spirits supplied to a guest resident in his house by a hotel keeper: *Procter* v. *Nicholson*, 7 C. & P. 67. If supplied to people dining at a tavern the small spirit items could not be recovered : *Barnoyat* v. *Hutchinson*, 5 B. & Ald. 241 ; *Hughes* v. *Done*, 1 Q. B. 294. Yet in some cases, though the demand was not recoverable, it would be allowed on a mutual settling of accounts : *Crooksbank* v. *Rose*, 5 C. & P. 19 ; *Dawson* v. *Remnant*, 6 Esp. 24. If a bill of exchange was given for the value under 20*s.*, the statute was a good defence : *Scott* v. *Gillmore*, 3 Taunt. 226. The vendor of spirits under 20*s.* might validly apply a payment made by the customer generally to satisfy this item, though it could not be sued for : *Philpott* v. *Jones*, 2 A. & E. 41.

By the County Courts Act, 51 & 52 Vict. c. 43, s. 182, no action

Appndx.

THE REVENUE ACT, 1863.

26 & 27 VICT. CAP. 33.

* * * * * *

1. *Licensed beer dealers may take out additional license to sell beer by retail not to be consumed on the premises.*] Any person who, in England or Ireland, shall have taken out an excise license to sell strong beer in casks containing not less than four-and-a-half gallons, or in not less than two dozen reputed quart bottles at one time, to be drunk or consumed elsewhere than on his premises, may take out an additional license on payment of the excise duty of one pound one shilling, and five per cent. thereon; and the same shall authorise such person to sell beer in any less quantity and in any other manner than as aforesaid, but not to be drunk or consumed on the premises where sold; and such additional license shall be granted without the production of any certificate or the possession of any other qualification than the license herein first mentioned.(*b*)

* * * * * *

---

shall be brought or be maintainable in any county or other court to recover any debt or sum of money alleged to be due in respect of the sale of any ale, porter, beer, cider, or perry, which was consumed on the premises where sold or supplied, or in respect of any money or goods lent or supplied, or of any security given for, in, or towards the obtaining of any such ale, porter, beer, cider, or perry.

(*b*) This retail license was subjected to a valuation qualification after 1870, by 33 & 34 Vict. c. 29, s. 10. But it is not necessary that the license holder reside on the licensed premises: *R.* v. *De Rutzen; R.* v. *Glamorganshire JJ.*, 1 Q. B. D. 55; 45 L. J. M. C. 57; 33 L. T. 726; 24 W. R. 343; 40 J. P. 150. At the same time the dealer's license and the retail license must apply to the same premises. The certificate of justices cannot now be obtained at a special transfer sessions, but only at the general annual licensing meeting: Licensing Act, 1874, section 31; 43 Vict. c. 6, s. 2.

Under the Act 32 & 33 Vict. c. 27, s. 8, a person already holding a beer license under 1 Will. 4, c. 64, was entitled also to apply in respect of the same premises for a beer dealer's additional retail license under this Act and *vice versâ*: *R.* v. *Blackburn JJ.*, 43 J. P. 111; 42 J. P.

18. *Licenses granted to refreshment house keepers to retail foreign wine to include the sale of sweets and made wines.*] Every license taken out under the provisions contained in the two several Acts, 23 Vict. c. 27, and c. 107, respectively, by a licensed keeper of a refreshment house, to sell therein by retail, foreign wine, to be consumed in such house or on the premises belonging thereto, shall authorise and include the sale of sweets, made wines, mead, and metheglin, by retail, to be consumed in the said house or on the said premises.(a)

19. *Alteration of duty on a victualler's occasional license.*] There shall be charged and paid the following duty; (that is to say,)—

> For and upon every occasional license to be granted to any person who shall be duly authorised to keep a common inn, alehouse, or victualling-house, and licensed to sell therein beer, spirits, wine, or tobacco, to sell the like articles for which he shall be so licensed at any such other place, and for and during such space or period of time not exceeding six days as shall be specified in such occasional license, the sum of two shillings and sixpence for every day so specified as aforesaid for which the same shall be granted :
>
> Provided always that when any person shall have taken out such an occasional license for six successive days, and shall desire to take out another occasional license for a time in immediate succession, or only separated by the intervention of Sundays and

---

775 ; *R.* v. *Over Darwen*, 39 L. T. 444. But now both or either can be refused at discretion : 43 Vict. c. 6 ; 45 & 46 Vict. c. 34.

The "two dozen reputed quart bottles" are merely used to denote quantity, being a supposed equivalent for 4½ gallons. And the dealer may use imperial pint bottles instead of reputed quart bottles, provided the total quantity sold at one time exceeds two dozen reputed quarts : *Fairclough* v. *Roberts*, 24 Q. B. D. 350 ; 54 J. P. 421 ; 59 L. J. M. C. 54 ; 62 L. T. 790 ; 38 W. R. 330.

It has been held that a person holding this retail license is disqualified from holding a game dealer's license, because he comes within the words in the Game Act, 1 & 2 Will. 4, c. 32, s. 18, licensed to sell beer by retail : *Shoolbred* v. *St. Pancras*, 24 Q. B. D. 346 ; 54 J. P. 231 ; 59 L. J. M. C. 63 ; 62 L. T. 287 ; 38 W. R. 399.

(*a*) A license to sell foreign wine, whether held by a refreshment house keeper or not, and whether by wholesale or retail, now includes sweets : 38 & 39 Vict. c. 23, s. 9.

holidays, then the duty chargeable for every license after the first, **Appndx.** and for any number of days not exceeding six, shall not exceed ten shillings.

20. *Alteration of the law relating to occasional licenses.*] Whereas it is expedient to alter and amend the conditions and restrictions upon and under which occasional licenses to sell beer, spirits, or wine may be granted and used, as provided by 25 & 26 Vict. c. 22, s. 13 : Be it enacted as follows :—

1. That the consent of one justice of the peace, as in the said section mentioned, only shall be necessary :

2. That the hours during which such occasional license shall authorise the sale of any beer, spirits, or wine shall extend from [such hour not earlier than sunrise until such hour not later than ten o'clock at night, as may be specified in that behalf in the consent given by the justice for the granting of such occasional license].

3. That upon the occasion of any public dinner or ball, it shall be lawful for the person who shall have obtained an occasional license under the provisions of the said Act to sell the said liquors during such hours before or after sunrise or sunset as shall be allowed and specified in that behalf in the consent to be given by the justice of the peace for the granting of such occasional license.(*b*)

21. Section 12 of 25 & 26 Vict. c. 22, not to prohibit persons licensed by the excise from selling beer, spirits, or wine at fairs or races.(*c*)

(*b*) The words within brackets were inserted by the Licensing Act, 1874, s. 19.
The consent of the justice here mentioned implies that he has a discretion, and that he does not act ministerially.

(*c*) The law as to fairs and races was further altered by 27 & 28 Vict. c. 18, s. 5, and Licensing Act, 1874, section 18, so that in all cases of fairs and races the party attending must get an occasional license from a justice.

THE INNKEEPERS LIABILITY ACT, 1863.

26 & 27 VICT. CAP. 41.

AN ACT to amend the law respecting the Liability of Innkeepers, and to prevent certain Frauds upon them.(a)
[13th July, 1863.]

* * * * * *

1. *Innkeeper not to be liable for loss, &c., beyond 30l., except in certain cases.*] No innkeeper shall be liable to make good, to any guest of such innkeeper any loss of or injury to goods or property brought to his inn, not being a horse or other live animal, or any gear appertaining thereto, or any carriage, to a greater amount than a sum of thirty pounds, except in the following cases ; (that is to say,)

(1.) Where such goods or property shall have been stolen, lost, or injured through the wilful act, default, or neglect of such innkeeper or any servant in his employ :

(2.) Where such goods or property shall have been deposited expressly for safe custody with such innkeeper :

Provided always, that in the case of such deposit it shall be lawful for such innkeeper, if he thinks fit, to require, as a condition of his liability, that such goods or property shall be deposited in a box or other receptacle, fastened and sealed by the person depositing the same.(*b*)

(*a*) See also 41 & 42 Vict. c. 38, *post*, as to lien of innkeepers.
(*b*) The word "wilful" applies to the word "act" only, and not to fault or neglect : *Squire* v. *Wheeler*, 16 L. T. 93.
An innkeeper is at common law liable for the safe keeping of the guests' goods, except for loss by the act of God or the king's enemies, or when the guest has been negligent : *Morgan* v. *Ravey*, 6 H. & N. 265 ; 25 J. P. 376 ; *Armistead* v. *Wilde*, 17 Q. B. 261 ; 16 J. P. 5 ; 20 L. J. M. C. 521 ; *Cashill* v. *Wright*, 6 E. & B. 891 ; 20 J. P. 678. It is sometimes difficult to know when the relation of guest begins : *Medawar* v. *Grand Hotel Company* (1891), 2 Q. B. 11 ; 55 J. P. 614. It is the fact of the person being a guest that makes the innkeeper liable to receive the goods, and horse and carriage, and to keep them safe : *Smith* v.

Appndx.
—
NOTE.

Dearlove, 6 C. B. 132. And while the guest is in the house the innkeeper is bound to take reasonable care so as to prevent any danger to him: *Sandys* v. *Florence*, 47 L. J. C. P. 598; 42 J. P. 712. But if in the middle of the night a guest wander about the hotel and fall down a shaft, the innkeeper may be guilty of no neglect: *Walker* v. *Midland Railway Company*, 51 J. P. 116. If an intending guest leaves goods with an innkeeper, but never becomes a guest, the innkeeper incurs no such liability for safe keeping: *Strauss* v. *County Hotel*, 12 Q. B. D. 27; 48 J. P. 69; 53 L. J. Q. B. 25; 49 L. T. 601; 32 W. R. 170.

Where the plaintiff, while a guest, had jewellery stolen from her room and neither she nor the innkeeper was negligent, and the notice was fixed in the room, it was held that the plaintiff was entitled only to recover £30: *Huntley* v. *Bedford Hotel Company*, 56 J. P. 53.

The compulsion upon an innkeeper to receive guests applies only to travellers: see 35 & 36 Vict. c. 94, s. 49, and notes, *ante*, p. 103. A hotel keeper is liable for the safety of the guests' goods, because he is usually an innkeeper: *Jones* v. *Osborn*, 2 Chitt. 433. A boarding-house keeper has not the liabilities of an innkeeper: *Dansey* v. *Richardson*, 3 E. & B. 144; 23 L. J. Q. B. 217. The keeper of a tavern, or place where people have sleeping and boarding accommodation, though not bound to receive any but travellers, yet has the innkeeper's lien on the guest's goods if he receives the guest and the goods: *Thompson* v. *Lacy*, 3 B. & Ald. 283.

The liability for the safety of the guests' goods arises out of the profession of keeping a common inn, which implies readiness to receive travellers if he has accommodation: *Holder* v. *Soulby*, 8 C. B. (N.S.) 254; 29 L. J. C. P. 246; 8 W. R. 438; 2 L. T. 219; see *Ultzen* v. *Nichols*, 1 Nov., 1893, Q. B. D. Part of a hotel may consist of a mere refreshment bar or victualling-house, as to which the innkeeper's usual liability does not attach: *R.* v. *Rymer*, 2 Q. B. D. 136; 41 J. P. 199; 46 L. J. M. C. 108; 35 L. T. 774; 25 W. R. 415.

Where the hotel belongs to a company, and the license is granted to the manager, the liability of an innkeeper lies on the company and not on the manager: *Dixon* v. *Birch*, L. R. 8 Ex. 135; 42 L. J. Ex. 135; 28 L. T. 360. And the keeper's liability would not be affected by any secret arrangement to divide his profits with a third person: *Day* v. *Bather*, 2 H. & C. 14; 32 L. J. Ex. 171; 8 L. T. 205; 11 W. R. 375.

An ordinary manager who orders liquors without authority cannot bind his principal: *Dunn* v. *Simmons*, 44 J. P. 264; 41 L. T. 783; 28 W. R. 129; and if the manager take on himself to give a customer into custody, the principal is not necessarily liable: *Abrahams* v. *Deakin* (1891), 1 Q. B. 516; 60 L. J. Q. B. 238; 55 J. P. 212; 63 L. T. 690.

F., a brewer and owner of a beerhouse, put in H. as manager and servant, and paid him weekly wages, supplying H. with beer and cigars to sell in the house for behoof of F. While H. was manager he ordered cigars from W., who supplied them to H., and W. credited H. alone, but afterwards discovering that H. was only a servant of F., sued F. for the

Appndx. **2.** *Obligation to receive property of guests for safe custody.*] If any innkeeper shall refuse to receive for safe custody, as before mentioned, any goods or property of his guest, or if any such guest shall, through any default of such innkeeper, be unable to deposit such goods or property as aforesaid, such innkeeper shall not be entitled to the benefit of this Act in respect of such goods or property.

3. *Notice of law, &c., to be conspicuously exhibited.*] Every innkeeper shall cause at least one copy of the first section of this Act, printed in plain type, to be exhibited in a conspicuous part of the hall or entrance to his inn, and he shall be entitled to the benefit of this Act in respect of such goods or property as shall be brought to his inn while such copy shall be so exhibited.(a)

---

price. Held, that as the cigars were such as a manager of such a business would have power to order as incident to the management, F. was liable for the price: *Watteau* v. *Fenwick* (1893), 1 Q. B. 246; 68 L. T. 831; 56 J. P. 839.

Questions have often arisen as to what acts of the guest will amount to negligence, so as to be a defence to the innkeeper, such as the not locking of his bedroom door before going to sleep: *Spice* v. *Bacon*, 2 Q. B. D. 463; 46 L. J. Q. B. 713; 42 J. P. 261; 36 L. T. 896; 26 W. R. 840; *Oppenheim* v. *White Lion Company*, L. R. 6 C. P. 515; 40 L. J. C. P. 93; 25 L. T. 93; *Herbert* v. *Markwell*, 45 L. T. 649; 46 J. P. 358. Where the guest has valuables in his possession, and omits to give them to the care of the innkeeper, this may be treated as negligence: *Jones* v. *Jackson*, 29 L. T. 399; 37 J. P. 776. How far a notice stuck up in each room as to this Act and the limit of 30*l.* protects the innkeeper, if goods are not deposited in his care, see *Medawar* v. *Grand Hotel* (1891), 2 Q. B. 11; 60 L. J. Q. B. 209; 55 J. P. 326; 64 L. T. 851.

(*a*) A mere verbal error in the copy will not vitiate the notice, if the material parts of the Act appear: *Spice* v. *Bacon*, 2 Ex. D. 463; 46 L. J. Q. B. 713; 36 L. T. 896; 42 J. P. 261.

As to the *lien of innkeeper*, see further notes to 41 & 42 Vict. c. 38, *post.*

See also as to signboard on premises of licensed persons, 9 Geo. 4, c. 61, s. 14, *ante*, p. 236.

Duties and taxes, and restrictions on innkeepers.] Some exceptional treatment is given to innkeepers in reference to taxes.

It shall not be necessary for a license to be taken out under 32 & 33 Vict. c. 14, by any hotel keeper, retailer of intoxicating liquor, or refreshment house keeper, for any *servant* wholly employed by him for the purposes of business: 36 & 37 Vict. c. 18, s. 4. And the term "male servant" shall not include a servant only employed for part of

4. *Interpretation of terms.*] The words and expressions Appndx. hereinafter contained, which in their ordinary signification have a more confined or a different meaning, shall in this Act, except where the nature of the provision or the context of the Act shall exclude such construction, be interpreted as follows; that is to say, the word "inn" shall mean any hotel, inn, tavern, public-house, or other place of refreshment, the keeper of which is now by law responsible for the goods and property of his guests; and the word "innkeeper" shall mean the keeper of any such place.

THE REVENUE (No. 1) ACT, 1864.

27 & 28 VICT. CAP. 18.

* * * * * *

5. *Occasional licenses may be granted to persons who have taken out licenses under 23 & 24 Vict. cc. 27 and 107 (Refreshment Houses and Wine Retailers); under 4 & 5 Vict. c. 85 (Beer Retailers); and under 6 Geo. 4, c. 81, (Tobacco Retailers).*] It shall be lawful for the Commissioners of Inland Revenue, whenever they shall consider it necessary for

---

each day, and not residing in the employer's house : 39 & 40 Vict. c. 16, s. 5.

As to the *inhabited house* duty, every inhabited dwelling house which, with the household and other offices, yards, and gardens therewith occupied and charged, is or shall be worth the rent of 20*l.*, or upwards by the year, which shall be occupied by any person who shall carry on in the said dwelling-house the business of a hotel keeper, or an innkeeper, or coffee-house keeper, although not licensed to sell therein by retail beer, ale, wine, or other liquors there, shall be charged for every 20*s.* of such annual value of any such dwelling-house the sum of *sixpence:* 34 & 35 Vict. c. 103, s. 31.

An innkeeper or victualler, or one licensed to sell beer by retail, and any one employed by such is not allowed to hold a license as a game dealer : 1 & 2 Will. 4, c. 32, s. 18. But any innkeeper or tavernkeeper may sell game for consumption in his own house, such *game* having been procured from some licensed game dealer : *Ibid. s.* 26.

Further restrictions on innkeepers and licensed persons as to allowing payment of wages, holding polls, bribery, disinfection, &c., are stated in 46 & 47 Vict. c. 31, and notes, *post.*

Appndx. the accommodation of the public, to authorise any officer of excise to grant (upon payment of the respective duties in that behalf mentioned in Schedule (B.) to this Act) an occasional license in the several and respective cases hereinafter mentioned; (that is to say,) to any person who shall have taken out an excise license under the Acts 23 & 24 Vict. cc. 27, 107, respectively, to keep a refreshment house, or to sell by retail in a refreshment house foreign wine to be consumed therein; or an excise license under the Act 4 & 5 Will. 4, c. 85, to retail beer to be drunk or consumed in or upon the house or premises where sold; or an excise license under the Act 6 Geo. 4, c. 81, to deal in or sell tobacco or snuff; and every such occasional license shall authorise any such person as aforesaid to exercise and carry on the same trade and business as he shall be authorised to carry on by virtue of the license granted under the said Acts respectively as aforesaid at any such place (other than the place for which his original license was granted), and for and during such space or period of time, not exceeding three consecutive days at any one time, as the said commissioners shall approve, and as shall be specified in such occasional license : Provided that the said occasional license shall not protect any such person in the carrying on of any such trade or business as aforesaid unless he shall produce such license whenever requested so to do by any officer of excise, or by any constable or police officer, at the time of exercising such trade or business; and provided also, that the conditions and restrictions contained in 26 & 27 Vict. c. 33, s. 20, relating to occasional licenses, shall apply to the occasional licenses to be granted under this Act (except in the case of occasional licenses to sell tobacco or snuff).(a)

(a) The duty fixed by Schedule (B.) was for occasional license to a refreshment house keeper, for each day *nil;* for same to retail foreign wine to be consumed on the premises, per day, one shilling; same to retail beer for consumption on the premises, per day, one shilling.

See further Licensing Act, 1874, sections 18, 19, *ante*, p. 197, and 25 & 26 Vict. c. 22, s. 13, *ante*, p. 295.

The occasional license here authorised to those holding retail wine and beer licenses is made subject to the conditions in 26 & 27 Vict. c. 33, s. 20, and one of those conditions is that the license is to be also subject to 25 & 26 Vict. c. 22, s. 13, which says the license is not to exceed three days. On the other hand, a publican's occasional license as authorised by 26 & 27 Vict. c. 33, s. 19, is not to exceed six days.

The consent of a justice is needed as well as the authority of the Commissioners of Inland Revenue: *Hannant* v. *Foulger*, L. R. 2 Q. B. 399; 36 L. J. M. C. 119; 8 B. & S. 425; 15 W. R. 787; 31 J. P. 628.

27 & 28 VICT. C. 64, S. 5.

Appndx.

THE PUBLIC-HOUSE CLOSING ACT, 1864.(b)

27 & 28 VICT. CAP. 64.

* * * * * *

[25th July, 1864.]

* * * * * *

1. *Short title.*] This Act may be cited for all purposes as "The Public-house Closing Act, 1864."

2. *Limits of Act.*] (c)

3. *Definition of "corporate body," &c.*] Repealed by 38 & 39 Vict. c. 66.

4. *Definition of "refreshment houses," &c.*] "Refreshment house" shall in this Act have the same meaning as it has in the Act 23 Vict. c. 27, s. 6.

Excisable liquor shall mean any spirits, foreign wine, beer, cider, sweets, or made wines, defined by the Acts relating to the excise.(d)

5. *As to the closing of refreshment houses.*] No person within the limits of this Act shall open and keep open any refreshment house or sell or expose for sale or consumption in any refreshment house any refreshments or any article whatsoever between the hours of [the night or morning at which premises

---

(b) This Act was *repealed* by Licensing Act, 1872, except as regards houses *not selling intoxicating liquors*. See Schedule, and section 24. The Act, so far as unrepealed, has to some extent been altered by Licensing Act, 1874, section 11, *ante*, p. 185. Thus it has been extended to the whole of England instead of being restricted to the metropolis.

The Licensing Act, 1872, schedule, also repealed the prior Acts as to the sale of liquors on the Lord's Day, viz., 11 & 12 Vict. c. 49, and 18 & 19 Vict. c. 118.

(c) Now extended to all England by 37 & 38 Vict. c. 49, s. 11.
(d) See 23 Vict. c. 27, s. 6, and notes, *ante*, p. 275.

licensed for the sale of intoxicating liquors by retail, situate in the same place as such refreshment houses, are required to be closed] and four o'clock in the morning.

Any person acting in contravention of this section shall be liable to a penalty not exceeding five pounds, to be recovered in a summary manner as provided by the Act 11 & 12 Vict. c. 43.(*a*)

* * * * * *

7. *Occasional license.*] If any keeper of a refreshment house as aforesaid within the limits of this Act applies to the local authorities hereinafter mentioned for a license exempting him from the provisions of this Act on any special occasion or occasions, it shall be lawful for the local authority, if in its discretion it thinks fit so to do, to grant to the applicant an occasional license exempting him from the provisions of this Act during certain hours and on a special occasion or occasions to be specified in the license; and no keeper of a refreshment house to whom an occasional license has been granted under this Act shall be subject to any penalty for a contravention of this Act during the time to which this occasional license extends, but he shall not be exempted by such occasional license from any penalty to which he may be subject under any other Act of Parliament.

8. *Definition of " local authority."*] The following persons and bodies of persons shall be deemed to be local authorities capable of granting occasional licenses for the purposes of this Act; that is to say :—

(1.) In the metropolitan police district, the commissioner of police for the metropolis, subject to the approbation of one of Her Majesty's principal Secretaries of State :

(2.) In the city of London and the liberties thereof, commissioner of city police, subject to the approbation of the Lord Mayor of the said city.(*b*)

9. *As to adoption of Act by corporate boroughs.*] *Repealed* by 38 & 39 Vict. c. 66.

(*a*) The words *within brackets* were inserted by the Licensing Act, 1874, 37 & 38 Vict. c. 49, s. 11, *ante*, p. 185. The other parts of this section were repealed by Licensing Act, 1872, sched. 2.

(*b*) Part of this section repealed by 38 & 39 Vict. c. 66. And the " local authority " was defined by 28 & 29 Vict. c. 77, s. 5, *post*, to mean two or more justices in petty sessions.

10. *Not to apply to sales at railway stations between one and four in the morning.*] Nothing herein contained shall apply to the sale at a railway station between the hours of one and four o'clock in the morning of refreshments to persons arriving at or departing from such station by railroad.(c)

Appndx.

THE PUBLIC-HOUSE CLOSING ACT, 1865.(d)

28 & 29 VICT. CAP. 77.

* * * * * *

[29th June, 1865.]

* * * * * *

1. *Short title.*] This Act may be cited for all purposes as "The Public-house Closing Act, 1865."

2. *Power to justices to grant licenses to refreshment house keepers suspending operations of recited Act.*] It shall be lawful for the licensing justices at the time of granting or renewing any license, upon the production of such evidence as they shall deem sufficient to show that it is necessary or desirable, for the accommodation of any considerable number of persons attending any public market, or following any lawful trade or calling, if, in the discretion of such justices, they shall think fit, to grant to any keeper of a refreshment house(e) whose place of business is in the immediate neighbourhood of such market, or of the place where the person follows such lawful trade or calling, a license exempting him from the provisions of the hereinbefore-mentioned Act between the hours of two and four o'clock in the morning, or any part of such hours, during such days, times, or

---

(c) See also Licensing Act, 1874, section 10, *ante*, p. 180.

(d) This Act was *repealed* by Licensing Act, 1872, as regards houses selling *intoxicating* liquor. As to refreshment houses it is still in force.

(e) As to what houses are refreshment houses within the meaning of these Acts of 27 & 28 Vict. c. 64, and 28 & 29 Vict. c. 77, see notes to 23 Vict. c. 27, s. 6, *ante*, p. 275.

Appndx. hours as shall be specified in such license; and no keeper of a refreshment house to whom such license has been granted under this Act shall be subject to any penalty for a contravention of the hereinbefore mentioned Act during the days or times to which such license extends, but he shall not be exempted by such license from any penalty to which he may be subject under any other Act of Parliament; provided that a printed notice stating the days and special hours during which, and the class of persons for whom, the house is open under such license shall be affixed in a conspicuous position outside the house.

3. *Power to withdraw such license.*] It shall be lawful for such justices, from time to time, as and when it may seem fit to them, either to withdraw such license altogether, or to alter, vary, or amend the same in such manner as such justices may deem necessary or expedient.

4. *Act to be in force in certain districts, &c.*] *Repealed* by 38 & 39 Vict. c. 66.(*a*)

5. *Justices of the peace to grant licenses.*] So much of 27 & 28 Vict. c. 64, s. 8, as defines the local authority to be a commissioner, superintendent, or other chief officer of police shall be repealed, and instead thereof the local authority shall be, in any district, city, or town where petty sessions are held, except in the metropolitan police district, two justices of the peace sitting in petty sessions, and in any other district, city, or town, two justices of the peace acting in the district, city, or town.

6. *Act to be construed with recited Act.*] This Act shall be deemed, construed, and taken as part of the said hereinbefore mentioned Act.

(*a*) The Act 27 & 28 Vict. c. 64, was by the Licensing Act, 1874, s. 11, extended to all England as regards refreshment houses not selling intoxicating liquors.

INLAND REVENUE ACT, 1867.

30 & 31 VICT. CAP. 90.

* * * * * *

17. *Penalty upon unlicensed persons (not being travellers for licensed persons) soliciting orders for spirits, wine, &c.*] If any person shall solicit, take, or receive any order for spirits, wine, or other article, for the dealing in, retailing, or selling whereof an excise license is by law required, without having in force a proper excise license authorising him so to do, he shall forfeit the penalty imposed by law upon a person dealing in, retailing, or selling such article without having an excise license in force authorising him so to do ; and in any case in which the place of business or residence of the offender shall not be known to the officer of excise who shall exhibit any information for the recovery of such penalty as aforesaid, or, if known, shall be out of the United Kingdom, it shall be sufficient service of the notice and summons required to be given to a defendant by any law of excise if the same be left at the house or place where the offender shall have solicited, taken, or received any such order as aforesaid, addressed to such offender : Provided always that nothing herein contained shall be deemed to apply to the sale of any spirits or foreign wine while the same shall be and remain in the warehouse or warehouses in which the same shall have been deposited, lodged, or secured according to law, before payment of duty upon the importation thereof, where such spirits or foreign wine shall be sold in a quantity not less than one hundred gallons at one time, or to impose a penalty upon a *bond fide* traveller taking orders for goods which his employer is duly licensed to deal in or sell.(*b*)

18. *Reduction of duty on licenses to retailers of methylated spirit.*] The annual duty payable upon a license to be taken out by a retailer of methylated spirit under the provisions contained in the Act 24 & 25 Vict. c. 91, shall be the sum of ten shillings.(*c*)

(*b*) See as to this Act, 1872, s. 3, and notes, *ante*, p. 4.
(*c*) See 43 & 44 Vict. c. 24, *post ;* 52 & 53 Vict. c. 42, s. 27. No duty is now payable : 53 Vict. c. 8, s. 31. The spirits must not be sold on Sunday : 52 & 53 Vict. c. 42, s. 26.

Appndx.

WINE AND BEERHOUSE ACT, 1869.

32 & 33 VICT. CAP. 27.

* * * * * *

[12th July, 1869.]

WHEREAS by the Acts relating to the general sale of beer and cider by retail in England ; (that is to say,)

(1.) An Act of 11 Geo. 4 and 1 Will. 4, c. 64 ;
(2.) An Act of 4 & 5 Will. 4, c. 85 ;
(3.) An Act of 3 & 4 Vict. c. 61 ;
(4.) An Act of 24 & 25 Vict. c. 21 ;

provision is made for the grant of licenses by the excise for the sale by retail of beer and cider upon the terms and conditions therein specified :(a)

And whereas by an Act of 26 & 27 Vict. c. 33, it is enacted, that any person who after the passing of that Act has taken out an excise license to sell strong beer in casks containing not less than four-and-a-half gallons, or in not less than two dozen reputed quart bottles, at one time, to be drunk or consumed elsewhere than on his premises, may take out an additional license on payment of the excise duties therein mentioned, and that the same shall authorise such person to sell beer in any less quantity and in any other manner than as aforesaid, but not to be drunk or consumed on the premises where sold, and that such additional license shall be granted without the production of any certificate, or the possession of any other qualification than the license therein first mentioned (26 & 27 Vict. c. 33) :

(a) The beer licenses mentioned in this recital whether those obtained under the Beerhouse Acts (1 Will. 4, c. 64 ; 4 & 5 Will. 4, c. 85 ; 3 & 4 Vict. c. 61), or those called the beer dealer's additional retail license obtained under 25 & 26 Vict. c. 33, or the table-beer license obtained under 24 & 25 Vict. c. 21, s. 3, have all been affected by later statutes (43 Vict. c. 6 ; 46 & 47 Vict. c. 34, *post*), which have the effect of giving the licensing justices the same discretion as they have always had with respect to alehouse licenses under 9 Geo. 4, c. 61. This is so as to all beerhouses, except those in-door houses continuously licensed since 1869 : 32 & 33 Vict. c. 27, s. 19; and except ciderhouses licensed under the Beerhouse Acts.

32 & 33 VICT. C. 27, S. 5.

And whereas provision is made for the grant of licenses by the excise for refreshment houses and for the sale of wine by retail, and for other purposes, by an Act of 23 & 24 Vict. c. 27 :

And whereas it is expedient to make better provision with regard to the granting of the licenses hereinbefore mentioned, and for regulating the houses and shops in which beer, cider, and wine are sold by retail.

Be it enacted by the Queen's most Excellent Majesty, by and with the advice and consent of the Lords Spiritual and Temporal, and Commons, in this present Parliament assembled, and by the authority of the same, as follows : (that is to say,)

Appndx.
—

1. *Application of Act.*] This Act shall not apply to Scotland or Ireland.

2. *Definition of " beer " and " cider."*] For the purposes of this Act the term " beer" shall include ale and porter, and the term " cider " shall include perry.(*b*)

3. *Short title.*] This Act may be cited as " The Wine and Beerhouse Act, 1869."

4. *Retail licenses not to be granted without certificate granted under this Act.*] No license or renewal of a license for the sale by retail of beer, cider, or wine, or any of such articles under the provisions of any of the said recited Acts, shall (save as in this Act otherwise provided) be granted except upon the production and in pursuance of the authority of a certificate granted under this Act.

Any license granted or renewed in contravention of this enactment shall be void.(*c*)

5. *Certificates by whom to be granted—9 Geo. 4, c. 61.*] Certificates under this Act shall be granted by the justices

---

(*b*) The word beer now includes botanic beer, or liquor brewed from sugar and water, which contains spirit to the extent of 6 or 7 per cent., and, therefore, an excise license is required for selling such liquor: 48 & 49 Vict. c. 51, s. 4 ; *Howarth* v. *Minns*, 51 J. P. 7. The former Act was otherwise : *Leah* v. *Minns*, 47 J. P. 198.

(*c*) The mode of obtaining the certificate is the same as in case of a license under the Act 9 Geo. 4, c. 61, s. 1, *ante*, p. 213. This certificate is not required for a wine dealer's additional retail license, or a spirit dealer's retail license under certain circumstances : Licensing Act, 1872, section 73, *ante*, p. 148.

WINE AND BEERHOUSE ACT, 1869, s. 7.

assembled at the general annual licensing meeting held in pursuance of an Act 9 Geo. 4, c. 61, or at some adjournment of such meeting held in pursuance of the said last-mentioned Act. [The rest of this section was *repealed* by 33 & 34 Vict. c. 29, s. 4.](*a*)

6. *Form of certificate*.] A certificate under this Act shall specify the name and address of the person thereby authorised to receive a license, the description of license or licenses authorised to be granted to him, and whether such license or licenses is or are to be granted for the sale of beer, cider, or wine to be consumed on or off the premises, and the situation of the house or shop in respect of which such grant is authorised. It shall be in force(*b*) for one year from the date of its being granted. [The rest of the section is *repealed* by Licensing Act, 1872; see Schedule.]

7. *Notice of application*.] Every person intending to apply to the justices for a certificate under this Act shall, twenty-one days at least before he applies,(*c*) give notice in writing of his

---

(*a*) This section is not directory but imperative. Hence where the justices, excise officers, and applicant were all ignorant of the repeal of a section and a license was granted under it by mistake, the license was held to be a nullity, and the holder liable for selling without a license : *Pearson* v. *Broadbent*, 36 J. P. 485.

The time of the general annual licensing meeting and its adjournments is stated in 9 Geo. 4, c. 61, ss. 1, 2, 3, 5, *ante*, pp. 212, 223. The Licensing Act, 1872, sections 37, 38, 50, modify the earlier statute.

As to adjournments, see 33 & 34 Vict. c. 29, s. 4, sub-section (4), and 33 & 34 Vict. c. 29, s. 11. See notes, *post*.

(*b*) This is now altered, and the beginning and ending of the year covered by the certificate is made uniform with publican's licenses. See 9 Geo. 4, c. 61, s. 13, *ante*, p. 227. See notes to 33 & 34 Vict. c. 29, s. 4 (5), *post*.

The forms of certificates or licenses have been altered by the Secretary of State, in pursuance of the Licensing Act, 1872, section 48. See the forms at the end of this volume.

(*c*) This is the section which now contains the general law as to notices before all applications for new licenses, for it was adopted and incorporated with an addition there declared into the Licensing Act, 1872, section 40, and made universal.

The time of the year for the application is specified in the Act 9 Geo. 4, c. 61, ss. 1, 2, 3, 5 ; and the time from which the notices are computed is the date of the general annual licensing meeting, or any adjournment thereof. Thus, if an applicant is not in time to give notice before the general meeting, he may yet be in time if the notices

32 & 33 VICT. C. 27, S. 7.

intention(*d*) to one of the overseers of the parish, township, or place in which the house or shop in respect of which his application is to be made is situate, and to [*the superintendent of police of the district*](*e*) and shall in such notice set forth his name and

Appndx.

---

are given before the adjournment day: *R.* v. *West Riding JJ.*, *Drake's Case*, L. R. 5 Q. B. 33; 34 J. P. 4; 10 B. & S. 840; 39 L. J. M. C. 17. In some cases he may fail at the general meeting, and be in time to give fresh notices for the adjournment, and apply on different materials. *R.* v. *Caulfield*, 46 J. P. 756; though he cannot usually apply again at the adjournment on the same materials: *Ex parte Rushworth*, 23 L. T. 120; 34 J. P. 676. See 9 Geo. 4, c. 61, section 3, and notes, *ante*, p. 221.

The mode of *computing* the twenty-one days for notice is to exclude the day of holding the general annual meeting or the adjournment day, and to exclude the day on which the notice is given: *R.* v. *Aberdare*, 14 Q. B. 856; *R.* v. *Shropshire*, 8 A. & E. 173; *Young* v, *Higgin*, 6 M. & W. 49; *Chambers* v. *Smith*, 12 M. & W. 2; *Robinson* v. *Waddington*, 13 Q. B. 753; *Norton* v. *Salisbury*, 4 C. B. 32; *Re Railway Sleepers Company*, 29 Ch. D. 204; *Mercantile Company* v. *International* (1893), 1 Ch. 484. And see Licensing Act, 1872, section 40, *ante*, p. 83.

As to the *notices* on the *church door*, any two consecutive Sundays may be selected within the twenty-eight days preceding the holding of the general annual meeting or adjournment day; but as to the twenty-one days a much longer notice would be equally good, the twenty-one days being the shortest time allowed. The church or chapel here mentioned means that of the Church of England; and if there is a notice board near the door, publication on such board will usually be sufficient: *Empson* v. *Metropolitan Board*, 25 J. P. 677; 3 L. T. 624.

The *situation* of the house need not be described so strictly as in a conveyance: *R.* v. *Penkridge Division of Staffordshire*, 56 J. P. 87. 66 L. T. 371; 61 L. J. M. C. 132.

(*d*) This notice may be served by post: 33 & 34 Vict. c. 29, s. 4; Licensing Act, 1872, section 70.

(*e*) The words in brackets were inserted by 33 & 34 Vict. c. 29, s. 4. Care must be taken to serve the superintendent either personally or by leaving the notice at his actual residence, and not merely at one of the police stations in the district: *R.* v. *Riley*, 53 J. P. 452.

Where a petty sessional division included a borough, and the borough had a chief constable of its own, and the rest of the division another superintendent of police, it was held that the notice was rightly served on the superintendent in whose part of the division the house was: *R.* v. *Birley*, 55 J. P. 87.

As to what is a new license, and what is a *renewal*, see notes to Licensing Act, 1872, section 74, *ante*, p. 157.

General effect of section 7.] The general effect of this section is, that in all cases whatsoever, twenty-one days' notice must be given to the

Appndx. address, and a description of the license or licenses for which he intends to apply, and of the situation of the house or shop in respect of which the application is to be made ; and in the case of a house or shop not theretofore licensed for the sale by retail of beer, cider, or wine, such person shall also within the space of twenty-eight days before such application is made cause a like notice to be affixed and maintained between the hours of ten in the morning and five in the afternoon of two consecutive Sundays on the door of such house or shop, and on the principal door or on one of the doors of the church or chapel of the parish or place in which such house or shop is situate, or, if there be no such church or chapel, on some other public and conspicuous place within such parish or place.

Where application is made to the justices for the grant of a certificate under this Act by way of *renewal* only, notice in pursuance of this section shall not be requisite.

overseer and superintendent of police of the first application to justices ; and if the house was not previously licensed for sale by retail the notice on the church door within the twenty-eight days must be superadded. But in future, if a certificate has been already given under this Act, and all that is wanted is renewal of the certificate to the same person and house, or in some cases to a different person and the same house, then neither of these notices need be given. As to renewals, see also Licensing Act, 1872, sections 42, 74.

This section now extends to the notices required for new alehouse licenses. See Licensing Act, 1872, section 40.

Where, as in many new churches, a notice board is placed near the door of the church on which miscellaneous notices are usually affixed, it will be sufficient, as already stated, to affix these notices on such board, provided the board is reasonably near the church door, and equal or greater publicity is thereby given. (See *ante*, p. 315.)

Over and above the notices above described there must, as to new licenses and certificates, be also a notice advertised in a local newspaper under Licensing Act, 1872, section 40.

Alteration of premises.] Where after a license has been obtained for premises used as an inn, the keeper of the inn buys an adjoining dwelling house and adds it to the inn by opening interior communications, he does not usually require to apply for a new license, provided the justices are likely to be satisfied that the premises are substantially the same as those formerly licensed : See *ante*, p. 158. And the same rule would apply to a certificate. Notice of any important changes in the structure should always be brought to the notice of the justices at the next general annual meeting ; and it may be prudent even beforehand to notify to them the intention to make such changes.

As to the forms of the notices, see notes to Licensing Act, 1872, section 40, *ante*, p. 82.

32 & 33 VICT. C. 27, S. 8. 317

8. *Provisions of 9 Geo. 4, c. 61, as to grants of certificates under this Act.*] (a) All the provisions of the said Act of the ninth year of the reign of King George the Fourth as to the terms upon

Appndx.
—

(a) *General effect of this eighth section as altered.*] This section formerly laid down the rule that, as to out-door licenses for wine, beer, cider (afterwards extended to (off) spirits and sweets by the Licensing Act, 1872), the discretion of justices in granting both a new and a renewal license, instead of being unlimited should be restricted to four grounds. That law existed till 1880 and 1883, when the restriction was abolished as to beer licenses, and the same general or absolute discretion was given to the licensing justices as they always enjoyed as regards publicans' licenses. But this section still governs the law as to off-wine, off-cider, off-sweets, and off-spirit licenses.

The applicant on each *renewal* is still bound, if challenged, and receiving proper notice under Licensing Act, 1872, section 42, to give evidence of good character, and if he has been convicted or been complained of during the previous year, and the objection is made, or stated in open court by justices (provided, in the latter event, time is given to answer the objection), the justices may refuse to renew the license or certificate under this head: *R.* v. *Birmingham JJ.*, 40 J. P. 132; *R.* v. *Merthyr Tydvil JJ.*, 14 Q. B. D. 584; 54 L. J. M. C. 78; 49 J. P. 213; *R.* v. *Lancashire JJ.*, 55 J. P. 580; 64 L. T. 562.

The justices have also a large discretion on all applications for *new* licenses of every description, as to the *quantum* or sufficiency of the evidence given by the applicant on each of the four grounds, and especially of his good character. And, in general, the applicant should not rest satisfied with assuming that nothing is to be said against him; he ought to be prepared to give affirmative evidence by witnesses and written testimonials as to his character: *R.* v. *Hanley JJ.*, 42 J. P. 102; 39 L. T. 444; *Ex parte Bendall*, 42 J. P. 88. In one case under a previous statute a question of good character arose, where the license holder was found to be cohabiting with a female: *R.* v. *Leader*, 16 C. B. (N.S.) 584; 33 L. J. M. C. 231; 28 J. P. 470. Sometimes opposition is based, not on the want of the applicant's character, but on that of a preceding holder of the license.

The valuation of premises.] The qualification referred to in the fourth ground means such restrictions or conditions as to the particular kind of license as are imposed by such statute, and does not mean mere suitability at the discretion of justices. Thus it is incompetent for justices to refuse an off-wine and off-spirit license, because the premises are under a certain value, or because a baker's shop is part of the premises: *R.* v. *Morison*, 55 J. P. 87. The Beerhouse Act, 3 & 4 Vict. c. 51, s. 1, also 23 Vict. c. 27, s. 8, and 33 & 34 Vict. c. 29, s. 10, prescribed the qualification referred to as regards the annual value of some premises, the meaning of which is further explained by the Licensing Act, 1872, sections 45, 46, 47. The sufficiency of the annual value is

Appndx. which, and the manner in which, and the persons by whom grants of licenses are to be made by the justices at the said general

estimated at the date of hearing the application: *R.* v. *Montagu*, 50 J. P. 55. There are also disqualifications as to the persons: as being a sheriff's officer, 1 Will. 4, c. 64, s. 2 : not being the real resident holder and occupier, 3 & 4 Vict. c. 61, s. 1 ; being convicted of felony or of selling spirits without license, 3 & 4 Vict. c. 61, s. 7 ; 23 Vict. c. 27, s. 22 ; 33 & 34 Vict. c. 29, s. 14 ; convicted of forging a certificate, 32 & 33 Vict. c. 27, s. 11 ; thrice convicted of selling without a license, &c., Act, 1872, section 3. See also Act, 1872, sections 15, 30.

Duty of justices as to four grounds.] It is the duty of the justices, on hearing all applications, to see that these several statutory requirements are satisfied, and to refuse the license if they are not satisfied, even though on other grounds the justices might be satisfied as to the person applying. Though these are still good special reasons for refusing licenses, yet the legislature has now, as above stated, conferred an absolute discretion on the justices to refuse all beerhouse licenses without stating any grounds whatever except as to in-door licensed beerhouses since 1869. This important change has been made by striking out of the section all beer licenses (except those mentioned in section 19, *post*), whether ordinary beer licenses or beer dealers' retail licenses, or table beer licenses, so that justices have now the same ample discretion as to all beer licenses, whether out-door or in-door, as they have and always had as to alehouse or public-house licenses. These changes have been made by the recent Acts, 43 Vict. c. 6, and 45 & 46 Vict. c. 34, *post*.

As to premises for which an alehouse license or a certificate under this Act for in-door consumption shall be hereafter applied for, see Licensing Act, 1872, section 45.

As to the meaning of the words "annual value," in 3 & 4 Vict. c. 61, and similar words in 23 Vict. c. 27, s. 8, and the mode of ascertaining it, see Licensing Act, 1872, sections 46, 47.

Stating grounds of decision.] Under this section, when it still applies, where the justices refuse to grant a certificate, they are bound to state upon which of the four grounds they have so refused, for otherwise the applicant may not know what is his remedy: *R.* v. *Sykes; R.* v. *Huddersfield*, 1 Q. B. D. 52 ; 45 L. J. M. C. 39 ; 40 J. P. 39 ; 33 L. T. 566 ; 24 W. R. 141. And if the justices refuse on some ground other than these four, a *mandamus* may be obtained to compel them to hear and confine themselves to such grounds: *R.* v. *Monmouthshire JJ.*, 38 J. P. 807 ; *R.* v. *Smith* or *Southport JJ.*, L. R. 8 Q. B. 146 ; 37 J. P. 214 ; 28 L. T. 129 ; 21 W. R. 382 ; *R.* v. *Redditch*, 50 J. P. 246 ; *R.* v. *King* or *Manchester JJ.*, 20 Q. B. D. 43 ; 52 J. P. 164 ; 58 L. T. 607 ; 36 W. R. 600 ; 57 L. J. M. C. 20 ; *R.* v. *Lancashire*, 55 J. P. 580 ; 64 L. T. 562. And the justices are bound, even though not asked, to state on what ground they refuse the license: *Ex parte Smith; R.* v.

32 & 33 VICT. C. 27, S. 8.

annual licensing meeting, and as to appeal from any act of any
justice, shall, so far as may be, have effect with regard to grants

Appndx.
—

Surrey JJ., 3 Q. B. D. 374; 47 L. J. M. C. 104; 42 J. P. 598; 26 W. R. 682; *R.* v. *Ashton-under-Lyne*, 37 J. P. 85; *Tranter* v. *Lancashire JJ.*, 51 J. P. 454.

The justices are, however, not bound to deliver in writing their reasons for refusing the license on the ground of not being duly qualified unless they are asked to do so: *R.* v. *Cumberland JJ.*, 8 Q. B. D. 369; 46 J. P. 7; 51 L. J. Q. B. 142; 30 W. R. 178.

The second of the four grounds may be compared with the offence in 35 & 36 Vict. c. 94, s. 14, *ante*, p. 29.

Terms or fees on which certificate granted.] The terms which are now declared by 33 & 34 Vict. c. 29, s. 4, to include the usual fees payable for licenses are the same for grant or transfer of certificates as of licenses under 9 Geo. 4, c. 61. The terms upon which the grant or transfer or renewal of an alehouse license is made are stated in 9 Geo. 4, c. 61, s. 15.

With regard to certificates granted by way of renewal, the only fees payable are 4*s.* to the justices' clerk, and 1*s.* for the constable serving notices. If the clerk demands or receives more, he will be liable to a penalty of 5*l.*: 33 & 34 Vict. c. 29, s. 4. The fees for renewal of an alehouse license are the same as for the original grant. To the above must also be added a fee of 1*s.* for the registration of each license under Licensing Act, 1872, section 36.

Manner in which, and persons by whom, grants made.] This section is now considerably modified by the Licensing Act, 1872, sections 37, 38. With regard to *new certificates*, these can only be granted in counties by the justices at the general annual licensing meeting or adjournments, and confirmed by the county licensing committee. In boroughs having ten justices, the grant of a new certificate must be by the borough licensing committee, and thereafter confirmed by the whole body of borough justices. In boroughs having less than ten justices, the grant of a new certificate must be by the borough justices, and confirmed by a joint licensing committee, consisting usually of three borough justices and three county justices. There is no appeal from the decision of these double bodies of licensing justices as to granting or refusing of a new certificate. But no confirmation is required for out-door licenses: Licensing Act, 1874, section 23.

As to grants of new certificates under the Wine and Beerhouse Acts, and the Licensing Act, 1872, for *wine or spirits, or sweets, or cider, not to be consumed on the premises*, the licensing justices will be bound by the conditions stated in the above section, that is to say, they can only refuse such a certificate on one of the four grounds specified: *R.* v. *Scott*, 22 Q. B. D. 401; 53 J. P. 119; 58 L. J. M. C. 78; 60 L. T. 281; 37 W. R. 301. And they will be equally bound by these conditions on applications for transfers: *Simmonds* v. *Blackheath JJ.*, 17 Q. B. D.

Appndx. of certificates under this Act, subject to this qualification, that no application for a certificate under this Act in respect of a license

---

765; 50 J. P. 742; 55 L. J. M. C. 166; 35 W. R. 167. And they would be equally bound on applications for renewal of the same licenses. But the last of the four grounds is inapplicable to houses having outdoor wine licenses (to which must be added out-door sweets, and out-door spirits, and liqueur licenses), for these were never subject to any valuation qualification. As to new certificates for in-door licenses, the discretion of justices is absolute and without appeal.

With regard to renewals of the in-door beer licenses for houses continuously licensed since 1869, the justices are still bound to observe the four grounds above specified if they refuse such licenses, see *post*, section 19. And there is always an appeal to quarter sessions against a refusal to renew or transfer any license.

The justices disqualified from acting are described in the Licensing Act, 1872, section 60.

The manner in which certificates are transferred is the same as in the case of alehouses: 9 Geo. 4, c. 61, ss. 4, 14; 5 & 6 Vict. c. 44; 33 & 34 Vict. c. 29, s. 4, sub-sect. (5).

As to renewal of certificates, see 32 & 33 Vict. c. 27, s. 19; and Licensing Act, 1872, section 42.

Appeal.] Any person aggrieved by any act of the justices, except as to the refusal of a new certificate, may appeal to the next general or quarter sessions of the peace holden for the county: see 9 Geo. 4, c. 61, s. 27, *et seq., ante*, p. 238. Hence a party whose certificate the justices refused, could once appeal to the quarter sessions, because this 8th section and 33 & 34 Vict. c. 29, s. 4, then incorporated all the sections of 9 Geo. 4, c. 61, relating to such appeals: *R.* v. *Smith* or *Southport JJ.*, L. R. 8 Q. B. 400; 37 J. P. 214; 28 L. T. 129; 42 L. J. M. C. 146; 21 W. R. 382. And the Licensing Act, 1874, section 27, *ante*, p. 204. only repealed such of these incorporated enactments as related to new certificates, leaving the appeal section in full force as regards *renewals* and *transfers*. If the refusal be by the justices of a quarter sessions borough within the Municipal Corporations Act, 1882, the appeal must be to the quarter sessions of the county, and not the recorder: see 9 Geo. 4, c. 61, s. 27, *ante*, p. 238, and cases cited. If the court of quarter sessions grant the certificate which the justices refused, the grant takes effect as from the date of its having been refused: 9 Geo. 4, c. 61, s. 27.

The extent to which at the court of quarter sessions an appellant waives an objection to jurisdiction is seen in *Whiffen* v. *Malling* (1892), 1 Q. B. 362; 66 L. T. 332; 40 W. R. 293; 55 J. P. 424; 56 J. P. 325; *R.* v. *Lancashire*, 55 J. P. 580; 64 L. T. 562.

Where the justices refuse to renew a license, and the applicant appeals to the quarter sessions, which court reverses the decision at special sessions, and the justices of special sessions do not appear to support

to sell by retail beer,(a) cider, or wine not to be consumed on the **Appndx.**
premises shall be refused, except upon one or more of the following grounds, viz. :—

(1.) That the applicant has failed to produce satisfactory evidence of good character :

(2.) That the house or shop in respect of which a license is sought, or any adjacent house or shop, owned or occupied by the person applying for a license, is of a disorderly character, or frequented by thieves, prostitutes, or persons of bad character :

(3.) That the applicant having previously held a license for the sale of wine, spirits, beer, or cider, the same has been forfeited for his misconduct, or that he has through misconduct been at any time previously adjudged disqualified from receiving any such license, or from selling any of the said articles :

(4.) That the applicant or the house in respect of which he applies, is not duly qualified as by law is required :

Where an application for any such last-mentioned certificate is refused on the ground that the house in respect of which he applies is not duly qualified as by law is required, the justices shall specify in writing to the applicant the grounds of their decision.

9.(b) As to *transfer* of certificates. *Repealed* by 33 & 34 Vict. c. 29, s. 4.

10. As to renewal of licenses in force in Middlesex and Surrey (*spent*).

11. *Penalty on forgery of certificate.*] If any person forge or tender, knowing the same to have been forged, any certificate authorised to be granted by this Act, he shall, on summary con-

---

their decision, or their decision is reversed, see 9 Geo. 4, c. 61, s. 29, *ante*, p. 243, as to costs.

(a) The word "beer" was struck out by 56 & 57 Vict. c. 54.

(b) This section has been repealed by 33 & 34 Vict. c. 29, s. 4, and now transfers of certificates are put on the same footing as transfers of licenses under the Alehouse Act, 9 Geo. 4, c. 61, ss. 4, 14. See 33 & 34 Vict. c. 29, s. 4, sub-sect. (5), *post*, and notes.

Y

viction before two or more justices, be liable to a penalty not exceeding twenty pounds, or, in the discretion of the justices before whom he is tried, to imprisonment for any period not exceeding six months, with or without hard labour. Any license granted in pursuance of such forged certificate shall be void, and any person making use of such forged certificate, knowing the same to have been forged, shall be disqualified from obtaining at any time thereafter a license for the sale of beer, cider, or wine by retail under any of the said recited Acts.(a)

12. Constables may *enter houses.* *Repealed* by Licensing Act, 1872. See Schedule, and section 35.

13. Proof of sale. *Repealed* by Licensing Act, 1872. See Schedule, and section 62.

14. *Sale on neighbouring premises.*] *Repealed* by Licensing Act, 1872. See Schedule, and section 6.

15. *Beer or cider* drunk at illegal times.] *Repealed* by Licensing Act, 1872. Schedule, and see Licensing Act, 1874, sections 3, 9.

16. *Houses open at illegal hours.*] *Repealed* by Licensing Act, 1272. See Schedule, and section 25.

17. *Second or third offence.*(b) *Repealed* by Licensing Act, 1872. See Schedule.

18. *Sale of table-beer.*] *Repealed* by Licensing Act, 1872. See Schedule.

(*a*) By this section any person knowingly making use of a forged certificate is disqualified for life from obtaining a license whether of the same kind or not. See as to disqualifications, Licensing Act, 1872, s. 3, *ante*, p. 6.

There being nothing said in this Act as to the application, &c., of penalties, the provisions of 11 & 12 Vict. c. 43, s. 19, *ante*, p. 113, will apply to the penalties under this section.

(*b*) As to mode of reckoning a second offence under this repealed section, see *Ex parte Short*, L. R. 5 Q. B. 174 ; 39 L. J. M. C. 63 ; 22 L. T. 94 ; 34 J. P. 599.

19. Existing in-door licenses to be renewed, except Appndx.
in certain cases.] Where, on the 1st May, 1869, a license, under any of the said recited Acts is in force [and has been renewed from time to time, whether held by the same person or not, or has been or may be transferred to any other person or persons : 33 & 34 Vict. c. 29, s. 7] with respect to any house or shop for the sale by retail therein of beer, cider, or wine to be consumed on the premises, it shall not be lawful for the justices to refuse an application for a certificate for the sale of beer, cider, or wine to be consumed on the premises in respect of such house or shop, except upon one or more of the grounds upon which an application for a certificate under this Act in respect of a license for the sale of beer, cider, or wine not to be consumed on the premises, may be refused, in accordance with this Act.(c)

(c) The Licensing Act, 1872 (Schedule), has repealed "so much of this section as relates to offences." This was somewhat ambiguous, but probably the result was to strike out the rest of this section, which accordingly has been omitted.

The section was altered as shown in the text by 33 & 34 Vict. c. 29, s. 7.

This section has not been affected by the recent Acts, 43 Vict. c. 6 ; 45 & 46 Vict. c. 34, having been probably overlooked, so that though the licensing justices have now an absolute discretion to refuse all other in-door and all out-door beer licenses, either new or old, they are restricted to the four grounds specified in section 8 as to in-door beer licenses which have been continuous since 1869. But it has been held that if the applicant has not applied for a transfer under 9 Geo. 4, c. 61, s. 14, until after the current license has expired, the justices will then have an entire discretion and not merely a discretion limited to the four grounds : *Murray* v. *Freer* (1893), 1 Q. B. 635 ; 62 L. J. M. C. 33 ; 67 L. T. 507 ; 57 J. P. 101, 583. Moreover, where a privileged beerhouse of 1869 has been compulsorily purchased for public purposes and the licensee applies under 9 Geo. 4, c. 61, s. 14, for a transfer of the license to another house, the jurisdiction of justices is no longer confined to the four grounds : *Traynor* v. *Jones*, 57 J. P. 724. It has been decided that the right to renew a license under this section must apply only to the same kind of liquor. Thus, if a license for beer only has since 1869 been held, he cannot demand to have a license on the same terms to include cider or wine, the words being read distributively : *R.* v. *King* or *Manchester JJ.*, 20 Q. B. D. 430 ; 52 J. P. 164 ; 57 L. J. M. C. 20 ; 58 L. T. 607 ; 36 W. R. 600.

The result of the enactments as to renewal of certificates under the Wine and Beerhouse Acts seems to be as follows :—

Renewing of certificates.—When the certificate is for a license to sell by retail wine or spirits, or sweets, or cider, *not to be consumed on*

WINE AND BEERHOUSE ACT, 1869, S. 20.

Appndx. **20.** *Nothing to affect privileges and rights therein named.*] Nothing in this Act shall be deemed to affect—

(1.) The privileges heretofore enjoyed by any university in England, or the chancellor, masters, and scholars of the same, or their successors:

---

the premises, then the justices cannot refuse the renewal, whether the license existed in 1869 or not, except upon one of the grounds stated in 32 & 33 Vict. c. 27, s. 8, and as to the last ground it is in such cases inapplicable, except as to cider. And he need not now give affirmative evidence of good character, for he has a right to rely on the expectation that nobody will oppose him on that or any other ground, unless he has got seven days' notice of some objection and the grounds thereof; Licensing Act, 1872, section 42; Licensing Act, 1874, section 26. This seven days' notice of opposition is a condition precedent to the refusing any renewal license. If the justices refuse on the ground that evidence as to good character is defective, the party may appeal to quarter sessions, and then give further and better evidence of good character, and if the quarter sessions are satisfied of the good character they are bound to reverse the judgment and grant the renewal: *R.* v. *Pilgrim*, 35 J. P. 169; L. R. 6 Q. B. 89; 40 L. J. M. C. 3; 23 L. T. 410; 19 W. R. 99. And there is the same right whatever may have been the ground of refusal to give additional evidence at quarter sessions. The renewal will take effect from the date of the previous refusal. If the justices refuse to renew a certificate there is always an appeal to quarter sessions. See notes to section 8, *ante,* p. 320.

Renewing on-certificates.] If the application is for renewal of a certificate for beer, cider, or wine, *to be consumed on the premises,* then the justices may refuse the renewal, as they may do with respect to a publican's license, without stating reasons, unless in case of a house licensed for beer, wine, or cider on 1st May, 1869. But in this, as in all cases, the renewal can only be refused if notice of opposition has been previously given. The license must have been continuous, for if there has been a forfeiture by the misconduct of an occupier at any time, or the license has been for any cause not renewed for a year, the next application is to be deemed an application for a new certificate so far as regards the grounds for refusal of the certificate: *R.* v. *West Riding JJ.*, 21 Q. B. D. 258; 52 J. P. 455; 57 L. J. M. C. 103; 36 W. R. 258; *Hargraves* v. *Dawson*, 35 J. P. 342; 24 L. T. 428; *R.* v. *Curzon*, 42 L. J. M. C. 155; L. R. 8 Q. B. 400; 37 J. P. 774; 29 L. T. 32; 21 W. R. 886. If the house was licensed on 1st May, 1869, and has been since licensed continuously, and the justices had not made any order under this 32 & 33 Vict. c. 27, s. 19, which, under the now repealed part of the section, took away the protection of such continuous license, then the justices cannot refuse to renew the certificate, except

32 & 33 VICT. C. 27, S. 21.

(2.) The privileges heretofore enjoyed by the masters, wardens, **Appndx.** freemen, and commonalty of the vintners of the city of London, except as to those freemen of the said vintners who have obtained their freedom by redemption only :(a)

(3.) The privileges heretofore enjoyed by the mayor or burgesses of the city of St. Albans in the county of Hertford, or their successors :

(4.) The right of any person who is duly authorised by justices of the peace to keep a common inn, alehouse, or victualling house to take out any excise license :

(5.) The grant of any occasional license, or the power of any person duly authorised by the excise to sell beer, spirits, or wine at any fair or public races.

21. As to repeal of Acts set forth in Second Schedule. *Repealed* by 46 & 47 Vict. c. 39.

---

on one of the four grounds set forth in 32 & 33 Vict. c. 27, s. 8 ; 33 & 34 Vict. c. 29, s. 7 ; and the appeal to quarter sessions, for not renewing a certificate, remains as before.

In *R.* v. *Curzon, supra,* a beerhouse license was in force in May, 1869, but the tenant had not renewed his license for three years owing to his rebuilding his premises. When they were rebuilt he applied for a renewal or a new certificate :—Held, that justices had a discretion to refuse the license though not on the four grounds, as it was a new license.

In *Hargraves* v. *Dawson, supra,* and *R.* v. *West Riding JJ., supra,* the beer license had been continuous since 1869, but the license holder forfeited his license, so that it ceased to exist, and the justices were held to be right in deciding that the next application could only be one for a new license.

A renewal of a certificate may in future (that is after 1872) be made by endorsement on the certificate : Licensing Act, 1872, section 48.

See also notes to Licensing Act, 1872, sections 42 and 74, *ante*, pp. 89, 154.

(*a*) These exceptions to the Act as to the universities and vintners of the city of London are the same as specified in 9 Geo. 4, c. 61, s. 36. See also Licensing Act, 1872, section 72. As to fairs and races, see Licensing Act, 1874, section 18.

FIRST SCHEDULE.

(Superseded by the Licensing Act, 1872, section 43.)

SECOND SCHEDULE.

[This schedule was twice *repealed* by 46 & 47 Vict. c. 39, and 56 & 57 Vict. c. 54, but is retained in order to show how it disposed of some of the prior enactments by repealing them. The extent of repeal follows each statute respectively.]

11 Geo. 4 and 1 Will. 4, c. 64 : So much of section 2 as required the grant of an excise license under the provisions of the Act to be made within ten days after the application has been made for the same.

4 & 5 Will. 4, c. 85 : Sections 2, 3, 8, and 9.

3 & 4 Vict. c. 61 : Sections 2, 3 ; so much of section 4 as enacts that in any extra-parochial place or places where no rates are made or collected for the relief of the poor a person applying for a license shall produce to and deposit and leave with the proper officer of excise granting such license a certificate in writing, signed by two inhabitant householders of the township or place, certifying that the party applying is the real resident in, and occupier of, the dwelling-house sought to be licensed, and also certifying the true and real annual value of the same with the premises occupied therewith, according to the best of their judgment and belief : sections 5 and 6.

23 Vict. c. 27 : Sections 13, 14, and 15.

24 & 25 Vict. c. 21 : So much of section 3 as renders it unnecessary that the person applying for a license shall produce any certificate.

THE WINE AND BEERHOUSE ACT AMENDMENT ACT (1870).

33 & 34 Vict. Cap. 29.

AN ACT to amend and continue the Wine and Beerhouse Act, 1869. [14th July, 1870.]

Be it enacted, &c., as follows :—

1. *Short title.*] This Act may be cited as "The Wine and Beerhouse Act Amendment Act, 1870."

2. *Extent of Act.*] This Act shall not extend to Scotland or Ireland.

33 & 34 VICT. C. 29, S. 4.

3. *Interpretation of terms.*] In this Act the words "the **Appndx.** principal Act," mean the Wine and Beerhouse Act, 1869, and the word "sweets" includes sweets, made wines, mead, and metheglin.

4. *Amendment of provisions of principal Act as to grants, durations, and transmissions of certificate.*] The provisions of the principal Act, with reference to the grant, duration, and transmission of certificates, shall be amended, as follows (that is to say) :—

(1.) The seventh section of the principal Act shall be read as if for the words "constable or police officer, acting within such parish, township, or place," there were substituted the words "the superintendent of police of the district," and the notice required by that section to be given to any overseer or constable may be served by a registered letter through the post :(*a*)

(2.) Where a certificate is now required to be signed by a majority of justices, it shall be sufficient if, instead of such signature, the concurrence of such majority be signified by means of an impression from an official seal or stamp, in such form as the justices may direct, affixed in the presence of the justices in sessions assembled, and verified in the case of each certificate by the signature of their clerk. Any seal purporting to be so affixed and verified shall be received in evidence without further proof ; and if any unauthorised person imitate or affix an impression of such seal on any certificate or imitation of a certificate, or knowingly use a certificate or imitation of a certificate falsely purporting to be sealed in pursuance of this section, he shall be guilty of forgery :(*b*)

(*a*) See 32 & 33 Vict. c. 27, s. 7, *ante*, p. 314, where the alteration here directed is made in that section. See also Licensing Act, 1872, section 40, *ante*, p. 82.

(*b*) The *form of certificate* has been settled by the Secretary of State under the Licensing Act, 1872, section 48. See the forms at the end of this volume.

The certificate may be stamped by an official stamp as here directed. The clerk must sign the certificate if so stamped, and the stamp must be affixed in presence of the justices or licensing committee.

This mode of official stamping has also been made applicable to alehouse licenses granted by justices: Licensing Act, 1872, section 40, *ante*, p. 82.

WINE AND BEERHOUSE ACT, 1870, S. 4.

(3.) For every certificate granted by way of renewal under the principal Act or this Act, there shall be payable to the clerk of the justices the sum of four shillings for all matters to be done by such clerk, and one shilling for the constable or officer for service of notices; and if any clerk of justices demand or receive any greater or further fee or payment in respect of any such renewal, whether for himself or for any other officer or person, he shall, upon summary conviction, be liable to a penalty of five pounds :(a)

(4.) It shall be in the discretion of the justices, to whom an application for a transfer is made, either to allow or refuse the application, or to adjourn the consideration thereof :(b)

(5.) [The proviso of the fifth section of the principal Act, and the ninth section of the principal Act shall be repealed, and] Subject to the provisions of this section, all the provisions of the Act 9 Geo. 4, c. 91, and Acts amending the same, relating to the time for which justices' licenses are to be in force, and relating to the fees payable for

---

(a) See as to fees for grant and transfer of certificate, 32 & 33 Vict. c. 27, s. 8, notes; also 9 Geo. 4, c. 61, s. 15, *ante*, p. 236.

(b) The application for a transfer is made under 9 Geo. 4, c. 61, ss. 4, 14, and 5 & 6 Vict. c. 44. See next sub-section.

See as to adjournment of the application for grant or renewal of certificate, 32 & 33 Vict. c. 27, s. 5, and notes; also this statute section 11.

This enactment must be understood to apply to the justices in special sessions sitting under 9 Geo. 4, c. 61, ss. 4, 14, and not to the justices in petty sessions sitting under 5 & 6 Vict. c. 44. And the enactment does not seem to apply to transfers of alehouse licenses.

This enactment does not give the justices an absolute discretion to refuse all applications for transfer of wine, spirits, cider, and sweets off-licenses and in-door beer, cider, and wine licenses continued since 1869, and is not inconsistent with the 8th and 19th sections of 32 & 33 Vict. c. 27. The words "in the discretion of the justices" do not imply an absolute discretion as regards the four grounds of refusal when these are applicable, for in applications for transfer the justices have the same limited discretion as they would have had on a renewal: *Simmonds* v. *Blackheath JJ.*, 17 Q. B. D. 765; 50 J. P. 742; 55 L. J. M. C. 166; 35 W. R. 167. But it has been held that the four grounds are no longer applicable if the current license has expired and no application for a transfer has been made till some time later: *Murray* v. *Freer* (1893), 1 Q. B. 635; 62 L. J. M. C. 33; 67 L. T. 507; 57 J. P. 101, 583. And see *Traynor* v. *Jones*, *ante*, p. 235.

such licenses, and relating to the transfer, removal, and transmission of such licenses, and the grant of licenses upon assignment, death, change of occupancy, or other contingency, and relating to copies of such licenses, and relating to grants or transfers of such licenses, without the attendance of any applicant who is hindered by sickness, infirmity, or other reasonable causes shall have effect with regard to certificates granted or to be granted under the principal Act and this Act :(c)

Appndx.

(c) The words within *brackets* were repealed by 46 & 47 Vict. c. 39, Schedule.
This enactment now modifies the enactment of the former Act (32 & 33 Vict. c. 27, s. 6), which declared the certificate to be in force for one year from the date of its being granted, no matter at what period of the year it was granted. The 9.Geo. 4, c. 61, s. 13, which has been above incorporated into this Act, and must now over-ride the principal Act, prescribes a definite beginning and ending for each certificate. In the counties of Middlesex and Surrey the certificate will be in force from the fifth day of April, and in other counties the certificates will be in force from the tenth day of October, after the granting thereof, " for one whole year thence respectively next ensuing and no longer "

Transfer of certificates.] The transfer of certificates is now regulated chiefly by the provisions of the Alehouse Act (9 Geo. 4, c. 61, ss. 4, 14), as to licenses, for all the provisions of that Act relating to transfers are incorporated in this Act.

Notice before transfer.] The notice before transfer is now regulated by the Licensing Act, 1872, section 40 ; and 9 Geo. 4, c. 61, ss. 4, 14. And see *ante*, p. 229.

Discretion of justices as to transfer and right of appeal.] The justices have a discretion either to allow or refuse the application for transfer, or to adjourn the consideration thereof (see this Act, section 4, sub-section 4, *ante*, p. 328). If refused, there is an appeal to quarter sessions (9 Geo. 4, c. 91, s. 27), for one of the leading provisions of the Act, 9 Geo. 4, c. 61, relating to the transfer, &c., of licenses, is that which gives the right of appeal. This section in effect imports into this Act all the provisions of the Act 32 & 33 Vict. c. 27, as well as the unrepealed parts of 9 Geo. 4, c. 61, relating to the grant, duration, and transmission of certificates. The justices must accordingly confine themselves in dealing with out-door wine, spirits, sweets, and cider licenses and all the in-door certificates existing in 1869 to the four grounds specified in 32 & 33 Vict. c. 27, ss. 8, 19, when those enactments apply. But see *ante*, p. 235.

Fees on transfer.] The fees are the same as upon grant of a certificate : see *ante*, p. 236, 328.

Appndx. 5. Provision as to *convictions*. *Repealed* by Licensing Act, 1872. See Schedule.

6. Provision as to certain offences. *Repealed* by Licensing Act 1872. See Schedule.

7. *Provision as to existing licenses.*] The *nineteenth* section of the principal Act (32 & 33 Vict. c. 27) shall extend to licenses granted by way of renewal from time to time of licenses in force on the first day of May, 1869, whether such licenses continue to be held by the same person or have been or may be transferred to any other person or persons. [The rest of the section was *repealed* by Licensing Act, 1872. See Schedule.](*a*)

8. Regulation as to *closing*, &c. *Repealed* by Licensing Act, 1872. See Schedule.

Time for granting transfer of certificates.] The special sessions appointed for transferring alehouse licenses are the times for applying for a transfer of certificates under this Act. (9 Geo. 4, c. 61, s. 4.) And by 5 & 6 Vict. c. 44, s. 1, the justices in petty sessions may by endorsement on any certificate continue it in force until the then next ensuing special session for transferring licenses and no longer.

Death, Bankruptcy, &c., of certificate holder.] This section extends the provisions of 9 Geo. 4, c. 61, s. 14, to the case of certificates in like circumstances, and the provision as to death of license holder is also contained in Licensing Act, 1872, section 3, *ante*, p. 11.

Personal application for certificate and transfer.] The provisions of 9 Geo. 4, c. 61, s. 12, dispense with personal application to the justices in some cases, and are here extended to certificates. In the case of renewal of certificates also, the applicant need not attend unless required: Licensing Act, 1872, section 42, *ante*, p. 87; Licensing Act, 1874, section 26, *ante*, p. 203.

Lost certificates.] When it is proved to the justices or magistrate, upon an application to transfer, &c., the certificate, that such certificate has been lost or mislaid, such justices or magistrate may receive a copy of such certificate, &c.: 5 & 6 Vict. c. 44, s. 2, *ante*, p. 271. And the same may be done in cases where the certificate has been wilfully withheld by the holder: Licensing Act, 1872, section 41, *ante*, p. 86. For every such certified copy, and every such endorsement a fee of 2*s* 6*d.*, and no more, shall be taken: 5 & 6 Vict. c. 44, s. 3.

(*a*) See 32 & 33 Vict. c. 27, s. 19, *ante*, p. 323.

33 & 34 VICT. C. 29, S. 11. 331

9. *Avoidance* of licenses. *Repealed* by Licensing Act, 1872. **Appndx.** See Schedule.

10. *As to beer dealer's additional retail license.*] A certificate for an additional license to the holder of a strong beer dealer's license to retail beer under the provisions of 26 & 27 Vict. c. 33, shall not, after the passing of this Act, except by way of renewal from time to time of a certificate in force at the time of the passing of this Act, be granted, unless upon the like proof of qualification according to rating, as is required in the case of licenses to retail beer for consumption on the premises under the provisions of the Acts recited in the principal Act for permitting the general sale of beer and cider by retail in England.(*b*)

11. *Power to justices to postpone applications for grants or renewals.*] Where any applicant for the grant or renewal of a certificate has through inadvertence or misadventure, failed to comply with any of the preliminary requirements of the principal Act or this Act, or any Act incorporated therewith, the justices may, if they shall so think fit, and upon such terms as they think proper, postpone the consideration of the application to an adjourned meeting, and if at such adjourned meeting the justices shall be satisfied that such terms have been complied with, they may proceed to grant or withhold such certificate as if the preliminary requirements of the principal Act had been complied with.(*c*)

(*b*) This section prevented any more certificates from being granted to beer dealers under 26 & 27 Vict. c. 33, *ante*, p. 299, to sell beer by retail, unless the house be of the same valuation qualification as required under the Beerhouse Acts. See notes to section 8 of 32 & 33 Vict. c. 27, and Licensing Act, 1872, ss. 45, 46, 47 ; also 3 & 4 Vict. c. 61, *ante*, p. 263. An exception, however, is made as to houses in respect of which a certificate was in force on the 14th July, 1870 ; and these are still under the old law, that is to say, no valuation or rating qualification was necessary. But these certificates cannot now be applied for at any special transfer sessions, for the Licensing Act, 1874, section 31, was repealed by 43 Vict. c. 6, s. 2, *post*.

(*c*) This section must be taken to extend and alter the provisions of the Alehouse Act, 9 Geo. 4, c. 61, so far as respects applications for certificates. By that Act the justices were bound to appoint the general annual licensing meeting in Middlesex and Surrey for one of the first ten days of March, and in every other county for some day between 20th of August and 14th of September, and the adjournment day was also restricted to March in Middlesex and Surrey, and to August or September in every other county. It was held in *R.* v. *West Riding of*

Appndx. **12.** Limit of *mitigation* of penalties. *Repealed* by Licensing Act, 1872. See Schedule.

13. Houses licensed to retail *sweets*. *Repealed* by Licensing Act of 1872. See Schedule.

14. *Persons convicted of felony disqualified from selling spirits by retail.*] Every person convicted of felony shall for ever be disqualified from selling spirits by retail, and no license to sell spirits by retail shall be granted to any person who shall have been convicted as aforesaid, and if any person shall, after having been so convicted as aforesaid, take out or have any license to sell spirits by retail, the same shall be void to all intents and purposes; and every person who, after being so convicted as aforesaid, shall sell any spirit by retail in any manner whatever shall incur the penalty for doing so without a license.(a)

Yorkshire JJ., L. R. 5 Q. B. 33; 34 J. P. 4; 39 L. J. M. C. 17; 10 B. & S. 840; 21 L. T. 490; 18 W. R. 259, that the justices might and ought to arrange the adjournment days so as to allow those who were not in time with their notices for the general annual licensing day to give these notices in time for the adjournment days. This section enables the justices to adjourn an adjourned meeting as well as the general annual meeting, and they may do so to a day beyond the respective months of March in Middlesex and Surrey, and of August and September in other counties, "if the applicant has through inadvertence or misadventure failed to comply with the Act." As the adjourned meeting here contemplated is distinct from the statutory adjournments mentioned in 9 Geo. 4, c. 61, the business will consist solely in disposing of cases entertained at the meeting which is so adjourned, and the notices as to adjourned meetings required by 9 Geo. 4, c. 61, s. 5, would not be necessary.

The above section does not apply to applications for transfers of certificates which are already similarly treated by section 4, sub-section 4, *ante;* nor does it apply to applications for the grant or renewal of alehouse licenses under 9 Geo. 4, c. 61, in like circumstances. But there seems nothing to prevent justices at a general annual meeting adjourning an application for an alehouse license in a similar manner.

(a) Where T. had been convicted of felony in 1865, and sentenced to three months' imprisonment, and in 1873 obtained by transfer an existing license which in September, 1873, was renewed at the general annual licensing meeting, and the previous conviction for felony was discovered in November, 1873, whereupon T. sought to transfer the license to V., the justices refused to transfer on the ground that the license in T.'s hands was utterly void. The court held that justices were right,

15. Visitation of suspected houses. *Repealed* by Licensing **Appndx.**
Act, 1872. See Schedule.

16. Section 6 of 5 Geo. 4, c. 54, section 2 of 6 Geo. 4, c. 81, and section 6 of 13 & 14 Vict. c. 67, so far as relates to brewers' retail licenses, repealed. *Repealed* by 46 & 47 Vict. c. 39. See Schedule.

17. Duration of the principal Act and of this Act. *Repealed* by Licensing Act, 1872. See Schedule.

THE BEERHOUSE ACT, 1870.

33 & 34 VICT. CAP. 111.

AN ACT to make provision in relation to certain Beerhouses not duly qualified according to law.

[10th August, 1870.]

WHEREAS in misapprehension of the provisions of an Act, 3 & 4 Vict. c. 61, licenses and certificates for the sale of beer and cider

---

for this enactment had a retrospective effect: *R.* v. *Vine ; Vine* v. *Leeds JJ.*, L. R. 10 Q. B. 196 ; 39 J. P. 213 ; 44 L. J. M. C. 60 ; 31 L. T. 842 ; 23 W. R. 649. But where II. had been convicted of felony, and received a free pardon under the sign manual, the court held that he was thereafter in the same position as if he had never been convicted, and therefore not disqualified from holding a publican's license : *Hay* v. *Tower Division*, 24 Q. B. D. 557 ; 54 J. P. 500 ; 59 L. J. M. C. 79 ; 60 L. T. 290 ; 38 W. R. 414. There is a similar disqualification as to beer and cider under the Beerhouse Acts, 3 & 4 Vict. c. 61, s. 7, and in respect of wine under 23 Vict. c. 27, s. 22. See also Licensing Act, 1874, section 15, as to a remedy for the owner. The owner may appeal under this last section against a refusal to transfer after a felony has been committed : *R.* v. *West Riding JJ.*, 11 Q. B. D. 417 ; 52 L. J. M. C. 99 ; 48 J. P. 149. But it seems he must follow the remedy given by Act, 1874, section 15, literally, as it is said to be the only remedy : *Stevens* v. *Green* or *Sharnbrook JJ.*, 23 Q. B. D. 143 ; 61 L. T. 240 ; 53 J. P. 423. See *ante*, p. 193.

Appndx. have been granted in respect of houses not duly qualified as by the first section of the said Act is required:

Be it enacted, &c., as follows :—

1. *Rating qualification and closing hours of beerhouses within townships where separate poor rate is or can be made.*] A dwelling-house, if situate within a township for which a separate poor rate is or can be made, or within a hamlet for which a separate poor rate is or can be made, shall, for the purpose of determining by reference to population, in accordance with the first section respectively of the said Act, the rating qualification as a house for the sale of beer or cider, be deemed to be within such township or hamlet, as the case may be, and not within any larger area of which such township or hamlet forms a part.(*a*)

2. *Restricted application of Act.*] This Act shall apply exclusively to houses in respect of which licenses under Acts to permit the general sale of beer and cider by retail in England are in force at the time of the passing of this Act, and to such houses so long only as such licenses or any renewal thereof shall remain in force.

3. *Short title.*] This Act may be cited for all purposes as "The Beerhouse Act, 1870."(*b*)

(*a*) Some words omitted, being repealed by the 46 & 47 Vict. c. 39, Schedule.

(*b*) *Rating qualification, and hours of closing of beerhouses.*] This Act was passed at the end of the session of Parliament, 1870, in order to correct what was considered an anomaly caused by the then recent decision of *Preston*, app., v. *Buckley*, resp., L. R. 5 Q. B. 391 ; 34 J. P. 372 ; 39 L. J. M. C. 105 ; 22 L. T. 653 ; 18 W. R. 1104. That decision was to the effect that where a parish consisted of townships, if the parish contained the amount of population specified in the Act 3 & 4 Vict. c. 61, ss. 1, 15, it was immaterial whether the particular township in which the beerhouse was situated contained the required amount of population; in short, that the population of the parish, and not of the township, governed the hours of closing the beerhouse. The Beerhouse Act, 1870 (which is, however, confined entirely to beerhouses for which a license was in force on 10th August, 1870, or for which such license has been renewed), alters the law, and now makes the township or hamlet, instead of the parish, the area of population, so as to govern the qualification in point of rating or annual value, provided

THE INNKEEPERS ACT, 1878.

41 & 42 VICT. CAP. 38.

AN ACT for the further Relief of Innkeepers.(c)

[8th August, 1878.]

WHEREAS it is just and expedient to give, in addition to the present right of lien, a power of sale under certain circumstances to keepers of hotels, inns, and licensed public-houses upon and in respect of goods and chattels deposited with them or upon the tenements and premises occupied by them:

Be it therefore enacted, &c., as follows ; that is to say,—

1. *Landlord, &c., may dispose of goods left with him after six weeks.*] The landlord, proprietor, keeper, or manager of any hotel, inn, or licensed public-house shall, in addition to his ordinary lien, have the right absolutely to sell and dispose by public auction of any goods, chattels, carriages, horses, wares, or merchandise which may have been deposited with him or left in the house he keeps, or in the coachhouse, stable, stable-yard, or other premises appurtenant or belonging thereunto, where the person depositing or leaving such goods, chattels, carriages, horses, wares, or merchandise shall be or become indebted to the said innkeeper either for any board or lodging, or for the keep and expenses of any horse or other animals left with or standing at livery in the stables or fields occupied by such innkeeper.

---

such township or hamlet has or may have a separate poor rate. If a separate poor rate cannot be made for the hamlet, then the law remains unaffected by this Act, and the population of the parish will (if not situate in a city, borough, or cinque port) still be the criterion for the hours of closing. It is to be observed, also, that this Act is confined to those beerhouses which had a license on 10th August, 1870, or which have since obtained a renewal license. Hence, if any new certificate has been granted since 10th August, 1870, the above Act will not apply, and the house will be subject to the Act 3 & 4 Vict. c. 61, as construed by *Preston* v. *Buckley* (*supra*), and as modified by Licensing Act, 1872, sections 46, 47.

(c) See the previous Act as to the liability of innkeepers, 26 & 27 Vict. c. 41, *ante*, p. 302.

Appndx. Provided that no such sale shall be made until after the said goods, chattels, carriages, horses, wares, or merchandise shall have been for the space of *six weeks* in such charge or custody or in or upon such premises without such debt having been paid or satisfied, and that such innkeeper, after having, out of the proceeds of such sale, paid himself the amount of any such debt, together with the costs and expenses of such sale, shall, on demand, pay to the person depositing or leaving any such goods, chattels, carriages, horses, wares, or merchandise the surplus (if any) remaining after such sale: Provided further, that the debt for the payment of which a sale is made shall not be any other or greater debt than the debt for which the goods or other articles could have been retained by the innkeeper under his lien.

Provided also, that at least *one month* before any such sale the landlord, proprietor, keeper, or manager shall cause to be inserted in one London newspaper and one country newspaper circulating in the district where such goods, chattels, carriages, horses, wares, or merchandise, or some of them, shall have been deposited or left, an advertisement containing notice of such intended sale, and giving shortly a description of the goods and chattels intended to be sold, together with the name of the owner or person who deposited or left the same where known.(*a*)

2. *Short title.*] This Act may be cited as "The Innkeepers Act, 1878."

(*a*) The innkeepers' lien at common law extends over such goods as the traveller usually takes with him, as bags, trunks, carriage, and effects: *Turrell* v. *Crawley*, 13 Q. B. 197; 18 L. J. Q. B. 155; *Smith* v. *Dearlove*, 6 C. B. 132; 17 L. J. C. P. 219; *Allen* v. *Smith*, 12 C. B. (N.S.) 638; 31 L. J. C. P. 306; 6 L. T. 459; 11 W. R. 440. And if he has horses the lien extends to the horses: *Mulliner* v. *Florence*, 3 Q. B. D. 484; 47 L. J. Q. B. 700; 38 L. T. 167; 42 J. P. 293; 26 W. R. 385.

The lien exists though the goods may be the property of a third party: *Snead* v. *Watkins*, 1 C. B. (N.S.) 267; 26 L. J. C. P. 57; 21 J. P. 263; *Threlfall* v. *Borwick*, L. R. 10 Q. B. 310; 39 J. P. 409; 44 L. J. Q. B. 87; 32 L. T. 32. And where husband and wife lived at an inn and the husband left and wife remained, her goods being separate property, the lien was held to attach to her property: *Gordon* v. *Silber*, 25 Q. B. D. 491; 63 L. T. 283; 59 L. J. Q. B. 507; 55 J. P. 134; 39 W. R. 111.

The lien does not, however, extend to a piano hired by the guest from a stranger: *Broadwood* v. *Granara*, 10 Ex. 407; 19 J. P. 39; 24 L. J. Ex. 1.

Appndx.

BEER DEALERS RETAIL LICENSES ACT, 1880.

43 VICT. CAP. 6.

AN ACT for amending the Law relating to the grant by Justices of Certificates for Beer Dealers Retail Licenses.

[19th March, 1880.]

WHEREAS by the enactments described in the schedule to this Act provision is now made for the holder of a strong beer dealer's wholesale excise license obtaining, on a certificate granted by justices, an additional license for the sale of beer by retail for consumption off the premises, and it is expedient that justices should be at liberty to exercise their discretion respecting the grant of such certificates, as they are in respect of their certificates for licenses for sale of beer to be consumed on the premises, and that such certificates should be granted at the general annual licensing meeting of justices, and not at any other time :

Be it therefore enacted, &c., as follows :—

1. *Justices to have discretion as to licenses for consumption of beer off the premises, 32 & 33 Vict. c. 27.*] Section eight of the Wine and Beerhouse Act, 1869 (32 & 33 Vict. c. 27),

---

The lien does not affect the person of the guest and clothes which are used by him : *Sunbolf* v. *Alford*, 3 M. & W. 248.

At common law, though the innkeeper could detain the horse and carriage of the guest under his lien, yet he could not use these : *Westbrook* v. *Griffiths*, Moor, 876 ; *Robinson* v. *Walter*, 3 Bulst. 270. Nor could the innkeeper sell the horse : *Jones* v. *Thurloe*, 8 Mod. 172 ; Str. 556 ; *Robinson* v. *Walter*, 3 Bulst. 270.

The fact of the innkeeper taking security from the guest for the bill incurred is no waiver of the lien : *Angus* v. *Maclachan*, 23 Ch. D. 330 ; 52 L. J. Ch. 587 ; 48 L. T. 863 ; 31 W. R. 641.

An innkeeper is not bound to receive and entertain a traveller if the latter, on request, gives no security to pay his bill : *Fell* v. *Knight*, 8 M. & W. 276 ; nor if he comes with a dog which causes reasonable alarm to inmates and visitors : *R.* v. *Rymer*, 2 Q. B. D. 136 ; 46 L. J. M. C. 108 ; 41 J. P. 199 ; 25 W. R. 415 ; 35 L. T. 774.

The lien arises by virtue of the innkeeper holding himself out to receive all travellers, and hence those who do not so hold themselves out have no such lien, but merely contract to give to persons whom they

Z

Appndx. is hereby repealed, so far as the qualification therein contained relates to grants of certificates for such additional licenses as aforesaid; and the licensing justices shall be at liberty either to refuse such certificates as aforesaid on any grounds appearing to them in the exercise of their discretion sufficient, or to grant the same to such persons as they, in the execution of their statutory powers, and in the exercise of their discretion, deem fit and proper.(a)

---

select certain accommodation, such as boarding-house keepers: *Dansey* v. *Richardson*, 3 E. & B. 144; 23 L. J. Q. B. 217: *Holder* v. *Soulby*, 8 C. B. (N.S.) 254; 29 L. J. C. P. 246; 8 W. R. 438; or coffee-house or tavern keepers, or victualling-house keepers: *Thompson* v. *Lacy*, 3 B. & Ald. 286; or restaurant keepers: *R.* v. *Rymer, supra.*

(a) The effect of this section was to strike out the beer dealer's retail off-license from the list of licenses as to which the licensing justices have only a limited power of refusal. The four grounds of refusal specified in 32 & 33 Vict. c. 27, s. 8, formed an exception to the original jurisdiction first given in dealing with publicans' licenses, as to which there was always an absolute discretion under 9 Geo. 4, c. 61. The Act 9 Geo. 4, c. 61, was made in 1869, to apply to beerhouse licenses, but was subject to the four restrictions mentioned. When the exception was now struck out, the original absolute discretion was at once restored. Hence the effect, shortly stated, of this section was to give to the licensing justices precisely the same absolute discretion which they always have had under 9 Geo. 4, c. 61, to deal with alehouse or publicans' licenses. That is to say, the justices can at discretion, and without being obliged to state any reason, refuse to grant an additional retail license to beer dealers.

And precisely the same absolute discretion was vested in the justices when dealing with *renewals* of these beer dealers' retail licenses, for under 9 Geo. 4, c. 61, the justices always had, and still have, the same absolute discretion in dealing with renewals as with grants of public-house licenses. The only qualification is, that before refusing a renewal the justices must now in all cases comply with the Licensing Act, 1872, 35 & 36 Vict. c. 94, s. 42, and the Licensing Act, 1874, 37 & 38 Vict. c. 49, s. 26, to this extent, that they are to see that no renewal is refused without first taking care that notice and an opportunity have been given to the licensed person to answer and obviate, if he can, all objections raised: *R.* v. *Justices of Essex*, 46 J. P. 761; *R.* v. *Merthyr Tydvil JJ.*, 49 J. P. 213; 54 L. J. M. C. 78; 14 Q. B. D. 584. And see Act 1872, s. 42, and notes, *ante*, p. 87. An in-door license for a beerhouse continued since 1869 is, however, still an exception, and cannot be refused except for one of the four grounds: *R.* v. *King* or *Manchester JJ.*, 20 Q. B. D. 430; 52 J. P. 164; 57 L. J. M. C. 20; 58 L. T. 607; 36 W. R. 600.

Another distinction between the discretion of justices in refusing grants and in refusing renewals under this and the Act 9 Geo. 4, c. 61,

43 VICT. C. 6, S. 3.

2. *Licenses at annual licensing meetings only*, 37 & 38 Appndx.
Vict. c. 49.] Section thirty-one of the Licensing Act, 1874, is
hereby repealed, as from and after the general annual licensing
meeting held in any licensing district next after the passing of
this Act; and thenceforth certificates for such additional licenses
as aforesaid shall be granted at general annual licensing meetings,
and not at any other time.(*b*)

3. *Short title; extent; construction*, 35 & 36 Vict. c. 94.]
This Act may be cited as "The Beer Dealers Retail Licenses Act,
1880," and shall not extend to Scotland or Ireland, and words
therein have the same meaning as in the Licensing Act,
1872.(*c*)

---

is, that there is no *appeal* to quarter sessions in respect of the refusal
of a grant, whereas there is always an appeal against the refusal of a
renewal, as the Licensing Act, 1872, did not repeal the appeal sections
as regards renewals and transfers.

(*b*) This section repealed the exception which had been introduced by
the Licensing Act, 1874, s. 31, of allowing the beer dealers' additional
retail licenses to be applied for at the special transfer sessions as well as
at the general annual meeting. These were the only kind of new licenses
that could be applied for at those intermediate sessions, and this exceptional advantage being now repealed, the result is that all new licenses
to sell intoxicating liquors by retail, and all renewals, must be applied
for at the general annual licensing meeting or its adjournment, and at
no other time.

(*c*) This Act is not declared to be read as one with the Intoxicating
Liquor Licensing Acts. But, as it professes only to alter one or two
sections in those Acts, the effect is precisely the same owing to the last
words in this section.

This Act dealt exclusively with the beer dealers' additional retail
license, which was an out-door license, and said nothing as to the other
two beer retail licenses, namely, those granted under the Beerhouse
Acts, 1 Will. 4, c. 64, and amending Acts, and the table-beer license
granted under 24 & 25 Vict. c. 21, s. 8. This omission was soon discovered, and in 1882, those two other kinds of beer licenses were also
put on the same level as public-house licenses by the next Act of 45 & 46
Vict. c. 34, *post*, which is a supplement to the present Act.

SCHEDULE.(a)

ENACTMENTS RELATING TO BEER DEALERS RETAIL LICENSES.

An Act for granting to Her Majesty certain duties of Inland Revenue, and to amend the laws relating to the Inland Revenue: 26 & 27 Vict. c. 33 (section one).
The Wine and Beerhouse Act, 1869.—32 & 33 Vict. c. 27.
The Licensing Act, 1874.—37 & 38 Vict. c. 49.

THE REVENUE ACT, 1880.

43 & 44 VICT. CAP. 20.

* * * * * *

[12th August, 1880.]

* * * * * *

33. *Provisions as to charge and payment of duty.*] (1.) The commissioners may, when they think fit, require a brewer, other than a brewer for sale, to verify the entries in the paper delivered to him by a declaration to be made by him before a justice of the peace or an authorised officer.

(2.) The charge of duty shall be made, and the duty shall be paid, at such times as the commissioners shall appoint.

(3.) Provided that if the annual value of the house occupied by the brewer does not exceed ten pounds, the beer brewed by him shall not be charged with duty.(b)

34. *Beer brewed to be for domestic use.*] (1.) A brewer, other than a brewer for sale, shall only brew beer for his own

---

(a) This Act did not affect the out-door wine licenses, which formerly stood on the same footing as off-beer licenses, and still retain that footing, for they can still only be refused for one of the four grounds: *R.* v. *Scott*, 22 Q. B. D. 481; 53 J. P. 119; 58 L. J. M. C. 78; 60 L. T. 231; 37 W. R. 301.

(b) It has been held that the brewer is exempt only if the house he resides in is under 10*l.* annual value, and he is not exempt merely if the house in which he brews is under that value: *Tippett* v. *Hart*, 10 Q. B. D. 483; 47 J. P. 199; 52 L. J. M. C. 41.

domestic use, or for consumption by farm-labourers employed by Appndx. him in the actual course of their labour or employment.

(2.) The brewer shall only brew on premises occupied by him, or, in case the brewer occupies a house of an annual value not exceeding ten pounds, on premises gratuitously lent to him by a brewer other than a brewer for sale.

(3.) If the brewer contravenes either of the foregoing provisions of this section, or sells, or offers for sale, any beer brewed by him, he shall incur the penalty of ten pounds.

35. *Power of entry.*] Any officer may at all reasonable times enter and inspect any premises used for the purposes of brewing by a brewer other than a brewer for sale, and examine the vessels and utensils used by him for the purpose of brewing.

* * * * * *

40. *Meaning of terms.*] For the purposes of this part of this Act, each of the following terms shall have the meaning assigned to it in this section.

"Cider" includes perry :

"Sweets" includes made wines, mead, and metheglin :(*c*)

"Beer" includes cider :(*d*)

"Wine" includes sweets.(*e*)

41. *Alteration of the duties on certain excise licenses.*] On and after 1 July, 1880, in lieu of the duties of excise now payable on the licenses mentioned in this section (except in the case of a license to sell wine by retail to be taken out by a grocer in Scotland), there shall be charged and paid the duties(*f*) following; (that is to say,)

(*c*) This is repeated in 52 & 53 Vict. c. 42, s. 28.

(*d*) Beer as used in this Act extends to any substitute for beer, which on analysis contains more than 2 per cent. of proof spirit : 48 & 49 Vict. c. 51, s. 4.

(*e*) A license to dealers or retailers of foreign wine includes sweets : 38 Vict. c. 23, s. 9.

(*f*) All these duties were in 1889 transferred to the county councils respectively, who have the same powers and duties as to levying and recovering the duties as the Commissioners of Inland Revenue : 51 & 52 Vict. c. 41, s. 20. And see 53 Vict. c. 8, s. 7.

Appndx.

	Duty.
	£ s. d.
On a license to be taken out by a person for the selling of *cider* by retail in England - - - -	1 5 0
On a license to be taken out by a retailer of *sweets* in the United Kingdom - - - - - -	1 5 0
On a license to be taken out by a person for the selling by retail in the United Kingdom of *beer* to be consumed on the premises- - - - - -	3 10 0
On a license to be taken out by a person for the selling by retail in England of *beer* not to be consumed on the premises - - - - - -	1 5 0
On a license (additional) to be taken out by a licensed dealer in *beer* in England or Ireland authorising him to sell by retail beer not to be consumed on the premises - - - - - - -	1 5 0
On a license to be taken out to sell *wine* by retail to be consumed on the premises - - - - -	3 10 0
On a license to be taken out by any person in England or Ireland for the sale by retail in any shop of *wine* not to be consumed on the premises - - -	2 10 0

42. *Duties on licenses for the retailing of beer and wine.*]
(1.) On and after 1 July, 1880, there shall be charged and paid upon licenses for the sale by retail of beer and wine to be taken out by any person in the United Kingdom who may be authorised to obtain the same, the duties of excise following; (that is to say,)

	Duty.
	£ s. d.
On a license for the sale by retail of *beer and wine* to be consumed on the premises - - - - -	4 0 0
On a license for the sale by retail of *beer and wine* not to be consumed on the premises - - - -	3 0 0

(2.) Every such license shall be in such form as the commissioners shall direct, and shall expire in England or Ireland on the tenth day of October, and in Scotland on the fifteenth day of May in each year.

43. *Alteration of duties on licenses to retailers of spirits.*]
(1.) On and after 1 July, 1880, in lieu of the duties of excise now payable on licenses to be taken out by retailers of spirits in the

United Kingdom, there shall be charged and paid the duties following ; (that is to say,) **Appndx.**

			Duty.		
			£	s.	d.
If the annual value of the dwelling-house in which the retailer shall reside or retail *spirits*, together with the offices, courts, yards, and gardens therewith occupied, is under 10*l.*			4	10	0
Is 10*l.* and under 15*l.*			6	0	0
„ 15*l.*	„	20*l.*	8	0	0
„ 20*l.*	„	25*l.*	11	0	0
„ 25*l.*	„	30*l.*	14	0	0
„ 30*l.*	„	40*l.*	17	0	0
„ 40*l.*	„	50*l.*	20	0	0
„ 50*l.*	„	100*l.*	25	0	0
„ 100*l.*	„	200*l.*	30	0	0
„ 200*l.*	„	300*l.*	35	0	0
„ 300*l.*	„	400*l.*	40	0	0
„ 400*l.*	„	500*l.*	45	0	0
„ 500*l.*	„	600*l.*	50	0	0
„ 600*l.*	„	700*l.*	55	0	0
„ 700*l.* or above			60	0	0

(2.) The holder of a license to retail *spirits* chargeable with duty under this Act shall not be required to take out any further or other excise license to enable him to sell *beer or wine* by retail. The holder of such license shall not be liable for any percentage, discount, or other charge more than the amount stated in the Act.

(3.) Any person applying for a *six days'* and *early closing* license for the sale of *spirits* as an auxiliary only to his business as a restaurateur or eating-house keeper, and not keeping an open drinking bar, shall be entitled to his license at a sum not exceeding thirty pounds, no such reduction to be made unless the licensing justices shall have certified by indorsement on their certificate that the nature of the business carried on by the applicant justifies the reduced scale of charge.

(4.) Where in the case of premises of the value of *fifty* pounds or upwards it shall be proved to the satisfaction of the commissioners that the premises are structurally adapted for use as an inn or hotel for the reception of guests and travellers desirous of dwelling therein, and are mainly so used, the amount of duty to be paid on a license to retail *spirits* shall not exceed twenty pounds. Provided that the relief under this sub-section shall not be given in case any portion of the premises is set apart and used

Appndx. as an ordinary public-house for the sale and consumption therein of liquors, and the annual value of such portion, in the opinion of the commissioners, exceeds twenty-five pounds.

(5.) The amount of duty to be paid for a license to retail spirits in any *theatre* granted under the provisions contained in 5 & 6 Will. 4, c. 39, s. 7, shall not exceed twenty pounds.(*a*).

(6.) The expression " retailer of spirits," as used in this section, does not include a spirit grocer in Ireland, as defined by section eighty-one of the Licensing Act, 1872, or a dealer in spirits selling spirits in bottle under an additional license authorising him in that behalf, or a grocer in Scotland as defined by section two of the Public Houses (Scotland) Act, 1853.

(7.) In the case of premises in Ireland, the annual value, upon which the duty on the license in respect of the premises to be charged, shall not exceed the amount of the value assigned thereto in the valuation in force under the Act 15 & 16 Vict. c. 63, with the addition of twenty per centum of such amount ; and the licensed person may appeal against the amount of annual value upon which the duty has been charged and paid to the chairman of the sessions of the peace for the county, or the recorder of the city or borough in which the premises are situate, and such chairman or recorder shall have power to hear and determine such appeal, and his determination shall be final. If, in accordance with such determination, there shall have been any over-payment of duty, the amount shall be repaid.

44. *Extension of six-day and early closing licenses to the United Kingdom.*] The provisions regarding six-day licenses and early closing licenses contained in section forty-nine of the Licensing Act, 1872, and sections seven and eight of the Licensing Act, 1874, shall be deemed to apply throughout the United Kingdom.(*b*)

45. *Duties on licenses for the sale of liquors and tobacco in boats.*] (1.) The duty now charged upon a license to supply, retail, and sell foreign wine, strong beer, cider, perry, spirituous liquors, and tobacco to passengers on board any *packet-boat* or other vessel employed for the carriage and conveyance of passengers, to be consumed in or on board such boat or vessel, shall

---

(*a*) See as to theatre licenses, Act, 1872, section 72, and notes, *ante*, p. 144.
(*b*) See as to these licenses, *ante*, pp. 102, 176, 178.

cease to be payable, and there shall be granted and paid the following duties of excise ; (that is to say,)

Upon a license to be taken out for the sale of spirits, wine, beer, and tobacco to be consumed on board a *boat* or vessel of any description employed for the carriage and conveyance of persons going as passengers from any place in the United Kingdom to any other place in the United Kingdom, or going from and returning to the same place on the same day,—

	Duty.
	£ s. d.
If the license is to be in force from the day of the date thereof until the thirty-first day of March next ensuing - - - - -	5 0 0
If the license is to be in force for one day only -	1 0 0

(2.) Such licenses shall be granted under and be subject to the enactments contained in the Act 9 Geo. 4, c. 47, as amended by 4 & 5 Will. 4, c. 75, s. 10, so far as such enactments are consistent with this Act and the terms of the licenses respectively.

Supplementary.

46. *Powers and provisions to be applied to excise duties, drawbacks, and licenses under this Act.*] The duties and drawbacks of excise charged and allowed by Parts II. and III. of this Act, and the licenses therein mentioned, shall be under the management of the commissioners ; and all the powers, provisions, regulations, and directions contained in any Act relating to excise duties, drawbacks, or licenses, or to penalties or forfeitures under excise Acts, and now or hereafter in force, shall respectively be of full force and effect with respect to the duties and drawbacks charged and allowed by Parts I. and II. of this Act and the licenses therein mentioned, and the penalties and forfeitures imposed by this Act, so far as the same are applicable and are consistent with the provisions of this Act, as fully and effectually as if the same had been herein specially enacted with reference to the last-mentioned duties, drawbacks, licenses, penalties, and forfeitures respectively.

47. *Construction of term "excisable" liquors in billiard license.*] The grant of a duty on beer by this Act shall not be deemed to bring beer within the expression "excisable liquors" as contained in the Third Schedule in the Act 8 & 9 Vict. c. 109.

Appndx. **48.** *Saving rights under certain charters.*] Nothing in this Act contained shall in anywise alter or affect the rights and privileges now existing under the charters of—
(1.) Any university in the United Kingdom, or
(2.) The master, wardens, freemen, and commonalty of the vintners of the city of London, or
(3.) The mayor or burgesses of the borough of St. Albans in the county of Hertford.

SPIRITS ACT, 1880.
43 & 44 VICT. CAP. 24.(a).

* * * * * *

[26th August, 1880.]

* * * * * *

96, 97. Retailers of spirits are subject to a penalty for interfering with the gauging of spirits and dipping-holes of casks and fittings; and must make entry with the excise of the places where they keep spirits.

* * * * * *

101. *Situation of dealer's and retailer's premises.*]
(1.) A dealer or retailer must not carry on his business upon any premises communicating otherwise than by an open public street or carriage road with any premises entered or used by a distiller, or a rectifier keeping a still.

(2.) A retailer must not be concerned or interested in the business of a distiller, or of a rectifier keeping a still, carried on upon any premises within two miles from the premises on which he is licensed to carry on the business of a retailer.

(3.) If a dealer or retailer contravenes this section he shall for each offence incur a fine of two hundred pounds.

102. *Restrictions on sale by dealers and retailers.*]
(1.) A dealer must not, unless he has an additional license authorising him so to do, or is also licensed as a retailer, sell, send out, or deliver spirits in any less quantity than two gallons of the same denomination at a time for the same person.

(*a*) See amendments to this Act: 53 & 54 Vict. c. 21.

(2.) A retailer must not, unless he is also licensed as a dealer, sell, send out, or deliver spirits to a rectifier, dealer or retailer, or buy or receive spirits from another retailer, not being also licensed as a dealer.

(3.) A dealer or retailer must not receive, send out, or have in his possession any British spirits of any strength exceeding that at which a distiller may send out spirits of the like denomination.

(4.) If a dealer or retailer contravenes this section he shall for each offence incur a fine of fifty pounds, and in case of the spirits being of unlawful strength they shall be forfeited.

103. *Penalty for excess in stock of dealer or retailer.*] (1.) An officer may at any time take an account of the quantity of spirits in the stock or possession of a dealer or retailer.

(2.) If the quantity of spirits computed at proof found on taking the account exceeds the quantity which ought according to the stock-book of the dealer or retailer to be in his possession, the excess shall be forfeited and the dealer or retailer shall incur a fine of twenty shillings for every gallon of the excess.

104. *Meaning of sale by retail.*] The sale of spirits in any quantity less than two gallons or less than one dozen reputed quart bottles shall be deemed sale by retail.

* * * * * *

112, 113. Every retailer must keep a stock-book and certificate book.

* * * * * *

126. A retailer of *methylated* spirits must make entry with the commissioners of the places where he keeps such spirits, and must not have more than fifty gallons in possession at one time.(*b*)

* * * * * *

141. An officer of Inland Revenue may at any time enter and examine the stock of spirits of any dealer or retailer.

* * * * * *

(*b*) These spirits are now exempt from duty : 53 Vict. c. 8, s. 31.

Appndx. **145.** *Arrest of and penalties on persons unlawfully removing spirits.*] (1.) Any officer or any officer of customs, and any officer of the peace having a commission from the commissioners, may stop and detain any person found carrying or removing any spirits, and may examine the spirits and require the production of a permit or certificate authorising the removal thereof.

(2.) If a permit or certificate is produced agreeing with the spirits in all respects the officer may endorse thereon the time and place of his examination thereof.

(3.) If any person is found carrying or removing any spirits exceeding the quantity of one gallon of the same denomination for the same person and does not, on request by any such officer, forthwith produce a permit or certificate authorising the removal of the spirits, he shall incur a fine of one hundred pounds, and the spirits shall be forfeited.

(4.) The sum to which the fine may be mitigated in Scotland or Ireland shall not be less than ten pounds.

(5.) In default of payment of the fine on summary conviction the offender shall be imprisoned with or without hard labour. The term of imprisonment in Scotland or Ireland shall be not less than one month nor more than six months.

(6.) Any officer may arrest any person found committing an offence against this section.

146. *Unlawful hawking and sale of spirits.*] (1.) If any person hawks, sells, or exposes to sale any spirits otherwise than in premises for which he is licensed to sell spirits he shall incur a fine of one hundred pounds, and the spirits shall be forfeited.

(2.) The sum to which the fine may be mitigated in Scotland shall not be less than twenty-five pounds, or, in Ireland, shall not be less than six pounds.

(3.) In default of payment of the fine on summary conviction the offender shall be imprisoned with or without hard labour. The term of imprisonment in Scotland or Ireland shall be not less than two months nor more than three months.

(4.) Any person may arrest a person found committing an offence against this section.

147. *Sale of spirits for unlawful purposes.*] If any person knowingly sells or delivers, or causes to be sold or delivered, any spirits to the end that they may be unlawfully retailed or consumed or carried into consumption, he shall, in Appndx. addition to any other penalty, incur a fine of one hundred pounds.

148. *Unlawful purchase of spirits.*] If any person receives, buys, or procures any spirits from a person not having authority to sell or deliver the same, he shall incur a fine of one hundred pounds.

149. *Penalty for possession of spirits on which duty has not been paid.*] If any person knowingly buys or receives, or has in his possession any spirits after they have been removed from the place where they ought to have been charged with duty and before the duty payable thereon has been charged and paid or secured to be paid or the spirits have been condemned as forfeited, he shall forfeit the spirits and incur a fine equal to treble the value of the spirits.

* * * * * *

Informers.

155. *Discharge and reward of informers.*] (1.) On the commission of any offence against this Act, the offender who, before any information is lodged against him in respect of the offence, first discovers and informs against any other offender, shall, on the conviction of the person against whom the information is given, be discharged and acquitted from all penalties or disqualification to which at the time of giving the information he may be liable by reason of the offence committed by him.

(2.) When, on the conviction of any person for an offence against this Act, the pecuniary penalty imposed for the offence is not paid and cannot be levied, or the person incurring the penalty is sent to prison in default of payment, the commissioners may cause such reward as they think fit, not exceeding in each case fifty pounds, to be paid in such shares and proportions as they think fit to the persons who appear to the commissioners to be entitled thereto as informers.

Procedure.

156. *Recovery of fines.*] Any fine for any offence against this Act may be sued for and recovered, and any goods, chattels, or commodities forfeited under this Act may be returned for condemnation and condemned in the manner provided by law for the recovery of fines or penalties and for the condemnation of goods forfeited under any Act or Acts for the time being in force relating to the revenue of excise or customs.

Appndx.

SUNDAY CLOSING (WALES) ACT, 1881.

44 & 45 VICT. CAP. 61.

AN ACT to prohibit the Sale of Intoxicating Liquors on Sunday in Wales. [27th August, 1881.]

WHEREAS the provisions in force against the sale of fermented and distilled liquors during certain hours of Sunday have been found to be attended with great public benefits, and it is expedient and the people of Wales are desirous that in the principality of Wales those provisions be extended to the other hours of Sunday :

Be it therefore enacted, &c., as follows :—

1. *Premises where intoxicating liquors sold to be closed on Sundays in Wales.*] In the principality of Wales all premises in which intoxicating liquors are sold or exposed for sale by retail shall be closed during the whole of Sunday.

2. *Application of Licensing Acts.*] The Licensing Acts, 1872—1874, shall apply in the case of any premises closed under this Act as if they had been closed under those Acts.(a)

(a) These two sections taken together are somewhat obscure, owing to the words "as if they had been closed under those Acts." The statute does not say that all the licensed houses in Wales shall be on the same footing as if they had been declared to be six-day licenses, pursuant to the Licensing Act 1872, section 49, for, if so, then the licensee would be prohibited by the Act, 1874, section 10, from selling any intoxicating liquor on Sunday to any person whatsoever not lodging in his house. And yet a six-day licensed house is the only house mentioned in the Licensing Acts which is closed under those Acts. The six-day licensees are exempted as well as prohibited from selling to *bonâ fide* travellers. And it cannot be supposed that the legislature intended to prohibit all the inns and hotels of Wales from supplying *bonâ fide* travellers. The result, therefore, is, that the Welsh licensed houses are not identical with the six-day licensed houses in the rest of England, but form a distinct class by themselves. Nothing is said as to whether the Welsh licensees are entitled to the same deduction from the Inland Revenue of one-seventh of the ordinary license duty, as the six-day licensees in England are entitled. And yet there is, on the other hand,

3. *Commencement of Act.*] This Act shall commence and come into operation with respect to each division or place in Wales on the day next appointed for the holding of the general annual licensing meeting for that division or place.(*b*)

Appndx.

4. *Sale of intoxicating liquors at railway stations.*] Nothing in this Act contained shall preclude the sale at any time at a railway station of intoxicating liquors to persons arriving at or departing from such station by railway.(*c*)

5. *Short title.*] This Act may be cited as "The Sunday Closing (Wales) Act, 1881."

---

no prohibition against Welsh licensees asking the justices for a six-day license, so as to put themselves on the same footing as the English six-day licensees are placed.

Christmas Day and Good Friday in Wales.] The statute says nothing directly or indirectly as to whether it alters the previous law in any way as regards Christmas Day and Good Friday. And the court has decided that the Act makes no alteration except as regards Sunday: *Forsdike* v. *Colquhoun*, 11 Q. B. D. 71 ; 49 L. T. 136; 47 J. P. 392.

The bearing on the point whether the holder of the license had a six-day license under 35 & 36 Vict. c. 94, s. 49, and whether it made any difference, did not require to be considered by the court in that case. If there is a six-day license, then the Act, 1874, section 3, makes the holder liable to close the house on Christmas Day and Good Friday as he does on Sunday. See notes to that section, *ante*, p. 170.

In Wales the licensees have the same option as in England to ask the justices for a six-day license, and if they obtain it they will be entitled to a deduction of one-seventh of the duty, and be prohibited as well as protected from supplying any *bonâ fide* travellers. If, on the other hand, those who keep inns do not ask for six-day licenses, but take the license such as the statute now gives it, they will be entitled to supply *bonâ fide* travellers, and indeed will be indictable if they do not.

(*b*) This somewhat obscure section was held to mean that the Act was not to come into operation till the general licensing day in 1882 : *Richards* v. *McBride*, 8 Q. B. D. 119; 46 J. P. 247.

(*c*) This section saves the previous practice as to railway stations : See Act, 1874, section 10, *ante*, p. 180, and notes.

Appndx.

BEER DEALERS RETAIL LICENSES (AMENDMENT) ACT, 1882.

45 & 46 VICT. CAP. 34.

AN ACT to amend "The Beer Dealers Retail Licenses Act, 1880." [10th August, 1882.]

WHEREAS by the Beer Dealers Retail Licenses Act, 1880 (43 Vict. c. 6), it is provided that the licensing justices shall be at liberty to exercise their discretion respecting the grant of certificates for such additional licenses for sale of beer by retail off the premises as are therein referred to, and that certificates for such additional licenses shall be granted at general annual licensing meetings, and not at any other time:

And whereas it is expedient to extend the provisions of the said Act to the granting of certificates for all licenses for sale of beer by retail for consumption off the premises.

Be it therefore enacted, &c., as follows:—

1. *Extension of discretion as to licenses for consumption of beer off the premises.*] Notwithstanding anything in section eight of the Wine and Beerhouse Act, 1869, or, in any other Act now in force, the licensing justices shall be at liberty, in their free and unqualified discretion, either to refuse a certificate for any license for sale of beer by retail to be consumed off the premises on any grounds appearing to them sufficient, or to grant the same to such persons as they in the execution of their statutory powers and in the exercise of their discretion deem fit and proper.(*a*)

(*a*) This section is almost identical in its expressions with the previous statute 43 Vict. c. 6, *ante*, p. 337, except that it applies to "any license for the sale of beer to be consumed off the premises." These words necessarily include the ordinary beer licenses granted under 1 Will. 4, c. 64, and the amending Acts, *ante*, p. 233, and also included the table-beer licenses granted under 24 & 25 Vict. c. 21, s. 3, *ante*, p. 291. And it produced precisely the same effect on these two last-mentioned licenses by assimilating the jurisdiction of justices, and conferring on them absolute discretion as regards all beer licenses, whether in-door or out-door, so as to put these on the same footing as

2. *Certificates at annual licensing meetings only.*] Certificates for any such licenses as aforesaid shall, notwithstanding anything in any Act now in force, be granted at general annual licensing meetings, and not at any other time.(*b*)

Appndx.

3. *Short title; extent; and construction of Act.*] This Act may be cited as "The Beer Dealers Retail Licenses (Amendment) Act, 1882"; and shall not extend to Scotland; and word therein have the same meaning as in the Licensing Act, 1872.

THE PAYMENT OF WAGES IN PUBLIC-HOUSES PROHIBITION ACT, 1883.

46 & 47 VICT. CAP. 31.

AN ACT to prohibit the Payment of Wages to Workmen in Public Houses and certain other places.

[20th August, 1883.]

WHEREAS by the Coal Mines Regulation Act, 1872, 35 & 36 Vict. c. 76, and the Metalliferous Mines Regulation Act, 1872

---

public-house licenses. It gave precisely the same jurisdiction, neither more nor less, not only as to new grants, but also as to renewals: *Kay* v. *Over Darwen*, 10 Q. B. D. 213; 52 L. J. M. C. 94; 31 W. R. 273; 47 L. T. 411; 47 J. P. 388. The exemption, however, from the new rule remains of in-door beer licenses which existed since 1869, and which cannot be refused to be renewed except on one of the four grounds: *R.* v. *King* or *Manchester JJ.*, 20 Q. B. D. 430; 52 J. P. 164; 57 L. J. M. C. 20; 58 L. T. 607; 36 W. R. 600.

It is true that there are inserted in this section the additional words not found in 43 Vict. c. 6, namely, "in their free and unqualified discretion," but these are mere surplusage. They do not imply, for example, that the appeal to quarter sessions has been taken away in respect of refusals to renew beerhouse licenses. If this had been so, the statute would have put the justices' discretion as to beer licenses on a far higher footing than it had always existed as to public-house licenses. Hence, as to these beer licenses, it has been decided that the appeal to quarter sessions against refusals to renew beerhouse licenses remains as before under the present Act: *R.* v. *Schneider*, 11 Q. B. D. 66; 52 L. J. M. C. 51; 47 J. P. 596; 48 L. T. 482.

(*b*) This section was superfluous, for no Act then in force authorised certificates for any such license to be granted at any other time than at the General Annual Licensing Meetings.

Appndx. 35 & 36 Vict. c. 77, the payment in public-houses, beershops, or other places in the said Acts mentioned of wages to persons employed in or about any mines, to which the said Acts apply, is prohibited, and it is expedient to extend such prohibition to the payment in public-houses, beershops, and other places in England and Scotland of wages to all workmen as defined by this Act:

Be it therefore enacted, &c., as follows :—

1. *Short title.*] This Act may be cited as "The Payment of Wages in Public-houses Prohibition Act, 1883."(a)

2. *Definition of workman.*] In this Act the expression "workman" means any person who is a labourer, servant in husbandry, journeyman artificer, handicraftsman, or is otherwise engaged in manual labour, whether under the age of twenty-one years or above that age, but does not include a domestic or menial servant, nor any person employed in or about any mine to which the Coal Mines Regulation Act, 1872, or the Metalliferous Mines Regulation Act, 1872, applies.(b)

(a) The Coal Mines Regulation Act, 1887, 50 & 51 Vict. c. 58, s. 11, enacts as follows: (1) No wages shall be paid to any person employed in or about any mine at or within any public-house, beershop, or place for the sale of any spirits, beer, wine, cider, or other spirituous or fermented liquor, or other house of entertainment, or any office, garden, or place belonging or contiguous thereto, or occupied therewith; (2) Every person who contravenes or fails to comply with, or permits any person to contravene or fail to comply with this section, shall be guilty of an offence against this Act; and in the event of any such contravention or non-compliance by any person whomsoever, the owner, agent, and manager of the mine shall each be guilty of an offence against this Act, unless he prove that he had taken all reasonable means by publishing, and to the best of his power enforcing, the provisions of this section to prevent the contravention or non-compliance. The penalty is stated *ibid.*, section 59.

The Metalliferous Mines Act, 1872, 35 & 36 Vict. c. 77, s. 9, contains a provision in nearly the same words. The penalty is stated *ibid.*, section 31.

(b) The definition of workman here given is nearly identical with that given in the Employers and Workmen Act, 1875, 38 & 39 Vict. c. 90, s. 10, but not quite so extensive. The decisions, however, under the latter Act will usually apply to this Act.

3. *No wages to be paid within public-house.*] From and after the passing of this Act no wages shall be paid to any workman at or within any public-house, beershop, or place for the sale of any spirits, wine, cider, or other spirituous or fermented liquor, or any office, garden, or place belonging thereto or occupied therewith, save and except such wages as are paid by the resident owner or occupier of such public-house, beershop, or place to any workman *bonâ fide* employed by him.

Appndx.

Every person who contravenes or fails to comply with, or permits any person to contravene or fail to comply with, this Act shall be guilty of an offence against this Act.

And in the event of any wages being paid by any person in contravention of the provisions of this Act for or on behalf of any employer, such employer shall himself be guilty of an offence against this Act, unless he prove that he had taken all reasonable means in his power for enforcing the provisions of this Act and to prevent such contravention.(*c*)

(*c*) The description of public-houses, &c., here is not quite so extensive as in the above quoted sections of the Mines Regulation Act, which contains the words "or other house of entertainment." The places for the sale of spirits, beer, wine, cider, &c., include houses which are licensed for consumption off the premises. The person who will be liable under this section will be the paymaster, whoever he be, and the employer will escape liability if he can show that he took reasonable means to prevent the contravention of the Act, and such means seem to be an express direction to his clerks, managers, &c., not to pay the workmen in such houses.

No parliamentary polls at inns.] No poll at any election for members of parliament in England and Wales shall be taken at any inn, hotel, tavern, public-house, or other premises licensed for the sale of beer, wine or spirits, or in any booth, hall, room, or other place directly communicating therewith, unless by consent of all the candidates expressed in writing: 16 & 17 Vict. c. 68, s. 6.

No borough justices' room to be at inn.] (1) The council of a borough having a separate commission of the peace shall provide and furnish a suitable justices' room, with offices, for the business of the borough justices. (2) No room in a house licensed for the sale of intoxicating liquors may be used for this purpose: 45 & 46 Vict. c. 50, s. 160.

At parliamentary elections no inns for committee rooms.] (*a*) Any premises on which the sale by wholesale or retail of any intoxicating liquor is authorised by a license (whether the license be for consumption

Appndx. **4.** *Penalties.*] Every person who is guilty of an offence against this Act shall be liable to a penalty not exceeding ten pounds

---

on or off the premises); or (*b*) any premises where any intoxicating liquor is sold or is supplied to members of a club, society, or association, other than a permanent political club; or (*c*) any premises whereon refreshment of any kind, whether food or drink, is ordinarily sold for consumption on the premises; or (*d*) the premises of any public elementary school, in receipt of an annual parliamentary grant, or any part of any such premises shall not be used as a committee room for the purpose of furnishing or procuring the election of a candidate at an election; and if any person hires or uses any such premises, or any part thereof, for a committee room, he shall be guilty of illegal hiring, and the person letting such premises, or part, if he knew it was intended to use the same as a committee room, shall also be guilty of illegal hiring. Provided that nothing in this section shall apply to any part of such premises which is ordinarily let for the purpose of chambers or offices, or the holding of public meetings, or of arbitrations, if such part has a separate entrance, and no direct communication with any part of the premises on which any intoxicating liquor or refreshment is sold or supplied as aforesaid: 46 & 47 Vict. c. 51, s. 20.

At municipal elections no committee rooms in inns, &c.] (1) (*a*) Any premises which are licensed for the sale of any intoxicating liquor, for consumption on or off the premises, or on which refreshment of any kind (whether food or drink), is ordinarily sold for consumption on the premises; or (*b*) any premises where any intoxicating liquor is supplied to members of a club, society, or association, or any part of any such premises, shall not, for the purpose of promoting or procuring the election of a candidate at a municipal election, be used either as a committee room or for holding a meeting, and if any person hires or uses any such premises, or any part thereof, in contravention of this section, he shall be guilty of illegal hiring, and the person letting or permitting the use of such premises, or part thereof, if he knew it was intended to use the same in contravention of this section, shall also be guilty of illegal hiring. (2) Provided that nothing in this section shall apply to any part of such premises which is ordinarily let for the purpose of chambers, or offices, or the holding of public meetings, or of arbitrations, if such part has a separate entrance, and no direct communication with any part of the premises on which any intoxicating liquor or refreshment is sold or supplied as aforesaid: 47 & 48 Vict. c. 70, s. 16.

Bribery or treating on licensed premises.] With respect to a person holding a license or certificate under the Licensing Acts (in this section referred to as a licensed person) the following provisions shall have effect:—

(*a*.) If it appears to the court by which any licensed person is

46 & 47 VICT. C. 31, S. 4.

for each offence; and all offences against this Act may be prosecuted and all penalties under this Act may be recovered by any person summarily in England in the manner provided by the

convicted of the offence of bribery or treating that such offence was committed on his licensed premises, the court shall direct such conviction to be entered in the proper register of licenses.

(*b*.) If it appears to an election court or election commissioners that a licensed person has knowingly suffered any bribery or treating in reference to any election, to take place upon his licensed premises, such court or commissioners (subject to the provisions of this Act as to a person having an opportunity of being heard by himself, and producing evidence before being reported) shall report the same; and whether such person obtained a certificate of indemnity or not, it shall be the duty of the Director of Public Prosecutions to bring such report before the licensing justices from whom, or on whose certificate the licensed person obtained his license, and such licensing justices shall cause such report to be entered in the proper register of licenses.

(*c*.) Where an entry is made in the register of licenses of any such conviction of or report respecting any licensed person as above in this section mentioned, it shall be taken into consideration by the licensing justices in determining whether they will or will not grant to such person the renewal of his license or certificate, and may be a ground, if the justices think fit, for refusing such renewal. And where the evidence shows any corrupt practice committed by a licensed person, the election commissioners are to report the case to the Director of Public Prosecutions: 46 & 47 Vict. c. 51, s. 38. This section was extended to bribery and treating at municipal elections: 47 & 48 Vict. c. 70, s. 23. The section was also extended to bribery and treating at elections for all members of local boards under the Public Health Act, members of improvement commissioners, of guardians, and members of school boards, except that as to these last elections, candidates' committees may be held in public-houses in districts not being urban sanitary districts, or not being in the metropolis: 47 & 48 Vict. c. 70, s. 36.

If debtor arrested not to be taken to public-house.] Where any officer whatsoever arrests or has in custody any person by virtue of any action, writ, or attachment for debt, such officer shall not (*a*) convey such person without his free consent to any house licensed for the sale of intoxicating liquors, &c., nor (*b*) charge such person with any sum for, or procure him to call or pay for any liquor, food, or thing whatsoever except what he freely asks for: 50 & 51 Vict. c. 55, s. 14.

Giving drink as part of wages.] The *Truck* Amendment Act, 1887, 50 & 51 Vict. c. 46, s. 4, provides that no contract with a servant in husbandry, to give intoxicating drink in addition to money wages shall be legal. [See *Gould* v. *Haynes*, 54 J. P. 405; 62 L. T. 732.]

Appndx. Summary Jurisdiction Acts, and in Scotland in the manner provided by the Summary Jurisdiction (Scotland) Acts, 1864 and 1881.

5. *Act not to apply to Ireland.*] This Act shall not apply to Ireland.

LICENSING (EVIDENCE) ACT, 1884.

47 & 48 VICT. CAP. 29.

AN ACT to extend section forty-one of "The Licensing Act, 1872." [28th July, 1884.]

WHEREAS by the 41st section of the Licensing Act, 1872, it is provided that magistrates or justices in petty sessions may, if the application is for the grant of a license, receive a copy of the license if the same has been wilfully withheld by the holder thereof, and it is expedient to extend the said section:
Be it enacted, &c., as follows:

1. *Extension of 35 & 36 Vict. c. 94, s. 41.*] Section 41 of the Licensing Act, 1872, shall be construed as if after the words "application is for the grant of a license" there were inserted the words "or for the transfer of a license."
Provided that the magistrates or justices shall be satisfied by evidence submitted to them that the license is withheld without any legal right to withhold the same.(a)

2. *Short title.*] This Act may be cited as "The Licensing (Evidence) Act, 1884."

Disinfecting rooms in licensed houses.] Any person who knowingly lets for hire any house, room, or part of a house in which any person has been suffering from any dangerous infectious disorder, without having such house, room, or part of a house, and all articles therein liable to retain infection, disinfected to the satisfaction of a legally qualified medical practitioner, as testified by a certificate signed by him, shall be liable to a penalty not exceeding 20*l*. For the purpose of this section the keeper of an inn shall be deemed to let for hire part of a house to any person admitted as a guest into such inn: 38 & 39 Vict. c. 55, s. 128. The same enactment is applied to inns by the Public Health (London) Act, 1891, 54 & 55 Vict. c. 76, s. 63.

(a) The words here directed to be inserted will be found within brackets in the 35 & 36 Vict. c. 94, s. 41, *ante*, p. 86. See notes to that section.

INTOXICATING LIQUORS (SALE TO CHILDREN) ACT, 1886.

49 & 50 VICT. CAP. 56.

AN ACT for the Protection of Children against the Sale to them of Intoxicating Liquors.

[25th June, 1886.]

WHEREAS it is expedient to protect young children against the immoral consequences resulting from their being permitted to purchase intoxicating liquors for their own consumption :

Be it therefore enacted, &c., as follows :

1. *Sale of liquors to children to be illegal.*] Every holder of a license who knowingly sells, or allows any person to sell, any description of intoxicating liquors to any person under the age of thirteen years for consumption on the premises by any person under such age as aforesaid, shall be liable to a penalty not exceeding twenty shillings for the first offence, and not exceeding forty shillings for the second and any subsequent offence.(*b*)

2. *Legal Proceedings.*] For the purpose of all legal proceedings required to be taken under the foregoing section, this Act shall be construed as one Act with the Licensing Acts, 1872, 1874.

3. *Extent of Act.*] This Act shall not extend to Scotland.

4. *Short Titel.*] This Act may be cited for all purposes as "The Intoxicating Liquors (Sale to Children) Act, 1886."

5. *Commencement of Act.*] This Act shall come into operation on 31st July, 1886.

(*b*) See this section in notes to Act, 1872, section 7, *ante*, p. 17.

PREVENTION OF CRUELTY TO, AND PROTECTION OF, CHILDREN ACT, 1889.

52 & 53 VICT. CAP. 44.

AN ACT for the Prevention of Cruelty to, and Better Protection of, Children. [26th August, 1889.]

*   *   *   *   *   *

3. *Restrictions on employment of children.*] (a) Any person who—

(a.) Causes or procures any child, being a boy under the age of fourteen years, or being a girl under the age of sixteen years, to be in any street for the purpose of begging or receiving alms, or of inducing the giving of alms, whether under the pretence of singing, playing, performing, offering anything for sale, or otherwise; or

(b.) Causes or procures any child, being a boy under the age of fourteen years, or being a girl under the age of sixteen years, to be in any street, or in any *premises licensed* for the sale of intoxicating liquor other than premises licensed according to law for public entertainment, for the purpose of singing, playing, or performing for profit, or offering anything for sale, between ten P.M. and five A.M.; or

(c.) Causes or procures any child under the age of ten years to be at any time in any street, or in any premises licensed

---

(a) A constable may take into custody without warrant a person within his view committing an offence under the Act. (Section 4.)

The accused and the wife or husband are competent, but not compellable, witnesses. (Section 7.)

The child's evidence may be admitted without oath. (Section 8.)

The defendant, if convicted, may appeal to quarter sessions. Section 10.)

The guardians of a union or parish may pay the costs and expenses of any proceedings. (Section 12.)

for the sale of any intoxicating liquor, or in *premises* Appndx.
licensed according to law for public entertainments, or
in any circus or other place of public amusement to
which the public are admitted by payment for the
purpose of singing, playing, or performing for profit, or
offering anything for sale,

shall, on conviction thereof by a court of summary jurisdiction in
manner provided by the Summary Jurisdiction Acts, be liable, at
the discretion of the court, to a fine not exceeding twenty-five
pounds or alternately, or in default of payment of the said fine,
or in addition thereto, to imprisonment, with or without hard
labour, for any term not exceeding three months.

Provided that any local authority may, if they think it necessary or desirable so to do from time to time by bye-law extend or restrict the hours mentioned in sub-section (*b*) of this section, either on every day or any specified day or days of the week, and either as to the whole of their district or as to any specified area therein.

Provided also, that in the case of any entertainment or series of entertainments to take place in premises licensed according to law for public entertainments, or in any circus or other place of public amusement as aforesaid, where it is shown to the satisfaction of a petty sessional court, or in Scotland the school board, that proper provision has been made to secure the health and kind treatment of any children proposed to be employed thereat, it shall be lawful for the said court or school board, anything in this Act notwithstanding, to grant a license for such time and during such hours of the day, and subject to such restrictions and conditions as it may think fit for any child exceeding seven years of age, of whose fitness to take part in such entertainment or series of entertainments without injury the said court or school board is satisfied, to take part in such entertainment or series of entertainments, and such license may at any time be varied, added to, or rescinded by the said court or school board, upon sufficient cause being shown; and such license shall be sufficient protection to all persons acting under or in accordance with the same.

A Secretary of State may assign to any inspector appointed, or to be appointed, under section sixty-seven of the Factory and Workshop Act, 1878, specially and in addition to any other usual duties, the duty of seeing whether the restrictions and conditions of any license under this section are duly complied with, and any such inspector shall have the same power to enter, inspect, and examine any place of public entertainment at which the employ-

Appndx. ment of a child is for the time being licensed under this section as an inspector has to enter, inspect, and examine a factory or workshop under section sixty-eight of the same Act.

Nothing in this section shall affect the provisions of the Elementary Education Act, 1876, or the Education (Scotland) Act, 1878.

So much of sub-section (c) of this section as makes it an offence to cause or procure a child to be in premises licensed according to law for public entertainment, or in any circus or other place of public amusement, for the purpose of singing, playing, or performing for profit, shall not come into operation until the first day of November, one thousand eight hundred and eighty-nine.

* * * * * *

FORMS.

GREAT BRITAIN.
DEALER'S LICENSE.

No.

———— Collection.

I, the undersigned, duly authorised by the Commissioners of Inland Revenue, hereby grant license to ———— to exercise and carry on the trades, and to sell the intoxicating liquors undermentioned in the manner hereinbefore described, at a house situate at ———— in the parish of ———— within the administrative county* ———— of ———— from the day of the date hereof, until and including the Fifth day of July next ensuing, he having paid for this license the undermentioned duties in respect of the several licenses to exercise the said trades, and which amount altogether to the sum of £————.

Dated this ———— day of ———— 18—.

	£	s.	d.
Dealer in spirits†			
(a) Ditto, to retail any quantity not less than one reputed quart bottle, to be consumed off the premises (to be granted in England only)			
Dealers in foreign wine, and in sweets or made wines			
Dealer in beer‡			
(b) Ditto, to retail beer to be consumed off the premises (to be granted in England only)			
Dealer in tobacco			
Total......£			

————————————
Collector of Inland Revenue.

(L. S.)

NOTE.—Any authority granted by this license which is founded upon a magisterial certificate will cease if the magis-

Appndx.

Forms.

terial certificate is forfeited in pursuance of "The Licensing Act, 1872," or become void under any of the provisions of that Act (see 35 & 36 Vict. c. 94, s. 63).

* If the residence is within an administrative county borough insert "borough."

† The spirit dealer's license does not authorise the sale of less than two gallons of spirits of the same denomination at a time to the same person.

‡ The beer dealer's license does not authorise the sale of less than four gallons and a half or two dozen reputed quart bottles.

N.B.—Where the person taking out the license does not intend to carry on all the enumerated trades, those which he does not intend to carry on must be struck out.

(*a*) Where the premises of the spirit dealer are not exclusively used for the sale of intoxicating liquors, or where the premises communicate with premises occupied by a person carrying on any other trade, the spirit dealer must obtain a magisterial license authorising him to hold the retail spirit license (this applies to England only).

(*b*) The beer dealer's retail license can only be granted upon the production of a magisterial license (this applies to England only).

FORM OF REFRESHMENT HOUSE LICENSE.

(23 & 24 Vict. cc. 27, 107, and Acts amending the same.)

I, the undersigned, duly authorised by the Commissioners of Inland Revenue, hereby grant license to ———— now being a householder, and dwelling in a house in ———— in the parish of ———— in the ———— of ———— to keep open the said house as a refreshment house, and to sell any victual or refreshment to be consumed therein, and in the premises thereunto belonging (provided that for the sale of any excisable or intoxicating liquor he shall have in force a proper license granted to him in that behalf), and for this license he hath paid the sum of ———— the said house and premises being ———— the value of thirty pounds a year; and this license is granted upon condition that the said ———— do not wilfully or knowingly permit any drunkenness, or any violent or quarrelsome, or other disorderly conduct, in his house or premises, or knowingly suffer any unlawful games or any gaming whatsoever therein, nor knowingly suffer or permit persons of known bad character to assemble and meet together therein, but do maintain good order and rule therein; And this license shall continue in force from the day of the date hereof until the first day of April next ensuing; and this license shall cease and determine, and shall become void, in case any of the conditions or regulations contained therein shall be transgressed or shall not be observed.

Dated this ———— day of ———— 18—.

(L.S.)

Collector of Inland Revenue.

FORMS OF LICENSES.

FORM OF PUBLICAN'S EXCISE LICENSE.

(6 Geo. 4, c. 81 ; 43 & 44 Vict. c. 20.)

Appndx.

FORMS.

I, the undersigned, duly authorised by the Commissioners of Inland Revenue, hereby grant license to ———— residing in a house situate at ———— in the parish of ———— in the ———— of ———— and known by the sign of ———— to exercise and carry on the trade or business of a retailer of spirits in the said house, and to sell by retail therein, spirits, wine, sweets, made wine, mead, metheglin, beer, cider, and perry, to be consumed either on or off the premises, from the day of the date hereof until and including the tenth day of October next ensuing, such house and premises being rented or valued at the rent or annual sum of £ ———— and I also hereby grant license to him to deal in and sell tobacco and snuff during the term above mentioned, he having paid for this license, being ———— license, the under-mentioned duties, amounting together to the sum of £————.

Dated this ———— day of ———— 18—.

	£	s.	d.
Retailer of spirits............	,,	,,	
Dealer in tobacco............	,,	,,	
Total	,,	,,	

(L.S.)

Collector of Inland Revenue.

NOTE.—This license, so far as it relates to the sale of intoxicating liquors, becomes void if the magisterial license granted to the licensee is forfeited in pursuance of "The Licensing Act, 1872," or becomes void under any of the provisions of that Act (see 35 & 36 Vict. c. 94, s. 63).

FORM OF JUSTICES' CONSENT FOR AN OCCASIONAL LICENSE.

(25 Vict. c. 22, s, 13 ; 26 & 27 Vict. c. 33, s. 20 ; 27 Vict. c. 18, s. 5 ; 37 & 38 Vict. c. 49, ss. 18—20 ; 37 & 38 Vict. c. 69, ss. 4—6.)

I, the undersigned, a justice of the peace, usually acting at the petty sessions for the petty sessional division within which the place of sale hereinafter mentioned is situated, hereby consent to the grant of an occasional license to ———— of(*a*) ———— in the county of ———— authorising him to sell(*b*)———— on the (*c*) ———— day of ———— 189—, between the hours of ———— o'clock in the forenoon and ———— o'clock in the afternoon (*being not earlier than sunrise nor later than ten o'clock at night, unless the occasion be a public dinner or ball*(*d*)) in a (*e*) ———— situate at ———— in the parish of

Appndx.
Forms.

——— on the occasion of (*f*) ——— he being a person duly licensed to sell the same at the premises first above-mentioned, Dated at ——— this ——— day of ——— 189—.

                     J.P.

This consent signed by a justice is to be produced with the proper duty, to the collector or supervisor of Inland Revenue, who thereupon will grant the occasional license.

The duty payable is as follows:—For a licensed victualler, 2*s.* 6*d.* a day; for a beer retailer and for a wine retailer, 1*s.* a day; for a tobacco and snuff dealer, 4*d.* a day. No duty is chargeable for the sale of refreshments only.

(*a*) Insert the premises for which the applicant is licensed.
(*b*) Insert the articles for sale of which the license is required.
(*c*) Insert the day or days for which the license is to be granted.
(*d*) An extension of the hours of sale is only allowed on the occasion of any public dinner or ball.
(*e*) Insert the place of sale, as "a tent," "a booth," "a stall," "a room," or according to the fact.
(*f*) Insert "an agricultural show," "public races," "a fair," "a cricket match," or according to the fact.

FORM OF OCCASIONAL LICENSE.

(25 Vict. c. 22, s. 13; 26 & 27 Vict. c. 33, ss. 19, 20; 27 Vict. c. 18, s. 5; 37 & 38 Vict. c. 49, ss. 18—20; 37 & 38 Vict. c. 69, ss. 4—6.)

I, the undersigned, duly authorised by the Commissioners of Inland Revenue, hereby grant license to ——— of, &c., in the county of ——— to sell ——— on the ——— day of ——— 189—, between the hours of ——— o'clock in the forenoon and ——— o'clock in the afternoon (*being not earlier than sunrise nor later than ten o'clock at night, unless the occasion be a public dinner or ball*), in a ——— situate at ——— on the occasion of ——— he being a person duly licensed to sell the same at the premises first above-mentioned, and having produced to me the consent of a justice of the peace for the grant of this license, as required by the enactments in that behalf.

Dated this ——— day of ——— 189—.

              s. *d.*
      Duty paid £ " "
             Collector.
                  (L.S.)
             Supervisor.

This license does not protect the person to whom it is granted, unless, at the time of sale, he produces it when requested to do so by any officer of Inland Revenue, or by any constable or police officer.

Appndx.

Forms.

FORM OF ORDER MADE UNDER SECTION 53 OF THE LICENSING ACT, 1872.

The ——— day of ——— 189—.

Upon reading the application of ———, dated the ——— day of ———, the Commissioners of Inland Revenue hereby order that ——— be permitted to carry on his business as a retailer of spirits, beer, and wine at the house and premises known as the ——— in ———, during the pendency of this appeal against the refusal of the justices to renew his license.

By the Commissioners,

_____ *Secretary.*

Appndx.
Forms.

FORMS OF LICENSES AND CERTIFICATES

Issued by the Secretary of State.

[See 35 & 36 Vict. c. 94, s. 48, *ante*, p. 101.]

I. FORM OF GRANT OF A NEW LICENSE, AND CONFIRMATION OF SUCH GRANT.

Licensing Act, 1872.

At the general annual licensing meeting [*or* an adjournment of the general annual licensing meeting] holden at ———, on the ——— day of ———, 188—, for the division of ———, in the county of ——— [*or* for the borough of :]

(*a.*) We, being ——— of the justices acting for the said division and being the majority of those at the said meeting assembled,

or,

(*b.*) We, being the majority of the members present of the borough licensing committee appointed for the said borough in pursuance of the Licensing Act, 1872,

or,

(*c.*) We, being ——— of the justices of the said borough, and being the majority of those at the said meeting assembled,

Hereby grant unto *A. B.*, of ——— [*here insert* a licensed victualler, beerhouse keeper, coffeehouse keeper, confectioner, eating-house keeper, licensed dealer in spirits, a refreshment house keeper, a wholesale spirit dealer, the holder of a strong beer license, *or as the case may be*], this license authorising him to apply for and hold ———.

[*Here insert A.,* or *B.,* or *C.* . . . . . *or M., as in the Appendix,* p. 371, *as the case may be.*]

The owner of the premises in respect of which this license is granted is *M. N.*, of ———.

This license shall be in force from the ——— day of ——— until the ——— day of ———.

Witness our hands. [*Signature of Justices.*]*

---

* NOTE.—A license may be authenticated by an official seal in lieu of signatures (35 & 36 Vict. c. 94, s. 40, sub-sect. 3), applying 33 & 34 Vict. c. 29, s. 4, sub-sect. 2. *In that case insert, instead of* "witness our hands"—"given under the official seal of the said justices in sessions assembled, which seal is hereto affixed in their presence by me, *C.D., Clerk of the licensing justices,*" *or as the case may be.*

FORMS OF LICENSES AND CERTIFICATES.

Confirmation.

At a meeting holden at ———, on the ——— day of ———,
(*a.*) We, being the majority of members present at the county licensing committee, appointed for the said county in pursuance of the Licensing Act, 1872, do hereby confirm the grant of the above license.
Witness our hands.*

or,

(*b.*) We, being ——— of the justices of the said borough, and being the majority of those at the said meeting assembled, do hereby confirm the grant of the above license.
Witness our hands.*

or,

(*c.*) We, being the majority of the members present of the joint committee, appointed for the said borough in ——— in pursuance of the Licensing Act, 1872, do hereby confirm the grant of the above license.
Witness our hands.

[*Signatures of Justices.*]*

Appndx.
———
FORMS.

II. FORM OF RENEWAL OF A LICENSE, 35 & 36 VICT. C. 94, S. 48.

Licensing Act, 1872.

At the general annual licensing meeting [*or* an adjournment of the general annual licensing meeting] holden at ——— on the ——— day of ———, for the division of ———, in the county of ——— [*or* for the borough of ———]:
(*a.*) We being ——— of the justices acting for the said division, and being the majority of those at the said meeting assembled,

or,

(*b.*) We, being ——— of the justices of the said borough, and being the majority of those at the said meeting assembled,
Hereby grant unto *A. B.*, of ——— [*here insert,* a licensed victualler, beerhouse keeper, coffeehouse keeper, confectioner, eating-house keeper, licensed dealer in spirits, a refreshment-house keeper a wholesale spirit dealer, the holder of a strong beer license, *or, as the case may be*], this renewal license authorising him to apply for and hold ———. [*Here insert A., or B., or C., . . . or M., as in the Appendix,* p. 371, *as the case may be.*]
The owner of the premises in respect of which this license is granted is *M. N.,* of ———.
This license shall be in force from the ——— day of ——— until the ——— day of ———.
Witness our hands.

[*Signature of Justices.*]*

2 B

Appndx.

Forms.

III. THE SAME BY WAY OF INDORSEMENT, 35 & 36 VICT. C. 94, S. 48 (2).

(*To be indorsed on the License, or on a copy thereof.*)

At the general annual licensing meeting [*or*, an adjournment of the general annual licensing meeting] holden at ———, on the ——— day of ———, for the division of ———, in the county of ——— [*or*, for the borough of ———]:

(*a*.) We, being ——— of the justices acting for the said division, and being the majority of those at the said meeting assembled,

or,

(*b*.) We, being ——— of the justices of the said borough, and being the majority of those at the said meeting assembled,

Hereby renew the license within contained, and such license as renewed shall be in force until the ——— day of ———.

The owner of the premises in respect of which the license is granted is *M. N.*, of ———.

Witness our hands.   [*Signature of Justices.*]*

IV. FORM OF TRANSFER LICENSE GRANTED AT SPECIAL SESSIONS, IN PURSUANCE OF 9 GEO. 4, C. 61, S. 4.

At a special session holden at ———, on the ——— day of ———, for the division of ———, in the county of ———, [*or*, for the borough of ———]:

(*a*.) We, being ——— of Her Majesty's justices of the peace acting in and for the said division, and being the majority of those at the said sessions assembled,

or,

(*b*.) We, being ——— of the justices of the said borough, and being the majority of those at the said meeting assembled,

Hereby, pursuant to section 4 of the Intoxicating Liquor Licensing Act, 1828, and the Acts amending the same, license one *C. D.*, of ———, and transfer to him* the license now held by *A. B.*, of ——— [*here insert* a licensed victualler, beerhouse keeper, coffeehouse keeper, confectioner, eating-house keeper, licensed dealer in spirits, a refreshment-house keeper, a wholesale spirit dealer, the holder of a strong beer license, *or as the case may be*], and granted on the ——— day of ——— last, authorising him to hold ———.

[*Here insert A., or B., or C. . . . or M., as in the Appendix* p. 371, *as the case may be.*]

*[*If by indorsement, say from the asterisk,**] the license within contained now held by the within-named *A. B.*

And we hereby authorise the said *C. D.* to apply for and hold [*in the cases of alehouses insert*, any of the said excise licenses, as now held, as well as those which were not held by the said *A. B.*:—*in other cases insert*, the said excise license so held by the said *A. B.*].

This transfer to be in force from this day until the ———.

Witness our hands.

                           [*Signatures of Justices.*]*

FORMS OF LICENSES AND CERTIFICATES.

V. FORM OF GRANT OF LICENSE AT SPECIAL SESSIONS, IN PURSUANCE OF 9 GEO. 4, C. 61, S. 14.

Appndx.
FORMS.

At a special sessions holden at ———, on the ——— day of ———, for the division of ———, in the county of ——— [*or* for the borough of ———]:

(*a*.) We, being ——— of the justices acting for the said division, and being the majority of those at the said sessions assembled,

or,

(*b*.) We, being ——— of the justices of the said borough, and being the majority of those at the said sessions assembled,

Hereby, pursuant to section 14 of the Intoxicating Liquor Licensing Act, 1828, and the Acts amending the same, grant unto *A.B.*, of ——— [*here insert* a licensed victualler, beerhouse keeper, coffeehouse keeper, confectioner, eating-house keeper, licensed dealer in spirits, a refreshment house keeper, a wholesale spirit dealer, the holder of a strong beer license, *or as the case may be*], this license authorising him to apply for and hold

[*Here insert A., or B., or C.,* . . . *or M. as in the Appendix below, as the case may be.*]

The owner of the premises in respect of which the license is granted is *M. N.*, of ———.

This license shall be in force from the ——— day of ——— to the ——— day of ———.

Witness our hands.   [*Signature of Justices.*]*

FORMS OF DESCRIPTIONS OF THE SEVERAL LICENSES (FOR INSERTION IN THE PREVIOUS SKELETON FORMS).

A.

Alehouse license (*on or off*).] Any of the excise licenses that may be held by a publican for the sale by retail, at a house situated at ———, known by the sign of the ———, of intoxicating liquor, to be consumed either on or off the premises.

If the license be a six-day license add as a separate paragraph:

The premises in respect of which this license is granted shall be closed during the whole of Sunday.

Appndx.
FORMS.

B.

Beerhouse license (off).] An excise license to sell by retail at a house situated at ——— beer, to be consumed off the premises, in pursuance of the Act 11 Geo. 4, and 1 Will. 4, c. 64, and Acts amending the same.

C.

Beerhouse license (on or off).] An excise license to sell by retail at a house situated at ——— beer, to be consumed either on or off the premises, in pursuance of the Act 11 Geo. 4, and 1 Will. 4, c. 64, and Acts amending the same.

If the license be a six-day license add as a separate paragraph:

The premises in respect of which this license is granted shall be closed during the whole of Sunday.

D.

Cider and perry license (on or off).] An excise license to sell by retail at a house situated at ——— cider and perry, to be consumed either on or off the premises, in pursuance of the Act 11 Geo. 4, and 1 Will. 4, c. 64, and Acts amending the same.

If the license is a six-day license add as a separate paragraph:

The premises in respect of which this license is granted shall be closed during the whole of Sunday.

E.

Additional license to strong beer dealers.] An additional excise license to sell by retail at a house situated at ——— beer, to be consumed off the premises, in pursuance of the Act 26 & 27 Vict. c. 33, s. 1.

F.

Table beer license (off).] An excise license to sell by retail at a house situated at ——— table-beer, to be consumed off the premises, in pursuance of the Act 24 & 25 Vict. c. 21, s. 3.

G.

Wine license to shopkeeper (off).] An excise license to sell by retail at a shop situated at ——— wine, to be consumed off the premises, in pursuance of the Act 23 Vict. c. 27, s. 3, and Acts amending the same.

FORMS OF LICENSES AND CERTIFICATES.

H.

License for wine to a refreshment house keeper, confectioner, or eating-house keeper (on or off).] An excise license to sell by retail at a house situated at ——— wine, to be consumed either on or off the premises in pursuance of the Act 23 Vict. c. 27, ss. 7 and 8, and Acts amending the same.

If the license is a six-day license add as a separate paragraph:

The premises in respect of which the license is granted shall be closed the whole of Sunday.

I.

A licensed dealer's additional spirit license (off).] An additional excise license to sell by retail at a shop situated at ——— spirits, to be consumed off the premises, in pursuance of the Act 24 & 25 Vict. c. 21, s. 2.

K.

License for liqueurs in shops (off).] An excise license to sell by retail at a shop situated at ——— liqueurs, to be consumed off the premises, in pursuance of the Acts 11 & 12 Vict. c. 121, and 23 & 24 Vict. c. 114, and Acts amending the same.

L.

License for sweets to a refreshment house keeper, confectioner, or eating-house keeper (on or off).] An excise license to sell by retail at a house situated at ——— sweets, to be consumed either on or off the premises, in pursuance of the Act 6 Geo. 4, c. 81, and Acts amending the same.

If the license is a six-day license add as a separate paragraph:

The premises in respect of which the license is granted shall be closed the whole of Sunday.

M.

Sweets license to shopkeeper (off).] An excise license to sell by retail at a shop situated at ——— sweets, to be consumed off the premises, in pursuance of the Act 6 Geo. 4, c. 81, and Acts amending the same.

Appndx.

FORMS.

Appndx.

HOUSE OF LORDS.

SHARP v. WAKEFIELD.

Licensing Acts—Discretion of justices as to renewals of publicans' licenses—Ground of opposition.

R., the holder of a publican's license, applied for renewal, and no ground of opposition being proved, except that the house was too far removed from police superintendence and was not needed,

Held, *the quarter sessions were justified in refusing the renewal on those grounds alone.*

Susannah Sharp, the owner of an inn called the Low Bridge Inn, Kentmere, Westmoreland, appealed to the quarter sessions against the refusal of a renewal license to her tenant, W. Ridding. Notice of opposition had been duly served on Ridding that his license would be opposed on the ground that the house was too remote from the police supervision, and that the house was not required in the locality and neighbourhood. The quarter sessions holding these grounds of opposition to be proved refused the renewal on those grounds alone. A case was, however, stated for the opinion of the Queen's Bench Division.

The Queen's Bench Division (consisting of FIELD, J., and WILLS, J.) held that the decision of quarter sessions could not be interfered with.

The Court of Appeal (consisting of Lord ESHER, M.R., FRY, L.J., and LOPES, L.J.) affirmed that judgment.

The case was then appealed to the House of Lords and was there reviewed.

Henn Collins, Q.C., *Candy*, Q.C., and *L. Sanderson*, for the appellants.

Addison, Q.C., *Poland*, Q.C., and *J. Paterson*, for the respondents.

Judgment was given on 20th March, 1891, as follows :—

Lord HALSBURY, L.C.—I do not think that at any period of the argument any of your lordships doubted but that this judgment must be affirmed. By the express language of the statute (9 Geo. 4, c. 61), which is still the governing statute, the grant of a license is expressly within the discretion of the magistrates. For reasons to be stated presently, I am of opinion that no legislation has ever altered that provision ; but if one were to argue *à priori*

what possible reason could there be for limiting the discretion of **Appndx.**
the justices to the first grant of the license? It is not denied —
that for the purpose of the original grant it is within the power
and even the duty of the magistrates to consider the wants of the
neighbourhood with reference both to its population, means of
inspection by the proper authorities, and so forth. If this is the
original jurisdiction, what sense or reason could there be in
making these topics irrelevant in any future grant? It surely
must have been in the contemplation of the legislature that the
circumstances of a neighbourhood might change; a population
might diminish or increase. Would it be argued, that, if the
population had very much increased at some point where by
reason of its previous want of population no such public accommodation had been hitherto granted, no license should be granted
because this additional grant might to some extent interfere with
the practical monopoly enjoyed by the persons already licensed?
This, of course, could not be argued, since it is the well-understood
practice to do this very thing. But can anything be more
unreasonable than the suggestion that the legislature had given
the discretion in one direction and withheld it in the other? In
real truth a great deal of the argument addressed to us on the
part of the appellant has been less addressed to us upon the true
construction of the Act of 1828 (9 Geo. 4, c. 61), or the statutes
which have followed it, than to some supposed injustice, which
the argument assumed would be so great, if the matter was left
to the discretion of the justices, that the legislature never could
have intended to have intrusted them with a discretion so wide.
I do not think if the injustice were so great as it is suggested by
the argument that that consideration could prevail over the plain
language of the legislature. But I am not able to assent to the
notion that the injustice is so great. An extensive power is
confided to the justices in their capacity as justices to be exercised
judicially, and discretion means, when it is said that something
is to be done within the discretion of the authorities, that that
something is to be done according to the rules of reason and
justice, not to private opinion (*Rooke's Case*, 5 Rep. 100a);
according to law, and not humour. It is to be not arbitrary,
vague, and fanciful, but legal and regular, and it must be exercised within the limit to which an honest man competent to
the discharge of his office ought to confine himself (*Wilson* v.
Rastall, 4 T. R. 757). So in the *Queen* v. *Boteler* (33 L. J., Mag.
Cases, 101; 4 B. & S. 959; 28 J. P. 453), where justices thought
proper not to enforce the law because they considered that the
act in question was unjust in principle, the Court of Queen's
Bench compelled them by a peremptory order to do the act
which nevertheless the statute had said was in their discretion

Appndx. to do or to leave undone. So, again, when overseers were required by 3 & 4 Vict. c. 61, to certify whether applicants for beer licenses were real residents and ratepayers of the parish, it was held that they were not entitled to refuse the certificate on the ground that in their opinion there were already too many public-houses, or that the beershop was not required (*R.* v. *Withyham*, 2 C. L. R. 1657). So a discretion which empowered justices to grant licenses to innkeepers, as in the exercise of their discretion they deemed proper, would not be exercised by coming to a general resolution to refuse a license to anybody who would not consent to take out an excise license for the sale of spirits (*The Queen* v. *Sylvester*, 2 B. & S. 322; 26 J. P. 151; 31 L. J. M. C. 93; 5 L. T. 794). Again, justices in Scotland were authorised to alter the hours for the sale of intoxicating liquors in any particular district, but it was held that, though this was a general discretion given to them, they had no right by virtue of a general resolution to alter the time in every case. They were required judicially to determine, although according to their discretion, what places in the honest exercise of their judgment required other hours for opening and closing than those specified. The question arose in the case to which I am referring on the proviso to section 2 of the 16 & 17 Vict. c. 67, which was in these words :—" Provided always, that in any particular locality within any county or district or burgh requiring other hours for opening and closing inns and hotels and public-houses than those specified in the forms of certificates in said schedule applicable thereto, it shall be lawful for such justices or magistrates respectively to insert in such certificates such other hours not being earlier than six o'clock or later than eight o'clock in the morning for opening, or earlier than nine o'clock or later than eleven o'clock in the evening for closing the same, as they shall think fit." Eleven o'clock at night was accordingly the hour appointed for closing public-houses in Scotland, and the magistrates of Rothesay issued an order closing them at ten o'clock instead of eleven. Lord SELBORNE, in giving judgment in the House of Lords in that case, makes these observations :—" Without meaning to deny that it is confided to the discretion of the magistrates to determine what particular localities require other hours for opening and closing than those specified, it is obvious that such discretion as they have is not an arbitrary discretion to define any locality they please, but they must be such localities as they consider in the honest and *bonâ fide* exercise of their own judgment to require a difference to be made. The participle 'requiring' is connected with the substantive 'locality,' and, therefore, it must be a requirement arising out of the particular circumstances of the place. The magistrates must, in the exercise of an honest and *bonâ fide* judgment, be of opinion that the 'particular locality' which they **Appndx.** except from the ordinary rule is one which from its own special circumstances requires that difference to be made" (*Macbeth* v. *Ashley*, L. R. 2 Scotch Appeals, 360). I do not feel, therefore, though the language of the statute and the power given by that language is so great and so unqualified, that the mischief or danger apprehended by the appellants is at all likely to arise. The legislature has given credit to the magistrates for exercising a judicial discretion that they will fairly decide the questions submitted to them, and not by evasion attempt to repeal the law which permits public-houses to exist, or evade it by avoiding a plain exposition of the reasons on which they act. I am very far, indeed, from saying that, assuming the complete discretion that I have indicated to exist, it would be likely that the persons exercising it would consider an original application in the same way as one which was applied for by the person who has already been licensed for one year. Of course, the justices would remember that a year before a license had been granted, and presumably, unless some change during the year was proved, they start with the fact that the topics to which I have referred have already been considered, and one would not expect that those topics would be likely to be reopened, unless, as I say, some change has been proved. This would be likely to limit the inquiry to the conduct of the house and the character of the licensee, and perhaps the condition of the house, but as matter of fact and not as matter of law at all. As to the question of law arising upon the language of all the statutes, it may, in my judgment, be very shortly disposed of. The first statute (9 Geo. 4, c. 61) to which one need go back it is admitted gives discretion. Does any Act passed since purport to withdraw it? Certainly not. On the contrary, the Acts referred to (35 & 36 Vict. c. 94, s. 42 ; 37 & 38 Vict. c. 49, s. 26) expressly retain it, subject to certain provisions which it cannot be pretended affect to exclude the topics, which it is argued are topics irrelevant to a renewal. Now, I do not mean to say that a repeal or qualification may not sometimes be implied by subsequent statutes enacting something inconsistent with a previous Act, but in a matter so constantly before the legislature as the licensing laws I cannot but think that if it was intended to alter the law in this respect it would have been done in plain and unambiguous language. Now, the Licensing Acts of 1872 and 1874, which are the Acts upon which reliance is placed, do not profess to limit the discretion, but enact certain new procedure, all of which procedure is perfectly consistent with the preservation intact of the discretion given to the magistrates. I do not think that it is necessary to go into details as to the alteration of procedure—it is merely procedure. It leaves the

Appndx. earlier Act absolutely untouched upon the subject now in debate, and I entirely approve of and adopt the decision of Chief Justice COCKBURN and Mr. Justice MELLOR, arrived at thirteen years ago in *R.* v. *Smith,* or *Smith* v. *Hereford,* 48 L. J. M. C. 38 ; 42 J. P. 295 ; 39 L. T. 606. I, therefore, think that this appeal ought to be dismissed with costs.

Lord BRAMWELL.—I think this a very plain case, and that the judgment should be affirmed. Houses of public entertainment and the sale of drink have been in this country and in many others the subject of regulation for police purposes : not for what one may call economic purposes, like the fixing of the price of bread, or the wages of labour, but for the maintenance of order. And, naturally, the buildings themselves, their character, their number, and their neighbourhood have been considered as well as the persons who should be permitted to carry on the trade or business. That certainly has been the case in England ; and it is undoubtedly so now with respect to licenses granted to sell drink on premises for the first time. This is so clear that the learned counsel for the appellants have not contended to the contrary. If an application is made for a license to sell drink on premises not before licensed it is certain that the magistrates may refuse it, and may refuse for the reason and no other than that they think the neighbourhood does not need it ; that none is needed, or none in addition to the houses already licensed. But it is said that this power or right in the magistrates does not exist where a license has been granted, and the question is whether it should be renewed. I am not sure that this contention might not be met by this : the magistrates have a discretion to refuse, they are not bound to state their reason, and, therefore, their decision cannot be questioned. But I think it better to say that, in my judgment, if they had to state their reasons it would be a good one in point of law, that they refused to renew on the ground of "the remoteness from police supervision and the character and necessities of the locality and neighbourhood in which the inn is situate." Of course the finding of the facts by the sessions is conclusive. Two objections are raised by the appellants. One is, that though by the Act 9 Geo. 4, c. 61, the above might be a good ground for the refusal of a license applied for for the first time, it is not so for a refusal of its renewal. Why, 1 know not. I quite agree that different considerations should operate on the minds of the justices, and, I doubt not, do so. The hardship of stopping the trade of a man who is getting an honest living in a lawful trade and has done so, perhaps, for years, with probably an expense at the outset, may well be taken into consideration, but it must be done so in conjunction with considerations the other way, and must be left to the discretion of the justices. The license is a renewal. That word has been criticised. It may be misleading, but is, I think, correct. It is a "renewal," *i.e.*, a new license, as we talk of a new lease being a renewal, though parties and terms may be wholly different. And one cannot help seeing this, that if the discretion was to be limited, as contended, in the case of a renewal, the legislature might have said so in terms, and has not. Whenever that is the case, it seems to me that courts ought not to put a limit on general words without almost a necessity for doing so. The other objection is, that subsequent legislation has shown that Parliament intended there should be a difference between the treatment of original applications for a license and applications for renewals, and has shown that it intended the license should be renewed except for objection to the license—at all events, that its renewal should not be refused for such a reason as is given in this case, and so the power to refuse on that ground has been taken away by the legislature. I cannot find this. I do find, indeed, that the legislature, in its subsequent Acts, contemplated that, as a rule, as a practice, licenses would be renewed. But there is nothing to show that the discretion to refuse is taken away. The word "personal," so much relied on, means "individual," as distinguished from the class to which he belongs. And I must repeat my remark that it could have been so enacted, and there is nothing to justify implying such a repeal. Indeed, I think this argument presents a consideration unfavourable to the appellants. The legislature has most clearly shown that it supposed—contemplated—that licenses would usually be renewed; that the taking away of a man's livelihood would not be practised cruelly or wantonly. True, and because it showed that plainly, it may have felt it safe to leave an absolute discretion with the justices, a discretion that would be discreetly exercised. And it has been so. I do not say in this case, I know nothing about it; I mean by justices generally. That is shown by what was mentioned by Mr. Poland—namely, that at the sessions when there used to be an appeal against a refusal of a first license the appellant began ; the burden of proof was on him, he had to make out that he ought to have a license. Where, on the other hand, the appeal is against a refusal to renew a license, the respondents begin ; the burden of proof is on them, they have to make out that the applicant ought not to have a license ; practically, that his license should be taken from him. This, Mr. Poland says, was the practice throughout England. One may well suppose this to be known to the legislature, and to be one cause why the justices are trusted with such extensive powers. For these reasons I think the appeal should be

Appndx.

Appndx. dismissed, thinking, indeed, that the legislature contemplated that, ordinarily, licenses would be renewed, and have most strongly shown that, but thinking also that that does not help the appellants to show, and that they have not shown, that a renewal may not be refused for the reason given in this case.

Lord HERSCHELL.—The sole question for decision in this case is, whether, where a license is applied for, by way of renewal, by one who already holds a license for the sale of intoxicating liquors, the licensing authorities are entitled to take into consideration the wants of the neighbourhood and the remoteness of the premises from police supervision, or whether their inquiry must be limited to the character and conduct of the applicant, and they can only refuse the applicant on the ground of his personal unfitness. It was admitted by the learned counsel for the appellants that there was authority for the proposition that a complete discretion had been vested in the justices to grant or withhold any application for a new license, though they somewhat faintly contended that, upon the true construction of the first section of 9 Geo. 4, c. 61, this discretion was confined to the question whether the applicant was a fit and proper person to hold the license, and whether the premises in respect of which he made the application were suitable for the purpose. It is, to my mind, abundantly clear that this is not a correct view of the statute. Giving to the language used its natural interpretation, I think it impossible to do otherwise than hold that the discretion of the justices is not in any way fettered. When once this conclusion is arrived at, it seems to me to follow that the justices had, under the statute of 9 Geo. 4, c. 61, the same discretion when the holder of a license applied for another license for the ensuing year. It is by virtue of the very same enactment that the justices are empowered to grant such a license. The statute makes no distinction between this case and the original application. The word "renewal" is never mentioned, and it is expressly provided that every license granted under the authority of the Act shall last for one year "and no longer." But it was argued that the law had been modified by subsequent legislation, and this was the point mainly insisted upon on behalf of the appellant. The Licensing Act of 1872 has, it is true, by section 42, altered in some respects the procedure provided in relation to applications for licenses by the statute of 9 Geo. 4, c. 61. But the alterations have reference to matters of procedure only. Under the earlier Act the applicant for a license was required to attend in person unless hindered by sickness, infirmity, or other reasonable cause. The Act of 1872 provided that in case of an application for the renewal of a license the applicant need not attend in person at the annual licensing meeting, unless required by the justices so to attend. It also contained enactments securing to the applicant for a renewal of his license notice that objection was taken to such renewal, and prescribed that no evidence with respect thereto should be received by the justices that was not given on oath. These provisions would obviously have left the discretion of the justices just what it had been before, even if the statute had not gone on, as it does, to provide that, subject thereto, licenses should be renewed, and the powers and discretion of justices relative to such renewal should be exercised as theretofore. But it was said that the amendment of section 42 of the Licensing Act, 1872, enacted by section 26 of the Licensing Act, 1874, had the effect of limiting the power of the justices and prohibiting them from refusing to grant a renewal of a license save from some cause personal to the applicant. The enactment in question certainly does not in terms contain any such provision, and I do not think it is possible to infer from the language used that the legislature intended thus to alter the law. The section, after reciting that it was enacted by section 42 of the Act of 1872 that an applicant for the renewal of his license need not attend in person at the annual licensing meeting, unless required by the licensing justices so to attend, enacts "that such requisition shall not be made save for some special cause personal to the licensed person to whom such requisition is sent." I think the object of this provision is obvious. Under the earlier Act the justices at any sessions might (or at the very least it was open to contention that they might) have required all applicants for a renewal to attend as before. The later Act prescribes that no such requisition is to be made except for some special cause personal to the recipient of the requisition. The cause, it will be observed, is to be a cause for requiring the individual to be present, and the fact that objection was taken to the renewal of his license would be such a cause. The language of the statute has no reference to the causes which, when the applicant attends in pursuance to the requisition, may operate in the minds of the justices to determine whether his application shall be acceded to or not. For these reasons I think that the judgment of the court below was correct and ought to be affirmed. There is one observation made by my noble and learned friend, the Lord Chancellor, to which I am not prepared to give my assent without qualification. I do not think that the fact, that a license had been granted for the previous year would be a sufficient ground for the justices presuming that the licensed house was then needed, and for considering only whether the circumstances had changed in the interval. It might well be that the attention of the licensing justices had not on a former occasion been called to the condition and wants of the neighbourhood.

Appndx.

Appndx. Lord MACNAGHTEN.—For the reasons which have been stated by my noble and learned friends, and which it is unnecessary for me to repeat, I also am of opinion that is is clear beyond the possibility of doubt or question that the Act of 1828 (9 Geo. 4, c. 61) conferred upon the licensing justices the same discretion in the case of an application for what is now termed a renewal as in the case of a person applying for a license for the first time, and that, although there has been an alteration in the procedure in favour of applicants for renewed licenses, there is nothing in the subsequent legislation to do away with, or impair or fetter that discretion.

Lord HANNEN.—I do not consider it necessary to occupy your lordships' time with observations on the Act 9 Geo. 4, c. 61. It was long ago decided, I think rightly decided, that the justices were under that Act entitled and bound to consider the needs of the neighbourhood on the application for a license to a person seeking to keep a house for the sale of excisable liquors, and that their discretion is equally wide in the case of a person already keeping such a house as in one where the application is by a person not before licensed (*R.* v. *Lancashire,* 35 J. P. 170 ; L. R. 6 Q. B. 97 ; 40 L. J. M. C. 17 ; 23 L. T. 461 ; 19 W. R. 204 ; *Smith* v. *Hereford, R.* v. *Smith,* 42 J. P. 295 ; 48 L. J. M. C. 38 ; 39 L. T. 606). But it was contended that the general discretion given by the Act of Geo. 4 was restricted by the Act of 1872 (35 & 36 Vict. c. 94), and by the Act of 1874 (37 & 38 Vict. c. 49). By the first of these Acts the renewal of licenses is dealt with, and by the 42nd section certain changes are made in the procedure where a renewal is asked for :—(1) The applicant need not attend in person unless required by the justices to do so ; (2) no objection to the renewal is to be entertained unless written notice of the intention to oppose, stating the general grounds of the opposition, has been served seven days before the meeting ; and (3) evidence with respect to the renewal shall be given on oath. But the section concludes : "Subject, as aforesaid, licenses shall be renewed, and the power and discretion of justices relative to such renewal shall be exercised as heretofore." This, therefore, clearly leaves the discretion of the justices unfettered where the provisions of the 42nd section have been complied with. The argument for the appellants was chiefly based on the qualification of the above-mentioned 42nd section of the Act of 1872, added by the first clause of the 26th section of the Licensing Act of 1874 (37 & 38 Vict. c. 49). That clause is as follows : " Whereas by section 42 of the principal Act, it is enacted that a licensed person applying for the renewal of his license need not attend in person at the general licensing meeting, unless he is required by the licensing justices

so to attend : Be it enacted that such requisition shall not be **Appndx.**
made save for some special cause personal to the licensed person
to whom such requisition is sent." Rightly to understand this
enactment, it is necessary to revert to the earlier legislation on the
subject of the personal attendance of applicants for licenses. By
the 12th section of the Act 9 Geo. 4, c. 61, only those applicants
were excused from personal attendance who could prove by sworn
testimony that they were hindered by sickness or infirmity or by
any other reasonable cause, in which case an authorised person
might attend for them. The 42nd section of the Act of 1872
excused the applicant for a renewal of his license from attendance
unless required by the justices. This left it in the power of the
justices to require the attendance of all applicants for renewed
licenses. This power might be exercised so as to cause inconvenience to applicants required to attend on grounds not having
reference to their particular case. Instances have been brought
before the superior courts where justices have expressed and
acted upon a general intention with regard to all licenses, whereas
it is their duty to consider each individual case on its own special
merits. The object of the 26th section of the Act of 1874 appears
to be to enforce this duty, and to require the justices to particularise the special ground on which they consider the personal
attendance of the applicant necessary. The word "personal" is
fully satisfied by construing it as meaning "for a cause in which
the applicant is personally interested, and not merely interested
as one of the general body of licensed persons." For these reasons
it appears to me that the judgment appealed from is correct, and
should be affirmed.

Appeal dismissed with costs.

INDEX.

A.

Access to places of public resort, 40.
Action against disqualified justice for penalty, 132; none for refusing license, 215.
    none for price of liquor consumed on premises, 298.
    to recover accounts for spirits, 297.
Address of person found in closing hours, 60.
    of person interested in premises, 141.
    of person found where liquors kept, 196.
Adjacent places to towns included, 209.
Adjoining, drinking on premises, 15.
Adjournment of application for renewal license, 87; when objection started to renewal, 88, 91.
    valuation of premises sufficient at, 100.
    of general licensing meeting, 221, 223.
    in Middlesex and Surrey, 221.
    re-hearing a case at, 222.
    giving notice of application in time for, 222.
    of appeal at quarter sessions, 241.
    of special transfer sessions, 222.
    to allow notices to be given, 221.
    notice of, to parties, 203, 223.
Admitting constable into premises, 194.
    into billiard rooms, 163.
    into refreshment house, 280.
Adulteration of liquor, 188; selling with label, 189; holding warranty, 192; defence as to, with water, 190; of beer, 190; penalties as to, 190; affixing notice as to mixing liquors, 190.
Advertising betting-house office, 52
    variation of Sunday hours, 174.
    notice of a new license, 82.
Affixing name on licensed premises, 21.
    inscription on music and dancing places, 35, 39
    notice of exemption order, 66.
    notice of six-day licensed house, 102.
    notice of billiard license, 163.
    notice as to mixing liquors, 190

Affixing hours of closing refreshment house, 185, 307.
    hours of closing night houses, 185.
    hours of early closing houses, 176.
    notice on church door of licensing meeting, 220, 316.
    notice on church door of new license, 316.
    notice on door of house to be licensed, 316.
Age of children buying liquors, 17, 359.
Agent for dealers in liquors, 4.
Aggrieved person as to license, who is, 117, 240.
    as to conviction, who is, 117.
    demanding case for High Court, 121, 242.
    seeking *certiorari*, 124, 217.
Aiding and abetting by servant, 28.
Alehouse is public place, 24.
    found drunk in, 25.
See "Public-house ;" " License."
Alehouse Acts, 9 Geo. 4, c. 61, 212.
    5 & 6 Vict. c. 44, 269.
See " License ;" " Renewal ;" "Transfer ;" " Notice."
Altering licensed premises, 7, 158.
    when new license required, 158.
    hours of exemption order, 61.
    hours of Sunday closing, 173.
Analysis of liquors adulterated, 188.
Analyst of adulterated liquors, 189.
Annual licensing meeting. *See* " General Annual," &c.
Annual value of future in-door licensed houses, 95, 99.
    of beerhouses before 1872, 99, 263.
    of wine houses (on), 276.
    how ascertained, 97, 99.
    rating not now needed for license, 100.
    sufficient if made so at adjournment, 100, 222, 317.
    for excise licenses, 343.
Appeal, fifteen days' notice before, 119, 238.
    against excise conviction, 10.
    against betting-house convictions, 54.
    against gaming-house convictions, 48.
    against refreshment-house convictions, 285.
    against conviction for harbouring thieves, 32.
    against conviction for billiard offence, 164.
    against refusal to renew, 93, 238.
    against any conviction, 116.
    none by landlord against tenant's conviction, 116.
    recognizance in conviction appeals, 118.
    if appeal against conviction succeeds, 120.
    none against refusing billiard license, 164.

INDEX. 387

Appeal, none against refusal of new certificates, 167, 204, 240.
    if owner can appeal against refusal of license, 240.
    adding restictions to right, 240.
    as to costs on licensing, 243.
    to county quarter sessions, 241.
    by refreshment house keeper, 285.
    constable prosecuting refreshment house keeper, 286.
    notices of, sent by post, 119.
    to House of Lords in *mandamus*, 217.
    to quarter sessions as to new grants, 167, 204, 243.
                as to transfers and renewals, 93, 231, 320.
                costs upon, 243,
                adjournment of, as to license, 241.
                temporary license during, 124.
                a case can be stated, 121, 242.
    to High Court by case stated, 121, 242.
    to justices by owner against disqualification, 128.
Application of penalties, 110, 116, 185 ; in boroughs, 138.
Apprehending drunken person, 25.
            persons found in closing hours, 59, 196.
Army Act, 1881, sections as to canteens, 147 ; billeting, 258.
Arrest of debtor ; not to be taken to inns, 357.
Assaulting constable entering premises, 194.
Assembling of prostitutes, 30, 31.
    of thieves, penalty, 31.
Assignee of license holder, 193, 227.
    of landlord enforcing covenants, 254.
Attempt to obtain liquor falsely, 60, 181.
Attendance for renewal of license, 86, 203.
    sickness excusing, 226.
Attending in person for license, 83, 226.
Authentication of licenses and certificates, 84, 327.

B.

Bagatelle included in billiards, 161.
Ball, a special occasion for exemption order, 66, 301.
    public, occasional license for, 301.
        refreshment house license for, 301.
Bankruptcy of licensee, 3, 11, 227.
    application to next transfer sessions, 3.
    how far license is property, 11.
Barter of liquor, 135.
Beer, definition of, 154.
    duty on license by publicans, 342.

2 c 2

Beer sale of spruce, or black, 144.
    sale by retail, 9, 159, 342.
    sale of, without excise license, 3, 249, 262.
    partners in license, 249.
    exemption orders near markets, &c., 63, 173.
    license to sell, includes cider and perry, 252, 341.
    excise duties on licenses, 341.
    dealer's additional retail license, 299, 331, 342.
    valuation qualification for, 97, 100, 263.
    when residence not necessary, 299.
    discretion of justices as to, 317, 352.
    sellers of, formerly not to sell spirits or wine, or sweets, 261; not now prohibited, 293.
        must usually be resident occupiers, 264.
        not liable to some penalties as to billiards, 164.
        absolute discretion of justices now as to, 352.
    fraud in obtaining excise license, 249.
    adulteration of, 190.
    in-door license since 1869, when cannot be refused, 317, 319.
    duration of license same as publican's, 294, 329.
    botanic beer, 313.
    cider may be separate from beer, 252.
    license for, in 1840 privileged, 268.
    occasional license to beerseller, 300; duty on same, 300.
    brewers making for domestic use, 340.
  See "Sunday;" "License;" "Wine and Beerhouse Acts."
Beerhouse Acts, 11 Geo. 4 and 1 Will. 4, c. 64, 247.
        4 & 5 Will. 4, c. 85, 258.
        3 & 4 Vict. c. 61, 263.
        33 & 34 Vict. c. 111, 333.
        43 Vict. c. 6, 337.
        45 & 46 Vict. c. 34, 352.
Betting-house, manager of, 49.
        using licensed houses for, 49, 50.
        inducing infants to bet, 53.
        playing for money in licensed houses, 46, 47.
        wager on game of billiards, 49.
        evidence of betting, 49.
        deposit on bet, 50.
        advertising betting, 52.
        warrant to search, 52.
Bicycle, if included in carriage, 24.
Bill of sale, lease with power of distress, a, 236.
Billeting soldiers in victualling-houses, 258; remedies as to, 259.
Billiard licenses, how applied for, 160.
        no appeal against refusal, 161.

INDEX.   389

Billiard licenses, form and duration of, 161.
    no excisable liquor to be consumed, 161, 345.
    penalty for unlicensed, 162.
    offences connected with, 163.
    constable to visit, 163.
    closing hours, 162.
    lodgers in licensed houses playing at, 164.
    appeal against conviction of licensee, 164.
    beersellers not liable to some penalties, 164.
Boarding house, keeper of, not liable for guest, 275, 303, 338.
Boats and packets, liquors in, 143, 272, 344.
    duties on sale in, 44.
Bond fide traveller, 61, 180 ; in Wales, 170, 351.
Boots allowing gaming, in licensed premises, 46.
Borough, definition of, 152.
    grant of new licenses in, 78.
    licensing committee in, 78.
        powers of, 80.
    licensing meetings, how held in, 78, 218.
        in quarter sessions boroughs, 218.
        in Cinque Ports, 219.
    county justices not to interfere in licenses, 80.
    brewers as justices in boroughs, 82.
    justices of, not to use licensed house, 355.
    penalties, how applied in, 138, 219.
    precept to constable in, 221.
    costs at quarter sessions in appeals, 243.
    joint committee, 80, 93, 202.
Botanic beer, license for, required, 313.
Break in license, 233.
Brewers, when disqualified as justices, 23, 82, 132.
    excise duties on brewers of beer not for sale, 340.
Brewster sessions, holding of, 213.
        when adjourned, 221, 223.
        notices when adjourned, 223.
Bribery by licensed person, conviction entered in register, 75, 357.
    of electors in inns, 356.
Bribing constable, penalty for, 44.
British sherry, license for, 274, 281.
    wine included in license for foreign, 281.
Brothel, evidence of once using as, 43.
    conviction for, avoids license, 42.
    indictment or summary proceeding, 43.
    licensed house, if used as, 42.
Burden of proof as to travellers, 110, 180.
    as to other matters, 110.

C.

Canteens, sale of spirits in, 147.
Card-playing in licensed houses, 46.
Carriage on highway driven by drunken person, 24; if carriage includes bicycle, 24.
Carrying liquor for consumption, 16.
    from licensed premises, 135.
    See " Wine and Beerhouse Acts," and " License."
Case stated for High Court in convictions, 121, 242.
    who may demand, and notices, 122.
    if stated as to licenses, 242.
Casting vote of chairman of joint committee, 81.
    in ordinary licensing sessions, 226.
Cattle, drunken person in charge of, 24.
Census, population as to, 137.
    using for declaring populous place, 209.
    as to (on) wine license, 277.
Certificates under Wine and Beerhouse Acts, 313.
    included in license under Licensing Act, 150.
    form and duration of, 313, 329, 368.
    fees for, 319.
    forgery of, 192, 321.
    appeal against refusal of, 320.
    some not to be refused, 318.
Certiorari as to convictions, &c., 125.
    where case stated for High Court, 121, 242.
    not allowed to quash, when, 126.
    quashing licenses, 217.
    none to quash excise license, 260.
Chairman of joint committee has casting vote, 81.
    of licensing sessions, 226.
Chamberlain, Lord, control of theatres, 145.
Change of occupancy of premises, 227.
Chapel, affixing notices of licensing meetings, 220, 316.
    notice of application for new license, 83, 316.
Character, additional evidence of, on appeal, 241.
    of applicant for license, 213, 317.
Children, sale of spirits to, 17, 359.
    proof of age of, 16, 17.
    employed in licensed houses, 360.
Chimney sweep, excluding from business, 55.
Christmas Day, closing premises on, 170.
    in Wales, 350.
    occasional licenses on, 296.
    for billiards, 163.

INDEX. 391

Christmas Eve, special exemption order for, 67.
Church door, notices on, 220, 316.
    of holding licensing meeting, 220.
    notice of applications for license on, 316.
    dissenting chapels not included, 316.
Cider, license to sell by retail, 249.
    all penalties as to beer apply to, 249.
    in-door license exemption order, 63.
    out-door refused on what grounds, 317, 352.
    in-door since 1869, when refusable, 318.
    duties on license, 342.
    is included in beer license, 252, 341.
    separate license for, 252.
    valuation qualification, 97, 100, 263.
Cinque Ports, how licensing meeting held, 219, 225.
    county justices not to act in, 225.
    statutes as to, 225.
Circulars as to betting-house, 52.
Clerk of licensing justices, 73, 76, 152.
    definition, 152.
    appointment, 73.
    to allow inspection of register, 73.
    unauthorised fees, 74, 78, 236.
    to enter convictions in register, to send notice of conviction, 73, 128, 130, 142.
    signing extracts of register, 131.
    justices to send notices to constables of licensing meeting, 220, 223.
    justices may stamp licenses, 327.
    charging excessive fees, 310, 328.
Clerk of peace to be clerk of county licensing committee, 76.
    costs at quarter sessions paid to, 243.
Closing of premises on Sunday and week-days, 170.
    varying hours on Sunday, 173.
    right of license holder as to, 102.
    as regards travellers, 102, 181.
    of theatre bars, 146.
    of billiard tables, 162.
    at railway stations, 182.
    persons found on premises during closing hours, 60.
    exemption order from, 61.
    notice stating exemption hours, 61.
    during special occasion, 66.
    on Sunday in Wales, 170, 350.
    under six-day licenses, 102, 170.
    under early closing license, 176.

Closing, penalty for infringing closing hours, 178.
    friends during, 184, 206.
    gift of liquor during, 206.
    of night-houses, 185, 307.
    places with occasional licenses, 301.
    right to close at any time, 102.
    in case of riot, 56.
    exception from, in favour of travellers, 56, 102.
    of refreshment houses not selling liquor, 65, 308.
            selling wine, 170, 179.
Clubs supplying liquors, 5.
    manager of sham, 5.
    proprietary, if license needed, 6.
Cock-fight in licensed premises, 33.
Combination, meetings for unlawful, 32.
Comedy, acting of, requires license, 145.
Commissioner of police granting exemption order, 62.
Commitment for non-payment, 113.
Committee, county licensing, 76; borough licensing, 78.
        joint committee as to borough licenses, 80, 199, 202.
Common gaming house, 47.
Communication, internal, with unlicensed places, 20.
        continuance of license, if forfeited, 192.
-Company or firm, license to, 215, 250.
        owners of hotel, 303.
Compensation for loss of license, 235.
-Computation of time includes Sunday on a case stated, 123, 315.
        as to appeal to quarter sessions, 118, 119, 240.
        as to notice for new license, 315.
Concurrent remedies, 131.
Conduct, disorderly, in licensed house, 29, 42, 54.
    in refreshment house, 284, 289.
Confectioner treated as victualling house keeper, 214.
    entitled to wine license, 276.
Confirmation of new licenses in counties, 75, 78.
    regulations as to, 78, 202.
    discretion of confirming authority, 75.
    in borough licenses, 78.
    opposition to, not allowed in some cases, 93.
    costs may be awarded on, 93.
    costs how recovered, 93, 115.
    for provisional license, 199.
    rules for, 202.
    required for removal, 105, 201.
    none required as to out-door licenses, 202.
Consent to drinking on premises, 15.

Consent of justice to occasional license, 301.
    to sell at fairs and races, 197.
Constable, harbouring, in licensed house, 44.
    closing premises during riot, 56.
    demanding license and exemption order, 66, 137.
    demanding name of persons found in premises, 60.
    duty as to excluding drunkards, 55.
    duty as to apprehending drunkards, 25.
    entering premises with search warrant, 194.
    entering refreshment houses, 280.
    entering gaming houses, 48.
    entering betting houses, 53.
    entering licensed premises to enforce Act, 195, 196.
    evidence of, as to using as brothel, 43.
    evidence of, as to prostitutes, 30.
    fee on serving precept and notices, 236, 328.
    gift of liquor to, 44.
    giving private information to justices as to renewals, 91.
    high constable, duty as to precepts, 220.
    may inspect register of licenses, 74.
    obtaining search warrant, 195.
    proof of knowledge that constable on duty, 44.
    prosecuting refreshment house keeper at quarter sessions, 287.
    punishment for assaulting, 194.
    taking charge of one found drunk, 25.
    to visit licensed billiard houses, 163.
    to serve and affix notices of general meeting, 220, 223.
    turning out visitors, 60.
Consumption of liquors on unlicensed premises, 12, 17.
    by drunken man, evidence of sale, 135.
    in refreshment house in closing hours, 64.
    some evidence of sale, 136.
Continuance of license during appeal, 124.
    if forfeited, 192.
Contracts as to sale of premises, 235.
Conviction, proof of previous, 32, 115, 131.
    as to serving child, 17.
    to be entered in register, 73.
    three recorded, cause disqualification, 67, 70.
    consequence of forfeiture for repeated, 67.
    to be entered on copies of license, 101.
    reversed by quarter sessions, 120.
    notice of same, sent to owners, 127, 129.
    several on one day, 130.
    disqualifying premises, 67, 68.

Conviction after five years, effect of, 71.
    recording of, on license, 126.
    punishment of first, 110, 186, 192.
    omission to record, 71.
    defacing record of, 72.
    certiorari, as to, 125, 217.
    for felony disqualifies to sell spirits, 192, 266, 281.
        also to sell beer and cider, 266.
        also to sell wine, 281.
Copy of license in cases of transfer, 86, 270.
        to contain endorsement of convictions, 101.
    of case for High Court, 124.
    of entries in register of licenses, 131.
Costs awarded by confirming authority, 93.
    other than on conviction, 115.
    in case of small fines, 112.
    in case of discharge without punishment, 112.
    on dismissal of charge, 113.
    on appeal to quarter sessions against refusal of license, 243.
    on appeal against conviction, 119.
    on appeal by refreshment house keeper, 286.
    taxing at quarter sessions, 244.
    of justices paid by county council, 244.
County council, some licenses transferred to, 33, 38.
    theatre licenses transferred to, 144, 146.
    allowing costs of justices defending their own acts, 244.
County quarter sessions, appeal on refusal of license, 243.
    definition of, 154.
    division of county for licensing, 212.
    justices issuing precept to hold general meeting, 219.
    grant of new licenses in, 75.
    licensing meetings in, 212.
    licensing committee in, 75.
    liberty of, 152, 213, 224, 247.
    treasurer, costs of licensing appeal paid to, 243.
Court of summary jurisdiction, 117, 153.
Covenants in leases against using as alehouse, 253.
        by tenant to do nothing to affect license, 25.
        to take beer from brewer, 256.
        not to erect house for liquor, 254.
        not to use house for, runs with land, 256.
        as to wine houses, 290.
Criminal information against justices, 216.
        offence, master liable for servant's, 27, 44, 46, 51
Curtilage as part of premises, 100, 195.

Custody of guests' goods in inn, 302, 335.
Customs as to closing hours abolished, 178, 295.
    as to fairs and races, 301.

D.

Dancing licenses, 35, 38.
  See "Music and Dancing."
      in public-house, 38, 41.
      in recreation rooms, 146.
Dealers in spirits, retail license, 139, 291, 343, 348.
    in wine, retail license for, 273.
    in beer, retail license, 299.
    grocer as wine dealer, 3.
    valuation required as to retailing beer, 331.
    no residence required for same, 299.
    in spirits, traveller for, soliciting orders, 4, 311.
Death of licensee, 3, 227.
    executors may continue business for a time, 3.
    of holder of beer license, 227, 266.
    of holder of wine license, 227, 278.
    transfer license, on, 227.
Debtor arrested not to be taken to public-house, 359.
Defacing record of conviction, 72.
Defendant, burden of proof on, 110, 180.
    and wife may be a witness, 109.
Definitions in Alehouse Act, 246.
    in Beerhouse Acts, 257.
    in Licensing Act, 1872, 149.
    in Licensing Act, 1874, 206.
Demand of case for High Court in convictions, 121, 242.
                   on refusal of license, 121.
    license and exemption order, 136.
Deposit on bet, 50.
    by guest in inn of his goods, 302.
Description of offence in summons, 110.
Detaining defendant till return of warrant, 113, 114.
Dinner, public, occasional license for, 66, 301.
Discharge of defendant without punishment, 112.
Dismissal of case, costs, 112, 113.
Discretion of justices as to new licenses, 213, 317; generally, 213.
    on renewal applications, 89, 337, 352.
    on re-hearing a case, 217.
    limited as to some out-door licenses, 318.
    as to evidence of character, 214, 317.
Disorderly person, permitting in licensed house, 29.

Disorderly, person keeping licensed house as, 29, 42, 54 ; liability for single offence as brothel, 43 ; a ground for refusing license, 318.
    conduct in licensed premises, 43 ; in refreshment houses, 284.
    excluding from licensed house, 54.
    refusing to quit refreshment house, 289.
Disqualification of premises, notice of, sent to owner, 69, 94, 127 ; for third conviction, 67, 69 ; notice of, to be served on owner, 127.
    order for, 67, 94.
    in what cases of repeated convictions, 69.
Disqualification of person for third conviction, 69 ; to be entered in register, 73.
    license to disqualified person void, 94.
    for selling without license, 2.
    for forging license, 192, 321.
    for using premises as brothel, 43.
    for repeated convictions, 69.
    in case of, license is void, 94, 237.
    notice of, sent to licensing justices, 127.
    of person, continuing license after, 192.
    of justices, 132.
    of persons to sell beer, 266.
    of persons to keep inns, 237.
    of persons to hold wine licenses, 281.
Disqualified person's license is void, 94, 237.
Distiller, when disqualified as justice, 132.
Distress for penalty, 113.
    issuing and mitigating warrant of, 114.
    apparel and tools not taken, 114.
    for liquor supplied, held a bill of sale, 236.
District, licensing, what is, 151.
Dog, visitor taking into premises, 55.
Domestic use, beer brewed for, 340.
Dominoes, playing at, in licensed houses, 46.
Door of church, notices upon, 220, 316.
    shop, notices on, 316.
Drinking on premises without license, 13.
    contrary to license, 14.
Drunk on highway, 24 ; meaning of public place, 24 ; drunk and riotous, 24.
    taking charge of drunken person, 25.
    drunk in metropolis, 25.
    selling to drunken person, 27.
    risk of serving drunken person, 27.

INDEX. 397

Drunk, what justices may hear charge for, 132.
Drunkards, turning out of houses, 54.
        conviction for refusing to quit, 55 ; refusing to quit refreshment house, 289.
        treated by a sober companion, 136.
        found in refreshment houses, 284, 289.
Drunkenness, permitting, in licensed house, 28.
        conviction for, by one justice, 107, 132.
Duration of license, 227
        of certificate, 329.
Duties on cider, sweets, beer, wine, spirits, 342.

E.

Early closing licenses, 176 ; affixing notice on premises, 177 ;
        remission of duty on, 177.
        extended to United Kingdom, 344.
        excise duties on, 342.
Eating-house keeper entitled to refreshment house license, 276.
        also to alehouse license, 214.
Elections not to be held in inns, 355.
Enclosed place near unlicensed premises, 16.
Endorsement of renewal of license, 101 ; of license at petty sessions, 269.
        of conviction on license, 126, 186.
        ·on each copy of license, 101.
Enlarging premises, 7, 158.
Entertainment, places of public, internal communication, 20, 192.
        harbouring thieves in, 31.
        public, require license for liquor, 146.
        closing of, on Sundays, 172.
Entry on premises by constable, 194 ; if object specific, 195.
        on gaming houses, 48.
        on betting houses, 51, 53.
        on billiard premises, 163.
        on refreshment houses, 280.
        of premises with excise by beerseller, 267 ; same by wine seller, 281.
Equally divided, effect of justices being, 215, 225.
Evasion of law as to unlicensed premises, 15, 16.
Evidence of sale of liquor, 135.
        of consumption of liquor, 14, 135.
        of endorsements and register, 131.
        defendant and wife may give, 109.
        Licensing Evidence Act, 358.

Evidence of conviction after five years not admissible, 71.
  of previous convictions, 32, 115.
Exceptions in summons for offence, burden of proving, 110.
Exchange of liquors, 135.
Excise license void when justices' license void, 136.
  penalty not under Licensing Acts, 9, 10.
  entry of premises with, 267, 281.
  selling without license of, 10.
  appeal to quarter sessions against, 10.
  commissioners altering forms, 101 ; form of, 368.
  officer may sue for any penalty, 4, 5, 108.
  officer demanding license or exemption order, 136
  closing of premises under license, 169, 178.
  several licenses included in one, 201.
  justices' license must precede, 237, 313.
  no *certiorari* to quash excise license, 260.
  death of license holder, 11, 227.
  officer entering premises, 267, 282.
  scale of duties for license, 342.
  prosecutions by, 4.
  inspecting register, 74.
  temporary license during appeal, 124.
Excisable liquor in billiard license, 161.
  in refreshment houses, 281.
Excluding drunkards, 54, 59.
Excursionists, supplying liquors to, 183.
Executor of licensee, how to proceed, 3, 227, 266, 278.
Exemption order for houses near markets, &c., 61.
  holder to produce, 136.
  for in-door beerhouses, 173.
  consent by wrong justice, 296.
  for refreshment houses, 66, 305.
Expelling drunkards, 54.
Expiration of license, 227, 329.
  applying for transfer before, 230.
Extent of licensed premises, 100, 127, 197, 215.
Extracts from register, 131.

F.

Fairs and races, special exemption order for, 67.
  occasional license for, 197, 305.
  sale of liquor at, 305.
False representation as to being traveller, 60, 171.

Fast day, occasional licenses on, 295.
Fee on inspection of register of licenses, 15.
    on grant of ale and beer license, 236.
    on registration of license, 74.
    on renewal of license, 237, 328.
    on renewal of certificate, 328.
    on certificates for beer and wine, 236, 328.
    on transfer of license or certificate, 236, 329.
    on indorsing copy of lost or withheld license, 271.
    of constable as to licenses, 236, 328.
Felony, conviction for, license is void, 192, 266, 281, 332.
    first conviction for, 192.
Festival, occasional exemption order for, 67.
Final order on provisional license, 200.
Fire-arms, drunken person having, 25.
Fire, premises consumed by, 228.
First conviction, 110, 186, 192.
Five years from date of conviction, 71.
Fixtures of licensed houses, 236.
Flower garden of premises in valuation, 100.
Forfeiture of license, effect of, 6, 136, 192.
    continuing license after, 192.
    of liquor, notice before, 8, 21.
    notice of, to justices' clerk, 8, 128.
    of illicit stores, 21.
    for harbouring thieves, 31.
    for seditious meetings in licensed houses, 32.
    for using as brothel, 43.
    temporary license on appeal against, 124.
    notice of, sent to owner, 127.
    for repeated convictions, 67.
    not caused by conviction of five years past, 71.
    to be entered in register, 73.
    how to be disposed of, 108.
    of excise licenses as well as justices, 136.
    of liquor found on unlicensed premises, 21, 195.
Forging justices' signature, 6.
    certificate, conviction for, 321.
    first conviction for, 192.
Forms of licenses and certificates issued by authority, 101, 368.
    of renewal, 369.
    of billiard license, 161.
    of excise license, 363, 365.
    of occasional license, 366.
    of renewal may be endorsed, 101.
    of refreshment house license, 364.

Found drunk, meaning of, 25.
    penalty for, 26.
    in public place meaning of, 25.
    on premises, in closing hours, 60.
    what justices may hear charge, 132.
    on unlicensed premises, 60, 196.
Four convictions against premises, 67.
Fraud in obtaining license, 249.
Frequenting of prostitutes, 30, 284, 289.
    of thieves, 31, 284.
    of disorderly persons endangering license, 54
Friends of publicans playing games, 47.
    entertained by license holder, 206.
    who may be deemed, 58, 135.
    of lodger entertained, 178, 206.

G.

Game-dealer, innkeeper not to be, 300.
Games, list of unlawful, 47.
    wagers on, 48, 53.
Gaming Houses Act, 48.
    warrant to search, 48.
    arrest for keeping, 48.
Gaming, permitting in licensed houses, 46.
    unlawful gaming house, 47.
Garden valued as part of premises, 100.
General annual licensing meeting, discretion of, 213.
    license not granted at, void, 6, 227.
    removal license to be applied for at, 105.
    adjournment of, 221.
    attendance at, if applicant sick, 87 226.
    giving notices to license holders of, 219, 223.
Gift of liquor to constable on duty, 44.
    to other persons, 135, 179.
Glass of beer not a standard measure, 18.
    measures for liquors, 19.
Good Friday, closing premises on, 170.
    varying closing hours, 173.
    of billiard tables on, 163.
    closing in Wales, 350.
Goods, other than wine, what, 274.
    distress on, 113, 114.
Goodwill of licensed house, 235.

INDEX. 401

Grant of license. *See* " License."
    provisional, 199.
Greenwich time adopted, 172.
Grocer, when not requiring justices' license, 3, 148, 170.
    when may open in closing hours, 59, 148.
    as a wine merchant exempt, 148.
    sale of retail spirits, 148.
    closing of premises, 170, 180.
Grounds of opposition to renewal, 87, 318.
    of refusing some licenses, 319.
Guest in inn, his person and goods, 302.
    locking his bedroom door, 304.
    his goods, when may be sold, 335.

H.

Hard labour not imposed for non-payment, 111, 114.
Harbouring constables, penalty for, 44.
    prostitutes, penalty for, 30, 43.
    thieves, penalty for, 31; appeal against conviction for, 32.
Hawking spirits, penalty, 8, 348.
High constable, precept to, as to licensing meetings, 221.
    abolition of office of, 220, 221.
    any constable may do duty of, 221.
Highway, drinking on, 13, 16.
    house taken for improvement of, 228, 235.
Hired premises, drinking on, 13, 16.
Holder producing license, 136.
Horse, drunken person in charge of, 24.
    of guest received by innkeeper, 302.
    when guest's, may be sold, 335.
Hotel, license as to, 335.
Hours of closing licensed houses, 169, 173, 178.
    music and dancing places, 36, 39.
    under exemption order, 61.
    under occasional license, 301.

I.

Illicit storing of liquor, 21.
Imperial measure, sale of liquor by, 18.
Imprisonment for selling without license, 2, 8, 9.

2 D

Imprisonment, when alternative punishment, 9.
          in default of distress, 8, 111, 114.
          if penalty not paid, scale of, 111.
Improvement Act district, definition of, 153.
Inhabited house duty on inns, 305.
Inadvertence, justices postponing for, 331.
Incapable of keeping inn, &c., transfer, 192, 228.
Indecency on licensed premises, 43.
Indictment and summary conviction on same facts, 131.
Injury to guest in inn, 302.
In-door license, if for six days, 102.
          for beer since 1869, when refused, 318.
Infant as license holder, 11.
     induced to bet, 53.
Information, criminal, against justices, 216.
Inland Revenue Acts:—
          24 & 25 Vict. c. 21, 291.
          24 & 25 Vict. c. 91, 292.
          25 & 26 Vict. c. 22, 295.
          25 & 26 Vict. c. 38, 297.
          26 & 27 Vict. c. 33, 299.
          27 & 28 Vict. c. 18, 305.
          30 & 31 Vict. c. 90, 311.
          43 & 44 Vict. c. 20, 340.
Inland Revenue officer may inspect register, 74.
          prosecutions by, 4.
Inmate on premises in closing hours, 59.
Inscription on music and dancing places, 35, 38.
          on licensed premises, 21.
          on six-day houses, 102.
          on billiard premises, 162.
          on refreshment-houses, 185, 307.
          on early closing houses, 176.
          on night houses, 185.
          on exemption houses, 66.
Inn, when requiring license, 102; right of traveller to be received, 103; traveller's right to liquors, 103.
Innkeeper's lien, 303.
          liability as to guest's goods, 303, 304.
          duties and taxes on, 305.
          tax on servant, 304.
          inhabited house duty, 305.
          not licensed as game dealer, 305.
          may sell guest's goods after notice, 335.
          relief as to duty for spirits, 343.
Inspection of register of licenses and fee, 74.

INDEX. 403

Inspector of measures, seizure by, 18, 19.
    procuring samples of liquor, 191, 192.
Instalments of penalty allowed to be paid, 111.
Insurance of licensed premises by tenant, 100.
Intent to evade license, 15.
Internal communication with unlicensed places prohibited,'20.
    first conviction for, 192.
Intoxicating liquor, meaning of, 150.
    Liquor Licensing Acts, meaning of, 149.
Ireland, what sections of Act apply to, 165.
Island uninhabited, license for sale in, 213.

J.

Joint committee for licensing in boroughs, 80.
    deficiency of justices, 199.
    to make rules as to confirmation, 202.
Jurisdiction, if none, *certiorari* granted, 217.
    over piers, rivers, 134.
Jury, defendant may demand, in certain cases, 113.
Justices varying hours of Sunday closing, 173.
    who may endorse license at petty sessions, 270.
    disqualification of and penalty, 132, 224.
    shareholder in hotel company, 132.
    as owner of licensed house, 132.
    one may convict of drunkenness, 107, 132.
    jurisdiction of, over piers and rivers, 134.
    licensing, who are, 151.
    at general annual licensing meeting, 212.
    cinque ports, 219, 225.
    at petty sessions transferring licenses, 269.
    at special sessions for transfer, 228.
    in liberties of counties, 213, 224, 246.
    action against for penalty, 132.
    origin of their jurisdiction, as to licenses, 212.
    license by, how far necessary, 212, 213.
    discretion of, as to licenses, 212, 213, 318.
    altering name of owner in register, 74, 205.
    license valid, though borough justices not qualified, 81.
    of county not to interfere in borough licenses, 81.
    hearing application for renewal of license, 87.
    starting objections to renewal, 91.
    granting exemption order, 61.
    two generally to hear informations, 107.

2 D 2

Justices imposing small fine, 112.
    discharging in trifling cases, 112.
    awarding costs, 113.
    issuing warrant of distress and commitment, 113.
    detaining defendant till warrant returned, 114.
    mitigating and postponing warrant, 114.
    demand of case for High Court, in convictions, 122.
    certiorari in case of conviction by, 125.
    demand by, of license and exemption order, 136.
    discretion in recording licenses, 186.
    consent to occasional license for fairs and races, 197, 305.
    form of consent, 365.
    borough, joint committee for, 80.
    granting provisional license, 199.
    granting one license for several liquors, 201.
    acting corruptly as to license, 216.
    re-hearing application under a *mandamus*, 217.
    majority of, to sign licenses, 226, 327.
    costs against, at quarter sessions, 243.
    reimbursing if refusal of license reversed, 244.
    costs of, by county council, 244.
    licensing theatres, 145.
    as to *quantum* of evidence, 214, 317.
    discretion at transfer sessions, 229.
    if not voting, 226.
    if equally divided, 215, 226, 241.
    bound to state grounds when, 318.
    to grant exemption to refreshment houses, 308.
    may use stamp or seal to licenses, 327.
    may postpone applications, 331.
    not to meet in licensed houses, 355.

K.

Keeping a brothel in licensed premises, 42.
    a licensed house, liability for servants, 27, 43, 46.
    gaming house on premises, 48.
    betting house on premises, 49.
    billiard table, 162.
    open during closing hours, 169, 178.
    license only granted to those about to keep inns, 214.
    an inn by a manager, 215.
Knowingly committing offences, 27, 43.
Knowledge of servant in licensed house, 27.

L.

Label on bottles of liquor, 191, 192.
Legal proceedings under Licensing Act, 107.
Letting room to unlicensed person, 7, 12.
Liberties of counties, licensing meeting, 224, 247.
    definition of, 152, 247.
License, definition of, 150.
    origin of justices' jurisdiction, 213.
    how far necessary, 213, 318.
    sale without, 2, 3.
    sale under when void, 6.
    when required by club, 5.
    to a dead man, 6.
    by justices in private, 6.
    under repealed enactment, 6.
    letting room to sell without, 7, 12.
    when premises enlarged, 7, 158.
    how far property, 11.
    drinking on premises contrary to, 12, 15.
    for music and dancing, 34, 38, 41.
    for metropolitan racecourses, 33, 37.
    recording convictions on, 68, 72, 186.
    omission to record on, 72.
    not void for disqualified borough justices, 81.
    if valid when no statutory notice given, 84.
    wilfully withheld or lost, 85, 271.
    to disqualified person or premises void, 6, 94.
    rooms required in new in-door premises, 96.
    regulations as to forms of, 101.
    removal of, to another part, 105.
    on a charge of offence, defendant must prove exceptions, &c., 110.
    when forfeited, notice to licensing justices, 127.
    when forfeited, forfeits excise also, 136.
    allowing liquor to travellers, 180.
    female holder, marrying, 231.
    covenant to do no act affecting, 253, 255.
    occasional, when granted, 197, 295, 305.
    offences on premises, with occasional, 198.
    for refreshment houses, 275, 307.
    forfeiture of, on repeated convictions, 67.
    register of, 73.
    defacing record of conviction on, 72.
    new, definition of, 150, 208.

License grant of new, in counties, 75 ; in boroughs, 78.
    notices before new, 83, 314.
    transfer of, notices before, 83, 84.
        in what cases, 228.
    renewal of, notice of objection to, 87, 91.
    confirmation of new county licenses, in-door, 75 ; of new in-door borough licenses, 78.
    valuation qualification of premises for new in-door, 95.
    for beer in-door before 1872, 99, 263.
    for new beer in-door, after 1872, 95.
    certiorari to quash, 217.
    one may include several, 201.
    in quarter sessions boroughs, 207, 218.
    in Cinque Ports, 219, 225.
    signature of, by majority of justices, 226.
    provisional, 199.
    wine in refreshment house, 276, 316.
    death of holder of excise wine license, 278.
    register of wine licenses, 279.
    form of licenses, in future, 101, 368.
    may be stamped or sealed, 327.
    partners holding beer, 250.
    to state owner's name, 73.
    six-day, application for, 102.
    deduction of duty by excise, 103, 342.
    notice of, to be affixed on six-day house, 103.
    turning six-day into seven-day, 104.
    early closing, 176, 342.
    to have a notice affixed, 177.
    remission of duty, 177.
    renewal of, no notice for, 82, 316.
    temporary, during appeal, 124.
    production of, by holder, 61, 66, 126, 137.
    retail spirit, by dealer, 139, 291.
    retail wine, by dealer, 148, 273.
    retail beer, by dealer, 299.
    exemptions from necessity of, 143.
    for billiards, 161.
    duration of alehouse, 227 ; of beerhouse and wine, 329.
    to sell liquor in boats or vessels, 143, 272, 344.
    to sell at theatres, 146.
    refreshment houses, 276, 316.
    occasional, for refreshment house, 308.
  See also "Certificate ;" "Wine and Beerhouse Acts."
Licensed persons, what, 151.
        liability for servant or manager, 27, 43.

Licensed person, liability as to travellers, 182.
    premises, definition of, 151.
Licensing Act of 1828, general effect, 213.
    defining populous place, 209.
Licensing committee, in counties, 75 ; in boroughs, 79.
    joint, in boroughs, 80, 202.
Licensing justices, definition of, 151, 173 ; stipendiary magistrates may be, 82.
    justices to fix days for advertisement notices, 83.
    to receive notice of forfeiture and disqualification, 127.
    varying closing hours, 173.
    justices may order names to be affixed, 21.
    district, exemption order, 61.
    occasional license in, 197, 295, 306.
    justices disqualified in, 132.
    district, definition of, 151.
    officer, definition of, 151.
Lien of innkeeper, when goods may be sold, 335.
Limited discretion of justices on renewals, 89, 92.
    as to some licenses, 318.
Liqueurs, retail license for, 140.
Liquor, intoxicating, meaning of, 150.
    consumption of, evidence of sale, 135.
    adulteration of, 188.
    search warrant for, 195.
    given to private friends, 47, 135, 206.
Loaded firearms, drunken person having, 24.
Local authority for exempting licensed houses, 61.
    may withdraw exemption order, 62.
    may grant occasional exemption orders, 62.
    for occasional license to beer and refreshment houses, 305, 308.
    government district, definition, 153.
    customs as to fairs and races, 308.
    as to closing hours, 178, 308.
Lodger, sale of liquors to, 178, 206.
    falsely pretending to be, 59.
    found on closed premises, 60.
    playing billiards, 162.
    in six-day licensed premises, 102, 182.
    in closing hours exempted, 181.
    as to gaming after closing, 59, 181.
    entertaining his friends, 178, 205.
London, local authority for exemption order, 62.
    for occasional exemption order, 62.

London, city of, time for obtaining licenses, 218.
Lost licenses, copy of, 86, 271.
        fee on endorsing copy, 271.

M.

Made wines. *See* "Sweets."
Majority of justices to sign licenses, 226.
Malt, maker of, when disqualified, 132.
Manager, license holder liable for, 27, 46.
    of Sunday public entertainments, 172.
    of betting house, 51.
    of gaming house, 48.
    of hotel and liabilities, 215, 302.
Mandamus to licensing justices, when granted, 215.
    to re-hear renewal application, 91, 215.
    return to, treated as defence, 216.
    discretion on a re-hearing, 215.
    for not stating grounds of refusal, 318.
Market, licensed houses near, 63.
    refreshment houses near, 63, 302.
Marriage of female licensee, 231.
Master responsible for criminal acts of servants, 27, 46.
Mayor, Lord, approving exemption order, 62.
        occasional license to refreshment house, 308.
Measure, sale of liquors by, 18.
Meeting-place of prostitutes, 30.
    of thieves, 31.
Merchant, wine, retail, 148.
Metheglin. *See* "Sweets."
Methylated spirits, no justices' license for, 147.
    duty on, 347.
Metropolitan district, who may grant exemption order, 63.
    valuation for new in-door licenses, 96.
    area of, where defined, 211.
    not within High Constable Abolition Act, 220.
    closing houses in, 169.
    petty sessions for transfer of licenses in, 270.
    police magistrates, when may be licensing justices, 82, 270.
    area, qualification of premises in, 96, 211.
    music licenses, 35, 37.

Midnight closing of premises, 169.
     of night-houses, 61, 185, 308.
Miners, paying wages in public-houses, 354.
Mistake of power in granting license, 6.
Mitigation of punishment, 110, 114.
  of penalties, 185.
Mixing one beer with another, 190.
Mortgagee of licensed premises, notice to, 73, 204.
     appeal by, 240.
Municipal Corporations Act, 138, 218, 221. *See* " Borough."
Municipal elections not to be in inns, 356.
Music and dancing license, 33, 36, 39, 41.
     license to sell liquors in, 35.
     no license for, in recreation room, 35, 146.
     does not include stage plays, 41, 145.
     as part of public entertainment on Sunday, 172.

N.

Name on licensed premises, 21.
 of holder and owner to be in register, 73.
 of those found on unlicensed premises, 196.
 penalty for giving false, 196.
 demand of, by constable, if found on licensed premises, 59.
 in register of licenses, 73, 205.
Neglecting to renew a license, remedy, 228.
Neighbourhood of markets, exemption order, 61.
New license. *See also* " License."
  definition of, 150, 208.
  notice before, 83, 315.
  distinguished from renewal, 155.
  when application must be made, 213.
  when premises have been altered, 158.
  no appeal against refusal, 240.
Newspaper, advertisement of notices, 83.
New Year's Eve, special exemption order for, 67.
Night, opening licensed houses during, 170, 178.
  closing of refreshment houses, 185.
  license to accommodate trades, 61.
Night-houses Act, 27 & 28 Vict. c. 64, 307.
     28 & 29 Vict. c. 77, 309.
Nine-pins, playing at, in licensed house, 46.
Notice, computation of time for applying for licenses, 315.

Notice, affixed on house with the exemption order, 66.
 of six-day license to be affixed, 102.
 of billiard license, 163.
 of disqualification of premises served on owner, 70.
    sent to licensing justices, 126.
 of forfeiture sent to licensing justices, 126.
 of conviction to person interested, 126, 127.
 to parties as to brewster sessions adjourned, 219.
 of opposition to renewal, 87, 202.
 of time of adjournment, 221.
 of general annual meeting, 219, 229.
 for a removal license same as for new, 105.
 board at church door, 219, 315.
 before new license to overseer and superintendent of police, 315.
 advertisement of new, 83.
 no notice required before renewal, 88, 316.
 proof of notice of opposition, 89.
 service of notices may be by post, 141.
 of innkeeper's liability for goods, 302.
 before selling guest's goods, 335.
 before transfer of licenses, 83.
 to owner before disqualification of premises, 69, 127.
 to mortgagee of premises, 205.
 before license to sell liquor and spirits by retail, 83.
 before retail license by dealers, 140.
 service of, in conviction appeals, by post, 119.
 of appeal to quarter sessions, 119, 239.
Notoriously bad characters in licensed house, 30, 31.

O.

Oath, evidence on, in renewal applications, 88.
Objections to renewals, notice of, 88, 203.
    adjourning to hear, 91.
  notice of, to removals, 106.
Obliterating record of conviction on license, 72.
Occasion, special, as to sale of liquor, 66.
    as to closing premises, 64, 65.
Occasional licenses, definition of, 66, 197, 295, 305.
    granted to publicans, 66, 295, 305; duty on same, 301.
    granted to refreshment houses and beer houses, 305.

Occasional licenses, one justice to consent to, 301.
    for refreshment house not selling liquor, 66, 308.
    local authority to grant, 306.
    at fairs and races, 66, 305.
    time for closing under, 198, 306.
    offences on premises with, 198.
Occupier of unlicensed premises, 15.
    agreement with unlicensed person, 12.
    to give notice of owner's name, 73.
Offence, description of, 110.
    two, on same facts, 131.
    disqualified justice trying, 132.
    notice of, to owner, 69, 126, 127.
    more than one, on one day, 130.
Office for betting, keeping, 50.
Officer, licensing, 151.
Off-license, drinking on premises, 12, 16.
    ordering liquor from premises, 16.
    no confirmation required, 202.
    limited discretion of justices, 317.
Omission to record convictions on license, 72.
Open court, justices stating objections in, 91.
Opening house in prohibited hours, 178. *See* "Closing."
Opposition to renewal license, notice of, 90.
    burden of proof of, 91.
    what are competent grounds of, 90.
Order disqualifying premises, 69, 94, 127.
    sanctioning removal, 105.
    directing conviction to be recorded, 186.
    of justices, varying hours of Sunday closing, 173.
    final, after provisional license, 199.
    declaring a populous place, 209.
    exemption from closing hours, 61.
    occasional exemption order, 305.
Ordering liquor and calling at premises, 179.
Orders, traveller soliciting, for spirits or wine, 4, 311.
Outhouse of licensed house is part of, 195.
Owner, definition of, 151, 205.
    to be named in register, 73.
    application to vary name in register, 73.
    may inspect register of licenses, 74.
    may demand to be registered, 205.
    protection of, against recorded convictions, 128.
    serving notice of disqualification on, 70, 129.

Owner to receive notice of removal of license, 106.
    to get notice of some convictions, 128.
    when he may appeal to quarter sessions, 240.
    cannot appeal against tenant's conviction, 117, 205.

P.

Packet boats, sale of liquors, 143, 272, 344.
    duties on, 344.
Parish, definition, for valuation qualification, 264, 333.
Parliamentary elections not to be in inns, 355.
Partners in beer license, 250.
Penalty, enforcement of, generally, 8.
    recovered under Summary Jurisdiction Acts, 109.
    not to be excise, as to application, 108.
    against disqualified justice, 133.
    imprisonment proportioned to, 111 ; payment of, by instalments, 111 ; recovery of, 115.
    Crown may remit, 137 ; excise not affected by Acts, 144.
    moiety of, to police superannuation fund, 137.
    mitigation of, 114, 185.
    payment of, in boroughs having quarter sessions, 138.
        in boroughs without quarter sessions, 137.
Permitting drunkenness, penalty, 26.
    brothel on premises, 42.
Personal service of notice of appeal against convictions on justices, 117.
    on justices in licensing appeals, 241.
    on owners of premises, 141.
Petty sessional division of county, 152, 212, 247.
Petty sessions, application for temporary license, 269.
    disqualified justices at, 272.
Picture, as signboard of inn, 236.
Piers, jurisdiction over, 134.
Place, public, meaning of, 24 ; penalty for found drunk, 25.
    populous, what, 209.
Plans for provisional licenses, 200.
Playing for money in licensed houses, 46.
    at billiards, 163.
Pleading under a writ of *mandamus*, 216.
Pleasure grounds as part of valuation of premises, 100.
Pledges given for liquor consumed, 297.
Police. *See* " Constable."
    authority defined, 62.

Police, commissioner of, granting exemption order, 61.
  superintendent to receive notice of new license, 315.
  superintendent, notice of transfer served on, 83.
  supervision, want of, as objection to license, 214.
  superannuation fund, part penalties applied to, 137.
Polls not to be taken in licensed houses, 355.
Poor rate for licensed premises not needed, 100.
  valuation, how far applicable, 99.
Population, regulating value for new in-door license, 95 ; for beer licenses, 264, 333.
  of populous place, 209 ; for (on) wine license, 276.
  of parish or place, 97, 264, 333.
  to be according to last census, 137.
Populous place, definition and order, 209.
Possession of liquor in unlicensed place, 3, 21, 195.
  of illicit stores, 21.
Post, service of notices as to appeals against conviction by, 119 ; on case stated for High Court, 123 ; of notices as to licenses, 141 ; notice by post to owner, 142.
Postponing applications by justices, 331.
Precautions as to travellers, 181.
Precept before general annual licensing meeting, 220 ; to justices' clerk, in boroughs, 220.
Premises, what are licensed, 151.
  varying size of, 158.
  enlarging when new license needed, 158.
  where liquor is sold, 14.
  drinking on highway adjoining, 15, 16.
  closing in case of riot, 56.
  recording convictions against, 69.
  qualification for new in-door licenses, 96.
  annual value for new in-door, 97.
  annual value for existing beerhouses, 97, 264.
  liberty to increase valuation, 98.
  include out-houses, 195.
  right of constable to enter, 194.
  sale in unlicensed, 3.
  disqualification for license, 69, 94.
  license for disqualified, void, 94.
  unlicensed, communicating with, 20.
  name on licensed, 21.
  permitting drunkenness, 26.
  drunken person on, 27.
  drunkards expelled from, 54.
  persons drinking on, during prohibited hours, 57.
  garden and curtilage included in valuation, 97, 158.

Premises, repairs and insurance of, by tenant, 96.
    occupied exclusively for liquor, 148.
    for billiard tables, 161.
    closing hours for all, 169, 178.
        of grocers, 170.
        of night houses, 185.
    early closing, 176.
    closing of places with occasional licenses, 198.
    provisional licenses for, 199.
    contract for sale of licensed, 235.
Prevention of Crimes Act, 31.
Previous conviction, how proved, 32, 115.
Private, justices granting licenses in, 6.
    justices hearing opponent of renewal in, 89.
    friends of license holder entertained, 135, 206.
Privity to consumption on unlicensed premises, 14, 16.
Production of license by holder to justices, 126, 136; penalty for not, 136.
Profit, drinking for, on unlicensed premises, 16.
Prohibited hours, selling in, 168, 178.
    varying on Sunday, 173.
Prohibition, writ of, to justices, 218.
Proof of consumption, 135.
    of sale, 5, 10, 135.
    of previous conviction, 8, 32, 115.
    of grounds of opposition to renewals, 90.
    of service of notices, &c., 116, 141, 241.
Prostitutes, harbouring, in licensed houses, 28; in refreshment houses, 284, 289.
    turning out, 54.
Provisional grant of license, 199.
    removal, 199, 201.
Public Entertainment Act, 36.
    places of, internal communication with, 20; hours for opening, 36, 39.
    regular license to sell liquors, 36; closing of, on Sunday, 172.
    See " License."
Public fast, billiard tables on, 163.
    occasional license on, 296, 301, 305.
Public-houses, paying wages in, 353.
Public improvement, licensed house pulled down for, 228, 235.
Public market, exemption order near, 61, 305.
Public place, drunk in a, 24; meaning of public place, 24.
Public resort, meaning of place of, 20, 24.

INDEX. 415

Publican. *See* " License."
    license, how granted, 213.
        eating-house keeper, entitled to, 214.
    occasional licenses, 197, 295, 305.
    form of excise license, 365.
    form of justices' license, 368, 371.
    no wages to be paid in house of, 353.
Publication of census as to populous place, 209.
    notices for licenses, 83, 314.
Punishment, discharge without, 112.
    two kinds for same facts, 132.
    twice for same offence, 132.
Purchasing for drunken person, 14, 27.
    liquors adulterated, 4, 190, 311.
    licensed premises, 235.

Q.

Qualification of premises for new licenses, 95, 100, 263.
    of present beerhouses, &c., 100, 263.
    of justices, 132.
Quarrelsome conduct in licensed house, 27.
    excluding such persons, 54.
Quarter sessions includes general sessions, 154.
    appeal to, in excise convictions, 8, 10.
        in betting-house convictions, 54.
        in gaming-house convictions, 48.
        in conviction for harbouring thieves, 32.
        in conviction of billiard licensee, 164.
    to appoint licensing committee in counties, 76.
    to make regulations for county licensing committee, 76.
    mandamus to appoint committee, 77.
    object of confirmation, 77.
    discretion of, limited in some cases, 320.
    may grant license, if reverse judgment, 243.
    of county to hear appeals against refusals, 241.
    no appeal for refusing new grant, 166, 241.
    appeal against convictions generally, 116.
    adjournment of appeal against refusal of license, 241.
    notice of appeal against refusal of license, 241.
    recognizance on licensing appeal, 239.
    power to adjourn licensing appeal, 241.
    temporary license during, 124.

Quarter sessions, giving notice of appeal against conviction, 119.
    recognizance on such appeal, 119.
    power to adjourn appeal against conviction, 118.
    power to state case for High Court, 121.
    appeals in refreshment-house cases at, 285.
    constable's costs allowed, when, 287.
Quay, jurisdiction of justices over, 134.
Quit, drunkards, &c., ordered to, 54.
    licensed tenants refusing to, 128, 156.
Quorum of county licensing committee, 76.
    of borough licensing committee, 79.

R.

Race, paying money on event of, 51.
Racecourse licenses, 37.
Races. *See* "Fairs."
Railway carriage, when deemed a public place, 24.
Railway station, a place of public resort, 20, 24.
Railway stations, no valuation qualification for, needed, 95.
    sale of liquor at, 182.
    refreshment-room at station, 95, 182, 309.
    exemption from night closing, 182, 309.
Ratepayer may inspect register of licenses, 73.
Rates and taxes of licensed persons, 100, 304.
Rating qualification for licenses not needed, 100.
Recognizance on appeal to quarter sessions, 118, 240.
    on case for High Court, 123.
Recorder of borough not to hear licensing appeal, 241.
Recording convictions and effect of third, 67, 186.
    of persons since 1872, 73.
    second, to count against premises, 69.
    to be entered in register, 73.
    discretionary in justices, 186.
    direction as to, 186.
    omission to record, 72.
    defacing, 72.
Recovery of penalty, 107, 185.
Recreation room, dancing license for, 34.
    when no license required for stage plays, 146.
Refreshment of prostitutes, permitting, 30.
    bar in hotel, 286.
Refreshment Houses Act, 23 Vict. c. 27, 273.
    form of license, 364.
    what is such house, 275.

Refreshment houses, value required for wine on-license, 99, 276.
    when license not required, 275.
    duty on, 274, 292.
    license for wine includes sweets, 341.
    obtaining exemption order, 61.
    guest consuming liquor in, 64.
    obtaining occasional exemption order, 66.
    penalty for offences in, 284.
    appeal against conviction, 285.
    harbouring thieves and drunkards in, 284, 289.
    constable prosecuting at quarter sessions, 287.
    not selling liquors, occasional license, 66, 308.
    local authority to grant occasional license, 308, 309.
    at railway station, without liquor, 309.
    occasional license for markets, 304.
    not selling liquor, closing of, 65, 398.
    closing by night, 185.
    occasional license for, 66.
    selling wine, closing of, 169.
    condition of closing at ten, 65, 275.
    who entitled to license, 277.
    who bound to take license, 275.
    selling by retail in, 274.
    confectioners selling wine, 276.
    valuation qualification for, 276.
    keeping without license, 277.
    duration of licenses, 328.
    death of licensee, 3, 278.
    list of licenses, 279.
    transfer of licenses, 227, 328.
Refusal of new license not appealable, 167, 204.
    of renewal license, 87.
    of transfer, 228.
Refusing to quit, drunken persons, 54.
    same in refreshment houses, 289.
Register of licenses, 73 ; inspection of, 74 ; retaining licenses for, 126 ; entries in, 74, 131 ; evidence of, 131 ; conviction for bribery to be entered in, 357.
Registered letter as service, 83, 105, 141.
Regulations as to procedure for confirming, 78, 93, 202.
    as to forms of licenses, 101, 368.
Re-hearing application for renewal license, 91.
    at adjournment of general meeting, 222.

2 E

418 INDEX.

Re-hearing application after *mandamus*, 216.
Remission of duty on early-closing and six-day licenses, 178.
Removal of license same as new license, 105.
    notice to owner, 106.
    of licensee, transferring of license, 228.
    of provisional license, 199, 201.
Renewal of licenses, definition of, 150.
    what is implied, 155.
    distinguished from new license, 155, 157.
    to a person not previously licensed, 156.
    when premises have been altered, 158.
    and certificates, no notice before, 82, 316.
    may be by endorsement, 101, 327.
    fee for certificates, 328.
    in name of dead person, 6.
    notice of objection to, 87.
    attendance of applicant when required, 88.
    what justices grant renewals, 89.
    what are grounds of opposition to, 90.
    justices starting objection to renewal, 91.
    as to some licenses discretion limited, 92, 318.
    appeal against refusal to renew, 91, 93, 166, 238.
    for wine and beer, 323.
    fees for, 237, 328.
Rent as valuation qualification of premises, 99, 100.
    now replaced by annual value, 100.
    for on-wine license, 276.
Repairs of licensed premises by tenant, 100.
Repeal of statutes, 160, 166, 210, 320.
Repeated convictions, 67.
Reputed prostitutes, harbouring, 30.
    thieves, harbouring, 31.
Resident occupier of beerhouse, 263.
    beer dealer's retail licensee need not be, 299.
Resort, place of public, internal communication, 20.
    what is, 20.
    habitual, for prostitutes, 30.
    habitual, for thieves, 31.
Restaurant, part of a hotel, 303, 343.
Retail, selling by, what is, 8, 159.
    as to different liquors, 8, 159.
    selling beer by, 262.
    valuation of premises for beer, 263.
    spirit license by dealer, 139, 148, 291, 297, 346.

Retail beer by dealer, 299.
    liqueurs and spirits license, 130.
    wine license, by dealer, 273.
Return by justices to *mandamus*, 216.
Revenue. *See* "Excise."
Riot, closing hours during, 56.
Riotous and disorderly persons drunk, 26.
    conduct in licensed persons, 23.
Rivers, jurisdiction over, 134.
Rooms required in new in-door licensed premises, 96.
    committee, at elections not to be in inn, 355, 356.

S.

Saint Albans, saving as to privileges, 143, 325.
Sale of Food Act, 186.
    procedure under, 188.
Sale, without license, 2, 3.
    in clubs, 5.
    by retail, what, 8.
    as to affixing name on premises, 21.
    to drunken persons, 27.
    in refreshment houses, 64, 65, 275, 284.
    money not necessary to prove, 135.
    distinguished from keeping open, 179.
    includes barter and exchange, 4, 135.
    by standard measure, 18, 19.
    of spirits to children, 17, 359.
    on Sundays and in prohibited hours, 170.
    by retail, what, definition, 8, 151.
    of liquor at railway stations, 95, 182, 309.
    in packet boats, 143, 272, 344.
    to travellers and lodgers, 180, 350.
    evidence of, 136.
    consumption is *primâ facie* evidence of, 136.
    of spruce or black beer, 144.
    of liquor at theatres, 146, 344.
    on special occasions, 66, 198, 295, 305.
    in canteens, 143, 147.
    at fairs and races, 66, 305.
    suing for price of liquors, 297.
    of licensed house, contracts as to, 235.
Saturday night, closing on, 169.
Saving of indictments, &c., under other Acts, 131.
Schedule of statutes as to repeal, 160, 166, 210, 326.
Scores for spirits, action for, 297.

Scotland, Licensing Acts do not extend to, 1.
Search warrant for liquors, 195.
    for betting houses, 53.
    for gaming houses, 48.
  of register, 73.
Sea shore, jurisdiction over, 134.
Second offence, how counted, 8.
Secretary of State, definition of, 154.
    licensing recreation rooms, 34, 146.
    approving exemption order, 62.
    issuing forms of licenses, 101.
    licensing canteen, 147.
Security, giving, for liquor consumed, 297.
    for non-payment of penalty, 111.
Seditious meetings in licensed premises, 32.
Seizing liquor found in unlicensed places, 195.
Servant, master's liability for, 27.
  on premises during closing hours, 57.
  consumption by, on premises, 135.
Service of notices of appeal against convictions by post, 119.
  of notice of case stated, 123.
  of notice of appeal as to license, 240.
  of notice to oppose licenses, 85, 141, 316.
Seven-day license contrasted with six-day, 102.
    turning into-six day, 104.
Several licenses included in one notice, 201.
  occupiers, license to one, 215, 250.
Shareholder in hotel company, justice being, 132.
Shed, drinking in unlicensed, 15.
Sheriff's officer disqualified for license, 237, 248.
Sherry, British, license for, 281.
Shop, keepers of, entitled to off wine license, 275.
Shore, jurisdiction over, 134.
Shutting up licensed house, 103.
Sickness hindering applicant attending for license, 86, 226, 328.
Signature of justices to license by stamp, 85, 327.
  if forged, 5, 321.
  by majority of justices, 226.
Signboard of inn goes with inn, 236.
Similar license, what is, 208.
Six-day license, application for, 102.
    only for in-door, 103.
    cannot afterwards be changed for seven days, 104.
    closing on Sunday, 105—170.
    if bound to receive travellers on Sunday, 104, 171.

INDEX. 421

Six-day license, remission of duty on, 178.
    extended to United Kingdom, 344.
    duties as to spirits, 343.
Skating rink, license for, 42.
Skittles in licensed houses, 46.
Small fines, costs in case of, 112.
Sober man treating drunken man, 27.
Soliciting orders for spirits and wines, 4, 311.
Special case for High Court on convictions, 121, 242.
    notices, how served for case, 123.
    case for High Court from licensing justices, 121, 242.
    from quarter sessions, 242.
    sessions for transfers, 229.
        See " Transfers."
    occasion for exemption order, 61, 66.
        for sale of liquor, 143, 197.
Spinster licensee marrying, 231.
Spirits, Tippling Act as to, 297.
    travellers soliciting orders for, 311.
    dealer having agencies for, 4.
    hawking, penalty for, 7, 348.
    sale of, to children, 17, 359.
    rooms required for in-door license, 96.
    wine sellers, having spirits in possession, 282.
    felony disqualifying license holder, 192, 266, 281, 332.
    methylated, sale of, 5, 147 ; duty on retailers abolished, 347.
    what is deemed, 281.
    sale by retail of, 8, 151, 347.
    no certificate required for, in certain cases, 148.
    retail license by dealer, 139, 291, 343, 348.
    excise duties on retailers, 342.
    certificate required for, in some cases, as for wine, 140.
    sale in canteens, 147.
    sale by beersellers, 140, 294.
    selling without license, 192, 266, 281, 332.
    first conviction for selling without license, 2, 192.
    possession of, by refreshment houses, 282.
    action to recover scores for, 297.
    situation of retail premises, 346.
    selling by retailer to retailer, 347.
    unlawful purchase of, 349.
    possessing, duty not paid, 349.
    reward to informers, 349.
    recovery of fines for condemnation, 349.
Spruce beer, sale of, not affected, 144.

Stage plays, license for, not included in music license, **41, 145.**
        meaning of, 145.
        require license, 145.
        copy of, sent to Lord Chamberlain, 145.
        regulated by London County Council, 146.
        allowed in recreation room, 146.
Stamping of liquor measures used, 19.
        of justices' signature to licenses, 84, 327.
Standard measures, sale by, 19.
Station. *See* "Railway Station."
Steam-engine in charge of drunken person, 23.
Stipendiary magistrates may be licensing justices, 82.
Storing of liquor, if illicit, 21 ; search for, 195.
Structural adaptation of new in-door licensed houses, 96.
Subsequent offence, penalty for, 8.
Summary Jurisdiction Acts, as to procedure, 109.
        as to appeals, 121.
        on being charged, if may demand a jury, 113.
        court of, 110, 153.
        proceedings as to convictions, 110.
        non-payment of penalty on, 113.
        procedure as to appeals, 119.
Summons to state that license must be produced, 126.
Sunday Acts for closing repealed, 167, 307.
        closing of all licensed houses during part of, 169.
        closing of billiards, 162.
        closing in Wales, 172, 350.
        notice on church door of new licenses, 83, 316.
        closing of six-day licensed houses on, 102, 171.
        notice of six-day license to be affixed, 103.
        of general annual licensing meeting, 220, 223.
        included in computing time, 123, 316.
        public entertainments, 172.
        power to vary closing in afternoon, 173.
Superannuation police fund, 138.
Superintendent of police to receive notice of license, 315.
        to get notice of transfer, 83.
Surety for good behaviour in trifling cases, 112.
Sweets, sale of, by wine sellers, 341.
        definition of, 9, 327, 341.
        sale by retail, what, 9.
        license for, necessary, 150.
        includes made wines and metheglin, 327, 341.
        same as for wine, 150.
        included in wine license, 327, 341.
        duties on, 342.

T.

Table-beer retail license, 291.
           duty for, 291.
           no valuation for, 291.
           justices' discretion absolute as to, 352.
Taxes on innkeepers, 304.
Taxing costs at quarter sessions, 244.
Tempest destroying inn, remedy, 228.
Temporary license from excise during appeal, 124.
           during forfeiture, 124.
           continuance of forfeited license, 192.
           at petty sessions till transfer sessions, 269.
Tenant, owner appealing against disqualification of premises, 127.
    refusing to leaving premises, 128, 157.
    covenant not to endanger license, 186.
    if landlord cannot get license, 86.
    removing from licensed house, 227.
    must be resident for beer license, 263.
    rates and taxes on licensed premises, 100, 304.
Tent or shed, drinking in, 16.
    occasional license to sell in, 197.
Theatres, exemption from closing of house near, 61.
    sale of liquors at, 146, 344.
    excise duty for licenses at, 344.
    licenses now by London County Council, 144.
    license by Lord Chamberlain, 144.
    license by justices, 145.
        granted only to manager, 145.
    penalty for unlicensed, 145.
    exemption order not allowed near, 173.
Thieves, harbouring, 31.
        in refreshment houses, 284.
Third conviction recorded, effect of, 67.
Three miles, as to *bond fide* traveller, 181.
Time for obtaining case for High Court, 122.
    computation of, as to notices, 85, 315.
    for appealing to quarter sessions against conviction, 117.
    against refusal of license, 241.
    computation as to closing, 172.
        for new licenses, 85, 315.
Tippling Act, 297.
Tithe rentcharge paid by license holder 100.
Title, vendor's, to public-house, 235.
Tools of trade not taken on distress, 114.

Town, definition of, 153, 207.
    population of, as to, 137, 209, 333.
        annual value in respect of, 97, 264.
Township, valuation for beer license, 264, 333.
Trades, exemption order, to accommodate, 61.
    occasional license for refreshment house, 301, 306.
Transfer, of licenses, definition of, 150, 228.
        in case of forfeiture, &c., 192.
        of wine excise license, 278.
        endorsing license for transfer sessions, 270.
        fees on, 236, 328.
Transfer of licensed house, contract as to, 235.
Transfer sessions, procedure on death of licensee, 3, 11.
    notice before application to, 85, 227.
    notice of time of holding, 222.
    number to be appointed each year, 222.
    when application too late, 233.
    temporary at petty sessions, 269.
    adjournment of hearing, 328.
    no new licenses granted at, 339.
Transparent measures for liquors, 19.
Traveller, falsely pretending to be, 58, 181.
    found on closed premises, 57.
    who is a, 183.
    in Wales, 350.
    right to be received in inns, 103.
    measuring the three miles, 183.
    servant's neglect as to, 182.
    custody of goods and horse at inn, 303, 335.
    soliciting orders for spirits, 311.
    sale of goods if left in inn, 335.
Treating voters in inns, 356.
Trial by jury, if three months' imprisonment, 7, 113.
Trifling charge, how to be treated, 112.
Truck Act, forbids drink as wages, 357.
Trustee of bankrupt licensee, procedure, 3, 10, 228.
    justice being, as to licensed house, 133.

U.

Universities, saving of privileges as to liquors, 143, 245, 264, 325.
Unlawful gaming in licensed houses, 48.

INDEX. 425

Unlicensed premises, internal communication with, 20.
    penalty for selling in, 3, 12.
    seizing liquors in, 195.
    agreement to allow sale without license, 12.
    if license forfeited, continuance, 192.
  music and dancing places, 34, 39.

V.

Vacancy in county licensing committee, 76,
    in borough committee, 79.
Valuation qualification of new in-door premises, 96.
    sufficient at date of application, 101.
    of premises for beer retailers, 96, 264.
    of premises for wine, 99, 276, 321.
    of beer dealer's retail, 299, 331.
    for retail of spirits, 343.
Value of premises, how estimated, 101.
    scale for excise duties, 343.
Vendor of public-house making title, 235.
Vessels, sale on board, 143, 272, 344.
Victualling-house, a confectioner's is, 214.
    billeting soldiers on, 258, 259.
    a refreshment house as, 214, 276.
Vintners, saving as to privileges of, 143.
Violent conduct in licensed house, 24, 29.
    excluding violent persons, 54.
Visitors on premises in closing hours, 58.
Void license, sale under, 5 ; to disqualified person void, 94 ; list of enactments as to disqualification, 95.
    for felony, 192, 266, 281, 332.
    excise license, when not, 265.

W.

Wagers on games unlawful, 48, 51, 53.
    loser of, recovering back money, 48.
Wages, paying in public-houses, 353.
    drink not to be part of, 357.
Wales, Sunday closing in, 172, 350.

INDEX.

Warrant to search gaming-houses, 48.
    to search betting-houses, 53.
    of distress and commitment, 113.
    justices mitigating and postponing, 114.
    to search for liquor in unlicensed places, 195.
Warranty of liquors if adulterated, 192.
Wearing apparel not taken in a distress, 113.
Week-days, closing of premises, 172.
Weights and Measures Act, 192.
Wholesale liquor not affected, 147.
Wife of license holder a witness, 109.
    as license holder, liable for husband, 109, 194.
Wilfully withholding license from owner, 86.
Wine, sale of foreign wine in refreshment houses, 276.
    what is deemed foreign wine, 274.
    license to sell, by beersellers, 293.
        includes sweets, 327, 341.
    duties on license, 342.
    occasional license and duty for, 305, 308.
    made wines or sweets, 327, 341.
    grocer when selling without justices' license, 9, 275.
    shopkeepers entitled to off-license for, 273, 319.
    residence not required for off-license, 274.
    who entitled to refreshment house license, 275.
    confectioners and eating-house keepers licensed, 276.
    register of licenses to be kept, 279.
    death of holder of excise license, 278.
    foreign, license for, includes British, 274.
    sellers of, having spirits in possession, 282.
    license void on conviction for felony, 281.
    transfer of excise license, 229, 278.
    certificate required for, 314.
        form of, 314, 368.
        when not required for, 3.
        no valuation qualification in some cases, 318.
    notice before certificate, 314.
    refusal of certificate for certain licenses, 317.
    appeal against refusal, 318.
    forgery of certificate, 321.
    transfer of certificate, 278, 329.
    renewal of certificate, 92, 322.
    duration of certificate, 329.
    signature of certificate, 328.

Wine, lost certificate, 86, 271.
    dealer's additional retail license, 9, 273.
    dealers entitled to off-license, 273.
    See "License."
Wine and Beerhouse Acts, meaning of, 149, 314.
        32 & 33 Vict. c. 27, 312.
        33 & 34 Vict. c. 29, 326.
        houses subjected to, 312.
Withdrawing exemption order, 61.
    occasional order for refreshment house, 306, 308.
Witness, defendant and wife may be, 109.
Workmen, paying wages to, in public-house, 353.
Worship, public, varying Sunday closing, 173.
Writ of *mandamus*, effect of, 215.
    certiorari and prohibition, 217.

Y.

Yard valued with licensed premises, 100.

www.ingramcontent.com/pod-product-compliance
Lightning Source LLC
Chambersburg PA
CBHW022104300426
44117CB00007B/583